IØØ99544

THE PLA AT HOME AND ABROAD:
ASSESSING THE OPERATIONAL CAPABILITIES
OF CHINA'S MILITARY

Roy Kamphausen
David Lai
Andrew Scobell
Editors

June 2010

*****

Published by Books Express Publishing
Books Express, 2011
ISBN 978-1-780395-23-4

Books Express publications are available from all good retail and online booksellers. For
publishing proposals and direct ordering please contact us at: info@books-express.com

CONTENTS

FOREWORD

It is a distinct honor to write the foreword to this volume dedicated to Ambassador James R. Lilley. I am proud that the George H. W. Bush School of Government and Public Service at Texas A&M University — along with the National Bureau of Asian Research and the U.S. Army War College — was one of the sponsoring institutions of the September 2009 Conference on the People's Liberation Army. For the 11th consecutive year, the event has been held at Carlisle Barracks, Pennsylvania.

It is entirely appropriate that this book of papers presented at the 2009 conference be dedicated to Jim's memory. He had been closely involved in this series of conferences from the very start; indeed, Jim was the driving force behind the instigation of this enterprise back in the early 1990s. Jim believed that it was important to gather leading specialists on China's military on a regular basis away from the hustle, bustle, and hype of Washington for serious, objective, and in-depth analysis of the subject. Jim was a man ahead of his time in that he recognized the importance of carefully monitoring and documenting the modernization of China's military. Moreover, he was committed enough to seek funding, commission experts to write research papers, and ensure the proceedings were published. The result is an entire bookshelf's worth of high quality edited volumes that are invaluable reference works for policymakers, analysts, scholars, and students.

This volume and many others stand as part of Jim Lilley's enduring legacy and as testament to the impact that a single determined individual can have on U.S. policy. With the passing of Jim Lilley in October 2009, the United States lost one of its most dedicated public servants and an extremely talented China hand. And I lost an old and loyal friend.

While Jim, of course, needs no introduction to the contributors to this volume and many readers, it is worth mentioning some of the highlights of his extremely eventful life and long history of selfless service to this country. Jim was a China hand literally from the day he was born in Shandong Province and grew up speaking Chinese. Jim's career of government service began in the military and continued in the intelligence community, with a major focus on China. Later, he shifted to a career as a diplomat. In the early 1980s Jim took the post of chief of the American Institute in Taiwan, the de facto U.S. Embassy in Taipei. Shortly thereafter, he ably served as U.S. ambassador in two Asian capitals at times of considerable political upheaval—for 3 years in Seoul, Korea, followed by 2 years in Beijing. The latter posting was during my administration and took place at an especially difficult time in America's relationship with China during the tragedy of Tiananmen Square and its aftermath. Simply put, Jim did an outstanding job.

After such a distinguished career, Jim richly deserved a restful retirement. But leaving government service in 1991 did not mean sitting back in a rocking chair. Jim lived in the Washington area, where he remained an active participant in policy debates on China and Korea and a keen sponsor and lively participant in this conference series.

While Jim never got to see this volume or attend last year's conference, I am confident that he would have been extremely satisfied with the results. I commend this fine collection to anyone interested in the military and security affairs of China.

GEORGE H. W. BUSH

CHAPTER 1

INTRODUCTION

David Lai

The final years of the 2000s turned out to be quite eventful for the People's Republic of China (PRC and China interchangeably) and its armed forces, the People's Liberation Army (PLA). While there were exciting events for them to celebrate, there were disturbing ones for them to worry about as well.

China's economic reform and phenomenal economic development had sailed on uncharted waters for 30 years. The Chinese Communist Party (CCP) leaders could not have wished for a better occasion than the 2008 Summer Olympics in Beijing to celebrate their accomplishments. The Beijing Olympics ceremonies were probably the most expensive in history; but China had plenty to spend. After all, its economic development had turned it into the world's third largest economy and trading nation, the largest holder of foreign exchange reserves and U.S. treasury bonds, and so on.

In 2009, the PRC turned 60. The CCP leaders staged a lavish celebration and held a spectacular national day armed forces parade that made similar ones in Moscow and Pyongyang look pale by comparison. "Commander-in-Chief" Hu Jintao followed the footsteps of his predecessors (the "core leaders" [领导核心] of the CCP's first, second, and third generations: Mao Zedong, Deng Xiaoping, and Jiang Zemin, respectively) to review PLA troops in Tiananmen Square. The PLA took the occasion to show off its defense modernization advances since its last parade in 1999.

1

Also in 2009, the PLA Navy (PLAN) and PLA Air Force (PLAAF) celebrated their 60th anniversaries. The PLAAF demonstrated its new air power during the October 1 national day parade. The PLAN held its birthday party earlier in April in Qingdao, the Headquarters of its Beihai Fleet (北海舰队 [Northern Sea Fleet]). Over 200 foreign naval dignitaries, most notably the U.S. Chief of Naval Operations and the Russian Navy Commander, were invited to the celebration. It was like an Olympics meeting for the international navies. President Hu Jintao and all the senior PLA leaders led the review of China's major warships, headed by two nuclear-powered and armed submarines (the first-ever public demonstration of China's strategic submarine fleet) and 21 warships from 14 other nations, especially major naval powers such as the United States, Russia, the United Kingdom, and France.

Behind these glittering numbers of China's economic development, the PLA parades, and the spectacular celebration fireworks, the world clearly saw an ambitious China edging its way to the center stage of international economic, political, and military affairs. However, a few other major events in the last 2 years came just in time to remind the Chinese leaders, and the world as well, that China still faced a challenging future.

- The global financial crisis was a wakeup call to China that its economy was vulnerable to a volatile world market that was still beyond its control. China's mercantilist export-oriented development strategy, while deserving credit for jump-starting China's economic development, was making China too dependent on the well- and ill-being of the outside world. The

Chinese government was aware of this problem and wanted to address it before the onset of the global financial crisis (see China's 11th Five-Year Plan for 2006-10 and Hu Jintao's report to the 17th CCP National Congress). The wakeup call thus put much urgency on China's agenda. The Chinese leadership hoped the $500 billion stimulus plan launched in December 2008 would be on target to help China restructure its economic development (a main portion of the stimulus fund was earmarked to develop China's domestic market and expand internal demand [发展国内市场, 扩大内需]).

- The large-scale riots in Tibet (March 2008) and Xinjiang (June 2009) highlighted the fact that while China had a monumental mission of unification with Taiwan and consolidating control of the disputed ocean territories in the East and South China Seas, it had not yet achieved internal harmony and national unity. China's homeland security is still at stake. Back in 2000, the Chinese government launched a "Great Development Program for the Western Regions (西部大开发计划)." It was an attempt to help China's backward western regions catch up with the rapidly approaching well-off societies in China's eastern coastal areas and improve the life of the Tibetans and Uyghurs who form the majority of the western region population so that they would not join their struggling compatriots-in-exile to fight for independence (East Turkistan for the Uyghurs). The riots indicated in part that this program had not quite borne fruit. The CCP leaders have vowed to step up their measures to improve the situation in the western regions.

- The severe winter storm and earthquake in 2008 showed the Chinese government that internal natural disasters could be just as destructive as external security threats for a nation racing to become rich. The call for the PLA to take on the nation's "diverse military tasks" and "military operations other than war" (多样化和非战争任务和行动) got the full attention of the CCP and PLA senior leadership. The PLA was tested during those disaster relief operations.

- The ongoing, and at times escalating, conflicts with Japan, the Philippines, Vietnam, and Malaysia over disputed islands and maritime territorial interests in the East and South China Seas in the last 2 years had generated an outcry in China and much pressure on the Chinese government and the PLA to take more forceful measures to secure those "stolen" territories.[1] The loudest of the Chinese people's calls for action were those demanding the Chinese government accelerate the construction of aircraft carrier battle groups and to modify China's policy of "shelving the disputes while pursuing joint development of ocean interests" (搁置争议, 共同开发海洋资源).

- The Somali pirate attacks on Chinese merchant vessels reaffirmed Chinese concerns that their expanding national interests were at stake. Although the PLAN took prompt action to set up escort operations in the Gulf of Aden and hence started the first-ever PLA overseas combat operation, China nevertheless remains concerned for the safety of its sea lines of communication and business operations in foreign countries.

- Over the last 2 years, China and the United States clashed over their claimed rights to operate in the 200 nautical mile Exclusive Economic Zones (EEZ) off China's coasts (the USNS *Impeccable* and USNS *Victorious* incidents in March and May 2009). These incidents reminded the Chinese, as well as the Americans, that the two great powers have much to learn and do before they can come to terms with the emerging new realities in their relations.

TO BUILD A PROSPEROUS COUNTRY WITH A STRONG MILITARY (富国强军)

Chinese leaders and the PLA have anticipated these daunting challenges. Indeed, China's *Defense White Papers* have repeatedly expressed concerns for China's security and wellbeing:

With the advent of the new century, the world is undergoing tremendous changes and adjustments. Peace and development remain the principal themes, and the pursuit of peace, development and cooperation has become an irresistible trend of the times. . . . However, there still exist many factors of uncertainty in Asia-Pacific security. The drastic fluctuations in the world economy impact heavily on regional economic development, and political turbulence persists in some countries undergoing economic and social transition. Ethnic and religious discords and conflicting claims over territorial and maritime rights and interests remain serious, regional hotspots are complex. At the same time, the United States has increased its strategic attention to and input in the Asia-Pacific region, further consolidating its military alliances, adjusting its military deployment and enhancing its military capabilities. In addition, terrorist, separatists and extremist forces are running rampant; and non-traditional security issues such as serious natural disasters crop up frequently. The mechanisms for security cooperation between countries and regions are yet to be enhanced, and the capability for coping with regional security threats in a coordinated way has to be improved.[2]

The question is: What should China do with these challenges? Chinese President Hu Jintao has a ready answer: accelerating modernization of the PLA and upgrading China's national defense. This is the CCP's strategic call made at its 17th National Convention in October 2007.

> Bearing in mind the overall strategic interests of national security and development, we must take both economic and national defense development into consideration and make our country prosperous and our armed forces powerful while building a moderately prosperous society in all respects (在全面建设小康社会进程中实现富国和强军的统一).[3]

In fact, this is the first time in its history that the CCP put the "prosperous nation with a strong military (富国强军)" call in its party platform. The call also found its way into China's 2008 *Defense White Paper*.[4] This is a very significant milestone in China's contemporary history and its ongoing modernization drive.

Ever since China's fall from grace in the mid 19th century, generations of ambitious Chinese leaders have wanted to restore the greatness of China. However, many of them failed. In all fairness, the CCP leaders have advanced this mission the most so far. Now with a rejuvenated and prosperous China within their reach, the CCP is ready to accelerate the buildup of China's military muscle. This move draws painful lessons from the past (i.e., 落后要挨打，弱国无外交 [backward nations get bullied and weak powers cannot conduct sound diplomacy]) and the hard reality of the present. As noted PLA analyst Wang Faan (王法安) observes, although Chinese leaders believe that peace and development are the main themes of the time, they also see that the world is still a dangerous place and hegemonic powers (read as the United States and its allies) continue to dominate world affairs. Moreover, as China seeks to become a great power with global reach, its growth will profoundly change the strategic makeup of Asia and the world; China undoubtedly faces resistance and even sabotage from the other great powers. In fact, among all the big nations of the world, China comes under the most serious security pressure from outside; yet unlike Germany and Japan, which restored their great power status under the U.S. umbrella, China must rely on itself to promote its welfare and security; in the face of this tough security environment, any illusion or neglect of its security will put China in danger.[5]

The prosperous-nation-strong-military initiative is very significant in setting the direction for China's defense modernization in the years to come. First, the prosperous-nation-strong-military initiative is in essence Part II of Hu Jintao's call for a New Mission for the PLA in the New Century (解放军新世纪新阶段历史使命). Part I was delivered in December 2004 as Hu's inaugural speech to the CCP's Central Military Commission (CMC) when he assumed the chairmanship of this powerful institution. The full text of Hu's speech was not released to the public; however, the key elements were expressed in the CCP's 17th National Convention platform (Hu's report) in October 2007 and in China's 2006 and 2008 *Defense White Papers*. As characterized by Chinese analysts, the PLA is tasked to carry out "three provides and one role" (三个提供，一个发挥). Specifically, it is to:

- provide an important source of strength for consolidating the ruling position of the CCP;
- provide a solid security guarantee for sustaining the important period of strategic opportunity for national development;
- provide strong strategic support for safeguarding national interests; and
- play a major role in maintaining world peace and promoting common development.[6]

The new mission indicates that Chinese leaders took note of the changes that have taken place and adjusted their strategy to meet the challenge of the time. Indeed, China's standard of living has improved. Most Chinese have moved beyond subsistence-level concerns. Chinese now care more about the opportunity and rights to development, a higher level of human needs.[7] In fact, the need for development has already caused the Chinese to pursue their interests everywhere in the world, into the open seas, outer space, cyber space, and other emerging areas. China now has an "interest frontier" that goes beyond the confines of its traditional territorial boundaries.

What is striking is that the CCP leaders have a great sense of urgency for China's development. On the one hand, they see that there is a fierce race to modernity in the world. Those nations that fail to keep up with the race will be marginalized and may never catch up. On the other hand, the CCP leaders believe that the world is still a dangerous place, and great power war remains a constant threat to world peace (and more pointedly, to China in particular). The CCP leadership made an assessment 30 years ago that great power war was not imminent and turned its attention from preparation for war (against the Soviet Union and the United States, in that order) to economic development. Chinese leaders felt fortunate that they had 30 uninterrupted years to turn China's economy around (even the political turmoil of 1989 at home and the fall of communism abroad in the following year did not hold it back). Now the Chinese leaders are looking at the next 30 to 40 years as a similar window of opportunity, a very critical stage where China is to "build a well-off society with Chinese characteristics in an all-round way (全面建设中国特色的小康社会)."[8] China's modernization plan assumes that it will take at least that many years to turn China (with its current level of modernity) into a true great power.[9] It took the West several hundred years to develop the well-off societies of today. It would be a miracle for China to do it in 60 to 70 years (with its size both in terms of territory and population larger than those of Europe). This opportunity is precious and critical. The CCP is tasking the PLA to ensure that the opportunity will not be compromised by internal or external obstacles. However, as a *PLA Daily* 2008 New Year's Day editorial points out, the PLA's "level of modernization is incompatible with the demands of winning a local war under conditions of informatization, and capabilities are still incompatible with the demands of carrying out the new historic mission (两个不相适应)."[10] The prosperous-nation-strong-military (富国强军) initiative thus is to substantiate the new mission call and to make the PLA commensurate with China's rising international status.

Second, the prosperous-nation-strong-military initiative is a strategic adjustment in China's development strategy. In 1978, the CCP made a switch in its central task from class struggle to economic development. China had long wanted to pursue "Four Modernizations," namely, industrial, agricultural, science and technology, and defense modernizations; however, it could not pursue all of them at the same time. Deng Xiaoping, the architect of China's reform, set the priority in the following order 30 years ago:

> The four modernizations include the modernization of defense. Without that modernization there would be only three [agriculture, industry, and science and technology]. But the four modernizations should be achieved in order of priority. Only when we have a good economic foundation will it be possible for us to modernize the army's equipment. So we must wait patiently for a few years. I am certain that by the end of the century we can surpass the goal of quadrupling the GNP. At that time, when we are strong economically, we shall be able to spend more money on updating equipment. We can also buy some from abroad, but we should rely on ourselves to conduct research and design superior planes for the air force and equipment for the navy and army. If the economy develops, we can accomplish anything. What we have to do now is to put all our efforts into developing the economy. That is the most important thing, and everything else must be subordinated to it.[11]

Thanks to its relentless pursuit of wealth in the last 30 years, China had more than quadrupled its gross national product (GNP) by the end of the 20th century (from $191 billion of 1978 to $1.25 trillion in 1998) and increased it to over 3 trillion U.S. dollars (USD) by 2008,[12] much along the lines of Deng Xiaoping and CCP leaders' projections. Now the question is, should

China continue with this strategy? Or should China unleash its hold on the defense modernization? The answer is clear. The prosperous-nation-strong-military initiative has turned on the green light for China's defense modernization.

However, CCP leaders understand that China's modernization is only a little over one-third of its way. China is looking to the year 2050 to complete this mission. Defense modernization can be put in a higher gear, but it must not overtake economic development to become the top priority. Indeed, Hu Jintao has made it clear that economic development will still be the overarching task in the years to come; defense modernization will be an integral part of this mission. The CCP's solution is to make economic and defense modernizations complementary to each other, but not compel a choice between guns and butter. 军民结合, 寓军于民 (integrating military with civilian development and embedding the military in the civilian sector) is the way to go. Moreover, the CCP leaders are mindful of the lessons from the former Soviet Union. They promise not to exhaust China's economy to develop its military. China will not engage in the trap of entering into an arms race with other great powers, especially the United States, but will develop its military according to its developmental needs.

The prosperous-nation-strong-military (富国强军) call, as the Chinese characterize it, is the CCP's timely adjustment to the changing situation and the advance of times (与时俱进). It is a well-thought-out and well-calculated move to advance the modernization mission. As Sun Kejia (孙科佳), a professor at the Chinese National Defense University puts it,

> This call reflects the elevation of the importance of national defense modernization in China's overall strat-

11

egy. National defense modernization was no longer an isolated issue. It is a systemic requirement of China's development. As China's development progresses, its national security content and outreach will expand from the traditional "national sovereignty security" to the "national interest security;" from the traditional territorial security to a wide variety of security in the nation's politics, system, economy, science and technology, social life, culture, information, ideology, and military. The level and quality of national defense and military power affect China's position in the evolving international strategic order and the historic process of China's peaceful development, and eventually the life and death of China.[13]

TRANSFORMATION IN MILITARY AFFAIRS WITH CHINESE CHARACTERISTICS

The new mission and prosperous-nation-strong-military calls give blessing to China's defense modernization that has been going on for close to 20 years under a different agenda—it is called 中国特色的军事变革 (transformation in military affairs with Chinese characteristics).[14]

The impetus for the early start of China's defense modernization is twofold; both are closely related to the United States. In a practical sense, China's confrontations with the United States during the 1996 Taiwan Strait crisis, the 1999 bombing of the Chinese Embassy in Belgrade, Yugoslavia, the EP-3 incident in 2001, and so on, stimulated the Chinese to upgrade the PLA's fighting power. Their efforts unavoidably jump-started China's long-awaited defense modernization.

At the strategic level, the U.S.-led revolution in military affairs (RMA) and its impressive demonstrations in the Gulf War of 1991, the Kosovo campaign of 1999, and the operations in Afghanistan and Iraq in 2001 and 2003 caused the Chinese to see fundamental changes taking place in military affairs and compelled them to ask hard questions: Where is the RMA leading the world? Can China afford to wait?

PLA analysts were quick to point out the following. First, the RMA started with the advanced industrial powers; it would get them further ahead of the less-developed nations. Second, over the centuries, China has missed several important revolutions in military affairs, the most critical of which were the transitions from cold-weapon warfare (with the use of mainly knives) to hot-weapon warfare (with the development of guns and firepower) and from hot-weapon warfare to mechanized warfare (with the employment of tanks, battleships, and airplanes, etc.). The consequences were devastating. When the well-armed Western powers forced their way into China 170 years ago, the Chinese were defenseless with their outmoded weapons (the Opium War of 1840 is a good example; the Boxer Rebellion is another). Third, when the Western powers developed mechanized weapons during and after World War II, China was in the midst of internal turmoil and suffered from foreign invasion (i.e., the Chinese Civil War and Japanese invasion); it did not have any capacity to keep up with the developments of the time. In fact, more than half a century since then, China is still trying to catch up with the mechanization of its armed forces. Finally, "reflecting on the past, Chinese have only sorrow and regrets. Today, an opportunity not seen in a hundred years is unfolding in its early stage, failing to catch the opportunity could put China another generation behind the Western powers. China must act."[15]

There is no regret this time. Unlike past Chinese rulers, who foolishly dismissed foreign ideas and advances, current Chinese leaders are quick to grasp the significance of the RMA and are supportive of the PLA's quest for transformation. Xiong Guangkai (熊光楷), a retired PLA general and former Deputy Chief of Staff of the PLA, recalls that, while the Gulf War of 1991 was still going on, Chinese President Jiang Zemin tasked the PLA to study it; shortly after the war in 1992, Jiang instructed the Chinese CMC to host seminars to discuss the key aspects and lessons learned from the American new fighting power. They subsequently published their study in a book entitled 海湾战争纵览 (*Aspects of the Gulf War*).[16] Jiang's following remarks also give China's efforts a sense of urgency:

> From now to the first 2 decades of the 21st century, we have a very critical time period. During this time period, the world's new revolution in military affairs will be at its early stage. If we can make good observation and take appropriate measures, we can achieve a big stride in our national defense and armed forces modernization, greatly reducing the gap between us and the world's advanced powers, and laying a solid foundation for our further development.[17]

In subsequent years, Jiang became instrumental in initiating major changes in the PLA's strategic design and setting the course for China's transformation in military affairs.[18] In December 1993 at an expanded CMC meeting, Jiang put forward a new military strategy guideline (军事战略方针) for the PLA to pursue the following: (1) China's defense strategy to move from sole protection of national boundaries to protect national unity, and however reluctant, to win a local war if forced to do so (read as by the United States and unmistakably over Taiwan); (2) China's defense forces to make two fundamental transformations (两

个根本性的转变), that are a change from a manpower-intensive military to a science and technology-intensive one, and a transformation from a quantity-based force to a quality-based military; and (3) China will develop its armed forces to handle limited war under high-tech conditions, possibly involving hegemonic powers (read as the United States and its allies).[19]

Two years later at another expanded CMC meeting, Jiang instructed the PLA to put the two fundamental transformations in action. To clear the way for this act, Jiang took the initiative to downsize the PLA. In what the PLA analysts call 瘦身 ("lose weight") exercises, Jiang brought the oversized PLA down from about 3.5 million to 2.3 million.[20] At the same time, the CMC also initiated reforms in the PLA's organization and education. A more professional military emerged from this reform in the first decade of the 21st century.[21]

In 1997, the CCP put forward a "Three-Stage" plan for the remainder of its modernization mission: (1) double China's 2000 gross domestic product (GDP) by the year 2010; (2) further improve the economy and various aspects of the society by 2020; and (3) bring about a prosperous, strong, democratic, and culturally advanced socialist China by 2050.[22] Later in the same year, Jiang instructed the PLA to follow the CCP's design to develop a "Three-Step (三步走)" plan as well. In 2002, the PLA came up with its roadmap for transformation. Specially, the PLA will lay a solid foundation for force informationization and mechanization by 2010, complete force mechanization and the initial stage of informationization by 2020, and complete informationization for all the services and national defense modernization by 2050.[23] Jiang Zemin characterized this as an "action plan for the PLA (解放军的行动纲领)."

Chinese leaders are well aware of the huge challenge in their endeavor. They do not have the luxury to follow what the Western powers have gone through in their RMA. First, Western powers made their militaries transition to the information age on the basis of their fully developed economies. China has to make the transition while at the same time trying to develop its economy. Second, Western military powers were highly mechanized when they added their informationized capabilities. China's force mechanization is only half-way completed. Yet China cannot afford to wait until the completion of force mechanization to make the transition to informationization. Its decision is to make a "leap forward development (跨越式发展)," striving to make mechanization and informationization mutually reinforcing and complementary.

"Learn from the U.S. Military (向美军学习)"

The revolution in military affairs started as speculations in the mid-1970s by the Soviet military leaders on future ways and means of waging war but has been turned into reality by the United States in the last 2 to 3 decades. The RMA has now come to mean the fundamental changes that have taken place, in the words of the Pentagon 1999 *Annual Report to the President and the Congress*, in military strategy, doctrine, training, education, organization, equipment, logistics operations, and tactics.[24]

The PLA follows closely the development of the RMA and learns from the experience of the U.S. armed forces in practically every aspect. The heading of this section is actually the title of a recent article by the PLA's Academy of Military Science Political Commissar, Lieutenant General Liu Yazhou (刘亚洲). It stands as a testimony to the PLA's learning business.[25] In the last 20 years, there has been so much learning from the United States and other advanced militaries that the PLA National Defense University tasked a group of diligent researchers headed by a major general to put together a book entitled *New Concepts in the Transformation in Military Affairs* (军事变革中的新概念),[26] with well over 200 entries, to keep the PLA informed about the new advances.

The PLA, however, does not take everything wholesale from the U.S. military. It selects the "good ones" while rejecting the "bad ones," especially those that are not "suitable" for China ("de-politicization of the military" for instance, see the discussion of this in Chapter 4 of this volume by You Ji and Daniel Alderman). Many PLA officers agree that learning the "smart things" from the U.S. military helps the PLA to "get more with less investment (投入少, 效益高)" and learning from U.S. mistakes helps the PLA avoid roundabout courses (少走弯路) and move faster in the transformation.[27]

It is interesting to note that the Chinese leaders at this critical time are mostly well-educated engineers (Jiang has a degree in electrical engineering and had further training at the automobile works in Moscow; he was also China's Minister of Electronic Industries in the early 1980s; Hu graduated from Tsinghua University [China's MIT equivalent] with a degree in hydraulic engineering). Other factors aside, their "engineer instinct" may be instrumental in making them enthusiastic about the advancements of science and technology and wholeheartedly embracing transformation in military affairs with Chinese characteristics. Since taking the helm of the CCP leadership, Hu Jintao has been equally, if not more, enthusiastic about China's transformation in military affairs. With this top-down support, the PLA has gradually initiated an across-the-board transformation in the last 15 years, establishing a professional officer education and promotion system; an integrated logistics supply system (联勤供应系统); new armament production and acquisition systems; a more effective medical support system; restructured military industry; integrated transportation; dual-use railroad, highway, water transport, and air transport systems; joint and combined military exercises; and many other initiatives.[28]

ASSESSING THE PLA'S CAPABILITIES

It is against this backdrop that the PLA conference took place in September 2009. More than 70 noted China observers gathered at the U.S. Army War College in Carlisle, Pennsylvania to share their assessments of the PLA transformation and its implementation. The discussion was structured as follows: in the opening section, three presentations set out to analyze China and the PLA's views on China's changing security landscape, the operational requirements of China's 2008 *Defense White Paper*, and China's changing civil-military relations and the impact of those relations on the PLA's new mission. The second section examines the PLA's performance at home, with emphasis on the PLA's developments in informationization and management of diverse military tasks (DMT) and military operations other than war (MOOTW). The third part of the volume looks at the PLA's interactions with foreign militaries and its first combat operation abroad, the anti-piracy operation in the Gulf of Aden. The final section examines the PLA's support systems. The two chapters look at China's efforts to transform its defense industry and logistics systems. The conference participants provided valuable critiques and shared their insights on the issues under study. The authors polished their presentations to produce this new volume as a timely study of the PLA.

Setting the Stage.

In Chapter 2, Paul H. B. Godwin provides an assessment of how the PLA views its roles and responsibilities amid a changing global security landscape. PLA leaders see China living in a tough neighborhood, surrounded by the largest number of neighbors, and, more pointedly, by the largest number of nuclear-weapon-possession states. Complicating this picture are China's territorial disputes with India on its western frontier, with some Southeast Asian nations in the South China Sea, with Japan in the East China Sea, and two of the world's conflict flashpoints, North Korea and Taiwan. A reading of China's official and unofficial assessments of its national security surroundings clearly indicates China's serious concerns about national security.

However, China's utmost security apprehension concerns the United States, the only foreign nation mentioned by name in China's *Defense White Papers*. China and the PLA hold that the strategic objective of the United States is to restrain the development of China's economic, diplomatic, and military capabilities, particularly in Asia. In Beijing's view, there is good reason to have such apprehensions. PLA researchers read of official U.S. documents where U.S. "hedging" against China's growing military capabilities is evident. Moreover, China sees that the U.S. build-up of its forces in the Western Pacific has a hostile purpose.

Indeed, the United States now deploys more than half of its nuclear-powered aircraft carriers and submarines, Aegis destroyers, and strategic bombers in the Asia-Pacific region. The apprehension about U.S. strategic intent, therefore, is the driver for much of the PLA's modernization programs and doctrinal evolution encompassing all realms of military operations from space to submarine warfare.

China's defense modernization, unfortunately and unavoidably, has in turn deepened U.S. apprehension about China's intent and the impact of China's growing power. It has also generated concerns from China's neighbors across Asia, a natural outgrowth of the security dilemma in international relations. China is aware of this negative impact. Chinese President Hu Jintao has taken measures to address this issue. One noted measure is to stress the PLA's non-war roles and responsibilities. The other is to promote Hu's calls for a "harmonious world" (in September 2005 at the United Nations (UN) 60th anniversary), and "harmonious oceans" (at the PLA Navy's 60th anniversary in April 2009).

Godwin closes the chapter with the observation that resolving U.S.-China mutual apprehension is important, for it involves more than the bilateral relationship between the two great nations. In essence, all of Asia is watching the dynamics of the Sino-American relationship. The United States can take advantage of the realities recognized by Hu Jintao and the PLA and systematically and deliberately build on the commitments Beijing has already made and to some extent implemented, namely, China's commitment to stay engaged with global affairs, China's promise that its defense modernization would not disturb the security arrangement in Asia, China's commitment to increase military transparency, China's need for a stable security environment in Asia, and its promise for peaceful development and the construction of a harmonious world.

In Chapter 3, Andrew Scobell offers a creative design to put PLA discourse about its new mission in perspective. From his analysis of the PLA's "multilevel" interactions and "multidimensional" discourses, Scobell has brought to light the key contradictions confronting the PLA. The most significant one is about the PLA's core military capability (核心军事能力) and its role in handling DMT and MOOTW.

DMT and MOOTW gained attention and significance in 2008 when the PLA was mobilized several times to help with China's natural disaster relief and the Beijing Olympics games security measures. Those were no small undertakings. As PLA Senior Colonel Li Daguang (李大光) puts it, 2008 could very well be the PLA's "Year of MOOTW."[29] Other PLA commentators complemented the PLA for its heroic acts, celebrating them as the PLA's return to its basic roots (回归本色). After all, the PLA, as its founder Mao Zedong put it, is always a fighting force, a propaganda team, and a work brigade (战斗队, 宣传队, 工作队).

However, PLA analysts do not deny the fact that the U.S. military was the first to coin the terms DMT and MOOTW and developed doctrines to regulate their applications.[30] Although some argue that the United States uses DMT and MOOTW as disguises for U.S. interference in other nations' internal affairs (human rights over sovereign rights and humanitarian interests, for instance),[31] most agree that DMT and MOOTW are broader in scope than the PLA's traditional functions, more complicated, and require legal measures to carry out these nonwar activities.[32] It is through their learning from the U.S. military that the PLA is making itself more professional in carrying out the DMTs and MOOTWs.

While many in the PLA are embracing DMT and MOOTW as "soft applications of hard power" (硬实力的软运用),[33] some are concerned that the efforts devoted to DMT and MOOTW will divert the PLA's attention from pursuing its core mission and capabilities. Their concerns have clearly reached the top echelon of the discourse. Indeed, Chinese President Hu Jintao came out on several important occasions to clarify these matters:

> The PLA must keep preparation for war as the leading force for defense modernization. The central focus is on strengthening core military capability (核心军事能力), the cutting-edge capability that will allow a military to win wars in a competitive military arena. With respect to the PLA, this capability means the ability to win local wars under conditions of informatization. This is the fundamental criterion to measure whether a military is strong or not. The ability to handle non-war military operation should be a byproduct of the core military capability.[34]

Although the PLA appears to hold the balance between its core mission and MOOTW, it nevertheless has to reconcile a number of other contradictions such as the PLA's expanding commitments and limited resources, mechanization and informatization, competing interests of different services and the tension between the "echelons" (the levels of officers as depicted in the analytical scheme), the contradiction between the PLA's ongoing robust program of modernization and Beijing's continuing campaign to persuade the rest of the world that China does not pose a military threat to anyone, and the "incompatibles" in the PLA's capabilities and the demands of its new mission.

In the years to come, while the PLA will continue to wrestle with these contradictions, it will nevertheless continue to refine its DMT and MOOTW capabilities. Indeed, the PLA's General Staff Department recently released a report that China has preliminarily established a MOOTW capability system that is based on the special forces for flood rescue, earthquake rescue, nuclear and bio-chemistry disaster rescue, transportation emergency, and international peacekeeping and supplemented with an integrated system of Public Security and People's Armed Police (PAP) national and local special teams. The report also mentioned that the PLA's next step would be to develop an emergency command system, joint operations, combined supply protection, and so on.[35]

In Chapter 4, You Ji and Daniel Alderman offer an analysis of the changing civil-military relations in China and the impact of those relations on the PLA's modernization. The most significant issue in China's civil-military relations is the CCP-PLA "symbiotic relations (休戚与共的关系)" under stress. China's transformation in military affairs is tearing apart the fabric of this relationship.

The symbiosis paradigm is built on four pillars in the CCP-PLA relationship: (1) a common ideological and revolutionary approach; (2) an overlapping personnel structure reflecting an integrated decision making process at the apex of power; (3) a nearly equal political status; and (4) shared mentality and vested interests in governance. The CCP and PLA penetrate each other's organization and affairs. Now this relationship is under pressure due to the professionalization of the PLA.

PLA professionalism creates a strong, subordinate, and noninterventionist military. It also allows the CCP

23

to gain an objective control measure to supplement its traditional subjective control mechanisms. However, true professionalism is possible only alongside a high level of de-politicization. The CCP has long engaged in a battle to fight against "Western attempts to corrupt the PLA" (through their examples of "delinking party-military ties," "de-politicization of the military," and "nationalized military"). This struggle will only intensify as the PLA's professionalization deepens. The danger to the CCP control of the gun is clear: Party control, based on ideational indoctrination, is progressively diluted as the PLA undertakes internal changes driven by Information Technology (IT)-RMA transformation. The CCP is clearly fighting a losing battle.

The change in this fundamental relationship between the CCP and PLA is making its subtle impact on such important matters such as the selection of the next generation of civil and military leaders and China's dealing with the Taiwan issue. The two authors point out that by embarking on building professionalism as a key organizational objective, the PLA will develop its own corporate identity and logic of operational autonomy. Therefore, as U.S. policymakers assess the long-term prospects for China's civil-military relations, the possiblity remains that dichotomous CCP-PLA institutional imperatives may create fault zones in the Party's control of the gun.

The PLA at Home.

In Chapter 5, Kevin Pollpeter offers an assessment of the PLA's transformation into an informationized force. He uses the PLA's ability to conduct joint operations as the metric for evaluating its level of informationization. The analysis finds that the PLA's drive to develop an informationized force began in the early 1990s and was a response to the revolution in military affairs and the performance of the U.S. military in Operation DESERT STORM. It reveals a learning curve (or step) that goes from command and control (C2) to command, control, and communications (C3) to command, control, communications, and intelligence (C3I) to command, control, communications, computers, intelligence, surveillance, and reconnaissance (C4ISR). It was in 2004 when the PLA began to refer to "our military's C4ISR systems" in its publications.

However, the analysis also finds that the PLA has made only desultory progress in establishing genuine inter-service institutions, technology, and training in the past 10 years. One main difficulty in establishing an integrative C4ISR system lies more with the approach the PLA has taken with C4ISR modernization than with the level of technology used. Stovepiping, for example, has been a major impediment. While the services have been good at establishing communications with subordinate units, they have largely ignored connectivity with their sister services.

Another hindrance to the development of integrative C4ISR technologies in the PLA is the lack of understanding of the exact nature of informationized war. Doubts or misunderstandings remain over the conduct of informationized war and how to fight it. The main reason for this is the PLA's lack of recent warfighting experience and the inability of PLA officers to accurately conceptualize the demands of modern war.

Finally, jointness is still largely anathema to the PLA, and it appears that the ground force continues to wield extraordinary power at a time when PLA writings on future wars depict a more prominent role for the other services.

From the previous observations one can say that the PLA's efforts in informationization transformation have largely failed. But these yardsticks may be too high. According to China's 2008 *Defense White Paper*, the PLA has the goal of laying a foundation for informationization by 2010, to make major progress by 2020, and to mostly reach the goal of informationization by 2050. By this measure, it appears that the PLA is meeting its own standards for joint reform.

Pollpeter also observes that the PLA is aware of the fact that informationization is a double-edged sword. It creates vulnerability for the PLA. Yet the PLA commitment to this transformation is undiminished. It will press on, much like the Chinese old saying of 明知山有虎, 偏向虎山行 (going undeterred by the dangers ahead). That said, it appears that the PLA possessing sophisticated C4ISR is only a matter of time. With this capability, the PLA will become a true global military power and pose a serious challenge to the United States.

In Chapter 6, Harold M. Tanner looks at the PLA's recent MOOTW experience. Tanner points out that the PLA has not seen combat since its brief "punitive war" against Vietnam in 1979. In the 30 years since, and particularly since the mid-1990s, the PLA has undergone substantial modernization, reorganization, and training; but while they have been trained and equipped for war, China's soldiers have been deployed time and again not to fight external enemies, but to respond to internal security issues such as natural disasters, violent mass demonstrations or "mass incidents," and episodes of ethnic unrest.

Tanner examines four recent cases of PLA MOOTW: the snow and ice emergency of January-February 2008, the Wenchuan earthquake of May 2008, the handling of four violent mass incidents in 2007-08, and the riots in Lhasa (March 2008) and Urumqi (July 2009). Tanner finds that many in the PLA treat mobilization for natural disasters similar to the mobilization for war. In this respect, the PLA's reaction to the winter weather emergency, and particularly the Wenchuan earthquake, indicates some significant institutional and operational weakness. On the institutional side, China continues to struggle with problems both in the legal framework, organization, and mobilization for internal MOOTW. Discussions in PLA writings indicate a strong interest in building a more complete corpus of legislation to define the duties and powers of the military as an emergency responder and in consolidating and improving China's national, provincial, and local emergency response plans.

It is interesting to note that prior to the Tiananmen Square incident and until the middle of the 1990s it never occurred to the Chinese leaders that they needed laws to govern the use of the PLA in domestic or any other situation. In addition to its duties to protect the country, the PLA is a political tool the CCP can use at will. Chinese leaders see the PLA as an integral part of the people. The relationship is "natural, as close as flesh and blood, bound by a common cause, and goes through thick and thin together (天然的, 血脉相通的, 休戚与共的紧密联系);" MOOTW has always been an "organic part of the PLA's mission (有机组成部分);" use of the military for domestic affairs is "right and proper (天经地义)." The CCP and the Chinese people generally expect the PLA to take care of both external and internal defense problems.[36] This tradition, however, is giving way to a more law-governed employment of the PLA in China's emerging MOOTWs.

In operational terms, the PLA's recent disaster relief experiences underline continued problems with equipment, logistics, airlift capability, and joint operations. Training, specialized rescue units, and equipment (both rudimentary and specialized) were all in short supply. The lack of heavy helicopter transport capability and the PLAAF's apparent inability to efficiently deliver large numbers of troops to the disaster areas are particularly striking. The PLA has been working to increase its force projection capabilities and its ability to perform joint operations. But the difficulties encountered in mobilizing and delivering forces for the earthquake disaster relief effort, and the vulnerability of south China's transportation and power infrastructure as seen in the snow and ice emergency, underline just how far the PLA has to go before it will be able to reliably project overwhelming force beyond its borders under challenging circumstances.

However, Tanner observes that the PLA's participation in MOOTW can be a valuable experience when it comes to dealing with a Taiwan scenario in which China successfully invaded and occupied Taiwan but then faced serious urban unrest or even insurgency. The PLA and PAP would presumably draw on the tactics and techniques that they have developed to prevent, contain, and suppress such unrest. In addition, PLA commentators generally draw direct parallels between the experience and lessons of their MOOTW and their wartime mobilization and operations. For example, PLA officer Yang Jinkui (杨金奎) writes in the *PLA Daily* that the PLA should reflect on what might happen if severe weather coincided with war. Stating that the United States had used cloud-seeding as a weapon during the Vietnam War, Yang argued that the PLA should be prepared for climate manipulation in wartime and take the experience of fighting the severe winter storm of 2008 as a lesson in overcoming the problems that such weather might bring to command, joint operations, and logistics.[37]

Other PLA analysts look at natural disaster rescue operations as a variety of joint operations. They suggest that the PLA's use of aerial reconnaissance, airborne remote sensing, and other advanced techniques in the earthquake relief operation brought to mind the American use of satellites, airpower, and special ground forces in Kosovo, Afghanistan, and Iraq.

It appears that although the PLA has concerns about its participation in MOOTW as discussed by Scobell in Chapter 3, Tanner finds no evidence suggesting that preparation for and participation in internal MOOTW has any negative impact on the PLA's core mission or its pursuit of modernization.

The PLA Abroad.

In Chapter 7, Andrew S. Erickson provides an assessment of the PLA Navy's operation in the Gulf of Aden with emphasis on the motivations and preparations for the mission; relevant operational details, including rules of engagement, equipment, personnel, and logistic support; degree of coordination with other militaries; domestic and international responses to the mission; and indications of the PLA's own assessment of its achievements regarding the deployment. The findings are:

- Reasons for China to act are crystal clear: its economic interests are under threat. PLA's new mission is key in this operation. The dispatch of this PLAN fleet clearly has implications for future operations outside of China. It also goes along with China's quest for maritime power. China is fortunate to have UN sanctions for this mission. It is able to conduct a "unilateral approach under a multilateral aegis."

- Limited U.S. response to piracy in the Horn of Africa arguably offered China a particularly useful strategic opportunity in this regard.
- Platform capability is adequate. China sends its best fleet; although a little oversized for the mission, it is nevertheless well suited for it. At the writing of this volume, China has rotated in five task forces and warships from a variety of classes have participated. See Table on p. 305.
- Rules of engagement are well observed. China strictly follows UN authorization and obtained Somalia government approval to act. It projects the image of a responsible stakeholder.
- The operation is a valuable training opportunity for the PLA Navy. Significant logistics capabilities constitute the vital backbone of the mission; their largely commercial nature suggests dynamism and sustainability that could make future efforts in this area both feasible and affordable.
- The PLAN tests a variety of capabilities such as satellite tracking and communication, sustained logistic support, and replenishment.
- China is attaining a new level of blue-water experience with a mission that requires rapid response, underway replenishment, on-station information-sharing, and calls in foreign ports to take on supplies and engage in diplomacy.

Sending an 800 crew-member surface action group five time zones away, with 70 special forces embarked and combat contingencies possible, presents unprecedented challenges and opportunities. PLAN personnel continue to learn new techniques, test their equipment, and can be expected to advocate improvements upon their return.

- An overseas supply base is now on the agenda. Without an overseas supply post, a PLAN long-term operation is still in question. Looking for a base on land will naturally follow.

Erickson maintains that in the years to come, China is likely to follow a two-level approach to naval development, with consistent focus on increasingly formidable high-end anti-access capabilities to support major combat operations in China's maritime close neighborhood (e.g., a Taiwan scenario), and relatively low-intensity but gradually growing capabilities to influence strategic conditions further afield.

In Chapter 8, Dennis J. Blasko provides an assessment of trends in the PLA's combined exercises with the ground forces of foreign militaries, both on Chinese territory and abroad. Blasko observes that since October 2002, Chinese PLA ground forces and the PAP units have conducted approximately 24 combined exercises with foreign military, law enforcement, or emergency rescue organizations. In the course of these exercises, Chinese forces have gained valuable experience in operating with foreign forces, command and control, staff planning procedures, long-distance rail or air deployment, logistics, and to a lesser extent actual battlefield tactics and combat methods. Although limited in number, these exercises contribute to China's foreign and security policy objectives.

However, Blasko also finds some shortcomings in the PLA's combined exercises. Exercise artificialities, such as compressing the battlefield so it can be observed from nearby reviewing stands, limited timeframes (often counted in minutes or hours), and daylight operations only are all problems with the PLA's current combined exercises with its foreign counterparts—they lack the reality of modern combat against either an unconventional enemy or larger, modern military opponent. In addition, most combined exercises China has conducted are tiny compared to the combined exercises NATO conducted during the Cold War or the U.S. and South Korea have done for decades.

Based on recent experience, the steady stream of exercises is likely to continue with scenarios becoming more challenging, complex, and realistic. As such, they will help the PLA tremendously. At the same time, they will present outsiders an opportunity to better understand both China's military capabilities and its intentions.

In Chapter 9, Heidi Holz and Kenneth Allen provide an assessment of recent trends in the pace, scope, goals, and degree of success of the PLA's military to military exchange activities. It has been 10 years since Kenneth Allen and Eric A. McVadon produced a comprehensive study of the PLA's foreign military relations.[38] This chapter is a timely addition to the previous study.

Through their analysis of the PLA's foreign military relations in the last 2 decades, Holz and Allen find that the PLA has interacted with the international community in more ways, more often, and more effectively. The increased frequency and sophistication of China's employment of military diplomacy as a tool of statecraft mirrors trends in the overall Chinese diplomacy as the PRC becomes increasingly engaged in the international community.

Holz and Allen present that the PLA has set a broad range of objectives for its diplomacy, nine categories ranging from national level strategic dialogue to naval port calls and humanitarian operations. China uses PLA military diplomacy as a tool of reassurance to offset the repercussions of China's rapid and extensive military modernization program, enhance China's image as a responsible member of the international community, gain access to foreign military technology and expertise, and deter threats to stability by demonstrating the PLA's improving capabilities. The knowledge, experience, and technology that the PLA gains through interactions with foreign militaries make it a more formidable fighting force.

The increasing scope and sophistication of PLA military diplomacy is representative of a larger trend in Chinese foreign relations. Since the mid 1990s, as China has become increasingly engaged in the international system and progressively more adept at promoting its influence, so too has the PLA. As a result, China can challenge U.S. interests more effectively than it has in the past. This is a serious challenge for U.S. policymakers in their consideration of future U.S.-China military relations.

The PLA's Support Systems.

In Chapter 10, Eric Hagt provides an assessment of China's efforts to transform its defense industrial complex. Hagt observes that China has embarked on a transformative change to its defense industry. The Chinese leadership's strategic sights are set on civil-military integration (CMI, [军民一体化]) as the centerpiece of this reform. CMI is described as the "integrated and coordinated development of the defense and civilian technology economies." The decision to pursue CMI is the result of a decade of intensive study of international trends and a comprehensive self-assessment that past efforts to retool the industry have not met the needs of the PLA in preparing for future warfare.

The measure of CMI's success will be in those areas where leap ahead and disruptive innovations are most likely to occur; that is, in C4ISR systems, advanced electronic components, high-end integrated circuits, next generation broadband wireless mobile communications, precision guidance and its tracking and targeting assets, situational awareness, connectivity, digital simulation facilities, etc. These technologies may adjust the power balance in a more fundamental way since, if successful, China would begin to compete (or close the gap) with the United States where it is strongest—such as advanced net-centric warfare, high-speed communication links, and interoperable data systems. It is these areas that will make by far the highest demands in human and monetary resources as well as industrial capacity, and where the dynamic and large scale of the civilian sector will be most critical.

However, the prospects for success of China's new strategic direction in defense industry reform remain decidedly uncertain, though not for lack of vision or effort. The highest rungs of leadership in the military, political, scientific, and industrial bureaucracies have committed to forge ahead with civil-military integration as the cornerstone of future defense reform. However, the difficulty of harmonizing the very disparate economies and cultures of China's closed, massive military industrial complex and its dynamic but vast civilian economy will hold significant barriers to fashioning a comprehensive and coherent strategy. To date, CMI is best characterized as "九龙治水 (nine dragons to tame the floods)," that is, an air of trial and error pervades the various attempts to mold policy, institutional, programmatic, and funding efforts into a feasible plan.

The above said, one must see that China's defense industry reform will continue. Hagt holds that as China's efforts in CMI pick up steam, new breakthroughs and advances in PLA capabilities will emerge with greater frequency. More importantly, advances in China's defense industry input will grow harder to detect and evaluate with several consequences. First, it will be increasingly difficult to parse the specific military application of China's highly dual-use space or telecommunications infrastructure. Moreover, China's growing capability to conduct information-based warfare will largely depend on breakthroughs in more amorphous C4ISR components, many of which will be difficult to assess. Finally, and perhaps most significantly, tracking technological progress for national defense purposes will be complicated as CMI blurs the lines between civilian and military entities participating in weapons research and development (R&D) and productions.

All of these factors will require additional methods to better measure and assess defense industry reform at a systemic level.

In Chapter 11, Susan M. Puska provides an overall assessment of the success and shortcomings of PLA logistics reform since the late 1990s. The author finds that China's logistics system is steadily moving toward providing concrete capability to China's armed forces in both the defense and the offense under informationalized conditions, but shortcomings continue to co-exist alongside improvements that provide contradictory indicators about the pace, scope, and potential intent of China's military modernization.

- Military logistics modernization now enjoys the highest priority it has had in the 30 long years of defense modernization in China. Consequently, developments in China's military logistics capacity will remain an important indicator of when and how well China would project power beyond its land borders.
- Based on the level of effort and trends of logistics modernization over the last 10 years, we should expect continued operational logistics improvements to support military operations outside China's border.
- Improvements can be accelerated with command decisions from above, increased sense of urgency to address perceived threats, and application of greater resources and heightened priority.
- China's civilian logistics system, which is concurrently modernizing and maturing at a significant rate, should help multiply the capacity of the military logistics system through direct support to mobilization and outsourcing. Additionally, a more robust and sophisticated civilian logistics system should also help improve China's military logistics over time, and continue to feed innovation and adaptation of new and improve logistics systems and practices into the military, as occurs in other countries.
- The PLA has made a good start on its ability to project force globally with the Gulf of Aden

mission. We should expect China to build on this to develop greater capacity for offshore operations and to protect its national interests around the world. Long-distance logistics support will require foreign base access for replenishment, which we can expect China to continue to develop.

- U.S. military logistics cooperation with China, which has been significantly constrained for most of the last 20 years since the Tiananmen Square incident, could provide an area for development of cooperation and mutual reassurance of intentions. Deep-seated distrust will continue to make the U.S. Government (especially the Congress) hesitate to open up to China on logistics cooperation. The main concern is that such cooperation will help the PLA to improve its logistics system. U.S. constraints will not prevent the PLA from moving forward, but it can slow it down. Perhaps this is something from which we can take comfort. China will continue to develop and improve. The PLA will continue to learn from the U.S. military as well.

The chapters presented in this volume have demonstrated first, Chinese and PLA leaders have a strong sense of mission and concern for China's security and well-being (使命感和忧患意识). Second, the PLA is committed to the transformation in military affairs with Chinese characteristics. Third, the PLA is eager to learn from the U.S. military to expand and improve its operational capabilities. Finally, the PLA has made progress in its transformation and operational capabilities.

For a long time, American leaders have been surprised with the PLA's advances. This volume (and many of the previous volumes from past PLA conferences) show that these advances did not come out of the blue. Although much of the learning and many of the improvements are still far from what is desired (from Chinese expectations and American critiques), and some of the learning has even created contradictions for the PLA, these persistent and diligent learning practices will eventually bring the PLA to a higher level of proficiency in its capabilities. The emergence of a much more sophisticated PLA in the coming years should not be a surprise.

ENDNOTES - CHAPTER 1

1. In the literature on the territorial conflicts in the Pacific, "disputed islands" is a standard term. However, in Chinese discussions the term "stolen" is often used, because the Chinese argue that these territories were taken from China when it was under foreign invasions.

2. *China's National Defense in 2008*, Beijing, China: The Information Office of China's State Council, January 2009, available from *merln.ndu.edu/whitepapers/china_endlish208.pdf*.

3. Hu Jintao (胡锦涛), "Report to the 17th Party Congress," October 25, 2007.

4. *China's National Defense in 2008*, p. 8.

5. Wang Faan, (王法安), "坚持富国和强军统一, 在更高起点上推进强军战略 上, 中, 下" ("Stressing the Unity of Building a Prosperous Nation and Strong Military, Pursuing the Strategy of Strong Military at a Higher Level, Parts I, II, and III"), 国防 (*National Defense*,) Vols. 1, 2, and 3, 2008.

6. *China's Defense White Paper, 2006*.

7. Chinese leaders have clearly learned about this idea from the works of Abraham Maslow, who explains the hierarchy of human needs from survival to self-actualization. See his works in "A Theory of Human Motivation," *Psychological Review*, Vol. 50, No. 4, 1943, pp. 370-396; and *Motivation and Personality*, New York: Harper, 1954.

8. This is the title of Jiang Zemin's "Report to the 16th CCP National Congress" in November 2002. The CCP believes that the first 30 years of economic reform have laid a solid foundation for China's modernization drive. The first 20 years in the 21st century will be very critical for China's all-out development for a well-off society. See Zhang Baijia (章百家), "改革发展进入关键时期的几点思考" ("Several Thoughts on Reform and Development Entering a Critical Stage"),中国党政干部论坛 (*China Party and Government Officials' Forum*), April 19, 2007, available from *theory.people.com.cn/GB/49150/49152/5638700.html*.

9. See the visions put forward by Jiang Zemin in the CCP's 16th National Party Convention and by Hu Jintao in the CCP's 17th National Party Convention. See also China's Modernization Reports (中国现代化报告) from 2001 on.

10. "新年献词：在党的十七大精神指引下开创国防和军队现代化建设新局面" ("New Year's Day Message: Promote a New Situation in National Defense and Military Building Modernization under the Driving Spirit of the 17th Party Congress"), *PLA Daily*, January 1, 2008.

11. Deng Xiaoping (邓小平), *Selected Works of Deng Xiaoping, Vol. III*, Beijing, China: The People's Daily Online, June 4, 1985, available from *www.people.com.cn/english/dengxp/*.

12. Data from *World Bank Development Indicators*, constant 2005 U.S. dollars.

13. Sun Kejia (孙科佳), "实现富国与强军相统一—学习党的十七大报告有关重要论述" ("Bring About Unification of Making the Country Wealthy and the Military Powerful—Studying the Relevant Important Discussions in the 17th CPC National Congress Report"), 学习时报 (*Study Times*), No. 417, December 2007.

14. Chinese leaders chose to use the term "transformation" rather than "revolution" for several reasons. First, revolution suggests complete change whereas transformation means adaptation. Second, revolution usually comes as a sudden change while transformation makes gradual progress. Finally, and as a corollary to the first two, China wants to transform the PLA while retaining its "core values" such as its loyalty to the CCP and so on. The decision to use this term came all the way from President Jiang Zemin. See Xiong Guangkai (熊光楷), "论世界新军事变革趋势和中国新军事变革" ("On the Trend of Change in the World's New Transformation in Military Affairs and China's New Transformation in Military Affairs"), 外交学院学报 (*Journal of China Foreign Affairs University*), No. 76, June 2004; and Fang Gongli (房功利), 中国国防战略演变研究 (*A Study of the Evolution of the PRC's Defense Strategy*), Ph.D. Dissertation, Beijing, China: 中共中央党校 (The Central Party School) 2004, pp. 197-198.

15. See the following writings on the PLA analysts' comments. Sun Kejia (孙科佳), "试论中国特色军事变革" ("On Military Reform with Chinese Characteristics"), 军事科学 (*Military Science*), Vol. 16, No. 1, 2003; Sun Keijia (孙科佳), "中国特色的军事变革" ("Military Transformation with Chinese Characteristics"), Beijing, China: Changzheng Chubanshe (长征出版社), 2003; Pi Mingyong (皮明勇), "关注与超越: 中国军事改革历史透视" ("Concern and Surpassing: Perspective of the History of Military Reform in China"), cited in 南方周末 (*South China Weekend*), June 12, 2003; Peng Guangqian (彭光谦), "迎接新军事变革的挑战" ("Embrace the Challenge of Transformation in Military Affairs"), 瞭望新闻周刊 (*Liaowang Weekly News*), June 9, 2003; Wang Baocun (王保存), Wu Yujin (吴玉金), and Ku Guisheng (库桂生), "直面军事变革—中国将军纵论机遇和挑战" ("On Transformation in Military Affairs—Chinese Generals Discuss Opportunities and Challenges"), 瞭望周刊 (*Liaowang Weekly*), July 16, 2003. Professor Sun Kejia also notes that in the mid 1990s, the PLA's basic trainings were still bayonet drills and hand grenade throwing. Sun Kejia (孙科佳), 中国特色的军事变革 (Transformation in Military Affairs with Chinese Characteristics), Beijing, China: Changzheng Chubanshe, 2003, p. 185.

16. Xiong Guangkai (熊光楷), "关于新军事变革问题" ("On the New Revolution in Military Affairs"), 军事历史 (*Military History*), No. 4, 2003; Yao Youzhi (姚有志), "世界新军事变革的战略特征和

影响" ("The Strategic Character and Impact of World New Revolution in Military Affairs"), 国防技术基础 (*National Defense Technology Foundation*), No. 3, 2004.

17. Jiang Zemin (江泽民), "论国防和军队建设" (*On National Defense and Armed Forces Building*), Beijing, China: PLA Publishing, 2003, pp. 288-89.

18. See also Wang Wenrong (王文荣), "学习贯彻江主席重大战略思想, 积极推进中国特色的军事变革" ("Study and Implement President Jiang's Key Strategic Thought, Actively Pursue Transformation in Military Affairs with Chinese Characteristics"), Introduction in Sun Kejia (孙科佳), 中国特色的军事变革 (*Transformation in Military Affairs with Chinese Characteristics*), Beijing, China: Changzheng Chubanshe, 2003; and Sun's work itself.

19. Jiang Zemin (江泽民), 论国防和军队建设 (*On National Defense and Armed Forces Building*), Beijing, China: PLA Publishing, 2003, p. 82.

20. *Xinhuanet*, "解放军历次重大精简整编：兵力总数降至230万" ("PLA Major Downsizing Measures: Total Number Down to 230,000"), *China's National Defense in 2004*, *Defense White Paper*, July 31, 2009.

21. See Roy Kamphausen, Andrew Scobell, and Travis Tanner, eds., *The "People" in the PLA: Recruitment, Training, and Education in China's Military*, Carlisle, PA: Strategic Studies Institute, U.S. Army War College, 2008.

22. Jiang Zemin (江泽民), "Report to the 15th CCP National Congress," September 1997.

23. *China's National Defense in 2006*.

24. William S. Cohen, Secretary of Defense, *Annual Report to the President and the Congress*, Washington, DC: U.S. Government Printing Office, 1999, p. 122.

25. Liu Yazhou 刘亚洲, Lieutenant General and Vice Chief of Staff, PLAAF, "向美军学习" ("Learn from the U.S. Military"), *Lingdao Wencui*领导文萃 (*Leadership Digest*), No. 10, 2007.

26. Su Xisheng (苏希胜) *et al.*, "解放军国防大学科研部" ("Scientific Study and Research Office, PLA National Defense University), 军事变革中的新概念 (*New Concepts in the Transformation of Military Affairs*), Beijing, China: PLA Press, 2004. See also Wang Baocun (王保存), 世界新军事变革新论 (*A New Analysis on the New Transformation on Military Affairs in the World*), Beijing, China: PLA Press (解放军出版社), 2003; and Sun Kejia (孙科佳), 中国特色的军事变革 (*Transformation in Military Affairs with Chinese Characteristics*), Beijing, China: Changzheng Chubanshe (长征出版社), 2003.

27. Wang Baocun (王保存), "抓住我军'跨越式'发展机遇" ("Catch the Our Army's 'Leap Forward' Development Opportunity"), 瞭望周刊 (*Liaowang Weekly*), July 16, 2003. See also Liu Jixian (刘继贤), "世界新军事变革形势与应对思考" ("Some Thoughts on the Situation in and the Response to the New Revolution in Military Affairs in the World—Understandings from Studying Hu Jintao's Thought on the Revolution in Military Affairs"), 学习时报 (*Study Times*), June 11, 2007.

28. *The PLA Daily* (解放军报), September 15, 2006; Liu Jixian (刘继贤), "国防和军队建设改革的回顾与思考" ("Reflection on National Defense Development and Military Transformation"), 军事经济研究 (*Military Economy Studies*), No. 1, 2009; Lin Yong (林勇), "中国特色国防研究30年—中国特色军事变革篇" ("30 Years of Study on National Defense with Chinese Characteristics—Transformation in Military Affairs with Chinese Characteristics"), 军事历史研究 (*Military History Studies*), No. 4, 2008.

29. *Xinhua Net*, "专家解读非战争军事行动力量体系构建完成" ("Expert on the Completion of MOOTW Capability System"), May 14, 2009.

30. See Zhu Zhijiang (朱之江), "论非战争军事行动" ("On MOOTW"), 南京政治学院学报 (*Journal of PLA Nanjing Institute of Politics*), Vol. 19, No. 5, 2003.

31. Jin Yinan (金一南), "非战争军事行动'成中国军事力量应用的重要方式" ("'MOOTW' has become an important method for the use of Chinese military power"), 中国青年报 (*Chinese Youth Daily*), August 1, 2008.

32. See *PLA Daily* Reports, "兵马未动，法规先行" ("Before Setting the War Machine in Motion, Establish Rules and Regulations"), "让法规先行成为常态" ("Let Laws and Regulations Become the Basic Requirements"), and so on, March 18, 2009.

33. Xiao Tianliang (肖天亮), "关于非战争军事行动的理论思考" ("Thoughts on MOOTW"), 国防大学学报 (*Journal of National Defense University*), No. 5, 2008.

34. JFJB Staff Commentator, "重点加强核心军事能力建设" ("Put Emphasis on Strengthening Building of Core Military Capabilities"), *PLA Daily*, March 18, 2009.

35. *Xinhua Net*, "中国军队非战争军事行动力量体系初步构建完成" ("Chinese Military Has Preliminarily Established Systems for MOOTW"), May 13, 2009.

36. Jin Yinan (金一南), "非战争军事行动'成中国军事力量运用的重要方式" ("MOOTW Has Become an Important Aspect of Chinese Use of Military Force"), 中国青年报 (*Chinese Youth Daily*), August 1, 2008.

37. Yang Jinkui (杨金奎), "假如战争中遇上雪灾" ("Suppose a snow emergency came during wartime"), 解放军报 (*PLA Daily*), April 21, 2008, p. 6.

38. Kenneth W. Allen and Eric A. McVadon, *China's Foreign Military Relations*, A Center, Report #32, Washington DC: October 1999.

CHAPTER 2

THE PEOPLE'S LIBERATION ARMY AND THE CHANGING GLOBAL SECURITY LANDSCAPE

Paul H. B. Godwin

INTRODUCTION

This chapter assesses People's Liberation Army (PLA) views on the roles and responsibilities of the armed forces in China's changing global security landscape. It does so by focusing primarily on the years since December 2004, when at an expanded meeting of the Chinese Communist Party (CCP) Central Military Commission (CMC) Chairman Hu Jintao revised the armed forces' "historic missions." It was at this meeting that Hu Jintao stressed the "diversified military tasks" required by the PLA to respond effectively to the changes in China's security environment and provide more extensive support for Beijing's foreign policy.

Hu Jintao's revisions broadened and extended PLA missions in two ways. First, they expanded the PLA's defense mission beyond defending China's international borders and territorial claims. This process had been underway for some years, but as CMC Chairman, Hu Jintao provided the authoritative source for continuing and extending this process. Second, they placed greater importance on the PLA's nonwar roles and responsibilities than had previously been the case.[1] In essence, Hu Jintao directed the PLA's roles and missions be adjusted to the growing complexities of China's interaction with the 21st century world.

This adjustment recognized that China's military modernization programs had raised apprehensions across Asia and beyond about Beijing's strategic intent. These apprehensions threatened to undermine Beijing's core foreign policy objective of sustaining an international environment conducive to the continued growth and modernization of China's economy.

Assessment of these issues is organized into six major components and concludes with some speculations and policy implications for the United States. The chapter first provides an overview of PLA responses to Hu Jintao's revisions of the armed forces' roles and missions. This is followed by a discussion of PLA estimates of the global security environment it confronted in 2008 and the defense policy adopted in response to these estimates. The chapter then broadens its focus by discussing the PLA's response to Hu Jintao's expansion of the armed forces' missions. This analysis is followed by a review of PLA responses to specific Asia-Pacific security issues. These are divided into near-term concerns and long-term strategic concerns. The specific cases addressed are Taiwan, the Korean Peninsula, South and Central Asia, maritime territorial and resource disputes, and the United States and Japan in maritime Asia.

THE PLA AND CHINA'S NATIONAL SECURITY

As a continental power with extensive land and sea borders, the defense demands on China's armed forces are extensive. China's neighborhood is huge, composed of Northeast Asia, Russian-Asia, Central Asia, South Asia, Southeast Asia and maritime Southeast and East Asia. All of Asia converges on China, and Beijing's national security assessments have to enfold extensive, changing local security environments. With land borders of more than 22,000 kilometers (km) and maritime borders exceeding 18,000 km, collectively, touching on 20 neighboring states when continental frontiers and countries on adjoining seas are included, the PLA faces a potentially daunting task.[2] For the most part, these frontiers are now quiet and resolved, but there are maritime resource and territorial claims in the East and South China Seas that remain unresolved, particularly the difficult extensive border disagreements with India. Moreover, with the acquisition and deployment of nuclear weapons by India and Pakistan, together with the half dozen or so weapons evidently held by the Democratic People's Republic of Korea (DPRK), the nuclear weapons environment surrounding China has become more complex. When these developments are joined with the U.S. ballistic missile defense (BMD) programs, China's nuclear deterrence strategy confronts an increasingly difficult environment.

The point is that from Beijing's perspective, no matter how important it may be, China's defense requirements are not myopically focused on a potential military conflict over Taiwan that would likely involve U.S. military intervention. The demands on the PLA are broader than this single contingency. Not the least of these demands is created by the continuing distrust of the U.S. strategic intent beyond potential U.S. military intervention in a military confrontation over Taiwan. There remains apprehension that American strategic intent is to prevent China from achieving what Beijing perceives as its proper role in Asia.

The current statements of the PLA's responsibilities in China's security environment stem primarily from Hu Jintao's December 2004 speech. In the years since Hu's address to the CMC, extensive assessments of the armed forces' responsibilities have occurred in the military news media providing a reasonably solid base for assessing PLA views.[3] Judging from these appraisals, Hu Jintao's speech directed the PLA to assume a more expansive role in an increasingly complex national security environment.[4] This environment required the armed forces to prepare for the "diversified military tasks" stemming from the emerging mix of what were defined as traditional and nontraditional security threats.

A December 2008 *PLA Daily* article described the PLA's responsibilities in this manner:

> The pluralism of security threats brings about the pluralism of military operations. Our Army's historical mission requires that we not only safeguard the national survival interest, but also safeguard national development interest; not only safeguard territorial land, territorial waters and airspace security, but also safeguard the oceans, space and electromagnetic space security, as well as other aspects of national security. [We must] not only safeguard national security, but also actively participate in international and regional security cooperation, the United Nations peacekeeping, international counterterrorism, international humanitarian aid, and other actions in order to contribute to the maintenance of world peace. In other words, the army's diversified military tasks include both war operations and nonwar operations.[5]

Counterterrorism, United Nations Peacekeeping Operations (UNPKO), international disaster relief operations, regional security cooperation, and nonwar military operations were not all missions freshly minted by Hu Jintao. China's contributions to UNPKO had been increasing in the years before 2004, as had regional security cooperation through such organizations as the Association of Southeast Asian Nations (ASEAN) Regional Forum (ARF), the Shanghai Cooperation Organization (SCO). Counterterrorism had also formally entered the PLA portfolio in the post-September 11, 2001 (9/11) era after many years of such operations in Tibet and Xinjiang.

Hu Jintao's speech evidently sought to extend and integrate these components into a cohesive image of how PLA missions could be revised to contribute to a national security strategy reflecting China's increasing involvement in world affairs. Moreover, under Hu Jintao's direction, nontraditional and nonwar missions were becoming of growing importance. Certainly the most noticed of China's nonwar missions is the late 2008 decision dispatching a small PLA Navy (PLAN) flotilla to contribute to counterpiracy operations in the Gulf of Aden. This is the furthest from China's shores the PLAN has ever conducted a sustained operation.

Even as articles dissecting the demands placed on the armed forces by the requirement to effectively conduct diversified military tasks were spun out, there was also a call from military publications for the PLA to remain focused on its "core" military capability—warfighting. The PLA's core military role is seen as "the capacity to win local wars under informatized conditions."[6] The concern expressed was straightforward. As the PLA prepared for an increasing number of diverse military tasks, it was too easy to "relax core military capacity building and misread the relationship between core military capacity and other capabilities."[7] Whereas the PLA does have to participate in international and regional security cooperation, UNPKO, international counterterrorism, international humanitarian aid, disaster relief, and make other contributions to secure and maintain world peace, "we must never depart from the main line of 'fighting a war.'"[8] An article in *China's Defense* stated that even though "diversified military tasks" include war and nonwar operations, it was possible that improving nonwar capabilities might diminish "core military capability." The author pointedly noted an unspecified U.S. Army training and evaluation center's conclusion that "nonwar military actions, particularly peacekeeping operations, can lower the performance of crucial skills for war fighting."[9]

A pattern emerged over the years following Hu Jintao's "historic missions" speech where military authors and authors in military publications while supporting the CMC Chairman's directive on the PLA's "diversified tasks" ultimately stressed that defending national sovereignty, security, integrity, national interests, deterring war, defusing crisis, and containing wars that do erupt depend on the PLA's military capabilities — capabilities that of necessity had to be improved. As a February 2009 *PLA Daily* author wrote:

> At present, on the foundation of the traditional superiority in people's war, our nation has formed powerful domestic defense capabilities, and we are set free from the threat of large scale invasion. However, there is still a relatively wide gap between our overall military capability and the needs of national security and development; the function scope of military capability cannot keep up with the steps of national interests' development, and there is the prominent issue that its functional strength could not eliminate various kinds of security threats.[10]

A lengthy article in *China's Military Science* published by the PLA's premier research institution, the Academy of Military Science (AMS), stressed the same point

2 years earlier. After tracking in detail the development of the CCP's national security "theory" from Mao Zedong through Hu Jintao's revised "historical mission," the director of the AMS War Theory and Strategic Research Department, Major General Shou Xiaosong, writes of the PLA's needs in "entering the new century":

> For instance, by adjusting to the trend of national interest expansion and modern war development and under the precondition of sticking to the defensive nature of military strategy, we need to appropriately develop strategic offensive force and strategic projection force, increase the depth of our strategic defense, expand from defending territory toward defending national strategic space, and plan as a whole the security of territorial land, territorial seas, and territorial air space as well as the security of oceans, outer space, and electromagnetic space; ...[11]

General Shou later repeats the common "two incompatibles" assessment found among PLA authors:

> Compared with safeguarding the strategic needs of national security and the military development trends around the world, there is obvious inadequacy in China's military strategic capability and incompatibility between the level of military modernization and the requirements for winning wars under informatized conditions, effectively dealing with various kinds of security threats, and accomplishing diversified military tasks.[12]

For General Shou and the vast majority of military assessments, Hu's adjustment of the PLA's historic missions in support of China's changing national security environment and strategy, and the diversified tasks this adjustment required, demanded a more capable and modernized armed forces than existed, including the need to enhance the PLA's ability to deter war. General Shou identifies three key areas as priorities for enhancement: space systems, naval forces, and strategic nuclear deterrence and counterattack capabilities. He viewed deterrence, both strategic and conventional, as demanding a higher military requirement than winning wars, for it is based on the potential adversary recognizing China's military strength.[13]

THE PLA AND CHINA'S GLOBAL SECURITY ENVIRONMENT

China's 2008 *Defense White Paper*[14] laid out the themes that had received emphasis since Hu's speech. The most pressing difficulties confronting China's defense forces were seen as consequences of the increasing influence of military power on international relations.[15] International military competition was seen as intensifying as science and technological advances were driving the revolution in military affairs (RMA) to new and higher levels. "Some major powers" (read as the United States) were building up their alliances, accelerating the "transformation" of their armed forces with advanced technology weapons and equipment. Strategic nuclear forces, astronautics, ballistic missile defense systems, and global and tactical reconnaissance and surveillance are among the top priorities of these powers. Moreover, "some developing countries" (India?) were seen as seeking and acquiring advanced technology capabilities to increase the strength of their armed forces. Moreover, supporting diplomatic strategy with military power had become the accepted policy of essentially all countries, leading to regional arms races and severe challenges to the international arms control and nonproliferation regimes.

Even though the security situation in China's immediate neighborhood, the Asia-Pacific region, was viewed as stable, this stability was threatened by several factors. The global economic crisis was creating political instability in some countries, ethnic and religious discontent was intense, and competing territorial and maritime rights and interests remained severe. The United States had sharpened its focus on the region, was strengthening its military alliances, and enhancing its regional military capabilities. Non-traditional threats generated by terrorists and "separatist" forces, and the consequences of serious natural disasters were troubling the region. These threats to regional stability were made even more serious by the lack of an effective mechanism for regional security cooperation and coordination.

China's security environment was perceived as improving, but continued to confront long-term and complex security challenges. These stemmed from developed countries' economic, science, technology and military superiority, and from strategic maneuvering designed to contain China even as it suffers internally from separatist and hostile forces, including the East Turkistan, Tibet and Taiwan independence movements. The latter exacerbated by continuing U.S. sale of arms to Taiwan in what Beijing views as violation of the three Sino-American joint communiqués.

CHINA'S DEFENSE POLICY[16]

China's primary strategic objective is to foster a security situation essential for China's "peaceful development." This is no doubt Beijing's highest priority, for nothing would have graver political consequences and undermine China's national development goals more than a major war. Thus, the second component of Beijing's defense policy, which is to "take the initiative" in defusing crises and deterring war, is seen as essential to achieve China's highest strategic priority. Deterrence includes nuclear and conventional deterrence, with strategic nuclear deterrence requiring a "lean" but credible deterrent force. In addition to its deterrence and crisis defusing functions, this military strength must be enhanced to ensure the PLA can:

- Win local wars under informatized conditions.
- Maintain China's maritime, space, and electro-magnetic space security.
- Carry out tasks of counterterrorism, internal stability, emergency rescue, international peacekeeping, and military operations other than war.
- Provide the military strength supporting the diplomatic, economic, cultural, and legal instruments Beijing will employ to achieve its security objectives.

To ensure the security environment remains advantageous to the primary strategic objective of sustaining the development so crucial to China's future, Beijing declares it will continue participation in international security cooperation, promote the establishment of confidence and security building measures, and that the PLA will persist in conducting a variety of international military exchanges.

THE PLA AND CHINA'S FOREIGN POLICY: AN OMNIDIRECTIONAL FOREIGN MILITARY DIPLOMACY

A major focus of Hu Jintao's 2004 speech had been to outline how the PLA was to enlarge its role supporting China's foreign policy. He gave particular emphasis to the armed forces' nonwarfighting missions in supporting this foreign policy. In December 2008, General Liang Guanglie, a CMC member and China's Minister of Defense, published a *PLA Daily* article[17] of some length surveying PLA military diplomacy since "reform and opening up" began in late 1978, and outlining future directions as the PLA pursued its "omnidirectional" foreign military diplomacy. This diplomacy, he stated, was designed to support China's foreign policy through relations with foreign defense establishments, regional security cooperation and multilateral dialogues, military transparency, and what is referred to as "contributing to world peace and development." General Liang sees the PLA's omnidirectional military diplomacy as a success. The PLA now has military relations with more than 150 countries, has military attaches in 109 countries, hosts 98 countries' attaches, sends 200 military delegations abroad annually, and receives at least 200 delegations annually.

Most of his article is devoted to the progress in expanding and developing relations with foreign defense establishments. Perhaps because on becoming Director of the PLA General Staff Department in 2002 General Liang supervised the development of foreign military relations strategy for the PLA when relations with the United States and Japan were in the "midst of setbacks," this article is a self-assessment of his strategy's success and deficiencies. Certainly throughout the article, General Liang makes no attempt to conceal that rebuilding military relations with the United States and Japan was and remains difficult. Nor does he conceal that the PLA has gained from foreign military contacts. General Liang refers to the RMA as creating the most profound changes in military development in the history of man. By establishing "professional technical communications" with foreign militaries at multiple levels including military research universities, "work units" and headquarters, General Liang states that the PLA has expanded its understanding of the RMA and its implications. This has not only helped in the development of weapons and equipment, but has given the PLA a greater understanding of the military environment in which China's armed forces exist.

Although declaring that the PLA's "military foreign relations" were undertaken with individual countries regardless of their size and whether their military was advanced or backward, General Liang's article established priorities. Of first importance were relations with the United States' defense establishment. Links with the Russian military were given second priority. General Liang then proceeds to systematically lay out both the problems and progress the PLA has made in developing its relationships with foreign military establishments. His longest discussion is of the problems effecting relations with the U.S. military, which he defines as of great importance because of their significance to world peace and stability. Beginning with the deterioration of relations created by the PLA Navy's F-8 fighter collision with the U.S. Navy's (USN) EP-3 reconnaissance aircraft in April 2001, he tracks the gradual restoration of Sino-American military relations with the visit of General Guo Boxiong, a CMC

Vice-Chairman and Politburo member in July 2006. General Liang concludes his assessment lamenting the factors that yet restrain relations, primarily arms sales to Taiwan, with the arms package announced in October 2008 being the most recent sale to "seriously disrupt" military relations.

Military relations with Japan receive similar treatment. Relations gradually improved following Prime Minister Abe's October 2006 visit to China with the military exchanges and reciprocal ship visits of 2007 and 2008. General Liang placed special emphasis on the aid for victims of the Sichuan earthquake provided by Japan's defense ministry and brought to China by the Japan's Maritime Self-Defense Force (MSDF) destroyer *Sazanami's* Guangzhou port call in June 2008. General Liang was quite open in his assessment that reaching even this minimal level of military relations with Japan was extremely difficult and that considerable patience will be required to more fully develop military relations between the two countries.

Despite the overall maturity of military relations with individual European countries, such as the United Kingdom (UK) and France, General Liang notes there is no direct military contact with the European Union (EU). Presumably, he is referring to the Military Committee of the European Union (EUMC), chaired by a four-star flag officer and staffed by EU members' chiefs of defense or their military representatives. In assessing why this is the case, General Liang lays out a litany of recent tensions between China and the EU that have delayed military relations and the development of any sense of strategic partnership and trust. They are, not surprisingly, EU criticism and pressure on such issues as Tibet and the Dalai Lama, Taiwan, human rights, climate change, energy resources, and even the interference with Beijing's Olympic Torch Relay. Future progress, General Liang states, depends on eliminating the misunderstanding and suspicion that now pervades China's relations with the EU.

Military diplomacy with China's neighbors is seen as successful. With Russia, "mutual trust" is deepening as cooperation in international and regional affairs continues to be strengthened — mutual trust is not a term used in assessing military relations with the United States. With other neighboring countries, cooperative ties with their armed forces have been enhanced together with consultations over coastal defense and disputes over land and maritime territories. Since 2002, security mechanisms and consultations have been established with Mongolia, Vietnam, Indonesia, Malaysia, the Philippines, Singapore, Pakistan, and India, all of which contribute to the building of trust in military affairs with China's major neighbors.

These bilateral relations with neighbors are complemented by PLA involvement in regional security dialogues and mechanisms. General Liang points to PLA participation in the ARF, SCO, the Western Pacific Naval Symposium (WPNS), and the annual Shangri-La Dialogue.

As progress has been made in the PLA's military diplomacy efforts, General Liang asserts China's military establishment has grown more confident and that this is reflected in the PLA's increasing transparency. Not the least of this increasing transparency is the steady opening of PLA exercises to foreign military observers and the PLA's now frequent participation in combined exercises with foreign armed forces. These are not only regional bilateral exercises but also multilateral exercises with armed forces from outside the Asia-Pacific Region.

PLA NEAR-TERM CONCERNS

With cross-Strait tensions eased by the policies pursued by Ma Ying-jeou following his election to Taiwan's presidency, Beijing's concern over the outbreak of a cross-Strait military confrontation has declined. Hu Jintao's speech marking the 30th anniversary of Jiang Zemin's "Message to Compatriots in Taiwan" reflected this reduced concern by raising the need for cross-Strait confidence-building measures (CBM). Point VI of his text stressed that there was a need to "mitigate military security apprehensions" and that "in due course" the two sides should explore how to create "a mechanism of mutual trust for military security."[18] In May 2009, Yang Yi, spokesperson for the Taiwan Affairs Office (TAO) of China's State Council repeated this recommendation stating that in "good time" the two sides can conduct military exchanges and explore ways to construct a "mechanism of mutual trust."[19] This is not to suggest the PLA no longer prepares for a possible military confrontation over Taiwan with potential, if not probable, U.S. military intervention. It does suggest, however, that a cross-Strait war is not a near-term concern. This is particularly so when the political and economic relations between Taiwan and China are quickly expanding.

The Korean Peninsula.

Of more immediate concern to the PLA is the tense situation on the Korean peninsula. It is evident Beijing found the political and security consequences of DPRK's satellite launch in April 2009 and the second nuclear test in May extremely unsettling. In response to the United Nations Security Council's (UNSC) condemnation of the satellite launch, Pyongyang declared it would withdraw from the Six-Party Talks, would not be bound by any agreements it had made during the Six-Party Talks and would restore its nuclear facilities to ensure the DPRK could sustain its nuclear deterrent posture. Pyongyang then ended its cooperation with the International Atomic Energy Administration (IAEA), dismantled the monitoring equipment, removed the seals at its Yongbyon nuclear plant, and expelled IAEA inspectors and the U.S. nuclear disablement inspection group. On April 25, Pyongyang stated it had begun reprocessing the Yongbyon reactor's fuel rods. April 29 saw Pyongyang declare the Six-Party Talks dead, and that a second nuclear test and a ballistic missile launch were in the offing. A second nuclear test was conducted on May 25, together with the firing of short-range missiles. Moreover, Pyongyang announced it would no longer abide by the Korean Armistice Agreement of 1953. In effect, Pyongyang had totally rejected Beijing's position that peace and stability of the Korean peninsula can only be restored with the resumption of the Six-Party Talks and the denuclearization of the Korean peninsula through these negotiations.

Initial PLA opinions were expressed in no uncertain terms. General Chen Bingde, the PLA Chief of Staff, expressed his opposition to the nuclear test and missile launches saying they complicated the Korean peninsula situation, could prompt the Republic of Korea (ROK) to develop its own nuclear weapons, and would grant the U.S. additional grounds to intervene in regional affairs.[20] Rear Admiral Yang Yi, formerly Director of the PLA-NDU's [National Defense University's] Institute for Strategic Studies, summed up the entire period with: "The whole world is astounded and shocked by these actions of the DPRK." He described China's opposition to the nuclear test as violating UNSC resolutions, degrading the effectiveness of the international nuclear non-proliferation regime, and disturbing the peace and stability of northeast Asia.[21] Retired Major General Peng Guangqian, formerly of the PLA Academy of Military Science, was equally, if not more, critical of the DPRK in a *Huanqiu Shibao* commentary. Major General Peng criticized the view perhaps held in Pyongyang that nuclear arms will improve its international standing and strengthen the DPRK's national security. Rather than achieve these objectives, he asserts that nuclear weapons will put the DPRK in a "more precarious position." DPRK nuclear weapons, Peng declared, will provide increased incentive for preemptive attacks on itself. Indeed, the DPRK's nuclear arms do not provide either a first-strike capability or second-strike capability They provide only "greater instability and uncertainty for the DPRK's own security." Reflecting a view likely held widely in Beijing, Major General Peng argues Pyongyang's efforts should be devoted to building the DPRK's crumbling economy. This would not only improve the people's quality of life, but would lay the groundwork for enhancing the country's national power. Developing nuclear weapons, he said, can only detract from the DPRK's ability to strengthen its national power.[22]

PLA views of the situation on the Korean peninsula were clear enough. What was not evident is how Beijing would ultimately respond to a DPRK that consistently pursues policies that not only serve to destabilize the Korean peninsula, but which threaten the peace and security of Northeast Asia. A nuclear-armed DPRK does not serve China's interests any more than it serves the interests of the region. This is especially so when Pyongyang confronts a possibly destabilizing succession crisis. There are indications that China's future policy toward the DPRK is in flux.[23] First, there is a more open debate on China's future policies toward the DPRK than has occurred in past years. Some express the view that Beijing's policies should not change because the DPRK remains a strategic asset. Other views propose that the DPRK has become a strategic liability; therefore Beijing must become much tougher on Pyongyang to make it more accommodating to Chinese interests.

What must be of most concern to the PLA, however, is what missions it could be required to perform should a succession crisis generate severe instability in the DPRK.[24] China would prefer any intervention to come under the auspices of the UN. If the UN cannot act quickly enough, then China could take unilateral action with the PLA assigned the missions of restoring stability and providing humanitarian relief for what would likely be a flood of refugees. The PLA is also reportedly concerned about the possibility that fissile materials and nuclear weapons could end up in the wrong hands, and that damage to nuclear facilities could result in nuclear contamination. An additional mission therefore would be to respond to any nuclear contamination problem and prevent fissile material and nuclear weapons from falling into unauthorized and potentially criminal control.

Such instability and potential chaos, however, could lead to more than the massive flow of refugees into China and the nuclear weapons and fissile materials danger Beijing fears. It could well result in the intervention of ROK forces and quite possibly forces of the United States deployed in the ROK. Even if not an effort to reunify the peninsula but a stabilizing and policing mission, Beijing would fear the intent was reunification. Indeed it would be difficult for the ROK government to explain that its forces had undertaken the intervention to help put the DPRK together again.[25] Given what is a most probable concern in Beijing, PLA intervention beyond restoring and sustaining order could be seen as countering a ROK and U.S. presence.

Despite what could well become a perilous situation, Rear Admiral Yang Yi was reflecting Beijing's risk-averse view on how to most effectively respond to the delicate situation Pyongyang has created when he recommended that all the countries involved in the current crisis remain calm and avoid any actions that might worsen the situation. Political and diplomatic means are declared the only way to resolve the dilemma created. Moreover, the DPRK's sovereignty must be respected, as must Pyongyang's security concerns. When Pyongyang has returned to the Treaty on the Non-Proliferation of Nuclear Weapons (NPT), the DPRK's right to the peaceful use of nuclear energy must be assured.[26] Put another way, Beijing's view seems to be that more forceful responses to Pyongyang's actions will make an extremely volatile situation even worse. Such an assessment was evident during General Liang's visit to the DPRK in November 2009. Despite earlier harsh words by senior and retired PLA officers, *China Daily* reported the Defense Minister's speech at the welcoming banquet as including "No force on Earth can break the unity of the armies and peoples of the two countries, and it will last forever."[27]

PLA LONG-TERM STRATEGIC CONCERNS

Once one moves beyond the situations across the Taiwan Strait and the Korean Peninsula, PLA concerns become more long-term and strategic in their focus. Whether these concerns originate in South and Central Asia, a potentially militarily powerful Russia in Asia, conflicting maritime and territorial claims in the East and South China Seas, a militarily assertive Japan, issues with the United States over what is legally permissible in terms of foreign military activities in China's maritime Exclusive Economic Zones (EEZ) and air space beyond the accepted 12-mile limit of sovereignty, the effectiveness of China's nuclear deterrent or United States' long-term intentions toward China, these are not issues where the PLA anticipates a near-term major military confrontation. Certainly, the PLA must be prepared for a show of force when Beijing believes it is necessary to demonstrate China's position on any particular issue, but not a war. These, however, are the strategic issues that appear to be of most concern to the PLA. It is these long-term strategic concerns that now drive China's military modernization programs and have driven much of the PLA's regional military diplomacy.

What China confronts is a classic "security dilemma" where what Beijing views as security policies and military modernization programs designed to equip and train the PLA to perform defensive missions are viewed by other governments as potentially if not probably offensive in their purpose. Beijing is fully aware of this dilemma and has been for a number of years as its constant battle against the "China threat" thesis demonstrates. Most recently, for example, in an assessment of Japan's 2009 *Defense White Paper*, a *PLA*

Daily article criticized the document's judgment that PLA modernization programs may threaten regional and Japanese security.[28]

Nonetheless, Beijing and the PLA must accept some responsibility for this condition. Senior PLA officers such as Major General Shou Xiaosong cited earlier[29] have been quite outspoken about China's need to strengthen its strategic offensive forces and force projection capabilities and to increase the depth of China's strategic defense, including outer space. Among the more worrisome concepts to emerge from Hu Jintao's revision of the PLA's "historic missions" is the commitment to "safeguard national development interest."[30] It is quite unclear where this mission takes the PLA. It certainly does not appear to be limited to defense of China's sovereignty. When these assessments are combined with PLA modernization programs, a potentially more aggressive China seems quite plausible. General Shou, however, was most likely not thinking in expansionist terms. His view would be driven by what he saw as the requirements for a more effective defense of China. That is, China's strategic nuclear force is being strengthened to retain its deterrent value in a more complex environment that includes not only ballistic missile defenses but also more nuclear powers. The need to increase the depth of China's defense perimeter will be seen as stemming from the increasing range and accuracy of advanced precision guided munitions. Strengthening PLA force projection capability will be driven by the simple fact that this capability is currently so limited, and space defense is needed to offset the capabilities of China's most powerful potential adversary—the United States whose capabilities are seen as currently dominating space. This dilemma will not be easily resolved. Most likely, China's long-term strategic concerns will heighten the consequences of the security dilemma.

South and Central Asia: India.

The suspicions infecting Sino-Indian relations are impossible to avoid. They are perhaps best illustrated by a reported March 2009 Indian military exercise at a time Sino-Indian relations were at a high point. The *Hindustan Times*[31] reported that India had conducted a secret 3-day exercise called "Divine Matrix" designed on the assumption that a "nuclear-armed China would attack India by 2017." Following a 6-month study of various potential scenarios, the scenario selected had China employing information warfare to disrupt India prior to launching a military offensive. It would not be a nuclear war but a short, quick conventional operation designed to grant China dominant position in the region. A week later, *China Daily* reported the Foreign Ministry spokesman, Qin Gang, at a press conference expressed surprise at the report because the leaders of China and India had already agreed that the two countries did not pose a threat to each other but would "treat each other as partners."[32] Even so, in an August 2009 lecture to the National Maritime Foundation in New Delhi, India's senior military officer, Chairman of the Chiefs of Staff Committee (COSC) and Chief of the Naval Staff (CNS) Admiral Sureesh Mehta, would state that "coping with China will certainly be one of our primary challenges in the years ahead." He specifically referred to China's growing footprint in the Indian Ocean region. Yet, in the same lecture he also recommends that cooperation with China rather than competition or conflict was the better policy because

India does not match China in economic strength, national infrastructure, or military spending. Nor, he declared, does India plan to match China's military capabilities in either conventional or nonconventional arms.[33]

The suspicions contaminating Sino-Indian relations derive from the competing territorial claims that led to a brief war in 1962. That war created the tensions that continue despite a steady improvement of relations set in motion in the 1980s, particularly with Indian Prime Minister Rajiv Gandhi's visit to Beijing in 1988. Sino-Indian border disputes show no sign of resolution today despite the confidence-building measures agreed to in 1996 and ratified in 1997 together with high-level meetings on border questions that have served to keep the frontier quiet despite frequent charges from New Delhi that Chinese forces violate Indian territory by crossing the Line of Actual Control (LAC). Relations suffered a setback in 1998 when India's nuclear weapons programs were defined as a deterrent against China following the tests of nuclear devices. *PLA Daily* responded by declaring that the nuclear tests exposed India's ambition to become the region's hegemon.[34] No doubt India's nuclear weapons programs continue as a source of concern for China as China's do for India, thereby adding to their mutual suspicions.

Pakistan has been India's bête noir since the day of its founding and the brutal transition period separating the two sovereignties, and China has been Pakistan's steadfast supporter for decades. Until the early 1990s, Beijing's strategic objective was to keep India occupied with a threat that would distract India's military from the northern border with China. China was crucial to Pakistan's nuclear weapons[35] and missile programs and a provider of Islamabad's conventional arms. Despite the more neutral stand Beijing has taken for more than a decade and more on such issues as Pakistan's claims to Kashmir, New Delhi remains concerned that China's relationship with Pakistan could once more change. This would depend on Beijing's view of India, which in turn depends upon China's political objectives in South Asia and the Indian Ocean.

India has the most powerful Asian naval presence in the Indian Ocean and clearly does not wish to see this change. Despite Beijing's participation as a "dialogue partner" in the Indian Ocean Rim Association for Regional Cooperation (IORARC),[36] China's naval focus has been and likely remains on the West Pacific. Beyond the possibility of a military confrontation across the Taiwan Strait where U.S. military intervention is possible, no matter how remote this may currently be, there is good reason for China's naval programs to remain focused on the West Pacific. There are maritime and territorial disputes in the East and South China Seas, and the U.S. forward posture in Asia largely depends on its naval presence and access to bases and facilities in the Western Pacific. But, from India's particular strategic perspective, China's energy flow from the Middle East and Africa, together with its commercial and trade developments with Africa, make the Indian Ocean of growing strategic interest to China.[37] Hence, New Delhi's worry that these interests and the consequent concern over China's sea lines of communication (SLOC) from East Africa to China's east coast ports will divert Beijing's strategic focus from the West Pacific to the Indian Ocean regions. Indeed, there is a segment of Chinese SLOC vulnerability analyses that does focus on India's potential threat to China's most important oil shipping lane.[38] For this reason, India pays close attention to any Chinese activities that would grant Beijing intelligence collection facilities and access to ports in the Indian Ocean region. Particular attention has been focused on reported naval facilities, radars, and signal-intelligence collection posts constructed by China along Myanmar's coast, on the Cocos Islands, and the new port of Gwadar on Pakistan's coast.

Beijing's strategic goals in South Asia writ large are difficult to discern. On the one hand, cooperating with India serves China's interests well. Beijing nonetheless obviously views India's deepening defense-related links with the United States with concern. China's response to these expanding defense ties has been one of making Beijing's unease clear while simultaneously avoiding the charge that India has become a U.S. ally. For example, on June 28, 2005, the U.S. Secretary of Defense and India's Minister of Defense signed the "New Framework for the U.S.-India Defense Relationship."[39] The English language edition of *People's Daily* on July 7 published an unsigned commentary on this development that had appeared a week earlier in the *Global Times,* a subsidiary of *People's Daily*, entitled "Washington Draws India in Against China."[40] The commentary asserts that the agreement is "partly intended to diminish China's influence in the region and to safeguard and expand U.S. strategic interest in Asia." Nevertheless, citing India's Defense Minister Pranab Mukherjee, the commentary continues by stating that India is suspicious of U.S. intentions and has no intention of joining an India-U.S. strategic alliance against China.

Beijing, perhaps partially in response to the U.S. initiative upgrading American defense links with India, signed a memorandum of understanding (MOU) with New Delhi in 2006 committing the two countries' military institutions to a program of combined exercises; an annual defense dialogue between the two defense establishments; and collaboration in anti-piracy and counterterrorism operations, search-and rescue exercises, and recurring military exchanges.[41] This MOU built on an already expanding pattern of Sino-Indian military contacts.[42] The two navies had conducted their first combined exercise off Shanghai in November 2003 — a search and rescue exercise. This was followed by another search and rescue exercise in the Arabian Sea off the Malabar coast in 2005, and Chinese observers were invited to the Indian Army's exercises that year. At China's invitation, India sent observers to the SCO's combined exercise "Peace Mission 2005," where Russian and Chinese units formed the largest contingents. 2007 saw yet another Sino-Indian combined naval exercise off Qingdao. Following the MOU, the first Sino-Indian defense dialogue was held in Beijing in November 2007, and their first ground force combined exercise, "Hand-in-Hand 2007," was held in Yunnan Province during December. Combined exercises and dialogue between senior military officers continue. These exercises parallel India's exercises with U.S. forces, suggesting that New Delhi has crafted a course of military diplomacy designed to enhance India's gains without offending either China or the United States.

It seems evident that both China and India see their mutual suspicions and potential strategic competition as best managed by close military and political ties. As New Delhi and Beijing know full well, military confrontation would serve neither country's interests. Close military and political linkages that encourage frequent dialogue allows both to keep a finger on the pulse of the other, even as suspicion of each other's long-term strategic intent remains. This is reflected in the recent decision by Beijing and New Delhi to raise the status of their long-standing border talks to a "strategic dialogue."[43] This agreement emerged from the 13th round of boundary talks held in August 2009 headed by India' National Security Adviser M. K. Narayanan and Chinese State Counselor Dai Bingguo. In these talks, boundary issues did not dominate the discussion but broadened to include the Afghanistan-Pakistan situation, global issues, trade, counterterrorism, and an agreement to establish a hotline between New Delhi and Beijing. With Dai Bingguo also heading the Chinese delegation to the U.S.-China Strategic-Economic Dialogue (SED), New Delhi is undoubtedly pleased that Beijing holds India in such high esteem. Moreover, closer Indian defense links with the United States did not trigger increased Sino-Indian tensions but contributed to improved relations.

Central Asia: The Shanghai Cooperation Organization.

China's contemporary security concerns with Central Asia emerged with the 1991 dissolution of the Soviet Union.[44] The disintegration of the Union of Soviet Socialist Republics (USSR) created both new states on China's inner Asian frontier and a weakening of Moscow's influence in the region. China sought and gained mutually agreed upon and demilitarized borders with Russia and the newly independent states of Kazakhstan, Kyrgyzstan and Tajikistan. The instrument created to implement China's strategy was the Shanghai Five formed in 1996 by China, Russia, Kazakhstan, Kyrgyzstan, and Tajikistan. Uzbekistan joined the five

when they renamed themselves the Shanghai Cooperation Organization (SCO) in 2001.[45] In following
years, Mongolia, Iran, Turkmenistan, Pakistan, and
India received observer status in the SCO. In 2009, Sri
Lanka and Belarus became the SCO's first "dialogue
partners." With these peripheral partners, the SCO's
range of associated members ranges from Central
Asia to Eastern Europe and the Indian Ocean.

Although far from a cohesive organization due to
differences among the members, the SCO has developed security programs focused on defeating terrorist
action or a mass uprising. All member states fear such
crises to some extent, and combined military exercises
to counter these emergencies have been held with China and Russia in the lead. The first combined exercise,
"Peace Mission 2005," was held in China's Shandong
Province. "Peace Mission 2007" was held on Russia's
Chelyabinsk military exercise area in southern Russia.
"Peace Mission 2009" was conducted on the PLA's
Taonan exercise area in Jilin Province. These exercises also demonstrated that China's relationship with
at least one of the four Central Asian SCO members
shows signs of being stressed. Chinese units from the
Lanzhou Military Region (MR) assigned to the SCO
military exercise "Peace Mission 2007" were denied
passage across Kazakhstan to reach the Chelyabinsk
exercise area on Kazakhstan's northern border—the
most direct route. With this denial, these PLA units
had to detour through China's northeast and Russia's
Trans-Baykal region to reach the exercise area.[46]

The war in Afghanistan adds to the SCO's troubles
through its combination of terrorism, drug trafficking,
and religious extremism that threaten the region's stability. While SCO member states do have an interest
in restoring Afghanistan's stability, their participation

in rebuilding the country has been limited despite Afghanistan President Karzai's call for their assistance. China is the largest investor along with Kazakhstan, which has also made some significant investment. China's largest venture is the U.S. $4 billion invested to develop the Aynak copper mines south of Kabul. Beijing's single military contribution to Afghanistan began only this year with the mine clearing training provided the Afghan National Army at the PLA University of Science and Technology in Nanjing.[47]

Notwithstanding their interest in a stable Afghanistan, both Russia and China view the U.S. presence in Central Asia with distrust.[48] It is not only a U.S. military presence that leads to Russian and Chinese suspicion. American support for democratizing regional political institutions is unwelcome by all SCO members. These suspicions and concerns led to the SCO's call at its June 2005 Astana, Kazakhstan, summit for a Washington timeline specifying when the United States would withdraw from Central Asia. This demand was followed almost immediately by Uzbekistan's ejection of U.S. forces from its Karshi-Kanabad air base.[49]

Base issues were to be a continuing U.S. problem. In February, 2009, after receiving $2 billion in aid from Russia, Kyrgyzstan informed the United States it was ending American access to Manas air base — the most important base facility the United States has in Central Asia for sustaining Afghanistan operations. The United States then paid $180 million to keep the base open. Moscow responded by successfully pressuring Bishkek for a second Russian base near Osh in southern Kyrgyzstan. Demonstrating the lack of common security views among the Central Asia states, Uzbekistan raised objections to a new Russia base, even though it is a member together with Tajikistan, Kazakhstan, Belarus, and Armenia in the Russian-dominated Collective Security Treaty Organization. Views in Tashkent were not only that a second Russian base was unnecessary, but the new base would be justification for closer U.S.-Uzbek cooperation.[50] Given that Uzbekistan had ejected the United States from the Karshi-Kanabad air base in 2005, opposition to a new Russian base in the region and suggestions of greater cooperation with the United States imply as much concern with a dominant Russian presence as American influence. Furthermore, all five Central Asia States are members of the North Atlantic Treaty Organization's (NATO) Partnership for Peace (PfP), with NATO providing security assistance to all of them, including the four SCO members.

China's security interests in Central Asia and the SCO's role in these interests seem clear enough, although Beijing's particular priorities within these interests are not so clear.[51] Beijing has made it evident that Russia cannot treat China as a junior partner in this arrangement. Moreover, the SCO provides Beijing an instrument by which China and Russia can coexist in Central Asia. Beijing has also demonstrated that it can form an international security mechanism not based on Western principles. China's perhaps overriding security interest served by the SCO is in preventing transnational terrorism taking root in the region and infecting Xinjiang, where Beijing faces serious potential unrest from Uighur separatists. Beyond the security interests, China's economic penetration into Central Asia through trade, investments, and especially its growing need for energy grants Beijing influence Moscow cannot match. In this sense, China now has a significant role in Russia's "near abroad."

The SCO nonetheless allows both to pursue their individual interest and concerns within a framework of cooperation.

Maritime Asia: Territorial and Resource Disputes.[52]

China is involved in a number of East Asian maritime territorial and resource disputes, with Taiwan joining China in Beijing's claims. In the South China Sea, China claims all the Paracel and Spratly Islands, as does Vietnam. The Philippines and Malaysia also claim some islands and reefs in the Spratlys. Brunei has claimed an "exclusive fishing zone" that includes a reef in the southern Spratlys but has made no claim to the reef itself. Indonesia does not claim any of the Spratly Islands, but the oil and gas fields surrounding its Natuna Islands extend into South China Sea waters claimed by China. Taiwan occupies and has built a paved 3,773-foot runway on the largest island in the Spratlys known as Taiping Dao by Chinese and otherwise as Itu Aba. This one-half mile square island has the only natural water supply in the Spratlys. China, Malaysia, the Philippines, and Vietnam occupy some 50 other South China Sea islets and reefs. Additionally, China and Vietnam have unresolved border disputes in the Gulf of Tonkin known as the Beibu Gulf to China. In the East China Sea, China's most serious dispute is with Japan over territorial and seabed resource claims that include the Diaoyu/Senkakus Islands and the Chunxiao oil and gas field.

Beyond the territorial claims and the important oil, natural gas, and fisheries resources they encompass, the South China Sea is a maritime crossroads for critical regional SLOCs serving the Koreas, Japan, and China as much as they do Southeast Asia's trading nations. More than half of the world's merchant ships cross the South China Sea transiting the Malacca, Sunda, and Lombok Straights. The cargo carried by this shipping is dominated by oil and liquid natural gas.

China's strategic interest in the South China Sea is reflected in the construction of a new naval base near Sanya on Hainan Island complementing the South China Sea air base on Woody Island. In addition to supporting surface combatants, the Sanya naval base has underground facilities for submarines, making the South China Sea a transit route for both nuclear-powered attack (SSN) and ballistic missile (SSBN) submarines. [53] Thus, although the South China Sea SLOC is critically important to all of maritime East Asia, and the resources it contains serve Southeast Asia as much they do China, Beijing has taken a course of action designed to affirm its military superiority in this regional sea.

China has entered into various bilateral agreements on joint development of South China Sea resources and to peaceful resolution of disputes, including an ASEAN-wide "Code of Conduct" where all 10 signatories agreed to pursue diplomatic solutions to territorial disputes. Nonetheless, in all these agreements Beijing's position has remained constant: China's sovereignty over the Paracel and Spratly Islands and their adjacent waters is indisputable.[54] Beijing thus agrees to negotiate while insisting that on sovereignty questions there is nothing to negotiate. What can be negotiated is joint development of South China Sea resources and scientific explorations. It seems that as the most powerful military force in the South China Sea, Beijing believes it can dictate terms because no regional state can or is willing to confront China militarily. Even so, Chinese press reports have bitterly warned against Vietnam's planned acquisition of 12 Su-30 MK2 aircraft and six Kilo-class submarines from Russia, complaining they threaten the Malacca Strait SLOC.[55] Thus no resolution to South China Sea disputes appears probable in the near-term. No doubt the Southeast Asian states welcome China's participation in the various ASEAN forums, the several bilateral "Defense and Security Conferences" it has arranged with Southeast Asian countries, and the professional exchanges generated by the PLA's military diplomacy. Thus far, however, these have made little or no contribution to resolving the South China Sea territorial and resource disputes that disturb the region.

Beijing's most contentious issues in the East China Sea are with Tokyo over seabed resources and competing claims to some small uninhabited islands and reefs known to China as the Diaoyu Islands but administered by Japan as the Senkaku Islands. The connection between these issues is the delimitation of Exclusive Economic Zones (EEZ) and continental shelf declarations by China and Japan.

Chinese and Japanese claims[56] to the Diaoyu/Senkakus are indicated by their inclusion in their respective 1996 EEZ and continental shelf declarations. China claims a continental shelf that extends to the Okinawa trough based on the prolongation of its land territory, thereby encompassing the Diaoyu/Senkaku Islands. Japan claims an EEZ that extends to the median line dissecting the East China Sea, thus encompassing the Senkaku/Diaoyu Islands. China does not recognize the Japanese median line. Because both delimitation methods are recognized under the UN Convention on the Law of the Sea (UNCLOS), it does not provide any resolution to this disagreement.

The Chunxiao gas field dispute emerges from this disagreement. Beijing argues that the Chunxiao gas field is five km west of even Japan's claimed EEZ, so it must be in the Chinese EEZ. Tokyo argues that the Chunxiao gas field and other related East China Sea gas fields extend to the east of the median line into its EEZ; therefore Japan is entitled to a share of the Chunxiao field's resources. Four years of negotiations led to a June 2008 agreement providing for a 2,700 km joint development zone (JDZ) that essentially bisects the median line used by Japan to establish its East China Sea EEZ. Joint exploration of this zone is to be conducted on the principle of "mutual benefit." As of November 2009, however, there has been no progress in either the conclusion of the treaty that would formalize the agreement or Japanese participation in exploiting the Chunxiao gas field.[57]

Despite the significantly improved relations between Tokyo and Beijing, including military relations to be discussed below, as with the South China Sea disputes it is highly unlikely that Japan and China will resolve the issues dividing them any time soon. What does seem evident is that China's naval programs are designed in part to ensure that Beijing's ability to defend its maritime interests in both the South and East China Seas is clearly recognized.

Maritime Asia: The United States.

While South and Central Asia present China and the PLA with long-term strategic concerns they cannot ignore, it is in maritime Asia they confront their most serious apprehensions. Here the primary concern is not the maritime territorial and resource disputes China has with various competing claims in the East and South China Seas, although these are important in terms of the PLA protecting China's sovereignty and resources. The PLA's primary apprehensions focus directly on U.S. strategic intentions toward the region and China's place in the region. As China's 2008 *Defense White Paper* stated the problem with an obvious but unstated reference to the United States:

> China is faced with the superiority of the developed countries in economy, science and technology, as well as military affairs. It also faces strategic maneuvers and containment from the outside while having to face disruption and sabotage by separatist and hostile forces from the inside.[58]

This statement reflects a perception widely held among Chinese policymakers and the PLA that the strategic objective of the United States is to restrain the development of China's economic, diplomatic, and military capabilities, particularly in Asia.[59]

In Beijing's eyes, there is good reason to have such apprehensions. PLA researchers read official U.S. documents where U.S. "hedging" against China's growing military capabilities are evident. Fan Gaoyue of the PLA-AMS [Academy of Military Science] and Rear Admiral Yang Yi of the PLA-NDU, reporting on the latest U.S. *National Defense Strategy* published in June 2008, saw the strategy as treating China as a potential threat. Rear Admiral Yang Yi was quoted as stating: "From US perspective, China's development is a threat to its hegemony."[60] Nor do the annual reports on China's military capabilities released by the Office of the Secretary of Defense provide any less of a menace. The "Executive Summary" of the 2009 report states:

China's ability to sustain military power at a distance remains limited, but its armed forces continue to develop and field disruptive military technologies, including those for anti-access/area-denial, as well as for nuclear, space, and cyber warfare, that are changing regional military balances and that have implications beyond the Asia-Pacific region.[61]

There is no question that those who drafted this report have reason to make such a judgment. But, from the PLA's point of view, they overstate its capabilities and demonstrate little recognition of the security environment perceived by Beijing. From the PLA's vantage point, the U.S. armed forces are not only vastly superior in all realms of military operations from space to ground warfare, but the technological distance between them and the PLA is increasing. Moreover, the U.S. build-up of its forces in the West Pacific has a hostile purpose, with one Chinese report noting that the United States now deploys more than half of its nuclear-powered aircraft carriers and submarines, Aegis destroyers, and strategic bombers in the Asia-Pacific region.[62] Such hostile intent, the PLA insists, can be seen in the constant aerial and ship-based surveillance conducted by the United States on China's maritime perimeter with particular focus on military facilities. China demonstrates its opposition to these reconnaissance missions conducted within its 200 mile EEZ by harassing them, often aggressively. In part this harassment reflects the PLA's frustration that when the issue is raised at meetings of the Sino-American Military Maritime Consultative Agreement (MMCA) the United States insists the missions are legal as the United States is exercising its freedom of navigation.[63] Most recently, Lieutenant General Ma Xiaotian, a Deputy Chief of the PLA General Staff, raised the issue at an

August 2009 meeting of the MMCA and received the U.S. response he no doubt anticipated, based on past experience.[64]

PLA perception that defending China from sea attack is difficult should not be overlooked. As *The Science of Military Strategy* states:

> Although China is a country with large territorial waters, our sea area is closed or half-closed. It is surrounded by the longest chain of islands in the world, including the Aleutian Islands, the Islands of Japan and Islands of the Philippines. And it is connected with the outside world through the Korean Strait, water channels of the Ryuku, Taiwan Strait, Bashi Channel, Strait of Malacca and Sunda Straits.[65]

China's strategic analysts view this island chain as blocking PLA Navy access to the open ocean, and the United States as the most probable naval power to invoke this blocking strategy. The deployment of more than 50 percent of U.S. Naval aircraft carriers, submarines, and destroyers to the Pacific Ocean area would be viewed by Chinese analysts as supporting this assumption.

Yet another important PLA apprehension is the consequence of advances in U.S. ballistic missile defenses for China's strategic deterrent[66] The apprehension expressed, for example by Professor Wang Zhongchun of the PLA-NDU and just about all other Chinese analysts, is that when the BMD system has been fully developed, the United States will have both a strategic offense and strategic defense capability that will undermine China's strategic deterrent, based as it is upon a small number of nuclear weapons. This, of course, is read by China as requiring mobile land-based and submarine-based weapons to ensure the credibility of its strategic nuclear deterrent. For the PLA, whether measured by conventional military arms or strategic nuclear weapons, the United States has far the most powerful and capable armed forces accessible to the Asia-Pacific region. Accordingly, whereas there is a renewed and lively debate among Chinese scholars as to whether U.S. power is declining because of its economic crisis and the invasions of Iraq and Afghanistan,[67] for the PLA American military superiority remains a continuing concern.

Maritime Asia: Japan.

The U.S. military posture in the Asia-Pacific region is significantly enhanced by its security link with Japan. The base facilities provided by Japan are essential for the United States to sustain its forward deployed forces. Japan thus presents a complex issue for China and the PLA. On one hand, the U.S.-Japan security alliance diminishes the possibility that Japan will emerge as a powerful independent and potentially nuclear-armed military force. On the other, there is the experience of Japan's wars with China going back to the late 19th century and the brutal behavior of Japan's occupying forces in World War II. This experience is exacerbated by what Beijing views as Tokyo's failure to fully apologize for its past invasions and vicious treatment of the Chinese people joined with Japanese school textbooks that tend to whitewash this behavior. Visits of Japanese officials to the Yasukuni shrine honoring Japan's war dead, but which also contains the remains of 14 Class A war criminals from World War II, serve to remind China of all its historical grievances. Ongoing territorial and resource conflicts in the East China Sea serve only to enhance China's wariness of Japan. Moreover, the PLA knows full well that Japan's defense forces remain the best equipped and best trained of Asia's armed forces. As a U.S. ally, Japan comes under the protection of U.S. strategic nuclear weapons, which nullifies whatever advantage the PLA's strategic forces may have had in countering Japan's conventional superiority.

Given the apprehension with which each eye the other, Beijing's increasing influence in Asia beginning in the 1990s, together with advances in China's military capabilities, were bound to create difficulties in Sino-Japanese relations. These developments were paralleled by Tokyo's closer security arrangements with the United States in the administrations of both Presidents Clinton and Bush, which would appear to expand Japan's strategic role in Asia. Japan's support for the United States by providing MSDF refueling capabilities in the Indian Ocean for U.S. Naval forces conducting Afghanistan operations and the 2004 deployment of Ground Self-Defense Forces (GSDF) to Iraq, even in a noncombat role, suggested a much more active Japanese security role outside its home waters.

The dilemma faced by Beijing, however, is that increased tensions with Japan do not serve China's interests. Beijing's national security strategy is grounded on the strategic objective of maintaining an international environment conducive to sustaining China's national development. In the Asia-Pacific region this is essentially a "good neighbor" policy. Tensions and competition with Japan do not serve this policy well. As Robert Sutter's assessment has observed, the deterioration in Sino-Japanese relations over the years 2001-06 can in part be attributed to the status given Japan in China's defense policies outlined in the *Defense White Papers* of 2004 and 2006.[68]

The contrast between the treatment of Japan in the 2006 and 2008 *Defense White Papers* on this point is notable. The 2006 *Defense White Paper* states that the United States and Japan are strengthening their alliance to achieve operational integration while Tokyo seeks to revise Japan's constitution to permit collective self-defense as it builds a more externally-oriented defense posture.[69] The 2008 *Defense White Paper*'s assessment of China's security situation does not even mention Japan. The United States is charged with "further consolidating its military alliance" without any reference to Japan.[70] It is unlikely that Beijing had a change of heart about Japan or the importance of the U.S.-Japanese security alliance. Nonetheless, the years 2006-09 demonstrate that Beijing took considerable effort to transform Sino-Japanese defense links and the PLA placed great emphasis on its military diplomacy with Japan's Self-Defense Forces (JSDF).

A clear indication of the new direction in the PLA's military diplomacy [71] was to occur in September 2006, when Japan's Defense Minister Shigeru Ishiba visited China, and in August 2007, when China's Defense Minister General Cao Gangchuan returned his courtesy — the first time in 10 years a Chinese Defense Minister had visited Japan. During his visit, General Cao invited Japanese officers to observe a PLA exercise that September — the first time Japanese officers ever observed a Chinese military exercise. The following November, the destroyer *Shenzhen* made the first port call any PLAN vessel had ever made in Japan. In March 2008, Japan's Vice-Minister of Defense, Kohei Masuda met with Deputy Chief of Staff Lieutenant General Ma Xiaotian in Beijing for the eighth Sino-Japanese defense security consultations that had been initiated in 1997. They reached an accord on the Taiwan issue and agreed to expand military exchanges and enhance high-level contacts between the two defense departments. In June, the first Japanese combat vessel since World War II made a port call in China when the destroyer *Sazanami* visited Guangzhou. The *Sazanami* brought with it relief supplies for the survivors of Szechuan's Wenchuan earthquake even as Japanese relief workers were seen on China's television pulling the living and the dead from collapsed buildings. In 2009, the two defense ministers agreed to restart the defense dialogues that had ceased after 2006. These developments complemented existing agreements whereby Chinese and Japanese military officers would attend their opposite number's highest level professional military education (PME) centers.

These military exchanges were paralleled by Sino-Japanese summitry expressing goodwill and cooperation between the two countries. Prime Minister Yasuo Fukuda visited China in December 2007 and President Hu Jintao made a return visit to Japan in May 2008. Notably, this was the first visit by a Chinese president to Japan since 1998, and Hu's longest visit to a foreign country since selection as president in 2003. At the summit's conclusion, the two political leaders signed a six-point joint statement committing China and Japan to strategic cooperation.[72]

Even as these positive elements in Sino-Japanese relations were emerging, long-standing territorial disputes continued to produce friction. In September 2007, Chinese air force bombers made some 40 sorties over 2 days into the airspace around the disputed Chunxiao gas field in the East China Sea. Japan scrambled fighters from an Air Self Defense Forces (ASDF) base on Okinawa in response.[73] Somewhat more than a year later in December 2008, two patrol boats from the Chinese Maritime Monitoring Corps entered the 12-mile limit of the disputed Diaoyu/Senkaku Islands in the East China Sea. This was the first time any vessels from a Chinese government agency had violated Japan's territorial waters around these islands despite Beijing's competing claim. Japan lodged a diplomatic protest with the Chinese government. A spokesman from China's Ministry of Foreign Affairs, of course denied the vessels' actions were provocative because they were in Chinese territorial waters.[74] Moreover, and as anticipated, the PLA's response to the critical assessment of the strategic intent behind PLA modernization across a wide range of capabilities from space to naval programs expressed in Tokyo's 2009 *Defense White Paper* was sharp. A *Liberation Army Daily* article concluded that Japan paid no attention to the PLA's increasing transparency, continued assessing the PLA through "colored glasses," and maintained its suspicions about China's armed forces, especially the navy.[75] It seems evident that improving Sino-Japanese relations, including military relations, are a function of pragmatic mutual interest and far from a reflection of mutual trust and confidence.

CONCLUSIONS, SPECULATIONS, AND POLICY IMPLICATIONS

The strategic objective of Beijing's security policy remains sustaining a security environment conducive to China's national development. Achieving this objective is crucial if China is to become a true global rather than regional power. Within this strategic objective, PLA perceptions of China's global security environment are marked by two underlying assessments. First, no major war involving the large-scale invasion of China is anticipated. Second, with the possible exception of the Korean peninsula and now only remotely Taiwan, there are no immediate threats to China's security that will require major PLA operations. PLA evaluations of China's security environment focus primarily on long-term strategic concerns. Given these perceptions, PLA priorities are to preserve China's current favorable security environment by deterring war and defusing military crises before they can evolve into major military confrontations. Nothing would more severely damage China's economic expansion and ever-increasing political influence than a major war. Nevertheless, despite China's efforts to deter war, they can erupt and the PLA must therefore be capable of conducting effective military operations under any circumstances.

With borders stretching across Asia from the Korean Peninsula in the northeast through Central and South Asia to Southeast Asia and from there northward in maritime Asia through the South and East China Seas to Japan, China has a complicated security environment embracing both continental and maritime requirements. This extensive security environment contains potential adversaries, both state and nonstate, with a wide range of capabilities and presenting variety of potential threats to China's security interests. Among these, the United States is the most militarily capable and the source of the PLA's primary strategic concern. This apprehension of U.S. strategic intent is the driver of much of the PLA's modernization programs and doctrinal evolution encompassing all realms of military operations from space to submarine warfare. China is therefore confronted with a security dilemma. Beijing seeks to have its security policy accepted as defensive—that Beijing has no other security objective than defending China's legitimate interests. Outside China, however, PLA modernization programs create uneasiness among China's neighbors over the strategic objective behind them. It is not only the increasing sophistication of the platforms and weapons being acquired that create concern, but the all-encompassing array of capabilities they include. The PLA is acquiring space capabilities, sophisticated strategic nuclear weapons, conventionally-armed ballistic and cruise missiles, nuclear-powered attack and ballistic missile submarines, advanced diesel-powered submarines, advanced surface combatants, large amphibious warfare ships, and air power composed of increasingly capable combat aircraft supported by a growing aerial tanker fleet and supporting aircraft. PLA ground forces are undergoing comparable modernization programs. Among those looking askance at these programs is the United States.

Hu Jintao's December 2004 revising the roles and missions of the PLA was, in part, a response to this dilemma. It seems evident that at the core of Hu Jintao's revision was concern that the PLA's increasing operational capabilities were becoming so disconcerting to China's neighbors that they threatened to undermine the strategic objective of China's foreign policy. China's security does require armed forces capable of effectively defending China's sovereignty and national interests, which requires a PLA capable of deterring war with China's potential adversaries, defusing crises should they erupt, and winning wars should they occur. To the extent developing these capabilities raised apprehensions among China's neighbors and further abroad, however, they jeopardized Beijing's primary strategic objective by creating the perception of China as a threat. Hu Jintao's emphasis on nonwar operations was clearly designed to direct the PLA to place greater emphasis on essentially all regional and international roles that could ease the image of China's military power as a potential threat. This same emphasis also served Beijing's interest in that nonwar operations assisted in projecting the image of China as a responsible member of the international community committed to ensuring global peace and stability.

Whether Hu Jintao's redirection of the PLA will have the results he seeks is questionable. China's military modernization programs are not designed to create a military capability limited to the defense of continental China and its territorial waters. They are programs designed to create a military capability that, although not global in reach, is certainly capable of defending China's interests against any challenge by any military power, including the United States. Assuming this assessment is correct, it raises quite complex policy issues for the United States and its allies and friends in the Asia-Pacific region. It also raises questions Russia has to contemplate, but which this chapter will not address.

Beijing has been quite unambiguous in its *Defense White Papers* that China has strategic concerns directly involving the United States, and that these concerns go beyond Taiwan. Beijing's underlying apprehension is that the United States perceives China's emergent political, economic, and military strength as preparation to supplant the United States in the Asia-Pacific region and therefore seeks to restrain China's growth. The U.S. dilemma is that although the "United States welcomes the rise of a stable, peaceful, and prosperous China" that contributes to strengthening the "global security architecture...,"[76] it so lacks confidence in understanding Beijing's strategic objectives in the Asia-

Pacific region that it "hedges" against a Beijing that may in the future challenge U.S. regional preeminence. This uncertainty is also found in the U.S. academic community, as the recent debate between Professors Robert S. Ross of Boston College and Aaron Friedberg of Princeton University demonstrates.[77]

Resolving this mutual apprehension is important, for it involves more than the bilateral relationship extant between the United States and China. In essence, all of Asia is watching the dynamics of the Sino-American relationship. Thus far, U.S. economic, political, and military power has more than offset China's growing strengths, allowing all of Asia to gain from the economic opportunities China provides. In short, the United States has provided the security umbrella under which Asia can engage China without undue concern. As China's military capabilities increase, however, will Asia's confidence in the American security umbrella diminish? If it does, how should the United States respond?

The United States should take advantage of the realities recognized by Hu Jintao some 5 years ago. First, as Hu Jintao's speech demonstrates, Beijing fully understands that to achieve its domestic development goals, it must stay engaged with global affairs. Second, Beijing fully understands that its military modernization programs disturb all of Asia—not just the United States. Third, Beijing recognizes that greater military transparency is necessary to counteract Asia's concerns over what is emerging as a major change in the regional balance of power. Fourth, Beijing needs a stable security environment and has committed itself to regional security cooperation and confidence-building measures. The United States should therefore systematically and deliberately build upon the commitments Beijing has already made and to some extent implemented. It should do so by building on the progress already made in the relationship between the two defense establishments. Despite all the problems that have occurred over the past 30 years, the groundwork has been laid. It may not be too stable, but the foundation exists and there has been recent promising progress.[78] The telephone link established in March 2008 has been used three times, the first round of a nuclear dialogue took place in April 2008, Defense Policy Coordination Talks (DPCT) have been restored, with the February 2009 meetings focused on regional and global security issues and possible areas of cooperation between the two militaries. This revitalized engagement strategy must build on the ground work completed and the elements of cooperation already recognized by Beijing as necessary to defuse the widespread apprehension over the strategic objectives of China's defense modernization programs.

Most importantly, the United States should make eminently clear that it has no intention of restraining the expansion of China's influence regionally or globally. Rather, that the United States will willingly accept and cooperate with a China dedicated to reinforcing and building regional and global architectures ensuring the peaceful settlements of international disputes. The United States must emphasize, however, that cooperation between Chinese and American defense establishments is not the ultimate purpose of U.S. policy. The United States should make quite clear it is not the objective of U.S. strategy to have China and the United States jointly dominate the Asia-Pacific region. The United States objective should be to join with China in constructing a multilateral security architecture where any government desiring to participate will be accepted.

ENDNOTES - CHAPTER 2

1. Assessments of the diversity of defense issues now confronting the PLA can be found in Roy Kamphausen *et al*, *Beyond the Strait: PLA Missions Other Than Taiwan*, Carlisle, PA: U.S. Army War College, Strategic Studies Institute, April 2009.

2. These numbers are taken from *China's National Defense in 2000*, Beijing: Information Office of the State Council, October 19, 2000, p. 14.

3. For an analysis of propagation of "new historic missions" throughout the PLA, see James Mulvenon, "Chairman Hu and the PLA's 'New Historic Missions'," *China Leadership Monitor*, No. 27, January 2009.

4. See Daniel Hartnett, "The PLA's Domestic and Foreign Activities and Orientation," testimony before Senate Hearing on China's Military and Security Activities Abroad, Washington, DC, March 4, 2009, for analysis of this expansion. Unless otherwise noted, this discussion draws extensively from his analysis.

5. Zhang Zhaoyin, "Make Ceaseless Efforts to Strengthen Core Military Capacity Building—Important Experience From 30 Years of Reform, Opening Up," *PLA Daily Online*, December 2, 2008.

6. *Ibid.*

7. *Ibid.*

8. *Ibid.*

9. Yu Jia, "Diversified Military Tasks: Nonwar Military Actions," *Zhongguo Guofang Bao Online*, December 11, 2008.

10. Wang Xingwang, "National Strategic Capability: The New Leverage Point for Dealing with Comprehensive Security," *PLA Daily Online*, February 12, 2009.

11. Major General Shou Xiaosong, "Views on the Innovative Development of the Party's National Security Strategic Theory," *Zhongguo Junshi Kexue*, August 20, 2007.

12. *Ibid.*

13. *Ibid.*

14. *China's National Defense in 2008*, Beijing, China: Information Office of the State Council, January 2009.

15. The following discussion is taken from *Ibid.*, Part I. The Security Situation.

16. *Ibid*, Part II. National Defense Policy.

17. This discussion draws extensively from Liang Guanglie, "Chinese Military Foreign Diplomacy Is in Step with the Times," *PLA Daily Online*, December 23, 2008.

18. Hu Jintao, "Join Hands to Promote Peaceful Development of Cross-Strait Relations; Strive With Unity of Purpose for the Great Rejuvenation of the Chinese Nation—Speech at the Forum Marking the 30th Anniversary of the Issuance of "Message to Compatriots in Taiwan," *Xinhua Domestic Service*, December 31, 2008.

19. Li Hanfang and Li Kai, "Taiwan Affairs Office of State Council: Two Sides of the Strait Can Explore Ways for Setting Up Mechanism of Mutual Trust on Military Security in Good Time," *Xinhua Domestic Service*, May 27, 2009.

20. Reported in Oleg Gorupay and Vladimir Kuzar, "Start Made to Mirnaya Missiya-2209," *Krasnaya Zvezda*, July 23, 2009.

21. Yang Yi, "Developments on the Korean Peninsula—A Chinese Perspective," in *Three Perspectives on Korean Developments*, PacNet #55, August 6, 2009, available from *csis.org/publication/pacnet-55-three-perspectives-korean-developments*.

22. Commentary by Peng Guangqian, Deputy Secretary General of the National Security Policy Committee of China Society

for Policy Study: "Nuclear Arms Will Harm the Fundamental Interests of the DPRK," *Huanqiu Shibao,* June 8, 2009.

23. The following discussion draws primarily from Bonnie S. Glaser, "China's Policy in the Wake of the Second DPRK Nuclear Test," *China Security,* Vol. 5, No. 2, July 2009.

24. The following discussion draws from Bonnie Glaser, Scott Snyder, and John S. Park, "Keeping an Eye on an Unruly Neighbor: Chinese views of Economic Reform and Stability in North Korea," *United States Institute of Peace Working Paper,* A Joint Report, Washington, DC: Center for Strategic and International Studies and the U.S. Institute of Peace, January 3, 2008.

25. I am grateful to Professor Thomas Christensen of Princeton University for bringing this point to my attention.

26. Yang Yi, "Developments on the Korean Peninsula."

27. "Defense chief hails ties with DPRK, "*China Daily,* November 24, 2009.

28. Jiang Xinfeng, "What Does Japan's Annual Defense White Paper Mention," *PLA Daily Online,* July 20, 2009.

29. Shou, "Views on the Innovative Development of the Party's National Security Strategic Theory."

30. Zhang Zhaoyin, "Make Ceaseless Efforts to Strengthen Core Military Capacity Building — Important Experience From 30 Years of Reform, Opening Up," *PLA Daily Online,* December 2, 2008.

31. Rahul Singh, "Indian Army Fears Chinese Attack by 2017," *Hindustan Times Online,* March 26, 2009.

32. Li Xiaokun, "Drill Report 'Surprises' Chinese Government," *China Daily,* April 1, 2009.

33. Special Correspondent, "China will be one of our primary challenges: Navy Chief," *The Hindu,* August 11, 2009.

34. Liu Yang and Guo Feng, "What is the Intention of Wantonly Engaging in Military Ventures—India's Military Development Should Be Watched Out For," *PLA Daily*, May 19, 1998.

35. The most recent report of this assistance is R. Jeffrey Smith and Joby Warrick, "A Nuclear Power's Act of Proliferation," *The Washington Post*, November 13, 2009.

36. Bernard D. Cole, *The Great Wall at Sea: China's Navy Enters the Twenty-First Century*, Annapolis, MD: Naval Institute Press, 2001, p. 35.

37. See, for example, Commodore Gurpreet S. Khurana, "China-India Maritime Rivalry," *Indian Defence Review*, Vol. 23, Issue 4, October 1-December 31, 2008, pp. 89-93.

38. Andrew Erickson and Lyle Goldstein, "Gunboats for China's New 'Grand Canals'? Probing the Intersection of Beijing's Naval and Oil Security Policies," *Naval War College Review*, Vol. 62, No. 2, Spring 2009, pp. 55-57.

39. Embassy of India, "New Framework for the U.S.-India Defense Relationship," Washington, DC, June 28, 2005.

40. "Washington Draws India in Against China," *Renmin Ribao WWW-Text* in English, July 7, 2005.

41. Christopher Griffin, "Containment with Chinese Characteristics: Beijing Hedges against the Rise of India," *Asian Outlook*, No. 3, September 2006, p. 4.

42. This discussion draws primarily from Bhartendu Kumar Singh, "Military Diplomacy: The Future of Sino-Indian Military Relations?" *China Brief*, Vol. 8, Issue 23, December 8 2008.

43. Indrani Bagchi, "NSA Gets Charge of Ties With China," *The Times of India Online*, August 9, 2009.

44. For a useful assessment of China's policy and strategy toward Central Asia see, Robert Sutter, "Durability in China's Strategy toward Central Asia—Reasons for Optimism," *China and Eurasia Forum Quarterly*, Vol. 6, No. 1, 2008, pp. 3-10.

45. For a brief history of the SCO and U.S, interests, see Andrew Scheineson, "Backgrounder: The Shanghai Cooperation Organization," *Council of Foreign Relations*, March 24, 2009. For a more detailed assessment, see Alyson J. K. Bailes, Pal Dunay, Pan Guang, and Mikhail Troitskiy, *The Shanghai Cooperation Organization*, SIPRI Policy Paper No. 17, Stockholm, Sweden: International Peace Research Institute, May 2007.

46. Aleksandr Khramchikhin, "Chinese Detour," *Izvestiya*, Moscow, Russia, August 20, 2007.

47. Peng Kuang and Zhang Haizhou, "Clearing the Way for Peace," *China Daily*, November 10, 2009.

48. For a Chinese view of the United States and Afghanistan, see Wu Shuhu, "US Troop Surge Can Hardly Completely Control the Situation in Afghanistan," *Dangdai Shijie*, May 5, 2009.

49. Griffin, "Containment with Chinese Characteristics," p. 6.

50. "Uzbekistan Warns Over Russian Base Plan," *RadioFreeEuropeRadioLiberty*, July 14, 2009.

51. The following discussion draws from Bailes *et. al*, pp. 10-14.

52. I am grateful to Professor Bernard D. Cole for allowing me to use chapter 4 of his revised edition of *The Great Wall at Sea* to be published by Annapolis, MD: Naval Institute Press, in late 2010. Much of my discussion is drawn from this chapter.

53. Hans M. Kristensen, "New Chinese SSBN Deploys to Hainan Island," *FAS Strategic Security Blog*, April 24, 2009.

54. Cole, *The Great Wall at Sea* (2001), p. 50.

55. Hai Yan, "Vietnam Military Expansion Threatens Malacca Strait," *Guoji Xianqu Daobao*, May 19, 2009.

56. Much of this discussion is drawn from James Manicom, "The Sino-Japanese Energy Dispute in the East China Sea: Strategic Policy, Economic Opportunities, and Cooperation," *The Economics of Peace and Security Journal*, Vol. 4, No. 2, 2009, pp. 38-44.

57. James Manicom, "China's Claims to an Extended Continental Shelf in the East China Sea; Meaning and Implications," *China Brief*, Vol. 9, Issue 14, July 9, 2009.

58. *China's National Defense in 2008*, "The Security Situation."

59. See also Evan S. Medeiros, *China's International Behavior: Activism, Opportunism, and Diversification*, Santa Monica, CA: RAND Corporation, 2009, p. 30.

60. See, for example, Fan Gaoyue and Yang Yi, "Latest US Defense Report Specifically Outlines Strategy Toward China," *Zhongguo Tongxun She Online*, Hong Kong, August 4, 2008.

61. *Annual Report to Congress: Military Power of the People's Republic of China*, Washington, DC: Office of the Secretary of Defense, March 25, 2009.

62. Lu Yuan, "Change of US Asian-Pacific Strategies — Concluded From 'RIMPAC [Rim of the Pacific Exercise] 2008," *Xinhua Wang*, July 16, 2008.

63. For a thorough assessment of this issue, see Eric A. McVadon, "The Reckless and the Resolute: Confrontation in the South China Sea, "*China Security*, Vol. 5, No. 2, Spring 2009, pp. 1-15.

64. "China Urges U.S. to Halt Surveillance Near Its Shores," *The New York Times*, August 27, 2009.

65. Peng Guangqian and Yao Youzhi, eds., *The Science of Military Strategy*, Beijing, China: Military Science Publishing House, 2005, p. 440.

66. This discussion draws from Wang Zhongchun, "Nuclear Challenges and China's Choices," *China Security*, Winter 2007, pp. 52-60.

67. For an assessment of this debate, see Bonnie S. Glaser and Lyle Morris, "Chinese Perceptions of U.S. Decline and Power," Jamestown Publication, *China Brief*, Vol. 9, Issue 14, July 9, 2009.

68. Robert G. Sutter, "The PLA, Japan's Defense Posture, and the Outlook for China-Japan Relations," in Andrew Scobell and Larry M. Wortzel, eds., *Shaping China's Security Environment: The Role of the People's Liberation Army*, Carlisle, PA: Strategic Studies Institute, U.S. Army War College, October 2006, pp. 183-185.

69. "The Security Environment," *China's National Defense in 2006*, Beijing, China: Information Office of the State Council, December 2006.

70. "The Security Situation,"*China's National Defense in 2008*, Beijing, China: Information Office of the State Council, January 2009.

71. Jiang Xinfeng, "Creating a New Situation in Interaction on Defense Affairs by China and Japan," *PLA Daily*, May 6, 2008.

72. "China, Japan Sign Joint Statement on Promoting Strategic, Mutually Beneficial Ties," *Xinhua*, May 7, 2008.

73. Tsuyoshi Nojima, "China's sudden show of force sends SDF jets scrambling," *Asahi Shimbun*, January 2, 2008.

74. "PRC FM Spokesman Denies Provoking Japan Over Disputed Isles," *Kyodo World Service*, December 9, 2008.

75. Jiang Xinfeng, "What Does Japan's Annual Defense White Paper Mention," *PLA Daily Online*, July 20, 2009.

76. "China's Military and Security Activities Abroad," Prepared Statement of The Honorable David S. Sedney Deputy Assistant Secretary of Defense for East Asia Testimony Before the U.S.-China Economic and Security Review Commission, March 4, 2009, p.1.

77. Aaron L. Friedberg, "Menace," and Robert S. Ross, "Myth," in "Here Be Dragons: Is China a Military Threat?" *The National Interest*, No. 103, September/October 2009, pp. 19-34.

78. The following discussion draws upon David Sedney's March 4, 2009, prepared testimony, pp. 3-4.

CHAPTER 3

DISCOURSE IN 3-D:
THE PLA'S EVOLVING DOCTRINE, CIRCA 2009

Andrew Scobell*

The release of the 2008 *Defense White Paper* provides an opportunity to assess current thinking in the People's Liberation Army (PLA) and its future trajectory. Of course, the white paper is a consensus document issued by the State Council, not the Central Military Commission (CMC) or any other military entity. Nevertheless, we know the PLA has substantial input.[1] This chapter considers PLA discourse on evolving doctrine circa 2009 in light of the 2008 White Paper. As important as the white paper is—providing valuable insights and useful nuggets of information—it is not the bible of Chinese defense policy and military modernization. One needs to look further afield and back in time before the People's Republic of China (PRC) began to publish white papers.

WHERE DOES PLA DOCTRINE COME FROM?

Doctrine is important because "it consists of the fundamental principles by which those planning the application of military force guide their actions."[2] So where does the PLA's doctrine come from? It does not come straight from *Defense White Papers*. Rather, doctrine comes from authoritative doctrinal pronouncements issued by the Chinese Communist Party (CCP) Central Military Commission (CMC), usually coming

*The author thanks Daniel Alderman of the National Bureau of Asian Research for his expert research assistance.

from the lips of the paramount political ruler who, by tradition, serves as chair of the Party CMC (and since 1982 simultaneously as chair of the State CMC).[3] The highest level directives are known as the "Military Strategic Guidelines" (军事战略方针— MSG) and outline the general direction for defense policy and military modernization. They tend to remain in effect for approximately 10-15 years until they are replaced by a new set of guidelines. During the period, modifications are invariably issued. While these modifications are significant and authoritative, they do not fundamentally change or negate the guidelines in effect. The MSG are "the highest level of national guidance and direction to the armed forces of China" and are roughly equivalent to the "National Military Strategy" issued by the U.S. military, although the Chinese version is better understood as a "rolling [or evolving] national military strategy" because of the number of periodic modifications.[4]

Since 1949, only five sets of MSG have been issued.[5] The most recent set was issued in 1993 in the name of the then paramount ruler, Jiang Zemin. The guidelines maintained the overall thrust of the 1985 guidelines issued in the name of the former paramount ruler, Deng Xiaoping, and restated that peace and development were the main trends in world and that a world war or similar type of all-out war was unlikely. Consistent with the 1985 MSG, the 1993 MSG stipulated that China's military should be prepared to fight a "local, limited war" (局部有限战争) on China's periphery; however, waging mechanized warfare was no longer enough. The performance of the U.S. military in Operation DESERT STORM (1991) convinced China's leaders that a sweeping revolution in military affairs (RMA) demanded a PLA that could wage war "under high technology conditions (在高科技条件下)." There have been at least three modifications to these guidelines since 1993. The first modification, issued in late 2002 during a major defense speech by Jiang Zemin, stipulated that the RMA had accelerated and information technology was now the defining character of modern warfare. Thus local limited warfare would henceforth be waged "under conditions of informatization (在信息化条件下)." A second modification was reportedly announced by the new paramount ruler, CCP General Secretary and PRC President Hu Jintao, at an enlarged CMC meeting in December 2004. Hu expounded a set of four "New Historic Missions." The third and most recent public modification to the 1993 MSG occurred in January 2009 with the official release of China's 2008 *Defense White Paper*.

This chapter looks at PLA discourse unleashed by the most recent modifications to the 1993 guidelines. The discourse has unfolded in three dimensions each with its own distinct arena and audience. The first dimension is a **vertical** one, the second is a **horizontal** plane, and the third extends **outward**, perpendicular to the other two dimensions. It is useful to think of the PLA as a pyramid-shaped organization consisting of three distinct echelons (see Figure 1). The majority of the PLA can be found at the base of the pyramid: this is the **Lower Echelon** consisting of the officers and men at the level of Group Army and below. This level can be dubbed the *'war-fighting PLA.'* Above this layer is the **Middle Echelon** which consists of the staffs of the four General Departments (general staff, general political, general logistics, general armaments), and four services (ground forces, navy, air force and strategic rocket forces). This level can be dubbed the *'administration PLA.'* The smallest layer is at the **Higher**

Echelon which consists of the Central Military Commission and associated offices and entities. This upper level can be dubbed the *'command PLA.'*

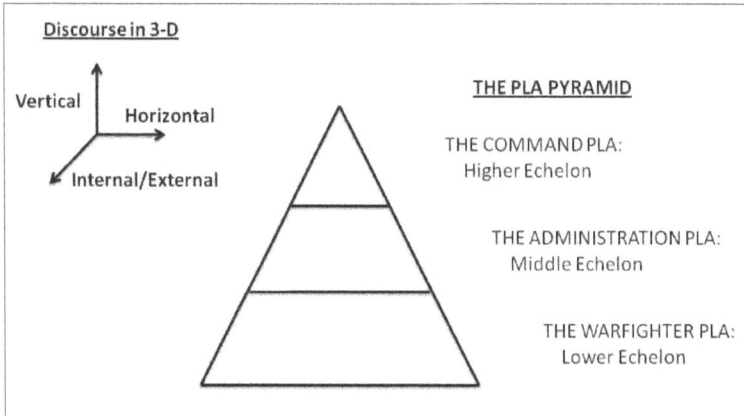

Figure 1. The PLA Pyramid and Doctrinal Discourse.

Discourse in the vertical dimension involves interaction between these three echelons; discourse in the horizontal dimension entails interaction within any one of these echelons; discourse in the outward projecting dimension consists of intercourse with audiences and actors external to the pyramid. While the PLA is clearly a military organization that has become increasingly distinct and differentiated from other entities and groups in China, fundamentally it remains a politico-military organism intertwined with the ruling political elite of the PRC. This key aspect of civil-military relations is especially important to understanding the configuration of the Higher Echelon. At the apex of the pyramid is the CMC, which is where the uppermost link in the politico-military chain of command is located. While the Communist Party is supposed to command the gun (as Mao famously insisted), the CMC has been dominated by men in uniform. In late 2009, membership of the commission was overwhelmingly military with only ONE of the 11 seats being occupied by a civilian. Of course, the civilian is none other than Hu Jintao, who chairs the CMC and concurrently serves as President of the PRC and General Secretary of the CCP. Hu is certainly the commander in chief, but he essentially depends on his colleagues in uniform for their military advice and counsel. So this key mechanism of civilian/party control of the military is very much a military entity. Nevertheless, all these soldiers are also senior members of the Communist Party. Thus, perhaps the most accurate word to characterize the relationship between the CCP and PLA is "interpenetration."[6]

Examination of this discourse in three dimensions will provide insight into key aspects of Chinese doctrinal development. An analysis of vertical and horizontal discourse will underscore both frustration among and maneuvering by uniformed personnel as they make sense of all these modifications, what these mean in concrete terms to the various constituent parts of the PLA and how to implement them effectively. An analysis of outward-directed discourse will highlight the PLA's effort to counter concerns abroad that China constitutes a military threat to any other country. I use the term "discourse" rather than "debate" because the former term seems to characterize more accurately what has been happening. The PLA is not debating the pros and cons of the New Historic Missions or whether to revise or junk them. Instead, Chinese soldiers are trying to make sense of the New Historic Missions and implement them in ways that will enhance rather than hamper PLA capabilities and operational effectiveness. Soldiers in various services and levels are attempting to leverage these modifications to further the interests of their own particular entity. Moreover, the PLA is working to package these changes to external audiences in advantageous ways. This multidimensional discourse involves reconciling contradictions and confronting challenges.

In the first part of this chapter I review what is new or significant in the 2008 *Defense White Paper* and then what roles and operational capabilities are specified. In the second part of the chapter, I examine the on-going three dimensional discourses on the PLA's evolving doctrine. In the third part of the chapter, I will identify the challenges faced by China's military before drawing conclusions and exploring some policy implications.

WHAT IS SIGNIFICANT OR NEW IN THE 2008 DEFENSE WHITE PAPER?

There are a number of significant or new features in the 2008 *Defense White Paper*. First, it is the latest authoritative restatement of the New Historic Missions first expounded by Hu Jintao in December 2004.[7] To recapitulate, the PLA is charged with four historic missions: The first is to guarantee Communist Party rule; the second is to safeguard national development; the third is to defend national interests; and the fourth is to protect world peace and common development. These are also referred to as the "three provides and one bring into play (三个提供, 一个发挥)."[8]

Second, the latest *Defense White Paper* reiterates the importance of "Diversified Military Tasks" — a term first used in 2006. Diversified military tasks was first introduced at the National People's Congress in March of that year and then first cited in a defense white paper in December 2006.[9] This laundry list of military tasks came on the heels of the expanded definition of national interests and elaboration of the dimensions of national territory and sovereignty in the New Historic Missions. Diversified Military Tasks appears to be an effort to reconcile the broader and intangible new historic missions with a narrower and more tangible conception of PLA duties (see Figure 2). The term diversified military tasks seems to be an umbrella concept to cover both the new historic missions and local war in conditions of informatization.

The relationship between New Historic Missions, Diversified Military Tasks, Military Operations Other Than War, and Local War In Conditions of Informatization can be expressed in the following equation:

$$DMT = LWICOI + NHM [MOOTW]$$

(2006)   (2002)   (2004)   (2008)

DMT = Diversified Military Tasks
LWICOI = Local War In Conditions of Informatization
NHM = New Historic Missions
MOOTW = Military Operations Other Than War

Figure 2. Doctrinal Algebra.

Third, the 2008 *Defense White Paper* is the first iteration of the biannual document to explicitly use the term "Military Operations Other Than War" (MOOTW). What is the real significance of MOOTW? Is it simply a new buzz word borrowed from the U.S. military lexicon, or is it something more significant? It appears that MOOTW amounts to a recycled subset of peacetime PLA duties repackaged for emphasis.[10] Use of the term may be an effort — like the introduction of the term "diversified military tasks" to make the new historic missions emphasis on peacetime responsibilities more military-like and hence more palatable to the PLA. In any event, use of these terms indicates that the PLA is expected to pay greater attention to noncombat functions such as disaster relief and peacekeeping. Indeed, the military's role in disaster relief has received growing coverage in authoritative publications and appears with increasing frequency in *Defense White Papers*. The term "disaster relief" is mentioned only once in the 2002 *Defense White Paper* — and then as a responsibility for the People's Armed Police (PAP). The term appears 14 times in the 2004 *Defense White Paper*, 22 times in the 2006 version, and 25 times in the 2008 *Defense White Paper*.

WHAT PLA ROLES AND OPERATIONAL CAPABILITIES ARE SPECIFIED?

There are three roles for the PLA identified in authoritative doctrinal publications. The PLA is charged with fighting "local wars in conditions of informatization," providing deterrence, and performing a wide array of domestic and foreign "diversified military tasks." The PLA's foremost task is to perform "integrated, joint operations" aimed at "winning local wars in conditions of informatization."[11] This mission requires:

> Meeting the requirements of confrontation between war systems in modern warfare and taking integrated joint operations as the basic approach. It [MSG] is designed to bring the operational strengths of different services and

arms into full play, combine offensive operations with defensive operations . . . refine the command system for joint operations, the joint training system and the joint support system, optimize the structure and composition of forces and speed up the building of a combat force structure suitable for winning local wars in conditions of informatization.[12]

Second, the PLA is charged with being effective in "deterring crises and wars." This requires "close coordination between military struggle and political, diplomatic, economic, cultural, and legal endeavors." Moreover, "[i]t [the MSG] strictly adheres to a position of self-defense, exercises prudence in the use of force, seeks to effectively control war situations, and strives to reduce the risks and costs of war. It [the MSG] calls for the building of a lean and effective deterrent force and the flexible use of different means of deterrence."[13] The most prominent manifestation of deterrence is the no first use principle in Chinese nuclear policy. But Chinese conceptions of what constitutes deterrence appear to be very broad and diverse—ranging from Chinese activities in space, such as the anti-satellite test in January 2007, to more down-to-earth displays such as military parades.[14]

These first two roles—warfare and deterrence—are long- standing missions of the PLA. What is relatively new to authoritative publications is the third role—performing a wide array of "diversified military tasks"—including peacetime tasks.[15] According to the Academy of Military Sciences' *The Science of Military Strategy*, "War-fighting and deterrence are the two basic functions of the armed forces."[16] The third task does not appear in this landmark volume first published in Chinese in 2001. How do diversified military tasks fit into the requirements stipulated for the PLA?

According to the 2008 *Defense White Paper*:

> This guideline [the MSG] focuses on enhancing the capabilities of the armed forces in countering various security threats and accomplishing *diversified military tasks*. With the focus of attention on performing the historical missions of the armed forces for the new stage in the new century and with raising the capability to win local wars in conditions of informationization at the core, it [the MSG] works to increase the country's capabilities to maintain maritime, space, and electromagnetic space security and to carry out the tasks of counter-terrorism, stability maintenance, emergency rescue and international peacekeeping. It [the MSG] takes military operations other than war (MOOTW) as an important form of applying national military forces, and scientifically makes and executes plans for the development of MOOTW capabilities.[17]

And how does the PLA define MOOTW? There does not seem to be a doctrinal definition but according to four officers from the Shenyang Military Region headquarters, writing in 2008, in *Chinese Military Science*, MOOTW:

> ... refers to the direct or indirect use of the armed forces in a non-violent manner ... to achieve certain political, economic and military purposes, safeguard national interests, maintain social stability, respond to natural disasters, and defend the people's peaceful labor, lives and property, or in certain conditions, military actions enforced with the use of limited violence.[18]

MOOTW encompasses internal security and external security missions and the range of tasks are numerous and challenging. According to the officers from the Shenyang MR, these MOOTW operations include:

. . . military deterrence, military diplomacy, struggles
for defense of land, maritime, and air frontiers, establishing restricted areas, soft battle strikes, military
trade and aid, peacekeeping operations, counter-terror
operations, crackdowns on organized crime and drug
trafficking, controlling and managing refugees, armed
escort, eliminating pollution from nuclear, biological,
and chemical agents, military control, civil assistance,
protecting and evacuating nationals in foreign trouble
spots, and managing crises. National defense and army
building are themselves forms of military operations
other than war, whereas military struggle is a routine
form of non-war military actions. The contents and
modes of military operations other than war will continuously witness new changes which will develop out
of practice.[19]

DISCOURSE IN 3-D: RECONCILING CONTRADICTIONS, CONFRONTING CHALLENGES

PLA writers continue to grapple with the challenges confronting Chinese military modernization
in the early 21st century. One particular challenge is
trying to make sense of the latest modifications to the
1993 MSG and what they mean to the PLA. A consistent theme of Chinese authors is the identification of
"contradictions" (矛盾). Here I outline a handful of
contradictions identified in the discourse triggered by
the New Historic Missions and 2008 white paper and
explore what each tells us about the discourse going
on within the PLA in 2009. The first and second contradictions are largely discussed vertically between
echelons; the third and fourth contradictions tend to
be discussed horizontally within echelons; the fifth
contradiction—is almost never explicitly stated—but
is clearly implicit in the on-going externally directed
discourse with other countries.

The First Dimension: Vertical Discourse.

Perhaps the most significant contradiction is between the costs of army building and the limited resources made available to the PLA for the undertaking. The New Historic Missions issued in late 2004 outline an extremely wide array of responsibilities for the armed forces and the PLA in particular. Assuming Chinese soldiers are prepared to take on additional responsibilities despite the daunting challenges involved (see below), the fundamental issue becomes one of receiving adequate funding. General Zhu Qi, Commander of the Beijing Military Region, addressing a wide audience at a higher echelon and outside the PLA pyramid, observed in mid-2005 in the pages of the CCP's most prominent journal: "We must soberly recognize that there are still some problems in the scale, structure, efficiency and balance of army building; indeed, there is a contradiction between the increasingly fast pace of army building today and the comparatively limited investment available."[20]

In this context, a Chinese general's wistful remark in 2007 takes on greater meaning. In front of a U.S. audience which included the author, the officer commented that China's extended period of largely uninterrupted sustained economic growth and peace has been a mixed blessing for the PLA. On one hand, he explained, this situation allowed for significant state funding for military modernization; but on the other, he lamented that this state of affairs provided no sense of urgency to drive the defense buildup anywhere fast enough as he would have liked.[21] Certainly military dissatisfaction with the size of the defense budget is neither unique to China or a new phenomenon in the post-Mao era. However, against the backdrop of a massive expansion of missions for the PLA this lament is of particular note.

In an effort to counter the frustration in the PLA with the New Historic Missions handed down by the CMC, Lieutenant General Wang Guosheng, Commander of the Lanzhou Military Region, reminded soldiers that while the missions of the PLA evolved over time, these were *always* consistent with the Party's historic tasks, the nation's security interests, the level of economic development, and the RMA. Writing in 2008 in the pages of the flagship journal of the Academy of Military of Sciences, Wang dubbed these the "four consistents" (四个一致). Coincidentally, these consistents are 'consistent' with the new historic missions. In the article, Wang reviews the evolving nature of PLA missions in various historical periods.[22]

Reading between the lines, Wang's message from the Middle Echelon to his fellow uniformed colleagues in the Lower Echelon is clearly discernible: Warfighters, you may be dissatisfied with the New Historic Missions and fear they are too much of a burden for the armed forces. Nevertheless, the PLA has always loyally shouldered the new missions it has been assigned by the CCP and its CMC whether soldiers liked them or not. "Missions are historically dynamic; they are always in flux. . . . New content has always been continuously added . . ."[23]

1 Contradiction; 2 Incompatibles. According to a 2008 New Year's Day editorial in the *Liberation Army Daily*: "At present and for a comparatively long time to come, the main contradiction in our army building will still be that our level of modernization is incompatible with the demands of winning a local war under conditions of informatization, and that our military capabilities are incompatible with the demands of carrying out the army's historic missions."[24] This contradiction is broken down into what have been dubbed "the two incompatibles" (两个不相适应).

The first "incompatible" is between the process of mechanization and the process of informatization.[25] In other words, as the first decade of the 21st century draws to a close, the PLA remains primarily a mechanized force rather than an informatized military. The overall level of information technology employed across the PLA is low and rudimentary despite pockets of high-tech information technology (IT) sophistry. Writing in 2009 in the pages of the *Liberation Army Daily*, Lieutenant General Wang Xixin, Commander of the 38th Group Army, contended: "The stove pipe issue (烟囱问题) is perhaps the greatest challenge we currently face in army capability building." From his position in the Lower Echelon addressing an audience at the Higher and Middle Echelons, Wang defined the problem as not having "strong systemic combat capability." The warfighter lamented that ". . . no matter how strong a single capability is, we will not be able to gain initiatives on a battlefield in which the fundamental feature is confrontation between systems."[26]

The second "incompatible" is one between the demands of war and nonwar missions. Indeed, the editors at the *Liberation Army Daily* have identified the existence of a contradiction between the demands placed on the PLA by "war and military operations other than war" (战争与非战争军事行动).[27]

The disgruntlement within the PLA prompted a response directly from the top. Hu Jintao gave a speech to the PLA delegation at the 2nd Session of the 11th National People's Congress in March 2009. In the address, he reportedly "clarified" (明确) the "relationship between construction of core military capabilities and construction of capabilities for military operations other than war." Hu apparently argued that "core military capabilities are the foundation for military operations other than war and MOOTW capabilities are an extension of core military capabilities; the two capabilities support each other and both are indispensible." Thus, a *Liberation Army Daily* editorial reporting on Hu's speech to the PLA NPC delegates asserted, "In essence, the 'two incompatibles' boil down to the incompatibility of the core military capabilities [with the winning of local wars]."[28] In other words, the "two incompatibles" are a misnomer, according to the *Liberation Army Daily* commentator. The Chinese military's most authoritative high-level open source mouthpiece was directing its message at the middle and lower echelons.[29]

The bottom line is that in the minds of many soldiers, the demands of modern warfare and MOOTW require very different capabilities. MOOTW generally call for lower tech and more manpower intensive capabilities than 21st century warfare. If the emphasis on MOOTW in the New Historic Missions remains, then additional significant manpower cuts seem unlikely.[30] This means that there will continue to be a "domestic drag" on China's military whereby the sheer number of uniformed personnel—in the active duty PLA, the reserves, the PAP, and the militia—will remain a brake on the PLA's ability to fight a "limited war under conditions of informatization (信息化条件下的局部战争)."[31] Personnel costs, which reportedly make up approximately two-thirds of the official defense budget is money not spent on equipment. Manpower matters will take money away from equipment and hardware purchases.[32]

The Second Dimension: Horizontal Discourse.

The PLA is grappling with MOOTW. Different services have different thinking about MOOTW. The PLA Navy (PLAN) and PLA Air Force (PLAAF), for example, see clear benefits for each service, while the ground forces appear more ambivalent. The discourse over MOOTW is primarily horizontal, although with clear vertical linkages.

The PLAN seems to be the most enthusiastic about MOOTW and best positioned and organized of all the services to exploit the concept for service interests. The PLAN has sought to highlight its value in MOOTW. Admiral Tian Zhong, concurrently commander of the Northern Fleet and deputy commander of the Jinan Military Region, began a major 2008 article in *China Military Science* with the following lead-in: "The 17th Party Congress Report states: 'Raise military capabilities to deal with many different security threats, and accomplish diversified military tasks,' [moreover, the report] emphasizes in international relations managing 'mutual trust, strengthening cooperation, strengthening peaceful means but not war methods to solve international disputes.' The PLAN can conduct strategic, comprehensive, and international military duties in vast maritime expanses to perform the New Historic Missions." Admiral Tian, writing from his perch in the Middle Echelon both to his colleagues in the Administration PLA as well as for the Higher Echelon Command PLA, focused on the "special characteristics" of the naval dimensions of MOOTW and capabilities required.[33]

The PLAAF also displays great interest in MOOTW and trumpets its advantages and contends it is poised to spearhead efforts in this area. According to five researchers at the Air Force Command Academy in Beijing, the PLAAF has "three dimensional mobility (立体机动) and is clearly the "vanguard" [先锋] of MOOTW. The researchers, writing in the July 2008 issue of the bimonthly journal of the PLAAF Political Department, assert that "the Wenchuan earthquake relief efforts demonstrate most clearly the meaning of modernized strategic air power (现代化战略空军), [and] revealed most intensely the demand for modernized strategic airpower to protect national security and development."[34] The PLAAF seems focused on actual air power capabilities relevant to specific aspects of nonwar operations. The researchers from the Air Force Command Academy, for example, focus on the role of air power in disaster relief operations in the aftermath of the May 2008 Wenchuan earthquake, including "air drops" (投送).[35]

In contrast to their uniformed colleagues in the air and naval services, the ground forces seem ambivalent about MOOTW. Indeed, the emerging doctrinal concept poses the greatest challenges and complications to the "muddy boots military." Ground force leaders have mixed feelings—they cannot seem to make up their minds as to whether MOOTW constitutes a boon or a boondoggle. For land power components, MOOTW present a dilemma: on the one hand, MOOTW served to justify many boots on the ground; on the other, MOOTW may detract from warfighting capabilities and readiness.

The members of the PLA's most important think tank on doctrinal matters, the Academy of Military Sciences (AMS), tend to be dominated by ground force personnel. These researchers are grappling with the significant and direct impact that a more central role for MOOTW will have on their land locked service. Three authors at AMS have identified two contradictions in MOOTW: The first is the contradiction between self and the enemy; and the second is contradictions among the people. As Senior Colonel Zhou Peiqing and two colleagues at the AMS wrote in a 2009 article on MOOTW in *China Military Science*:

> In particular, in performing the tasks of combating terrorism, maintaining stability, preserving rights, and coping with emergencies, we are often faced with situations in which there are contradictions between the enemy and ourselves, and contradictions among the people, nationalities problems, and religious problems, and overt struggles intertwined with covert struggles. In such situations, our troops have to withstand extremely stern political tests.[36]

The larger point is that such missions are very important but very complicated. As such, "[a]lthough military operations other than war are not combat operations, because they occur abruptly, require arduous duties and involve perilous circumstances of fairly long duration, the demands they place on the fighting spirit of officers and men is no less than wartime operations."[37] Moreover, these are often linked to larger political, economic, social, or international issues note the AMS researchers. Writing from their roost in the higher echelon as a CMC-affiliated research institute, the authors are addressing all three layers of the PLA pyramid: "Most military operations other than war, such as emergency rescue, disaster relief, anti-terrorism, and stability maintenance, are closely linked to the international and domestic situations, and have a bearing on the national image, the nation's economy and the people's livelihood, and social stability."[38]

MOOTW performed inside the country involve close coordination with CCP organs, including grass-roots party entities, government entities, and "the People." "To win victories in war, the armed forces must rely on the support of the people."[39] According to Senior Colonel Zhou and his co-authors,

> This is so in war operations, and also in military operations other than war. Without the ardent support of local governments and the masses, it is hard for the armed forces to accomplish anything whether the military operations are war or non-war. An important part of the political work in non-war military actions is to do a good job in maintaining the unity and cooperation between the military and the government, and between soldiers and civilians. [Moreover,] in carrying out the tasks of combating terrorists and maintaining stability in areas inhabited by national minorities, it is necessary to do a good job of providing personnel support in such aspects as national minorities, religion, language, and offering psychological counseling for soldiers . . . .

Outside the country the PLA also would encounter challenges. Knowledge about "foreign languages, laws, culture, and folkways in specific regions" is vitally important.[40]

Third Dimension: Discourse Beyond the PLA Pyramid.

There is a fundamental contradiction between debunking the "China Threat Theory" and the continued "rapid rise of China's national military power."[41] This contradiction is rarely, if even openly, acknowledged; however, the clearest indication that it exists is the ongoing efforts underway since the mid-1990s to counter the rising "China threat." Indeed, Chinese leaders are making considerable efforts to persuade other countries that China does not pose a threat to them. The double digit growth in the official defense budget over the past 20 years, along with periodic provocative acts by the PLA and some incendiary rhetoric by military men, combine to call into question whether there may be a "civil-military gap" in China's peaceful rise.[42] Beijing has become increasingly aware of perceptions of a China threat in other countries and adopted increasingly sophisticated approaches to countering this international concern. Promotion of a "New Security Concept" in the 1990s morphed into projection of the "peaceful rise" slogan in less than a decade. The latter term was quickly amended to the less ominous "peaceful development."[43]

The PLA dimension to this public relations campaign has slowly ramped up. One of the first indications was the appearance of biannual defense white papers (preceded by a white paper on arms control in 1995) starting in 1998. Squarely aimed at a foreign audience, the document has become gradually more sophisticated, detailed, and lengthy. The aim is to respond to demands that China become more transparent in defense matters. The 2008 *Defense White Paper* highlights the efforts of China's armed forces in humanitarian assistance and disaster relief activities, especially but not exclusively domestically. The latest iteration marks the emergence of the acronym "MOOTW." The acronym also appears on the Ministry of National Defense's website. Significantly, the term appears alongside a peace sign icon only on the English language version of the webpage and is absent from the Chinese language version.[44] This strongly suggests that use of the acronym is directed externally toward foreign audiences. Perhaps the primary purpose of the visit of General Xu Caihou to the United States in October 2009 was to highlight the numerous nonwar activities and heavily domestic focus of China's armed forces in recent years to American audiences. The Vice Chairman of the CMC gave considerable prominence to internal security concerns, including the multiple challenges Beijing faced in western China.[45] The message Xu sought to get across was: China does not pose a military threat to anyone, including the United States.

CHALLENGES

There are a number of significant challenges that become evident from the above contradictions. The horizontal contradictions in MOOTW are real but do not seem to be at the forefront of controversy within the PLA. The vertical contradictions may become more acute in the future but for now they remain manageable (see Challenge #3 below). The main contradiction at the center of the ongoing discourse among members of the PLA is encapsulated in the so-called "two incompatibles." The outward contradiction will also be a challenge.

Challenge # 1: Can the PLA Stay Focused?

The PLA may be unable to focus, be spread too thin, and thereby "lose its way." Indeed, this appears to be a significant fear within China's military. This expansion of missions and operational capabilities may be an inevitable consequence of the PLA beginning to move beyond a consuming focus on the Taiwan scenario.[46] But the process of formally defining these missions and capabilities has come much sooner and in a more accelerated fashion because of the confluence of certain events in 2008—dramatically improved cross-strait relations (following the March election of Ma Ying-jeou), PLA prominence in disaster relief operations (January snow storm rescues and May Wenchuan earthquake relief operations), armed forces involvement in the August Beijing Olympics (performance participation and internal security), growing participation in peacekeeping operations (including more than 300 soldiers to the African Union/ United Nations Hybrid Operation in Darfur, Sudan [UNAMID]), and the December decision to dispatch an anti-piracy task force to the Gulf of Aden.

The PLA is experiencing mission creep writ large. Repeatedly PLA authors stress the necessity of soldiers focusing on the "core (核心)" mission or capabilities: warfighting. Indeed, regular and authoritative utterances of this mantra seem to be aimed at reassuring Chinese soldiers. The party and military leadership have gone to great lengths to stress this point — perhaps reflecting the degree to which they sense that this is a burning issue among Chinese soldiers. As the *Liberation Army Daily* staff commentator stated in the wake of Hu Jintao's talk to PLA delegates at the NPC in March 2009: "The military's raison d'être is warfighting. Throughout history . . . the fundamental duty of the military has always been to prepare for wars, curb wars, wage wars, and win wars."[47]

A concentration on Taiwan contingencies helped PLA modernization by providing a clear target. A Taiwan scenario provided a tangible focus for the PLA to direct training, equipment, and force structure requirements. If this scenario recedes into the background or is relegated to the sidelines, the focus is lost. The value of a single scenario and challenge absorbing PLA thinking was that it enabled the military to make significant leaps in strategy, force planning, and operational capabilities. As James Q. Wilson noted, when an organization can concentrate wholeheartedly on overcoming the challenges of one problem, significant and rapid progress can be forthcoming. A corollary of this propensity is that too many missions can sap an organization's vitality and make it lose focus.[48]

Challenge # 2: Can the PLA Handle the Frustrations?

The expansion of missions and tasks is a recipe for frustration within the PLA. Following from the above analysis, too many demands may result in the PLA feeling completely overwhelmed. There is clearly already a widespread sense of frustration among some Chinese soldiers who feel they are being asked to do too much. In May 2009, editors at *Liberation Army Daily* asked: "Fundamentally, what are the kinds of capabilities that the military needs? Just what kinds of requirements need to be brought to the forefront of core military capabilities?" The questions came in the introduction to an important article intended to provide some authoritative answers to the readers of the newspaper.[49] Titled "Forge Military Capabilities in Sync with the Times," the article was written by someone who would seem to have the respect of his comrades in arms in the Lower Echelon and whose words would likely carry weight with them—55-year-old Major General Wang Xixin (王西欣), a warfighter who commands one of the PLA's most prominent units, the 38th Group Army stationed in the Beijing Military Region.[50]

The bottom line is that the PLA does not want to be distracted from its "core" mission of warfighting and the senior political and military leadership have waged a campaign of rhetoric to reassure the officer corps that this will not be a problem. Moreover, they have attempted to make the new historic missions and MOOTW more palatable to China's soldiers. According to one set of authors writing from their location in the Shenyang Military Region headquarters of the Middle Echelon, "MOOTW expands the traditional scope of army tasks and enable the military forces to play a greater role in a broader scope of time and space." The authors opined: "Relatively speaking, understanding of the military strategic guidelines has focused more on preparing for and winning wars . . . and insufficient attention has been given to MOOTW. This is not only because the strategic position of MOOTW has not been explicitly specified, but also that the strategic guiding principle for MOOTW has not been clarified." The authors tentatively suggest the concept of "selective active participation" rather than trying to do everything.[51]

Challenge #3: Can the Warfighters and their Politico-Military Chain of Command Mitigate/Manage the Tensions?

Among the unintended consequences of this for civil-military relations could easily be growing tensions between the PLA and Party-State. While New Historic Missions provide expansive justification for continued defense spending, they can also raise unrealistic expectations among civilian leaders (and even among the Chinese people) of what the PLA can or should be able to do. Certainly these new missions preempt the possibility of a peace dividend looming in the absence of a Taiwan imperative.[52] As tensions in the Taiwan Strait recede and perhaps even gradually disappear, there may be voices claiming that less funding for defense is necessary, and these monies can be allocated to other worthy projects. However, unlikely as this eventuality may be, the New Historic Missions require significant defense outlays. Defense spending is rarely — if ever — deemed by military professionals to be adequate to meet programs considered essential to national security (hence the existence of the first contradiction identified above).

Yet, equal if not greater aggravation may be directed at the wide spectrum of MOOTW that threatens to place ever-increasing demands on the PLA. In conversations this writer had with PLA researchers in the aftermath of the Wenchuan earthquake, for example, they appeared perturbed by the demands placed upon the military in relief operations. When this writer was asked what he thought of the PLA response to the disaster, he answered that he was full of admiration for the heroism and herculean efforts of Chinese soldiers. Nevertheless, it seemed to him that the armed forces were ill-equipped to handle the scope or scale of the disaster. The PLA researchers readily agreed remarking on the factors that had hampered rescue efforts including a lack of appropriate equipment and transportation. In particular, they cited a lack of helicopters. One officer remarked that if only China had a "FEMA" (Federal Emergency Management Agency) equivalent organization then this would lessen the onus on the PLA.[53]

Challenge #4: Can the PLA Disarm Its Foreign Critics?

The PLA has an ongoing global PR campaign to persuade other countries that China does not pose

a military threat: China is peaceful and defensive-minded. Chinese soldiers stress that the double-digit annual growth in the defense budget does not mean that China is girding for war or territorial conquest. The PLA's growing capabilities are regularly documented in annual U.S. Department of Defense (DoD) reports on Chinese military power, constantly analyzed by researchers and analysts in open source publications such as this conference series, as well as scrutinized by the media. The absence in recent years of military provocations in the Taiwan Strait can help but continued inflammatory rhetoric by senior soldiers and on-going incidents between Chinese forces and those of other countries—notably the United States and Japan—directly contradict the image of a peaceable and non-threatening rising power that Beijing desires to promote.

CONCLUSION

Different entities and echelons within the PLA are faced with reconciling contradictions, confronting challenges, and maneuvering around doctrine as they grapple with the 2003 MSG and subsequent modifications. The New Historic Missions pose daunting dilemmas for China's ground forces. But one of the greatest challenges across the PLA will be to maintain focus, something many soldiers seem to recognize. Other challenges to be confronted are managing the competing interests of different services as well as the tensions between echelons. Top level politico-military leaders appear aware of these and are engaged in trying to mitigate these frustrations. The PLA will also need to reconcile a number of contradictions. The most fundamental contradiction is the one between the demands of military modernization and the limited resources provided by the party-state. A second set of contradictions are between mechanization and informatization, and between the requirements of warfare and MOOTW. Further contradictions are spawned by the complex operational challenges of MOOTW which are of particular concern to the ground forces: contradictions between self and enemy, and contradictions among the people. Lastly, there is the implicit contradiction between the PLA's ongoing robust program of modernization and Beijing's continuing campaign to persuade the rest of the world that China does not pose a military threat to anyone.

To conclude, the core contradictions that the PLA has been grappling with in the past few years are the second set. It is this set of contradictions—dubbed the "two incompatibles" that has been the focus of PLA discourse. The message to China's soldiers—delivered in 2009 by none other than Hu Jintao himself—is that the contradictions are not as severe as some have made them out to be. According to Hu and others, the key focus of the PLA ought to be on honing its military capabilities to wage war. In sum, while MOOTW is important, most important is being ready to fight and win China's future wars.

What can one say about the larger significance of this analysis? First of all, the research offers important hints as to where the PLA is heading and differences within the military. The study provides a key window into the formulation and development of military doctrine. It is the PLA itself that seems to play the dominant role in formulating doctrine. If the discourse in recent years over the New Historic Missions is any indication, doctrine is developed through a dialectic process with significant vertical and horizontal dimensions as well an internal/external dimension. However, the involvement external to the PLA pyramid appears to be very limited. What little nonmilitary input within China that might occur would be at the apex through CMC Chair Hu Jintao. But since Hu has no appreciable military experience or expertise this is likely to be only of a very general broad brush variety. External input may also penetrate from outside of China via the internal/external dimension, but this discourse may be only one-way traffic — going outward.

There is also significant continuity in the PLA's doctrinal evolution and traditions. Doctrine appears to evolve gradually with considerable continuity with the past. The New Historic Missions announced by Hu in 2004, seem consistent with the "peacetime guidelines" outlined in the *Science of Strategy* (战略学) published in 1999 by the National Defense University Press.[54] The recent changes are the latest developments in an on-going gradual transformation, which began in the mid-1980s, away from a consuming focus on war, along with increasing doctrinal sophistication and complexity. Moreover, the noncombat missions of the PLA identified in the first decade of the 21st century hark back to the PLA's long-standing traditions as a productive force and an educative force.

Close monitoring of this doctrinal discourse can provide a valuable indicator of whether the PLA is becoming more or less threatening. It allows one to peek at the future trajectory — to discern where China's military is headed. It is a data point for identifying trends in intra-PLA relations and in civil-military relations. Lastly, it can suggest fruitful opportunities for other countries to draw the PLA out of its shell for military-to-military exchanges.

ENDNOTES - CHAPTER 3

1. *China's National Defense 2008*, Beijing, China: Information Office of the State Council, January 2009. Moreover, for the first time a military entity held a press conference to officially launch the white paper. On January 20, 2009, Senior Colonel Hu Chang-ming of the recently established Ministry of National Defense Information Office briefed the media on the contents of the document. For more on this new office, see Matthew Boswell, "Media Relations in China's Military: The Case of the Ministry of National Defense Information Office," *Asia Policy*, Vol. 8, July 2009, pp. 97-120.

2. Paul H. B. Godwin, "Change and Continuity in Chinese Military Doctrine, 1949-1999," in Mark A. Ryan, David M. Finkelstein, and Michael A. McDevitt, eds., *Chinese Warfighting: The PLA Experience since 1949*, Armonk, NY: M. E. Sharpe, 2003, p. 24. For key works of scholarship on Chinese doctrine, see other writings by the same author. See also James Mulvenon and David Finkelstein, eds., *China's Revolution in Doctrinal Affairs: Emerging Trends in the Operational Art of the Chinese People's Liberation Army*, n.p.: n.d.; Yao Yunzhu, "The Evolution of Military Doctrine of the Chinese PLA from 1985 to 1995," *The Korean Journal of Defense Analysis*, Vol. 7, Winter 1995, pp. 57-80; and Georges Tan Eng Bok, "Strategic Doctrine," in Gerald Segal and William T. Tow, eds., *Chinese Defense Policy*, Urbana and Chicago, IL: University of Chicago Press, 1984, pp. 3-17.

3. There can be a time lag during a leadership succession of at least several months before the new paramount ruler assumes the chair position on both of the CMCs. On one occasion, this situation dragged on for considerably longer. For details, see Andrew Scobell, "China's Evolving Civil-Military Relations: Creeping Guojiahua," *Armed Forces and Society*, Vol. 31, No. 2, Winter 2005, pp. 229-230.

4. For more discussion of military strategic guidelines, see David M. Finkelstein, "China's National Military Strategy: An Overview of the Military's Strategic Guidelines," in Roy Kamphausen and Andrew Scobell, eds., *Right-Sizing the PLA: Exploring the Contours of China's Military*, Carlisle, PA: Strategic Studies Institute, U.S. Army War College, 2007, pp. 69-140. The quotes are on pp. 82 and 95.

5. New MSGs have been issued in mid-1950s, mid-1960s, early 1970s, mid-1980s, and in 1993. See Finkelstein, "China's National Military Strategy," p. 93.

6. Andrew Scobell, "Why the People's Army Fired on the People: The Chinese Military and Tiananmen," *Armed Forces and Society*, Vol. 18, No. 1, Winter 1992, pp. 194-195. The term is that of Robin Allison Remington who used it to describe the communist era armed forces of Yugoslavia. See her "Political-Military Relations in Post-Tito Yugoslavia," in Pedro Ramet, ed., *Yugoslavia in the 1980s*, Boulder, CO: Westview Press, 1985, p. 57. Typically, civil-military relations in communist party-states have been described as approximating a "penetration" model in which the party controls the military by penetrating it. This term is Eric Nordlinger's. See his *Soldiers in Politics: Military Coups and Governments*, Englewood Cliffs, NJ: Prentice-Hall, 1977, pp. 15-18.

7. For a comprehensive treatment of the New Historic Missions, see Daniel M. Harnett, *Toward a Globally Focused Chinese Military: The Historic Missions of the Chinese Armed Forces*, Alexandria, VA: CNA Corporation, 2008. While the preferred term in Chinese official translations is "historical," this author—consistent with Harnett—prefers "historic." For a Chinese elaboration of the New Historic Missions, see, for example, Zheng Weiping and Liu Mingfu, eds., 军队新的历史使命论 (*On the Historic Missions of the Military*), Beijing, China: Renmin Wujing Chubanshe, 2005.

8. See, for example, Wang Xixin, "打造与时代同步的核心军事能力 ("Forge Core Military Capabilities in Sync with the Times"), 解放军报 (*Liberation Army Daily*), May 2, 2009, p. 6.

9. James Mulvenon, "Chairman Hu and the PLA's New Historic Missions," *China Leadership Monitor*, No. 27, Winter 2009, p. 7.

10. Perhaps a more apt term would be "MOOTW with Chinese characteristics." Whether the PLA's conception of MOOW is significantly different to the U.S. military understanding of the term is an open question to be answered by further research. I am indebted to Kevin Lanzit for deepening my understanding of this concept.

11. *China's National Defense in 2008*, Beijing, China: State Council Information Office, January 2009, pp. 8-9.

12. *Ibid.*

13. *Ibid.*, p. 9.

14. See, for example, Bao Shixiu, "Deterrence Revisited: Outer Space," *China Security*, Vol. 5, Winter 2007, pp. 2-11; and Dennis J. Blasko, "Military Parades Demonstrate Chinese Concept of Deterrence," *China Brief*, Vol. IX, Issue 8, April 16, 2009, pp. 7-10.

15. *China's National Defense in 2008*, p. 9.

16. Peng Guangqian and Yao Youzhi, eds., *The Science of Military Strategy*, Beijing, China: Military Science Publishing House, 2005, p. 213.

17. *China's National Defense in 2008*, p. 9.

18. Liu Xiangyang, Xu Sheng, Xiong Kaiping, and Zhong Chunyu, "非战争军事行动探要" ("An examination of MOOTW"), 中国军事科学 (*China Military Science*), No. 3, 2008, p. 1. Unless otherwise noted translations are my own.

19. Liu Xiangyang *et al.*, "非战争军事行动探要" p. 4.

20. Zhu Qi, "坚持科学发展观，推进部队全面建设" ("Uphold the scientific development concept, promote comprehensive army building"), 求是 (*Qiushi*), No. 14, July 16, 2005, internet version.

21. Andrew Scobell, "Is There a Civil-Military Gap in China's Peaceful Rise?" *Parameters*, Vol. XXXIX, No. 2, Summer 2009, p. 9.

22. Wang Guosheng, "对我军历史使命的认识与思想" ("Understanding and thinking about our military's historic missions"), 中国军事科学 (*China Military Science*), No. 5, 2008, p. 64-66.

23. Wang Guosheng, "对我军历史使命的认识与思想" p. 63.

24. New Year's Day Message, "在党的十七大精神指引下开创国防和军队现代化建设新局面" ("Promote a new situation in national defense and army building modernization under the driving spirit of the 17 Party Congress"), 解放军报 (*Liberation Army Daily*), January 1, 2008.

25. Editorial note, "打造与时代同步的核心军事能力" ("Forge core military capabilities in sync with the times"), 解放军报 (*Liberation Army Daily*), May 2, 2009. There are apparently others but these are not identified.

26. Wang Xixin (王西欣), "打造与时代同步的核心军事能力" ("Forge core military capabilities in sync with the times"), 解放军报 (*Liberation Army Daily*), May 2, 2009.

27. Editorial note, "打造与时代同步的核心军事能力" ("Forge core military capabilities in sync with the times"), 解放军报 (*Liberation Army Daily*), May 2, 2009.

28. Staff Commentator, "重点加强核心军事能力建设" ("Emphasize strengthening the building of core military capabilities"), 解放军报 (*Liberation Army Daily*), March 18, 2009.

29. The *Liberation Army Daily* is published by the General Political Department, but articles by "staff commentators" tend to be a vehicle to transmit messages from the CMC to the rest of the PLA.

30. Thus, a 2 million-man reduction of the militia (from 10 million to 8 million) occurring under the 11th Five Year Plan (2006-10) is unlikely to be followed by cuts of a comparable magnitude. *China's National Defense in 2008*, p. 37.

31. This "domestic drag" is a result of the enduring legacy of the long-standing internal security and nonmilitary functions historically performed by the armed forces in the communist era in the periods both before and after 1949. This term overlaps with the idea of a "Maoist drag" identified by Solomon Karmel in 1998. However, "domestic drag" is broader and more all-encompassing in scope and significance. On the earlier term, see Solomon Karmel, "The Maoist Drag on China's Military," *Orbis*, Vol. 42, No. 3, Summer 1998, pp. 375-386.

32. According to the 2009 *Defense White Paper*, "Expenses for personnel, training, and maintenance account for two-thirds of the defense expenditure," *China's National Defense in 2008*, p. 46.

33. Tian Zhong, "海军非战争军事行动的特点类型及能力建设" ("Special characteristics, categories, and capabilities of naval military operations other than war"), 中国军事科学 (*China Military Science*), No. 3, 2008, p. 25.

34. Wang Mingliang, Yang Yujie, Wei Dexing, Pang Xu, and Wang Suying, "非战争军事行动观察报告" ("Survey report on military operations other than war"), 中国空军 (*China Air Force*), July 2008 pp. 62, 64.

35. *Ibid.*, pp. 61-62.

36. Zhou Peiqing, Gan Xuerong, and Wang Xintian, "非战争军事行动政治工作特点规律研究" ("Research on the special characteristics and laws of political work in military operations other than war), 中国军事科学 (*China Military Science*), No. 6, 2009, p. 68.

37. *Ibid.*, p. 69.

38. *Ibid.*, p. 68.

39. *Ibid.*, p. 69.

40. *Ibid.*, p. 70.

41. See Contradiction #7 in Huang Renwei, "试论中国在世纪之交国际环境中的深层矛盾" ("On China's deep contradictions in the international system at the turn of the century"), 上海社会科学院季刊 (*Quarterly Journal of the Shanghai Academy of Social Sciences*), No. 1, 1997, pp. 10-11.

42. See, for example, Scobell, "Is there a Civil-Military 'Gap' in China's 'Peaceful Rise'?"

43. See, for example, Yong Deng, " Reputation and the Security Dilemma: China Reacts to the China Threat Theory," in Alastair Iain Johnston and Robert S. Ross, eds., *New Directions in the Study of China's Foreign Policy*, Stanford, CA: Stanford University Press,

2007, pp. 186-216; and Bonnie S. Glaser and Evan S. Medeiros, "The Changing Ecology of Foreign Policy-Making in China: The Ascension and Demise of the Theory of 'Peaceful Rise'," *China Quarterly*, Vol. 190, June 2007, pp. 291-310.

44. The website address is *www.mod.gov.cn*. The author thanks Greg Stevenson for drawing this to his attention.

45. Address at Center for Strategic and International Studies delivered by Gen. Xu Caihou, Vice Chairman, Central Military Commission, PRC, October 26, 2009, available from *www.mod.gov.cn*; and personal communications, Washington, DC, Fall 2009.

46. See, for example, Roy Kamphausen, David Lai, and Andrew Scobell, eds., *Beyond the Strait: PLA Missions Other Than Taiwan*, Carlisle, PA: Strategic Studies Institute, U.S. Army War College, 2009.

47. Staff Commentator, "重点加强核心军事能力建设" ("Emphasizing strengthening the building of core military capabilites").

48. James Q. Wilson, *Bureaucracy: What Government Agencies Do and Why They Do It*, New York: Basic Books, 1989, pp. 5-6, 14-18. For discussion of this in the context of the PLA and Taiwan, see Andrew Scobell, *China's Use of Military Force: Beyond the Great Wall and the Long March*, New York: Cambridge University Press, 2003, p. 190.

49. "Editorial Note," 解放军报 (*Liberation Army Daily*), May 2, 2009.

50. Major General Wang, born in 1954, joined the PLA in 1974 and the CCP in 1978. He is a veteran of the 1979 Vietnam conflict, a member of the PLA delegation to the National People's Congress, and an author of regularly published articles on military matters. Biographical data provided by Daniel Alderman of NBR.

51. Liu Xiangyang *et al.* Quotations are from pages 4 and 5.

52. Mulvenon, "Chairman Hu and the PLA's 'New Historic Missions'," p. 9.

53. Conversations with PLA researchers, Beijing, China, Summer and Fall 2008. I cautioned that the existence of a FEMA did not guarantee a quicker or more effective governmental response to a disaster (Hurricane Katrina and New Orleans, for example); moreover, the military was probably destined to bear the brunt of a response in any natural disaster no matter what the official bureaucratic responsibilities were.

54. See, for example, the discussion in M. Taylor Fravel, "The Evolution of China's Military Strategy: Comparing the 1987 and 1999 Editions of *Zhanlue Xue*," in James Mulvenon and David Finkelstein, eds., *China's Revolution in Doctrinal Affairs*, p. 96.

CHAPTER 4

CHANGING CIVIL-MILITARY RELATIONS IN CHINA

You Ji

Daniel Alderman

The People's Liberation Army (PLA) celebrated its 82nd birthday in August 2009. Compared with earlier milestones in 1927 and 1949, the PLA today is very different. Among the many changes that the PLA has undergone, its dramatic change vis-à-vis the PRC's civilian leadership has been most visible.[1] This can be concretely tested by Hu Jintao's way of commanding the military, which represents a sharp contrast with all his predecessors. Simply put, he is the first Chinese Communist Party (CCP) leader whose power consolidation is not through first controlling the gun. He is the first post-Mao leader whose control of the gun is based on first establishing a high level of popularity in the Party and society and then acquiring military compliance; and he is also the first leader who commands the military without first creating a structural personnel network within the Party and the PLA to manage powerful generals. Are these novelties permanent features of a new kind of civil-military relations in the making in China, or are they just an isolated development due to the personal leadership style of one particular Party leader?[2] Whatever the answer is, it further intensifies the on-going debate in the field about the continued relevance of the concept of symbiosis (休戚与共), the analytical framework that PLA analysts have applied to the study of CCP/PLA relations for many years.[3] If the concept of symbiosis has indeed become obsolete, what new theoretical framework should we use to guide our study on this important issue?

This chapter will assess the changes in China's civil-military relations as part of its overall political transformation. In order to assess these changes, this chapter analyzes the major trends that are taking place within China's civil-military relations as China's traditionally symbiotic relationship undergoes a period of transition. When placed together, the elements of the symbiotic framework in transition form a relationship in which the PLA seems to be wielding increasing autonomy over its modernization and national security decisionmaking, while civilian leadership is primarily exerted at the pentacle of power in Hu Jintao and the Central Military Committee (CMC).[4] This chapter will use two case studies to highlight these changes: Hu's command of the PLA and his Taiwan policy.

CIVIL-MILITARY RELATIONS BEYOND SYMBIOSIS

Until recently, the concept of symbiosis captured the essence of CCP/PLA relations. For a long time, the two most powerful institutions in China were fused in the governing process. And, the lack of functional differentiation and clear institutional boundaries between the two underlined their unique ties. The Party in uniform informs the nature of communist civil-military relations,[5] and symbiosis has traditionally been the foundation for communist rule worldwide.

Civil-Military Symbiosis: Identifying the Changes and Continuities.

How has post-Mao reform altered this pattern of CCP/PLA interaction? The obsolescence of symbiosis as a defining concept is now a common view.[6] The diversification of Party/PLA interests has exerted strong impact on Party/army interaction and led prominent scholars to explore replacement of symbiosis as the dominant theoretical paradigm.[7]

The paradigm *symbiosis* is built on four pillars in Party/PLA relations: (1) a common ideological and revolutionary ferment; (2) an overlapping personnel structure reflecting an integrated decisionmaking process at the apex of power;[8] (3) a nearly equal political status; and (4) shared mentality and vested interests in governance. These four pillars have historically provided channels for Party penetration into the military and for PLA intervention in civilian politics (相互渗透). As a result, the PLA acquired a political role.

Changes have taken place in all of these four parameters, giving rise to a new pattern of civil-military interplay. First, revolution is no longer an organizational objective for the PLA. It simply describes its willing subordination to the Party with no forced ideological hold on soldiers. Second, the overlapping personnel structure is basically undone. There is no politician in uniform in the country.[9] The minimized PLA presentation at the apex of power has become largely functional. The Party owns the procedural control over the appointments of the top brass, but these appointments are mainly based on CMC nominations.[10] Third, the military's status in the political system is crucial, as it holds the final say to the settlement of most serious Party disputes, proven by its role in 1966, 1976, and in 1989. Yet one major change in China's political system is despecialization of PLA status in both state apparatus and society, partly due to the design of CCP leaders learning the lesson of the Cultural Revolution, and partly due to the PLA's own choice of reducing its involvement in nonprofessional affairs. In the public's eye, the PLA is one of the important institutions in government, not above any other in the system, such as the State Council.

The changes in the fourth category are subtler. The PLA shares the Party's determination to maintain the existing system and makes itself available to answer the Party's call for actions against any organized opposition. Therefore, the remnants of symbiosis are still visible, and today the Party and the PLA firmly stick together. The military supports the CCP, which respects the military's voice on major national issues and provides it with the best resources possible. Thence, the PLA has little incentive or need to disobey the Party when its privileges are guaranteed. At a time short of crisis, the current formula of the PLA backing the civilians' political agenda in exchange of their support to its modernization will continue to hold.

Within civilian-military relations, many long-term and strategic challenges lie in the domestic front, namely how the PLA positions itself in the tripartite relations between the Party and society, in which the latter two are not always in harmony. The number of organized protests in China is mounting.[11] But these protests have been social and economic in nature, posing no immediate pressure on the military to make a choice. However, given the nature of the country's stressful state/society relations, when these protests are resolved, they are social and economic, but when they become hard to suppress, they become highly political. The prospects that the PLA is ordered to do the mission of cleaning the street remain constant. China has entered a risky period of transformation.[12] The Tiananmen event has made PLA officers reluctant to be drawn into a clampdown on large-scale civic protests.[13] This shows that the real test would come only when a major social crisis occurs. The PLA's unconditional support to the Party is a foregone conclusion in a symbiotic relationship, but as the nature of this relationship changes over time, such a conclusion cannot be drawn with high confidence in a situation of major social crisis.

A hypothesis can be raised that *symbiosis* is a transitional phenomenon, found in transitional regimes and reflecting a course of gradual transformation. In the Union of Soviet Socialist Republics (USSR), the ties between the ruling party and the military seemed to be symbiotic in peacetime. Yet once they no longer saw their common survival in the same boat, the military placed its own interests above those they used to share.[14] This was a natural and an unavoidable choice under enormous internal and external pressure, as the Soviet Red Army decided in 1991 that defending the Party would be too costly and fundamentally jeopardize its own key interests. A painful divorce occurred. The Soviet case revealed that the symbiotic civil-military relationship is neither a given, nor unshakable. This divorce was the result of a military embracing professionalism, deemphasizing ideology and protecting its own prestige. The trigger for this is often irreconcilable confrontation between the state and society, which imposes the ultimate choice upon communist armed forces.

China's case is a lot more complicated. However, similar catalysts for change are discernable in most societies in transition. Organizational atrophy is a rule for all political institutions. This is especially logical for a ruling party, which is huge in size and possesses enormous resources, but is under no effective system of checks and balances. The pace of Party atrophy is logically faster than that of a professional, highly disciplined, and relatively small organization like the PLA. This organizational logic is further enhanced by the inherent contradictions in a symbiotic civil-military relationship — the military being the one servant serving two masters: the Party, which remains monolithic; and the society, which becomes increasingly more pluralistic. Indeed, the PLA defines itself as a Party's army, a people's army, and a professional army.[15] However, these three features may clash against each other, especially during a time of crisis. The factors that drove traditional dynastic cycles present themselves in present time, and are mostly embodied in official corruption and state/society tensions. In the long run, dichotomous institutional imperatives may create fault zones in Party control of the gun. Moreover, there has been no permanent symbiotic civil-military relationship in China's recorded history.

Conceptualizing Emerging Trends: Shared PLA/ Party Interests?

The changes mentioned above are significant, but at the present time they are embedded in continuities of close CCP/PLA bondage of 82 years of mutual support. Military subordination to the civilians remains a strong tradition in Chinese military culture,[16] which has been reinforced by the Party with numerous new ways of organizational and spiritual control over the soldiers. Despite all the changes in civil-military relations, the traditions of the old guard linger on in the post-Deng era. For instance, the first thing a new conscript does after entering the barracks is to express an oath in front of the Party banner, shouting that he would sacrifice everything to protect the Party. The Party's psychological hold on soldiers should not be underestimated, as the majority of them take obedience to the Party for granted throughout their service career.

There are several cases that exemplify this trend. In a 1993 trip to the Association of Southeast Asian Nations (ASEAN), General Chi Haotian announced that, at the request of the Party, the PLA pledged not to use force to settle the South China Sea disputes when other claimants continued to occupy islets there. Again in 2002, China's signing of the ASEAN Treaty of Amity legally tied the PLA's hands for further actions. In the early 1990s, the PLA was doubtful about Lee Tenghui's intention to conduct secret contact with Beijing,[17] but it followed Jiang's peace initiative toward Taiwan embodied in his 1995 8-point declaration, whose emphasis on "Chinese do not fight Chinese" amounted to half-way discarding the use of military means to resolve the Taiwan issue. Yet it backed Jiang anyway. When the PLA's research for upgrading land and sea-based long-range nuclear missiles was at a crucial stage, it accepted the civilian order to terminate nuclear tests in 1996, which probably delayed warhead miniaturization. Furthermore, answering the call of the Party, the PLA gave up its vast economic and commercial machine in 1998. After the EP-3 incident in 2001, the PLA ordered its combat units monitoring U.S. military spy activities in both the South and

East China Seas to exercise maximum restraint, again following the Politburo's decision.[18] Furthermore, there is a long lasting discrepancy between civilian and military interests over the military's budget. The PLA's structural shortfall in funding has stimulated PLA strategists to persistently require an increase in the military's share of 1.7 percent in the gross domestic product (GDP) total to 3 percent, and from 8 percent in government expenditure to 12-15 percent.[19] Apparently, the civilian leaders have not budged. The fact that no matter how reluctantly the PLA has swallowed what is imposed upon it indicates that it is very conscious of civilian supremacy over it.

On the other hand, PLA subordination has been rewarded in this relationship of shared interests with the Party that defines the relationship today. Actual civil-military interest-sharing has served as a political foundation for the PRC's political system from which each organization benefits enormously. Additionally, interest-sharing is grounded on their shared national goal of making China socially stable, economically prosperous, and militarily powerful (富国强兵).[20] In addition, the PLA actively embraces the Party's promotion of nationalism, concretely expressed by their shared determination to safeguard Beijing's sovereignty over domestic governance and territorial integrity. For instance, anti-Taiwan independence has become a key ideological anchorage for Party/military interaction. The PLA's focus on external threats is enhanced by its deeply rooted anti-Americanism that has translated into support for the Party's goal of power consolidation at home and preparation for international conflict.

In 1999, the Party decided to accelerate preparation for war and made military modernization a top national priority, paralleling Deng's principle of economics in command, much to the delight of PLA generals. War preparation has enhanced the PLA's special place in China's overall development.[21] On the other hand, military transformation serves CCP efforts to raise China's international profile, which in turn enhances the Party's popularity with the soldiers. Inevitably, building a capable fighting force entails sustained inputs of resources. Although short of PLA expectations, CCP leaders have ensured the rise of defense expenditures in keeping with the GDP growth rate. The *National Defense Law* provides the legal basis for the double-digit military budget increase in the last 2 decades. The special interest-sharing relations between the CCP and the PLA are reflected in the fact that few ruling parties in the world are as nice as the CCP is to the PLA and vice versa.

Conceptualizing Emerging Trends: Promoting PLA Professionalism.

The ultimate interests sought by the PLA as a key power group concern the improvement of its combat capabilities and corporate identity. Preparation for war is now the center of all its work, and everything else serves the goal of winning the next war.[22] This has made irreversible the trend of PLA professionalization, which has a profound impact on long term civil-military ties. At the moment, a delicate balance has been struck by the two sides: if professionalism helps create a strong, subordinate, and noninterventionist PLA, it serves the best interests of the Party: protecting the CCP's hold on power, while allowing the PLA to concentrate on its professional pursuits.

What CCP leaders have done in this regard is similar to what civilians in other states do: have soldiers obsessed more with the high-tech "toys" than with elusive politics. The outcome of this arrangement is the joint CCP/PLA promotion of military professionalism as a way for the former to use objective control measures to supplement its traditional subjective control mechanisms.[23] Promoting PLA professionalism thus serves as a practical point of departure from Maoist strong-man control based on factional manipulation, overt ideological indoctrination and routine politicization.

There is consensus in the field that the PLA is rapidly professionalizing. However, true PLA professionalization is possible only alongside a high level of depoliticization (去政治化). Here debate arises on how depoliticized the PLA has become.[24] There are signs of depoliticization in the PLA, based on a relatively narrow perspective that the officers have largely taken a noninterventionist approach to the Party's internal strife and to civilians' decisionmaking process on non-defense matters.

In further exploring this professionalization, it is important to note that the PLA's information technology (IT)/revolution in military affairs (RMA)-driven transformation has made the PLA a high-tech force, increasingly unsuitable for domestic missions involving street control. The rapid changes within the composition of the PLA's personnel structure, as reflected by ever-rising proportions of returned students from foreign countries, graduates from civilian universities, and noncommissioned conscripts, contributes to the PLA's "expertise and corporateness."[25] In the West, the military has basically curbed its influence within the national security policymaking process.[26] The question for the PLA is whether its trend of nonintervention on matters other than defense can be institutionalized so that the generals' noninterventionism can go beyond being a self-imposed choice to being a self-conscious culture, producing soldiers of political neutrality. Such an end will depend on several conditions. First, on-going gradual political change continues to derevolutionize the Party and reshape the military's objectives, e.g., from internally oriented to externally focused. Second, this popular depoliticization continues to influence new conscripts who are changing the PLA from within, e.g., graduates from civilian universities bringing a worldly middle class mentality to the officer corps. Third, China's zeal for globalization and the PLA's study of Western military science and technology help it accept international norms for civil-military relations. There is no doubt that western military science has been the dominant paradigm shaping Chinese military thinking since the early 1990s. IT/RMA insights now guide the PLA in formulating national defense strategy and combat doctrines of all four services. It is doubtful, however, whether western ideas of objective control, especially in the form of state, not partisan, command of the gun, have deeply penetrated the minds of officers. Although they eagerly embrace western military thinking, the majority of them simply do not distinguish the Party from the state.

On the other hand, relatively apolitical technocrats, e.g., graduates from civilian universities, have started to take over command within the lower levels of the PLA hierarchy, a sign of rising professionalism within the officer corps. This will increasingly have an impact on the "red" (loyal to the Party) versus "expert" (commitment to professionalism) discourse. The former is often a Party imposition upon soldiers for how to think and behave, and the latter is often

a natural requirement for officers operating sophisticated high-tech equipment. PLA history has proved
that this discourse is inherently self-contradictory and
underlies the Party's continuous call for the PLA to
resist western ideas of "delinking party-military ties,"
"depoliticization," and "nationalizing" the PLA.[27] The
danger to CCP control over the gun is clear: Party
control, based on ideational indoctrination, is progressively diluted as the PLA undertakes internal changes
driven by IT/RMA transformation. This explains why
the CCP continues to emphasize its "absolute control
over the gun."

Specifically, rising PLA professionalism can be
gauged by the military's retreat from societal politics,
as it is no longer an organ of CCP grass-roots mobilization. Furthermore, the PLA has relinquished "people's war doctrine" and related combat models, as
these are irrelevant to its future mode of engagement:
no land invasion of China is imaginable for a long
time to come. Thus, these events gradually undercut
the so-called natural ties between a revolutionary
military and a politicized population that previously
enhanced the symbiotic civil-military relationship in
the name of a "nation-in-arms." The PLA has ridded
itself of many nonprofessional missions that impeded
it from exercising its primary functions of national defense. Increasingly, professionalism defines the value
judgments of PLA soldiers and encourages them to be
preoccupied with the business of war. Indirectly the
emphasis on "expert" erodes a foundation of "red."
Additionally, corporate identity is a double-edged
sword for civil-military relations in all transforming
societies: a united military contributes to the ruling
party when both sides share strategic interests, but
this could become a problem if their interests diverge

over major issues. To the CCP, an exclusive PLA corporate identity as a result of officer unity undermines the foundation of the Maoist divide-and-rule method of control, which is still useful for the Party to counter the possibility of a powerful and politically ambitious general. Gradually, new rules have emerged governing the changing civil-military relations in the post-Deng era. Apparently, these rules are inherently at odds with symbiosis.

Conceptualizing Emerging Trends: Codifying CCP/PLA Interaction.

PLA professionalism has been instrumental in allowing the CCP and the PLA to institutionalize (制度化) their relations during the post-Mao period. Institutionalization is a rule-based control mechanism, and it is the best weapon to curb interventionist tendencies from both civilian and military leaders.[28] The essence of China's post-Mao military reform is to regulate the PLA's political role in the country's political and social system, based on a CCP/PLA understanding on the danger of military interventionism in domestic politics. At the same time that Party officials are officially barred from intruding into PLA affairs, they are especially prohibited from forging any unauthorized contacts with PLA generals for the purpose of political lobbying.[29] To the CCP, the significance of institutionalization is that it can help avoid the worst of Mao's practice of using the gun to settle internal party disputes.

Ironically however, the best institutional safeguard for the CCP and the PLA that creates a good fence between them is Mao's formula of 政治局议政, 军委议军 (the Politburo takes charge of political affairs and the CMC military affairs). This has been codified in order to govern the interactions between these two most powerful institutions.[30] These codified rules are sanctioned by an emerging culture in civil-military relations, which has created a deeply rooted taboo in the minds of both civilian and military leaders not to step beyond this red line.[31] The leaders who intrude into areas of responsibility other than their own have been punished politically, as seen by the lesson of Yang Shangkun (杨尚昆) and Yang Baibing (杨白冰) who in 1992 used the PLA to back up Deng's way of reform without CMC approval. This unauthorized PLA interference with civilian leadership was the immediate cause for their removal from PLA top command. Since then, no such case has been repeated. Clearly, this lesson has been learned with sincerity from both sides. Indeed, institutionalization cuts both ways for the CCP and the PLA, and it has placed the commander in chief in a most advantageous position for moving between exerting party leadership over the PLA and soliciting military support for his policy initiatives. Jiang and Hu have effectively used existing civilian institutions for control and to compensate for their weakness vis-à-vis the generals and have had PLA support for their major policies.

In principle, the decisionmaking process concerning matters of national defense and national security is now structured in regular and formal meetings of the relevant parties after lengthy consultations and debate among different interests.[32] Less known, however, are the concrete channels of communication between the PLA and state agencies over specific cases that have strong domestic and international significance. One example is the PLA shooting down *Feng Yun-1C*, a meteorological satellite, on January 11,

2007. Because of the foreign ministry spokesman's ignorance of the event during a news conference at the time, some analysts believed that it was an independent PLA act.[33] This chapter argues that this is not the case. There is no doubt that the antisatellite weapon (ASAT) proposal came from the CMC, where Hu's approval was crucial and needed to be cleared by civilians in the Politburo Standing Committee (PSC). This conforms to Hu's leadership style, which stresses collective responsibility and civil-military coordination on key national security matters that are of grave international consequence. Technically, the satellite was owned by a civilian body, the Central Meteorological Bureau under the State Council. It is inconceivable that the PLA could knock it down without any prior consultation with the State Council, because the political consequences were simply too huge. Moreover, the PLA needed specific data from the Bureau in its long preparation for the operation, e.g., data acquisition of the satellite. Therefore, the PLA could not do the test without civilian assistance. The question is at what level the bureaucrats were notified about it. It is apparent that neither the Ministry of Foreign Affairs nor the State Meteorological Bureau was senior enough to be involved in the decisionmaking process, but this does not mean that their top heads were not informed before the missile launch.

The civilians at various state agencies are not in a position to monitor, still less oppose, any PLA initiative proposed by the CMC, approved by the PSC and pursued in the name of national security. Their role is simply to help the PLA implement the initiative, as seen from the PLA's missile exercises in 1996 and the Sino-Russo joint exercise in 2005. Yet civil-military coordination on matters that could have a deep impact on China's relations with major world powers, especially with the United States, are taken seriously in regard to anticipated or unforeseen events, such as the U.S. Naval Ship (USNS) *Impeccable* encounter. To the PLA, it was electronic warfare, not just a diplomatic incident, as the ship was perceived to be stealing vital information about China's nuclear submarines. Therefore, advanced counter plans (预案) have been formulated to deal with this quasi-war situation. Yet in order to lower the intensity of confrontation, it was the militia that was dispatched to the scene with PLA back-up. Therefore, civilians' assistance was important. Like the U.S. aircraft EP-3 event before it, Chinese action was carefully executed according to the predetermined rules of engagement, and thus it was unlikely independent behavior by the soldiers at the front line. During the EP-3 incident, Wang Wei may have implemented the plan with more zeal than necessary, but it was not likely a breach of discipline.

Conceptualizing Emerging Trends: Guaranteeing Military Autonomy.

The post-Deng leaders have realized that institutionalized civil-military relations can be achieved only when civilians and generals strike a balance between effective civilian control and sufficient military autonomy. Without the former, the military may be tempted to maximize its gains at the expense of other political and social interests. Without the latter, civilian control can be intrusive and bilateral relations become unstable. Only when the military has enough autonomy, will it become less interventionist in inner party politics. In the post-Deng era, the trend toward promoting military autonomy has been a focus of institutionalization within civil-military relations. In other words, a level of autonomy is the precondition for the PLA to reshape of the relationship of symbiosis with the Party.

At the organizational level, thanks to the unparalleled power of the CMC, which is made up entirely by professional soldiers except for its chair, the military has achieved a relatively independent status vis-à-vis the center of state power. This can be seen from the following points. In terms of the decisionmaking process, the CMC is under the Politburo in the Party's hierarchical chain. However, in actuality it operates largely outside the latter's reach under the formula of "政治局议政, 军委议军 (the Politburo takes charge of political affairs and the CMC military affairs)," as mentioned earlier. Unless invited, no civilian Politburo member can sit in CMC weekly meetings where key decisions are decided by the top brass. But, some of the key decisions may be presented to weekly Politburo or PSC meetings for approval. The next step is normally a formality, as CMC proposals are already agreed to by the General Secretary. On personnel matters, the CC Central Organizational Department formally transferred PLA cadre management responsibility to the PLA General Cadre Department on August 14, 1950, at Mao's order.[34] This amounted to severing the Party's command chain over the PLA's personnel system. According to the current "PLA Active Duty Officer Appointment Regulations and Procedures," with the CMC chair's authorization in the form of his signature, the CMC can automatically appoint commanders up to the level of heads of the *Dadanwei* (大单位): headquarters departments, military regions, three special services, and the People's Armed Police (PAP). No word is mentioned about the role of the

Party Center (党中央).[35] This simply follows the tradition and privilege of Mao and Deng in selecting top PLA commanders without any need to seek Politburo opinion, not to say approval.[36] The difference in the post-Deng era is that selection and approval of CMC members has to come through the Politburo process. However, this is exclusively based on CMC recommendations because, first, members in the PSC are not personally familiar with PLA generals; and, second, they know personnel power is seriously guarded by the CMC chair. Moreover, ties between top civil and military leaders are predominantly business oriented, leaving little room for personal preference. Thus, Hu has further strengthened the CMC's autonomy. Under Hu, PLA nominations have basically become professional and functional, with fixed terms and little connection to civilian factional networks and major policy debates. Therefore, there is little need for PSC members to oppose any particular appointee. Today, this pattern of PLA appointment has taken the form of a tradition—a norm and rules of the game. Both civilian and PLA leaders know that any serious breach of this tradition could be both disruptive to civil-military interaction and politically expensive. Therefore, few people are likely to rock the boat.

The lack of reinforceable organizational means over PLA personnel matters has resulted in CCP political leadership over military affairs in the form of Party leadership in providing ideological guidance and the Party line to the PLA.[37] The rhetoric *Party Center* has gradually become an abstract concept to soldiers, as compared with the word CMC. The state administration has no agency overseeing military affairs. This political division of power erects a firewall that allows the top brass to concentrate on military management.

At the policy level, while the Politburo is theoretically the ultimate forum for approving key military decisions, it is the PLA that creates policy initiatives for policies. This shows the Party's respect for professional inputs. One example of this is that, since the 1950s, the Party has never interfered with PLA efforts to formulate and revise national defense strategies. On issues of national security that involve both civilian and military interests, the Politburo incorporates views from both sides. Key PLA leaders participate in these meetings and exchange views with representatives from state agencies. It is a foregone conclusion that most military matters submitted to the Politburo will be approved automatically because the green light has already been given by the Party boss at a CMC forum.[38] This paves the way for the CMC to exercise decisionmaking power in a highly autonomous manner. At the administrative and operational levels, the PLA has gained the most autonomy, including personnel nomination and promotion, transfer, and punishment of senior officers; allocation of the military budget to the services; research of new weapons systems; reviews of defense strategies; salary and social welfare matters; and so on. Additionally, the PLA's legal and discipline authorities assume full autonomy in handling their own criminal and other related cases. None of these, however, can be compared with the effect of the passage of Party and military elders who took it for granted to move across the civilian/military boundaries. Now, an unprecedented level of autonomy in managing its own affairs has presented the PLA with a decreased need and will to get involved in civilian politics.

HU JINTAO AND CHINA'S CHANGING CIVIL-MILITARY RELATIONS

Hu Jintao's authority construction since the 16th Congress has been very impressive and testified to many novel developments in the country's social-political transformation in general and its civil-military relations in particular. From his example, it can be seen that Hu now exerts the principle civilian control over the PLA. Specifically, through both his rise to power and time in office, the emerging trends of civil-military relations outlined above can be seen.

Hu Jintao has solidified his position as the top leader in charge of China's military. In a report on the Wenchuan Earthquake rescue operations by the General Engineering Corps of the Second Artillery in June 2008, it was advocated that the whole PLA should work hard to enhance Hu's power of appealing (感召力) and soldiers' centripetal force (power) toward him (向心力). This new vocabulary was immediately captured by the PLA's General Political Affairs Department (GPAD). It sent out a directive in the same month, asking all PLA units to embrace the spirit of these two powers of Hu's.[39] Use of this kind of language of worship has not been seen for quite some time, certainly not in the Jiang era, and was not even used to praise Deng. Another concrete measure to test the PLA's stance toward Hu is the quickness of PLA top commanders to voice their personal support to his political initiatives. Immediately after Hu put forward his New Deal on harmonious society and scientific development in the CMC annual meeting in December 2005, the whole PLA was mobilized to study the call. All PLA headquarters quickly convened high level meetings to formulate measures of implementation. The vocabulary is familiar, as it was expressed to support Mao and Deng before. The PLA Air Force Party Committee made it clear that supporting Hu's idea of scientific development was a matter of political attitudes on the part of soldiers.[40] In other words, this symbolized the PLA's loyalty to the new civilian leadership. Other services also pledged similar allegiance.[41]

Dealing with Transitional Uncertainties.

Upon assuming office, Hu, like Jiang before him, confronted a huge challenge in authority building vis-à-vis the PLA. At the core of this challenge is the reality that the old method of strongmen control, the way of Mao and Deng, is no longer viable. Yet the new method of control in the form of erecting institutionalized safeguards is still far from complete. If not handled properly, a transitional vacuum may emerge with military strongmen or ambitious politicians inclined to manipulate the civil-military relations to their advantage. This has happened many times in Chinese history. The many firsts about Hu's power consolidation, mentioned at the beginning of the chapter, may have shown that the challenge has been coped well with, although it is still too early to conclude that a pattern has been molded for his successors to follow in the future. In a way, Hu's new method of commanding the gun continues Jiang's effort to turn the PLA into a professional and noninterventionist force, although still loyal to the Party. It keeps abreast with the Party's own institutionalization of power.

Hu's succession and consolidation strategy has attributed to his quick ascendance as a powerful commander in chief. This strategy minimized any unpredictability in his interaction with Jiang before he was confirmed as CMC chair in 2004. Primarily, he has timed his execution of control over the PLA correctly. For instance, Hu has been careful about what he should not do prematurely. Although as part of the succession plan he oversaw the PLA's daily management since the beginning of 2004, he inspected its Western Hills Strategic Command Center only a few days after he was confirmed as CMC chair. This means that he avoided stepping into the areas of top operational command (i.e., the nuclear button), which is the institutional privilege of the CMC chair under the CMC one-man command system. Following the principle that key military power should not be divided, all vice CMC chairs lead only under authorization of the chair.[42] On major decisions, they are just top advisors to the chair. Hu observed this tradition and strict regulations carefully.[43] This is what Jiang's emphasis on "understand politics" (讲政治) was about.

However, as soon as Hu took the helm, he exercised his institutional power without any hesitation. He issued his strategic guidance for PLA development, namely "three provides and one role": provide the CCP with a political guarantee for its hold on power, provide the state with the security guarantee for its governance, and provide the nation with military capabilities to protect its best interests. The key role is to maintain world peace and regional stability.[44] He wields his power of troop deployment and personnel appointment with determination. For instance, the troop deployment for the Wenchuan rescue was strictly under his authorization, normally through General Cao Gangchuan (曹刚川) rather than Wen Jiabao (温家宝).[45] One of the reasons for Hu to cut short his trip to Italy for the G-8 meeting in July was that he had to order PAP reinforcement to Xinjiang personally, upon listening to the situation report.

Generally speaking, Hu's power consolidation strategy has the following features. Firstly, he maintained unity in the Politburo where Jiang's appointees made the majority. To counter a lopsided equilibrium in their personnel line-up, Hu made a number of smart moves. He has allied with Wen on the basis of policy. Therefore, his support to Wen's economic policy was reciprocated by Wen's support to Hu's idea of social harmony and scientific development. This helps prevent the emergence of major policy disagreement, which is the most fatal threat to a new leader in the process of power consolidation.[46] At the same time, Hu has managed a delicate equilibrium between Jiang's nominees and other Politburo members. Hu cooperated well with Zeng Qinghong over personnel matters and supported non-Jiang appointees in their daily work. Therefore, Hu has been seen as posing no threat by most of Hu's Politburo colleagues. The result is that no major factional strife has happened since Hu became the Party boss.[47] This fundamentally removed the source of military intervention in Party factional politics.

Second, Hu has chosen consolidation of his Party position as the precondition for controlling the gun, not the other way around. Deng and Jiang proved that with dominant authority in the Party, it is highly unlikely they would be challenged by the PLA. However, in building these two mutually supporting mechanisms of control, Hu's sequence is unusual. All of Hu's predecessors used the PLA to command civilian politics. Hu is probably the first leader in CCP history to reverse this practice. Certainly what Hu has done was not his choice. The arranged succession denied his control over the gun at the same time he became Party leader. Yet, that he was able to turn something negative into positive shows his political maturity. In a way, this also reflects the changing nature of China's civil-military relations.

Third, soliciting popular support as a means of civilian control of the gun is not new, but neither Deng nor Jiang was able to achieve this at a high level, as they remained controversial among large sections of the population. Hu is the only key CCP leader against whom I have never heard something negative among Beijing's taxi drivers.[48] This is largely due to Hu's revisionist social policy agenda that leans public finance towards under-privileged classes.[49] This has resulted in his rising popularity among the masses, which has helped him lay a firmer civilian foundation to control the military. This outside-in method of commanding the gun turned out to be a more effective take-over plan than hasty penetration into the armed forces through creating a pro-Hu personal network. Traditionally, the latter way is a common practice for party leaders to control the gun. From Mao to Jiang the PLA was their primary power base and a short cut for power accumulation.[50] However, this brought about unintended consequences: the factionalized top brass and increased military influence in domestic politics, to name a few. Hu's reliance on the leader's popular legitimacy as a method of civilian control over the gun is less risky than the tactics of divide-and-rule.

Finally, Hu takes good care of PLA interests and is thus welcome by the military. One of his early efforts was to iron out a Party consensus on the IT/RMA as a way of PLA transformation. His first formal speech on military affairs in a rare Politburo study session in May 2003 was designed to prepare for his final takeover of PLA command. The IT/RMA theme of the speech reflected his commitment to helping quicken PLA transformation and war preparation.[51] Subsequently, this commitment to PLA reforms was concretely translated into his support of the PLA's plan to build a blue water navy, strategic air force, reliable second strike missile force, and an army capable of joint warfare with other services. His support for the PLA's war-preparation strategy, its selection of senior officers, and its request for a budgetary increase furthers its professionalization and operational autonomy. He went to additional lengths in arranging two salary increases to officers in the last 4 years, in having dumplings with foot soldiers in remote border posts in every Spring Festival holiday and in bringing PLA uniforms to world standards. In discussing the new food and nutrition standards for first line solders that were implemented on July 1, 2009, Hu intervened a few times to pick the options that give the men better supplies. For instance, each soldier can have a daily portion of 400 grams of meat, increased from 280 grams. Even the proportion of lean meat is carefully worked out, something that has never happened to PLA foot soldiers before.[52] Politics of the dinner table (饭桌上的政治) are connected to the politics of civilian interaction with the military. During the Wenchuan operations, Hu personally received 162 generals working in the front line and discussed with them urgent matters on the spot. Many of them were deeply moved. Hu's strong support to PLA transformation and his kind treatment to the rank and file of PLA soldiers have won him almost unconditional PLA support to his domestic policies, as shown by its support to his Taiwan policy.

Challenge Ahead: In Search of the Next Commander in Chief.

Hu's smooth command of the gun is based on his efforts to build a relative balance of different groupings at the apex of power. Additionally, his ability to avoid major policy disputes also makes it easier for his control of the military. At the moment and in the next few years, the biggest challenge for Hu to run the military is the selection of a new commander in chief acceptable to PLA soldiers, which has become routine with unavoidable cycles of succession. In a way, leadership consensus on social and economic policies is comparatively easy to reach but not on the issue of choosing an heir-apparent, which is more strategic and forces every top leader to take a position, as it would have a major impact on faction interests. What has not been discussed is one important reason for Hu's smooth consolidation of power, that is, there had existed a general consensus on his succession arrangement in the whole Party prior to his takeover. Now, this is not the case, as there has not emerged an undisputed "Mr. Right" to succeed him. Time is growing short.

The first uncertainty is about the speculated Xi Jinping (习近平)-Li Keqiang (李克强) race. Clearly, Xi is strategically positioned to become the successor. He ranked number one in the CC's primary vote for Politburo candidates in the lead-up to the 17th Party Congress and this gave him a good deal of legitimacy for the top job.[53] However, this top vote has not been translated into a consensus on Xi's ascent, which may have an unpredictable impact on his final confirmation. One of the reasons for Hu's successful succession is that he did not belong to any particular faction. Nor was he inclined to form his own faction when in charge of the Party's organizational affairs. Although Xi has tried to imitate Hu, there has been talk of him placing his former inferiors in leadership positions. His image as a key member of the princelings grouping is widely believed, and rightly or wrongly, generates difficulty for public acceptance of him as the ultimate leader.[54]

The inclusion of Li in the PSC was well anticipated. When all of the criteria were considered, he seemed to have no contender: he enjoys the closest personal ties with Hu that can be traced back in the early 1980s; he is the only person among the nine new Politburo members who served two full terms as a CC member; and he held full ministerial/provincial posts for 10 years. Therefore, he has the best seniority. Very importantly, he had the ideal age of a bit over 50 in 2007, which would be crucial if Hu has to go for a third term completely or for a proportion of it. Prior to the primary vote, he seemed to be the sole candidate for the top job.

In a way, listing Xi ahead of Li in the PSC was a surprise. Xi was just appointed to be Shanghai's party boss a few months earlier. It has been extremely rare for this kind of quick transfer to happen in CCP history. If it was decided for him to take over Party affairs from Zeng Qinghong in October and ultimately the Party's helm, it would have been more logical to transfer him to Beijing directly from Zhejiang in April to assist Zeng in personnel matters for the 17th Congress, a platform constructed to groom Hu in the 15th Congress. Logically, the decision on Xi was made promptly, but this was not helpful for a consensus to be brewed on him as the successor.

It may well be a historical accident that Xi was placed ahead of Li. Xi is basically a politician versed in Party affairs. In contrast, Li is basically a Party technocrat, interested more in China's economic management as shown by his choice of studying economics as his Ph.D. major. Going for the job of executive premier in charge of the national economy was his own suggestion to the Party leadership.[55] Xi and Li have got the jobs that suit them well, although the difference is huge when it comes to the finalization of the succession plan. If the claim is true that Li volunteered to go for the post of premier, he might have already given up the race, and this might have resolved a major challenge in the arranged succession and avoided a potential power struggle inherent in the dual candidature.

On the other hand, it may also be an accident that Xi ranks fifth and Li sixth in the 17th Supreme Peoples' Court (SPC), as traditionally the person running Party daily affairs is bureaucratically placed before the person running daily affairs of the State Council. In a way, it is not Xi ahead of Li, but his portfolio ahead of Li's. This means that if the final choice is sought on an individual basis, Li is not yet out of the race. Today, Li's job is probably tougher than Xi's in that China's economy has been at a crossroads. If a strong first vice premier capably assists a relatively weak premier in the next few years and succeeds in rectifying China's economic ills, he remains a viable contender.[56] Yet as time passes, swapping the sequence of the first and second candidates would cause an even more tremendous backlash against the Party. Li's chances are becoming increasingly smaller.

The second uncertainty is the PLA's position on Xi. Logically, this will remain unknown until Hu makes his final decision. Certainly, Hu will constantly consult with the senior officers in the process. The Fourth Plenary Session of the CC (September 15-18) did not nominate Xi as the first deputy CMC chair, against the speculation of many analysts. This means that Xi may not have been involved in managing PLA affairs.[57] In fact, this was in agreement with the Party tradition that before the final card is opened all potential candidates should keep away from PLA affairs, which serve as the indicator for the settlement of the issue. A premature involvement would complicate the whole process. The challenge is that the successor's participation in CMC affairs cannot be delayed too much either. It is an art for Hu to get the timing correct for bringing either Xi or Li on board.

The PLA's position is important in that it could reduce the negative impact on the unity of the Politburo due to the sensitive nature of this issue, even if the heir-apparent is not indisputable. For a huge Party like the CCP with many leadership groupings, it is almost impossible for a fast consensus on one particular candidate to emerge. Hu, as a rare exception may not be repeated for a long time to come. Succession is unfolding constantly in disputes and even in factional strife. But Hu's case shows that it can be well managed. If the PLA backs up Xi, these problems may be easily overcome. Xi has the closer ties with the military than all fifth generation leaders. His father, commissar of the First Field Army (第一野战军), enjoyed a similar status with PLA marshals in the PLA. The 1st Group Army (第一集团军), which has provided a good number of the current PLA leaders (for instance, former chief of staff Fu Quanyou (傅全有), former deputy chief of staff Wu Xuquan (吴旭全) and the current chief of staff Chen Bingde (陈炳德), was under his command in the Civil War. In the early 1980s, Xi served as the personal secretary to General Geng Biao (耿飚), who ran PLA daily affairs as CMC

Secretary General. This is a position at the divisional rank, better than most incumbent CMC members at that time. In terms of seniority, he is not inferior. More importantly, his CMC experience familiarized him with the skills of running PLA daily affairs, such as the procedures for cadre nomination and promotion, troop redeployment, budgetary allocation to different services, and nuclear launch procedures. As none of any other possible fifth generation leaders (born in the 1950s) had any military experience, Xi is clearly in the best position to take over the CMC helm. This was one of the considerations of Zeng Qinghong who went to additional lengths to nominate Xi as his replacement.

Yet the final say is Hu's, given his now undisputed power vis-à-vis the PLA. His own choice was allegedly Li, whom he had groomed since 1982. Hu's leadership style on personnel matters is to select appointees with minimal controversies. Clearly, Li is better than Xi in this regard. On the other hand, he is serious about the Party norms of collective leadership and majority rule. This was the reason why he could have blocked Zeng's suggestion for a primary vote or later disregarded its result, but he chose not to do so. The failure of the incumbent leaders from Jiang to Hu in nominating their favored successors demonstrates the extent to which institutionalization of elite politics has evolved. But in Xi's case, Hu would have to pay a high level of attention to PLA opinions.[58] After all, the ability of the successor to secure PLA cooperation decides the fate of the CCP.

TAIWAN AS A TEST TO CHINA'S EVOLVING CIVIL-MILITARY RELATIONS

As mentioned earlier, the continuation of the current smooth civil-military relations depends on some preconditions. Prominent among them is the absence of major policy disagreement between these two powerful institutions and, of course, within the Politburo. Therefore, this seemingly uneventful civil-military relationship is not a given. Among the issues that may generate policy strife is the Taiwan challenge, especially at this moment when Beijing is substantially adjusting its Taiwan policy as a result of the regime change in Taipei in May 2008. The ease of tension provides both new opportunities and challenges to joint CCP/PLA management of Taiwan affairs.

Civil-Military Convergence on a Taiwan Policy.

There has been a broad civil/military consensus on a Taiwan policy, which has been defined by war avoidance. But at the same time, civilians' lofty rhetoric contrasts with tough PLA remarks. This is particularly true in Hu's case, who has seldom used any threatening language in commenting on Taiwan affairs.[59] The usual talk about a discord between civilian and military leaders over the Taiwan issue has been exaggerated. They share a strategic view that anti-independence efforts have to be firm and persistent.[60] Beijing's Taiwan policy is built upon two bases: peaceful inducement for reunification, and threat of force against independence. It is only natural that civilians emphasize the former and officers the latter. Any discussion of the PLA's role in Beijing's Taiwan policy process needs to trace the sources of their functional differences that are often times interpreted as policy differences.

Institutionally, it is hard for major policy disagreement to emerge. The Party's Small Leading Group on Taiwan Affairs(对台工作领导小组) largely runs Taiwan Affairs on behalf of the CMC. Put another way, Hu is chair of the Group more because he is commander in chief than because he is the Party boss.[61] Ultimate PLA control of Beijing's Taiwan policy could be traced back to a deliberate design of Mao in the 1950s when Taiwan affairs were exclusively military affairs. The report on Taiwan affairs by civilian agencies was sent to the CMC. The Small Group was established in 1978 when Beijing decided that the Taiwan challenge should not be dealt with by military means only. Contacts with old Kuomintang (KMT) friends/ foes needed to be restored as a platform for a new Taiwan policy pronounced by Ye Jianying (叶剑英) in 1979. This highlighted the Group's missions of united front work. Yet, the bulk of the Taiwan affairs were handled by military and state security bodies in PLA Headquarter Departments. Since the 1980s, Taiwan affairs have become multidimensional, incorporating economic, cultural, and legal matters. Jiang and Hu have laid more emphasis on political and economic aspects of Taiwan affairs in the open, with military issues to be handled in the background. However, war or peace is the ultimate concern in Beijing's Taiwan policy, and all other aspects of cross-Strait interaction service this consideration. So the military's leadership is strategic and directional, although not too visible in Beijing's daily running of Taiwan affairs. Even when Deng Yingchao (邓颖超), widow of Zhou Enlai (周恩来), was the nominal head of the Group in the early 1980s when united front work was made central to the

Taiwan policy, Deng transferred a PLA general Yang Side (杨思德), (his man in the 2nd Field Army [第二野战军]) to lead the Taiwan Affairs Office. The PLA involvement in Taiwan affairs is traditionally both deep and dominant. And the PLA has a decisive say, if not the final say, in setting the overall direction of Beijing's Taiwan policy. This was clearly reflected by the drafting process of the Anti-Secession Law in 2005, which was basically a PLA process with civilian legal support.[62]

On the other hand, simply due to the CMC's one-man responsibility system (一长制) under the Party leader, it is difficult for the PLA to exert itself excessively in the top decisionmaking process. Normally, the commander in chief finalizes his Taiwan policy in the meetings of the Politburo Standing Committee (PSC) rather than at the August First Building (八一楼). But he listens to his CMC colleagues extensively over any major Taiwan policy. In this process, Hu can wear different hats. In the meetings of the PSC he can be representative of the armed forces, and in the CMC meetings discussing Taiwan issues, he can be the Party boss. Since 1999 when Hu was entrusted to oversee the running of the Small Leading Group of Taiwan Affairs (对台工作领导小组), he has gradually developed his distinctive leadership style: compared with Jiang, he can be softer when wielding an olive branch and harder when employing military pressure. Generally, he is more masterful in doing the former than the latter.[63] Thanks to the complicated nature of cross-Strait relations, Hu has to make prompt controversial decisions against agency inputs, such as how to respond to Ma's approval of the Dalai Lama's visit to Taiwan in August. This requires the power of decision on Taiwan affairs to be highly concentrated and integrated

in Hu's hands. Lengthy debate is not allowable. Therefore, most major decisions bear Hu's personal traits,
although embedded in a collective process.[64] As a result, the PLA's support to Hu is essential for any consensus to be forged. In return, the PLA's role is well
respected.

In policy terms, the management of the Taiwan
problem has been integrated into Hu's overall national development strategy that focuses on domestic stability and economic growth.[65] The PLA has followed
Hu's strategic guidance. As pointed out by Lieutenant General Liu Jixian (刘继贤), "Since Chairman Hu
took over the CMC, he has scientifically evaluated
the PLA's historical stage of development and runs
military affairs from a political height and within the
broad sequence of national interests."[66] More concretely, the interaction between Hu and the PLA in
managing Taiwan affairs is oriented toward matching
PLA support to Hu's domestic priority and enhancing
its vested interests in accelerating war preparation.
Ma Ying-jeou's anti-independence stance has allowed
this match to be preserved.

Beijing's Policy Evolution Since May 20, 2009.

The regime change in Taipei has substantially
altered the strategic nature of cross-Strait relations.
Simply put, if Beijing's Taiwan policy is bottom-lined
on anti-*de jure* independence, it has achieved an over-
night victory almost without a fight. In the foreseeable future, say up to 2016 if Ma has a second term,
Beijing is automatically in a "no-defeat" position. This
sudden sea-change creates a wider range of policy
choices as Beijing attempts to build a gradual prepon-
derance over Taiwan.[67] Since May 2008 Beijing has

taken a reluctant but positive-sum response toward Ma's requests in economic and diplomatic areas. Yet all of Beijing's compromises so far seem to have been tactical by nature in comparison with its new strategic gains.

The strategic significance for Beijing of the *Kuomintang* (KMT) in power can be concretely seen from the following points.

1. It gives Beijing an extended "strategic opportunity period" until 2016. This would be a further extension of 8 years that Beijing has already obtained, thanks to the War on Terrorism since 2001. By 2016, the PLA will be closer to achieving mutual assured destruction (MAD) capabilities vis-à-vis the United States, which would complicate Washington's decisionmaking process on whether to participate in a Taiwan war. By then, China's economic power will have reached a new height and delivered much greater military transformation.

2. The likely *decombatification* (去战争化) in the Strait helps reduce the level of militarization in the Sino-U.S. relations. As Taiwan is the only cause for the pair to see each other in a war,[68] peace in the Strait on the basis of maintaining the status quo, the core of Ma's mainland policy, may help remove the most likely trigger for armed conflict between the two nuclear powers. Without a drag such as the Taiwan issue on China's diplomacy, Beijing can deal with challenges posed by some countries with a relatively freer hand, as seen by its tough response to Canberra's visa permit to Rebiya Kadeer (a Uyghur political dissident in exile).[69]

3. Reduced level of tension in the Strait helps Hu concentrate his time and energy on handling his priority concerns over domestic stability. One of these

is how to pursue the next round of CCP succession. Without an overt disruption by a Taiwan challenge, arranged succession can be conducted with a reasonable level of smoothness.

4. Taiwan's creeping independence lost momentum when it lost state sponsorship. For a long while, Beijing had no effective countermeasures against the salami independence moves, which convinced many strategists of an inevitable war in the Strait.[70] Now the situation is reversed in that an elected leader helps curb the trend from within. Ma's de-de-Sinification (去去中国化) effort has given Beijing precious time in a race to build a more solid foundation for its long-term effort of reunification.

5. Taiwan's economic dependence on Beijing will have deepened significantly by 2016 as the current quickened pace of integration between the two sides continues, driven by three-direct-links and the Economic Cooperation Framework Agreement (ECFA). When half of Taiwan's economic activities are tied to that of the mainland, according to a Chinese economist, *de jure* independence will almost become an unrealizable concept.[71]

The list expands. Predictably, as long as Ma's non-independence stance holds, concessions from Beijing will be further expected. Beijing's gesture of goodwill to improve bilateral relations will be integrated into its practical effort to help the KMT win a second term in 2012. The immediate policy challenge, however, is how to recalibrate the existing hierarchical order of the two-pronged policy: peace inducement and threat of force. Although in disguised form, the latter moved to the central place in Beijing's Taiwan policy toward Chen's second term in office but at a high cost: mili-

170

tary pressure alienated the majority of Taiwanese, affected Beijing's international image, and resulted in an increased financial burden on the state budget. It was high time that there should be a change in approach, if not in texture.

The Benefits for the PLA.

Ma's no-independence policy has brought about an emerging trend of *decombatification* in the Taiwan Strait. *Decombatification* has been the largest common denominator in the strategic concerns of Washington, Beijing, and Taipei. The Democratic Progressive Party's (DPP) promotion of *de jure* independence upset a strategic framework for the status quo upheld by all three capitals. Today, the three parties have restored this strategic framework. In a way, the most visible beneficiary is, however, the PLA. This can be seen from the points listed below.

First, the trend of *decombatification* has allowed the PLA to break away from a sub-state of war for the second time in its history since the late 1960s when Sino-USSR military tensions forced it to prepare for an imminent war. Large quantities of sub-standard arms were promptly produced and quickly became obsolete, a huge waste of resources.[72] In the first half of this decade, the history repeated itself, though with qualitative differences. After the Politburo passed the resolution to accelerate war preparation in 1999, the Chinese defense industries received an unprecedented number of orders, and this even stressed the transportation system. Beijing saw the DPP's promised referendum for a new Constitution in 2006 as the trigger of a Taiwan war that seemed to be more imminent than common sense judgment would have convinced people. For the sake of maintaining a high level of deterrence and for the planning of a war with U.S. involvement, the PLA had no other choice but to introduce many conventional weapons systems that, it knew, would soon become obsolete. Yet without these arms, the PLA could not effectively cope with worse case scenarios in the minds of its leaders. Without a better option, the CMC chose the lesser evil but at a higher cost.

In the meantime, Russia became the chief beneficiary of the PLA being in a sub-state of war. Since the 1990s, the PLA has procured a substantial amount of advanced but near obsolete Russian weapons to fulfill this dangerous transitional vacuum where its second generation weapons were of little battlefield use but most of its designs of third generation weapons had only undergone laboratory experiments. Yet the PLA is also clear that foreign arms cannot resolve the fundamental challenges of its IT/RMA transformation, and are too costly as well. Now with this transitional cycle gradually coming to an end and particularly due to the ease of tension in the Taiwan Strait, the PLA can afford to greatly reduce its reliance on Russian arms and develop its own weapons of North Atlantic Treaty Organization (NATO) standards.[73] Apparently, the preparation for a Taiwan war was the driver for the PLA to purchase this "pocket of excellence" for its first units.

The PLA is now in a much better position to project its comprehensive transformation based on the strategic guidance of "double leap-forward" (双重跨越).[74] This would have an enormous impact on many crucial issues of army-building. For instance, with the pressure to acquire emergency capabilities eased, more allocations could be directed to boost the efforts of PLA informatization, such as command, control, communications, computers, intelligence, surveillance, and reconnaissance (C4ISR) architecture and military space programs. The opportunity for adjusting the overall equipment guidelines also becomes a possibility. This would induce a change in arms production from aiming at specific battle scenarios in the Strait to aiming at production for the purpose of raising the PLA's overall capabilities so that it could be better equipped to deal with all situations, including the possibility of a Taiwan conflict. Within each service, more money could also go toward research and development of future generations of weapons without substantially weakening their current level of readiness. One specific example is the ongoing debate among naval planners. After the completion of the 18-New Ship Project, they are facing a key choice: to add a few more 053 destroyers and 054 frigates, or to concentrate on fourth generation combatants. Taking the former choice is logical, as these ships (052C, 053B, and 053C) can be regarded as experimental. Adding follow-ups is explainable. However, if the pressure of a Taiwan war is not high, it is more sensible that the PLA Navy (PLAN) chooses the second choice. Japan's new carrier destroyers stimulate the PLAN and its feeling that these destroyers should be matched. Furthermore, the carrier project may also get a boost.[75]

Secondly, China confronts multiple security threats, but in the last 2 decades, it has had to concentrate on building a relative superiority vis-à-vis Taiwan.[76] Security threats from other strategic directions, e.g., along China's land borders, could not be given the due attention they deserved until now. The new challenges in Xinjiang and Tibet call for immediate countermeasures through more force deployments.

Terrorist threats remain real, although not strategic by nature. For a long time to come, the PLA's overall deployment guidance of defensive defense in the north and defensive offense in the south (北守南攻) will not change.[77] This entails the strategic guidance of the 1.5 war scenario: waging an offensive war against Taiwan independence and a defensive counterattack along land borders due to the "chain reaction of a Taiwan war by China's hostile land neighbors."[78] Yet the defensive posture in the northwest and the southwest can now be better taken care of with strengthened redeployment against India's stationing of 60,000 more soldiers in the Zangnan region (藏南地区), North Korea's increased hostility toward China, and clashes along sections of the Sino-Burma border.[79] This continental defense has been comparatively less emphasized up to now in order to put limited resources along the eastern flank. Now, if the CMC wants to adjust the force strength in the two directions, *decombatification* in the Taiwan Strait may offer an unprecedented opportunity. For instance, when the missiles deployed across the Strait are reduced in number, they can be moved elsewhere to counter new threats.[80]

Civilian-Military Responses to the New Taiwan Situation.

The strategic gains for the PLA, mentioned above, in the new Taiwan situation provide the foundation for PLA support to Hu's efforts to fine-tune the two-pronged Taiwan policy. Concretely, this means Beijing's constant concessions to Ma in order to boost his chances to win the second term and in return prolong China's strategic opportunity period. Yet this is easier said than done. The major source of tension lies in the fact that the two sides are still in a state of war and hostility, which many Taiwanese feel toward the mainland, that is deeply entrenched. Despite the visible ease of tension in the Strait, huge uncertainties lie ahead and are serious enough to put the PLA on constant alert. The PLA researchers are particularly concerned about the prospects of the DPP coming back to power in the future.[81]

This is reflected by the so-called Ma Ying-jeou dilemma in Beijing's Taiwan policy.[82] To many PLA officers, the analysis by David Gompert before May 2008 that "Imaging a future moment in which Beijing concludes that Taipei is using practical cooperation and political dialogue with China as a smoke screen for the pursuit of perpetual separation and de facto independence" may be more relevant now under Ma's "mutual non-denial" (互不否定) guidance than under Chen's creeping independence.[83] Even if "mutual non-denial" is a framework within "one China" rhetoric, it is clearly a notion of two Chinas.[84] When this notion is operationalized in Taipei's efforts to enlarge its international space, it is more linked to ultimate secession than to reunification. In the view of many mainlanders, Taipei got a real bargain as through one vocal commitment to none-independence, Beijing allows for unprecedented concessions: (WHA), tourism, investment, and its positive response to a so-called "diplomatic truce," to name a few. Ma's Three-Noism is a recycled expression of U.S. advocacy. More seriously, in this three-Noism, resisting reunification is deliberately tasked prior to shelving independence. In addition, Ma has changed a long term KMT definition about Taiwan's future status from belonging to the people across the Strait to belonging to the Taiwanese only. Beijing's Taiwan specialists are troubled by a strategic question of whether Ma's Strait vision converges with Lee Teng-hui's.[85]

So far Beijing has elected not to employ such an interpretation, wisely and correctly. To maintain the momentum of anti-independence and opportunities created by Taipei's rhetorical adherence to the 1992 accord, a maximum level of ambiguity has been exercised as a strategy to guide Beijing's response to the Ma Ying-jeou dilemma. The question is whether Hu can sustain this top consensus, which is by no means firm, as ambiguity is a hotbed for controversies by itself. This is especially true when Ma continues to raise controversial issues, such as the Dalai's Taiwan visit in August, which forced Hu to make the tough decision to retaliate or to "swallow it."[86] Not all leaders see Beijing's strategic gains from Ma's claim on nonindependence to have exceeded its tactical concessions.

So far, the PLA shows no sign of disagreement with Hu's employment of an olive branch toward Taiwan, although its rank and file members question the wisdom of softening pressure too quickly.[87] The CMC has actually supported Hu's call for building mutual military and security trust with Taiwan in his 6-point declaration. It has refrained from commenting on the provocations from Taipei, such as Ma's 6-points in March 2008 which started with a personal attack on Wen Jiabao, threatened to boycott the Beijing Olympic Games, and supported the Dalai Lama and Chinese dissidents. Certainly, there is the occasional use of tough language over some issues, such as criticism of U.S. arms sales to Taiwan.[88] Major General Luo Yuan (罗援) has been the only senior official to criticize Ma by name over his approval of the Dalai Lama's visit to Taiwan.[89] On the other hand, the PLA consistently backs Hu's Taiwan policy that expresses Party support to PLA transformation centered on a Taiwan war or other conflict. Second, the Party's preferential budgetary treatment to the PLA will remain persistent; and third, PLA autonomy will be guaranteed, especially in the areas of operational planning, engagement codes, and troop deployment. It can be well anticipated that there will be a high level accord between the CCP and the PLA on the three conditions. So far the level of mutual support is high.

CONCLUSION AND POLICY IMPLICATIONS

In summary, the changes and continuities of China's civil-military relations can be analyzed through the dialectical interaction between the PLA's old guard traditions and its new historical missions. The former informs the PLA's continued subordination to the Party. The latter refers to PLA transformation being driven by its preparation for war, which consolidates PLA professionalization.

Policymakers should first recognize that the emerging trend of PLA noninterventionism is the outcome of a CCP/PLA consensus that the military entering the Party's internal politics harms the long-term prospects for Party leadership, but this does not contradict the PLA's willingness to protect the CCP's maintenance of leadership over China. Therefore, the implication of this arrangement is that it continues to give the PLA a key role in the country's political process. For instance, the PLA was not in a position to press for its choice in China's recent succession process, but in 2002, it helped Jiang retain his title as CMC chair. This shows that the institutionalization that has taken place to date is still reversible.[90] But policymakers should also note that such intrusive behaviour is no longer routine, especially given the fact that the succession cycle emerges only once in a decade, and more recent behaviour has been within permissible limits, such as comments on state affairs in the annual NPC sessions or plenary CC meetings. The remarks of PLA generals exert pressure on CCP leadership, but open PLA criticism on major CCP political lines and policies has been virtually unheard of in the Jiang-Hu eras.

Second, policymakers must take into account that deepening PLA professionalism is a natural result of the military's pursuit of IT/RMA transformation as its organizational objective. This is further driven by the PLA's current accelerated pace of war preparation. At the same time, rising PLA professionalism is also contributing to the unprecedented level of autonomy that the PLA has achieved since the end of the Deng era. However, this autonomy has been by and large confined to the administrative and operational realms. Due to its subordinate position vis-à-vis the Party, the PLA has obeyed the CCP on most of the strategic issues that have had a profound impact on China's diplomacy and Beijing's Taiwan policy. Yet a military embarking on building professionalism as a key organizational objective will develop its own corporate identity and logic of operational autonomy. Therefore, as policymakers assess the long-term prospects for China's civil-military relations, the prospect remains that dichotomous CCP/PLA institutional imperatives may create fault zones in the Party's control of the gun.

ENDNOTES - CHAPTER 4

1. This chapter follows in a long tradition of articles assessing the changes that have occurred in China's civil-military relations following the reform and opening movement of the 1980s. Ellis Joffe "The Military and China's New Politics: Trends and Counter-Trends," in James C. Mulvenon and Andrew N.D. Yang, eds., *The People's Liberation Army in the Information Age*, Santa Monica, CA: The RAND Corporation, 1999, serves as one key work that set the stage for the next decade's analyses. In addition, David Shambaugh's work, particularly his chapter titled, "Civil-Military Relations" in his book, *Modernizing China's Military: Progress, Problems, and Prospects*, Berkeley, CA: University of California Press, March 2003, pp.11-55, provides a thorough overview of the symbiotic relationship that has traditionally occurred in China's civil-military relations. For an overview of the manner in which this topic has traditionally been studied, Thomas J. Bickford's "A Retrospective on the Study of Chinese Civil-Military Relations Since 1979: What Have We Learned? Where Do We Go?" in James C. Mulvenon and Andrew N. D. Yang, eds., *Seeking Truth from Facts: A Retrospective on Chinese Military Studies in the Post-Mao Era*, Santa Monica, CA: RAND Corporation, 2001, pp. 1-38, provides a detailed background, and, two more recent edited volumes, *Chinese Civil-Military Relations: The Transformation of the People's Liberation Army*, Nan Li, ed., Abingdon, UK: Routledge, 2006; and *Civil-Military Relations in Today's China: Swimming in a New Sea*, David Finklestein and Kristen Gunness, eds., Alexandria, VA: The CNA Corporation, 2007, provide sizeable contributions to this field.

2. You Ji, "Hu Jintao's Succession and Power Consolidation Strategy," John Wong and Lai Hongyi, eds., *China's Political and Social Change in Hu Jintao Era*, Singapore: World Scientific, 2006, pp. 33-60.

3. Li Nan, "Changing Functions of the Party and Political Work System in the PLA and Civil-Military Relations in China," *Armed Forces & Society*, Vol. 19, 1993.

4. Here the debating point is whether the CMC is basically a Party body or a top military command. This chapter argues that the latter is closer to the reality.

5. Amos Perlmutter and William LeoGrande, "The Party in Uniform: Toward a Theory of Civil-Military Relations in Communist Political Systems," *American Political Science Review*, Vol. 76, 1982.

6. Shambaugh; and Li.

7. For instance, Mulvenon used an analytical framework of *conditional compliance* to highlight the bargaining dynamics in CCP/PLA interaction, "China: Conditional Compliance," in Muthiah Apalagapa, ed., *Coercion and Governance in Asia: the Declining Political Role of the Military*, Palo Alto, CA: Stanford University Press, 2001; and Ellis Joffe, "The PLA and the Succession Problem," in Richard Yang, ed., *China's Military: The PLA in 1992/1993*, Boulder, CO: Westview Press, 1993.

8. In 1956, Mao decided that when PLA generals at the 6th Grade (the rank of Lieutenant General) were transferred to civilian posts, they did not need to be retired from the Army. PLA generals were reluctant to leave the military. This was partially because the military's salary was 20 percent higher, which remains true to this day, and they enjoyed more privileges in the PLA, such as additional body guards and better cars. The last person following this rule was General Yu Qiuli, who returned to the PLA as its head of General Political Affairs Department in the 1980s, from the post of vice premier in charge of China's heavy industries. Yang Shangkun was the last civilian leader to wear a PLA hat.

9. In preparing for restoration of military ranks in 1985, some senior Party leaders suggested that since local party secretaries concurrently held the position of the first political commissar of the regional garrison, they should be granted a military rank. Deng personally vetoed this motion.

10. At the beginning of Deng's reign, he often personally appointed senior officers without consulting with the CMC, but after he firmly established his command of the gun, he gradually delegated the power of nomination to the CMC, with the Yang brothers as the main initiators. According to his daughter, Momo, throughout the 1980s, he worked only 2 hours a day, which did not allow him to take detailed care of the personnel matters below

the CMC level. A pattern started to emerge. Jiang and Hu continued this, as they had little personal contacts in the PLA prior to their assumption as the commander in chief. According to my research in Beijing over the years, normally the CMC presented a list of a few candidates for the chair to choose one from. It is not that Jiang or Hu did not make personal nominations, but the professional inputs from the CMC make the majority of personnel decisions.

11. Politburo member Zhou Yongkang (China's public security chief) revealed that in 2004 over 80,000 such protests occurred. During the next year, the number went up to 100,000. But since 2007, no such figures have been published.

12. Sun Liping (孙立平), "中国社会结构转型的中近期趋势与隐患" ("Trends and hidden dangers in China's social structure in transition"), 战略与管理 (*Strategies and Management*), No. 5, 1998, pp. 1-17.

13. Murray Scott Tanner, "How China Manages Internal Security Challenges and its Impact on PLA Missions," in Roy Kamphausen, David Lai, and Andrew Scobell, eds., *Beyond the Strait: PLA Missions Other Than Taiwan*, Carlisle, PA: Strategic Studies Institute, U.S. War College, 2009.

14. Gerald Segal, "China and the Disintegration of the Soviet Union," *Asian Survey*, September 1992.

15. Major General Zhang Weibing (张卫兵), "构建和培育当代革命军人核心价值观之我见" ("On cultivating core values of contemporary soldiers"), 中国军队政治工作 (*Political Work in Chinese Military*), No. 7, 2008, p. 70.

16. Ray Huang, *1587, A Year of No Significance*, New Haven, CT: Yale University Press, 1981.

17. This referred to a series of secret meetings between Zeng Qinghong and Su Zhicheng, a good friend of Lee's son, in Hong Kong that paved the way for Wang/Gu talks in Singapore in 1993. Su Chi (苏起), 危险边缘：从两国论到一边一国 (Brinkmanship: From the two-state thesis to one country on each side), Taipei, China: Bookzone 天下远见出版有限公司, 2004, p. 12.

18. The U.S. Secretary of State confirmed in Beijing that the Chinese military had stopped tailing U.S. spy planes in the South and East China Seas. See the transcript of his speech from the news conference in Beijing during his first China visit as Secretary of State in July 2001.

19. The Writing Group of the PLA NDU, 国防发展战略学教程 (The textbook for teaching the course of development strategy of national defense), Beijing, China: The PLA NDU Press, 1990, p. 232; and Ku Guisheng (谷贵生), "社会主义市场经济与国防建设" ("The socialist market economy and the military development"), 中国人民解放军国防大学学报 (*The Journal of the PLA National Defence University*), No. 6, 1993, p. 46

20. On July 25, 2004, the Politburo convened a meeting to formulate the country's grand national development strategy. 富国强兵 (prosperous nation and powerful military) was confirmed as the foundation for the strategy that has tremendous effect to unite the Party and the military in search of a world power status. *The PLA Daily* and *Xinhua News Agency*, 26 July 2004.

21. General Qian Guoliang (钱国梁), "全面贯彻司令部建设条例" ("Comprehensively implement the guideline of headquarters construction"), 中国人民解放军国防大学学报 (*Journal of the PLA NDU*), No. 6, 2000, p. 4.

22. Major General Zhang Ruilin (张瑞林), "大力加强领导干部队伍作风建设" ("Greatly improve the working style of the military cadre"), 中国军队政治工作 (*Political Work of the Chinese Military*), No. 1, 2008, p. 14.

23. In fact, Jiang Zemin and Hu Jintao are the primary initiators and supporters for PLA IT/RMA transformation. Hu has especially pushed PLA joint training as one of his key measures of commanding the gun. Jiang Zemin, "国际形势和军事战略方针" ("The global situation and military strategy"), in 江泽民文选 (*Selected Works of Jiang Zemin*), Beijing, China: Reminchubenshe, 2006, Vol. 1; and on Hu's call for enhancing joint military training as a strategic leverage for PLA transformation, see Major General Gao Donglu (高东路), "实现部队建设又快又好发展需要处理好几个关系" ("Several key relationships affecting the PLA's fast and all-round development"), 中国军队政治工作 (*Political work in Chinese military*), No. 7, 2008, p. 6.

24. Andrew Scobell put forward the concept of the PLA as a nationalized military to analyze the long term trend of China's civil-military relations. See his article, "China's Evolving Civil-Military Relations: Creeping *Guojiahua*," in Nan Li, ed., *Chinese Civil-Military Relations*, London, UK: Routledge, 2006.

25. According to PLA sources, the PLA recruited 130,500 graduates from civilian university in 2009 alone. "Daily Military Report," *PLA Channel, CCTV*, December 22, 2009. The deputy chief for military administration at GSD, Major General Chen Dongdeng, revealed that the number of noncommissioned officers in the PLA would reach 900,000 by the end of the current reform of the non-commissioned officer system, which is about half of its total personnel, making the PLA a truly professional military. Focus on the reform of non-commissioned officer. See 军事一周热点档案 (*The weekly key issues for the PLA*), No.2, July 2009.

26. Richard Kohn, "Out of Control: the Crisis in Civil-Military Relations," *National Interest*, Vol. 35, 1994, pp. 3-17.

27. Qiu Shenghong (邱圣宏), "论新时期我军坚持党对军队绝对领导的基本经验" ("The basic lessons of Party absolute leadership over the PLA in the new era"), 中国军队政治工作 (*Political work in Chinese Military*), No. 10, 2008, p. 26.

28. Samuel Huntington, *The Soldier and the State*, Cambridge, MA: Harvard University Press, 1957.

29. For instance, Politburo members are not supposed to inspect local PLA garrisons when they visit localities, and the local military leaders are not requested to accompany them without the specific instruction of the CMC General Office.

30. Mao reiterated this formula in a Politburo meeting in December 1972 that decided on the transfer of eight MR Commanders. Interestingly, at a time of great political uncertainty, Mao added that the PLA should also involve itself in political affairs. 解放军生活 (*The PLA Life*), August 20, 2009.

31. In 1975 Jiang Qing inspected a company of the 20th Army in Zejiang without CMC approval, one of the serious crimes she was charged with later. This has become a classic case to warn ci-

vilian leaders what they should not do, as the case is continuously mentioned today.

32. On this process, see Bonnie Glaser and Philip Saunders, "Chinese Civilian Foreign Policy Research Institute: Evolving Roles and Increasing Influence," *China Quarterly*, No. 171, 2002, pp. 597-616.

33. For instance, Craig Covault, "Chinese Test Anti-Satellite Weapon," *Aviation Week & Space Technology*, January 17, 2007.

34. Mu Song (慕崧), "毛泽东与总干部部的组建" ("Mao Zedong and the creation of the PLA General Cadre Department"), 解放军报 (*PLA Daily*), September 14, 2009.

35. "The Active Duty Officer Appointment Regulations and Procedures of the PLA," promulgated and implemented on January 14 2002.

36. Cadre Department of the GPAD, 中国人民解放军干部制度概要 (The PLA institutions of cadre management), Beijing, The PLA Academy of Military Science Press, 1988, p. 158.

37. The Party History and Party Building Research and Teaching Group of the PLA National Defense University, 总队新时期军队思想建设的依据 (*The guidance for enhancing the PLA's political and ideological work in the new era*), Beijing, China: National Defence University, 2000, p. 307.

38. Without the signature of the CMC chair, no proposal can be presented to Politburo meetings. For instance, the 232th PSC weekly meeting in January 1992 approved the 921 Project (Shenzhou, manned space-ship) proposed by the PLA. TV Documentary 撼天记 (Shaking the sky), September 28, 2008.

39. "总政治部关于转发二炮工程总队抗震救灾总结的通知" ("The Directive of the GPAD on the Second Artillery's report on the Wenchuan quake relief operations"), 火箭兵报 (*Newspaper of Soldiers in the Rocket Force*), June 27, 2008, p. 1.

40. "空军党委扩大会议召开" ("The Enlarged PLAAF Party Committee in Session"), 空军报 (*The PLA Air Force Newspaper*), January 12, 2006, p. 1.

41. "海军党委扩大会议召开" ("The Enlarged PLA Navy Party Committee in Session"), 人民海军报 (*The PLAN Newspaper*), March 23, 2006, p. 1.

42. *The PLA Daily*, September 26, 2004.

43. Here is a telling example of this tough regulation. In 1969 Lin Biao summoned General Chen Shique, commander of PLA Engineering Corps, to brief him about nuclear construction projects. When Chen got to know that Mao did not know about this meeting, he became extremely nervous. After a few sleepless nights, he reported this to Mao and got Mao's praise. Chen Renkang (陈任康), 一生追随毛泽东 (*Following Mao Zedong for the whole of his life*), Beijing, China: Renmin Chubanshe, 2005. This tradition holds ground to this day. It is politically dangerous for any senior PLA commanders to intrude into commanding areas other than their own.

44. On the "three-provide and one-guarantee," see Lieutenant General Liu Jixian (刘继贤), "学习贯彻胡锦涛军队政治工作思想的认识" ("Understanding Hu Jintao's thinking on the political work of the PLA, Part Two"), 中国军队政治工作 (*Political Work in Chinese Military*), No. 11, 2008, p. 7; and *Xinhua*, September 20, 2005.

45. I have read hundreds of articles written by PLA Officers about PLA Wenchuan operations. The standard language is "troops are deployed and activities are implemented under the leadership of the CC, the CMC, and Chairman Hu." Virtually no mention was made to Wen Jiabao and the State Council's Wenchuan Rescue Headquarters. Soldiers were unhappy at Wen's unnecessary reprimand to the PLA Air Force for its failure to parachute in Beichuan due to bad weather. Clearly, in their minds it was Hu, rather than anyone else, that they should unconditionally obey. See Lieutenant General Wu Cangde (吴唱德) , director general of the Political Affairs Department of the Chengdu Military Region, "从抗震救灾看非战争军事行动中的政治思想工作" ("Political work in military operations short of war in earthquake relief"), 中国军队政治工作 (*Political Work in Chinese Military*), No. 8, 2008, pp. 11-14.

46. Wen's power lies in the State Council's premier responsibility system that allows the premier to exercise dominant authority in economic management and state administration.

47. The purge of Chen Liangyu, Politburo member and Shanghai's Party secretary, was an exceptional case, but this happened after Hu's consolidation. Hu also took great care not to implicate other Party leaders of Shanghai origin.

48. Beijing's taxi drivers are famous for bad-mouthing senior officials, so their attitudes can be evaluated as a true indicator of popularity of the leader. Each time I take a taxi in Beijing, I ask their opinions about state leaders and their policies. I also ask my friends to talk to the taxi drivers for this purpose. Hu commands a high level of respect among them, in contrast to their relatively low regard to Jiang whose pretentious style makes him unpopular.

49. Jin Renqing, China's former finance minister, was summoned by Hu and Wen a number of times in 2006 to discuss how state expenditure should be prioritized. Under the new ideological guidance Hu and Wen reset the rules of appropriation: leaning toward the poor; the western regions; and the peasants. Specifically, 700 billion *Yuan*, the bulk of the increased central revenue in 2006, would be mostly spent on creating a safety net for the rural and urban poor. Tuition fees for 150 million rural children will be spared. Medical care will be enlarged from covering 50 percent of peasants in 2005 to 80 percent in 2008. Each farmer receives an annual 50 *Yuan* insurance plan (individual contribution of 10 *Yuan*; 40 *Yuan* from local and central governments) for hospital visits. Jin's interview with Wu Xiaoli, *Phoenix TV*, March 3, 2007.

50. For more comments on this point, see You Ji, "Leadership by 'Lines': China's Unresolved Succession," *Problems of Communism*, Vol. 39, January 1990, pp. 28-44.

51. See Hu Jintao's speech on RMA to the enlarged Politburo meeting on May 24, 2003, *The PLA Daily*, May 25, 2003.

52. Ni Eryan (妮尔砚), "解放军伙食有新标准" ("The PLA has New Food Standards"), 大公报 (*Takung pao*), July 1, 2009.

53. The vote was based on a list presented for CC members by the Politburo. Although it was nonbinding, the people receiving best votes eventually entered the Politburo. Talk with former vice president of the Central Party School, Beijing, China, September 2008.

54. In fact, Xi does not belong to any factions. He has for a long time tried to keep a distance from other so-called princelings figures, as all these figures do the same. I really doubt whether there is such a thing as the princelings faction at the top leadership. In fact, Huang Jing (first husband of Jiang Qing), father of Yu Zhengsheng and Xi Zhongxun, father of Xi Jingping did not get along well. And Xi Zhongxun and Bo Yibo, father of Bo Xilai, did not enjoy good relations in the State Council in the 1960s.

55. Oral sources in Beijing. It has been a long Party tradition that before such a key appointment is finalized, the candidate would be approached about his opinion on job choices, although the Party's preference is made known to him.

56. Since Huang Ju's illness, the State Council's economic management had been greatly weakened. On several major issues, such as the duration of oil price hike, of the inflation, of America's subprime crisis, the leadership judgment was not sound, which has adversely affected Hu's overall management of state affairs.

57. There are cases to suggest otherwise. For instance, he was the leader in charge of the Beijing Olympic Games, so he maintained close contacts with the PLA over the security related matters of Games. On October 26, 2009, Xi received Senior General Li Wenyong, Director general of the General Political Affairs Department of the Vietnam armed forces. "Xi Jinping Meets with Vietnam Delegation," *The PLA Daily*, October 27, 2009, p. 1. Normally, CCP leaders meet with foreign visitors according to their specific division of labor in the PSC.

58. Oral sources from Beijing, China, July 2009.

59. In comparison, Jiang stressed peaceful means to solve the Taiwan issue when addressing civilian audiences, but he highlighted the necessity of the use of force when talking to PLA leaders.

60. You Ji, "Taiwan in the Political Calculations of the Chinese Leadership," *The China Journal*, Vol. 36, July, 1996, pp. 117-125.

61. Information obtained from people with deep knowledge of PLA elite politics in Beijing.

62. Xin Qi (辛旗) and his organization, a think tank associated with the 2nd department of the GSD (总参二部), played a crucial role in the drafting process.

63. From 1999, Hu began to preside over the annual national TAO conference, normally held in December each year. He also presided over the meeting where Qian Qishen announced the "new three-sentence."

64. It is said that few matters have captured Hu's personal attention more than Taiwan affairs. For instance, he has personally called leaders of the TAO for their prediction on the outcome of a major forthcoming election in Taiwan. As many issues in the bilateral negotiation may have a profound impact on Beijing's long-term Taiwan policy, he also has to make decisions himself, often in a prompt manner.

65. This is best revealed by Hu's speech to his first news conference as the Party's new leader on November 15, 2002, *Xinhua New Agency*, November 16, 2002.

66. Liu Jixian (刘继贤), "学习胡锦涛军队政治工作思想的认识" ("Understanding Hu Jintao's thinking on the political work of the PLA, Part One"), 中国军队政治工作 (*Political Work in Chinese Military*), No. 10, 2008, p. 2.

67. As the balance of power has decisively shifted in favor of the mainland, Beijing has more options against Taiwan's challenge. See a roundtable discussion by Asia Policy on the concept of healthy balance across the Taiwan Strait, *Asia Policy*, No. 8, 2009.

68. James Thomson, "US Interests and the Fate of Alliances," *Survival*, Vol. 45, No. 4, 2003-04, p. 214.

69. Beijing has cancelled a number of diplomatic programs with Australia. Its position to Canberra's application for a UNSC seat seems to be even more elusive now. Without Beijing's support, it seems Canberra does not need to bother making such an attempt.

70. Yan Xuetong, "Reasoning for containing Taiwan independence through use of force," *Zhanliu yu guanli*, No. 3, 2004, p. 1. You Ji, "China's New National Defence Strategy, Naval Transformation and The Taiwan Conflict," *Stockholm Journal of East Asian Studies*, Vol. 15, 2005, pp. 75-88.

71. Talk with a Chinese bank executive in Sydney in May 2008. In addition, the pace of integration has accelerated since Ma came to power. Now the proportion of Taiwan's university graduates who have an intension to work in the mainland has risen from 51 percent to 73 percent. 两岸开讲 (Talks Across Strait), CTV (Taipei), September 5, 2009.

72. Li Ke and Hao Shengzhang (李克, 郝慎彰), 文化大革命中的人民解放军 (*The PLA in the Cultural Revolution*), Beijing, China: Zhongguo dangshi ziliao chubanshe, 1989.

73. For more analysis on China's purchase of Russian arms, see You Ji, "Friends in Needs or Comrades in Arms: Sino-Russo Military Cooperation," Andrew Tan, ed., *The Global Arms Trade*, London, UK: Routledge, 2009.

74. You Ji, "Revolution in Military Thinking," in Bo Huldt and Masako Ikegami, eds., *China Rising*, Stockholm, Sweden: The Swedish National Defence College, and Helsinki, Finland: The Finnish National Defence University, 2008, pp. 335-364.

75. I doubt if the PLA is really serious about building carriers for combat purposes. There is no evidence that any decision on this project has been made.

76. The mentioning of this multiple nature of external threats has become more frequent, as seen from Hu's speeches and PLA documents, such as the *Defense White Paper* in 2008.

77. This is by the traditional Chinese geographic definition that uses the Yellow River as the dividing line.

78. Liu Yongxin, "连锁反应背景下边境防御战役指导" ("Guiding principle for defensive campaigns in the border regions under the background of armed conflicts elsewhere"), 军事学术 (*Military Studies*), No. 3, 2003, p. 39. For more analysis on this, see You Ji, China's New Diplomacy, Foreign Policy and Defense Strategy," in Stuart Harris, Qin Yaqing, and Pauline Kerr, eds., *China's New Diplomacy: Tactical or Fundamental Change?* New York: Palgrave Macmillan, 2008.

79. For instance, after Burma shelled inside the Chinese border and killed and wounded over a dozen Chinese, General Liang Guanglie, defense minister, told a high level meeting in Kunming that Southwest China was a key strategic direction and the task for war preparation was very heavy. *PLA Daily*, August 29, 2009.

80. Jiang Zemin told Clinton that it was not impossible for the number of missiles to be reduced. Similar remarks were also made by former Chinese U.S. Ambassador Zhou Wenzhong, *the Voice of America*, November 11, 2008.

81. Major general Peng Guangqian's remarks in a talk-show on *Phoenix TV*, February 4, 2009.

82. For an analysis of Beijing's dilemma, see Alan Romberg, "A Confederacy of Skeptics," *China Leadership Monitor*, No. 29, 2009.

83. David C. Gompert, "Strategic Context," in Stuart E. Johnson and Duncan Long, eds., *Coping with the Dragon: Essays on PLA Transformation and the US Military*, Washington, DC: National Defense University, 2007, p. 21.

84. This is common of China's Taiwan specialists. See for instance, Yan Anlin (嚴安林), "Reflection on political positioning of the Mainland and Taiwan" ("海峡两岸政治定位问题的回顾与思考") paper to the 18th Annual Conference on Cross-Strait Relations （第十八屆「海峽兩岸關係學術研討), Nanjing, August 4, 2009,.

85. Chairwoman Shin-yuan Lai (Minister, Mainland Affairs Council) made it clear that the Republic of China is an indepen-

dent sovereign state without a need to announce independence. In her first news conference upon accepting Ma's nomination, *China Times* (中国时报), May 2, 2008.

86. Ma's permit was issued when Beijing tried hard to raise money to help Taiwan's Typhoon rescue in August 2009. The Chinese media regarded it as stabbing Beijing in the back. "Allowing Dalai's entry is like a very sick patient seeking hurried medical treatment," *Oriental Daily* (东方日报), May 29, 2009.

87. In the defense internet forums, the majority view is that as long as Ma continues to identify Beijing as the primary security threat, the PLA should remain vigilant and tough toward Taipei.

88. General Chen Binde, chief of staff, used tough remarks to the visiting U.S. Army chief of staff in regard to U.S. arms sales to Taiwan in August 2009.

89. "On military and security mutual trust across the Strait," *Phoenix TV*, September 2, 2009. (Luo's father Luo Qingchang (罗青长), was in charge of the security aspects of Taiwan affairs for decades under Zhou Enlai).

90. In the long lead-up to the 16th Party National Congress PLA leaders repeatedly lobbied for Jiang's staying on. For instance, Major general Zhu Chenghu (朱成虎), director of the Institute for Strategic Studies of the PLA National Defence University made a speech to the Beijing Institute of Contemporary International Relations on October 15, 1999, calling Jiang to stay after the Congress, on the grounds that China encountered unprecedented domestic and international security challenges (the U.S. bombing of Chinese embassy and Lee Denghui's push for Taiwan independence).

CHAPTER 5

TOWARDS AN INTEGRATIVE C4ISR SYSTEM: INFORMATIONIZATION AND JOINT OPERATIONS IN THE PEOPLE'S LIBERATION ARMY[1]

Kevin Pollpeter

INTRODUCTION

The People's Liberation Army (PLA) views information superiority — the use of information and its denial to adversaries — as the main determiner of success on a high technology battlefield. While much attention has been paid to the PLA's development of modern weaponry, less attention has been paid to its development of a comprehensive command, control, communications, computers, intelligence, surveillance, and reconnaissance (C4ISR) system. While the PLA follows Chinese leaders' guidance, namely Chairman Hu Jintao's addresses and the recent *Defense White Papers*, to develop overall information capability, it also sees the development of a networked C4ISR system capable of locating and tracking targets and fusing intelligence into a coherent battlefield picture as essential to carrying out the long-range precision strikes necessary to attack Taiwan and keep the U.S. military at bay.

This chapter conducts an assessment of the PLA's transformation into an informationized force. In conducting this examination, the chapter will not focus on the development of technologies but will instead primarily focus on the capabilities that such technologies are intended to provide. To this end, it uses the PLA's ability to conduct joint operations as the metric for evaluating its level of informationization. As the PLA trains for a potential conflict in the area around and well beyond Taiwan, its navy, air force, and Second Artillery will play larger roles and may even command operations. As a result, information must be brought together through an organizational and technological system that facilitates jointness.

This chapter is organized into four parts and is confined to the 10-year period beginning in 1999, the year the PLA issued a *gangyao* (纲要)[2] that formally instituted joint operations into PLA warfighting. The chapter first looks at the theoretical foundation for informationization and the PLA's policies to turn itself into a network-centric force capable of winning future wars. It will then examine the PLA's progress in developing C4ISR technologies with the goal of supporting network-centric operations by offering representative examples of PLA technology development. The third section takes joint operations as the metric for PLA informationization and analyzes PLA progress in organizing and training for joint operations. The chapter concludes that the PLA has made only desultory progress in establishing genuine interservice institutions, technology, and training in the past 10 years. This lack of progress in joint capabilities renders the PLA incapable of carrying out true joint operations. PLA analysts admit this fact and by extension, the PLA's inability to win informationized wars. The PLA's modernization goals, however, do not require it to be able to win an informationized war in the near term and China's 2008 *Defense White Paper* only commits the PLA to lay a solid foundation by 2010. The year 2009, however, will most likely be seen as a pivotal year in the PLA's quest for joint operations. In 2009 the General Staff Department (GSD) provided training objectives that for the first time fully committed the services to joint operations. At the same time, the services have also been admonished for their lack of attention to joint reforms. These regulations and exhortations were followed up by the first war zone-level joint exercise in the PLA in June 2009. Consequently, while the PLA has much work ahead to realize true interoperability, recent efforts have laid a foundation that positions the PLA for reforms in the decades ahead.

INFORMATIONIZATION THEORY AND POLICY: NETWORK-CENTRIC WARFARE

The PLA's drive to develop into an informationized force began in the early 1990s and was a response to the revolution in military affairs (RMA) and the performance of the U.S. military in Operation DESERT STORM. The superiority of airpower, precision guided munitions, and high technology stirred debate within the PLA on its ability to fight and win modern wars in terms of both technology and operational doctrine. PLA theorists concluded that the source of U.S. military strength was based on the RMA, which PLA authors stressed was mainly a technological revolution in which information technology (IT) would play a central role. In the words of one group of authors, "If information technology is the vanguard of the new technological revolution, then information warfare will be the core of the new military revolution."[3]

A major component of PLA transformation is the development of a networked C4ISR system. The PLA in this regard has largely been guided by the U.S. concept of network-centric warfare (NCW). The term net-work-centric warfare was first coined by Chief of Naval Operations Admiral Jay Johnson in 1997 and later popularized by the late Admiral Arthur K. Cebrowski when he headed the Pentagon's Office of Force Transformation. Network-centric warfare remains ill-defined, but involves translating an information advantage characterized by a shift in focus from platforms to networks, information sharing, and shared situational awareness into a warfighting advantage characterized by knowledge of commander's intent, self-synchronization, and increased combat power.[4] Network-centric warfare is intended to "enable a shift from attrition-style warfare to a much faster and more effective warfighting style" characterized by speed of command. The resulting increase in the speed of command is intended to foreclose enemy courses of action and disrupt the enemy's strategy.[5]

The decision to build a network-centric force occurred in the early 1990s when the PLA determined that it required an integrated C4ISR system. This assessment occurred at the same time that the U.S. military was making similar assessments, the difference being that the U.S. military stressed space-based and ground-based system integration whereas China only stressed ground-based systems.[6]

It was not until 2000, however, that the PLA issued a *gangyao* on the building of "command automation systems." Command automation systems are defined by the *Chinese People's Liberation Army's Command Automation Regulations* (中国人民解放军指挥自动化条例) as "military information systems that possess command and control, intelligence and reconnaissance, early warning and surveillance, communications, electronic countermeasures, and other operational and information support capabilities with computers as the core."[7] They have also been described as "an important yardstick for measuring an armed force's operational capabilities."[8]

While the official definition of command automation systems does not appear to have changed since 2000, the practical understanding of the term appears to have changed as the PLA has modernized. In fact, PLA writings indicate that the practical understanding of command automation was expected to change as PLA technology levels improved, just as the U.S. military changed its understanding of command systems from C2 (command and control) to C3 (command, control, and communications) to C3I (command, control, communications, and intelligence) to C4ISR (command, control, communications, computers, intelligence, surveillance, and reconnaissance). As one source states, "The content of military command automation systems is not unchanging, and it will continually be developed, enriched, and expanded along with military technology."[9]

In a reflection of this, writings around the time of the issuing of the command automation *gangyao* often referred to command automation as equivalent to the term C3I.[10] An article from 1999, for example, states that Chinese command automation systems are mainly made up of networks, databases, and command posts and does not mention surveillance or reconnaissance technologies.[11] In the years following the issuing of the command automation *gangyao*, the PLA began to develop and field airborne and space-based ISR technologies, and it was during this time that Chinese military analysts began to consider the requirements and applications of C4ISR systems to be used by the PLA.[12] By at least 2004, articles began referring to "our military's C4ISR systems,"[13] with other sources explicitly linking the PLA's practical understanding of command automation to mean C4ISR systems.[14]

The command automation *gangyao* "laid down the guidelines for the development of command automation systems, and set objectives and implementation measures."[15] Xu Xiaoyan, then head of the GSD Communications Department, described the *gangyao* as a "herculean mission" that would have "an enormous impact on bringing about a fundamental change in the construction of the Chinese armed forces' command automation systems from being a spontaneous, disorderly endeavor to one that is regulated by law; and on turning separate, independent systems into integrated systems."[16]

The *gangyao* proposed "four adherences" to guide the PLA in the development of command automation systems.

1. **Integration** is described as the inevitable trend of the development of command automation systems and the essential measure for improving the overall efficiency of these systems.

2. **Dual Peacetime/Wartime Use** is adherence to the basic principle of combining peacetime and wartime needs and being prepared for offensive and defensive operations. The PLA is urged to develop a system for use in wartime that can also meet peacetime needs. The PLA must also be prepared to defend the command automation network from attacks using information technology and to prepare to attack the enemy's command automation systems.

3. **Centralization** means that command automation systems must be built according to centralized plans and according to the same regulations and standards.

4. **Innovation** consists of making leap-frog developments and breakthroughs in key areas.[17]

OVERALL STRATEGY

The *gangyao* also led to the development of a four-part overall strategy to implement informationization in the PLA. The four parts of this strategy include: correct recognition of informationized warfare requirements, technology development, leveraging civilian information technology for military use, and leap-frog development.

Correct Recognition of Informationized Warfare Requirements.

One of the primary hindrances to the development of integrative C4ISR technologies in the PLA is the lack of understanding of the exact nature of informationized war. Doubts or misunderstandings remain over the conduct of informationized war and how to fight it. The main reason for this is the PLA's lack of recent warfighting experience and the inability of PLA officers to accurately conceptualize the demands of modern war.[18] In broad terms, the PLA is to expand into three new operational areas that will require it to develop six capabilities: rapid response, precision strike, information offense and defense, situational awareness, command decisionmaking, and precision support.[19] The three new operational areas that these capabilities are to support are:

1. Information: The PLA is to use information technology to improve operations;

2. Outer Space: The PLA is to develop military space technologies and equipment to seize the high ground of space before the enemy; and,

3. Blue water: The PLA is to develop capabilities to defend its maritime interests well-beyond its shores.

Technology Development.

The PLA must develop so-called "assassin's mace" weapons that are supported by a combination of ISR assets and integrated information transmission and processing technologies.[20] Chinese analysts argue that the sensors and weapons required for over-the-horizon attacks are often possessed by multiple services, and that multiple reconnaissance platforms and services must be used in concert to both maximize strengths and minimize weaknesses.[21] According to PLA analysts, C4ISR systems based on NCW will be completely networked, and will use a variety of communications means to link strategic, campaign, and tactical levels of command with every unit having access to the same information.[22] Operations will be characterized by an expanded operational battle space which encompasses the ground, sea, air, space, and electromagnetic spheres. Information from ISR assets in these spheres will be fused into a large, seamless intelligence system that is designed to provide commanders with all-weather and all-dimensional information.[23]

Leverage Civilian Information Technology for Military Use.

Because economic development is the main concern of the Chinese Communist Party (CCP), national defense construction must be subordinate to economic development. At the same time, national defense construction will continue as long as financial resources increase. In developing information technology, the PLA will leverage information technology developed in the civil/private/commercial sectors, but will concentrate its own research on developing operational command and weapons systems, and rely on commercially-provided technologies for other systems.[24]

Leap-frog Development.

The PLA will exploit advances by other countries in information technology to assist its own development. The PLA can acquire foreign technology, improve existing foreign technology, learn from the experience of foreign militaries, and use foreign technologies as benchmarks.[25] Leap-frog development is facilitated by the ease with which information technology can be easily purchased (or copied), unlike other types of military technologies, such as missiles.[26] Moreover, the PLA should avoid the U.S. military's mistake in first building stove-piped systems that then had to be integrated by developing those integrative technologies later.[27]

The PLA's commitment to leap-frog development is represented in the "twin important historic tasks (双重历史任务) of transforming from a half-mechanized force into a mechanized and informationized force. These taskings explicitly acknowledge that the PLA is not a fully mechanized force, yet is required to work simultaneously to become a mechanized and informationized force. This requirement was based on the realization that if the PLA waited until it became a fully mechanized force to develop into an informationized force, then it would fall too far behind the U.S. military. On the other hand, PLA technology limitations render it unable to transition directly into an informationized force.[28]

TECHNOLOGY ADVANCES

The PLA has made great strides since 1999 in developing the technological basis for a comprehensive C4ISR system. The PLA uses a variety of communication means, including fiber optic lines, wireless communications, and satellite communications. In fact, PLA communication systems are broad-based and extensive. At the strategic level, for example, the PLA has established the All-Army Cultural Propaganda Information System (全军宣传文化信息网),[29] an All-Army Military Training Information Network (全军军事训练信息网),[30] an All-Army Long Distance Telephone Network, an All-Army Command Automation Network (全军指挥自动化网),[31] an All-Army Teleconferencing Network (全军电话会议网络),[32] and an All-Army "310 Office Net" (全军 "310办公网").[33]

At the Military Region (MR) level, the Chengdu MR is said to use a combination of optical fiber networks, satellite networks, program-controlled switched telephone networks, computer networks, and teleconferencing networks. Optical fiber cables now cover 98 percent of the units at the regiment or battalion level and above, as well as key border defense posts and entry ports. Military program-controlled switched telephone network and satellite networks cover all units at the company level and above. Regional computer networks and teleconferencing systems have been established in combat units at the regimental level and above. In addition, a digitized broadband communications network connects all campaign and tactical level units horizontally and vertically.[34]

The Nanjing MR has also extensively developed its C4 system over the past 30 years, which one article breaks down into three stages:

1. In 1978, a phase-one network established a computer network linking the GSD's Operations Department with the MR Operations Department.

2. In 1985, work began on a phase-two network establishing a computer network linking the GSD with MR combat units at and above the division and brigade level. This network was put into service in 1992.

3. In 1998, the MR began the third phase which raised the MR units' networking, informatization, and joint operations capabilities. In 2004, the MR built a network that appears to be equivalent to a Non-classified Internet Protocol Router Network (NIPRNet) that extends from the Central Military Commission (CMC) and the GSD to units at and above the regiment level. This network is used for videoconferencing, hosting websites and online forums, sending emails, and broadcasting movies, as well as for hosting specialized networks for political work; materials supply; petroleum, oil, and lubricants management; transportation; and frequency spectrum management. Presently, 100 percent of combat brigades and regiments, 93 percent of organic battalions, and 86 percent of companies are connected to the all-army and MR political networks. This phase also involved establishing a security and encryption system in early 2008. [35]

ISR systems and procedures have also been improved. For example, China has launched a number of new satellites, including imagery and synthetic aperture radar satellites and is developing the KJ-200 and KJ-2000 airborne early warning and control (AEW&C) aircraft. The PLA is also training to use these new resources. New procedures were developed by a unit of the South Sea Fleet in 2009 entitled, "Stipulated Technical Procedure for Maritime Terrain Digitized Satellite Surveying and Mapping," that is said to be able to meet the needs of wartime operations.[36] Another 2009 article states that a Guangzhou MR surveying and mapping unit used satellite imagery to establish the PLA's first digitized production network for map making.[37] In April 2009, the GSD Surveying and Mapping Bureau held an exercise to support joint operations that used satellite imagery and navigation and precision information to provide targeting information.[38]

The PLA and the commercial sector have also joined hands in maintaining elements of military command systems by having civilian organizations maintain key telecommunication lines and having joint PLA/commercial repair teams fix telecommunications lines.[39] During times of need the PLA has also reportedly taken over or rented civil telecommunication lines from the commercial sector.[40] The Nanjing MR reportedly uses railroad communication lines to send encrypted messages to subordinate logistics units when the military communications network is down.[41]

The PLA has also made progress in developing integrative technologies. Perhaps one of the most important technical advances is the development and possible fielding of a joint operational datalink system called the Triservice Tactical Information Distributed Network (三军战术数据分发系统), abbreviated by Chinese sources in English as TIS. This network is described as being similar to the U.S. Joint Tactical Information Distribution System (JTIDS), a system that provides jam-resistant digital communication of data and voice for command and control, navigation, relative positioning, and identification that allows units using different technologies to communicate with each other. TIS is said to operate over line-of-sight ranges up to 500 nautical miles and operates in the

960-1,215 MHz frequency band.[42] As with JTIDS, TIS uses frequency hopping and direct sequence spread spectrum to prevent jamming, though sources differ on their effectiveness.

Chinese articles describe TIS as being limited by a lack of over-the-horizon capabilities and requiring a relay mechanism to transmit data over long distances. One article suggests using aircraft to relay communications, but acknowledges that in the case of a conflict over Taiwan, these aircraft will be subject to attack from Taiwanese and U.S. air forces. It notes hopefully, however, that as China's air defense capabilities improve, the utility of TIS will increase.[43]

Another article describes a system of systems in which multiple TIS nodes are located throughout a theater and linked via satellites, fixed communication networks (e.g., fiber optic lines), service communication networks, and tactical networks to provide theater-wide communications and situational awareness beyond visual range. In using this network, the article concludes it would be possible for the campaign command headquarters, service-level units, and tactical-level units to both provide inputs and access information from TIS in order to obtain a common theater-wide battlefield picture.[44]

The extent to which TIS is integrated into current PLA operations is unknown. A 2000 article states that TIS was under development and that service technologies facilitating intra-service communications may be merged with TIS.[45] An article 7 years later stated that the networking of TIS into a system of systems had already achieved some success.[46] It is unclear, however, how comprehensive this system may be. While a 2008 *PLA Navy* article boasts that a "tri-service connection via one network" was used during an exercise, the manner in which the joint communications system was established casts doubt on this claim. The article reports that in order for the services to communicate with each other, ground force communication personnel, with their equipment, were stationed aboard ships to facilitate communication between the services.[47]

Other reports reveal that individual MRs have established or are working on their own joint C4 systems and it is unclear if these technologies involve TIS. In 2009, it was reported that the Jinan MR held a meeting on the construction of a "new type of theater joint command information system" designed to join the services.[48] Similarly, a 2009 article stated that the Nanjing MR in the past 2 years had established the PLA's first theater C4ISR system.[49] This system is said to have broken the communication barriers between services and solved the MR's challenges with joint operations command, real-time air intelligence, joint firepower attack, and precision support.[50] Again, as with other technologies, the development of theater-wide C4ISR systems by individual MRs suggests that a standardized C4ISR system has not been established by the PLA or, at the least, that standardization is not being enforced.

Despite the many successes in developing C4ISR technologies, the PLA admits that its technologies cannot yet fully support joint operations. However, the PLA's main difficulty in establishing an integrative C4ISR system lies more with the approach the PLA has taken with C4ISR modernization than with the level of technology used. Stovepiping, for example, has been a major impediment. While the services have been good at establishing communications with subordinate units, they have largely ignored connectivity with their sister services.

Communication problems have also arisen due to the incompatibility of technology. Units use different models and generations of weapons and equipment and there are differences in the technology levels of services and combat arms or even between different operational units within a service or combat arm.[51] One of the main sources of this incompatibility is the decentralized nature of PLA technology development where individual units are provided funding to develop their own technology but pay no attention to connecting with other units. A main communications station of the Navy, for example, was praised in a *PLA Daily* article for building a 600,000 yuan comprehensive training center using indigenously designed software.[52]

The goal of establishing an automated command system is not just to make systems automated, but also to make them integrated into a synergistic whole in which "1 plus 1 is greater than 2."[53] While technology is required, it is also more important to have the mindset, organization, and training to use it correctly.[54] This requires organizational and training reform to conduct operations that can fuse together separate resources from multiple services to locate and track targets, such as opto-electronic and radar imagery satellites, over-the-horizon radar, early warning aircraft, and more traditional assets such as visual location and tracking by aircraft, ships, or ground personnel that facilitates the technological foundation stressed in NCW. The information collected from network-centric forces needs to be communicated to a central location where it is fused into a common battlefield picture that enables commanders to make informed decisions. This capability is best illustrated by the PLA's ability to conduct joint operations, which will be evaluated in the following sections.

NCW CAPABILITY: JOINT OPERATIONS

Joint operations are fundamental to carrying out the PLA's strategy of active defense and winning local wars under informationized conditions. Indeed, China's 2008 *Defense White Paper* describes winning local wars in conditions of informationization as inherently relying on jointness. It states:

> This guideline aims at winning local wars in conditions of informationization. It takes into overall consideration the evolution of modern warfare and the major security threats facing China, and prepares for defensive operations under the most difficult and complex circumstances. Meeting the requirements of confrontation between war systems in modern warfare and taking integrated joint operations as the basic approach, it is designed to bring the operational strengths of different services and arms into full play, combine offensive operations with defensive operations, give priority to the flexible application of strategies and tactics, seek advantages and avoid disadvantages, and make the best use of our strong points to attack the enemy's weak points. It endeavors to refine the command system for joint operations, the joint training system and the joint support system, optimize the structure and composition of forces, and speed up the building of a combat force structure suitable for winning local wars in conditions of informationization.[55]

In 1999, the PLA issued a *gangyao* on joint operations that instituted the concept in PLA warfighting, and since 2000 the GSD has given increased priority to joint operations in its annual military training objectives.[56] The PLA's concept and practice of joint operations has evolved since 1999 from emphasizing joint operations to integrated joint operations (一体化

联合作战). This transition from joint to integrated revealed fundamental flaws in the PLA's conception of joint operations. The main impediment to achieving interoperability was the 1999 joint operations *gangyao* itself, which only required the services to form coordinating relationships rather than foster true interoperability.[57] In fact, some PLA sources from this early period stress "joint operation coordination" (联合作战协同).[58] Under this construct, each service remained independent with respect to operational forces, weapons and equipment, communications networks, and logistics, albeit under a unified command.[59]

Ultimately, the codification of coordination over true jointness has come to impede PLA capabilities. Instead of centralizing personnel into one organization, coordination requires each service to exchange personnel between each of the service commands at the campaign, *juntuan* (军团), and tactical levels.[60] Not only does such a system slow the transition to a wartime command, this process requires different services with their own cultures to mesh their own ways of operating at every level of the campaign. The addition of new personnel also taxes every service command unit to provide computers, communication equipment, and other types of equipment to newly arrived personnel. Indeed, one author asked "if every operational *jituan* (集团) sends a liaison group and there are 5 to 7 operational groups, then there are 20 to 30 new people who all require command equipment. Where does it come from?"[61]

By 2003, the PLA leadership recognized that coordinated joint operations would not achieve the level of interoperability required by modern war. As a result, PLA analysts began to reconceptualize joint operations into a new framework called "integrated joint operations."[62] It appears that the PLA has not officially defined integrated joint operations, but generally they are described as "an advanced stage of joint operations," in which the command organization is not a coordinating body but, in fact, has the authority to make decisions. Integrated joint operations are thus "not the simple combining of service operations but are the organic merging of the planning and command of separate service operations in order to form a more powerful comprehensive operation."[63]

ASSESSING PROGRESS IN INTEGRATED JOINT OPERATIONS

This section will evaluate the PLA's progress in two critical areas: organization and training.

Organization.

The PLA has made some progress in creating a joint organizational structure over the past 10 years, but major hurdles remain. The main reason for the lack of progress is the historical predominance of the ground force and its predilection to control PLA doctrine, organization, and operations. The predominance of the ground force has led to a lack of permanent joint structures, which has stymied a culture of jointness and the technology needed to support it. As one Navy author writing on the dominance of the ground force complained, "military region leadership organizations cannot say that they are a real command organization and this makes it difficult to meet the needs of commanding multi-dimensional operations under high technology conditions."[64] The lack of a permanent joint organization at the MR level has been the fundamental impediment to fostering interoperability. Without a joint organization, it has been difficult to develop the technologies to connect the organizations or to train the personnel in joint operations.[65]

The PLA has made some progress in establishing joint organizations, however. For example, since 2004 each service has been represented at the CMC, but it appears that little effort has been made to go beyond this level of jointness. Only ground force officers have become vice chairmen of the CMC or held the position of Chief of the General Staff. Only one nonground force officer has held the rank head of the General Political Department, General Logistics Department, or the General Armament Department. Li Jinai, current head of the GPD, spent much of his career in the Second Artillery.

Moreover, jointness is limited at the staff officer levels of the four General Departments. For example, at the deputy commander level, the General Staff, Political, and Logistics Departments are each staffed by three ground force officers and one Air Force officer. The staffing of the General Armament Department at the deputy commander level is more nuanced with representation coming from career armament department officers who have served in nonservice specific positions working in the ground, aviation, missile, and space fields. No Navy or Second Artillery officer holds the position of deputy director for any of the four General Departments, and below the deputy director level, jointness appears to be less prevalent.

The PLA also lacks a permanent joint organization at the MR level. Indeed, in a run-up to a war, the MR must transition to a joint warfighting organization called the war zone. The lack of jointness at the MR level is reflected in the fact that only ground force officers have served as MR commanders. While some deputy commander positions are occupied by the Air Force and Navy, no Second Artillery or PAP officers occupy deputy commander positions.

The PLA has made progress in the area of joint logistics. The PLA officially instituted a joint logistics department (JLD) system in 2000, but a true joint system was not formed until 2004 when the Jinan MR was selected as a test bed for an enhanced JLD.[66] The enhanced JLD provides both common use supplies, defined as supplies used by all services, and service-specific supplies instead of routing supplies through each service. The Jinan MR formally adopted this system in 2007, but Hu Jintao postponed expansion of the JLD system pending additional research and evaluation.[67]

Training.

While training has also had modest successes since 1999, PLA sources indicate that progress has not been sufficient. As one source states, the PLA trains to "fight a battle jointly, yet exercises separately."[68] Training is said to either lack jointness or is insufficiently joint. An exercise may only be joint for certain segments rather than throughout its entirety. Moreover, no standards or criteria have been established to evaluate jointness. Training also needs to be expanded to include "topic training" on joint offensive and defensive operations, joint command and control, joint logistics, and joint information support.[69]

As with wartime joint operations, the main obstacle to conducting joint training is the lack of a permanent joint training structure at the MR region and below. While the GSD had conducted some joint training, such training has been done on a temporary and ad hoc basis with limited long-term results. In addition, because there is no permanent joint training structure, the services do not have a mechanism to discuss how joint training should be conducted or evaluated. Consequently, the PLA still lacks clear and sufficient regulations and standards regarding joint training.[70]

The main attempt to establish an organization for joint training has been the formation of "coordination zones" in 2003. A training coordination zone is described as:

> A place where units of various arms and services having similar future combat missions are relatively concentrated, and where a zone of mutually coordinated military training is set up. This is aimed at effective integration and sharing of training resources, so that units of the various arms and services can rely on the coordination zone to accomplish integrated, joint training, and exercises.[71]

The designation of these training areas as "coordination zones," however, belies the PLA's propensity for coordinated operations rather than true interoperability. Indeed, PLA sources lament that training in coordination zones is characterized by "communication" plus "consultation" instead of true jointness.[72]

Despite structural impediments, the PLA has made some progress in joint training. For example, one article notes that a motorized infantry division now has an Air Force ground controller attached to it.[73] But the joint training praised in PLA publications is often rudimentary or superficial. For example, one report stated that ground force and Navy units in a training coordination zone practiced ship loading and unloading and ground force units practiced loading aircraft onto railcars for the Air Force.[74] Another report praised the "jointness" of an exercise which merely brought together the top leaders of each service via video teleconferencing.[75] Other efforts described as joint are really combat arms exercises. The Navy appears particularly egregious in this matter and frequently touts training between surface, subsurface, and aviation units as "joint."[76]

A review of the PLA's training goals from 2002-09 shows incremental improvements in joint training as training requirements moved from amorphous calls to conduct joint training to the study of the theoretical underpinnings of joint training, to the creation of test points, to the focus on specific joint training subjects, and finally to the first war zone level joint exercise. In detail, the Outline of Military Training and Evaluation (OMTE) for these years is discussed.

The 2002 training goals described joint operations as a key training objective and directed all units to strengthen their understanding of joint operations. However, the training goals directed the PLA to carry out "coordinated training" against the background of joint operations.[77]

The 2003 training goals paid little attention to joint operations and only directed the PLA to carry out training under the guidance of the joint operations concept, but did not specifically mandate what actions should be taken.[78]

Integrated training was formerly introduced into the 2004 training goals. The year 2004 was obviously a "building year" in which emphasis was placed on study as units were urged "to create the substance, methods, and mechanisms of integrated training and to develop a model of integrated training."[79]

The 2005 training goals stressed "incremental progress" in carrying out integrated training. For the first time, the training goals identified the formation of joint training organizations as a key requirement. Theoretical progress was also stressed, as the Academy of Military Science was directed to conduct theoretical study of integrated training. The integration of specific tasks was also mentioned for the first time. In this case, the strengthening of command and control of intelligence, support, and live fire exercises.[80]

The 2006 training goals stressed practical application and directed the PLA to continue its theoretical study of integrated operations. Whatever progress was made in 2005 was meant to be refined in 2006, as the 2005 tasks do not appear to have been expanded. Instead, the PLA was asked to study the "pathway" to combined arms and joint training as well as "to give prominence to joint training, and to strive to build and further improve institutions and mechanisms conducive to joint training so as to boost the integrated fighting capability of the army."[81]

The year 2006 also saw the convening of an all-Army meeting to discuss training under conditions of informationization. This meeting is said to be the first meeting to unify thought, resolve problems, and promote the development of informationized training. The meeting resulted in the CMC issuing a document entitled "Decisions on Strengthening Military Training During the New Period of the New Century," which issued five instructions to the PLA:

1. Deepen the content of training and promote the establishment of military training systems under informationized conditions. The main efforts were to build a force able to use information, accomplish different tasks, promote joint training, and conduct

realistic training with the goal of accomplishing the New Historic Missions and improving the ability to conduct joint operations under informationized conditions.

2. Take improving joint operations capabilities as the main line. Establish a complete joint training system focused on completing missions and taking strategic and campaign training as the core. Joint training will include support from integrated command platforms and will abide by the principles of the main force taking the lead.

3. Increase the ability of units to work in a complex electromagnetic environment. The PLA was instructed to study the requirements of fighting in a complex electromagnetic environment with a focus on training communication, radar, and electronic countermeasure units.

4. Train joint operations personnel and strengthen the quality of military personnel. Joint training will become part of the educational requirements for personnel and training at military schools will be improved. Education will focus on personnel involved in joint operations, information technology, and new equipment.

5. Take informationized construction as the foundation and develop training methods that are adaptable to the new combat power. The PLA is to focus on training bases and operational laboratories of schools.[82]

Despite the importance of the year 2006 for setting training goals, press reports on the 2007 training goals merely directed the PLA to "continue to explore integrated training" and to fully use what had been achieved at integrated training test points and to "promote the healthy and orderly development of integrated training" as well as to explore a path to regional joint training methods.[83]

The building and exploration that occurred from 2005-07 appears to have been successful as the 2008 training goals became more specific in its requirements for joint training. In fact, 2008 was an important year in which 163 primary level units were involved in developing new training and evaluation standards. In June 2008 the GSD issued 1,522 training publications reflecting achievements in training reform, and in late 2008, the PLA held an all-Army video and teleconference to formally institute these guidelines into PLA training.[84] Interestingly, the training goals did not discuss integrated training, but did identify joint training as a key objective. The training goals specifically mentioned that joint training should be carried out in regards to intelligence, command and control, and communications. The 2008 training goals also encouraged the PLA to organize units and commands by missions and to deepen regional coordinated training.[85] This last requirement suggests progress towards joint training commands organized around particular missions rather than missions carried out by individual services.

The training guidelines developed in 2008 were implemented in 2009. Indeed, the year 2009 appears to be a pivotal one in which the PLA began to address the fundamental barriers to jointness. In fact, the PLA is putting its foot down and ordering all the services to cooperate and institute joint training reforms. In March 2009, the *PLA Daily* published the minutes of a meeting held by the Jinan MR in which the leadership exhorted the services in no uncertain terms to make joint training work. The organizers of the meeting criticized the services for treating joint training as merely the topic *de jour* rather than as a fundamental reform, stating "the road of joint training must be taken. We have no choice . . ." The leadership also described joint operations as essential to victory, stating "the isolated battle of a single service will never achieve what it wants" and that "every military has acutely recognized that the one who starts joint training first and who does a great job at joint training will have the key to victory." The services were also urged to continue joint training despite disputes because it is only through continued training that problems can be resolved.[86]

To carry out the 2009 training goals, the PLA appointed the Jinan MR to be a test bed for joint training and established the first joint training command organization on February 23, 2009.[87] This step was described as signifying "that joint training at the theater level started to step into a new development stage."[88] The Jinan MR may be the joint reform test bed for several reasons. The Jinan MR, along with the Nanjing and Guangzhou MRs, is one of three MRs that has representation from all services as well as fleet headquarters, and for this reason joint training can be conducted more easily with higher level service units. The PLA, however, may want to limit the negative effects of experimentation on units in the Nanjing and Guangzhou MRs due to their proximity to Taiwan and probable use in a Taiwan conflict. Finally, the MR has been the site of large-scale military exercises, including the China-Russia "Peace Mission 2005," which has given the MR more experience with dealing with dissimilar forces.

According to one source, in setting up its joint training command mechanism, the Jinan MR will make overall plans for joint training, but each year a different service will command the training in which one core issue is highlighted and one subject is practiced. The culmination of these joint reforms to date has been the 8-day exercise "Joint-209" which was held in the Jinan MR and involved all of the services and the People's Armed Police (PAP), and was the first joint war zone exercise for the PLA. The exercise was said to have focused on four areas:

1. The inclusion of Army, Navy, Air Force, Second Artillery, and PAP forces in the war zone in the exercise for the first time.

2. The inclusion of local governments into training.

3. The inclusion of local national defense mobilization organizations into the war zone joint training system.

4. The use of an integrated command platform to organize joint training for the first time.[89]

CONCLUSIONS

The 10-year history of PLA informationization reveals a pattern of limited progress stymied by service rivalry, inadequate doctrinal development, and technological shortcomings. In pursuing informationization, the PLA has simultaneously taken a bottom up and a top down approach. Technological improvements have mainly followed a bottom-up process in which even units at very low levels have been given funds to develop their own systems. While individual services have managed to develop robust vertical command and control systems that link superior with subordinate units, they have not taken the initiative to develop integrative technologies that connect them with their sister services. As a result, the CMC and

GSD have had to take a top down approach to force jointness upon the services in the form of doctrine and regulations. These efforts, however, have resulted in limited improvements in establishing an organizational structure capable of supporting joint operations. While the CMC has been made joint and a Joint Logistics Department established, the four General Departments and the military regions continue to lack jointness and it is unclear how joint the JLD system is Army-wide. The PLA has also done little joint training.

Jointness, it seems, is still largely anathema to the PLA, and it appears that the ground force continues to wield extraordinary power at a time when PLA writings on future wars depict a more prominent role for the other services. Without a permanent joint structure, it will continue to be difficult to build suitable technology systems and to change the mindset of single service domination. In fact, the PLA continues to delay making the hard decisions concerning joint reform. There has been no discussion of making the four General Departments truly joint nor do the 2009 training reforms indicate that the MR headquarters itself will be made joint. They only require the formation of a permanent joint training organization. While the PLA focuses on establishing jointness at the CMC and MR levels, the U.S. experience in forming a joint military suggests that joint organizations must be formed from the strategic to the tactical levels. In this regard, the lack of jointness at the General Department level appears to be a critical shortcoming of joint reform as these organizations are the working bodies of the CMC. The prominence of ground force officers in the four General Departments suggests that, at worst, service rivalry continues to retard joint reforms and, at best, suggests that a lack of a basic understanding of the requirements and capabilities of their sister services by ground force officers limits reforms. Either way, jointness at the General Department level appears to be an essential measure in altering institutional interest and the mindset of the top PLA leadership, and, without that change in mindset, it seems difficult to enforce joint reforms at lower levels.

But how should we judge PLA progress to date? We could judge progress by whether the PLA can conduct joint operations. By this measure, the PLA has failed. Even PLA authors are clear that the PLA is incapable of carrying out true joint operations.[90] But this standard is probably too high. Jointness is difficult. The U.S. military in World War II was joint in many respects, especially in the Pacific Theater, but it lost that interoperability and fought the Korean and Vietnam Wars with minimal jointness. It was not until the passage of the Goldwater-Nichols Act in 1986 that the U.S. military began the path that has led to its current level of jointness and that jointness has been forged by fighting two wars for the past 8 years. By this measure, the PLA has a long and difficult road ahead to become an effective joint force. These efforts will be made more difficult without warfighting experience.

PLA authors have also attempted to establish benchmarks by which to measure PLA progress in joint reform. Noted information warfare expert Dai Qingmin describes three stages of informationization.

> The first stage is the standalone construction stage in which individual services build their own information systems and move from a stage of mechanization to informationization as traditional weapons are integrated with information systems.

The second stage is the comprehensive development stage in which information systems are horizontally integrated and changes are made in a military's organizational structure, training, and education. The U.S. military is described as being in the middle to later part of this stage.

The third stage is the overall transformation stage. This stage reflects a maturation of the informationization process in which a military carries out system-to-system attacks around the information flows on the ground, the sea, the air, the space, the electromagentic domain, the network, and the sensory dimensions.

Dai concludes that the PLA is in the beginning stages of comprehensive development or in the transition between the first stage and the second stage. Dai also concludes that the PLA is in the preliminary stages of constructing an informationized organization management system that has focused on top-level design, improved regulations and standards, infrastructure, and making breakthroughs in key points.[91]

The PLA's own timetable offers a final metric by which to judge progress in jointness. According to the 2008 *Defense White Paper*, the PLA has the goal of laying a foundation for informationization by 2010, to make major progress by 2020, and to mostly reach the goal of informationization by 2050. The establishment of a joint CMC, a Joint Logistics Department, a joint training structure test bed, and the conducting of the first war zone-level joint exercise has been conducted. Moreover, individual services and MRs have made impressive gains in technology, including the first joint war-zone C4ISR system established by the Guangzhou MR. By this measure, it appears that the PLA is meeting its own standards for joint reform.

Despite the emphasis on informationized operations, informationization does pose dangers for the PLA. By developing into a networked force just like the U.S. military, the PLA opens itself up to the same sorts of vulnerabilities that it hopes to exploit in the U.S. C4ISR system. This reduction of asymmetry could be advantageous to the U.S. military and remains a contradiction largely unaddressed in PLA writings. Dai Qingmin admits that informationization is a double-edged sword that will cause it "danger and hidden troubles," but he also recommends that at its current stage of development the PLA should pay more attention to its beneficial effects and ignore its disadvantages.[92] This is most likely because the PLA, and China, have no other alternative. China desires to become a major power and can only do this by becoming modern, and modernity depends on a reliance on information technology. To remain as a largely mechanized force forever dooms the PLA to being a second-rate military and China a second-rate power. Consequently, the PLA must transform into an informationized force even if this creates vulnerabilities in the short to medium term.

PLA writings also do not discuss another paradox of a network-centric force: the tendency of commanders to centralize control. Ostensibly, the benefit of NCW is its ability to increase the ability of lower-level officers to make decisions. Technology, however, could further centralize command by enabling senior commanders to monitor and direct small units. Considering the PLA's predilection for heavily centralized command, command automation systems may strengthen the role of the campaign commander at the expense of limiting subordinates' freedom of action. These problems will eventually need to be addressed, but for now what emerges from PLA writings is that they are trying to harness new technology to abide by the tenets of NCW.

The PLA commitment to jointness is undiminished, and it appears will only increase. Could information-ization, however, be derailed by the global economic crisis? The PLA's modernization drive depends upon advancements in civilian information technology, and with China's export-oriented economy it is possible that a downturn in global demand could negatively affect China's IT sector, which could then negatively affect military modernization. Here the answer is less certain, but it appears that the drive for informationiza-tion will continue unabated. The Chinese government has an immense and expanding amount of money on which to draw from to aid economic recovery. China's foreign currency reserves reached U.S. $2.13 trillion at the end of the second quarter of 2009.[93] In December 2008, China devoted U.S. $586 billion to a stimulus plan. Of this, 4 percent, or U.S. $23.44 billion, went to technology advances and industrial restructuring.[94] The stimulus has had an effect, with economic growth up 8.9 percent in the third quarter of 2009.[95] Nor has the economic crisis affected military spending. China's official defense budget increased 14.9 percent in 2009.

In fact, it is possible that the economic crisis could be beneficial for the PLA. Additional stimulus money may be used to spur technological innovation. Ad-ditionally, the threat of higher unemployment may make military careers more attractive for those with high tech backgrounds. China's large cash reserves could also give it the ability to acquire struggling for-eign companies at bargain prices. While no high pro-file mergers or acquisitions have been reported since the economic crisis, Chinese companies are willing to explore opportunities. These efforts in the past, however, have been blocked by the national security concerns of home countries. Huawei, for example, was blocked in its attempts to acquire Marconi by the British government in 2005 and by the U.S. Government in 2008 to acquire a stake in 3Com.

It is more certain that the PLA's drive to informationize will have a profound effect on U.S. military operations. The PLA already possesses or is working on weapons systems that threaten or could threaten the U.S. military. These include advanced air defense systems, especially "double digit SAMS;" long range cruise missiles; and anti-ship ballistic missiles (ASBM). While each of these systems poses a threat, they become even more formidable when networked to form a system of systems. While much analysis has been done on individual PLA weapon systems, it is C4ISR systems which will facilitate PLA efforts to deny the U.S. military access to a theater. For example, improved C4ISR systems could improve attacks against U.S. forces and bases in the region by precisely and in a timely manner locating targets and conducting battle damage assessments. Improved C4ISR systems could also greatly improve attacks against U.S. naval forces. PLA authors writing on attacks against aircraft carrier strike groups discuss swarm attacks in which surface, subsurface, and aviation attacks would be conducted simultaneously. A comprehensive C4ISR system would also be integral to ASBM attacks against aircraft carrier strike groups as data from space-based ISR, over-the-horizon radar, and aviation or surface assets would need to fused to form actionable intelligence. Ultimately, this could enable China to become more forceful in its dealings with the United States, Taiwan, or its neighbors.

Over the longer-term, the development of an integrative and comprehensive C4ISR system will enable the PLA to project power globally. As China's relations with Africa deepen and as its energy needs increase, a robust C4ISR system will permit China to defend its global interests by supporting forces well beyond its borders. China's C4ISR developments will then be one indicator of China's rise as a global power.

ENDNOTES - CHAPTER 5

1. This is the first paper that discusses PLA organizational and training reform and technological advances within the context of joint operations and the first paper that takes joint capabilities as an overall indicator of the PLA's level of informationization. For discussions of the PLA's conceptualization of joint operations, see Dean Cheng, "The PLA and Joint Operations: Moving From Theory to Practice" in Michael D. Swaine, Andrew N. D. Yang, and Evan S. Medeiros, eds., with Oriana Skylar Mastro, *Assessing the Threat: The Chinese Military and Taiwan's Security*, Washington, DC: Carnegie Endowment for International Peace, 2007, pp. 55-83; and Dean Cheng, "*Zhanyixue* and Joint Campaigns," in James Mulvenon and David Finkelstein, eds., *China's Revolution in Doctrinal Affairs: Emerging Trends in the Operational Art of the Chinese People's Liberation Army*, Alexandria, VA: CNA Corporation, December 2005, pp. 101-118.

2. Gangyao has been defined as "outline" or "regulations." This chapter will leave the term *gangyao* undefined since the exact contents of *gangyao* are unknown.

3. Zhang Qinsheng and Li Bingyan, "Complete New Historical Transformation – Understanding Gained From Studying CMC Strategic Thinking on 'Two Basic Transformations,'" 解放军报 (*PLA Daily*), January 14, 1997.

4. *The Implementation of Network-Centric Warfare*, January 5, 2005, Washington, DC: Office of Force Transformation, February 14, 2005, pp. 3-4.

5. Vice Admiral Arthur K. Cebrowski, U.S. Navy, and John J. Garstka, "Network-Centric Warfare: Its Origin and Future," *U.S. Naval Institute Proceedings*, Vol. 124, No. 1139, January 1998.

6. Liang Zhenxing, "对指挥自动化系统一体化体系结构的理解（上）" ("Understanding the Integrated Structure of Command Automation Systems [I]"), in *C4ISR 系统现状与发展* (*The Current Situation and Development of C4ISR Systems*), Virginia Beach, VA: The Naval Equipment Demonstration Research Center Command Automation Research Institute, 2002, p. 133.

7. Zhao Jie, ed., 指挥自动化教程 (*A Course on Command Automation*), Beijing, China: Military Science Press, 2002, p. 2.

8. Xu Xiaoyan, "坚定不移的走依法建设之路，学习中央军委颁发的《指挥自动化建设纲要" ("Follow Through the 'Outlines,' and Proceed with the Development According to the Law"), 解放军报 (*PLA Daily*), September 26, 2000.

9. Zhao, p. 8.

10. *Ibid.*, p. 6.

11. Zhang Peigao, "对加强我军军队自动化建设和运用的探索" ("Strengthen Our Army's Construction and Implementation of Automation"), 军事系统工程 (*Military Systems Engineering*), 1999/2, p. 19.

12. See, for example, a series of books published by The Naval Equipment Demonstration Research Center Command Automation Research Institute in 2002 on command systems that emphasize the study of C4ISR systems: *C4ISR 系统现状与发展* (*The Current Situation and Development of C4ISR Systems*), 联合作战中的指挥自动化建设 (*Joint Operation's Command Automation System Building*), and 军事运筹与系统工程 (*Military Planning and Systems Engineering*).

13. Liu Jing, Yuan Weiwei and Luo Xue-shan, "C4ISR 领域本体研究初探" ("Research of the Ontology Used in the C4ISR Systems"), 情报指挥控制系统与仿真技术 (*Intelligence, Command, and Control Systems and Simulation Technology*), February 2004, p. 16.

227

14. See, for example, Wang Wangzhun and Lu Lihua, eds., *Joint Campaign Operations Command*, Beijing: National Defense University Press, 2000.; and Yu Bin, Duan Caiyu, and Rao Dehu, "C4ISR 系统军事需求描述概念模型" ("A Conceptual Model for Describing C4ISR Military Requirements"). 国防科技大学学报 (*Journal of National University of Defense Technology*), 2008/2, p. 112.

15. *Ibid.*

16. *Ibid.*

17. *Ibid.*

18. Xu Xiaoyan, ed., 军队信息化概论 (*An Introduction to Military Informationization*), Beijing, China: Liberation Army Press, 2005, p. 61.

19. *Ibid.*, p. 153.

20. *Ibid.*, p. 63.

21. Kan Yabin and Xue Jianfei, "反舰导弹攻击指挥与战术决策的超视距跨越" ("Command and Tactical Decision For Over-The-Horizon Leap of Anti-ship Missile Attack"), 飞航导弹 (*Winged Missiles*), May 2004, pp. 12-16.

22. Wang Wen and Huang Duanxin, "浅谈一体化联合作战指挥的几点要求" ("A Preliminary Discussion of Several Operational Command Requirements for Integrated Joint Operations"), 战士报 (*Soldier News*), April 7, 2005, p. 3.

23. Yang Hong, "一体化联合作战指挥特征" ("The Special Characteristics of Integrated Joint Operations Command"), 战士报 (*Soldier News*), October 28, 2004, p. 4.

24. Xu, *An Introduction to Military Informationization*, p. 64.

25. *Ibid.*, pp. 65, 140.

26. *Ibid.*, p. 140.

27. *Ibid.*, p. 146.

28. *Ibid.*, p. 138.

29. Zhou Ming, "全军宣传文化信息化信息系统通过鉴定" ("All Army Cultural Propaganda Information System Approved"), 解放军报 (*PLA Daily*), September 28, 2000.

30. Information available from *www.lw23.com/lunwen_956 7922/*.

31. Information available from *www.hunan.gov.cn/tmzf/xxlb/ zwxx/200909/t20090905_170401.htm*.

32. "Guangxi Military District Builds Information Superhighway," 战士报 (*Soldier News*), April 25, 2002.

33. Jia Yuntong, "联合作战应建立高效后勤指挥系统" ("Need to Set up Highly Efficient Logistics Command System to Support Future Tri-Service Joint Operations"), 战士报 (*Soldier News*), January 15, 2002.

34. 战旗报 (*Battle Flag*), February 14, 2006.

35. He Rong, Chen Xiangdi, and Cai Haibing, "军网纵横" ("A Tightly Knit Military Web"), 人民前线 (*People's Frontline*), December 11, 2008, p. 4.

36. Wu Xiaofeng and Deng Ping, "《海上数字化地形卫星测绘技术规程》通过专家评审" ("Stipulated Technical Procedure for Maritime Terrain Digitalized Satellite Surveying and Mapping' Passes Experts' Evaluation — Provides Powerful Support for Wartime Maritime Terrain Surveying and Mapping"), 人民海军 (*PLA Navy*), June 6, 2009, p. 1.

37. "聚焦军官：热浪滚滚正是练兵好时节" ("Officer Focus: A Rolling Heat Wave is Really a Good Time to Train Troops"), 解放军报 (*PLA Daily*), June 14, 2009.

38. Liu Jihong and Zhu Da, "'经纬 2009' 测绘保障训练在南京落幕" ("The 'Jingwei 2009' Surveying and Mapping Exercise in Nanjing Concludes"), 解放军报 (*PLA Daily*), May 1, 2009.

39. Zhang Fuyou, "军事通信在军民结合中跨越腾飞" ("Military Communications Are Rapidly Becoming Military-Civilian Use"), 解放军报 (*PLA Daily*, September 27, 2000.

40. *Ibid.*

41. "Merger of Military and Civilian Communications Networks," 解放军报 (*PLA Daily*), February 15, 2000.

42. Xu Lei, Wang Rong, and Yao Minli, "TIS系统的弱实施多任务网管的设计" ("Windows NT-based Research On Soft Real-time Multi-task Gateway of TIS," 电光与控制 (*Electronics Optics and Control*), August 2007, p. 16.

43. Sun Jingfang, "信息战条件下水面舰船编队通信网络技术发展与分析" ("Surface Ship Formation Communication Network Technology Under Information Warfare Conditions Development and Analysis"), 舰船电子工程 (*Ship Electronic Engineering*, 1999/4, p. 31.

44. Xu, Wang, and Yao, "Windows NT-based Research On Soft Real-time Multi-task Gateway of TIS," p. 16.

45. Li Min, "21世纪初我国海军海上编队'协同作战系统'的构想" ("A Vision for Our Navy's Naval Units 'Cooperative Operation System' in the Early 21st Century"), 舰船电子工程 (*Ship Electronic Engineering*), 2000/1, p. 17.

46. Xu, Wang, and Yao, "Windows NT-based Research on Soft Real-time Multi-task Gateway of TIS," p. 16.

47. Yuan Zhenjun, Zhang Xinxin, Li Taowei, and Cui Xiaolong, "Why Do Sounds of Drums and Trumpets Not Reach Others in Ship-Aircraft Joint Operations? Communication 'Dialects' Hinder Intercommunication—Serial Reports From Theater by Renmin Haijun Staff Reporters, Part 3," 人民海军 (*PLA Navy*), October 31, 2008, p. 2.

48. Liu Hongtao and Han Zongcheng, "联战先联建，联训先联通—战区新型联合指挥信息系统建设系统会在济举行" ("Joint Construction Before Joint Combat, Joint Communication Before Joint Training—Coordination Meeting for Construction of New

Type of Theater Joint Command Information System Held in Ji-nan"), 前卫报 (*Frontline Defense News*), April 2, 2009, p. 1.

49. Zhong Yongguo and Zhang Kejin, "广州战区三军部队构建联训'准战场" ("Guangzhou Theatre Sets up Close-To-Real Battlefield for Joint Training"), 解放军报 (*PLA Daily*), February 27, 2009.

50. Zhong Youguo, Li Huamin, Zhang Kejin, and Yan Deyong, "构建联合训练'大特区' 解释广州战区探索三军部队联战联训的实践历程" ("Build a Joint Training Big Special Zone—Analysis of Guangzhou Theaters Exploration of Joint Operations and Joint Training Process of its Three Branches"), 解放军报 (*PLA Daily*), March 2, 2009.

51. Pan Ningyong, "联合训练有如一部结构严整的大机器，其运转速度的快慢及效率的高低取决关键性链条的牢固与否—强化联合训练的'结构链" ("Joint Training Is Like a Big, Tightly Structured Machine; Its Operational Speed and Efficiency Are Determined by Whether Its Crucial Chains Are Strong—Strengthening the 'Structural Chains' of Joint Training"), 解放军报 (*PLA Daily*), February 26, 2009.

52. Yu Guimin, "Group of Noncommissioned Technical Officers with Superb Skills Excels in Shooting Range at Sea," 解放军报 (*PLA Daily*), January 17, 2009, p. 1.

53. Zhang Peigao, ed., 联合战役指挥教程 (*Joint Campaign Command Teaching Materials*), Beijing, China: Military Science Press, 2001, p. 46.

54. *Ibid.*, p. 45.

55. *China's National Defense in 2008*, Beijing: Information Office of the State Council of the People's Republic of China, January 2009, p. 11, available from *Ndu.edu/whitepapers/China_English2008.pdf*.

56. See, for example, Wang Wenjie and Su Ruozhou, "进一步推动我军军事工作跨世纪发展" ("Further the Promotion of the Development of Our Army's Cross-century Military Work"), 解放军报 (*PLA Daily*), November 13, 1999.

57. Zhang, *A Course in Joint Campaign Command*, p. 7. The quote from the *gangyao* is identified by the source as taken from the PLA's 1999 *Joint Campaign Gangyao* (联合战役纲要).

58. See, for example, An Weiping, Peng Buwen, and Zhou Xiaozi, eds., 联合作战新论 (*A New Theory on Joint Operations*), Beijing, China: National Defense University (NDU) Press, 2003, pp. 212-236.

59. Ji Gong, "Several Important Training Tasks Are Accomplished Before the End of the Year with High Standards," 战士报 (*Soldier News*), October 18, 2003, p. 2.

60. Zhou Huan and Zou Hanbing, "第二炮兵在联合作战中的协同问题" ("Coordination Issues of the Second Artillery Corps in Joint Operations"), 军事学术 (*Military Art*), July 2004, p. 71.

61. Jiang Fangran, "联合作战控制与联合作战协调" ("Joint Operations Control and Joint Operations Coordination"), 军事学术 (*Military Research*), March 2004, p. 32.

62. See, for example, the criticism of the PLA's conception of jointness in Bai Fengkai, Fang Jiayin, and Bai Haiwei, "装备联合能力一体化研究" ("Study on Equipment Joint Capabilities Integration"), 装备指挥技术学院学报 (*Journal of the Academy of Equipment Command & Technology*), June 2005, pp. 11-14.

63. Cui Shizeng and Wang Junyi, "解析'一体化'联合作战" ("Analysis of 'Integrated' Joint Operations"), 解放军报 (*PLA Daily*), July 7, 2004.

64. Hua Xiaoping, "对建立我军联合作战指挥体系的探讨" ("An Examination of Establishing Our Military's Joint Operations Command System"), 联合作战中的指挥自动化系统建设 (*Joint Operation's Command Automation System Building*), Virginia Beach, VA: The Naval Equipment Demonstration Research Center Command Automation Research Institute, 2002, p. 105.

65. Zhou Daoan, Zhang Dongge and Chang Shuchu, "基于 n-宗派的C2 协作型分析" ("Collaboration Quantitative Analysis of C2 Organizations Based on n-Clans"), 指挥控制与仿真 (*Command and Control and Simulation*), August 1, 2008, p. 13.

66. Zhang Liansong and Liu Jing, "从军兵种自我保障到军联合保障" ("From Individual Service Support to Joint Support"), 军事历史研究 (*Military History Research*), April 2004, p. 40.

67. Liao Xilong, "亲历济南战区大联勤改革" ("Personally Experiencing Jinan Theater's Major Joint Logistics Reform"), 解放军报 (*PLA Daily*), December 16, 2008.

68. Li, Zhang, Ding, and Zhang, "Take the Initiative to Take the Momentum."

69. Pan.

70. *Ibid.*

71. Li Zhaocheng, Zhang Yuntao, and Bi Jiankui, "一体化训练阔步向前" ("Marching in Step: A Set of News Reports from the 'Weifang Military Training Coordination Zone'"), 前卫报 (*Frontline Defense News*, December 10, 2004, p. 2.

72. Pan.

73. Zou Qiuyue, Cui Yongchang, and Liu Yi, "步兵营长调来了飞机" ("Infantry Battalion Commander Summons Aircraft"), 前进报 (*Frontline Defense News*), November 22, 2008, p. 1.

74. Li, Zhang, and Bi.

75. Fan Qingjun and Liu Xuenong, "三军联手渡天堑硝烟末散康报传" ("Hand in Hand, the Three Service Arms Cross the River; the Report Is Spread Before the Smoke Has Cleared"), 前卫报 (*Frontline Defense News*), September 26, 2008, p. 1.

76. Yu Zifu, Dong Xiaobo, and Li Yibao, "大批联合作战指挥人才脱颖而出" ("A Large Number of Command Personnel for Joint Operations Reveal Themselves—Large-Scale Selection, Multi-Channel Training, and Strengthening through Practice"),人民海军 (*PLA Navy*), December 8, 2008, p. 1.

77. Yang Huicheng and Su Ruozhou, "总参部署新年度军事训练和院校教育工作" ("GSD Lays Out New Year Military Training and School Education Work"), 解放军报 (*PLA Daily*), January 11, 2002.

78. Sun Kaixiang and Su Ruozhou, "总参部署全军新年度军事训练工作" ("GSD Lays Out New Year Military Training Work"), 解放军报 (*PLA Daily*), January 17, 2003.

79. Wu Jianhua, "总参部署全军新年度军事训练工作强调打赢信息化战争" ("The GSD Stresses Winning Informationized Wars In Signing the New Year All Army Military Training Work"), 解放军报 (*PLA Daily*), February 1, 2004.

80. Liu Chunjiang and Su Ruozhou, "总参部署新年度军事训练工作全面提高部队战斗力" ("The General Staff Headquarters Makes Plans for This Year's Military Training Work in a Bid To Comprehensively Enhance Units' Combat Power"), 解放军报 (*PLA Daily*), January 17, 2005.

81. Yang Huicheng and Li Xing'an, "总参部署全军新年度军事训练工作" ("The GSD Issues New Year All Military Training Work"), 解放军报 (*PLA Daily*), January 18, 2006.

82. Liu Xiaohua, Wu Dilun, Liu Jian'an, and Wu Tianmin, "具有战略意义的深刻改革 — 我军军事训练从机械化向信息化转变" ("Possessing a Strategically Significant and Deep Reform – Our Military's Training Transformation From Mechanization to Informationization"), available from *www.mod.gov.en/*

83. Liu Chunjiang and Liu Xing'an, "总参部署新年度军事训练工作强调积极推进军事训练向信息化条件下转变" ("GSD Lays out New Year Military Training Work and Stresses: Actively Promote Military Training towards Transformation under Information-ized Conditions"), 解放军报 (*PLA Daily*), January 12, 2007.

84. Liu, "Possessing a Strategically Significant and Deep Re-form."

85. Wu Dilun and Liu Feng'an, "总参部署新年度军事训练工作" ("GSD Lays out New Year Military Training Work"), 解放军报 (*PLA Daily*), January 21, 2008.

86. Li Yadong, Zhang Xicheng, Ding Feng, and Zhang Guoyu, "主动作为乘大势殚精竭虑抢先机 — 济南战区联合训练试验论证筹划会纪要" ("Take the Initiative to Take the Momentum, Make Every Effort to Seize the Preemptive Opportunities Minutes on the

Demonstration and Planning Meeting for Joint Trainings Test in Jinan Theater"), 解放军报 (*PLA Daily*), March 26, 2009.

87. Huang Chao and Meng Bin, "全军首个战区联合训练领导机构运行" ("The PLA's First War Zone Joint Training Leadership Organization Put Into Operation"), 解放军报 (*PLA Daily*), February 25, 2009.

88. Li, Zhang, Ding, and Zhang, "Take the Initiative to Take the Momentum."

89. Hong Bin, Jia Han, and Zhang Guangquan, "军民一体三军一体，战训一体—联合-2009拉开我军首次战区机级联合训练帷幕" ("Civil-Military Integration, Tri-service Integration Training Integration—Our Army's First War Zone level Joint Training Commences"), 前卫报 (*Frontline Defense News*, June 30, 2009, p. 1.

90. Xie Shibao, "Two Mistaken Opinions on Bringing Into Play Integrated Training," 战士报 (*Soldier News*), January 7, 2005, p. 4.

91. Dai Qingmin, "Ensure Historical Orientation and Promote Comprehensive Innovation of Military Informationization," 中国军事科学 (*China Military Science*), 2007/1, p. 78.

92. *Ibid.*, p. 83.

93. "China's foreign reserves top $2tn," BBC, July 15, 2009.

94. Information available from *www.chinaenvironmentallaw. com/2009/03/07/chinas-stimulus-package-pie-chart/*.

95. "China's Economy Expands by 8.9 Percent," *Associated Press*, October 21, 2009.

CHAPTER 6

THE PEOPLE'S LIBERATION ARMY AND CHINA'S INTERNAL SECURITY CHALLENGES

Harold M. Tanner

INTRODUCTION

The People's Liberation Army (PLA) has not seen combat since its brief "punitive war" against Vietnam in 1979.[1] In the 30 years since, and particularly since the mid-1990s, the PLA has undergone substantial modernization, reorganization, and training. But while they have been trained and equipped for war, China's soldiers have been deployed time and again not to fight external enemies, but to respond to internal security issues such as natural disasters, violent mass demonstrations, or "mass incidents," and episodes of ethnic unrest.

In prosecuting these "military operations other than war" (MOOTW), the PLA works in cooperation with the People's Armed Police (PAP), the militia, and the reserves. As these forces carry out internal security operations, their mutual relations and responsibilities develop and are clarified, strengths and weaknesses are revealed and addressed, and lessons are drawn, both for the Chinese military and for civilian government officials. For PLA and PAP officers, MOOTW, particularly emergency response and disaster relief operations, involve sudden deployment in challenging environmental conditions (flood, extreme cold, earthquake zones, fire zones, and scenes of chemical spills for example). Response often requires rapid decisionmaking under difficult circumstances. Psychological pressure can be intense for officers and, perhaps more so, for young soldiers dealing with civilian casualties during disaster rescue operations. MOOTW also require a high level of cooperation between military officers and civilian government and Party officials — a level of cooperation that is apparently difficult for some officers to accept.[2]

This chapter uses openly published Chinese sources to examine selected recent internal security operations and the lessons that China's military draws from those operations.[3] We will be looking specifically at disaster rescue and relief as seen in the snow and ice emergency of January-February 2008 and the Wenchuan earthquake of May 2008, at the handling of four violent mass incidents in 2007-08, and at the riots in Lhasa (March 2008) and Urumqi (July 2009). To begin with, however, we will look at the legal framework within which the PLA, the PAP, the militia, and reserve forces responsibilities for MOOTW are delineated.[4]

MILITARY OPERATIONS OTHER THAN WAR: LEGAL AND INSTITUTIONAL INFRASTRUCTURE

The Chinese military's internal security responsibilities fall within the broad category of "diversified military tasks." The concept of "diversified military tasks," first introduced at least as early as 2004 and emphasized at the Chinese Communist Party's Seventeenth Congress in 2007, calls for the PLA, the PAP, the militia, and the reserves to be prepared to handle a range of responsibilities far wider than simply deterring and if necessary defending against aggression by foreign armed forces.[5] Although the concept is only loosely defined, commentators in China understand it as including both the wide variety of tasks that a modern army would have to perform in conducting "local wars in conditions of informatization" and a number of responsibilities that fall under the rubric of "military operations other than war."

MOOTW cover a wide range of responsibilities including conduct of operations meant to deter foreign aggression, border control, counterterrorism, response to serious incidents of mass violence, emergency response, rescue, humanitarian aid, participation in United Nations (UN) peacekeeping operations, and even drought alleviation measures such as cloud-seeding.[6] All of these MOOTW and other "diversified tasks" are seen as being related. China's leaders see themselves and their military as facing a world in which "Issues of existence security and development security, traditional security threats and nontraditional security threats, and domestic security and international security are interwoven and interactive."[7]

The legal basis for the Chinese armed forces' internal missions is ultimately derived from Article 29 of the Constitution of the People's Republic of China (PRC). After stating that the purpose of the armed forces is to "strengthen national defense, resist aggression, [and] defend the motherland," Article 29 goes on to assign three other broadly defined tasks: "safeguard the people's peaceful labor, participate in national reconstruction, and work hard to serve the people."[8] This flexible definition of the tasks of the armed forces supplies a constitutional basis for virtually any internal deployment of military force for the accomplishment of any specific task that the Chinese leadership might wish to accomplish.

The PRC only began to build a formal emergency response management system in the post-Mao era. Prior to that, emergency response was handled largely on an ad hoc basis by the Communist Party leadership on all levels, who tended to employ temporary crisis management small groups to lead "mass movement" style of social mobilization to deal with crises. Since 1979, economic reform, the growth of a market economy, greater respect for property rights, an increasingly complex bureaucracy, and greater awareness of models of emergency response in other countries have combined to move China toward the development of a specialized emergency response system. A growing body of law seeks to define the Chinese military's roles and responsibilities and its relations with the state, society, and economy.[9] One of the regular complaints emerging in the Chinese literature on the PLA's internal security missions is that this body of law is still woefully inadequate. As the Asian Development Bank pointed out in its report on the Wenchuan earthquake response: "the Chinese government does not have a stand-alone disaster risk management agency with a dedicated disaster risk management function."[10] However, there are a number of laws and emergency response plans that lay out some of the internal security roles and responsibilities of the PLA, the PAP, the militia, and the reserves.

China's laws describe "contingencies" or "public emergencies" (突发事件, 突发公共事件) as including natural disasters, accidental disasters, public hygiene incidents, and social security incidents.[11] Contingencies are classified into four levels: I - Very Severe; II - Severe; III - Relatively Severe; and IV - Average. In general, the laws and contingency or emergency response plans envisage local police, militia, and reserves as the initial and, in lower-grade incidents, only necessary responders to contingencies. However, in severe and very severe incidents, the PAP and/or the PLA are called upon to operate as "shock troops" and even as the main forces in handling natural disasters and other emergency situations.

The Emergency Response Law of the PRC states the military's role in typically flexible terms: "The Chinese People's Liberation Army, the Chinese People's Armed Police Force, and militia join in emergency response, rescue, and management in accordance with this law and other relevant laws, administrative regulations, and military laws and the commands of the State Council and the Central Military Commission."[12] The "Regulation on army participation in disaster rescue and relief" describes the PLA's role in disaster rescue and relief as that of a "strike force," and its responsibilities as rescuing, transferring, or dispersing victims; protecting the safety of important targets; rescuing and transporting important materials; participating in specialized tasks including repair of roads, bridges, and tunnels, rescue at sea, nuclear, chemical, and biological rescue, control of infectious disease, preventing or controlling other serious dangers or disasters, and when necessary, assisting local government in reconstruction.[13] The PLA began formally including rescue and disaster relief operations in its training programs in 2002.[14]

While the PLA and the PAP (as well as militia and reserve forces) have been called upon to respond to natural disasters and other emergency situations, the PLA has, since 1989, been reluctant to participate in the management of mass incidents, preferring to leave that task almost exclusively to the PAP.[15] Laws including the Law on Martial Law (戒严法) clearly indicate

that the primary responsibility for maintaining or restoring public order resides with the police and the
PAP: "where necessary, the State Council may propose
to the Central Military Commission (CMC) for decision that the People's Liberation Army be dispatched
for assisting to enforce the martial law."[16] The PAP is
specifically designed for response to internal security
problems. Organized in 1983 and reorganized in 1995,
the PAP is reported to have had around 700,000 troops
as of 2008.[17] The PAP has a wide range of responsibilities, most of which (such as guarding government
buildings, foreign embassies, television and radio stations, important transportation hubs, border security,
and firefighting, among others) are beyond the scope
of this chapter. What concerns us here is the PAP's
role in emergency response and in suppressing social
unrest. The PAP has 14 mobile divisions. They come
directly under the command of the CMC and can be
deployed anywhere in the country and function as the
front-line troops in handling serious social unrest.[18]

LESSONS LEARNED: DISASTER RESPONSE
AND HUMANITARIAN AID

By 2008, China had constructed an emergency response system designed to facilitate and coordinate
response to natural disasters and other emergencies.
In that year, those plans were put to the test by two
major natural disasters: the snow and ice storms of
January-February and the Wenchuan earthquake
of May. How did China's military respond to these
emergencies, and what lessons did they derive from
their experience?

China was hit by unusually cold weather and severe winter storms from mid-January through Febru-

ary 2008. The areas south of the Yangzi River were especially hard-hit. Heavy snow, ice, freezing rain, and unusually cold temperatures affected 19 provinces in all. The severe weather and accumulations of ice on power lines cut off electricity. In China south of the Yangzi, where passenger and freight trains were pulled by electric locomotives, the electricity outage paralyzed transportation and stopped the shipment of coal to power plants. The effects of the storms and cold weather on the transportation system were magnified by the fact that the crisis coincided with the Lunar New Year festival, one of the peak periods for domestic road, rail, and air travel. Snow and ice accumulations also caused roads and bridges to be shut down and buildings to collapse. Millions of seasonal or migrant workers who were taking their annual trips to their family reunions in the countryside were all stuck in the major hubs of transportation in those provinces, creating a mass human disaster situation everywhere.

Government response to the snow, ice, and cold weather emergency was slower than desired and hampered by lack of equipment. The problems began with a failure to forecast the unusual winter storms. Part of the government response to the severe winter weather disaster was to mobilize regular PLA troops, PAP troops, reserve troops, and militia forces. As of early February 2008, 306,000 soldiers had been deployed, along with 1.07 million militia and army reservists.[19] The PLA roles in this disaster relief operation included air transport of food, medicine, quilts, and clothing to affected areas, crowd control in places like railway stations, and supplying skilled and unskilled labor to repair power grids, open roads, and restore railway traffic.[20]

As they considered the lessons learned from the ice and snow emergency, writers in *Guofang* (国防 *National Defense*) and other publications pointed to the importance of PLA, PAP, militia, and reserves having the right equipment and the right training to deal with emergencies. During the snow and ice emergency, Nanjing was able to keep its major bridges across the Yangzi open because 10 years earlier, they had set aside funds to purchase snow-plows.[21] Most areas of the south, however, did not have snow and ice removal equipment: PLA, PAP, militia, and reserve personnel often had to rely on simple tools and hard manual labor.[22] Even in Liaoning Province in the Northeast, PLA soldiers assigned to take part in disaster relief after a snowstorm had to rely on shovels and pickaxes. Local governments in Liaoning did have snow and ice removal equipment, but the army units assigned to assist in this disaster relief effort did not.[23]

The lack of equipment was tied to larger issues of preparation and mobilization. The experience of the ice and snow emergency was used to argue for the importance of better emergency response planning and the need to build technically specialized units within the militia and reserves — units that would be prepared to deal with tasks ranging from repair of electrical generation and transmission facilities, first-aid and rescue, transportation, and other specialized areas.[24] Beyond that, some commentators pointed to the snow and ice emergency's implications for the PLA's preparedness to fight local wars under informatized conditions. Pointing to an alleged 1999 RAND Corporation scenario for war between the United States and China which had envisioned the American air strikes cutting China's north-south transportation lines and electrical grid so as to paralyze south China and cause internal chaos, two staff officers from Jiangxi province, writing in *Guofang*, argued that the snow and ice emergency showed how such a scenario might work in practice.[25]

Given that south China's transportation and communications infrastructure would play an important role in military operations in the Taiwan Strait or the South China Sea, PLA analysts Cui and Li recommended that China's defense planning put more emphasis on building capacity to carry out rapid repairs on transportation and power infrastructure and that future construction of transportation and communications infrastructure be done in such a way as to ensure multiple lines of transportation and communication and with an eye to dual civilian and military use.[26] Yang Jinkui, an officer in the Chengdu Military Region (MR), writing in the *PLA Daily* (解放军报) suggested that the PLA should reflect on what might happen if severe weather coincided with war. Stating that the United States had used cloud-seeding as a weapon during the Vietnam War, Yang argued that the PLA should be prepared for climate manipulation in wartime and take the experience of fighting the severe winter weather of 2008 as a lesson in overcoming the problems that such weather might bring to command, joint operations, and logistics.[27]

In January and February 2008, it seemed that the winter weather emergency would become a defining moment in the PLA's experience of disaster response and relief and a major source of lessons to be learned regarding relief and rescue operations. However, the severe weather emergency was soon eclipsed by a disaster of far greater magnitude: the Wenchuan earthquake. The earthquake, with a magnitude of 7.9, occurred at 2:28 p.m. on May 12, 2008, with its epicenter in Wenchuan County in the western part of Sichuan province.

The government's response to the earthquake, which included mobilization of units from all of China's seven military regions and the Second Artillery, drew praise not only within China, but also from the international media. According to reports at the time, by 5:00 p.m. 50,000 PLA troops had been mobilized for earthquake relief, of which 20,000 had arrived in the area affected.[28] As the rescue and relief operation continued, the PLA, the PAP, and the Chinese media continued to pile up and report impressive statistics: 133,000 PLA and PAP officers and soldiers and 45,000 militia and reserve personnel mobilized as of May 28; 1.6 million pieces/sets of clothing and 32,000 tons of fuel distributed by May 31.[29] Since it was perceived as a success, the earthquake relief effort had tremendous propaganda value. It could be used both to demonstrate the superiority of China's socialist system and economic reform program to the Chinese people at large and to drive home to the PLA the importance of obeying the Party and understanding the significance of being prepared to accomplish not only traditional defense missions, but also "diverse military tasks."[30] Coverage of the earthquake relief effort thus focused almost exclusively on the roles of the PLA and the PAP, with little attention being paid to civil society support or to international aid.[31]

The overwhelmingly favorable spin put on the military's contributions to disaster relief and humanitarian aid in response to the earthquake has led participants and observers to draw a number of positive lessons from the armed forces' response to the earthquake.[32] Commentators are particularly proud of the speed of the response. Sichuan provincial military command state that half an hour after the earthquake, they had contacted seven prefectural and city military commands and ordered each city or prefecture to organize 500-man disaster relief battalions from their militia forces, equip them with transportation and engineering equipment, and get them on the way into areas affected by the earthquake. Three hours after the quake hit, after they had gained a clearer understanding of the situation, they ordered reserve divisions, brigades, and regiments to gather their forces and head for the affected areas. These reserves, following on the militia, made up a second wave of response to the disaster. The Sichuan Military District (MD) leaders attributed their rapid response to their having had in place a dual-use (war and emergency response) defense mobilization plan that involved the MD leadership and the provincial, prefectural, and county-level governments.[33] Other authors, too, pointed to the utility of existing national defense mobilization plans and to successes in transferring troops and equipment to the earthquake zone.[34]

In addition to the speed of response, another area of much-publicized positive lesson had to do with air power. The People's Liberation Army Air Force (PLAAF) played roles including aerial monitoring and reconnaissance, airborne insertion of troops and supplies, and communications (the use of the Beidou satellite positioning system, for example).[35] Much was made of the exploits of 15 soldiers who parachuted into a remote village cut off from the outside world under difficult conditions. Advocates of army aviation also made a very strong case for the utility of helicopters (and the need to purchase more helicopters) as one of the lessons of the disaster relief effort.[36]

While there was much to celebrate about the earthquake relief effort, commentators also pointed to a number of weak points from which they argued that the PLA, PAP, militia, and reserves might derive valuable lessons. These areas included emergency response planning, speed, and efficiency of the mobilization of human and material resources, equipment, and training. As with the lessons derived from the ice and snow emergency response, some commentators drew direct parallels between the experience and lessons of the Wenchuan earthquake disaster response and their relevance not only for MOOTW, but also for wartime mobilization and operations.

While the Sichuan MD leaders cited above attributed their successful, rapid early response to existing mobilization plans, much of the criticism of the response to the Wenchuan earthquake revolved around the questions of emergency response planning, preparedness, and mobilization. Some observers found serious problems with the mobilization of material resources: supplies were insufficient and transportation of material to the front lines of the disaster areas was too slow.[37] Despite the celebratory claims of the PLA's ability to move large numbers of troops to the earthquake zone quickly, some commentators argued that the air force had, in fact, performed poorly. Shen Dingli, a scholar at Fudan University, was particularly harsh in his criticism: "[T]he air force should have been able to get troops to Wenchuan in 2 hours. It took them 44 hours. If it took them 10 hours, that's understandable. But 44 hours is shameful."[38] The poor performance of the PLAAF in this respect suggests that China's military would have serious difficulty in carrying out rapid long-distance deployment of large numbers of troops in wartime.[39] While not pointing explicitly to any failings on the part of the PLAAF, other commentators suggested that the experience of the Wenchuan earthquake showed that the PLAAF needed to undergo a fundamental "transformation" in its theoretical understanding of its roles and responsibilities in MOOTW, to establish appropriate emergency response plans and mechanisms, and to integrate these with the emergency response plans and mechanisms of the civilian government.[40]

These criticisms of the PLAAF and of the mobilization of resources for the earthquake relief effort came in the context of an on-going discussion of the weaknesses of China's emergency response system. One of the main themes appearing in this discussion is that if the PLA, PAP, militia, and reserves are going to be regularly called upon as emergency response forces under the rubrics of diversified military tasks and MOOTW, there needs to be a comprehensive, integrated national defense/emergency response mobilization system, backed up by appropriately organized, equipped, and trained military units and operating under an effective command and control system. Some of the critiques of PLA/PAP/militia/reserves performance in the Wenchuan earthquake relief effort focused on lack of search and rescue, communications, and engineering equipment, even stating flatly that China's emergency response and rescue techniques are "primitive."[41]

Other critiques focused not on equipment but on the organization of China's emergency response and its relation to the national defense mobilization system. At one level, this involves the idea that China's national defense mobilization system needs to be thoroughly reorganized to create an integrated "dual response" system that would be prepared to mobilize military and civilian resources (human, material, and financial) for both war and for peacetime emergency response.[42] This would also involve standardizing, unifying, and streamlining a plethora of sometimes overlapping and mutually contradictory national, provincial, and local defense mobilization and emergency response plans and bureaucracies.[43] Some suggested that the emergency response systems of foreign countries, including the United States, could be useful models from which China could learn.[44]

At another level, ideas for improvements in the PLA's ability to perform emergency response duties relate more directly to force recruitment, organization, training, and equipment. A number of authors put particular emphasis on the need to expand the roles of the militia and reserves as first responders to natural disasters and other emergency situations and call for improved training of militia and reserve forces and the building of units with specialized skills for addressing different types of emergency situation — floods, earthquakes, chemical and industrial accidents, forest fires, etc. — based on the needs of their communities.[45]

The interest in increasing the responsibilities and the competence of the militia and reserve forces for performance of disaster relief duties touches on another issue which, though subtly addressed, appears evident in some of the open-source discussion of the lessons of Wenchuan and China's emergency response and disaster relief: just how much of a role should the PLA play in MOOTW, and how do they relate to the PLA's primary mission of national defense?[46] Some argue that participation in MOOTW like the earthquake relief effort is, in fact, good training for military operations and thus contributes directly to the furtherance of the PLA's primary mission. For example, Zhao Guoqi, a senior colonel and political commissar in the Communications Command Academy in Wuhan, compared the damage done by the Wenchuan earthquake to that which would be done by a nuclear weapon and argued that the task of mobilization for earthquake relief under those conditions was similar to, and in some respects more difficult than, mobilization in wartime.[47]

Others argued that the participation of various units in earthquake relief was a variety of joint operations, and thus bore directly on the PLA's efforts to develop its joint operations capability for combat operations, or suggested that the PLA's use of aerial reconnaissance, airborne remote sensing, and other advanced techniques in the earthquake relief operation brought to mind the American use of satellites, airpower, and special ground forces in Kosovo, Afghanistan, and Iraq.[48] But while acknowledging the importance of MOOTW, some commentators emphasize that training for and participation in MOOTW must always be done with an eye to building the PLA's core national defense capabilities, and that training and carrying out MOOTW should be assigned to regular and specialized PLA units that are not already heavily burdened with national defense duties.[49]

LESSONS LEARNED: MASS INCIDENTS

Response to mass incidents is another facet of the Chinese military's responsibilities for MOOTW. By "mass incidents," the Chinese authorities mean large-scale demonstrations, which have the potential to develop into violent stand-offs between crowds of demonstrators and the authorities, or violent attacks on government organs, factories, or other property. Mass incidents have been an increasing problem throughout the reform era. Wang Erping, of the Chinese Academy of Social Sciences' Institute of Psychology, cites government statistics that indicate over 10,000 mass incidents in 1995, 60,000 in 2005, and 80,000 in 2007.[50] With mounting unemployment at least part of which can be associated with the global economic crisis, Chinese experts expected that rising unemployment and increased social tension in both rural and urban areas would lead to an increase in mass incidents in 2009.[51]

Most mass incidents are resolved peacefully or relatively peacefully by local officials and local public security forces.[52] Some, however, develop into large-scale violent clashes between masses of citizens and the authorities. When these clashes, which can involve hundreds, thousands, or even upward of 10,000 people, get out of control, local government is forced to turn to the PAP to restore order. Thus the PAP has a strong interest in analyzing the causes of mass incidents and developing strategies, procedures, and equipment to handle such events.[53]

Some authors link social instability to "foreign enemy forces" trying to "Westernize China."[54] But for the most part, Chinese analysts attribute mass incidents to domestic causes: unemployment, the precarious economic and living situations of rural migrants in China's cities, social tensions associated with the increasingly unequal distribution of wealth, and, particularly, dissatisfaction with and alienation from local government, which often seems to be in cahoots with wealth and power and callousness toward the needs and feelings of local people.[55] Both members of the Chinese People's Political Consultative Committee and Chinese Academy of Social Sciences (CASS) sociologists have suggested that mass incidents tend to occur in places where there are no open channels of communication between local people and their government and Party leaders, and where the local government and Party leaders tend to respond to petitioners and demonstrators by suggesting that they have been "manipulated by a small number of bad people with ulterior motives" or are "enemies of the people" — both ideological justifications for the use of overwhelming coercive force.[56]

Not all mass incidents require the use of coercive force: many are resolved in such a way as to achieve a "soft landing."[57] There are, however, many instances in which local governments have called upon the PAP to handle mass incidents. The immediate causes of these mass incidents are varied. Many concern grievances generated when powerful industrial or real estate developers, operating with the protection of local government, seize land for development.[58] In addition to disputes over land use, development, and resettlement, other common causes of mass incidents include anger over failed investment schemes, protests at environmental damage caused by industry or mining, and popular dissatisfaction with the authorities' handling of sensitive legal cases such as rape, homicide, or unexplained death.[59]

In 2008-09, four mass incidents in particular were publicized as examples from which the PAP and (even more so) local government could learn some valuable lessons. These were, the Weng'an Incident in Guizhou Province, the Menglian Incident in Yunnan Province, the Longnan Incident in Gansu Province and the Shishou Incident in Hubei. We will look briefly at these four incidents, and then consider the lessons that Chinese observers, the Chinese government and the PAP have drawn both from these particular incidents and from the handling of mass incidents in general.

Both the Menglian and Longnan incidents were sparked by citizen concerns over land and property rights. The Menglian incident involved a protest by rubber farmers in Yunnan Province's Menglian County. The farmers complained that a local rubber company was violating their land rights. On July 19, 2008, after the local government had refused to consider their concerns, 500 farmers clashed with police or, as the newspaper *Caijing* (财经，*Financial Times*) put it: "the farmers rose up to defend their rights, and the local government used police to suppress them."[60] In the Longnan incident of November 17-18, 2008, city officials turned away a group of around 30 farmers petitioning for compensation for their forced removal from their houses and fields. That afternoon, the disagreement between the petitioners and the officials developed into a riot in which thousands of angry citizens (far outnumbering the original petitioners and having no vested interest in the farmers' complaint) broke into the city government office compound, smashing, looting and burning, and fighting with the police and PAP who were deployed to restore order.[61]

The Weng'an (瓮安) Incident was sparked by controversy over the death of a young woman in Guizhou's Weng'an County—a poor area with a record of crime, social tensions, and popular resentment against the local government. On June 22, 2008, Li Shufen, 16 years of age, was out for an evening with friends, including her boyfriend, a man of 21, when she talked of suicide and then jumped from a bridge into a river. Her friends, unable to save her, called the police, who recovered her body. The police report held that Li Shufen had committed suicide, that the cause of death was drowning, and that she had not engaged in sexual activity in the hours prior to her death.[62] Li's family, however, believed that she had been raped and killed by the two young men with whom she and another girl had gone out with, that they had dumped her body into the river to cover up their crime, and that the authorities had bungled the investigation and were protecting the young men because they had relatives in the public security office. The authorities' demand that Li Shufen's body be interred immediately further incensed her family and public opinion.

On June 28, public security officials turned away a demonstration of 500 students in support of Li's family. With bystanders joining in, the demonstration quickly developed into a riot. Over a period of 7 hours, some 30,000 people attacked government and Communist Party offices in Weng'an, smashing and burning vehicles and buildings. Regular police and PAP forces finally restored order and made arrests of individuals accused of being instigators or leaders of the rioting. Enthusiastic (although not always accurate) coverage and commentary by bloggers and users of Twitter ensured that reports, photographs, rumors, and commentary spread rapidly, drawing national and international attention to the incident.[63]

Like the Weng'an incident, the Shishou (石首) incident was sparked by an apparent suicide, this one of a young man who was reported to have jumped from the third floor of a hotel where he was employed in the kitchen. Fuelled by the knowledge that the hotel had a reputation for being a center for drug deals, that the owner had connections with the city authorities, and that there were reports of at least one similar suicide having occurred at the same hotel, the deceased man's family demanded a new investigation and autopsy. As in the Weng'an incident, a stand-off ensued over possession of the body and, as in Weng'an, the local authorities heightened tensions when they insisted that the family cremate the body by a certain deadline. Similar to the Weng'an and Longnan incidents, supporters and people with no vested interest in the original dispute itself quickly transformed a confrontation between local authorities and the family and friends of the deceased into a violent riot involving tens of thousands of people. According to one report, 10,000 armed police were deployed to bring the situation under control.[64]

We know that the handling of mass incidents is one of the PAP's tasks, and that PAP forces have been involved in bringing some of the most serious and highly publicized mass incidents under control. But what, specifically, are the PAP's tasks in that regard, and what lessons might the PAP have derived from its experiences? Unfortunately, openly published accounts of mass incidents have little specific to say about the precise roles played and techniques employed by the PAP in restoring order. Photographs, videos, and descriptions indicate the use of large squadrons of armed police equipped with protective helmets and riot shields advancing on (and sometimes being driven back by) crowds of rioters and refer to and/ or show the use of water cannon, police batons, what appear to be iron bars, and firearms. In the Shishou incident, armed police are described as advancing in waves, four rows of soldiers to a wave, retaking and sealing off the city streets.[65]

The reluctance to address PAP operations at any level of concrete detail is accompanied by a general lack of specific operational lessons to be learned from the handling of mass incidents. Some authors writing in professional journals suggest that lack of appropriate equipment is a problem.[66] One, for example, argues that armed police are sometimes reluctant to fire the high-velocity military weapons (handguns, rifles, and submachine guns) with which they are equipped for fear that the bullets will pass through the suspect and still have sufficient velocity to kill or injure innocent bystanders. China, he suggests, needs to develop lower-velocity weapons and use dum-dum bullets in order to make it safer for police to fire on suspects under chaotic and crowded conditions.[67]

While not forthcoming about operational details, openly published descriptions and analyses of the handling of mass incidents are often willing to draw general lessons on the appropriate use of police (including PAP) power. Most of these lessons are directed more at the government than the police or PAP themselves. The major theme emerging from the treatment of these incidents is that local authorities should be judicious in their use of police power and do their utmost to prevent delicate situations from developing into mass incidents which the police and the PAP then have to bring under control. Commentators including academics and local, provincial, and national level government and Party officials suggest that when dealing with sensitive events that may lead to a mass incident or when in the initial stages of handling a mass incident, local officials should explore ways of defusing the tension. They should use the media to communicate the government's position clearly to the people, avoid class-struggle style rhetoric which brands petitioners or demonstrators as "masses who are ignorant of the truth, instigated by a small number of bad people" and refrain from politicizing events by suggesting that they are caused by "evil forces in society" or even by foreign agitators.[68]

Another area in which the PAP has derived lessons from the handling of mass incidents is that of the policy and legal framework for the military's carrying out of internal security tasks. Among the observations made at a national conference on public security work in 2008 were that there was a need for advance contingency plans for dealing with sudden incidents, that command and control relations and authority in handling mass incidents needed to be clarified, and that there be plans in place for early detection, early reporting, and early control in order to bring mass incidents under control before they could grow into major events.[69] The recently passed law on PAP handling of mass incidents very likely incorporates lessons learned from these incidents.[70]

LESSONS LEARNED: TIBET AND XINJIANG

Openly published literature is less than forthcoming on lessons learned from the PAP's involvement in handling mass incidents: it is nearly mute on the lessons that the PAP and the PLA might learn from their participation in internal security operations in the PRC's Tibetan ethnic areas (the Tibet Autonomous Region [TAR], Qinghai province, and parts of Gansu, Sichuan, and Yunnan Provinces) and in the Xinjiang Uyghur Autonomous Region. In these areas, the same economic tensions and alienation of ordinary people from overbearing and corrupt local government is exacerbated by ethnic tensions between the minority Tibetan and Uyghur populations on the one hand, and the Han Chinese who command superior economic and political power, on the other.

To complicate matters further, the Chinese Communist Party and the Han Chinese public are, to a high degree, conscious of the fact that Britain, the United States, and Russia/Union of Soviet Socialist Republics (USSR) and India all, at various times in the past, have given moral and material encouragement (including money, weapons, and military training) to forces that sought to separate Tibet and Xinjiang from the former Qing Empire and, after 1912, from the weak new Chinese nation-state.[71] The political, ethnic, and international dimensions of Tibet and Xinjiang make any discussion the PLA/PAP's internal security responsibilities in these areas particularly sensitive. It is reasonable to assume that the PLA and PAP have drawn lessons from their operations in these areas, and particularly from the suppression of the riots in Lhasa in March 2008 and in Urumqi in July 2009. However, in the open press, we have only vague hints, at best, as to what those lessons may be.

TIBET: THE LHASA RIOT, MARCH 2008

The severe rioting that broke out in Lhasa, the capital of the TAR, in March 2008 has been described and analyzed by a number of scholars. The root causes of the incident clearly lie in failed ethnic and economic policies that have left young Tibetans unhappy and alienated. When the unrest broke out in Lhasa, a slow police response then allowed a volatile situation to spin out of control.[72] Reports from Lhasa all support the conclusion that it was PAP forces, not PLA soldiers, who were directly responsible for restoring order. The role of the PLA itself is difficult to gauge with any degree of accuracy. There is some indication that PLA units from Chengdu and perhaps elsewhere were sent to Lhasa, where their main role is thought to have been logistical support.[73] At least one foreign reporter observed "military looking vehicles with telltale license plates covered up or removed," and troops there wore uniforms that were distinctly lacking in the usual insignia of either the police or the riot police."[74] Such evidence suggests the possibility of PLA participation in operations to restore order in Lhasa, but the vehicles and troops could also have belonged to PAP or militia units.

What lessons, if any, did the PAP and the PLA derive from the experience of suppressing the riots in Lhasa? Openly published literature is exceedingly reticent on this point. Given the paucity and the rather vague nature of the sources available, we can only speculate. In June 2009, the TAR authorities opened a new "Tibet Emergency Response Communications Bureau" in Lhasa, equipped with new emergency response vehicles, portable Inmarsat satellite equipment and other advanced communications equipment.[75] In June 2008, two authors from the Tibet military command writing in *Guofang* suggested that reserve forces in border areas such as Tibet needed further emphasis on political indoctrination and training in tasks like containing riots and sealing off urban areas in order to guarantee that they would be politically reliable and professionally qualified to work effectively at counterterrorism tasks.[76] From these hints, one might speculate that the need for a more timely application of coercive force, better response and communications, better training and political reliability of local reserve and militia forces may have been among the lessons the PLA/PAP learned from the Lhasa riot of March 2008.

One area in which we see more direct evidence of the lessons of the Lhasa riots is in the new People's Police law which the Standing Committee of the National People's Congress approved in August 2009. This law defines the scope and nature of the PAP's responsibilities, including its responsibility for handling "riots, large-scale violent crimes and terrorist attacks."[77] In providing legal of the PAP's powers and responsibilities, the law moves to address a concern raised time and again in the openly published literature on the Chinese internal security tasks under the rubric of MOOTW: the lack of a clear legal framework.

On the other hand, the new law is purposely vague in the way it addresses another common concern: the need for clear, centralized command and control over military forces involved in emergency response, disaster relief, and handling of mass incidents. As seen in the discussion of the handling of mass incidents, many Chinese analysts believe that local authorities have been too quick to mobilize police and PAP in response to mass incidents, and that the result has been to exacerbate the levels of violence. When considering the question of what level of government should have the power to mobilize the PAP, some members of the NPC SC apparently argued that the power to deploy the PAP should be reserved to the State Council and the CMC, while others would give that power to county level governments. Each position has its merits: reserving the power to deploy the PAP to the center would address the problem of local governments turning too quickly to the use of coercive force and using the PAP to defend or disguise their own corruption or incompetence. On the other hand, depriving localities of the power to deploy the PAP could, in some cases, result in dangerous delays in the deployment of necessary force. As finally approved by the NPC SC, the armed police law neatly sidestepped the question by stating that the State Council and the CMC will make concrete rules regarding the deployment and use of PAP forces.[78]

XINJIANG: THE URUMQI RIOT

When it revised the draft armed police law to state clearly that the PAP is responsible for handling "riots, large-scale violent crimes, and terrorist attacks," the NPC SC was drawing not only on the experience of the Lhasa riots, but also on the more recent serious rioting in Urumqi, the capital of the Xinjiang Uyghur Autonomous Region (XUAR).[79] Xinjiang, like the TAR, is an area beset by deep-set ethnic tensions which are exacerbated by Han Chinese migration into traditionally non-Han areas, educational, religious, and economic policies that often relegate Uyghurs to second-class status (particularly in regards to economic opportunity), and a pervasive underlying "great Han chauvinism" which ascribes cultural and even moral inferiority to Uyghur and other non-Han ethnic groups.

The Chinese military's numbers, capabilities, and internal security operations in Xinjiang are shrouded in mystery. Historically, the central government has maintained relatively low troop levels in Xinjiang, and those troops units stationed in there were often of inferior quality.[80] Currently, Xinjiang is a part of the Lanzhou MR which is, then, responsible for both border security and for any internal security challenges that might arise in the XUAR. The military region's greatest internal security challenge is any expression of ethnic unrest, including the activities of Uyghurs advocating or taking action in support of greater autonomy or even the separation of Xinjiang from the PRC. In the post-September 11, 2001 (9-11) world, China has, with some success, recast its struggle against ethnic separatism (which has, thus far, been driven more by Uyghur nationalism than by Islamic extremism) as a part of the global war on terror.

There is little evidence of any large-scale, organized terrorist activity in Xinjiang. There have, however, been sporadic incidents of violence, including attacks on public transportation and on police installations, some of which may be characterized as terrorist. For example, in April 1990, PLA troops using air power were deployed to deal with a reported 200 or so armed Uyghur men who had clashed with police in Baren County, near Kashgar.[81] In February 1992, two bombs exploded on public buses in Urumqi, killing three and wounding 23. There were further bombings in public places in Urumqi, Kashgar, and other cities in Xinjiang from February 1992 through September 1993. More bombings and attacks, generally aimed not at public places, but rather at oil installations, public security and other government offices, and the homes of public security officers, have been reported in April-May 1996, February-April 1998, 1999, January 2000, and more recently in 2008, when armed men attacked a public security office in Kashgar on the eve of the Beijing Olympics.[82]

Xinjiang has also seen a number of mass incidents involving violent clashes between large groups of Uyghurs and security forces including PAP and PLA units. In early 1997, the arrest of two religious students in Yining (also called Gulja) precipitated a series of demonstrations and violent clashes between demonstrators and security personnel. In a major clash on February 5, PAP and/or PLA troops using fire hoses, tear gas, dogs, and live ammunition faced over a large number of Uyghur demonstrators and followed up by sealing the city off for 2 weeks and making large numbers of arrests.[83] On March 23, 2008, police and militia forces successfully contained a smaller protest in Hetian, apparently without much difficulty.[84] What lessons, if any, the PLA/PAP and the Chinese government in general may have derived from these past internal security operations in Xinjiang are not clear. Whatever those lessons may have been, they did not prepare local authorities in Xinjiang for the massive outbreak of violence that occurred in Urumqi in July 2009.

The demonstrations and rioting that took place in Urumqi in July 2009 were sparked when tension between Han Chinese and Uyghur workers at a toy factory in Guangdong province's Shaoguan city broke out into violence. In the Shaoguan incident, rumors that Uyghurs had raped Han Chinese women led a number of Han men to attack their Uyghur co-workers at the factory dormitory. A slow police response allowed the violence to continue for some hours. At least two Uyghur men were reported dead.[85] On the afternoon of July 5, thousands of Uyghurs took to the streets in Urumqi, ostensibly in protest over the Shaoguan incident.[86] According to a timeline released by the Chinese government, police responded quickly to an initial protest of some 200 Uyghurs at People's Square, following an existing plan for handling mass incidents, and taking 70 alleged protest leaders into custody.[87]

Subsequent gatherings of thousands of Uyghur protestors and various points across the city, including the Grand Bazaar and the South Gate, broke into violence. According to both government and independent reports, serious rioting began around 8:00 p.m. Beijing time (6:00 p.m. in the unofficially observed local time in Xinjiang).[88] It was at this point that the police appear to have lost control. On the northern edge of Urumqi's Uyghur quarter, fighting broke out between PAP troops and Uyghur demonstrators. In other areas, including the Grand Bazaar and several ethnically mixed neighborhoods, there was little or no police or PAP presence.[89] For hours, there was chaos in the streets as Uyghurs overturned and destroyed buses and other vehicles; smashed and burned shops and other buildings; and attacked, beat, and sometimes killed Han Chinese, apparently at random. The delay in the police and PAP response to the rioting led Han Chinese, too, to take to the streets both to defend themselves and to take revenge against Uyghurs.[90]

The slowness of the police and PAP response to the violence in Urumqi, coming little more than a year after a slow response had contributed to the rioting in Lhasa, indicates a failure to learn some valuable lessons. Foreign observers suggest that the slow response in Urumqi was at least partly due to two factors: a failure of intelligence, and the need to act first to secure high-risk targets such as government buildings, financial institutions, radio stations and other strategic points.[91] Standing regulations may have contributed to this problem: the PRC's Contingency Response Law, Article 50, places specific emphasis on the need to protect likely targets of unrest including government and military buildings and installations, communications centers, and radio and television broadcast facilities.[92] Another possible factor is that the PAP simply did not have enough personnel in and around Urumqi to handle such an unexpected, large-scale incident. As the seriousness of the situation became evident, President Hu Jintao returned from the G-8 meeting in Italy to take charge. PAP and also PLA units were reportedly transferred to Urumqi from other points within the Lanzhou MR.[93] According to one report, 14,000 PAP troops and 490 tons of equipment were also transported by air from Jiangsu, Henan, and Fujian Provinces.[94]

When they did move in to reassert control, the PAP acted, according to at least one foreign observer, effectively, with discipline and professionalism.[95] PAP troops used armored vehicles, water cannon, electric batons, tear gas, riot shields, and live fire (both warning shots and direct fire) to bring Uyghur and Han rioters under control.[96] As in the case of the unrest in Lhasa in 2008, the issue of coordination and respective roles of the PAP and the PLA remain unclear. Most reports strongly suggest that PAP units bore the responsibility for restoring order.[97] Some reports, however, do suggest that the PLA was deployed in response to the events in Urumqi, with PLA units acting (as they had in Lhasa) in a support capacity and perhaps being used to secure key installations.[98] Clearly following some of the lessons drawn from the experience of dealing with the Lhasa riots and other mass incidents, the authorities worked hard to manage the flow of information. On the one hand, internet and cell phone service were cut off in Urumqi, and problematic internet sites (such as Youtube, Facebook, and Twitter) were shut down all over the country in an attempt to stifle unofficial sources of information. At the same time, the authorities took the initiative to manage, rather than simply suppress, news media coverage. In addition to publishing news through the state-controlled news media, the authorities also allowed foreign journalists to report from Urumqi, while doing their best to guide such foreign reporting into avenues considered suitable by the government.

CONCLUSION: CHINA'S INTERNAL SECURITY, THE PLA, AND POLICY IMPLICATIONS FOR THE UNITED STATES

China's military—PLA, PAP, militia, and reserves—has faced severe internal security challenges over the past 2 years, including natural disasters, mass incidents, and ethnic unrest in Tibetan areas and in Xinjiang. Overall, what can the Chinese military's reactions to these challenges and the lessons that they have learned from them tell us about its operational capabilities? What implications do these experiences and lessons have for American policy makers?

First, as a number of Chinese analysts have observed, mobilization for natural disasters shares some similarities with mobilization for war. In this respect, the PLA's reaction to the winter weather emergency and particularly to the Wenchuan earthquake indicates some significant institutional and operational weaknesses. On the institutional side, China continues to struggle with problems both in the legal framework, organization, and mobilization for internal MOOTW. Discussions in *China National Defense*, *PLA Daily*, and other openly published news media indicate a strong interest in building a more complete corpus of legislation to define the duties and powers of the military as an emergency responder and in consolidating and improving China's national, provincial, and local emergency response plans.

There appears to be particularly strong interest in unifying war mobilization and emergency response plans and institutions. It is worth noting that some Chinese analysts suggest that the United States (along with Japan and Russia) might serve as a useful model for China's emergency management and for the role of the military in an emergency management system.[99] It is likely that some of the lessons derived from these experiences have contributed to the drafting of the new law on military mobilization.[100] The interest in constructing a more efficient emergency response system and in learning from the United States suggests that the U.S. Government and the American military could use cooperation with China in emergency response and disaster relief as a way of pursuing mutually beneficial engagement with the PLA.[101] Possibilities include short-term assistance during natural disasters, but also training in techniques and equipment, small-scale joint exercises in disaster relief and rescue operations, and consultation regarding emergency response law, planning, training, and institutional frameworks. The absence of Chinese forces during the tsunami disaster of 2004 and the Chinese role in similar situations in the future are also topics of discussion in China. Joint exercises on international disaster response and rescue are another area in which the United States could engage the PLA.[102]

In operational terms, the PLA's recent experiences in disaster relief underline continued problems with equipment, logistics, airlift capability, and joint operations. Training, specialized rescue units and equipment (both rudimentary and specialized) were all in short supply. The lack of heavy helicopter transport capability and the PLAAF's apparent inability to efficiently deliver large numbers of troops to the disaster are particularly striking. The PLA has been working to increase its force projection capabilities and its ability to perform joint operations. Exercises including Peace Mission 2007 (a joint exercise with Russia and other members of the Shanghai Cooperation Organization) involved carefully planned airlift and force projection exercises involving hundreds of troops and were (at least in public propaganda) hailed as brilliant examples of PLA prowess. But the difficulties encountered in mobilizing and delivering forces for the earthquake disaster relief effort and the vulnerability of south China's transportation and power infrastructure as seen in the snow and ice emergency underline just how far the PLA has to go before it will be able to reliably project overwhelming force beyond its borders under challenging circumstances.[103]

While the PLA's performance in disaster response indicates some serious weaknesses which should be of interest to American policymakers, the military response to mass incidents and ethnic unrest represents a very different facet of the PLA's domestic security responsibilities, and a less straightforward set of implications for U.S. policy. China's handling of mass incidents and ethnic unrest tells us relatively little about the PLA's operational capabilities, but the incidents themselves do have potential significance for American policymakers.

The Chinese military's response to mass incidents and to the unrest in Lhasa and Urumqi shows that China's military still remembers the lesson of 1989: the PAP appears on the front lines, hitting the streets to restore order, while the PLA itself remains in the background, playing a supporting role. When deployed in sufficient numbers and with appropriate rules of engagement, the PAP (perhaps with some support from the PLA in particularly serious incidents) has the training, the equipment and the capability of controlling violent mass incidents, ethnic and nonethnic. In any hypothetical scenario in which China successfully invaded and occupied Taiwan and was faced with serious urban unrest or even insurgency, the PLA and

PAP would presumably draw on the tactics and techniques that they have developed to prevent, contain, and suppress urban mass incidents in cities ranging from Shishou to Lhasa to Urumqi. These include securing sensitive installations, sealing off problem areas, retaking city streets block by block, and controlling and/or shutting down electronic means of communication.[104]

These techniques for handling mass incidents, while successful, have not been without problems. One of the challenges of handling mass incidents is the control of information, including the domestic and foreign media, cell phones, and the internet. Chinese specialists and practitioners disagree on the correct approach toward information control. The standard response (seen in a particularly extreme form with the clampdown on Twitter and social networking sites like Facebook in the response to the events in Urumqi) has been to attempt to limit or even shut down cell phone and internet services in the affected areas. But some Chinese commentators argue that shutdowns of electronic communications and media blackouts only contribute to the circulation of inaccurate information. They suggest that the authorities should place more emphasis on using and channeling media and communications in order to ensure that state-approved information gains dominance.[105]

A second challenge involved in response to mass incidents concerns the matter of timing. On the one hand, some Chinese analysts criticize local officials for being too quick deploy police and PAP units, thus fanning the flames of popular anger and bringing more people into the streets. On the other, there have clearly been incidents, including in Lhasa in March 2008 and in Urumqi in July 2009 when a slow response by internal security forces allowed riots to spiral out of control, at the cost of substantial property damage and loss of innocent civilian lives. Getting the response right—neither too slow nor too fast—is a challenge that, ultimately, requires accurate and timely intelligence (something that seems to have been notably lacking in the handling of unrest in Lhasa and Urumqi), acute judgment, rapid decisionmaking, and a coordinated command structure at the base level.

On the whole, China's mass incidents and ethnic unrest and the military's role in handling them offer few opportunities for American policy. In wartime, it is possible (particularly if the war were going poorly for China) that social, economic, and ethnic tensions might weaken the Chinese government from within. In this respect, mass incidents are further indication of the "fragility" of China's body politic—a factor that the Chinese regime would need to consider in deciding whether or not to engage a foreign power (Taiwan and/or the United States in the Taiwan Strait, or India on the Sino-Indian border) in military action.[106] American policymakers, too, should give some consideration to the potential for internal unrest in China in mind. In general, however, it would be a mistake to interpret nonethnic mass incidents as evidence of broad-based resistance to or alienation from the central government. These incidents are generated by local problems, and their primary targets are local Party and government officials and local police.

Mass incidents with an ethnic dimension are more complex, being generated by a combination of economic issues, the styles and policies of local leaders, and an ethnic and religious sense of difference from the Han Chinese majority. Like nonethnic mass incidents, the unrest in Lhasa (and other Tibetan areas) in

2008 and in Urumqi in 2009 is indicative of a broader source of internal instability which could have a negative impact on China's unity in times of war. Suppression of incidents like that in Lhasa or Urumqi, in which the PAP has played the leading role, says much about the PAP's ability to control isolated incidents of internal unrest, but little about the PLA's warfighting strengths or weaknesses. The occurrence and the suppression of mass incidents that have an ethnic dimension does present American politicians and the U.S. State Department with opportunities (many of them justified) for criticizing China's human rights record. Such criticism makes a certain amount of sense in domestic politics within the United States, but it is of little or no assistance to Tibetans or Uyghurs in China and is of debatable utility for the furtherance of the U.S. national interest in East Asia.

Finally, do internal MOOTW responsibilities represent a significant and growing burden on the PLA? Will these responsibilities detract from the PLA's ability to prepare for, train for, and carry out its central mission of national defense (including preparation for possible conflicts in the Taiwan Strait and the South China Sea)? Can the United States expect to be dealing with a PLA that is increasingly focused on internal security issues and therefore has fewer resources to devote to the development of force projection capabilities?

The short answer to those questions would be: no. It is true that China's military faces serious and probably increasing internal security challenges over the next 5 to 10 years and beyond. In early 2009, Chinese analysts predicted that the effects of the global economic downturn would lead to an increase in violent mass incidents in China. China's relatively rapid economic recovery may have prevented such an increase, but any future rise in economic and environmental pressures could cause an upswing in nonethnic and ethnic mass incidents. At the same time, global climate change and its attendant consequences, including increases in extreme weather and rising sea levels can be expected to contribute to more frequent large-scale natural disasters. The PLA is not alone among the world's militaries in having to play a significant role in emergency response and disaster relief. Scholars note a growing trend toward military involvement in disaster response and relief, both within individual countries and on an international scale.[107] The question is: What impact does that involvement have on military budgets, training, and preparedness for warfighting?

Faced with the apparently mounting challenges of internal security and disaster relief, some within the PLA have expressed concern that preparation and training for MOOTW such as disaster relief may be a distraction from the PLA's core mission of national defense.[108] Perhaps in response to these concerns, it appears that China places a good deal of emphasis on improving the overall quality of the militia and reserves and training and equipping specialized militia and reserves units to deal with specific types of disaster (industrial, forest fire, earthquake, and so on). These moves suggest a division of labor in which the militia, reserves (and also specialized PAP units including firefighting units) would be first responders to major natural and man-made disasters, with the PLA acting as a second echelon to be deployed in instances of major disaster.

Aside from these concerns, however, we have no evidence that preparation for and participation in internal MOOTW has, in fact, had any negative impact on the PLA's core mission or its pursuit of modernization. Furthermore, while some within the PLA seemingly resent the burden of MOOTW, others argue that MOOTW actually contribute to the PLA's ability to perform its core mission. PLA commentators appear to be particularly interested in establishing a unified wartime and emergency response mobilization system. If designed in a way that guaranteed a leading role for the PLA, such a unified system could conceivably enhance the PLA's power by providing a legal and institutional basis for PLA access to social, economic, financial, and human resources, and by preventing the establishment of a competing stand-alone civilian emergency response system.

No matter what the outcome of China's internal debate on emergency management, we can expect the PLA, the PAP, the militia, and the reserves to continue to play significant roles in maintaining domestic security, responding to natural and man-made disasters, and delivering disaster relief. American scholars can continue to gain further insight into some of the operational capabilities and weaknesses of the PLA and some of China's domestic social and infrastructural vulnerabilities by further observation and analysis of the growing legal and institutional frameworks for and prosecution of internal MOOTW. There are, however, no grounds to conclude that MOOTW represent a fundamental distraction from the PLA's main mission or that China's mass incidents and ethnic unrest represent a fatal internal weakness. China may be more adaptable and less fragile than it sometimes appears.

ENDNOTES - CHAPTER 6

1. I am discounting subsequent minor incidents along the China-Vietnam border and in the South China Sea and brief engagements in the context of UN peacekeeping missions.

2. Li You, "努力提高部队干部执行非战争行动的能力" ("Strive to improve army cadres' ability to carry out MOOTW"), 国防 (*National Defense*), Vol. 3, 2009, p. 6; Dong Zhijun and Ding Shaoxue, "构建精干高效的政治工作运行机制" ("Build a crack, high-efficiency political work mechanism"), 中国国防报 *Zhongguo guofangbao*, December 22, 2008, p. 3; Liu Demao, Zhang Yuejun, Li Zhao and Li Xucheng, "挑起非战争军事行动的重担" ("Shoulder the heavy burden of military operations other than war"), *(China National Defense Daily)*, October 23, 2008, p. 3. A reading of the many openly published articles on MOOTW indicates that PLA officers often find MOOTW challenging, that there is some debate within the PLA as to the relative importance of MOOTW, but I have seen nothing to suggest that PLA officers faced with MOOTW responsibilities do anything other than carry out their assigned tasks.

3. The reliance on openly published sources such as academic journals, magazines, newspapers, and websites carries severe limitations. Much (or all) of what appears in these formats is cautiously written, carefully vetted, and deals with issues at a fairly high level of abstraction. Specific details and concrete examples are few and far between.

4. For useful overviews of the PLA's internal security responsibilities, see David Shambaugh, *Modernizing China's Military: Progress, Problems, and Prospects*, Berkeley: University of California Press, 2004, pp. 20-22, 170-75; and Dennis J. Blasko, *The Chinese Army Today: Tradition and Transformation for the Twenty-First Century*, London: Routledge, 2006, pp. 171-78. In looking at "lessons learned" from internal security operations, this chapter further discusses some of the issues addressed by Murray Scot Tanner (no relation to the present author), "How China Manages Internal Security Challenges and its Impact on PLA Missions" in Roy Kamphausen, David Lai, and Andrew Scobell, eds., *Beyond the Strait: PLA Missions Other Than Taiwan*, Carlisle, PA: Strategic Studies Institute, 2009, pp. 39-98. Murray Scot Tanner's many publica-

tions on policing and internal security, including "China Rethinks Unrest" *The Washington Quarterly*, Summer 2004, pp. 137-56; and "Challenges to China's Internal Security," Testimony presented to the U.S.-China Economic and Security Review Commission, February 3, 2006, are particularly useful sources on internal security matters. Other valuable work on internal security includes Andrew Scobell, "The Meaning of Martial Law for the PLA and Internal Security in China After Deng," in James Mulvenon and Andrew N.D. Yang, eds., *A Poverty of Riches: New Challenges and Opportunities in PLA Research*, Santa Monica, CA: RAND, 2003, pp. 169-91; and Tai Ming Cheung, "Guarding China's Domestic Front Line: The People's Armed Police and China's Stability," *China Quarterly*, June 1996, pp. 525-47. On internal security challenges in Xinjiang, see Martin Wayne, *China's War on Terrorism: Counter-insurgency, Politics, and Internal Security*, New York: Routledge, 2009. There are no major studies in English on the PLA's role in disaster relief and rescue operations.

5. James Mulvenon, "Chairman Hu and the PLA's 'New Historic Missions,'" *China Leadership Monitor* Vol. 27, Winter 2009, available from *media.hoover.org/documents/CLM27JM.pdf*. Lt. General Guo Hongchao, "适应多样化军事任务, 推进战区民兵预备役工作" ("Adapt to the demands of diversified military tasks, move forward with military district militia and reserves work"), 国防 *(National Defense)*, Vol. 12, 2008, pp. 4-8; Hu Jintao, "Hold High the Great Banner of Socialism with Chinese Characteristics and Strive for New Victories in Building a Moderately Prosperous Society," October 15, 2007, available from *www.china.org.cn/english/congress/229611.htm#9*.

6. Yu Jia, "多样化军事任务 ≠ 非战争军事行动" ("Diverse military tasks does not equal military operations other than war"). 中国国防报 *(China National Defense Daily)*, December 11, 2008, p. 3; Zhao Zongqi, "完成多样化任务, 我们需要什么能力" ("What capabilities do we need to perform diverse tasks?"), 解放军报 *(PLA Daily)*, June 17, 2008, p. 11; Dong Qiang, "抗旱救灾, 中国军人依法行动" ("In Countering drought, and providing disaster relief, China's soldiers operate according to law"), 解放军报 *(PLA Daily)*, February 18, 2009, p. 6.

7. Information Office of the State Council of the People's Republic of China, "China's National Defense in 2008," "Preface," January 2009, available from *www.china.org.cn/government/central_government/2009-01/20/content_17155577_3.htm*.

8. Constitution of the People's Republic of China, Article 29, available from *www.english.peopledaily.com.cn/constitution/constitution.html.*

9. Lonnie D. Henley, "The Legal and Regulatory Basis for Defense Mobilization in China," RAND/CAN Conference on Chinese Mobilization, Warrenton, VA, February 2005, available from *www18.georgetown.edu/data/people/ldh28/publication-32841.pdf.*

10. Jiang Lingling, Wang Jiexiu and Liu Lianyou, *People's Republic of China: Providing EmergencyResponse to Sichuan Earthquake*, Asian Development Bank, 2008, p. 1, available from *www.reliefweb.int/rw/RWFiles2008.nsf/FilesByRWDocUnidFilename/LSGZ-7PCGC2-full_report.pdf/$File/full_report.pdf.*

11. Major legislation and contingency response plans consulted for this paper include "中华人民共和国突发事件应对法" ("Contingency response law of the People's Republic of China"), passed by the National People's Congress Standing Committee (NPC SC) on August 30, 2007, available from *www.gov.cn/flfg/2007-08/30/content_732593.htm.;* "军队参加抢险救灾条例" ("Regulation on army participation in disaster rescue and relief"), issued by the State Council and the Central Military Commission (CMC) June 7, 2005, available from *www.gov.cn/yjgl/2005-10/09/content_75376.htm.;* "四川省突发公共事件总体应急预案" ("Sichuan province overall public emergency response plan"), March 22, 2006, available from *www.202.123.110.5/yjgl/2006-03/22/content_233837.htm.;* "安徽省人民政府突发公共事件总体应急预案"（"试行"）("Anhui provincial people's government overall public emergency response plan, provisional"), passed April 10, 2006, available from *www.ahta.com.cn/News/Html/09/05/090516142917.html.*

12. "中华人民共和国突发事件应对法" Chap. 1, Article 40.

13. "军队参加抢险救灾条例" Article 3.

14. "Rescue, Disaster Relief Included in Military Training" Xinhua News Agency March 13, 2002, available from *www.china.org.cn/english/archiveen/28738.htm.*

15. See Dennis J. Blasko and John F. Corbett, Jr., "No More Tiananmens: The People's Armed Police and Stability in China," *China Strategic Review*, Spring 1998, pp. 88-89.

16. "Martial Law of the People's Republic of China" promulgated March 1, 1996, Article 8, available from *www.asianlii.org/cn/legis/cen/laws/ml100/*.

17. James Hackett, ed., *The Military Balance, 2009*, London: International Institute for Strategic Studies, 2009, p. 387. Another source estimates PAP strength in 2008 at 660,000. See *Sinodefense.com*, "People's Armed Police Internal Troops," available from *www.sinodefence.com/army/organisation/pap-internal*. James Hackett, ed., *The Military Balance, 2008,* London: International Institute for Strategic Studies, 2008, p. 380, put PAP strength in 2007 at 1,500,000 It is unclear whether the reduction from 1,500,000 in 2007 to 700,000 in 2008 is a function of budget-cutting, elimination of inferior and unneeded units, or if it is related to power struggles within and/or concerning control over the PAP.

18. Lu Siqing, "Chūgoku 'busō keisatsu' ni hisomu antō" ("Internal struggle underlying China's 'armed police'"), *Tokyo Facta*, March 1, 2009, pp. 70-73; *Sinodefense.com*, "People's Armed Police Internal Troops."

19. "306,000 Soldiers Mobilized to Combat Snow Disasters," *Xinhua*, February 2, 2008, available from *www.news.xinhuanet.com/english/2008-02/02/content_7549276.htm*.

20. Examples may be seen in stories from the *People's Liberation Army Daily* available online from "Chinese Servicemen in Fight Against Snow Chaos," available from *english.chinamil.com.cn/site2/special-reports/node_16079.htm*.

21. Sun Xianglin, Liu Zhongcheng, and Li Jinchuan, "大力推进国防动员应急应战一体化建设" ("Strongly advance the integration of national defense mobilization for emergency response and war"), 国防 (*National Defense*), Vol. 11, 2008, pp. 11-13.

22. *Ibid.*

23. Yang Zurong and Zou Weirong, "Pay Close Attention to the Building of Equipment Support for Military Operations Other than War," 解放军报 (*PLA Daily*), May 11, 2009, p. 1.

24. Zhu Yi and Wei Huayong, "组织民兵预备役部队抗雪救灾的几点启示" ("A few lessons from organizing militia and reserve

troops for disaster relief in the snow emergency"), 国防 *(National Defense)*, Vol. 5, 2008, pp. 28-9.

25. Cui Chen and Li Changrong, "从抗击冰雪灾害中透析我军交通运输保障" ("Safeguarding our army's transport and communications as revealed in the fight against the ice and snow disaster"), 国防 *(National Defense)*, Vol. 4, 2008, pp. 49-51. I have not been able to locate the RAND document to which the authors refer.

26. *Ibid.*

27. Yang Jinkui, "假如战争中遇上雪灾" ("Suppose a snow emergency came during wartime"), 解放军报 *(PLA Daily)*, April 21, 2008, p. 6.

28. Gu Yong and Cao Zhe, "进五万子弟兵奔赴灾区救急救难" ("Nearly 50,000 people's soldiers rush to the relief of the disaster area"), *Xinhuanet*, May 14, 2008, p. 1.

29. Department of Defense, "China: PLA Activities Report 1-15 Jun 08," July 14, 2008, pp. 2, 5.

30. Wang Jinxiang, "抗震救灾事件：主体教育的生动教材" ("The experience of earthquake resistance and rescue: vibrant material for theme-centered education"), 解放军报 *(PLA Daily)*, June 13, 2008, p. 6. For a representative example of the celebratory treatment of the earthquake relief effort, see "总政治宣传部" ("General Political Propaganda Department"), ed. "惊天动地战汶川" (*"The magnificent and earth-shaking battle of Wenchuan"*), Beijing, China: 解放军出版社 (PLA Press), 2008.

31. One analysis of the role of civilian volunteers described them as enthusiastic, but amateurish and of little real assistance and suggests that China formulate laws, regulations, and training programs for civilian volunteers willing to work in disaster relief efforts. Ma Shuangjun and Wang Dongping, "造就一支应战应急的轻骑兵" ("Forge a 'light cavalry' for wartime and emergency response"), 中国国防报 *(China National Defense Daily)*, May 19, 2008, p. 3.

32. As James Mulvenon notes, earthquake response helped the PLA to improve its image. James Mulvenon, "The Chinese

279

Military's Earthquake Response Leadership Team." *China Leadership Monitor* Vol. 25, summer 2008, pp. 1-8, available from *www.hoover.org/publications/clm/issues/20100024.html.*

33. Chen Long, "国防动员让汶川救灾更有力" ("National defense mobilization imparted greater strength to Wenchuan disaster relief operations"), 中国国防报 *(China National Defense Daily)*, May 29, 2008, p. 3. This praise for a provincial-level dual use wartime/emergency management mobilization system may also be part of the ongoing debate regarding the design of China's emergency response mobilization system—a debate in which many in the PLA have been arguing strongly for instituting such a dual-use system at the national level.

34. Wang Yongxiao, Hu Junhua and Li Hongxing, "完成多样化任务需要多样化能力" ("Completion of diversified tasks requires diversified capabilities"), 解放军报 *(PLA Daily)*, June 11, 2009, p. 3.

35. Wang Mingliang, Yang Yujie, Xu Pang and Wang Suying, "非战争军事行动观察报告" ("Observation report on military operations other than war"), 中国空军 *(China Air Force)*, July 1, 2008, pp. 60-64.

36. Gan Bo, "汶川救灾直升机优势独特" ("The unique advantages of helicopters in the Wenchuan earthquake relief effort"), 大众科技报 *(Popular Science and Technology Daily)*, June 12, 2008, p. A01.

37. Sun Xianglin, Liu Zhongcheng and Li Jinchuan, pp. 11-13.

38. Quoted in Jake Hooker, "Quake Revealed Deficiencies of China's Military," *The New York Times,* July 7, 2008, available from *www.nytimes.com/2008/07/02/world/asia/02china.html.*

39. Nirav Patel, "Chinese Disaster Relief Operations: Identifying Critical Capability Gaps," *Joint Force Quarterly*, Vol. 52, 2009, pp. 111-117.

40. Wang Mingliang, Yang Yujie, Pang Xu, and Wang Suying, pp. 60-64.

41. Sun Xianglin, Liu Zhongcheng, and Li Jinchuan, pp. 11-13; Wang Yuxin, "汶川地震对我国应急救援建设的启示" ("The Wenchuan earthquake's lessons for the development of our emergency response and rescue"), 人民公安报, 消防周刊 (*PAP Daily, Fire Department Weekly*), July 23, 2008, p. 3; Ai Husheng, "从非战争军事行动需要看民兵预备役建设" ("Viewing the building of militia and reserve forces from the needs of MOOTW"), 中国国防报 (*China National Defense Daily*), October 30, 2008, p. 3.

42. For example, see Che Ruijin, "抗击地震灾害对加强国防动员建设的启示" ("Lessons from the struggle against the Wenchuan earthquake disaster for strengthening our construction of national defense mobilization"), 国防 (*National Defense*), Vol. 7, 2008, pp. 12-14.

43. Sun Xianglin, Liu Zhongcheng and Li Jinchuan, pp. 11-13.

44. Che Ruijin, pp. 12-14.

45. *Ibid.*

46. A related, but much more difficult question would be how disaster relief and other internal security missions affect the PLA's budget. Enhancement of disaster relief and anti-terrorism capability are reported to have been part of the 17.6 percent increase in China's 2009 defense budget over that of the previous year. See Wendell Minnick, "China Increases defense budget," *Defense News*, March 4, 2009, available from *www.defensenews.com/story.php?i=3973307*. However, given our lack of detailed information on China's defense budget, there is no reliable quantitative data to indicate what kind of burden disaster relief and other MOOTW might be putting on the PLA's financial resources.

47. Zhao Guiqi, "Enlightenment Gained from Wenchuan Earthquake Relief Operation in the Perspective of National Defense Mobilization," 中国军事科学 (*China Military Science*), March 2008, pp. 7-13.

48. Wu Tianmin and Dong Haiming, "关键是打造核心军事能力" ("The key is building core army capabilities"), 解放军报

(PLA Daily), June 9, 2008, p. 1; Wei Qiujiang and Liu Xin, "抗震救灾实践对加强军队完成多样化军事任务能力建设的启示" ("The lessons of earthquake resistance and relief for the construction of military capability for carrying out diversified military tasks"), 国防 *(National Defense)*, Vol. 10, 2008, pp. 18-19; Wang Yongxiao, Hu Junhua and Xia Hongqing, "完成多样化任务需要多样化能力" ("Completion of diversified tasks requires diversified capabilities"), 解放军报 *(PLA Daily)*, June 11, 2009, p. 3.

49. Wu Tianmin and Ding Haiming, p. 1; Yi Qiaoping and Yan Feng, " 汶川抗震救灾对我军遂行非战争军事行动能力建设的启示" ("The Wenchuan earthquake resistance and rescue's lessons for our army's building of capabilities of carrying out military operations other than war"), 国防 *(National Defense)*, Vol. 7, 2008.

50. Cited in Liao Haiqing, "就业危机或致群体性事件发生几率增加" ("Employment crisis could lead to an increase in the rate of mass-type incidents"), *China Elections and Governance* March 10, 2009, available from *www.chinaelections.org/printnews.asp?newsid=144902*. For an earlier overview of mass incidents and police response to them, see Murray Scot Tanner, "China Rethinks Unrest," *Washington Quarterly*, 2004, pp. 137-156, available from *www.twq.com/04summer/docs/04summer_tanner.pdf*.

51. Chang Hongxiao, "陈锡文：约2000万农民工失业，须直面相关社会问题" ("Chen Xiwen: around 20 million rural migrant workers unemployed, must face related social problems"), 财经 *(Financial Time)*, February 2, 2009, available from *www.caijing.com.cn/2009-02-02/110051988.html*; Tan Ailing, "'散步' 是为了避免暴力——社科院专家单光鼐解析2008年群体性事件" ("'taking a stroll' to avoid violence—social sciences academy expert Dan Guangnai analyzes the mass incidents of 2008"), 南方周末 *(South China Weekend)*, January 14, 2009, available from *www.hi.baidu.com/dycxing/blog/item/fd3c6d3f1fa2fac87d1e7191.html*; "正确处理群众性事件" ("Correctly resolve mass incidents"), 中国新闻周刊 *(Chinese Newsweek)*, February 9, 2009. Since China has made a relatively rapid recovery from the global financial crisis, these predictions may turn out to have been overly pessimistic.

52. Tan Ailing, "'散步' 是为了避免暴力."

53. Zhang Shengzhi, "加强对群体性事件的研究演练" ("Strengthen research and training in handling mass incidents"), 人民论坛 (*People's Forum*), Vol. 6, 2009, available from *paper.people.com.cn/rmlt/html/2009-03/16/content_213819.htm*.

54. Zhang Shuling, "民兵预备役要充分做好参与维稳准备" ("Militia and reserve forces must do a good job of participating in preparations for maintaining social stability"), 国防 (*National Defense*), Vol. 11, 2008, pp. 23-4.

55. For example, a recent CASS study found that 69.4 percent of those surveyed thought that government officials (as opposed to business persons) had benefited the most from economic development. *China Youth Daily*, September 12, 2008, cited in BBC Monitoring: China Social Unrest Briefing, September 4-17, 2008, September 17, 2008, p. 1.

56. Liu Chang, "委员建议处理群体性事件慎用警力" ("Committee members suggest caution when using police force to handle mass incidents"), 北京青年报 (*Beijing Youth Daily*), November 3, 2009, available from *www.cyol.net/zqb/content/2009-03/11/content_2576501.htm*; Tan Ailing, "'散步' 是为了避免暴力."

57. Xiao Shu, "群体性事件矛头为何总指向政府?" ("Why are mass incidents always directed against the government?"), 南方周末 (*South China Weekend*), November 27, 2008, available from *www.infzm.com/content/20482*. The Chongqing taxi cab driver strike of the fall of 2008 is cited as an example of how appropriate action by local government officials can defuse a crisis which had the potential to develop into a violent mass incident. In this case, when taxi drivers went on strike over management fees, low base fares, fuel shortages, and competition from unlicensed "black cabs," the city's Communist Party leadership took steps to address the cab drivers' concerns, held multiple press conferences to get the government's point of view across, disciplined lower-level officials in the city transportation commission, held a televised discussion with representatives of the taxi drivers, and agreed to the formation of a taxi drivers' union. See Li Weiao and Deng Hai, "Chaotic Taxi Strike Pays Off in Chongqing," *Caijing*, November 15, 2008, available from *www.english.caijing.com.cn/2008-11-15/110028781.html*; Liao Haiqing, "就业危机或致群体性事件发生几录增加."

58. For example, on September 5, 2008, 4,000 middle school students besieged a county government building in Henan province, breaking doors and windows and setting fires (quickly extinguished) after the developer of the "European Garden" real estate development project tore up their school playground. Several hundred regular police and PAP officers clashed with the students, injuring 20. The issue was resolved when local officials agreed to negotiate with the developer on behalf of the students. Information Centre for Human Rights and Democracy, September 5, 2008, cited in BBC Monitoring: China Social Unrest Briefing, September 4-17, 2008, September 17, 2008, pp. 3-4.

59. Yu Jianrong and Yu Debao, "China Civil Society Report: Mass Incidents in China," *Policy Forum Online* 08-065A, August 26, 2008, available from *www.nautilus.org/fora/security/08065YuYu. html*.

60. Yu Jianrong, "Anger in the Streets," *Caijing*, July 7, 2009, available from *www.english.caijing.com.cn/2009-07-07/110194431. html*.

61. Zhou Zhejun and Li Feng, "陇南通报武都区群体性上访事件" ("Longnan reports mass petitioners incident in Wudu district"), 甘肃日报 (*Gansu Daily*), November 20, 2008; Andrew Jacobs, "Thousands Battle Police in China's Northwest," *The New York Times*, November 18, 2008, available from *www.nytimes. com/2008/11/19/world/asia/19china.html?ref=asia*. For a series of photographs taken during the incident, see *www.zonaeuropa com/20081122_1.htm*. See also videos of the Longnan incident, available from *www.globalvoicesonline.org/2008/11/19/china-protest-and-repression-at-earthquake-area-gansu-lungnan/*.

62. For a full statement of the official position on the Li Shufen case and riots, see "贵州省召开新闻发布会解瓮安6-28 事件真相" ("Guizhou provincial government holds press conference, reveals the truth of the 6-28 Weng'an incident"), available from *news.xinhuanet.com/video/2008-07/02/content_8473735.htm*. On the Weng'an incident in general, see also: Zhou Zhongwei, "瓮安事件对处置群体性事件的启示" ("The Weng'an incident's lessons on handling mass incidents"), 江西公安专科学校学报 (*Jiangxi Public Security School Journal*), 6: 126, November, 2008), pp.

22-25; Wang Tai Peng, "Lessons from the Weng'an riots," *AsiaInc*, September 4, 2008, available from *www.asia-inc.com/china/145-sep-oct-2008/277-lessons-from-the-wengan-riots.html*; Jim Yardley, "Chinese riot over handling of girl's killing," *The New York Times*, June 30, 2008, available from *www.nytimes.com/2008/06/30/world/asia/30iht-30riot.14086300.html?_r=1*; "China jails rioters, criticizes officials," *Reuters*, November 14, 2008, available from *www.in.reuters.com/article/worldNews/idININdia-36508820081114?pageNumber=2&virtualBrandChannel=0&sp=true.*

63. For a description and analysis of the Weng'an incident, see also Joseph Fewsmith, "An 'Anger-Venting' Mass Incident Catches the Attention of China's Leadership," *China Leadership Monitor*, No. 26, Fall 2008, available from *www.media.hoover.org/documents/CLM26JF.pdf.*

64. Yu Jianrong, "泄愤事件的后续效应" ("The after-effects of anger-venting incidents"). 南风窗 (*Nanfengchuang*), July 25, 2009, available from *www.nfcmag.com/articles/1577*; "湖北石市酒店命案几万民众打退上千武警" ("Hubei Shi city hotel death case—tens of thousands of citizens fight off over a thousand armed police"), available from *bbs.news.163.com/bbs/photo/140982378.html*; For a series of news stories, photographs and videos, see *www.zonaeuropa.com/20090621_1.htm.*

65. He Qing, "石首事件清场纪实：上万军警喊口号包围围观群众" ("Record of how the streets were cleared in the Shishou incident: over 10,000 soldiers and police shouting slogans surrounded on-looking masses"), 亚洲周刊 (*Asia Week*), June 28, 2009, available from *www.dwnews.com/gb/MainNews/Forums/BackStage/2009_6_28_3_3_28_918.html.* See also the photograph from 南方周刊 (*Southern Weekly*), available from *www.zonaeuropa.com/200906c.brief.htm#014.*

66. Nie Zhijian, "公安民警在处置群体性事件中伤亡的原因及对策" ("Death and injury of public security militia in handling mass incidents: causes and countermeasures"), 广西警官高等专科学校学报 (*Guangxi Police Senior Officers School Journal*), Vol. 1, 2007, pp. 19-20.

67. "作品相关武警装备2" ("Regarding products—armed police equipment 2), March 5, 2009, available from *www.vip.book.sna.com.cn/book/chapter_61691_56364.html.*

68. Yu Jianrong, Yang Huijing and Xie Feng, "处置群体性械斗事件的协同方法" ("Coordinated techniques for handling incidents of mass armed fighting"), 国防 (*National Defense*), Vol. 5, 2008, pp. 69-70; Liao Haiqing, "就业危机或致群体性事件发生几录增加."

69. Liu Yanghuai, "繁荣应急警务研究履行平安建设职责—2008 警察临战论坛综述" ("Envigorate police emergency response research, peacefully fulfill the construction of professional duties—summary of the 2008 conference on police emergency response in China"), 湖北警官学院学报 (*Hubei Police Officer College Journal*), Vol. 2, 2009.

70. "内地拟立法明确武警平息骚乱职责" ("Mainland prepares to pass legislation clarifying armed police role in pacifying riots"), 中国新闻网 (*China News Net*), August 24, 2009, available from *news.ifeng.com/mainland/200908/0824_17_1316479.shtml*.

71. The fact that governments and society in Western countries and India continue to offer asylum, moral and financial support for Tibetan and Uyghur dissident organizations and their leaders, including the Uyghur leader Rebiya Kadeer and Tibet's Dalai Lama further confirms the Chinese leaderships' perception (a perception shared by many, if not most, Chinese) that foreign powers are still actively interested in weakening or ending China's control over large areas of the territory of the PRC.

72. For an extended discussion, see Murray Scot Tanner, "How China Manages Internal Security Challenges," pp. 64-81. On the causes of the unrest in Lhasa, see Fang Kun, Huang Li, and Li Xiang, "藏区3.14事件经济成因调查报告" ("Report on investigation of the social and economic causes of the March 14 incident in the Tibetan areas"), Beijing, China: 公民法律研究中心 (Center for Citizen Legal Studies), 2008, available from *www.docs.google.com/Doc?id=df4nrxxq_91ctcf6sck*. See also Sebastian Veg, "Tibet, Nationalism, and Modernity," Vol. 3, 2009, available from *www.cefc.com.hk/download.php?fnom=cp_2009-3_ca1_veg*.

73. Zhu Ze, "First Armed Police Law Set to Pass." *China Daily*, August 25, 2009, available from *www.chinadaily.com.cn/china/2009-08/25/content_8610543.htm*; Murray Scot Tanner, "How

China Manages Internal Security Challenge," p. 73. For another, less objective point of view, see "Elite People's Liberation Army Troops Enter Lhasa," March 21, 2008, available from *www.phayul. com/news/article.aspx?id=19930&t=1.*

74. "Transcript: James Miles interview on Tibet," CNN, March 20, 2008, available from *www.cnn.com/2008/WORLD/asiapcf/03/20/ tibet.miles.interview.*

75. Wang Kaiwen, "西藏：遇突发事件通信永不中断" ("Tibet: when meeting with unexpected incidents, communications will never be cut off"). 西藏商报 (*Tibet Financial Daily*), June 18, 2009, available from *xz.people.com.cn/GB/139190/9500021.html.* The Tibet Emergency Response Communications Bureau could be designed primarily to deal with natural disaster response, to respond to ethnic unrest, or both.

76. Wang Guanghui and Li Jun, "努力提高边疆地区后备力量的应急维稳能力" ("Strive to improve the border area reserve forces' emergency response and stability maintenance capabilities"), 国防 (*National Defense*), Vol. 6, 2008, pp. 40-41.

77. Zhu Ze, "First armed police law set to pass."

78. "武警平息暴乱职责拟立法明确" ("Armed police responsibilities for riot control to be clarified in legislation"), 华夏都市报 (*Huaxia dushibao*), August 25, 2009, p. 6.

79. *Ibid.*

80. See the discussion in Yitzhak Shichor, "The Great Wall of Steel: Military and Strategy in Xinjiang," in S. Frederick Starr, ed., *Xinjiang: China's Muslim Borderland*, Armonk: M. E. Sharpe, 2004, pp. 120-160.

81. James A. Millward, "Violent Separatism in Xinjiang: A Critical Assessment," Washington, DC: The East-West Center, 2004, pp. 10-22. See also James A. Millward, *Eurasian Crossroads: A History of Xinjiang*, New York: Columbia University Press, 2007, pp. 322-334. The following overview of violent incidents in Xinjiang draws on Dr. Millward's work. For another interpretation

of the nature and seriousness of the threat that Uyghur separatist activities have posed to China, see Martin I. Wayne, *China's War on Terrorism: Counter-insurgency, Politics, and Internal Security*, London, UK: Routledge, 2008.

82. Fiona Tam and Chi-yuk Choi, "They Hacked Police with Machetes, then They Threw Grenades," *South China Morning Post Online*, June 8, 2008.

83. James Millward, "Violent Separatism in Xinjiang: A Critical Assessment," pp. 16-17; "Remember the Gulja massacre? China's crackdown on peaceful protesters," *Amnesty International*, January 2, 2007, available from *www.amnesty.org/en/library/asset/ASA17/002/2007/en/dom-ASA170022007en.html*; a video purporting to show footage from the Yining (Gulja) incident may be viewed at *www.youtube.com/watch?v=4RUCOrg2Pb0*. Amnesty International suggests that "(h)undreds, possibly thousands, lost their lives or were seriously injured" in this incident. Another source reports that 192 were killed in the crackdown, of which 100 were PAP officers. See Shinchen Wong and Andrei Chang, "Riots of Ethnic Minorities Challenge China's General National Defence Strategies," *Kanwa Asian Defense Review* Vol. 46, August 31, 2008, pp. 20-22.

84. "官方证实新疆和田三月发生分裂分子闹事事件" ("Officials affirm the March occurrence of a separatist incident in Xinjiang's Hetian"), 中国新闻网 (*China News Net*), April 4, 2008, available from *www.chinanews.com.cn/gn/news/2008/04-04/1211861.shtml*; Michael Anderson, "Breaking News - The CCP blocks news and represses mass protests in Hetian, Xinjiang," *Sohnews.com*, April 2, 2008, available from *www.sohnews.com/2008/04/03/breaking-news-the-ccp-blocks-news-and-represses-mass-protests-in-hetian-xinjiang/*.

85. Edward Wong, "China Locks Down Restive Region After Deadly Clashes," *The New York Times*, July 6, 2009, available from *www.nytimes.com/2009/07/07/world/asia/07china.html*; Jonathan Watts, "Old Suspicions Magnified Mistrust into Ethnic Riots in Urumqi," *The Guardian*, July 10, 2009, available from *www.guardian.co.uk/world/2009/jul/10/china-riots-uighurs-han-urumqi*; Kathleen E. McLaughlin, "Fear Grips Shaoguan's Uighurs," *Far Eastern Economic Review*, July 17, 2009, available from *www.feer.com/politics/2009/july58/Fear-Grips-Shaoguans-Uighurs*.

86. The Chinese government has suggested that the demonstrations and subsequent rioting were instigated and organized from abroad by the Uyghur dissident leader Rebiya Kadeer and her World Uyghur Congress, but has offered no conclusive proof of these allegations. See "China for unequivocal stand against ethnic separation," *The New Nation,* July 9, 2009, available from *www.nation.ittefaq.com/issues/2009/07/09/news0324.htm*; Li Wei, a terrorism expert at China's Institute of Contemporary International Relations, was quoted as saying: "I have not found any proof that points to linkage between the riot and other terrorist groups. …" Quoted in Ariana E. Cha, "China, Uighur Groups Give Conflicting Riot Accounts," *The Washington Post,* July 25, 2009, available from *www.washingtonpost.com/wp-dyn/content/article/2009/07/24/AR2009072403648.html.*

87."新疆披露打砸抢烧杀暴力犯罪事件当日发展始末" ("Xinjiang publishes timeline of developments on the day of the violent criminal beating, smashing, looting, burning, killing incident"), *Chinanews.com,* July 6, 2009, available from *www.chinanews.com.cn/gn/news/2009/07-06/1762907.shtml.*

88. "新疆披露打砸抢烧杀暴力犯罪事件当日发展始末" ("Xinjiang publishes timeline of developments on the day of the violent criminal beating, smashing, looting, burning, killing incident"); Tania Branigan and Jonathan Watts, "Muslim Uighurs riot as ethnic tensions rise in western China," *The Guardian,* July 5, 2009, available from *www.guardian.co.uk/world/2009/jul/05/china-uighur-riots-xianjing*; Ariana E. Cha, "China, Uighur Groups give Conflicting Riot Accounts"; Edward Wong, "Riots in Western China Amid Ethnic Tension," *The New York Times,* July 5, 2009, available from *www.nytimes.com/2009/07/06/world/asia/06china.html.*

89. Edward Wong, "Chinese Question Police Absence in Ethnic Riots," *The New York Times,* July 17, 2009, available from *www.nytimes.com/2009/07/18/world/asia/18xinjiang.html.*

90. Tania Branigan and Jonathan Watts, "Muslim Uighurs riot as ethnic tensions rise in western China"; Shai Oster and Gordon Fairclough, "Ethnic Tensions Escalate in China's Xinjiang Region," *The Wall Street Journal,* July 8, 2009, available from *www.online.wsj.com/article/SB124695275387404741.html.*

91. Murray Scot Tanner, quoted in Edward Wong, "Chinese Question Police Absence in Ethnic Riots," *The New York Times* July 17, 2009, available from *www.nytimes.com/2009/07/18/world/asia/18xinjiang.html.*

92. "中华人民共和国突发事件应对" ("Contingency response law of the People's Republic of China"), passed by the National People's Congress Standing Committee (NPC SC) on August 30, 2007, available from *www.gov.cn/flfg/2007-08/30/content_732593.htm.*

93. Wu Zhong, "No Question, Hu's in Charge of Xinjiang," *Asia Times Online,* July 10, 2009, available from *www.atimes.com/atimes/China/KG10Ad01.html.*

94. "武警赴疆维稳部队航空输送计划表" ("Air transport planning table for Xinjiang-bound stability-maintenance PAP troops"), *Ziqu xinwen (Free More News),* July 7, 2009, available from *www.freemorenews.com/2009/07/10/armed-police-force-air-transportationschedule/;* Total numbers of PAP and PLA troops deployed to Urumqi are unclear. Some reports mention "at least 20,000 troops," while others mention "thousands." Human Rights Watch, "China: Security Build-up Foreshadows Large-scale Crackdown." July 10, 2009, available from *www.hrw.org/fr/news/2009/07/10/china-security-build-foreshadows-large-scale-crackdown;* Jane Macartney, "China in deadly crackdown after Uighurs go on the rampage," *Times Online,* July 5, 2009, available from *www.timesonline.co.uk/tol/news/world/asia/article6644574.ece.*

95. Peter Foster, "Urumqi: Criticism and Credit for Chinese Police," *Telegraph,* July 9, 2009, available from *www.blogs.telegraph.co.uk/news/peterfoster/100002643/urumqi-criticism-and-credit-for-the-chinese-police/.*

96. Barbara Demick, "Chinese riot police, Muslims clash in northwestern city," *Los Angeles Times*, July 6, 2009, available from *www.articles.latimes.com/2009/jul/06/world/fg-china-protest6;* "Police kill 2 Uighur men, wound 3rd in west China," July 13, 2009, available from *www.abcnews.go.com/International/wireStory?id=8066645;* Edward Wong, "Riots in Western China amid Ethnic Tension."

97. For examples, see the sources cited above. See also the Nelson Report, July 8, 2009, and the many news articles and videos compiled on the blogsite Eastsouthwestnorth, available from *www.zonaeuropa.com/weblog.htm*.

98. Wu Zhong, "No Question, Hu's in Charge of Xinjiang;" Peter Foster and Malcolm Moore, "Chinese province of Xinjiang teeters on the edge of fresh violence," *The Telegraph*, July 8, 2009, available from *www.telegraph.co.uk/news/worldnews/asia/china/5774908/Chinese-province-of-Xinjiang-teeters-on-the-edge-of-fresh-violence.html*. This apparent division of responsibilities confirms earlier analyses, which argue that the Chinese approach to controlling incidents of unrest in Xinjiang evolved from an emphasis on military action in the early 1990s to an approach that placed more emphasis on the use of regular police and the PAP from around 1995 onwards. See Wayne, *China's War on Terrorism*, pp. 80-81.

99. Ma Minyue, "国外特警训练模式研究及启示" ("Research on and lessons from foreign special police training models"), 公安教育 (*Public Security Education*), Vol. 5, 2009, pp. 70-72; Duan Yao, "美国突发事件应急处置系统探悉" ("Analysis of the American emergency response and management system"), 武警学院学报 (*PAP College Journal*), Vol. 24, No. 3, March 2008, pp. 40-44; Lu Lihong, Shang Kaoding, and Zhang Xuekui, "发达国家突发公共事件管理对我国的启示" ("Enlightenment for China from advanced countries' public emergency response and management"), 武警学院学报 (*PAP College Journal*), Vol. 24, No. 10, October 2008, pp. 5-8.

100. "China mulls draft law on military mobilization," *Xinhua*, April 20, 2009, available from *www.chinadaily.com.cn/china/2009-04/20/content_7695424.htm*.

101. Others have previously suggested this as a possible area for American engagement with the PLA. For example, see Shambaugh, *Modernizing China's Military*, p. 351.

102. Japan and China are already moving in this direction, having agreed in November 2009 to conduct joint exercises for natural disaster relief and at-sea rescue sometime in 2010. Peng Kuang, "Japan, China agree to defense exchanges," *China Daily*, November 28, 2009, available from *www.chinadaily.com.cn/cndy/2009-11/28/content_9068608.htm*.

103. Patel, "Chinese Disaster Relief Operations," p. 114. The 2-month "Stride 2009" exercises involving 50,000 troops conducted in the summer of 2009 were in part designed to address the PLA's weakness in the area of force projection. Trefor Moss, "PLA takes largest ever exercise in its 'stride'," *Jane's Defence Weekly*, August 13, 2009.

104. Clearly, the scale and challenges of a hypothetical PLA occupation of Taiwan could be far greater than anything that the PLA and PAP have experienced in dealing with isolated mass incidents in China or even with the endemic underlying unrest in Tibet and Xinjiang.

105. Wu Sha, "大力加强群体性突发事件处置工作全力维护社会政治稳定" ("Resolutely strengthen handling of mass incidents, go all out to protect social and political stability"), 公安研究 (*Public Security Studies*), Vol. 12, 2004, pp. 48-53; Zhou Zhongwei, "瓮安事件对处置群体性事件的启示" ("The Weng'an incident's lessons on the handling of mass incidents"), 江西公安专科学校学报 (*Jiangxi Public Security Officer School Journal*), Vol. 6, No. 126, November 2008, pp. 22-25; Liu Chang, "委员建议处理群体性事件慎用警力" ("Committee member suggestion caution when using police force to handle mass incidents"), 北京青年报 (*Beijing Youth Daily*), November 3, 2009.

106. For a discussion of regime fragility and its implications for American policy, see Susan Shirk, *China: Fragile Superpower*, New York: Oxford University Press, 2008.

107. Charles-Antoine Hofmann and Laura Hudson, "Military responses to natural disasters: last resort or inevitable trend?" *Humanitarian Exchange Magazine*, Vol. 44, September 2009, available from *www.odihpn.org/report.asp?id=3030*; Kathleen J. Tierney, "Recent Developments in U.S. Homeland Security Policies and Their Implications for the Management of Extreme Events," in Haridán Rodriguez, Enrico Louis Quarantelli, and Russell Rowe Dynes, eds., *Handbook of Disaster Research*, New York: Springer, 2006, pp. 410-411. Following the disastrous landslides caused by typhoon Morakot, Taiwan President Ma Yingjiu suggested that Taiwan's military would play a much larger role in disaster relief in the future and that Taiwan would need to establish a modern national

disaster prevention agency. "China not main enemy: Ma," *Straits Times*, August 18, 2008, available from *www.straitstimes.com/ Breaking%2BNews/Asia/Story/STIStory_418306.html.*

108. It should be noted that the debate on MOOTW and the PLA's role in emergency response is paralleled by a debate within China's civilian bureaucracy on how to improve China's ability to handle domestic crises. With regard to natural disasters, public management specialists argue that military mobilization is very inefficient and that China should learn from organizations such as FEMA and also learn to incorporate NGOs and benefit more from their targeted, specialized expertise. I would like to thank Elizabeth W. Hague for bringing this to my attention.

CHAPTER 7

CHINESE SEA POWER IN ACTION: THE COUNTERPIRACY MISSION IN THE GULF OF ADEN AND BEYOND

Andrew S. Erickson*

The dramatic rise of piracy in the waters off of Somalia in 2008, combined with United Nations Security Council (UNSC) resolutions designed to empower other nations to fight that piracy, presented the Chinese with an historic opportunity to deploy a naval force to the Gulf of Aden. This chapter offers an assessment of the PLA Navy's (PLAN) mission and its implications. Emphasis is placed on the motivations and preparations for the mission; relevant operational details, including rules of engagement, equipment, personnel, and logistic support; degree of coordination with other militaries; domestic and international responses to the mission; and indications of the PLA's own assessment of its achievements regarding the deployment. The chapter then uses this case study to probe broader implications for the PLAN's role in defending China's expanding economic interests;

* The views expressed here are solely those of the author and in no way represent the official policies or estimates of the U.S. Navy or any other organization of the U.S. Government. He thanks Daniel Alderman for his helpful research assistance; James Lewis for sharing valuable research on replenishment; Nan Li for suggesting sources and offering important guidance concerning organizational and civil-military issues; William Murray for explanations of surface vessel capabilities; and Bernard Cole, Gabriel Collins, Edward Fiorentino, M. Taylor Fravel, Lyle Goldstein, Jesse Karotkin, Daniel Kostecka, David Polatty, Kathleen Walsh, and Christopher Weuve for their useful comments on earlier versions of this and related papers. It draws on previous work of the author's, including that copublished with Michael Chase, Lyle Goldstein, and Justin Mikolay. A preliminary partial version of the present argument was published earlier as Andrew Erickson and Justin Mikolay, "Welcome China to the Fight Against Pirates," U.S. Naval Institute *Proceedings*, Vol. 135, No. 3, March 2009, pp. 34-41.

its prospects for future participation in the global maritime regime; and associated implications for U.S. policy.[1]

UNCHARTED WATERS

For the first time in its modern history, China has deployed naval forces operationally (as opposed to representationally) beyond its immediate maritime periphery to protect merchant vessels from pirates in the Gulf of Aden.[2] Supported by a supply ship, two PLAN vessels are escorting ships from China and other nations; the 1,000th was escorted on October 24, 2009.[3] A week later, China's navy began the fourth deployment. What explains this unprecedented instance of long-distance, sustained operations?

MOTIVATIONS

Growing Sea Lines of Communication Security Imperatives.

China's leadership has identified the security of China's seaborne imports and exports as critical to the nation's overall development, and hence a vital and growing mission for the PLAN. The last two of the four "new historic missions" (新的历史使命) with which President Hu Jintao charged the People's Liberation Army (PLA) in 2004 reflect new emphases, and the fourth is unprecedented; all but the first may be furthered by naval development,[4] provided that the operation is UN-led, multilateral, and targeted at nontraditional threats.[5] Hu has also stated specifically: "As we strengthen our ability to fight and win limited wars under informatized conditions, we have to pay even more attention to improving non-combat military operations capabilities."[6] In an attempt to transform Hu's general guidance into more specific policy, articles in state and military news media have argued that to safeguard China's economic growth, the PLA must go beyond its previous mission of safeguarding national "survival interests" (生存利益) to protecting national "development interests" (发展利益).[7] High level PLAN officers are now conducting sophisticated analysis of the "nonwar military operations" needed to promote these interests.[8]

This guidance and policy implementation is informed by clear economic realities — themselves of particular importance for a leadership that has staked its political legitimacy on maintaining roughly 8 percent growth of an economy that remains reliant on extremely high levels of resource imports and manufactured goods exports. China depends on maritime transportation for 90 percent of its imports and exports. By some metrics, China has more seafarers, deep sea fleets, and ocean fishing vessels than any other nation.[9] As of 2006, maritime industries accounted for $270 billion in economic output (nearly 10 percent of gross domestic product [GDP]).[10] Already at least tied with South Korea for status as the world's largest shipbuilder, China aims to become the largest by 2015.[11] Chinese oil demand, growing rapidly, has reached 8.5 million barrels per day (mbtd) even amid the global recession.[12] China became a net oil importer in 1993, and will likely become a net gasoline importer by the end of 2009. While still a very significant oil producer, China now imports half of its crude oil, with 4.6 mbpd in imports as of July 2009. Seaborne imports, which even ambitious overland pipeline projects lack the capacity to reduce, constitute more than 80 percent of this total.[13] At present, therefore, 40 percent of China's oil comes by sea.

Why Beijing Had to Act.

Security of the sea lines of communication (SLOC) around the Horn of Africa is especially critical to major Chinese economic interests. China imports 16 percent of its overall energy (including one-third of its oil), as well as numerous strategic resources critical to manufacturing, from Africa. China is the European Union's (EU) second largest trading partner, the EU is China's largest, and much of their trade transits the Red Sea and Indian Ocean via container ship. Of the vessels transiting the Indian Ocean, 40 percent are Chinese.[14] Some of China's 2,000 distant water fishing vessels, subsidized by Beijing, balance East Asia's dwindling fish stocks by exploiting the more numerous ones off the Horn of Africa.[15]

Perhaps nothing exemplified this vulnerability and Beijing's inability to address it more directly than two incidents at the end of 2008.[16] On November 14, Somali pirates captured the fishing boat *Tianyu 8* and held its 24-member crew captive for 3 months.[17] On December 17, nine men attempted to pirate the tanker *Zhenhua 4*, using makeshift rocket-launchers and AK-47 assault rifles. An otherwise defenseless crew unnerved the pirates with improvised Molotov cocktails,[18] but it was a Malaysian military helicopter that compelled the attackers to retreat.[19] All told, a fifth of the 1,265 Chinese -owned, -cargoed, or –crewed ships transiting Somali waters in 2008 faced piracy, and seven were attacked.[20] This was part of a growing international problem that showed no sign of abating: of the 100 attempted piracies in 2008, 40 were successful, including the capture and detention of the VLCC *Sirius Star*.[21]

Official Explanations. China's government portrayed its decision to deploy naval vessels as a responsible solution to an unexpected but tangible challenge to its sovereignty, security, and commerce.[22] "Piracy has become a serious threat to shipping, trade, and safety on the seas," Foreign Ministry spokesman Liu Jianchao explained. "That's why we decided to send naval ships to crack down."[23] This was part of a carefully-orchestrated campaign. Various Chinese strategists floated "trial balloons" in the news media in mid-December, giving the government a chance to gauge possible international reactions.[24] As part of a larger effort to increase foreign perceptions of Chinese transparency, the Ministry of National Defense Information Office (MNDIO), conceived in late 2007 and active from January 8, 2008, plays new role both at home and abroad in interfacing with the outside world and consolidating public consensus.[25]

On December 17, 2008, MNDIO office director and chief spokesman Senior Colonel Hu Changming told the *Financial Times* that "China would likely deploy warships to the Gulf of Aden." On December 20, he stated officially that three vessels would depart in a week's time. Then, on December 23, Senior Colonel Huang Xueping, MND Secondary Spokesman and MNDIO Deputy Director, convened a news conference at MNDIO's News Release Office.[26] There he and two other PLA representatives stressed that the primary goal of the mission—to safeguard Chinese shipping—represented neither a shift in noninterventionist foreign policy nor a commitment to further blue-water operations. In the words of the director of the Operations Department at PLAN Headquarters, China wants to protect "ships of international organizations [such as the UN World Food Program] that are carrying humanitarian supplies to Somalia."[27] This allows China to shift from being the only permanent member of the UNSC not to have contributed to international maritime security operations toward becoming a responsible power that makes all types of contributions.[28] Of course, as repeated Chinese statements underscore, the central purpose of the mission is to escort Chinese ships. As criminal law researcher Huang Li, who has published one of the few Chinese books available thus far on the deployment, emphasizes, "sending warships on an escort mission is one's own business, as the country which joins the escort operation is the boss of its own. This is a transition of status from the employee to the boss."[29]

Unofficial Explanations. The above rationales are accurate, but incomplete. First, all easier options had been exhausted. Second, Beijing was under mounting popular pressure to act. Third, deploying naval vessels offered a politically-safe opportunity to do what many decisionmakers likely regarded as a logical next step in China's military development.

The heart of the matter was lack of further options to solve the piracy problem indirectly. According to Huang Li, "It took nearly a whole year to find a solution to this problem."[30] Unable to afford high private security fees, Chinese ships had started to detour around the Cape of Good Hope, raising shipping rates and risking the loss of market share if Chinese merchant ships broke contracts.[31] This, in turn, risked making China's government look ineffectual. Preoccupied with the May 12, 2008, Wenchuan Earthquake and the August 2008 Olympics,[32] Beijing tried a variety of alternatives to muddle through, but all failed; hence its pursuit of a unilateral approach under a multilateral aegis.

China's 3 decades of involvement in international organizations and a decade of increased military spending present a double-edged sword: They offer more options for safeguarding Chinese interests, but raise expectations among the public at home, and policymakers abroad. China's leadership was undoubtedly concerned about retaining legitimacy in the eyes of its citizens, some of whom expressed in Internet postings increasing frustration at governmental inability to protect Chinese shipping.[33] Reportedly, in mid-October, the PLAN "launched a feasibility study of an operation 'to send troops to Somalia on an escort mission',"and in mid-November, the PLA General Staff Department initiated a related study.[34] Unusually rapid and effective interagency coordination between China's Ministry of Transportation, Ministry of Foreign Affairs, and Navy (following an initial meeting between the first two in mid-October 2008) succeeded in laying the groundwork for the counterpiracy deployment;[35] these agencies and the Ministry of Commerce reportedly held a joint symposium on December 2.[36] Meanwhile, on November 15, 261 students of four PLAN academies aboard the training vessel *Zheng He* participated in an anti-piracy exercise in Southeast Asia. On December 4, Major General Jin Yinan, director of the National Defense University's Institute for Strategic Studies, advocated PLAN participation to "gain experience" both in "fighting piracy" and "carrying out ocean-going quasi-combat missions."[37]

Although its decisionmaking process appears to be long term and gradual, China's State Council and Central Military Commission (CMC) likely approved the Aden mission in part to exercise the PLAN's growing naval capability. "Apart from fighting pirates, another key goal is to register the presence of the Chinese navy," states Senior Captain Li Jie, a prominent expert at the Navy Military Studies Research Institute in Beijing. His institute, the PLAN's strategic think tank,[38] and the PLAN more generally,[39] had earlier analyzed relevant maritime legal issues and found nothing to prevent such a mission. The relatively limited U.S. response to piracy in the Horn of Africa arguably offered China a particularly useful strategic opportunity in this regard. As Huang Li put it, "to achieve 'peaceful' entry into the Indian Ocean, we need[ed] a legitimate cause so that other people could not criticize [us]."[40]

RELEVANT OPERATIONAL DETAILS

Platform Capabilities.

On December 26, 2008, China deployed two South Sea Fleet destroyers—*Wuhan* (DDG-169 052B Luyang) and *Haikou* (DDG-171 Type 052C Luyang-II)—and the supply ship *Weishanhu* (#887 Qiandaohu/Fuchi class) 10,000 kilometers (km) from their homeport in Sanya, Hainan Province. After about 3 months, the destroyer *Shenzhen* and the frigate *Huangshan* were dispatched to replace them, while the supply ship *Weishanhu* remained on station. This second escort fleet conducted operations for about 112 days before being relieved by a third escort fleet composed of the frigates *Zhoushan* and *Xuzhou* and another supply ship, *Qiandaohu*. Three months later, frigates *Ma'anshan* and *Wenzhou* relieved their predecessors and joined *Qiandaohu* in the Gulf of Aden. On March 4, 2010, missile destroyer *Guangzhou* and supply ship *Weishanhu* left Sanya to join missile frigate *Chaohu* in a fifth task force.

The PLAN chose some of its newest, most advanced (and indigenously constructed) vessels and most distinguished, experienced officers and crew to carry out this mission. This suggests that it is serious about using this opportunity to test some of its foremost systems and gain modern seafaring experience. For the first two deployments, the PLAN selected vessels from the South Sea Fleet, closest to the theater of operations. The next two deployments have come from the East Sea Fleet, which suggests a broader effort to expose as many units as possible to new experiences. Beijing reportedly sent large, impressive vessels for four reasons: to withstand difficult sea states, to compensate for lack of overseas military bases, to preclude a "mistaken bombing" of China's assets à la that of its Embassy in Belgrade in 1999, and to preempt perceptions of subsequent deployment escalation if it had to send major vessels in the future.[41]

Consider the first deployment. The flagship *Wuhan*, and even the newer *Haikou* (constructed in 2003), were never previously dispatched this far. Each displace 7,000 tons, have a maximum speed of 30 knots, and can carry a helicopter for patrol and surveillance.[42] For this mission, both ships embarked a Ka-28 *Helix* from the East Sea Fleet,[43] and piloted them with senior colonels with several thousand hours of flight experience.[44] The selection of East Sea Fleet helicopters to accompany warships from the South Sea Fleet on the initial rotation of the anti-piracy mission was likely due to the fact that the *Helix* is superior platform to the Chinese built Z-9.[45] *Wuhan* boasts anti-ship and surface-to-air missiles and a close-in weapon system. *Haikou*'s first generation phased-array radar and vertically launched long-range air defense missile system offer the fleet area air defense previously unavailable to the PLAN. Additionally, the 052B class destroyers (168 and 169) are outfitted to serve as task group command ships; *Wuhan*, though less advanced, reportedly served as the task group flagship because of its "operational tasks" and "arrangement of equipment."[46]

The 23,000-ton *Fuchi*-class *Weishanhu*, China's largest supply ship and one of its three newest, has a maximum speed of 19 knots, can carry two helicopters, is armed with eight 37 mm guns, and carries 130 crew members. It was China's most experienced replenishment ship, having participated in Sino-British Friendship 2007 exercise near the English Channel and Sino-French Friendship 2007 exercise in the Mediterranean.[47] Table 1 provides further details for vessels deployed in the first four task forces.

Vessel	Hull #	Class	Type	Displacement (tons)	Builder	Laid Down	Launched	Commissioned	Home Port
Wuhan	169	Luyang I (052B)	destroyer	7,000	Jiangnan Shipyard, Shanghai	2001	September 9, 2002	July 18, 2004	Sanya, SSF
Haikou	171	Luyang-II (052C)	destroyer	7,000	Jiangnan Shipyard, Shanghai	November 2002	October 23, 2003	July 20, 2005	Sanya, SSF
Shenzhen	167	Luhai (051B)	destroyer	6,100	Dalian Shipyard	July 1996	October 16, 1997	January 4, 1999	Sanya, SSF
Huangshan	570	Jiangkai II (054A)	frigate	3,900	Huangpu Shipyard, Guangzhou	2006	March 18, 2007	2008	Sanya, SSF
Zhoushan	529	Jiangkai II (054A)	frigate	3,900	Hudong-Zhonghua Shipyard, Shanghai	2006	December 21, 2006	2008	Zhoushan, ESF
Xuzhou	530	Jiangkai II (054A)	frigate	3,900	Huangpu Shipyard, Guangzhou	2005	September 30, 2006	January 29, 2008	Zhoushan, ESF
Ma'anshan	525	Jiangkai I (054)	frigate	4,053	Hudong-Zhongua Shipyard, Shanghai	Late 2002	September 11, 2003	February 18, 2005	Zhoushan, ESF
Wenzhou	526	Jiangkai I (054)	frigate	4,053	Hudong-Zhongua Shipyard, Shanghai	N/A	30 November 2003	26 September 2006	Zhoushan, ESF
Weishanhu	887	Fuchi	replenishment	23,000	Huangpu Shipyard, Guangzhou	N/A	July 1, 2003	April 2004	Sanya, SSF
Qiandaohu	886	Fuchi	replenishment	23,000	Hudong-Zhongua Shipyard, Shanghai	N/A	March 2003	April 2004	Zhoushan, ESF

Table 1: Vessels Deployed in the First Four Task Forces.[48]

305

Rules of Engagement.

Following the careful interagency coordination and PLAN legal preparations noted above, Beijing has reaffirmed the practical reasons for the deployment, and stressed that China has explicit UN authorization for its presence in the region. The UN Convention on the Law of the Sea of December 10, 1982, provides specific legal authority for the international effort to fight piracy outside a coastal state's territorial sea. The Security Council, necessarily with Beijing's support, has passed four relevant resolutions under Chapter VII of the UN Charter (authorizing states to take "all necessary measures"): 1816, 1838, 1846 (on December 2, 2008), and 1851 (on December 16).[49] Affirmed under that umbrella, UNSC resolution 1846 authorizes participating states to engage pirates within the 12-nautical mile territorial waters off the coast of Somalia.[50]

Resolution 1851, passed unanimously by the UNSC, authorizes international navies to pursue pirates from the Gulf of Aden to the shores of Somalia and—if conditions warrant—to engage in related activities "in Somalia" itself.[51] Beijing also voted in favor of Resolution 1816, which authorizes members of the international community to "enter the territorial waters of Somalia for the purpose of repressing acts of piracy and armed robbery at sea."[52] But China's government, having obtained from Mogadishu's ambassador to China, Ahmed Awil, a specific request to participate,[53] emphasized that international assistance "should be based on the wishes of the [Somali] Government and be applied only to the territorial waters of Somalia."[54] To build on this somewhat exceptional sense of legitimacy with Chinese characteristics, Beijing's official news media constantly publishes appreciation from Somali officials and civilians.[55]

The PLAN itself has pledged a cautious, reactive approach limited to defense of its ships and any vessels under their escort. The explicit objective is to escort Chinese vessels (and those of other nations on a case-by-case basis) and thus deter pirates from attacking them in the first place, not to actively search for pirates and engage in combat with them. PLAN forces will not even "take the initiative to search for captured vessels and personnel at sea and carry out armed rescues."[56]

Moreover, according to Senior Colonel Ma Luping, director of the navy operational bureau under the headquarters of the General Staff, PLAN forces will not normally enter another nation's national territorial seas (within the internationally recognized 12 nautical-miles limit) to chase pirates.[57] At a press conference accompanying the departure of the Chinese destroyer contingent on December 26, 2008, the high-ranking lead commander of the first deployment, South Sea Fleet Chief of Staff Rear Admiral Du Jingcheng, said the ships would "independently conduct escort missions" and not land on Somali shores.[58] According to a senior Chinese military official: "For us to use force is a very complex matter . . . it is not just a simple question based on an operational requirement. . . . There are political questions — and these are not issues dealt with by military commanders alone. Our warships off Somalia are very well aware of this. We are fully prepared to use force, but we do not take that step lightly."[59] It thus seems clear that China wants to avoid using force in another nation's land or territorial sea[60] to avoid setting a precedent that might later be used against it. Huang Li emphasizes that, according to

307

Article 107 of UNCLOS, "warships, military aircraft, or other aircraft or vessels carrying clear markings of service for a government may pursue, attack, and detain all pirate ships. . . ."[61] However, there have not been any signs yet that the PLAN is permitted even to board and inspect suspicious ships. Beyond basic escort duties, PLAN vessels have pursued two of the following three modes of emergency operation:

1. *On-call support*: "Rapid and flexible actions" that the task force takes after receiving a request for support from vessels passing through high-risk zones or anticipating pirate attacks. If the PLAN detects a "suspicious vessel," it will deploy a helicopter for surveillance and reconnaissance. Only after that will the Chinese ship(s) approach the vessel in question.

2. *Pirate deterrence*: After the fleet receives emergency rescue signals from vessels under attack but not yet controlled by pirates, PLAN platforms take air and sea deterrence measures. This typically entails helicopter deployment—with potential for engagement, at least in theory. It can also involve having a PLAN vessel approach the pirates, if available and close enough to arrive in time. In the event that pirates are seizing a ship and the PLAN vessels are close enough to stop it, the fleet commander will give orders based on his evaluation of the situation.

3. *Vessel rescue*: sustained pressure and rescue actions that the fleet takes when it receives calls for help or instructions that pirates have seized vessels. In the unlikely event that pirates attack, the PLAN ships with their overwhelming firepower—which they practice regularly at sea—will engage in "self-defense." Underscoring this defensive posture to an extreme, Chinese Rear Admiral Xiao Xinnian stressed: "[If] our naval vessels are ambushed by pirate ships, we will resolutely fight back to protect our own safety."[62]

These very cautious rules of engagement (ROE) suggest that Beijing wants to support the efforts of the UN, but does not want to have its forces subordinate to (or appear subordinate to) those of any other nation; that it wishes to avoid political and legal issues associated with engaging pirates directly if possible; and that it probably wishes to avoid capturing them for fear of the responsibility involved, the lack of viable legal options, and the possibility of negative political ramifications internationally, particularly in the Muslim world. Huang Li adds that killing pirates could lead to harming of crew members and targeting of Chinese vessels for revenge, neither of which is currently a problem.[63] To the extent that Beijing takes risks in any of these areas, it would almost certainly be to defend crewmembers of a Chinese vessel in the absence of other options.

Deployment, Operations, and ROE Employment.

The PLAN offers three methods of protection against pirates: "area patrol," "accompanying escort," and "on-ship protection." Area patrol, the method least-used (at least as a discrete approach), involves monitoring relevant zones. PLAN has maintained two rendezvous points 550 nautical miles apart, at 100 nautical miles north of Yemen's Socotra Island and 75 nautical miles southwest of Port Aden, and seven patrol zones along the main shipping route in the sea area east of the Gulf of Aden.[64]

Accompanying escort, in which PLAN ships travel next to or near groups of commercial vessels, is by far the most-used method. Through the China Ship Owners' Association, Beijing now accepts applications from ship owners in mainland China, Hong Kong, Macau, and Taiwan for the PLAN to escort their vulnerable ships through the Gulf of Aden.[65] Foreign ships may apply on a case-by-case basis. The Ministry of Transportation (MoT), which is subordinate to the State Council, processes the applications, determines ship-specific requirements, and suggests a method of escort to the PLAN. After the PLAN determines the proper plan, the MoT then guides the ships to be escorted to the predetermined location where they are to meet the relevant PLAN vessel(s).[66]

China has already escorted a wide variety of Chinese, and even some foreign, ships in an area west of longitude 57 degrees east and south of latitude 15 degrees north.[67] Even in the first deployment, *Wuhan* and *Haikou* worked around the clock and could escort multiple ships simultaneously in opposite directions.[68]

In response to initial problems with commercial ships not adhering to the details of escort procedures during the first month, the PLAN now offers pre-scheduled group escorts. Starting after the 2009 Spring Festival, escort was offered based on marine traffic conditions, as determined by PLAN and MoT research. Now this has become routinized, like a train schedule. Announcements posted on the China Ship Owners' Association's website before the 15th of each month announce "fixed escort times" (e.g., weekly) and merchant ships must make arrangements accordingly.[69] The PLAN must be notified a week in advance regarding ships which are slower than 10 knots/hour or have other special requirements.[70]

The configuration of the escort formation is generally determined by the number of merchant ships to be escorted. They are divided into one or two columns, organized to facilitate communication, and separated at a standard distance. For single-column escort, the

PLAN warship(s) will maintain similar speed and course from a position outside the column. For double-column escort, a single warship would operate on the inside, whereas two warships would each take one side. Occasionally one ship will be relieved by another coming in the opposite direction, as in a "relay race." Escort columns can incorporate more than a dozen ships and extend over a dozen km.

To save fuel and wear and tear on PLAN vessels on routes that are less traveled, with ships that travel fast enough to better evade pirates, the PLAN relies on embarked special forces and helicopter operations. On-ship protection involves stationing special forces personnel on one or more vessels in a group of civilian ships. Here the PLAN draws on its 70-90 highly trained Marine Corps Special Operations Forces. Building on earlier land-based training, during transit to the Gulf of Aden, members of a special force unit aboard the warships carry out anti-piracy training with a ship-borne helicopter, from which they rappel onto the deck to simulate landing on hijacked or pirate vessels. The helicopters also practice nighttime landing operations at sea, a new area for the PLAN.

The special forces are sufficient to protect at least 7 convoys of merchant ships. The typical procedure is to use helicopters to embark 5-7 special forces on the first and last ships of a convoy. With a range of up to 2,000 meters, their deck-mounted grenade launchers enable them to destroy pirate boats before the pirates could threaten them. They are also equipped with a variety of shorter range weapons, including Type-56 assault rifles, QBZ-95 automatic rifles, and QBU-88 sniper rifles, as well as infrared night-vision equipment. In emergencies, civilian crewmembers may be allowed to use some of the weapons.[71]

ENCOUNTERS WITH PIRATES

While the PLAN has sought to minimize contact with pirates during all three types of operations, it has encountered, and demonstrably deterred them, on several occasions. Of all PLAN platforms, helicopters have made the closest and most numerous encounters. On January 18, 2009, *Tianhe*, a vessel owned by China Ocean Shipping Company (COSCO), radioed to *Wuhan* that two speedboats were chasing it and — following suspicious communications breakup — requested immediate assistance. Task Group commander Admiral Du Jingcheng ordered the ships to assume battle formation, with helicopters readied. *Wuhan* approached the speedboats, chasing them away. The fleet received a similar distress call earlier that day from a mainland cargo ship, which evaded speedboats without needing PLAN assistance.[72] On February 6, seven embarked special operations forces organized crew members of *Oriental Oil Explorer 1* against an oncoming pirate speedboat, fired three warning shells, and prepared to fight when the speedboat, deterred, sped away.[73] On February 24, *Lia*, a Liberia-flagged Italian merchant ship, had to leave a *Haikou*-escorted formation to repair an engine. Almost immediately, in response to two rapidly-approaching speedboats, it requested help from *Haikou*. *Haikou* dispatched a helicopter with three special forces and a photographer. The helicopter fended off the speedboats by circling and firing two signal flares at each of them.[74] A similar procedure, this time using *Huangshan* as well, was used on July 13 to protect Liberian oil tanker, *A. Elephant*, and Maltese merchant ship, *Polyhronis*.[75] On August 6, *Zhoushan* "expelled several suspected pirate ships and guarded the Chinese merchant ship *Zhenhua 25*."[76] A further helicopter deterrent mission on November 12 also succeeded, even though pirates had already fired and attempted to board COSCO vessel *Fuqiang*, injuring two of its crew in the process.[77]

THE DEXINHAI INCIDENT: LOGICAL RESULT, OR EVIDENCE OF ONGOING LIMITATIONS?

A dramatic incident has called into question the extent to which Beijing can, and will, use naval means to safeguard civilian ships. *Dexinhai*, a Chinese-flagged bulk carrier which had failed to register according to Chinese procedures, was pirated 700 NM east of Somalia on October 19, 2009. Early rumors that *Zhoushan* and *Xuzhou* were steaming to its rescue[78] gave way to reports that as of November, *Dexinhai* and its 25 crew members were trapped in the pirate stronghold of Hobyo on the central Somali coast. Liang Wei, South Sea Fleet deputy chief of operations, reportedly explained that *Zhoushan* and *Xuzhou* had been too far away (over 1,000 nautical miles, according to another source)[79] to reach the pirates during the 3 days they piloted *Dexinhai* to shore. Apparently, the PLAN did convene an emergency meeting on October 21.[80] Fudan University professor Zhang Jiadong predicted that because the priority is to save lives, not fight pirates, China would establish communications with Somali government and warlords; approach the site with naval ships for deterrence and control; and pay the pirates to release the hostages.[81]

China's official press seemed to convey a sense of relief when *Dexinhai* entered Somalia's territorial waters because it provided a rationale for inaction. While UNSCR 1846 and 1851 authorize operations within Somalia's territory to include land, waters, and airspace, they were passed by the Security Council unanimously. This highlights the cautious approach that Beijing is taking although to be fair to the Chinese, other nations are taking a fairly conservative approach as well. Anthony Wong Dong, president of the International Military Association in Macau, offers an additional Chinese consideration: "If Beijing fails to save the Chinese crew, it will set a bad example for Chinese laborers who are working in energy-rich countries."[82] Huang Li adds more generally that China's deployments are "conducted under the watchful eyes of the whole world and any small error will be magnified over a hundred times . . . it will be an irretrievable loss if one hostage is injured or dead."[83] One Chinese analyst sees the incident as revealing not just political caution *per se* but also deficiencies in Chinese ISR, force scale, quick response, and calls for more robust "far seas presence," as well as overseas bases.[84]

Chinese Shipowners' Association secretary general Zhang Zuyue has reported that Chinese representatives were engaged in secret negotiations with the pirates.[85] Meanwhile, the Chinese task force "enhanced helicopter patrols, observation, lookout, guard, and patrols by small boats."[86] On December 28, 2009, *Dexinhai* and its crew were released after a reported $4 million ransom payment. While this caution is understandable, Beijing's apparent pursuit of a separate peace with pirates — without seeking publicly to confer with other maritime stakeholders — risks leaving other vessels worse off.

EQUIPMENT, PERSONNEL, AND LOGISTICS SUPPORT

At-Sea Replenishment.

In what might be considered the linchpin of the entire mission, the PLAN handled the logistics and supply requirements associated with the counterpiracy deployments through a combination of underway replenishment and port visits (see Table 2).

Port	Date	Vessel	Vessel Type	Purpose/Details
Port Aden, Yemen	February 24, 2009	*Weishanhu*	replenishment	replenishment
	April 25, 2009	*Weishanhu*	replenishment	replenishment
	July 23, 2009	*Weishanhu*	replenishment	replenishment
Port Salalah, Oman	June 21- July 1 2009	*Shenzhen*	destroyer	rest and replenishment
	June 21- July 1 2009	*Huangshan*	frigate	rest and replenishment
	June 21- July 1 2009	*Weishanhu*	replenishment	replenishment
	mid-August 2009	*Zhoushan*	frigate	rest and replenishment
	mid-August 2009	*Xuzhou*	frigate	rest and replenishment
	mid-August 2009	*Qiandaohu*	replenishment	rest and replenishment
Kochi, India	August 2009	*Shenzhen*	destroyer	good will; four-day visit
Karachi, Pakistan	August 5-7, 2009	*Huangshan*	frigate	three-day visit; joint exercises
Karachi, Pakistan	August 5-7, 2009	*Weishanhu*	replenishment	three-day visit; joint exercises

Table 2. Port Visits through August 2009.

First Deployment: Three PLAN vessels (*Wuhan*[87] and *Haikou*[88] destroyers and the replenishment vessel, *Weishanhu*[89]), commanded by Rear Admiral Du Jingchen and his deputy Rear Admiral Yin Dunping,[90] departed Sanya on December 26, 2008, and arrived in waters off of Somalia on January 6, 2009. On December 30, 2008, transiting the Strait of Malacca, *Weishanhu* performed its first at-sea replenishment.[91] *Wuhan* and *Haikou* spent 124 days at sea before returning on April 28 but did not make any port visits. *Weishanhu* made two brief replenishment stops at Port Aden, Yemen (February 24 and April 25).

Second Deployment: In April 2009, a destroyer and a frigate (*Shenzhen* and *Huangshan*), under the command of Rear Admiral Yao Zhilou, replaced the first two combatants. They conducted separate rest and replenishment port visits at Port Salalah, Oman, between June 21 and July 1, 2009. Resupply vessel *Weishanhu* made one more replenishment stop at Port Aden on July 23, as well as rotating Rest and Repenishment port visits to Port Salalah, Oman, between June 21 and July 1. Rotation ensured that five groups of 54 merchant ships were escorted during this time. This first ever shore rest for crew involved with the anti-piracy missions entailed group shopping and sightseeing and recreational activities with civilians.[92] On its way home in August, *Shenzhen* conducted a 4-day port visit in Kochi, India. The crew visited the Southern Naval Command's training facilities and interacted with their Indian counterparts.[93] Concurrently, *Huangshan* and *Weishanhu* visited Karachi, Pakistan, on August 5-7, 2009, to engage in joint exercises with Pakistan's navy simulating a variety of combat situations.[94] The task force returned to its home port on August 21.[95]

Third Deployment: Combatants *Zhoushan* and *Xuzhou*, along with replenishment vessel *Qiandaohu*, left Zhoushan, Zhejiang Province on the morning of July 16, 2009, under ESF deputy commander Wang Zhiguo.[96] They relieved the second trio on August 1.[97] All three vessels made alternating Rest and Replenishment port visits to Port Salalah, Oman, in mid-August.[98] Like *Weishanhu*, *Qiandaohu* has significant medical facilities.[99]

Fourth Deployment: On October 30, 2009, missile frigates *Ma'anshan* and *Wenzhou* left Zhoushan under the command of the East Sea Fleet Deputy Chief of Staff Qiu Yuanpeng to join replenishment vessel *Qiandaohu* in the Gulf of Aden. The task force has two helicopters and a crew of more than 700, including a special forces unit.[100]

The initial destroyer deployment made PLAN history in numerous ways. It was:

- The first time multiple naval service arms, including surface vessels, seaborne aircraft, and special forces, were organized to cross the ocean and execute operational tasks;
- The first long-term ocean task execution that did not include port calls throughout its entire course, breaking records in continuous time underway and sailing distance of a PLAN vessel formation and in flight sorties and flight time of seaborne helicopters;
- The first execution of escort tasks with the navies of multiple countries in the same sea area and holding of shipboard exchanges and information cooperation;
- The first sustained, high-intensity organization of logistical and equipment support in unfamiliar seas far from coastal bases, accumulating comprehensive ocean support experience;
- The first organization of base-oriented logistical support using commercial methods in a foreign port;
- The first time civilian vessels delivered replenishment materials for a distant sea formation;
- The first all-dimensional examination of multiple replenishment methods, including un-

derway, alongside connected, helicopter, and small vessel replenishment;

- The first long-range video transmission of medical consultations and humanitarian assistance such as medical care for casualties from other vessels conducted on the ocean.
- In addition to these, this first escort formation set a record of 61 days for the longest sustained support of a formation at sea, without calling at port for replenishment, and also set a record for the longest number of days of sustained support of a combatant vessel at sea without calling at port.[101]

The most significant sign from the Gulf of Aden mission is that the PLAN was able to keep the ships underway and steaming for this length of time.[102] Previously, PLAN ships transiting to the AMAN-07 and AMAN-09 exercises had refueled in Colombo, Sri Lanka, but China had little other experience on which to draw. As of November 2009, however, the replenishment vessels have been able to supply food and water, as well as ammunition, on smooth and even somewhat choppy seas. Fuel and spare parts are supplied both in this manner and via port calls; the latter is true for personnel rotation.[103]

Little information is available on maintenance and repairs, which are essential on a taxing mission of this duration. The situation appears to be far better than that during the 2002 global circumnavigation, when German technicians had to be flown in to repair imported MTU diesel engines on the Type 052 destroyer *Qingdao* (DDG 113);[104] this time, the PLAN even helped a civilian vessel fix its own engine problems. According to Senior Colonel Xie Dongpei, deputy director of the PLAN headquarters general office, vessels deployed for anti-piracy operations would go to Karachi, Pakistan, for major repairs if needed.[105]

Replenishment progress builds on China's developing combined civilian-military logistics system.[106] Here, China's commercial sector is already a tremendous asset. Two of China's top shipping companies, China Shipping Development and China Ocean Shipping (Group) Company (COSCO), have established several logistics-based joint operations with power and mining companies in China.[107] China Ocean Shipping and China Shipping Container Lines have also launched their own logistics operations, which support their mainstream shipping ventures. The West Asia division of COSCO Logistics, which has been rated China's biggest logistics firm in revenue terms 5 years running, has played a major role in supporting the current missions.[108] Smaller companies such as Nanjing Yuansheng Shipping Co. Ltd. have also been used.[109]

Satellite Tracking and Communications.

Unprecedented and innovative use of satellite communications has been a major highlight of China's deployment. While the United States and most Western (as well as the former Soviet) navies have engaged in related operations for years, this is a new and important step for the PLAN. Satellite communications has played some role in previous counterpiracy efforts. According to Director-General Ju Chengzhi, International Cooperation Department, MoT, on December 17, 2008, the captain of fishing vessel *Zhenhua 4* requested the MoT's Maritime Search and Rescue Center's assistance via maritime satellite. There, the rear command team directed *Zhenhua 4* to engage in self-defense, then secured the assistance of Malaysian warships via the International Maritime Bureau's anti-piracy center.[110] However, there has also been concern that unsecure communication via maritime satellite in the past meant that "secrets were divulged in PLA exercises"; subsequent use of the *Beidou* navigation satellite system's "short messaging" and "time service and position locating functions" has "solved the problem of secrets being divulged in communication to a certain extent."[111]

Now, apparently for the first time, China is relying on its own capabilities from start to finish. From the first counterpiracy deployment, PLAN Control Center (海军指挥中心) and MoT's China Search and Rescue Center (中国海上搜救中心) track all relevant Chinese merchant ships, on which the MoT has installed devices to support a maritime satellite-based ship movement tracking system (船舶动态跟踪系统). Supported by freshly developed software, this permits "all-dimensional tracking (全方位跟踪)" and video-based communications "at all times."[112] Here Beijing's ability to locate PRC-flagged vessels clearly benefits from the China Ship Reporting (CHISREP) System, which requires "all Chinese-registered ships over 300 GT engaged in international routes" to report position daily to the PRC Shanghai Maritime Safety Administration.[113] At least one drill has been conducted, and MoT is confident that "sufficient preparations have been made."[114] Rear Admiral Yang Yi was paraphrased as saying that communications between ships of different nations should not be difficult: "Surface ships are visible and usually tracked to avoid collisions. They are sometimes monitored by both satellite and surveillance aircraft."[115]

The most dramatic innovations in satellite applications are in PLAN operations themselves. At a April 29 symposium to welcome the first deployment home, General Political Department Director and CMC member Li Jinai praised the PLAN for "active exploration of the new 'shore and ship integrated' political work mode." This has entailed shifting from transmission of political materials via "plain code telegraph" (明码电报) (a process that once took as long as an entire day during a month-long deployment) to more sophisticated satellite communications. The deployment witnessed many other firsts, including "a communication satellite [being] used to provide 24-hour coverage for the oceangoing formation . . . shipborne helicopters [being] used to provide surveillance on battlefield situations, and . . . the formation [being] connected to the Internet."[116] A web-based IP communication network was developed to allow crewmembers to call any land line or cell phone in mainland China.[117]

In 2002, the PLAN sent *Luhu*-class guided-missile destroyer *Qingdao* (#113) and composite supply ship *Taicang* (#575), and 506 crew members on a global circumnavigation. During their 132-days, 33,000 kilometers voyage, "the Navy utilized telecommunications technologies for the first time to send domestic and international news to the formation." The PLAN refers to this new information transmission method as "cross-ocean 'information supply'" ("跨越大洋的 '信息补给'").

For the December 2008 mission, Wu Shengli and Liu Xiaojiang, PLAN Commander and Political Commissar, demanded "comprehensive coverage, all-time linkage, and full-course support" (全面覆盖, 全时链接, 全程保障). The PLAN Political Department worked with the PLAN Headquarters Communications Department and the State Information Center to improve the "shore and ship integrated" political work platform that integrates a land base information collection and transmission system, an information integration and distribution system, a shore-to-ship information wireless transmission system, and an information terminal receiving system. They also sent technical personnel to Sanya to conduct satellite receiving equipment debugging, system installation, and personnel training on the three combat ships that were about to set sail for escort operations. Moreover, they specially developed and improved a total of seven information processing software programs, which can send text, images, as well as video and audio documents quickly.[118] PLAN vessels support command and coordination during escort missions by "releasing for use high-frequency Chinese and English channels," and maintain constant communication with escorted vessels "through emails and satellite faxes."[119]

Communicating more effectively at sea, in part by increasing reliance on space-based assets, appears to be a major step for the PLAN. This could allow a PLAN task force commander to act more independently of other navies in a tense political situation, in part by receiving clear real time directions from civilian authorities in Beijing.

Coordination with Other Militaries.

Most of the 14 nations that have sent ships to conduct counterpiracy operations in the Gulf of Aden region do so under five types of Combined Maritime Forces (CMF): two multi-national ones, and those from the North Atlantic Treaty Organization (NATO) and the EU, which coordinate with their multinational counterparts. Combined Task Force 151 (CTF-151) was established on January 8, 2009, under U.S. leadership, specifically to combat piracy in the Gulf of Aden.[120] The Commander of CTF-151, Rear Admiral Terry McKnight, has indicated that he will continue to recruit partner nations to expand the current 14-nation, 20-ship effort.[121] A separate German-led coalition of NATO and EU allies, along with other willing participants, conduct Maritime Security Operations in the region under the broader charter of CTF-150.

From the outset, Beijing has been "ready to exchange information and cooperate with the warships of other countries in fighting Somalian pirates," according to MNDIO deputy spokesman Huang Xueping.[122] Admiral Du Jingcheng, commander of the first deployment, said his forces would "not accept the command of other countries or regional organizations," but rather "facilitate exchanges of information with escort naval vessels from other countries."[123] There has been gradual increase in communications with vessels from the United States and over 20 other countries and several shipboard exchanges of commanding officers and CTF 151 staff.[124] Email exchanges have increased markedly over time, with over 300 exchanged with foreign vessels during the first deployment alone. The PLAN uses a Yahoo email account and "unclassified chat" on an instant messaging system.[125] Methods for sea and air coordination and intelligence sharing have been exchanged, with exchange of relevant videos and photos, as well as best practices on identifying and handling pirate vessels discussed.[126] According to a U.S. destroyer commanding officer in the Gulf of Aden: "[We] talk with the Chinese destroyers by VHF radio to coordinate search patterns and to exchange information on suspicious ships. [We] also have coordinated Chinese helicopter flight operations with the ScanEagle launches and recoveries. The exchanges are professional, routine and positive. . . ."[127] On September 10, 2009, China began its first ever joint global security action with Russia on the world stage. All three vessels from the PLAN's third deployment will work with Russian vessels similarly deployed. As part of joint Blue Peace Shield 2009 exercises, the two navies have conducted "tests of communications links, simulated missions to identify ships from helicopters, coordinated resupply efforts, and live firing of deck guns."[128]

CLOSER COOPERATION?

Despite shared goals, China—like India and Russia—has yet to join any of the multinational counter-piracy efforts.[129] Instead, starting in mid-October 2009, Beijing made an official proposal that waters around the Horn of Africa be apportioned into discrete zones in which participating nations exercised responsibility for security to better cover the unexpectedly broadening of Somali pirate attacks beyond the 60th meridian in the more dangerous waters to the south and east.[130] In November, China convened a conference to promote the proposal. Despite extremely positive overtures in Shared Awareness and Deconfliction (SHADE) meetings and other venues and optimistic expectations from EU officials and Commodore Tim Lowe, deputy commander, CTF-150, China appears to have "deftly parried appeals . . . to lead" existing CTF initiatives. At the same time, at least one Chinese analyst states that while China's proposal would reduce costs and increase effectiveness, relative gains concerns on the part of other nations may well prelude its implementation.[131]

So why is Beijing making this effort? Rear Admiral Yin Zhuo, director of a naval expert committee, explains that China lacks formal relations with NATO.[132] Closer cooperation "would involve the sharing of intelligence codes, which is a sensitive military and political issue."[133] There are several broader potential explanations for China's hesitation: lack of experience and preparation, sensitivity regarding sovereignty, and concerns about revealing Chinese capabilities (or lack thereof). For example, there appear to be some Chinese concerns that their vessels will be subject to scrutiny. Rear Admiral Yang Yi states that "some secretive reconnaissance does take place"; Sr. Captain Li Jie of the Naval Research Institute adds that "As long as all parties keep their activities to a minimum, military powers will not engage in disputes."[134]

The author is concerned that the "patrol zone" approach, if adopted, is unlikely to be effective. First, dividing the sea among different nations evokes a sort of "Cold War" mentality, just as post-war Germany was divided into different sectors that later led to a painful and prolonged national division. Second, some sea areas are much busier than others, so this would result in an inefficient distribution of forces. Third, some nations navies may be more capable and/or experienced than others, so there is a risk that some areas might be less-secured than others. This could be very difficult to solve, as it might be very difficult for any nation to acknowledge that its forces were not able to perform adequately. Fourth, such a "distributed unilateral" approach seems regrettable when there is sufficient support in the international community for a genuine "cooperative multilateral" approach.

For all these reasons, a far more effective approach would be to support the truly cooperative Combined Task Force-151. CTF-151 has been led by a Pakistani

Admiral, so it is a genuinely multilateral initiative. Unlike other approaches, CTF-151 offers the flexibility needed to combat pirates: it allows for deployment of assets to sea areas where they are most needed, and withdrawal of assets from areas where they are not needed. At least 10 of the 14 nations that have deployed vessels to fight piracy in the Gulf of Aden have participated in CTF 150 and/or CTF-151; this is the vast majority. Perhaps most importantly, it meets general principles for cooperation with the United States in multilateral frameworks, as outlined by Rear Admiral Yang Yi: "all activities should be strictly within the framework of U.N. authorization and consistent with international laws; the sovereignty and territory of other countries must be respected and the use of force in order to intervene in a country's affairs shall be avoided; the target of the activity should be nontraditional security threats . . .; efforts should be made to increase mutual understanding and promote deeper cooperation. . . ."[135] With all these advantages, such an approach is widely accepted and is worthy of careful consideration. The United States and other participating nations would certainly welcome the PLAN into CTF-151.

What, then, are the prospects for China joining CTF-151 or a related cooperative action? One academic and retired PLA officer suggested optimistically that the United States publicly invite China to join CTF-151.[136] But another individual of similar background was more measured in his assessment:

> China knows that the U.S. is willing to lead, and the PLAN is prepared operationally, but China is not ready politically. The overall political climate is not ready: there are still misunderstandings and mistrust resulting from many issues, especially Taiwan. Differences in po-

litical systems and ideology are at the very roots of the problem.[137]

This individual believed that "anti-piracy cooperation on the high seas should be separated" from these issues, but that there were still many "hardliners" who disagreed.[138] In Huang Li's view, if China joined CTF-151,

> the naval commander of China has the chance to be the commander of a few dozen warships from various countries, including those of the sea powers of the day. In this way, [he] will not only develop ability to direct the concerted actions of large-sized squadrons of many countries, but also gain the chance of directly communicating and cooperating with the U.S. Navy. Of course, when not serving as the commander of the combined force, we also need to accept the directions of others, and that may be something which we are most unwilling to do.[139]

REACTIONS TO THE MISSION

Responses to the mission both at home and abroad appear to have exceeded the expectations of China's leadership and analysts. For the PLA, for which these dimensions are intimately connected, this is particularly good news. As a party army, it must rely to an unusual degree on the support of both China's increasingly sophisticated and informed public — who have been disenchanted by the PLA's involvement in government corruption and crises since the 1980s — and its civilian leaders, who must grapple increasingly with how other nations view China's rapid military development even as they count on the PLA to safeguard their rule and defend the nation's security interests.[140]

International.

Surveying relevant academic and media sources, as well as interviews with Chinese interlocutors,[141] suggests that foreign responses to the missions were far more encouraging than many expected. One Chinese source does see a "China threat theory," and questions the need for warships to address the piracy issue.[142] But the vast majority of assessments are far more positive. Fudan University scholar Shen Dingli states that "China's 'harmonious diplomacy' has been well received by countries in the region."[143] According to a mainland-owned Hong Kong newspaper, "the current expedition by Chinese naval vessels to Somalia has not stoked the 'China threat theory' in the West; quite the contrary, China is being seen as a 're-sponsible global player'."[144] Two professors from Lanzhou University's Central Asia Studies Institute have categorized piracy, with terrorism, as collective evils that a great power like China must oppose.[145]

Domestic.

The Chinese public has expressed great pride in the missions' success. PLA analysts have seized on this precedent to call for relevance to other military operations. Many suggest that such missions should increase in the future, and that therefore better plat-form capabilities, and even improved access to over-seas port facilities, are needed. Major General Peng Guangqian (Ret.), who played a significant role in shaping PLA strategy as an adviser to China's pow-erful CMC and Politburo Standing Committee, states that deploying to Somalia will teach the PLAN how to interoperate with other navies.[146] Major General

Zhang Zhaoyin, deputy group army commander, Chengdu MR, argues that the PLA should use missions other than war to increase warfighting capabilities.[147]

PLA(N) Assessments.

On May 25-27, 2009 the PLAN used the occasion of the first group's return to convene a high-level conference to assess the mission. Admiral Wu Shengli, PLAN Commander, proclaimed it a success, which "rendered a satisfactory answer to the party and the people, and won extensive praise at home and abroad." He stated that such missions should become "a routine function of the navy," and called for "further raising the Navy's capability of performing missions in the open ocean."[148]

China is attaining a new level of blue-water experience with a mission that requires rapid response, underway replenishment, on-station information-sharing, and calls in foreign ports to take on supplies and engage in diplomacy. Sending an 800-member crew surface action group five time zones away, with 70 special forces embarked and combat contingencies possible, presents unprecedented challenges and opportunities.[149] PLAN personnel continue to learn new techniques, test their equipment, and can be expected to advocate improvements upon their return.

This is likely to catalyze breakthroughs in logistics, intelligence, and communications. Such routine operations as at-sea replenishment will allow Chinese sailors to develop best practices for use in future operations. According to a "Professor Zhang" at China's National Defense University, reportedly a senior PLAN figure, "It is also a very good opportunity to rehearse sea rescue tasks and telecommunication with other military forces."[150] The value of air support is becoming clear, perhaps accelerating prospects for Chinese deck aviation development (e.g., ships that can accommodate larger numbers of helicopters as well as an increased number of shipboard helicopters): "The experiences of the naval forces of other countries show that the helicopters carried onboard the naval vessels and small-caliber artillery systems will play an important role."[151] Even more important, the Aden deployment opens up new ideas and discussions that were unthinkable in PLA even 1 year ago, such as the advocacy of overseas bases.

Although the deployment represents a breakthrough for the PLAN, the amount of time each of the escort fleets can spend in the area is constrained by logistics and supply limitations. This mission has therefore been viewed by some Chinese strategists as insufficient to safeguard Beijing's growing maritime interests. According to PLA Air Force (PLAAF) Colonel Dai Xu, "The Chinese expeditionary force in Somalia has been attracting a lot of attention from around the world, but with only a single replenishment oiler, exactly how much long-term escort time can two warships provide for commercial vessels from various countries?"[152] As such missions become more common place, China will need to carry them out in wider areas, at lower costs, and over longer periods of time. According to Dai, "moves toward establishing an overseas base are a logical extension of this line of thinking." Similarly, Senior Captain Li Jie, a strategist at the PLAN's Naval Research Institute, has recommended establishing a supply and support center in East Africa to facilitate PLAN operations in the region. Li argues that the setting up a support center in the area is a real possibility, given that the PLAN has already set the precedent of conducting resupply and maintenance activities in African ports and China has very good relationships with some countries in the region[153] (e.g., Pakistan, Bangladesh, and Sri Lanka).

Future Equipment, Personnel, and Logistics Capabilities.

Now that the PLAN has begun moderate blue water deployments in the form of counterpiracy missions, what are its prospects for developing power projection capabilities by 2020, the projected end of Beijing's "strategic window of opportunity,"[154] and beyond? Broadly speaking, at least theoretically, the PLAN's future force posture may progress along a continuum defined by the ability to sustain high intensity combat under contested conditions at progressively greater distances from China's shores, as represented in Table 3.

Posture	Sea Denial	Sea Control	Scope and Nature
Regional Anti-Access	X		China's maritime periphery (within First Island Chain)
Extended Blue Water Anti-Access	X		Maritime periphery and approaches thereto (out to Second Island Chain, full extent of South China Sea)
Limited Expeditionary		X	Noncombatant Evacuation Operations (NEO) and Marine Interception Operations (MIO), when necessary, in Western Pacific and Indian Ocean
Blue Water Expeditionary		X	Core strategic areas (e.g., Persian Gulf)
Global Expeditionary		X	Major strategic regions of world

Table 3. Potential Future PLAN Force Postures.

The first two benchmarks fall under the rubric of "sea denial," or the ability to prevent opponent(s) from using a given sea area without controlling it oneself. The second three benchmarks may be considered variants of "sea control," or command of the sea sufficient to allow one's own vessels to operate freely in a given sea area by preventing opponent(s) from attacking them directly. Most naval theorists would differentiate these two approaches, the latter of which is far more demanding than the former and requires a much broader range of capabilities, even for operations within the same geographic area—it is not simply a question of "being able to do more from further away." As such, the first benchmark is arguably within China's grasp today; there is no guarantee that the last will ever be pursued.

China's naval development thus far has been focused largely on developing a variant of regional anti-access to prevent Taiwan from declaring independence, in part by developing credible capabilities to thwart U.S. forces should Washington elect to intervene in a cross-Strait crisis. Taiwan's status remains the most sensitive, and limiting, issue in U.S.-China relations. But Taiwan President Ma Ying-jeou's March 2008 landslide election, and his pragmatic policies, have greatly reduced the risk of conflict. Now, with cross-Strait relations stable and China continuing to grow as a global stakeholder, China's navy is likely to supplement its Taiwan and South China Sea-centric access denial strategy that its current naval platforms and weaponry largely support with "new but limited requirements for protection of the sea lanes beyond China's own waters, humanitarian assistance/disaster relief, and expanded naval diplomacy."[155] Table 4 outlines the PLAN's current order of battle.

Platform	North Sea Fleet	East Sea Fleet	South Sea Fleet	Total
Nuclear Attack Submarines	4	0	2	6
Nuclear Ballistic Missile Submarines	2	0	1	3
Diesel Attack Submarines	20	19	14	53
Destroyers	10	8	8	26
Frigates	8	22	18	48
Amphibious Ships	9	19	30	58*
Missile Patrol Craft	15	32	33	80+
Mine Warfare Ships	N/A	N/A	N/A	40
Major Auxiliaries	N/A	N/A	N/A	50 (5 are fleet AORs)
Minor Auxiliaries and Service/Support Craft	N/A	N/A	N/A	250+

Table 4. China's Naval Order of Battle (2009).[156]

According to Scott Bray, Senior Intelligence Officer-China, Office of Naval Intelligence, "Between 2000 and 2009, the number of major surface combatants capable of carrying long-range ASCMs (anti-ship cruise missiles) has tripled from 12 to 36. Additionally, the PLA(N) has built more than 50 small combatants with long-range ASCMs." Still, this is part of an emphasis on improving quality and anti-access capability; the PLAN as a whole remains far from supporting a substantial SLOC security posture.

There appears to be leadership support for a least a gradual increase in long-range Chinese naval capabilities of lower intensity. Hu requires the PLA "to not only pay close attention to the interests of national survival, but also national development interests; not only safeguard the security of . . . territorial waters . . .

but also safeguard . . . the ocean. . . ."[157] On December 27, 2006, in a speech to PLAN officers attending a Communist Party meeting, Hu referred to China as "a great maritime power (海洋大国)" and declared that China's "navy force should be strengthened and modernized" and should continue moving toward "blue water" capabilities.[158] China's 2008 *Defense White Paper* stated that "the Navy has been striving . . . to gradually develop its capabilities of conducting cooperation in distant waters."[159] Chinese defense policy intellectuals who are not directly connected with the PLAN also generally consider SLOC security to be a major issue.[160]

China may already be pursuing the ability to project naval power further than would be necessary in a Taiwan contingency. China's 2008 *Defense White Paper* for the first time treats the ground forces as a distinct service equivalent to the Navy, Air Force, and Second Artillery,[161] and there are increasing indications that the PLA may abandon the present configuration of military regions in favor of a more streamlined and outward-looking organizational posture.[162] These emerging developments, and the gradually increasing though still disproportionately low representation of PLAN officers on the CMC, CCP Central Committee, and at the helm of PLA institutions suggests that the ground forces are becoming less dominant within the military and that the PLAN may grow correspondingly over time in funding and mission scope.

As the most technology intensive,[163] comprehensive, strategic-level (day-to-day), multirole, multidimensional, diplomatically-relevant, and naturally internationally-oriented of the services, the PLAN might stand to benefit most from such an increasingly "externalized" orientation.[164]

To be sure, proponents of SLOC defense as a mission for the PLAN are not the only ones contributing to what seems to have become a robust debate within China. Some Chinese views acknowledge the costs and difficulty of building the power-projection capabilities necessary to carry out credible SLOC defense missions (e.g., aircraft carriers), as well as the potential for balancing against China by regional neighbors and the political costs that would likely occur in the event that China procured a carrier battle group. Many writers express similar or related reservations, either directly or indirectly. Moreover, there are competing priorities: enhanced expeditionary capabilities (e.g., LPDs, LHAs, helicopters) to protect overseas Chinese workers may be more important over the next decade. It could well be argued that China is more likely to need to conduct a NEO somewhere in the Indian Ocean littoral than protect its SLOCs against a major naval threat.[165] The presence of these views within China may help explain why the arguments for energy/SLOC-defense missions have not yet gained greater traction.

Chinese writings suggest a range of views on how to organize the PLAN for operations further afield. A sustained movement of assets to the South China Sea could imply a PLAN mission beyond Taiwan, in pursuit of genuine, if limited, SLOC protection capability. Increased PLAN presence in key SLOC areas could also have a valuable "shaping" function, as it can "strengthen [China's] power of influence in key sea areas and straits" in peacetime and thereby decrease the chance of its interests being threatened in war.[166]

Here hardware acquisition and deployment is a useful indicator, because it is relatively easy to monitor. To be sure, modern warships are capable of performing many missions, and hence are not restricted to a specific role in specific waters. Their political masters presumably find them useful to perform a variety of missions in a wide range of circumstances and locations (e.g., both a Taiwan context and deployments farther afield). But to fully pursue robust long-range capabilities, new platforms and force structures would be needed. With respect to force structure, indicators of a more ambitious Chinese naval presence, particularly in the area of SLOC protection, would likely include the following, as Table 5 indicates.

Capability	Approach
Anti-Submarine Warfare	Construction of nuclear attack submarines and deployment of additional units of these and other platforms with significant demonstrated ASW capabilities.[167]
Long-range Air Power	Development of carriers, aircraft and/or helicopters to operate off them, and related doctrine and training programs.[168]
Military Ship Production	Establishment of new, modern shipyards dedicated to military ship production or expansion of areas in coproduction yards that are dedicated to military ship production.[169]
At-Sea Replenishment	Expansion of the PLAN auxiliary fleet, particularly long-range, high-speed oilers and replenishment ships.[170]
Remote Ship Repair	Development of the ability to conduct sophisticated ship repairs remotely, either through tenders or overseas repair facilities.[171]
Operational Readiness	Steady deployment of PLAN forces to vulnerable portions of the sea lanes to increase operational familiarity and readiness.
Overall Capacity	Maturation of advanced levels of PLA doctrine, training, and human capital.

Table 5: Indicators of Emerging PLAN Blue Water SLOC Protection Capabilities.

The PLAN's capabilities in key areas (assets, trained personnel, and experience) are currently insufficient to support long-range SLOC defense missions, but it may gradually acquire the necessary funding and mission scope. China's growing maritime interests and energy dependency may gradually drive more long-ranging naval development; indeed, repeated reports of imminent aircraft carrier development seem to represent an initial step in this direction. China is likely to develop some form of deck aviation capability, both for national prestige and for limited missions beyond Taiwan.[172] ONI estimates that China's former Ukrainian *Kuznetsov* class aircraft carrier *Varyag* will become operational as a training platform by 2012, and "the PRC will likely have an operational, domestically produced carrier sometime after 2015."[173] Developing the necessary forces, training, and experience for true blue water combat capabilities would be extremely expensive and time-consuming, however. Building an aircraft carrier is one thing; mastering the complex system of systems that enable air power projection costs years and precious lives.[174]

Overseas Facilities Access?

Perhaps the strongest indicator of Chinese intentions to develop blue water power projection capabilities would be pursuit of reliable access to overseas air and naval bases. At present, China appears far from having overseas naval bases of its own.[175] But recent debate among PLA scholars and other analysts suggests that China may be actively reconsidering its traditional approach of avoiding "power politics and hegemonism" by avoiding any kind of overseas military facilities.[176]

PLAAF Colonel Dai Xu, for instance, has openly advocated Chinese development of "overseas bases (遠洋基地)" to "safeguard commercial interests and world peace."[177] Specifically, Dai argues that support facilities are required not only to protect China's growing global economic interests, but also to enable PLA participation in peacekeeping missions, ship escort deployments, and humanitarian assistance and disaster relief operations.[178] Moreover, Dai argues that overseas bases or support facilities are required if China is to "effectively shoulder its international responsibilities and develop a good image." Perhaps anticipating the possibility that setting up overseas bases would heighten international concerns about China's growing power, however, Dai states that Chinese bases would not be part of a global military competition and "would not require long-term stationing of large military equipment or large-scale military units." Furthermore, Dai suggests that a strategic communications campaign would help to alleviate concerns about China's intentions.[179] As a first step, Dai advocates the establishment of a prototypical "test" base in the strategically vital South China Sea,[180] presumably in addition to existing facilities at Woody Island and Mischief Reef. Future bases should then be established in other areas where China has important strategic interests; when possible, bases should be located in countries with which China already has what Dai—perhaps somewhat optimistically—characterizes as "friendly, solid relationships."

While there are indications of growing Chinese influence in the South Pacific for commercial and perhaps even signals intercept purposes,[181] it is the Indian Ocean with its rich littoral resources[182] and busy energy SLOCs that seems the most likely future area of Chinese naval power projection. A range of Chinese analyses state that from ancient times through the Cold War, the Indian Ocean has been a critical theater for great power influence and rivalry.[183] Some PLA analysts argue, for instance, that it should be perfectly acceptable for China to advance to the Indian Ocean with changes in its national interests.[184] A second assessment in China's official news media suggests that to protect its newly emerging interests, China should learn from the United States, develop several overseas bases (e.g., in Pakistan, Burma, and Sudan), and build three or four aircraft carriers.[185] Huang Li states that as other nations become accustomed to the PLAN making "frequent appearances" in the Indian Ocean, "to look for a base on land will naturally follow" (物色陆上基地也就顺理成章了).[186]

It must be emphasized, however, that any change is likely to be gradual, and that many countervailing factors are likely to be at work. Countless debates over security policy issues have failed to produce change. Some powerful individuals are likely to resist changing the status quo, citing concerns about cost, impact on competing priorities, image, and departure from historical precedent/ideology in the form of self-imposed prohibition on foreign basing, outside of UN missions. Moreover, the PLAN's use of civilian and commercial (both Chinese and host country) entities to support its ships in the Gulf of Aden, both during port visits as well as at sea, demonstrates that China does not need a *military* presence/basing to support military operations.

It thus seems likely that China will not establish a "string of pearls," with extremely expensive and hugely vulnerable "bases."[187] While the Chinese government's anti-overseas basing statements appear to be less strident and frequent than in the past, this would not necessarily alter Beijing's position on foreign "basing." This is most in keeping with Chinese tradition and ideology and will be seen by Beijing's leadership as less threatening; China will be aware of the implications for its international image. Change is likely to be incremental.[188]

Instead, the most likely approach may be to pursue access to "overseas support facilities" capable of supporting expanded PLA participation in nontraditional security missions such as anti-piracy and humanitarian assistance and disaster relief operations in a very modest version of the U.S. "places, not bases" strategy. These support centers could presumably handle the requirements of nonwar military operations—such as food, fuel, and maintenance and repair facilities—without the prepositioned munitions and large-scale military presence typically associated with full-fledged overseas bases. In theory, any port in any country could do this, so long as the host country agrees. In practice, however, Beijing is likely to want access in countries that it considers politically reliable and immune to pressure from such potential competitors as the United States and India. China has been making small steps in this direction since around 2000, including participation in UN peacekeeping operations (PKOs).

In the absence of the ability to win a naval battle in the Indian Ocean, China is seeking to influence in areas proximate to Indian Ocean sea lanes through diplomacy, trade, humanitarian assistance, arms sales, and even strategic partnerships with countries in the region—including several nations traditionally hostile to India (e.g., Pakistan and Bangladesh). This "soft power" approach is designed to maximize access to resource inputs and trade in peacetime, while attempting to make it politically difficult for hostile naval powers to sever seaborne energy supplies in times of crisis, as they would be harming regional interests in the process.[189] Greater access to regional port facilities may be one outcome of China's soft power initiatives.

For several years now, China has been developing a number of what Kamphausen and Liang refer to as "access points," or "friendly locations" that are intended to enhance the PLA's ability to project power in Asia.[190] Pakistan's port of Gwadar and Sri Lanka's port of Hambantota represent possible candidates. China has invested significantly in their development, and has made contributions over the years to the welfare of their host governments in the areas of politics, economics, and infrastructure.[191] Perhaps the PLAN is making greatest progress in Burma, where it has reportedly assisted in the construction of several naval facilities (their precise nature undefined) on the Bay of Bengal.[192] A major entrepôt sitting astride key transit lanes, with a large ethnic Chinese population and good relations with the PRC, and with its primary security concerns Malaysia and Indonesia, not a rising China, Singapore might ultimately allow the PLAN some form of access.[193] Table 6 details tentatively some of the potential ports to which the PLAN might attempt to gain some form of special, if limited, access in the future.

Port	Country	Relations with China	Chinese Investment in Facility	Type	Development Status	Draft Limits (m)	Quality of Repair Facilities
Salalah	Oman	Long-term stable and significant; China imports 250-300,000 BPD of oil from Oman and is purchasing LNG	None yet; 10 PLAN counter-piracy task force visits through January 2010; Chinese unofficial media reports bilateral negotiations to establish facility	Deep water, major container transshipment port for Persian Gulf	Already well-established; construction of new port-side fuel bunkering facility under way, massive container terminal expansion plan contracted out	15.5	Only small craft facilities currently available
Aden	Yemen	Short-term but developing steadily; recent energy, trade, and commercial agreements	None yet; visited by many PLAN counter-piracy task forces; reportedly under consideration for Chinese supply access; some security concerns	Container and bulk cargo	Modest port; berth extension planned	16 outer channel; 6-20 outer harbor anchorage	National Dockyard Company offers range of limited facilities and services
Djibouti	Djibouti	Long-term stable and positive	None; home to French and American defense facilities, Japan permitted to base P-3C aircraft for counter-piracy patrols; visited by PLAN counter-piracy task force	Principal port for Ethiopian cargo transshipment; containers and bulk cargo	Container terminal under construction	12	Small repairs possible
Gwadar	Pakistan	Long-term strategic	$198MM, technicians and skilled workers	Large commercial port with conventional and container cargos (operated by Port of Singapore on 40 year contract) Pakistan navy	Already well-established, but potential for further development	12.5	500 acre shipyard. 2 600kdwt drydocks planned VLCC ULCC construction planned
Karachi	Pakistan	Long-term strategic	N/A	Pakistan's largest port	Already well-established; Bulk Cargo Terminal and other expansion underway	9.75 upper harbor, 12.2 approach channel; being increased to 13.5; developing 16 m container terminal	PLAN's current Indian Ocean port of choice for repairs. Two drydocks available, one for up to 25,000DWT
Hambantota	Sri Lanka	Short-term strategic	$360MM export buyer's credit from China's EXIM Bank "built by Chinese enterprises"	Commercial; export of essential goods, vehicle reexports	To be constructed in 3 stages over 15 years	16-17 (future)	Ship serving capabilities planned
Chittagong	Bangladesh	Long-term friendly	N/A	Bangladesh's main seaport: 6 general cargo berths, 11 container berths (3 dedicated with gantry crane)	Completed	7.5-9.15	Private repair yards available. Drydock available for vessels up to LOA 170m and 16,500DWT
Sittwe	Burma	Long-term strategic	Assisting (India helping too)	Large rice exporting port	Under development over 3 years	7.6	N/A
Singapore	Singapore	Long-term friendly, emerging strategic	N/A	Large, sophisticated, commercial ports, busiest in world: 1 terminal, 9 sub-ports. Military ports.	Already well-established, but potential for further development	22	Excellent

Table 6: Selected Potential "Places" for Access.[194]

i. "Chinese-Assisted Pakistani Gwadar Deep-Water Port Starts Operation," Xinhua, May 20, 2007, OSC CPP2007/0320968174; "Editorial: Gwadar's Strategic Aspects are Still Relevant," Daily Times, Lahore, Pakistan, December 23, 2008, OSC SAP2008122310105.

ii. "China-Pakistan Friendship Lasts Forever," People's Daily, October 20, 2008, OSC CPP2008102170102.; iii. Khaleeq Kiani, "$60bn Income Likely from Mega Projects," Dawn, Karachi, Pakistan, October 27, 2007, OSC SAP2007102709003.

iv. "Sri Lanka Inaugurates Port Project in South," Xinhua, October 31, 2007, OSC CPP2007/031968251., v. "Chinese Delegation Vies for Dedicated Zone in Sri Lanka," Daily Mirror Online, Colombo, Sri Lanka, May 20, 2009, OSC SAP2009052054902.

vi. Zhang Xin, "Rumors on Ties with Sri Lanka Dismissed," China Daily, July 4, 2009, OSC CPP2009070456802. vii. Kamphausen and Liang, p. 130.

342

In the future, any facilities that China did establish or plan to use would have to be defended effectively in the event of conflict. Gwadar, for instance, has been designed in part to "serve as an alternate port to handle Pakistani trade in case of blockade of existing ports," however, and Pakistan might be reluctant to grant the PLAN access during a conflict.[195] Gwadar, like any other potential port for PLAN use on the Pakistani coast, the Saudi peninsula, or the East Africa coast is located west of India and is thus too easily interdicted for any significant use by PLAN forces — unless India agrees to such use.[196] While it is easy to look at a map of the Indian Ocean and make shallow historical analogies to Mahan and the age of navalism a century ago, in this era of long range precision strike, a series of exposed and nonmutually supporting bases is unlikely to pay off in the event of war.

IMPLICATIONS

China's leaders approved the Gulf of Aden deployment to protect Chinese ships, which were being attacked and sometimes captured by pirates, under the aegis of furthering international security. This does not necessarily signify a change in Beijing's sensitive approach to national sovereignty issues: four UN resolutions and the Somali Transitional Federal Government itself explicitly support these missions. Instead, it represents China's debut as an international maritime stakeholder, and a vital training opportunity for its navy. Significant logistics capabilities constitute the vital backbone of the mission; their largely commercial nature suggests dynamism and sustainability that could make future efforts in this area both feasible and affordable. In sum, the PLAN is clearly attaining

343

a new level of blue-water experience; it remains to be seen how that knowledge will be spread throughout the service, and to what ends Beijing will put the new capabilities that result.

The PLAN's evolving role in defending China's expanding economic interests, as demonstrated in its ongoing Gulf of Aden deployments, has broader implications. For now, China seems to be pursuing a two-level approach to naval development, with consistent focus on increasingly formidable high-end anti-access capabilities to support major combat operations on China's maritime periphery (e.g., a Taiwan scenario), and relatively low-intensity but gradually growing capabilities to influence strategic conditions further afield (e.g., Indian Ocean) in China's favor.

Some expect Beijing to pursue a more ambitious approach. One American scholar believes that "the main disadvantage from Washington's perspective could be that, should Chinese leaders consider the Somali mission a success, they would likely prove more willing to promote the continued growth of China's maritime power projection capability."[197] Robert Ross envisions Chinese "construction of a power-projection navy centered on an aircraft carrier."[198] One predeployment Chinese analysis advocates just such a redirection of PLAN strategy: priorities from a submarine-centric navy to one with aircraft carriers as the "centerpiece."[199] Such a shift would have major domestic and international implications. Internally, it would mean that the PLAN would likely capture a much larger portion of the defense budget, especially as the carriers themselves would need a complement of aircraft and a dedicated fleet of escort vessels to be useful in actual combat conditions. Its internal clout would be further enhanced by the fact that aircraft carriers might rapidly become an important diplomatic instrument for projecting Chinese presence and influence in Asia, and perhaps (eventually) globally.

By this logic, moving toward a carrier-centric navy could prompt other navies in the region and further afield to upgrade their own forces in anticipation of China's taking a more assertive stance regarding naval power projection. Despite efforts both to channel China's maritime development in a peaceful direction and to portray it accordingly to the rest of the world, history suggests that any major military modernization program is likely to antagonize other powers. Internationally, moving toward a carrier-centric navy could prompt other regional and global navies to upgrade their own forces in anticipation of China's taking a more assertive stance regarding naval power projection.

I foresee a very different trajectory for China's navy. While China will no doubt build as many as several carriers over the next decade, its two-level approach to naval development is likely to persist for some time, with parallel implications for American security interests. China's military has achieved rapid, potent development by maintaining an anti-access posture along interior lines and exploiting physics-based limitations inherent in the performance parameters of U.S. and allied platforms and C4ISR systems.[200] This should be of tremendous concern to Washington. But dramatic breakthroughs here should in no way be conflated with developments further afield: the core elements of this approach cannot easily be transferred to distant waters. In perhaps the most graphic example of this strategic bifurcation, the Chinese military, as it develops increasing capabilities to target aircraft carriers, is likely becoming acutely aware of their vulnerabilities—and hence reluctant to devote more than a modest level of resources to their development.

Just as these limiting factors increasingly threaten U.S. platforms operating in or near China's maritime periphery, they likewise haunt China's navy as it ventures further afield—a navy that is still far, far behind that of the United States in overall resources and experience. Thus far, Chinese decisionmakers, having carefully studied the lessons of Soviet overstretch, seem unlikely to expend overwhelming national resources to fight these realities. Despite their growing concerns abroad, they have too many imperatives closer to home that demand ongoing funding and focus. Additionally, in two separate articles, one in written in 2007 and one in 2009, Admiral Wu Shengli, the commander of the PLAN, clearly states that the PLAN will continue to develop into a force that is smaller in quantity, yet greater in quality. In the 2009 article, he also states that naval modernization must be put within the overall context of national modernization as well as the overall context of military modernization. This suggests an honest acknowledgement of the reality that resources allocated to the PLAN are and will continue to be finite.[201] Given ongoing requirements for the PLAN to provide security for Chinese interests in the South and East China Seas, it is highly unlikely that a PLAN that is smaller in quantity will be able to sustain the sort of robust footprint in the Indian Ocean that some Western analysts claim it is moving toward, no matter how much greater in quality it may be.

It thus seems likely that for the foreseeable future China will have limited capabilities but significant shared interests with the United States and other nations in the vast majority of the global maritime commons. In fact, the prospects for China to participate further in the global maritime regime as a maritime strategic stakeholder look better than ever, now that Beijing increasingly has the capabilities to do so substantively.[202] The United States, in accordance with its new maritime strategy, has welcomed China's deployment to the Gulf of Aden as an example of cooperation that furthers international security under the concept of Global Maritime Partnerships. Admiral Timothy Keating, Commander, U.S. Pacific Command, has vowed to "work closely" with the Chinese task group, and use the event as a potential "springboard for the resumption of dialog between People's Liberation Army (PLA) forces and the U.S. Pacific Command forces."[203] In this sense, the Gulf of Aden, with no Chinese territorial claims or EEZ to inflame tensions, may offer a "safe strategic space" for U.S.-China confidence building measures and the development of "habits" of maritime cooperation.[204]

Washington's real security challenges in the Asia-Pacific, for now, are fostering stability and development while preventing transnational terrorism in southwest Asia; preserving peace in the Taiwan Strait; reassuring U.S. allies; and cooperating with China and other nations to restrain North Korea's reckless brinksmanship. Beyond that, the United States and China have considerable shared interests in maritime security and prosperity. In the words of Sun Zi, they are "crossing the river in the same boat, and should help each other along the way" (同舟共济). There is a lot the two great powers can accomplish together, if both sides do their part.[205]

ENDNOTES - CHAPTER 7

1. Existing literature on this subject falls into several categories. For PLAN development, see 张世平 (Zhang Shiping), "中国海权" ("China Sea Power"), Beijing, China: 人民日报出版社 (*People's Daily Press*), 2009; Nan Li, "The Evolution of China's Naval Strategy and Capabilities: From 'Near Coast' and 'Near Seas' to 'Far Seas'," *Asian Security*, Vol. 5, No. 2, May 2009, pp. 144-169. For piracy, see Martin Murphy, *Small Boats, Weak States, Dirty Money*, New York: Columbia University Press, 2009. For naval operations in the Gulf of Aden, see Gary J. Ohls, *Somalia . . . From the Sea*, Naval War College *Newport Paper*, No. 34, 2009.

2. See Bernard D. Cole, Ph.D., Testimony before the U.S.-China Economic and Security Review Commission, "China's Military and Security Activities Abroad," March 4, 2009, p. 4.

3. Guo Gang, "Escort by Military Vessels: Chinese Naval Escort Formation Gathered Representatives of Escorted Merchant Ships Together to Exchange Views on and Discuss Escort Safety," *Xinhua*, October 26, 2009, OSC CPP20091026354006.

4. At an expanded CMC conference on December 24, 2004, Chairman Hu introduced a new military policy that defined the four new missions of the PLA: first, to serve as an "important source of strength" for the Chinese Communist Party (CCP) to "consolidate its ruling position"; second, to "provide a solid security guarantee for sustaining the important period of strategic opportunity for national development"; third, to "provide a strong strategic support for safeguarding national interests"; and fourth, to "play an important role in maintaining world peace and promoting common development." See "Earnestly Step up Ability Building within CPC Organizations of Armed Forces," 解放军报 (*Liberation Army Daily*), December 13, 2004, available from *www.chinamil.com.cn*; "三个提供, 一个发挥" ("Three Provides and One Bring Into Play"), available from *news.sina.com.cn*. The second mission entails continued military modernization to enhance the credibility of deterrence against threats on China's periphery (e.g., the possibility of Taiwan independence). The resulting strategic stability ensures a peaceful external environment for economic development, globalization and integration of China into the global economy at a time when China can

benefit from diversion of U.S. attention to countering terrorism. According to a subsequent article in the PLA's official newspaper, the third includes maritime rights and interests. 刘明福 ，程钢, 孙学富 (Liu Mingfu, Cheng Gang, and Sun Xuefu), "人民军队历史使命的又一次与时俱进" ("The Historical Mission of the People's Army Once Again Advances with the Times"), 解放军报 (*Liberation Army Daily*), December 8, 2005, p. 6. See also 杨毅, 主编 (Yang Yi, chief editor), 国家安全战略研究 (*Research on National Security Strategy*), Beijing, China: 国防大学出版社 (National Defense University Press, 2007, p. 323. For further background, see Cole, p. 1; James Mulvenon, "Chairman Hu and the PLA's 'New Historic Missions'," *China Leadership Monitor*, No. 27, Winter 2009, available from *www.hoover.org/publications/clm/issues/37362924.html*.

5. Daniel M. Hartnett, "The PLA's Domestic and Foreign Activities and Orientation," Testimony before the U.S.-China Economic and Security Review Commission, "China's Military and Security Activities Abroad," Washington, DC, March 4, 2009.

6. 沈金龙 (Shen Jinlong, Commander of a North Sea Fleet Support Base), "海军非战争军事行动—面临的挑战及对策" ("Naval Non-Combat Military Operations—Challenges Faced and Countermeasures"), 人民海军 (*People's Navy*), December 1, 2008, p. 4.

7. "Our economic development generates the need of overseas resources and markets, and there are hidden dangers in the security of our development," explains a Nanjing Army Command College political commissar, Major General Tian Bingren. "With the deepening of economic globalization and increasingly frequent flow of . . . energy sources, an outside local war or conflict will influence the development and construction of a country." 田秉仁 (Maj. Gen. Tian Bingren), "新世纪阶段我军历史使命的科学拓展" ("The Scientific Development of the Historical Mission of Our Army in the New Phase of the New Century"), 中国军事科学 (*China Military Science*), October 2007, pp. 21–27, OSC CPP20080123325001. Writing in a PLA newspaper, the recently retired Major General Peng Guangqian—who has served as a research fellow at China's Academy of Military Sciences and who, as an adviser to China's powerful Central Military Commission (CMC) and Politburo Standing Committee, has enjoyed signifi-

cant influence in the shaping of PLA strategy—warns that "some of the foreign hostile forces" may "control the transport hubs and important sea routes for China to keep contact with the outside, and curb the lifeline China needs to develop." 彭光谦 (Peng Guangqian), "从着重维护生存利益到着重维护发展利益—对国家安全战略指导重心转变的一点思" ("From the Focus on Safeguarding the Interests of Survival to the Focus on Safeguarding the Interests of Development"), 中国国防报 (*National Defense News*), January 17, 2007, OSC CPP20070119710012. These statements may allude to concerns about potential great power competitors, but they could also apply even to non-state actors like pirates.

8. 田中 (Rear Admiral Tian Zhong), "海军非战争军事行动的特点, 类型及能力建设" ("Characteristics, Types, and Capability Development of Naval Non-War Military Operations"), 中国军事科学 (*China Military Science*), No. 3, 2007; 沈金龙 (Shen Jinlong) "海军非战争军事行动面临的挑战及对策" ("Naval Non-War Military Operations: Challenges Faced and Coping Strategies"), 人民海军 (*People's Navy*), January 20, 2009, p. 4. Tian is the commander of the North Sea Fleet, Shen is commander of a North Sea Fleet support base.

9. China has 260 shipping companies. Its flagged merchant fleet ranks fourth in the world, with 400,000 mariners crewing 3,300 ocean-going ships of 84.88 million deadweight tons. 张庆宝 (Zhang Qingbao), "'海外经济利益应由自己来保护' 一本报记者专访国家交通运输部合作司司长局成志" ("'We Should Protect Our Overseas Economic Interests': An interview with Director-General Ju Chengzhi of the International Cooperation Department under the Ministry of Transportation"), 人民海军 (*People's Navy*), January 9, 2009, p. 4.

10. "10% of GDP Now Comes from Sea, Says Report," *China Daily*, April 10, 2007, available from *www.chinadaily.com.cn*.

11. Between January-October 2009, Chinese shipyards won 2.7 million compensated gross tons of total global ship orders, or 52.3 percent of the world total.

12. Skyrocketing car ownership will hamper efforts to make China's economy less petroleum-intensive.

13. Andrew S. Erickson, "Pipe Dream—China Seeks Land and Sea Energy Security," *Jane's Intelligence Review*, China Watch, Vol. 21, No. 8, August 2009, pp. 54-55.

14. Wu Jiao, "Navies Seeking Better Ways to Battle Pirates," *China Daily*, November 6, 2009, p. 1. It is unclear whether this means Chinese owned, Chinese flagged (or both), or simply carrying goods to China.

15. Alison A. Kaufman, *China's Participation in Anti-Piracy Operations off the Horn of Africa: Drivers and Implications*, conference report, Alexandria, VA: CNA Corporation, 2009, p. 8. Interestingly, it is just this sort of (probably illegal) fishing that the Somalis site as the reason they have turned to piracy, yet "China has thus far refused to ratify the U.N. Fish Stocks Agreement." Lyle Goldstein, "Strategic Implications of Chinese Fisheries Development," *Jamestown China Brief*, Vol. 9, No. 16, August 5, 2009, available from *www.jamestown.org/single/?no_cache=1&tx_ttnews%5Btt_news%5D=35372*.

16. "China to Bolster Image as Responsible Big Nation," *People's Daily*, December 24, 2008, available from *english.people.com.cn/90001/90780/91342/6561221.html*.

17. Pirates released the crew unharmed on February 8 after negotiations with Chinese diplomats. "Somali Pirates Release Chinese Boat After 3 Months in Captivity," *Agence France Press*, February 8, 2009.

18. "Pictured: Desperate Chinese Sailors Fight off Somali Pirates with Beer Bottles and Molotov Cocktails," *The Daily Mail*, December 23, 2008, available from *www.dailymail.co.uk/news/worldnews/article-1098125/Pictured-Desperate-Chinese-sailors-fight-Somali-pirates-beer-bottles-Molotov-cocktails.html*.

19. "Chinese Ship Rescued in Gulf of Aden, Pirates Retreat," *Xinhua*, December 17, 2008, available from *www.chinadaily.com.cn/china/2008-12/17/content_7315328.htm*.

20. Wu Jiao and Peng Kuang, "Sailing to Strengthen Global Security," *China Daily*, December 26, 2008, available from *www.chinadaily.com.cn/china/2008-12/26/content_7342612.htm*.

21. For the importance of oil tanker security to China, see Andrew Erickson and Gabriel Collins, "Beijing's Energy Security Strategy: The Significance of a Chinese State-Owned Tanker Fleet," *Orbis*, Vol. 51, No. 4, Fall 2007, pp. 665-84.

22. Beijing has acknowledged publicly that its increasingly global interests will require a presence abroad—at least in the commercial and humanitarian dimensions. Since China opened up to the world in 1978, this has taken the form first of diplomacy, development efforts, and trade, then UN Peacekeeping missions, and now counterpiracy efforts.

23. Wu Jiao and Peng Kuang, "Sailing to Strengthen Global Security," *China Daily*, December 26, 2008, available from *www. chinadaily.com.cn/china/2008-12/26/content_7342612.htm*.

24. Richard Weitz, "Operation Somalia: China's First Expeditionary Force?" *China Security*, Vol. 5, No. 1, Winter 2009, p. 37.

25. Unless otherwise specified, all MNDIO data cited are derived from Matthew Boswell, "Media Relations in China's Military: The Case of the Ministry of National Defense Information Office," *Asia Policy*, No. 8, July 2009, pp. 97-120.

26. Two other PLA representatives presented conditions and answered reporters' questions on the PLAN's escort mission to the Gulf of Aden, including Rear Admiral Xiao Xinnian, Deputy Chief of Staff, PLAN; and Senior Colonel Ma Luping, Director of the Navy Operations Department in the General Staff Headquarters Operations Department, PLAN. China Ministry of *National Defense News* Conference, December 23, 2008, available from *military.people.com.cn/GB/1076/52984/8565326.html; www.gov.cn/xwfb/ 2008-12/23/content_1185458.htm*.

27. 李韬伟 (Li Taowei), "今日长缨在手—海军司令部作战部长沈浩答本报记者问" ("Today We Hold the Long Cord in Our Hands—Shen Hao, Director of the the director of the Operations Department at PLAN Headquarters, Answers Our Reporter's Questions"), 人民海军 (*People's Navy*), December 27, 2008, p. 3.

28. In response to charges that China should do more to further collective security close to home, PLA spokesmen state that

China is not similarly involved in Southeast Asia because the situation in Malacca is different from that in the Gulf of Aden. Piracy in the Malacca Strait is already controlled through the joint efforts of the coastal states Indonesia, Thailand, Singapore, and Malaysia. In Somalia, by contrast, the problem is more rampant—with 10 times as many attacks in the past year—and sea conditions around the Gulf of Aden are more complex. "出兵索马里海域护航 国防部介绍情况" ("Dispatching Forces to Escort in the Somalia Sea Area—The Ministry of National Defense Presents the Situation"), 中评社 (Zhongping News Agency), December 23, 2008. See also Huang Li, pp. 175-76. For further MNDIO updates on the missions, see "Chinese Naval Frigate Comes to Escort Released Filipino Tanker in Somali Waters," *Xinhua*, April 26, 2009; Central People's Government of the People's Republic of China, January 20, 2009, available from *www.gov.cn/wszb/zhibo300/*; Jiao Wu and Kuang Peng, "No Threat from Military Development," *China Daily*, January 16, 2009, available from *www.chinadaily.com.cn/china/2009-01/16/content_7403124.htm*; "胡昌明: 护航行动是在联合国框架下履行国际义务" ("Hu Changming: Ship Escort Activities Are Carried Out under United Nations Framework"), *Renmin Wang*, December 25, 2008.

29. 黄立 (Huang Li), 剑指亚丁湾: 中国海军远洋亮剑 (Sword Pointed at the Gulf of Aden: The Chinese Navy's Bright Far Seas Sword), Guangzhou, China: 中山大学出版社出 (Zhongshan University Press), 2009, p. 174. Dr. Huang Li is a professor at South China Normal University Law School, where he teaches international criminal law to master's students. He is a also a member of the China branch of the International Criminal Law Association, and Vice President of the Guangdong Province Criminal Law Institute. Huang worked in China's public security system for twelve years, achieving the rank of third class police inspector. He has conducted extensive research, and his reports have been praised by the Ministry of Public Security leadership. Huang is an influential expert in China on organized crime. His publications include the 2008 monograph, "Crack Down on Speculation and Profiteering, Eliminate the Loathsome Cancer Uprooting the Harmonious Society." While Huang acknowledges that he lacks naval operational expertise, his book is a useful compilation of open source information and displays incisive critical analysis.

30. *Ibid.*, p. 168.

31. Chinese shippers have seized a significant portion of the global shipping market by coming from the market that most drives growth in global bulk commodity and container shipping, and by minimizing crewing and other costs. No shippers from any country have been eager to spend money on private security fees, as this would affect their margins significantly and make them less competitive.

32. Huang Li, pp. 170. During the concurrent Russia-Georgia War, Moscow reportedly invited Beijing to send ships to fight pirates, but Beijing feared becoming implicated in an anti-NATO "alliance."

33. *Ibid.*, pp. 169. Eighty-six percent of respondents to a Chinese news media survey agreed that "China should send warships to fight international pirates and protect cargo ships of China." But some Chinese feared the potential for a new "China Threat Theory," the potential for PLAN secrets to be revealed, and the potential for disproportionate cost; and advocated a free-riding approach.

34. *Ibid.*, p. 170.

35. The author is indebted to Nan Li for these insights.

36. Huang Li, p. 170.

37. *Ibid.*

38. See "Head of International Cooperation Department of Ministry of Transportation Reveals Origins of Decision on Naval Escort," 三联生活周刊 (*Sanlian Life Weekly*), January 16, 2009, available from *www.lifeweek.com.cn*; "Military Law Precedes Movement of Troops and Horses—The Chinese Military Also Needs the 'Cover' of Law," 南方周末 (*Southern Weekend*), April 2, 2009. The author thanks Nan Li for directing him to these sources.

39. 李韬伟 (Li Taowei), "今日长缨在手—海军司令部作战部长沈浩答本报记者问" ("Today We Hold the Long Cord in Our Hands—Shen Hao, Director of the the director of the Operations Department at PLAN Headquarters, Answers Our Reporter's Questions"), 人民海军 (*People's Navy*), December 27, 2008, p. 3.

40. Huang Li, p. 178.

41. *Ibid.*, pp. 216-19.

42. "Chinese Navy Sends Most Sophisticated Ships on Escort Mission off Somalia," *Xinhua*, December 26, 2008, available from *news.xinhuanet.com/english/2008-12/26/content_10565179.htm*. While the PLAN has lagged historically in helicopter capabilities, Scott Bray, Senior Intelligence Officer-China, Office of Naval Intelligence, states that it "already employs shipboard helicopters, the MINERAL-ME radar, and datalinks on board a significant portion of its fleet. As more of these systems are fielded and operator proficiency increases, the PLA(N)'s capacity for OTH-T operations will continue to grow." This and all related quotations obtained from ONI Public Affairs Office.

43. Available from *cnair.top81.cn/mi-17_sa-342_s-70.htm*.

44. Senior Colonel Sun Ziwu, pilot of the Ka-28 on Wuhan, has participated in many foreign visits and military exercises. In the 2004 Sino-French naval exercise, he landed on the French ship. Huang Li, p. 211.

45. "Chinese Navy Sends Most Sophisticated Ships on Escort Mission off Somalia."

46. Huang Li, p. 208.

47. *Ibid.*, pp. 214-16.

48. Data from *Jane's Fighting Ships*, Jane's Information Group, available from *www.janes.com*; *China's Defence Today*, available from *www.sinodefence.com*; Huang Li, pp. 203-216.

49. Commander James Kraska, JAGC, U.S. Navy, "Fresh Thinking for an Old Problem: Report of the Naval War College Workshop on Countering Maritime Piracy," *Naval War College Review*, Vol. 62, No. 4, Autumn 2009, p. 141.

50. "Resolution 1846 (2008)," adopted by the Security Council at its 6026th Meeting, December 2, 2008.

51. "Resolution 1851 (2008)," adopted by the Security Council at its 6046th Meeting, December 16, 2008. Resolution 1851 also encouraged creation of a multinational Contact Group on Piracy off the Coast of Somalia. This group of more than 20 nations met for the first time in January 2009. Kraska, p. 141.

52. Report of Security Council 5902nd Meeting (PM) of June 2, 2008, available from *www.un.org/News/Press/docs/2008/sc9344.doc.htm*.

53. Huang Li, p. 169.

54. *Ibid*.

55. Abdurrahman Warsameh, "Somalis Express Support for China's Naval Operation Against Piracy," *Xinhua*, January 8, 2009, available from *news.xinhuanet.com/english/2009-01/08/content_10625418.htm*.

56. 石华, 张倍鑫 (Shi Hua and Zhang Beixin), "中国海军索马里护航不收费" ("Chinese Navy Will Protect Ships Free of Charge"), 环球时报 (*Global Times*), December 24, 2008, available from *world.huanqiu.com/roll/2008-12/322933.html*.

57. "Warships to Set off on Friday for Somalia Pirates," *China Radio International*, December 23, 2008, available from *english.cri.cn/6909/2008/12/23/189s435892.htm*.

58. Bai Ruixue and Zhu Hongliang, "Commander of the Chinese Flotilla for Escort Missions Says: At Present, the Flotilla Does Not Have a Disembarkation Plan," *Xinhua*, December 26, 2008.

59. Greg Torode, "For PLA, Firing on Pirates is a Political Issue," *South China Morning Post*, November 15, 2009.

60. Interestingly, Somalia lacks an EEZ, instead claiming a territorial sea out to 200 nm. Beijing has avoided calling attention to this anomaly. The author thanks Peter Dutton for this point.

61. Huang Li, pp. 252-53.

62. "Piracy Draws China Back to the Ranks of Maritime Giants," *Agence France-Presse*, December 24, 2008, available from *www.google.com/hostednews/afp/article/ALeqM5jStNCMD_SCFJWIPuB0J4LUeVVfd0w*.

63. Huang Li, pp. 258-62.

64. Sun Zifa, "Chinese Navy Escort Fleet to Adopt Three Modes of Action in Escort," *Zhongguo Xinwen She*, January 3, 2009.

65. "Hong Kong, Macau, Taiwan Ships Can Request Escort of Chinese Mainland Navy," *Xinhua*, January 6, 2009.

66. "Head of International Cooperation Department of Ministry of Transportation Reveals Origins of Decision on Naval Escort," 三联生活周刊 (*Sanlian Life Weekly*), January 16, 2009, available from *www.lifeweek.com.cn*. The author thanks Nan Li for recommending this source.

67. "Chinese Navy Completes 15 Escort Missions in Gulf of Aden," *Xinhua*, February 6, 2009.

68. Qian Xiaohu and Tian Yuan, "Three Chinese Warships Work Independently in Escort Mission," *Liberation Army Daily*, January 19, 2009.

69. "战斗篇" ("Chapter on Combat"), 当代海军 (*Modern Navy*), July 2009, pp. 10-11.

70. Lieutenant Commander Xie Zengling led the unit on the first deployment. Huang Li, pp. 222, 224.

71. Unless otherwise specified, all data in this section from *ibid.*, pp. 226-236.

72. *Liberation Army Daily*, January 18, 2009.

73. Huang Li, pp. 234-236.

74. The PLAN photographs events to provide legal evidence for its activities. *Ibid.*, p. 253.

75. Xia Hongping and Cao Haihua, "Mayday, Mayday, We are Attacked by Pirates," *Liberation Army Daily*, July 15, 2009.

76. Guo Gang, "Third Chinese Escort Flotilla on Task," *Xinhua*, available from *english.chinamil.com.cn*.

77. Stephen Chen, "Brave Crew of HK-Flagged Ship Holds Pirates at Bay," *South China Morning Post*, November 14, 2009.

78. 雷志华 (Lei Zhihua), "我护航编队正高速赶往事发海域营救被劫货轮" ("Our Escort Formation is Steaming at High Speed to the Area of the Incident to Rescue the Plundered Cargo Ship"), 环球网 (*Global Net*), October 20, 2009, available from *www.dehong.gov.cn/news/homenews/2009/1020/news-28789.html*.

79. Guo Gang, "(Escort by Military Vessels) Chinese Naval Escort Formation Gathered Representatives of Escorted Merchant Ships Together to Exchange Views on and Discuss Escort Safety," *Xinhua*, October 26, 2009, OSC CPP20091026354006.

80. "China Mute on Hijacking Dilemma," *People's Daily*, October 22, 2009, available from *www.english.people.com.cn/90001/90776/90883/6790222.html*.

81. "张家栋:目前首要目标是救人—最快两周内有消息" ("Zhang Jiadong: At Present, the Most Important Goal is to Save Lives—There Will be News within Two Weeks at the Earliest"), 中国网 (*China Net*), October 19, 2009, available from *mil.huanqiu.com/china/2009-10/609253.html*.

82. Greg Torode *et al.*, "Showdown with Somali Pirates a Test of PLA's Might," *South China Morning Post*, October 22, 2009.

83. Huang Li, pp. 239.

84. "'德新海' 号敲警钟—中国需要 '远洋存在'" ("'Dexinhai' Sounds the Alarm Bell—China Requires 'Far Seas Presence'"), 国际先驱导报 (*International Herald Leader*), October 28, 2009, available from *cn.chinareviewnews.com/doc/7_0_101117202_1.html*.

85. "China Ready to Pay Ransom to Free COSCO Bulker," *Seatrade Asia*, October 28, 2009, available from *seatradeasia-online. com/News/4788.html*.

86. Guo Gang.

87. Commanding officer: Captain Long Juan; political commissar: Captain Yang Yi.

88. Commanding officer: Captain Zou Fuquan; political commissar: Liu Jianzhong.

89. Commanding officer: Captain Xi Feijun; political commissar: Captain Yuan Zehua.

90. Deputy Director, South Sea Fleet Political Department.

91. Huang Li, p. 213.

92. Huang Shubo and Su Yincheng, "Chinese Naval Escort Taskforce Berths in Port Salalah for Rest," *Liberation Army Daily*, July 2, 2009, OSC CPP20090702702030.

93. "Chinese Warship Docks at Kochi," *The Hindu*, available from *www.hindu.com/thehindu/holnus/002200908081832*.

94. "Chinese Naval Ship Formation Visits Pakistan," *Liberation Army Daily*, August 6, 2009, available from *eng.chinamil.com. cn/news-channels/china-military-news/2009-08/06/content_4018615. htm*.

95. "*PLA Navy*'s 2nd Escort Formation Returns from Gulf of Aden 21 August," *Military Report*, CCTV-7, August 21, 2009, OSC CPM20091014013011.

96. CCTV-1, July 18, 2009, OSC CPP20090718338001.

97. Zhu Da and Yu Zifu, "Interview of Commander of Third Chinese Naval Escort Taskforce," *Liberation Army Daily*, July 16, 2009, OSC CPP20090716702013.

98. For details, see *Liberation Army Daily*, July 16, 2009, available from *www.chinamil.com.cn/site1/images/2009-07/16/jfjb04b716b0c*.

JPG; Guo Gang, "(Escorts by Naval Vessels) 'Zhoushan' Frigate from the PLAN's Third Escort Formation Conducts First In-Port Rest and Consolidation," *Xinhua,* August 16, 2009, OSC CPP20090816136005.

99. Zhu Da and Xu Yeqing, "Qiandaohu Supply Ship Becomes Logistics Support Base of Escort Taskforce," *Liberation Army Daily,* November 23, 2009, available from *eng.mod.gov.cn/ DefenseNews/2009-11/23/content_4106306.htm.*

100. "Chinese New Naval Flotilla Sets Sail for Gulf of Aden While Merchant Vessel Still Held by Pirates," *Xinhua,* October 31, 2009, available from *eng.chinamil.com.cn/news-channels/ china-military-news/2009-10/31/content_4071693.htm;* Xu Yeqing and Li Yibao, "China's Escort Action Heads Toward Regularization," *China Miliary Online,* October 30, 2009, available from *www.chinamil.com.cn.*

101. Wording taken directly from 孙彦新, 朱鸿亮 (Sun Yanxin and Zhu Hongliang), "军舰护航)中国海军首批护航编队开创人民海军历史上多个" ("Naval Vessel Escort First Chinese Navy Escort Formation Achieves Multiple 'Firsts' in History of People's Navy"), 新华社 (New China News Agency), April 28, 2009. In first bullet, "naval" was added and "jointly" was removed to prevent U.S. readers from assuming mistakenly that non-PLAN forces were involved.

102. Chinese deployments average 3 months in duration, half the U.S. length. This may be attributed to their lack of basing access. Huang Li, p. 213.

103. Alison A. Kaufman, *China's Participation in Anti-Piracy Operations off the Horn of Africa: Drivers and Implications,* conference report, Alexandria, VA: CNA Corporation, 2009, p. 11.

104. Gabriel Collins and Michael Grubb, *A Comprehensive Survey of China's Dynamic Shipbuilding Industry: Commercial Development and Strategic Implications,* China Maritime Study, Vol. 1, Newport, R.I.: Naval War College Press, 2008, p. 32.

105. Goh Sui Noi, "China Not Planning Sri Lanka Naval Base," *Straits Times,* June 24, 2009, OSC CPP20090624094001.

106. See several articles on "Research on the Concept of Military and Civil Integrated Development," in *China Military Science*, No. 2, 2009, pp. 26-50; Fan Jichang, "A Study of the Strategy of Building a Logistic Support System Bases on Military and Civilian Integration With Chinese Characteristics," *China Military Science*, May 2008, pp. 86-94, OSC CPP20090324563001.

107. Such companies as Liugong have long shipped large amounts of heavy equipment equivalent in size and weight to large tanks and armored personnel carriers to locations as far away as Africa.

108. For details, see Guo Gang, "(Escorts by Naval Vessels) 'Zhoushan' Frigate from the PLAN's Third Escort Formation Conducts First In-Port Rest and Consolidation," *Xinhua*, August 16, 2009, OSC CPP20090816136005.

109. Yu Zhangcai and Li Tang, "Merchant Ship Provides Supplies to First Escort Naval Ship Formation," *People's Navy*, April 13, 2009, p. 2.

110. 张庆宝 (Zhang Qingbao), "'海外经济利益应由自己来保护': 本报记者专访国家交通运输部合作司司长局成志" ("'We Should Protect Our Overseas Economic Interests': An interview with Director-General Ju Chengzhi of the International Cooperation Department under the Ministry of Transportation"), 人民海军 (*People's Navy*), January 9, 2009, p. 4.

111. 黎云, 刘逢安, 武天敏 (Li Yun et al.), "'跨越—2009': 一场贴近实战的大练兵——全方位点评 '跨越－2009' 系列跨区实兵检验性演习精彩看点" ("'Stride 2009': A Major Exercise Sticking Close to Actual War"), 解放军报 (*Liberation Army Daily*), August 11, 2009, p. 1.

112. 张庆宝 (Zhang Qingbao), "'海外经济利益应由自己来保护' —本报记者专访国家交通运输部合作司司长局成志" ("'We Should Protect Our Overseas Economic Interests': An interview with Director-General Ju Chengzhi of the International Cooperation Department under the Ministry of Transportation"), 人民海军 (*People's Navy*), January 9, 2009, p. 4; "Head of International Cooperation Department of Ministry of Transportation Reveals Origins of Decision on Naval Escort," 三联生活周刊 (*Sanlian Life Weekly*), January 16, 2009, available from *www.lifeweek.com.cn*.

361

113. "China Ship Reporting System," PRC Shanghai Maritime Safety Administration, available from *www.shmsa.gov.cn/news/200702095400641785.html*. This also allows Beijing to summon civilian vessels for national purposes; in January 2008, following the paralyzing snowstorms that caused many parts of China to run short on coal, the Ministry of Transportations requisitioned bulk carriers from China Shipping Group and COSCO and pressed them into service hauling coal to help replenish stockpiles that were depleted during the storms. "Coal Prices Jump, Hit by the Perfect Storm," *SeaTrade Asia*, January 30, 2008, available from *www.seatradeasia-online.com/print/2264.html*.

114. Zhang Qingbao, "'We Should Protect Our Overseas Economic Interests': An interview with Director-General Ju Chengzhi of the International Cooperation Department under the Ministry of Transport," *People's Navy*, January 9, 2009, p. 4.

115. Cui Xiaohuo, "Cooperation in Gulf Mission 'Smooth'," *China Daily*, February 19, 2009, OSC CPP20090219968021.

116. Zhang Rijun, "One Network Connects the Three Services, and We are Close Like Next Door Neighbors Although We are in Different Parts of the World," *Liberation Army Daily*, September 25, 2009, p. 5, OSC CPP20091116088002.

117. Tang Bo and Zhang Rijun, "Oceanic Warships Covered in Day-to-Day Communications," *Liberation Army Daily*, November 4, 2009, available from *eng.mod.gov.cn/DefenseNews/2009-11/04/content_4101031.htm*.

118. Unless otherwise specified, data for this and the previous two paragraphs are from 虞章才 (Yu Zhangcai), "生命线在大洋上延伸—海军探索 '岸舰一体' 政治工作新模式纪实" ("Lifeline Extended at Open Sea—Record of Navy Exploring New Mode of 'Shore-Ship Integrated' Political Work"), 人民海军 (*People's Navy*), June 1, 2009, p. 3.

119. Huang Li, pp. 243.

120. "Navy Counter-Piracy Task Force Established," Commander, Combined Maritime Forces Public Affairs Office, January 8, 2009, available from *www.navy.mil/search/display.asp?story_id=41687*.

121. Lt. Jennifer Cragg, "Navy Task Force, Partner Nations Deter Pirate Attacks," *Armed Forces Press Service*, January 30, 2009, available from *www.navy.mil/search/display.asp?story_id=42236*.

122. "Warships to Set off on Friday for Somalia Pirates," *China Radio International*, December 23, 2008, available from *english.cri.cn/6909/2008/12/23/189s435892.htm*.

123. Bai Ruixue and Zhu Hongliang, "Commander of the Chinese Flotilla for Escort Missions Says: At Present, the Flotilla Does Not Have a Disembarkation Plan," *Xinhua*, December 26, 2008.

124. "Commander of Chinese Naval Escort Taskforce Visits U.S. Guided-missile Cruiser Chosin," *Liberation Army Daily*, November 23, 2009, available from *eng.mod.gov.cn/DefenseNews/2009-11/23/content_4106280.htm*; "美国151特混编队指挥官访问 '舟山' 舰" ("U.S. CTF 151 Commander Visits the 'Zhou-shan'"), *Xinhua*, November 2, 2009, available from *news.xinhuanet.com/photo/2009-11/02/content_12372253.htm*.

125. Andrew Scutro, "Communication Key for Anti-Pirate Fleet."

126. 孙彦新, 朱鸿亮 (Sun Yanxin and Zhu Hongliang), "'军舰护航' 中国海军首批护航编队开创人民海军历史上多个" ("'Naval Vessel Escort' First Chinese Navy Escort Formation Achieves Multiple 'Firsts' in History of People's Navy"), 新华社 (New China News Agency), April 28, 2009.

127. Cole, p. 6.

128. "Russia, China Holding Anti-pirate Exercise off Horn of Africa," *Interfax* (Moscow), September 18, 2009, OSC CEP20090918964128; "China, Russia Navies on Joint Anti-Piracy Patrols," *Associated Press*, available from *www.seattlepi.com/national/1104ap_as_china_russia_piracy.html?source=rss*.

129. Alison A. Kaufman, *China's Participation in Anti-Piracy Operations off the Horn of Africa: Drivers and Implications*, conference report, Alexandria, VA: CNA Corporation, 2009, p. 3.

130. Guo Gang, "(Escort by Military Vessels) Chinese Naval Escort Formation Gathered Representatives of Escorted Merchant Ships Together to Exchange Views on and Discuss Escort Safety," *Xinhua*, October 26, 2009, OSC CPP20091026354006.

131. "专家：中国货轮被海盗劫持凸显护航盲区" ("Expert: Pirates' Commandeering of Chinese Cargo Ships Has Made Apparent Blind Spots in Escort Areas"), 国际先驱导报 (*International Herald Leader*), October 27, 2009, available from *www.chinareviewnews.com*.

132. Zhang Haizhou, "Team Anti-Piracy Fight Urged," *China Daily*, November 20, 2009, available from *www.chinadaily.com.cn/china/2009-11/20/content_9007337.htm*.

133. Wu Jiao, "Navies Seeking Better Ways to Battle Pirates," *China Daily*, November 6, 2009, p. 1.

134. Cui Xiaohuo, "Cooperation in Gulf Mission 'Smooth'," *China Daily*, February 19, 2009, OSC CPP20090219968021.

135. Rear Admiral Yang Yi, "Engagement, Caution," *China Security*, Vol. 3, No. 4, Autumn 2007, p. 38.

136. Interview, Shanghai, 2009.

137. *Ibid.*

138. *Ibid.*

139. Huang Li, p. 182.

140. Matthew Boswell, "Media Relations in China's Military: The Case of the Ministry of National Defense Information Office," *Asia Policy*, No. 8, July 2009, pp. 110-112.

141. Author's discussions in Shanghai and Beijing, June 2009 and Newport, RI, July and September 2009.

142. Hua Zhengmao, "'China Threat' Theory Resurfacing with Deployment of PRC Naval Vessels to Gulf of Aden, Somali Coast," *Wen Wei Po*, December 26, 2008, available from *www.wenweipo.com*.

143. Phoenix TV, July 23, 2009; James Holmes and Toshi Yo-shihara, "Is China a 'Soft' Naval Power?" *China Brief*, August 17, 2009.

144. Zhang Jingwei, "China Adjusts Its Maritime Power Strategy at the Right Moment," *Ta Kung Pao*, December 29, 2008, available from *www.takungpao.com*.

145. "海洋运输大国—中国岂能姑息海盗" ("A Great Ocean Transport Power—How Could China Possibly Appease Pirates?"), 中评社 (Zhongping News Agency), January 31, 2009, available from *www.chinareviewnews.com/doc/1_0_100871833_1_0131083717.html*.

146. "彭光谦: 中国海军赴索马里打击海盗完全有信心" ("Major General Peng Guangqian: Has Complete Confidence in China's Navy Going to Somalia to Attack Pirates"), 新浪军事-东方网联合报道 (Joint Report by Sina.com Military Affairs and Oriental Network), December 18, 2008, available from *www.chinareviewnews.com*.

147. 张兆垠, 少将, 成都军区驻滇某集团军副军长 (Major General Zhang Zhaoyin, deputy group army commander, Chengdu MR), "坚持不懈地加强我军核心军事能力建设" ("Strengthen Unremittingly Our Army's Core Military Capacity Building"), 解放军 (*Liberation Army Daily*), December 2, 2008.

148. Liu Xiang and Zhang Xinxin, "Navy Holds Meeting to Sum Up Experience in the First Escort Mission, Calling for Raising the Capability of Performing Open Ocean Missions from a New Starting Point; Commander Wu Shengli and Political Commissar Liu Xiaojiang of the Navy Speak at the Meeting," *People's Navy*, May 29, 2009, p. 1.

149. "Backgrounder: International Community's Response to Piracy off Somalia," *Xinhua*, January 6, 2008, available from *news.xinhuanet.com/english/2008-12/26/content_10564566.htm*.

150. Maureen Fan, "China to Aid in Fighting Somali Pirates," *The Washington Post*, December 18, 2008, available from *www.washingtonpost.com/wp-dyn/content/article/2008/12/17/AR2008121703345.html*.

151. 李大光 (Li Daguang, National Defense University), "专家: 出兵打海盗可检验中国海军的远洋战力" ("Expert: Sending Troops to Fight Pirates Can Test Chinese Navy's Overseas Capabilities"), 环球时报 (*Global Times*), December 23, 2008, available from *mil.huanqiu.com/Observation/2008-12/322668.html*.

152. Dai uses the PLA's one week limit on offensives during the Korean War as an analogy to current logistical limitations. "Colonel: China Must Establish Overseas Bases, Assume the Responsibility of a Great Power," *Global Times*, February 5, 2009, available from *www.chinareviewnews.com/doc/7_0_100877861_1.html*. It should be noted that most participating countries only have a ship or two operating in the area and few have sent an AOR along with their destroyers and frigates.

153. Li Jie is cited in "军事专家: 中国应考虑在非洲设陆上支援中心" ("Military Expert: China Should Consider Establishing a Land-based Support Center in East Africa"), 中评社 (Zhongping News Agency), May 21, 2009, available from *gb.chinareviewnews.com/doc/4_16_100975224_1.html*.

154. This refers to the idea that a peaceful external environment for economic development globalization and integration of China into the global economy allow China to benefit from diversion of U.S. attention to countering terrorism.

155. *The People's Liberation Army Navy: A Modern Navy with Chinese Characteristics,* Suitland, MD.: Office of Naval Intelligence, July 2009, p. 45.

156. *Ibid.*, pp. 13, 18, 20.

157. 刘明福, 程钢, 孙学富 (Liu Mingfu, Cheng Gang, and Sun Xuefu), "人民军队历史使命的又一次与时俱进" ("The Historical Mission of the People's Army Once Again Advances with the Times"), 解放军报 (*Liberation Army Daily*), December 8, 2005, p. 6. See also 杨毅, 主编 (Yang Yi, chief editor), 国家安全战略研究 (Research on National Security Strategy), Beijing, China: 国防大学出版社 (National Defense Univ. Press), 2007, p. 323.

158. For "great maritime power," 丁玉宝, 郭益科, 周根山 (Ding Yubao, Guo Yike, and Zhou Genshan), "胡锦涛在会见海军

第一次党代表会代表时强调: 按照革命化现代化正规化相统一的规则, 锻造适应我军历史使命要求的强大人民海军" ("When Hu Jintao Met with the Naval Delegates at the 10th Party Congress, He Emphasized Building a Powerful People's Navy That Meets the Requirements to Accomplish Historical Missions of Our Army in Accordance with the Principle of Unifying Revolutionization, Modernization, and Standardization"), 人民海军 (*People's Navy*), December 28, 2006, p. 1. For "strengthened and modernized," "Chinese President Calls for Strengthened, Modernized Navy," *People's Daily*, December 27, 2006. For "blue water," "Chinese President Calls for Strong Navy," *VOA News*, December 28, 2006, available at voanews.com.

159. "China's National Defense in 2008." China's 2006 Defense White Paper further states that China's "navy aims at gradual extension of the strategic depth for offshore defensive operations and enhancing its capabilities in integrated maritime operations." Information Office of the State Council, People's Republic of China, "China's National Defense in 2006," December 29, 2006, available from *www.fas.org/nuke/guide/china/doctrine/wp2006.html*. See also the statements in the official journal of the Central Committee by PLAN commander Wu Shengli, and Political Commissar Hu Yanlin, including, "To maintain the safety of the oceanic transportation and the strategic passageway for energy and resources . . . we must build a powerful navy." 吴胜利, 胡彦林 (Wu Shengli (PLAN commander) and Hu Yanlin (PLAN political commissar), edited by Wang Chuanzhi), "锻造适应我军历史使命要求的强大人民海军" ("Building a Powerful People's Navy that Meets the Requirements of the Historical Mission for our Army"), 求是 (Seeking Truth), No. 14, July 16, 2007, www.qsjournal.com.cn, OSC CPP20070716710027. A major study advised by such influential policy makers as Dr. Qiu Yanping, deputy director of the Chinese Communist Party (CCP) Central Committee's National Security Leading Small Group Office, emphasizes the importance of securing China's sea lines of communication. Yang Yi, pp. 274, 289, 323–24. While such statements serve these individuals' bureaucratic interests, they must nevertheless coordinate their statements with PLA and CCP leadership; such naval advocacy would have been impermissible previously.

160. The PLA's first English-language volume of its type, *The Science of Military Strategy*, emphasizes that SLOC security

is vital to China's long-term development. Peng Guangqian and Yao Youzhi, eds., *The Science of Military Strategy*, Beijing, China: Military Science Press, 2005, p. 446. An edited volume emphasizing the importance of SLOC and maritime oil security has been published by China Institute of Contemporary International Relations (CICIR). See 张运成 (Zhang Yuncheng), "能源安全与海上通道" (Energy Security and Sea Lanes), in 海上通道安全与国际合作 (Sea Lane Security and International Cooperation), 杨明杰 (Yang Mingjie, ed.), Beijing, China: 时事出版社 (Current Affairs), 2005, p. 103.

161. Information Office of the State Council, People's Republic of China, "China's National Defense in 2008," January 2009, available from *www.gov.cn/english/official/2009-01/20/content_1210227.htm*.

162. In an interview, M. Gen. Peng Guangqian, Academy of Military Science, and Zhang Zhaozhong, National Defense University, state that in the future China's ground forces will be downsized, the PLAN will be enhanced and become the second largest service, the PLAAF and Second Artillery will stay the same, and there will be new services such as space and cyber forces. Sr. Capt. Li Jie says that China's approach to carriers will be incremental and that once acquired, they will be deployed to important sea lanes and strategic sea locations for conventional deterrence and also deployed for non-traditional security missions. 马振岗 (Ma Zhengang), "'中国模式' 会取代 '美国模式'" ("Can the 'Chinese Model' Replace the 'American Model'?"), 人民网 (People's Daily Net), October 22, 2009, available from *cn.chinareviewnews.com/doc/50_1074_101111301_2_1022081349.html*. See also 责任编辑: 吴茗, 邱丽芳 (Wu Ming and Qiu Lifang, duty editors) 七大军区的划分 (The Division of the Seven Military Regions), 新华网 (Xinhua Net), April 8, 2008, available from *news.xinhuanet.com/mil/2008-04/08/content_7939418.htm*.

163. The PLAAF may be seen as equally technologically intensive, but is not on a par with the PLAN in the other characteristics listed here. Thus, it is hardly surprising that the PLAN is deploying far from China's shores, while the PLAAF has not been deployed abroad since the Korean War.

164. The author must credit Nan Li with these points. This process might be facilitated by gradual development and consolidation of China's civil maritime forces, which could then assume missions within China's coastal waters and EEZ that previously occupied the Navy.

165. Andrew S. Erickson, "International Rescue—China Looks After its Interests Abroad," *Jane's Intelligence Review*, China Watch, Vol. 21, No. 4, April 2009, pp. 50-52.

166. This entire paragraph is drawn from Zhang Yuncheng, "Energy Security and Sea Lanes," p. 124.

167. Because of their lower cost, smaller size, and potentially very quiet operation (e.g., under air-independent propulsion) if neither great speed nor range are not required, diesel submarines are best for littoral operations. The superior speed and range of nuclear submarines (and relative stealth within these demanding performance parameters), together with their ability to support formidable antiship weapons systems, make them essential for blue-water SLOC defense. However, their still-high cost and their need for highly trained crews and sophisticated maintenance facilities make them worth acquiring in substantial numbers only if SLOC defense is prioritized. For detailed explanation of these points, see Andrew Erickson and Lyle Goldstein, "China's Future Nuclear Submarine Force: Insights from Chinese Writings," *Naval War College Review,* Vol. 60, No. 1, Winter 2007, pp. 54–79, and Andrew Erickson, Lyle Goldstein, William Murray, and Andrew Wilson, *China's Future Nuclear Submarine Force*, Annapolis, MD.: Naval Institute Press, 2007.

168. China already has more deck and hangar space on various combatants than it has helicopters and currently the gap is growing. Carriers, more LPDs or even an LHA or two along with more hospital ships and modern DDGs and FFGs call for a dramatic increase in rotary wing force structure. This will also mean more pilots, more mechanics, and the attendant support infrastructure for these systems. For a discussion of potential future steps in Chinese aircraft carrier development emphasizing the difficulties and opportunity costs that would likely be involved, see Nan Li and Christopher Weuve, "China's Aircraft Carrier Ambitions: An Update," *Naval War College Review*, Vol. 63, No. 1,

Winter 2010, pp. 17-35. For indications that China may have decided to devote more resources to deck aviation development, see 邓佑标 (Deng Youbiao), "海军大连舰艇学院首次招收飞行学员" ("Dalian Naval Vessel Academy Recruits Flight Students for the First Time"), 解放军报 (*Liberation Army Daily*), September 5, 2008, p. 5, available at www.chinamil.com.cn, or in English as "Dalian Naval Academy Recruits Pilot Cadets for the First Time," *Liberation Army Daily*, September 5, 2008, english.chinamil.com.cn.

169. For detailed analysis, see Gabriel Collins and Michael Grubb, *A Comprehensive Survey of China's Dynamic Shipbuilding Industry: Commercial Development and Strategic Implications*, *China Maritime Study* 1, Newport, R.I.: Naval War College Press, 2008.

170. Here China appears to have shipyard capacity but not yet the intention to use it in this fashion. Two of China's 5 fleet AORs are approaching obsolescence. At some point in the next decade, they will have to be replaced. If China intends to support more than limited long range operations, more will need to be added.

171. If China wishes to maintain a limited posture that is focused on day to day operations in peacetime or the ability to participate in MOOTW type scenarios, it will not need tenders. The U.S. has this capability because of its large forward presence and a requirement to conduct a full range of combat operations with its fleet. Unless the Chinese are going to go that route, they only need the capability to conduct minor repairs; any ship needing sophisticated repairs could be sent back to China. In the absence of tenders, a navy determined to conduct significant blue-water SLOC security missions would probably need either the ability to bring technicians along in some capacity, access to technologically sophisticated port facilities, or both.

172. Following the 2004 Indonesian tsunami, for instance, Beijing was unwilling or unable to send ships, but witnessed the United States, India, and Japan receiving significant appreciation for their deck-aviation-based assistance.

173. *The People's Liberation Army Navy: A Modern Navy with Chinese Characteristics*, Suitland, MD: Office of Naval Intelligence, July 2009, p. 19. Scott Bray adds: "ONI bases its assessments of the timeline for operationalization of KUZNETSOV CV Hull 2 (commonly referred to as the former Russian carrier VARYAG) on a

number of factors, including observations of renovations ongoing at Dalian. Reporting from Chinese open sources indicates that the J-15, which is based on the Russian Su-33, is being developed for China's aircraft carrier program. Chinese interest in purchasing the Su-33 appears to have waned in light of indigenous development of J-15. While China has yet to officially announce the existence of an aircraft carrier program, numerous Chinese military officials have made public comments on the program. China likely intends to use aircraft carriers to bring the air component of maritime power to the South China Sea and other regional areas to protect Chinese sea lanes, shipping, and enforcing maritime claims. Additionally, an aircraft carrier would likely be used in regional humanitarian assistance and disaster relief missions."

174. If China's indigenous design mirrors the *Kuznetsov* class (i.e., ski jump vs. catapults) then the vessel will likely have a relatively limited capability, particularly in terms of the type of AEW platform the ship can operate as well as the warloads the fighters can carry.

175. An Indian naval officer, Commander Gurpreet Khurana, assesses, "China and the IOR (Indian Ocean Region) countries involved maintain that the transport infrastructure being built is purely for commercial use. There is no decisive evidence at this point to assert otherwise because these facilities are in nascent stages of development." Gurpreet S. Khurana, "China's 'String of Pearls' in the Indian Ocean and Its Security Implications," *Strategic Analysis*, Vol. 32, No. 1, January 2008, p. 3.

176. This section draws on Michael S. Chase and Andrew S. Erickson, "Changing Beijing's Approach to Overseas Basing?" Jamestown *China Brief*, Vol. 9, Issue 19, September 24, 2009.

177. "Colonel: China Must Establish Overseas Bases, Assume the Responsibility of a Great Power," *Global Times*, February 5, 2009, available from *www.chinareviewnews.com/doc/7_0_10087 7861_1.html*.

178. Dai warns that "If we make things difficult for ourselves in this matter by maintaining a rigid understanding of the doctrines of nonalignment and the non-stationing of troops abroad, then it will place a lot of constraints on us across the board. Not

only would we be unable to make use of our influence in international affairs, but even insignificant pirates and terrorists would create large amounts of trouble for us, and our route to revival would most certainly be fraught with more difficulties." *Ibid.*

179. Specifically, Dai recommends that Chinese foreign affairs and propaganda specialists should advance a new "Chinese contribution theory" to counteract the "Chinese expansion theory" and "China threat theory." *Ibid.*

180. Dai states that the base should be "suitable for comprehensive replenishment" and suggests that it could be used to promote common development with neighboring countries. *Ibid.* Several factors suggest that Dai may be using a very modest conception of a "base" here. Development of port facilities in other nations, be they places or bases, to support naval deployments tend to be very different facilities from the type of bases the Chinese have or might develop on such South China Sea islands, which would assist Chinese forces deployed there to enforce Chinese claims. Their small size and lack of fresh water limit their ability to help sustain naval forces on long range deployments.

181. Roy D. Kamphausen and Justin Liang, "PLA Power Projection: Current Realities and Emerging Trends," in Michael D. Swaine, Andrew N. D. Yang, and Evan S. Medeiros, with Oriana Skylar Mastro, eds., *Assessing the Threat: The Chinese Military and Taiwan's Security*, Washington, DC: Carnegie Endowment for International Peace, 2007, pp. 131, 136.

182. The Indian Ocean region contains 62 percent of the world's proven oil reserves, 35 percent of its gas, 40 percent of its gold, 60 percent of its uranium, and 80 percent of its diamonds; as well as other important minerals and industrial raw materials, such as iron, titanium, chromate, lithium, bauxite, cobalt, nickel manganese, rubber, and tin. *BP Statistical Review of World Energy*, June 2009, p. 6, available from *www.bp.com/statisticalreview*; "Indian Ocean," *CIA World Factbook*, Washington, DC: Central Intelligence Agency, 2007, available from *https://www.cia.gov/library/publications/the-world-factbook/geos/xo.html*.

183. Senior Captain Xu Qi, PLAN, "Maritime Geostrategy and the Development of the Chinese Navy in the Early 21st Century," *China Military Science*, Vol. 17, No. 4, 2004, pp. 75-81. For related Western arguments, see Robert Kaplan, "Center Stage for the 21st Century: Power Plays in the Indian Ocean" *Foreign Affairs*, Vol. 88, No. 2, March-April 2009, pp. 16-23; Thomas Culora and Andrew Erickson, "Arms and Influence at Sea," letter to editor, *Foreign Affairs*, Vol. 88, No. 4, July/August 2009, p. 164.

184. Wang Nannan, ed., "Expert Says China's Advancement toward the Indian Ocean Concerns National Interests and Gives No Cause for Criticism," *Xinhua*, June 10, 2008, available from *news.xinhuanet.com/mil/2008-06/10/content_8338128.htm*.

185. Sun Ruibo, ed., "The U.S. Military Strengthens Forces on Guam—For What Purpose?" *Xinhua*, July 4, 2008, available from *news.xinhuanet.com/mil/2008-07/04/content_8489422.htm*.

186. Huang Li, pp. 214.

187. Only the permanent stationing of military troops in another country constitutes a base. A facility may be smaller, have a lower profile—particularly if it is manned primarily by locals, and be more focused on support activities. There is also the issue of who "owns" the facility. For example, Al Udeid Air Base in Qatar is a Qatari Air Force Base. However, while there are probably only 100 or so Qatari personnel stationed there, the facility hosts over 10,000 U.S. personnel but technically it is not a U.S. base. The author thanks M. Taylor Fravel and Daniel Kostecka for these points.

188. Bases do not necessarily constitute a requirement for a major military presence or a desire to project a large regional footprint. France has four naval/air bases in the Indian Ocean: in Djioubti, Reunion, Mayotte, and the United Arab Emirates, but Paris is not accused of attempting to dominate the region.

189. In Mauritius, for example, Chinese media sources report, "China's first overseas special economic zone" has been established. Known officially as the Tianli Economic and Trade Cooperation Zone, the state-guided project could capitalize on the historically warm relations between the two nations. Lei Dongrui,

ed., "Unveiling Our Country's First Overseas Special Economic Zone: Mauritius Tianli Trade Zone," *Guangzhou Daily*, June 10, 2008, available from *news.xinhuanet.com/overseas/2008-06/10/content_8338093.htm*.

190. Kamphausen and Liang, pp. 111-50.

191. Senior Captain Xu Qi, PLAN, "Maritime Geostrategy and the Development of the Chinese Navy in the Early 21st Century," *China Military Science*, Vol. 17, No. 4, 2004, pp. 75-81.

192. A Chinese Southeast Asia expert notes that Sino-Burmese military and security relations have strengthened, with China assisting in the construction and modernization of Burmese naval bases by repairing and constructing radars and fuel facilities. Burma's leaders, he claims, have pledged to support China if it needs to defend its interests. 林锡星 (Li Xixing), Jinan University Institute of Southeast Asian Studies, "中缅石油管道设计中的美印因素" ("The Influence of the U.S. and India on the Sino-Myanmar Oil Pipeline Proposal"), 东南亚研究 (*Southeast Asian Studies*), No. 5, 2007, p. 34. For a more skeptical assessment, see Andrew Selth, "Burma, China and the Myth of Military Bases," *Asian Security*, Vol. 3, No. 3, September 2007, pp. 279–307.

193. See Lin Zhaowi, "China Offers Help on Strait Security—Malacca Strait Safety Among Possible Areas of Cooperation with S'pore," *Straits Times*, November 13, 2009, OSC SEP20091113118002; and "Singapore and China Sign Defense Pact," *Straits Times*, January 8, 2008, OSC CPP20080108094003.

194. Unless otherwise specified, data from this table are from Sean Gibson, ed., *Ports & Terminals Guide 2009-10*, Vols. 1-4, Surrey, UK: Lloyd's Register-Fairplay Ltd., 2008.

195. "Gwadar Port," *Gwadar News & Business Source*, available from *www.gwadarnews.com/gwadar-port.asp*.

196. The author thanks Bernard Cole for this point.

197. "A well-executed (Gulf of Aden) operation might tip the balance in favor of those Chinese strategists who want their country to acquire aircraft carriers, large amphibious ships, more effec-

tive attack submarines, many more replenishment and refueling vessels, and other naval instruments to defend Beijing's overseas interests." Richard Weitz, "Operation Somalia: China's First Expeditionary Force?," *China Security*, Vol. 5, No. 1, Winter 2009, p. 38.

198. Robert S. Ross, "China's Naval Nationalism: Sources, Prospects, and the U.S. Response," *International Security*, Vol. 34, No. 2, Fall 2009, p. 46.

199. 高月 (Gao Yue), "海权, 能源 与安全" ("Maritime Rights, Resources, and Security"), 现代舰船 (Modern Ships), December 2004), p. 7.

200. According to Scott Bray, "much of (the) 'remarkable rate' of capability growth for the surface combatant force is the result of improved ASCM range and performance. Similar ASCM improvements also impact the submarine force, naval air force, and coastal defense forces. ASBM development has progressed at a remarkable rate as well. . . . China is developing the world's first ballistic missile for targeting ships at sea. China has elements of an OTH network already in place and is working to expand its horizon, timeliness and accuracy. . . . In a little over a decade, China has taken the ASBM program from the conceptual phase to nearing an operational capability." Quotation obtained from ONI Public Affairs Office.

201. 吴胜利, 胡彦林 (Wu Shengli, PLAN commander) and Hu Yanlin (PLAN political commissar), edited by Wang Chuanzhi, "锻造适应我军历史使命要求的强大人民海军" ("Building a Powerful People's Navy That Meets the Requirements of the Historical Mission for Our Army"), 求是 (*Seeking Truth*), No. 14, July 16, 2007, p. 72, OSC CPP20070716710027. "A New Voyage Toward Scientific Development—Central Military Commission Member and Navy Commander Wu Shengli Answers Questions From Jiefangjun Bao, Zhongguo Qingnian Bao Reporters," *Liberation Army Daily*, April 18, 2009, OSC CPP20090420701001.

202. See, for example, Yang Yi, "Thirty Years of Tremendous Change in the PLA," *Contemporary International Relations*, Vol. 19, No. 1, January/February 2009, pp. 1-8.

203. Donna Miles, "U.S. Welcomes Chinese Plans to Fight Piracy, Admiral Says," *American Forces Press*, December 18, 2008, available from *www.defenselink.mil/news/newsarticle/aspx?id=52386*.

204. As Huang Li emphasizes, "China has no territorial ambitions in the Indian Ocean, nor are there any historical complications involving China." Huang Li, p. 177.

205. For examples, see Andrew S. Erickson and Wei He, "U.S.-China Security Relations," in *Task Force Report – U.S.-China Relations: A Roadmap for the Future*, Center for Strategic and International Studies Pacific Forum, *Issues & Insights*, Vol. 9, No. 16, August 20, 2009, pp. 7-12.

CHAPTER 8

PEOPLE'S LIBERATION ARMY AND PEOPLE'S ARMED POLICE GROUND EXERCISES WITH FOREIGN FORCES, 2002-2009

Dennis J. Blasko

Since October 2002, Chinese People's Liberation Army (PLA) ground forces (i.e., Army units) and People's Armed Police (PAP) units have conducted approximately 24 combined exercises with foreign military, law enforcement, or emergency rescue organizations.[1] The general trend lines observed include an increasing number of relatively small-scale, short-duration exercises, conducted mostly with forces from China's immediate neighbors, in nontraditional security missions that support Beijing's larger foreign policy objectives.

PLA and PAP units from all over the country, with the exception of Nanjing Military Region (MR), have participated in these exercises.[2] The official scenarios for all combined exercises have been described as nontraditional security missions, not directed at any third party.[3] Most exercises have been designed as anti-terrorist operations, with a few disaster relief, humanitarian assistance, anti-drug smuggling, border security, and emergency response exercises also included.

The annual number of combined exercises in the first years after 2002 was low (one or two per year), but in 2006 the pace picked up, reaching its current high point of nine training events in 2009 (2008 was an exception to that trend due to China's hosting of the Olympics). With one exception, combined ground force exercises have involved relatively limited numbers of personnel, numbering from a few dozen to a few thousand. The largest exercise was the combined and joint Sino-Russian "Peace Mission-2005" with approximately 10,000 total participants of which about 8,000 were Chinese. Exercise duration varies from a day (or less) to more than a week (not counting deployment, acclimation, and redeployment times).

In the course of these exercises, Chinese forces have gained valuable experience in operating with foreign forces, command and control, staff planning procedures, long-distance rail or air deployment, logistics, and to a lesser extent actual battlefield tactics and combat methods. The operational phase of most exercises is relatively brief, small in scale, and heavily choreographed. Many exercises highlight Special Operations Forces (SOF) operations. Frequently live firepower demonstrations are the climax of the exercises followed by parades and reviews as friendship-building components.

When enemy forces are part of the scenario, they are carefully calibrated to be comparatively small terrorist or criminal forces, usually with only limited, if any, high-technology weapons and equipment. Realistically, many exercise take place in mountainous regions where many actual terrorist organizations operate. At times, the enemy may have access to radioactive, biological, or chemical weapons, or the combined forces may have to respond to chemical emergencies and accidents. Portrayal of the enemy in such small numbers with minimal advanced weaponry lends credence to the official terrorist scenarios. Moreover, no PLA Second Artillery units have been involved in these combined exercises whereas the featured SOF participation is appropriate for anti-terrorist operations.[4]

Though limited in number, these exercises contribute to China's foreign and security policy objectives.[5] In particular, China's exercise partners conform well with Hu Jintao's four-tiered diplomatic agenda: the "great powers are the key, neighboring areas are the primary task, developing countries are the basic work, and multilateral relations are an important stage."[6] The majority of exercises have been conducted with Russia (the largest number overall) and the neighboring Shanghai Cooperation Organization (SCO) members (Kazakhstan, Kyrgyzstan, Tajikistan, and Uzbekistan). Other partners include forces from the bordering countries of India, Pakistan, and Mongolia, as well as the more distant Thailand, Singapore, Gabon, and Romania. So far, the U.S. military and Chinese forces have not conducted combined land training. That may change in the future with some sort of bilateral humanitarian assistance and disaster relief exercise as discussed during the visit of the Chief of Staff of the U.S. Army to Beijing in August 2009.[7]

In addition to the variety of combined exercises PLA Army and PAP units have conducted since 2002, Chinese ground forces also have had other contacts with foreign militaries beyond routine military diplomatic visits and exchanges. For example, PLA personnel have participated in and held multinational training seminars, attended foreign military schools, and conducted military training overseas. Though not the subject of this chapter, a few of those training events will be mentioned after more detailed discussion of the combined ground force exercises executed since the turn of the new century.

The Appendix to this chapter summarizes the 24 combined exercises conducted since 2002, including names, dates, participants, location, number of personnel, and major Chinese units involved. (In nearly all cases, *complete* PLA or PAP units *did not* participate in these events. Rather, the only elements, i.e., component parts, of larger units deployed.) Figure 1 charts the number of exercises by year. Figure 2 enumerates the training partners; and Figure 3 identifies which PLA Military Regions or PAP provided the main forces for the exercises. It is noteworthy that not just "the best" or "showcase" units in the PLA and PAP have participated in these exercises.

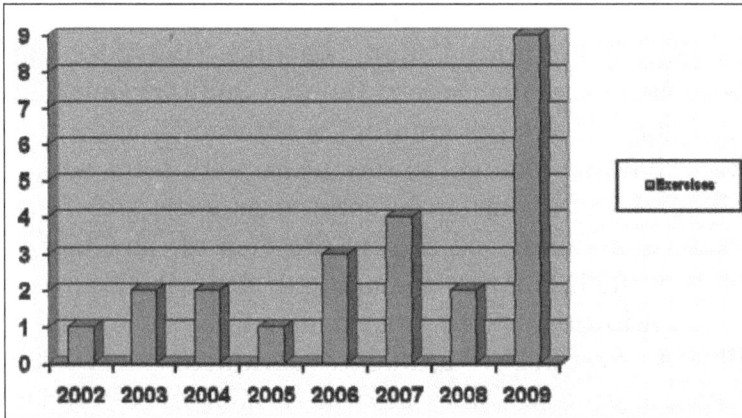

Figure 1. Yearly Number of Combined Ground Exercises.

Russia	6
Multiple SCO Members	4
Kyrgyzstan	1
Kazakhstan	1
Tajikistan	1
Pakistan	2
India	3
Mongolia	1
Thailand	2
Singapore	1
Gabon	1
Romania	1

Figure 2. Training Partners.

Lanzhou MR (Xinjiang MD)	5
Chengdu MR (Tibet MD)	4
Guangzhou MR	3
Shenyang MR	3
Beijing MR	2
Jinan MR	1
Nanjing MR	0
Unknown	2
PAP	4

Figure 3. Military Regions/PAP Providing Chinese Forces.

THE EARLY EXERCISES (2002-04)

Without much fanfare, Chinese and Kyrgyzstan forces executed a bilateral, combined anti-terrorism exercise, "Exercise 01," in the border area of the two countries on October 10-11, 2002.[8] Unlike the media attention provided later exercises, little was written or broadcast about the exercise at the time. Little also is known about the national-level decisionmaking process that led to the reversal of the decades-old policy of not training with foreign militaries. Such a decision would likely have to be made within the Central Military Commission (CMC), probably with the consent of the Chinese Communist Party Politburo and/or the Foreign Affairs Leading Small Group. While the terrorist attacks of September 11, 2001, (9/11), probably added impetus to this decision, the Chinese government previously had been concerned about the threat of terrorism and other non-traditional security challenges. For example, as early as the first White Paper on National Defense in 1998 the government had identified "terrorism, arms proliferation, smuggling and trafficking in narcotics, environmental pollution, waves of refugees, and other transnational issues" as "new threats to international security."[9] In March 2000, the defense ministers of the "Shanghai Five" (the precursor to the SCO) declared:

> They would never tolerate national separatism, religious extremism or terrorism, and that they would resolutely oppose any activity by such forces on their respective territory against other countries. They pledged to jointly take effective measures to crack down on such activities so as to safeguard regional peace and stability. The five agreed that they would further study the possibility of strengthening confidence- building measures in the military field, promote cooperation between frontier departments, and jointly combat transnational crimes, stage joint exercises in preventing dangerous military activities, combating international terrorists and carrying out emergency rescue and disaster relief, share peace-keeping experiences and coordinate with each other in their peace- keeping operations.[10]

The post-9/11 threat of al-Qaida and other terrorist organizations on China's western borders provided additional incentive to prepare for potential anti-terrorist operations in the region. Having no recent experience in conducting operations as part of a military alliance, China's decision to hold such exercises seeks to identify early-on problems inherent in multilateral operations while also learning from the experience of other countries. The American and NATO use of bases in Central Asia to support military operations in Afghanistan also may have encouraged Beijing to further cement military ties with SCO members.

Held in the Pamir-Alay mountain range, "Exercise-01" involved "several hundred men of the two countries' border defense units and more than 10 armored combat vehicles and numerous helicopters." The scenario posited that "more than 100 'terrorists' had secretly assembled on the Kyrgyz side of the border with a great quantity of weapons and ammunition, and were attempting to take advantage of the complex terrain to sneak into China. After consultations, the Chinese and Kyrgyz forces launched a joint operation to surround and annihilate these 'terrorists'." Using "hammer and anvil" tactics, the Kyrgyz border defense troops attacked the terrorists forcing them to flee into China. There their retreat was cut off and they were mopped up by the combined forces of both countries.[11] The exercise also included a live-fire phase. Friendly and enemy forces in this exercise were constructed according to attack ratios found in any basic military doctrine. Attackers outnumbered defenders at a ratio of at least 3:1 ("several hundred" Chinese and Kyrgyzstan troops versus about 100 terrorists). The Chinese coalition also had more advanced weapons (in this case, armor and helicopters) than the terrorists. Similar doctrinally sound force ratios will be included in future combined exercises against other theoretical terrorist threats.

The first low-level, small-scale military exercise with Russian forces took place in January 2003. In an unnamed, unpublicized training event, Chinese and Russian border units carried out a small combined exercise along the Heilongjiang border aimed at the "apprehension of illegal border crossers."[12] No further details of the exercise are available, and one must assume the PLA force involved was a Shenyang MR/ Heilongjiang Military District (MD) border defense unit.[13] This exercise was so small, it was not included in the list of nontraditional security exercises in the 2004 White Paper, nor was it included in other lists of "Major PLA-related joint anti-terror military trainings" published by *PLA Daily* because it was neither "major" nor was it an "anti-terrorist" exercise. As will be seen, other small-scale exercises along the border also receive only minor press coverage.

Less than a year after "Exercise-01," five SCO member countries (Uzbekistan had recently been admitted and did not participate) held the first multilateral SCO combined anti-terror exercise, "Coalition-2003" (also called "Joint-2003"), in the border areas near Ucharal, Kazakhstan and Yining (Ili) in Xinjiang from August 6-12, 2003. In total, about 1,300 troops of all five countries participated, with the majority, some 700 personnel, coming from China. The Xinjiang MD provided PLA main force units composed of mechanized infantry, tanks, artillery, helicopters, and SOF. Significantly, consistent with PLA doctrine, PAP, civilian special police forces, and militia personnel from the Xinjiang Production and Construction Corps also participated.[14] Coalition forces responded to a scenario in which "a group of international terrorists [about 25] hijacked a plane in a country, took hostages and invaded the air space of Kazakhstan. At the same time, some international terrorists [more than 100] secretly entered the Ili region of Xinjiang, China. They formed an armed base and sought opportunities to commit terrorist and violent acts."[15] A Joint Counterterrorism Central Headquarters, manned by the commanders and staff from all countries, directed the operations. The exercise emphasized intelligence collection and reconnaissance (including satellite and electronic surveillance and human intelligence such as gathering information from local civilians), electronic warfare (jamming terrorist communications), psychological operations (dropping leaflets), helicopter movement, special operations including hostage rescue, medical evacuation, and application of massive firepower as necessary.

China had proposed holding such a multilateral SCO anti-terrorist exercise in November 2002. At the time SCO members responded positively with the final decision for the exercise made at the March 2003 meeting of the SCO general headquarters in Moscow. In April, military representatives from all five countries met in Astana and Moscow. On April 29, the five ministers of defense signed a memorandum to conduct the exercise. A final preparatory meeting was held in July.[16] This was a fairly rapid planning cycle for such a complex exercise. Other combined exercises could take a year or more from initial proposal to execution.

A year after Coalition-2003, China and Pakistan held their first combined anti-terrorist exercise, "Friendship-2004," in Tajik County, Xinjiang, on August 6, 2004. The two countries deployed about

200 total personnel to hunt down "several dozen international 'terrorists'" who had "fled to the China-Pakistan border from a third country, carrying light weapons and explosive devices" where they "constructed hasty fortifications." After establishing a joint command post, reconnaissance forces (which may or may not have been special SOF troops) found the enemy hideout. Chinese and Pakistani forces, supported by a psychological operations vehicle, mortars, and recoilless rifles, attempted to surround and destroy the "terrorists," using the reconnaissance element to block enemy movement. After the terrorists ignored an offer to surrender, the Chinese and Pakistani units, acting as separate units, assaulted the enemy in a coordinated attack from the flanks. Following their link-up, the troops of the two countries "held a dignified troop review ceremony."[17]

Probably in an effort to balance relations with Pakistan and India, shortly after "Friendship-2004" on August 15, 2004 (India's Independence Day), a 46-member Chinese border defense troop delegation visited an Indian armed forces frontier station to celebrate the occasion. (Similar cross-border good will visits have been reported with other countries.[18]) Then on August 24, 2004:

> A dozen or so smiling Indian soldiers entered the Chinese territory through the Chang La Pass [Lipu-Lekh Pass on the Indian side] to participate in the Chinese-Indian border defense forces' joint mountaineering training that took place in Purang County on that day. At 1500, 12 capable mountain climbers from each side, selected by the border defense forces on either side, set off from a location 4,412 meters above sea level, traversed a 3,000-meter-long mountainside strewn with riprap, and smoothly completed the joint training. In their exchange, the soldiers from the two countries hit it

off with each other just like old friends and found each other's company natural and easy-going. . . .[19]

Like the January 2003 border exercise with Russia, this "joint mountaineering training" is not listed by some Chinese sources as an official combined exercise with India. It is, however, the type of exchange that allied or friendly forces routinely conduct with each other as part of their annual training schedules. Such low-level training allows troops to hone specialized skills, build confidence in their abilities, and gain exposure to foreign forces. Exactly what level of headquarters within the PLA does the detailed planning for such small-scale, cross-border exchanges or training is unclear, but it seems reasonable that the CMC and General Staff Department would have to approve the general concept of the operation which is then supervised by MR and MD headquarters.

THE MID-YEARS (2005-07)

Following what would have likely required some months of extensive lower level preparations and negotiations, on July 6, 2004, CMC Vice Chairman Guo Boxiong signed a Memorandum of Understanding with Russian Defense Minister Ivanov concerning combined (joint) military exercises to be conducted by China and Russia. By the end of the year, Minister of Defense Cao Gangchuan and his Russian counterpart agreed that "the first joint military exercise between the two countries was an important event in relations between the two countries and their military forces."[20] The timing of these high-level agreements would allow the General Staff Department to insert a major combined exercise into the annual training schedule for 2005 and commit appropriate resources for planning and execution. The exercise, "Peace Mission-2005," was to be conducted based on the United Nations (UN) Charter and in accordance with "generally recognized international laws and the principle of respect for the sovereignty and territorial integrity of other countries." At the end of January 2005, the Russian first vice minister for national defense declared the hypothetical enemy was "terrorists on a global scale."[21]

The scenario for "Peace Mission-2005" involved Countries N (Russia) and V (China) responding to the aid of Country S. According to Russian reporting, as a result of the "sharp worsening in the domestic-political situation on political, economic, interethnic, and religious grounds, the confrontation of the two main peoples populating the country [S] was starting to turn into total mutual destruction." After "opposition forces and armed formations seized a number of cities and rural regions in the western part of the state and established their own government there. . . . Country S turned to the international community with an initiative on adopting measures to prevent the internal conflict from possibly escalating into a local war." The mission of forces from Countries N and V was to restore "constitutional order effectively and with the least losses in the territory of State S."[22] With respect to Beijing's foreign policy principle of "noninterference" in the internal affairs of other countries, "Peace Mission's" intervention in Country S's affairs was "legal" because "the international community," i.e., the UN, approved Country S's appeal for help. With some local modifications, such a scenario could arguably apply to real-world situations found in Lebanon, Somalia, or Afghanistan.

After the air forces had attained dominance in the air, naval forces sought to blockade Country S from the sea on first day of the exercise (August 23). This prepared the battlefield for an amphibious assault conducted by elements of the PLA Navy's 1st Marine Brigade supported by airborne and SOF operations on the second day. (Russian ground forces included naval infantry and airborne forces of the same size as Chinese Marine and Airborne units involved.) On the third day, a PLA Air Force (PLAAF) airborne mechanized infantry company dropped with 12 armored fighting vehicles and helicopter-inserted SOF forces linked up with elements of the "Ye Ting" Regiment of 127th Light Mechanized Infantry Division. The exercise culminated in a live-fire ground and air pounding of the enemy who had retreated to defensive positions in what was termed a "forced isolation" drill.[23]

Exercise artificialities in timing and locations were imposed upon this exercise as they are on most such events, so that visiting dignitaries from both countries could watch the events from viewing stands along the side of the battlefield. The approximately 8,000 PLA Army, Navy, and Air Force personnel who took part in "Peace Mission-2005" were the largest number of PLA troops yet to participate in a combined exercise. (No Second Artillery units were involved.) Though other significant events occurred in 2005, such as the joint Army-Air Force "North Sword-2005" which allowed 40 military observers from 24 countries to attend the final phase, "Peace Mission-2005" was the highpoint of the PLA's training year.

A full year would pass before the next combined exercises. The first of three combined exercises in 2006 featured Xinjiang PAP border troops and a PAP Anti-Terror Reconnaissance Unit in what was billed as "the first antiterrorism exercise held by the Chinese law enforcement and security departments together with the relevant departments of a foreign country, and it is also the first joint antiterrorism exercise held by the two countries of China and Kazakhstan within the SCO framework."[24] "Tianshan-1" was conducted in two phases, beginning with indoor drills in Almaty Province, Kazakhstan, on August 24, 2006, and then with live force maneuvers in Yining, China, on August 26. Government forces from the two countries conducted a five-part operation against the terrorist enemy: (1) reconnaissance and positioning of forces, (2) multidirectional encirclement and three-dimensional blockade, (3) psychological operations, (4) sudden attack, and (5) battlefield clearance and withdrawal from combat. In addition to ground forces using armored vehicles, armed helicopters, patrol dogs, and artillery were employed.[25] Senior public security officials from both countries and observers from Russia, Kyrgyzstan, and Uzbekistan attended the exercise.

"Coordination-2006," China and Tajikistan's first joint anti-terrorism exercise, followed from September 22-23, 2006, in Kulyab, Tajikistan. In another "first," for "the first time the Chinese Air Force has flown outside China's borders to deliver an organic unit; a 150-soldier reinforced special operations company of Xinjiang MD's Special Operations Battalion" to Tajikistan. An unknown number of PLA Army Aviation helicopters from the Army Aviation Regiment in Xinjiang MD also self-deployed to support the SOF unit.[26] The 2-day exercise consisted of "a command post exercise and live rehearsal." *PLA Daily* reported that training "difficulties" included "rapid delivery, communication across a language barrier, adapting to the environment of another country, and logistical support."[27] The live-fire portion of the exercise appeared to be mainly a series of small unit demonstrations on a training range against a notional enemy.[28] "Coordination-2006" was probably about as rudimentary as a combined exercise can be.

The year 2006 concluded with the second Sino-Pakistani combined exercise, "Friendship-2006." This time the exercise was conducted in Abbottabad, Pakistan, from December 11-18. The Chengdu MR "Cheetah" SOF Group sent 100 personnel to the event.[29] Other than its focus (an "anti-terror operation in mountainous terrain"), the use of helicopters, and the fact it ended with "a colorful closing ceremony with an impressive display of hang, para, and motorized gliding mark[ing] the end of the 8-day long joint exercises," details of the exercise scenario were not published. Chinese television carried reports on the exercise.[30]

"Strike-2007," the first combined exercise with a non-contiguous neighbor, was held at the Military Sports Comprehensive Training Base, Guangzhou MR, from July 15-31, 2007, with Thailand. In an English-language report on the exercise, Guangzhou MR commander Zhang Qinsheng used the word "combined" to describe the event (or the translator used the word "combined," which was attributed to Zhang). The report made the following distinction between "combined" and "joint" exercises: "Compared with joint military exercises, the combined training means cooperation in a deeper sense," he said. As a combined training generally lasts longer than a joint military exercise, it offers trainees more opportunities to have a closer observation of other military forces, regarding arms equipment, campaign-related thinking, and personnel quality, Zhang said.[31]

Zhang's explanation (the Chinese version of this interview is not available) does not conform to the U.S. definition of "combined" training (between two countries). What Zhang did not say specifically here, but probably is an important difference from prior exercises with other countries, was that in "Strike-2007," "the Chinese and Thai sides each sent 15 people to participate in the training. They formed up into two mixed groups, one with a Chinese leader and the other with a Thai leader. The participants 'ate together, lived together, and trained together'."[32] Unlike other exercises where each nation's forces maintained their national integrity while operating in coordination with each other, here the Chinese and Thai were combined into mixed small units. After preparatory training that included "climbing, shooting, combat techniques, jungle crossing, and study on tactics of special forces," the teams executed two live exercises in which they first rescued teachers and students held hostage by an international drug smuggling organization and then attacked the smugglers' camp. A *Guangzhou Ribao* report goes into some detail of the tactics (deception, snipers, psychological operations, etc.) used in these exercises. Of note, "the Chinese and Thai sides communicated mainly with gestures and simple English."[33] In subsequent reporting about combined exercises, Chinese sources continued to use the word "joint," even when the forces were integrated into multinational units so the use of "combined" here appears to be an anomaly.

In August 2007, the second multilateral SCO exercise, "Peace Mission-2007," was held in Chelyabinsk, Russia. Although it was smaller in personnel size (more than 7,500 total personnel including 1,600 Chinese) than "Peace Mission-2005," more countries participated (all six SCO members). The PLA deployed elements from two Mechanized Infantry Divisions in the Xinjiang MD, an airborne mechanized infantry company, an SOF company, and elements of two Army Aviation Regiments, one from Lanzhou MR (Xinjiang MD, 16 transport helicopters, probably Mi-17 series) and the other from Beijing MR (16 WZ-9 helicopters).[34]

According to the 2008 White Paper, "this was the first time for the PLA to participate in a major land-air joint exercise outside the Chinese territory."[35] Defense Minister Liang Guanglie described the anti-terrorist exercise as follows:

> After the exercises began, adopting such methods as railroad and air transport and flight transitions, we organized and implemented - for the first time in our army's history-large-scale, organizational-system-based [involving full-scale original army units: corps, brigades, etc.], transnational long-distance maneuvers involving different services and arms, and carrying heavy weapons and equipment. The practice improved our military's strategic transportation and campaign maneuvering capabilities. In Chelyabinsk, we and other SCO member state armed forces trained jointly in such combat operation patterns as firepower assaults, special assaults, aerial landings under attack, and airborne attacks.[36]

Based on media reports, the largest single PLA unit to deploy was probably a reinforced infantry battalion. Significantly, "before leaving for Russia, Chinese soldiers underwent about 60 days of intensive training in the Gobi desert in Xinjiang."[37] Chinese reports noted positive aspects of the exercise, such as "the first time Chinese Army Aviation helicopters have transported foreign soldiers in an exercise. And the two sides had only trained together twice prior to this joint airlanding."[38] On the other hand, some Russian reports were considerably more condescending:

393

Following the 2 hours of field firing and the departure of the presidential motorcades, the military eased up and confessed in a whisper that there had been surprises. The Chinese, for example, refused for a very long time to rehearse the assault. Wrongfully, it turned out. During the general run-through and at the exercises themselves directly five of the servicemen's parachutes failed to open. . . .

But we observed with interest how every day, armed with pans, the Chinese strewed with crushed stone the places where their armored equipment passed: our hillocks were too much for their light six-wheel APCs. . . .

And one further story: at one rehearsal an absent-minded Chinese tank driver accidentally pulled the trigger. In the adjacent village the blank shell destroyed a barn, fragments of which killed three geese. So casualties were not avoided, for all that. . . .

Foreign reporters viewed all this and hastened to share their conclusions with the viewers and readers. Each of them probably observed that "the armies operated very formidably, and the peaceful population had practically no chance of survival in such concentrated carnage. . ."[39]

There is a language barrier between the Russian and Chinese military servicemen. . . . The national military contingents are guided by their commanders in their native language, but there are 200 interpreters who are helping to overcome the language barrier during interaction between the military of the two countries. . . . Russian military converse with their colleagues from other SCO countries exclusively in Russian. . . .

The official also said that the first joint training of the military contingents of Russia, China, and Kazakhstan on August 6 had shown that "we have certain complaints about how China's army aviation approaches the targets and strikes to destroy the enemy."[40]

Observers frequently hear similar statements from Russian military personnel about their PLA counterparts reflecting cultural tensions and suspicions between the two countries. Other comments expose the kinds of problems that exercises are intended to reveal so that they may be fixed on future exercise and battlefields. Nonetheless, the safe movement of such a large force over such distances in the heat of summer is not a trivial accomplishment. The Chinese were serious about the mission and accomplished it successfully.

Shortly after the PLA's participation in "Peace Mission-2007," the PAP sent approximately 600 personnel from the "Snow Leopard Commando" unit to Moscow for the bilateral anti-terrorist exercise, "Co-operation-2007." The 3-day, three-phase event culminated on September 6 with "a surprise assault on the 'sanatorium' occupied by the 'terrorists' and successfully rescued the kidnapped 'hostages'."[41] Prior to the exercise, in a relatively rare instance of the military media officially providing the true unit identifier for a unit, the Chinese text of a *PLA Daily* article identified the unit as the PAP Beijing Zongdui 13th Zhidui Special Duty Group.[42] PAP commander Wu Shuangzhan traveled to Moscow and told reporters the exercise was "carried out within the framework of the 'Year of China in Russia,' was not targeted at any third country and did not infringe on the interests nor pose any threat to any third state."[43]

In order to provide balance in China's relationships with Pakistan and India, 2007 ended with a bilateral Sino-Indian anti-terrorist exercise, "Hand-in-Hand-2007." Held outside of Kunming from December 19-27, 2007, a company of Indian infantry paired up with a reconnaissance company from the 14th Group Army in the Chengdu MR.[44] The exercise elements were reinforced by PLA tanks, armed helicopters, and a electronic warfare unit to jam the terrorists' communications. A Chinese Unmanned Aerial Vehicle also performed reconnaissance.[45] Like "Strike-2007" where PLA and Thai troops formed integrated units, the Chinese and Indian forces also formed two mixed companies for the drills and exercises.[46]

"Strike-2007" was the last combined exercise of a year that saw the highest number of combined exercises up to that time. In 2008, there would be fewer activities with foreign militaries than in 2007 due to the PLA and PAP's participation in Olympic security and ceremonial missions. It is possible that Sichuan earthquake disaster relief efforts caused the cancelation or postponement of previously planned events (though no evidence to support such a possibility has been found). Even so the PLA sent units to two combined training exercises to reciprocate for events held in China the previous year. Then in 2009, the number of combined activities reached its high water mark to date.

RECENT YEARS (2008-09)

It seems reasonable that much of the negotiation and planning for "Strike-2008" and "Hand-in-Hand-2008" occurred as part of a package during the initial work for "Strike-2007" and "Hand-in-Hand-2007" (with subsequent adjustments made due to lessons learned and changing circumstances). In both cases, forces similar to the type that participated in the original exercise traveled to the partner country.

"Strike-2008" took place exactly a year after its predecessor exercise, this time, though, in Chiang

Mai, Thailand. "Strike-2008" was a week longer and involved about twice as many personnel (34) from the Guangzhou MR SOF Group than the 2007 exercise. Once more, the two sides formed mixed units and engaged in multiphase training consisting of basic training, skills training, combat tactics training, and a comprehensive exercise.[47]

Likewise, "Hand-in-Hand-2008" was executed a year after its predecessor, with an infantry company (137 personnel) from the 14th Group Army travelling to Belgaum, India (via two PLAAF aircraft) for about a week. Again, the Chinese and Indian units formed mixed companies commanded by their respective battalion headquarters.[48] The exercise consisted of three phases: equipment display with technical and tactical exchanges; joint training; and a comprehensive anti-terrorist exercise, which included a heliborne assault using Indian helicopters.[49] The PLA battalion commander expressed surprise that "the Indian side did not prepare slogans and banners to welcome the Chinese side"; nonetheless, he felt "the Indian Army looked upon our arrival with great importance. Not only did the Indian side have everyday living needs ready for us, such as mosquito nets, bedsheets, and mattresses, they are even providing us with network access free of charge!"[50] The Chinese participants appeared also to appreciate the military professionalism displayed by their Indian hosts:

> The Indian Army has also embodied high efficiency in training and administration. An example of that could be seen in a training coordination meeting which took place last night. When explaining plans and arrangements for training in the coming days, the information presented was brief yet clear, and the multimedia courseware we were shown was concise and all-encompassing.[51]

Though there have been more PLA and PAP combined exercises with foreign countries in 2009 than any other year, many of the exercises were short, small-scale events, or the Chinese participants were only minor players on a larger canvas. As always, however, there were a series of "firsts" for China.

With the threat of cross-border terrorism, smuggling, and drug trafficking in mind, on February 26, 2009, Heilongjiang MD border troops and frontier forces of the Border Defense Bureau of the Russian Far East Federation Area conducted a "joint border blockading and controlling military exercise" along the Amur River between Heihe, China, and Blagoveschensk, Russia. Though it lasted only for the morning, the exercise was "the first joint border blockading and controlling military exercise" conducted between China and Russia.[52] The event appeared to have entailed increasing alert levels at sentry posts, establishing check points (or blockades), additional patrolling, and heightened communications among commanders with joint mobile command. Little else is known about this exercise.

Similarly, in August 2009, two more brief low-level exercises were conducted between Chinese and Russian government organizations on the river between Heihe and Blagoveschensk. On August 18, undefined Chinese and Russian agencies held a river emergency exercise. The exercise included ship rescue and fire fighting operations, which *might* have involved PAP forces.[53] Two weeks later, PAP border security patrol boats were among the participants in a "bilateral port emergency situation" involving 14 boats and 240 personnel. The exercise was described as the first-ever "drill between the two countries to promote cooperation in dealing with cross border crimes."[54] This may have been the "first" such event for the PAP, differing from the land-based PLA exercise in February. The two events in August were more like functional drills than full-fledged exercises. It would not be surprising for more such low-level, short emergency drills to be conducted along border areas between government forces without much media attention.

The exercises on the Russian border received minimal media coverage, as did two other combined exercise Chinese forces participated in April and May. Four more combined exercises in June and July received much greater coverage and scored several more "firsts" for China.

Chinese troops (possibly a small element of an SOF unit) were among the supporting elements in the "Nurek-Antiterror-2009" exercise held in April at Fakhrabad, south of Dushanbe, Tajikistan. Russian and Tajik troops formed the main exercise contingent, while Kazakhstan, China, and Kyrgyzstan sent fewer personnel. The scenario required the SCO troops using combat aircraft, helicopters, and armored vehicles to rescue hostages taken by terrorists who had entered Tajikistan from Afghanistan.[55] No details are available about the role played by the Chinese force in this exercise.

In May, a 20-man contingent from the from the China International Search and Rescue Team and China Emergency Fire Rescue Team traveled to Moscow to participate in the "Bogorodsk Disaster Relief Exercise." This event was called "the first joint disaster relief exercise to be held since the establishment of the SCO."[56] The Search and Rescue Team is composed of personnel from the China Earthquake Administration, a PLA engineering unit, and the PAP General Hospital.[57] The Fire Rescue Team is composed of

PAP personnel from the Shanghai Firefighters Special Duty Force.[58] The exact composition of the Chinese contingent was not disclosed, but exercise events included reaction to a serious earthquake, fire, explosions, and chemical leaks, as well as procedures for personnel rescue from collapsed buildings, tunnels, and traffic accidents. Observers at the exercise judged the Chinese team's chemical disaster capability to have reached "advanced level of the world."[59]

Defense officials from China and Gabon agreed in 2007 to conduct a joint humanitarian medical operation. "Peace Angel-2009," conducted from June 17-30, 2009, was "the first medical service joint operation conducted by the Chinese military with [a] foreign military and the first bilateral joint operation co-organized by the Chinese military with an African country in Africa." Some 60 PLA medical personnel and epidemic prevention personnel from the Bethune International Peace Hospital and the Academy of Military Medical Sciences traveled to Ogooué-Ivindo Province in Gabon to take part in a three-part operation consisting of professional training, a rescue exercise, and medical aid consisting of providing free medical services to the local people. The rescue exercise scenario involved a mine collapse and included poisonous gas detection, medical rescue, classification of wounded, and evacuation elements.[60] The humanitarian assistance aspect of the deployment was very busy as "the participants both from China and Gabon diagnosed and treated 18,000-odd patients and performed more than 300 operations in 4 different areas in Gabon."[61]

At the same time as "Peace Angel-2009" was underway in Africa, chemical defense and medical personnel from China and Singapore were executing "Cooperation-2009" at the Guangzhou MR Comprehensive Training Base, Guilin. Sixty-one PLA personnel from a Chemical Defense Regiment and the Center for Diseases Control and Prevention from the Guangzhou MR worked with a like number from the Singapore Armed Forces (SAF) 2nd People's Defense Force, and the SAF Chemical, Biological, Radiological, and Explosives Defense Group focused on "the prevention and emergency handling of nuclear, chemical and biological terror attacks."[62] After holding seminars, the PLA and SAF forces formed mixed teams to conduct hands-on training.

Rounding out activities, from June 26 to July 4, Chinese and Mongolian forces conducted "Peacekeeping Mission-2009," the "first joint peacekeeping exercise China has held with another country, as well as the first joint military training between China and Mongolia." The exercise included lectures, joint training, and comprehensive simulation drills, such as "transport and defensive missions against the backdrop of a simulated United Nations peacekeeping mission." In that exercise, the participants formed a peacekeeping company. A total of 91 personnel from both countries participated, with China providing 46 troops.[63] The Chinese contingent likely included personnel from the Engineer Brigade stationed in Beijing that has sent forces to several UN missions. The exercise was probably conducted at the newly opened PLA "Peacekeeping Training Center" in Huairou, northeast of Beijing.[64]

The third in the "Peace Mission" series of exercises was another bilateral Sino-Russian event (though other four SCO member states sent observers). A 1-day "strategic consultation" phase held in Khabarovsk preceded the live troop phase from July 24-26, 2009, at the Taonan Combined Arms Training Center in Jilin. "Peace Mission-2009" was the smallest exercise of the series, with a total of about 2,600 personnel, half of which were Chinese. The main participating PLA ground force units were elements of the 190th Mechanized Infantry Brigade, the 9th Army Aviation Regiment, and the Special Operations Group of 39th Group Army, Shenyang MR, supported by a PLAAF battle group of 20 fighters (J-8II), ground attack aircraft (Q-5), and fighter-bombers (JH-7), along with an air defense missile and radar unit.[65]

According to Senior Colonel Lu Chuangang, head of the PLA's command group in the exercise directorate, "The preparation time for the joint exercise has been shortened from 10 months in the previous exercises to 4 months this year, which show how Chinese and Russian armed forces can mobilize and deploy to a location within a very short time."[66] The exercise scenario was constructed around actions to rescue hostages taken by an armed terrorist group in an urban setting and included blowing up a chemical plant. In particular, the enemy was said to have "a certain degree of organization and combat capability rather than disbanded militants who could be easily put to rout."[67] The terrorists used man-portable surface-to-air missiles in their defense and had access to some sort of aircraft (exact specifications unknown). As a result, for the first time in a "Peace Mission" exercise, PLA and Russian forces were required to integrate air and air defense operations, including the use of their own surface-to-air missiles.[68] Senior Colonel Lu also indicated that despite the smaller number of personnel involved, the exercise used "few to represent many" suggesting that the units on the exercise field may have been smaller than would actually be used in a combat scenario.[69]

The live demonstration phase of the exercise lasted only 1 hour and 20 minutes, but a lot of action was packed into that time period. SOF operations were highlighted, including helicopter insertions, reconnaissance activities, use of snipers, and close quarters combat. The ground assault on the terrorists in the village of "Kunshan" emphasized Russian lessons learned in Chechnya. Several PLA leaders acknowledged that the PLA had much to learn from Russian experience. For example, 190th Brigade Commander Hua Yi stated:

> . . . during the plan consultation, the Chinese side proposed that armored vehicles advance into city blocks to provide firepower coverage, which was quickly and specifically denied by the Russian side. According to them, once entering city blocks, armored vehicles would become targets and would be quickly destroyed. The offense should be launched with special forces as the lead, the infantry as the main force, and armor providing the coverage.[70]

Guo Yaodong, commander of the 9th Army Aviation Regiment observed:

> . . . in every shooting with live ammunition, Russian helicopters always entered at extremely low altitude, fired at extremely low altitude, and exited at extremely low altitude. Such an assault method was capable of thoroughly making use of a helicopter's advantage in launching attacks from a treetop level and rapidly and stealthily engaging the enemy.
>
> From the exercise, I felt that in our regular flight training, we must further enhance the training according to actual combat, transform from seeking stable flights to rapid mobility, accurate strikes and effective command of the air, and test the training quality according to the requirements of actual combat.[71]

The difference in helicopter attack profiles was mentioned in another article noting "the Chinese and Russian sides each used helicopters in its own way. In attacking the enemy, the Chinese helicopters would generally pull up, then dive and fire, then pull up again and withdraw. Russian helicopters would generally go straight in and straight out, fire directly at the enemy, and then depart on a level flight path."[72]

Pan Liangshi, commander of the 39th Group Army, "was deeply impressed by the Russian military's 'taking everything seriously.' The Russian military strictly follows regulations and rules. . . . When cleaning and maintaining equipment, the Russian troops did not miss any key parts in the equipment that could determine its tactical and technical performance. The maintenance was meticulous and thorough. But they did not care too much about a clean and beautiful appearance of the equipment."[73]

The Chinese side expended great efforts in providing a comfortable base camp for the Russian visitors. The large tent city was equipped with television, 24-hour hot water, a bank, and two "supermarkets."[74] Naturally, "slogans and banners" were prepared to welcome their guests.

Planning is underway for "Peace Mission-2010" to be held in Kazakhstan from September 9-17, 2010. According to Moscow Interfax, "up to 10,000 personnel" will be involved with the largest number provided by the Kazakh armed forces. "Russia and China's contingents will be large, too."[75] *People's Daily* quotes the "famous Russian military commentator Vladimir Muhin":

> . . . the separatism issue that emerged in Xinjiang also exists in Kazakhstan to some extent. The Kazakh gov-

ernment has cracked down on several separatist organizations set up by 'Eastern Turkestan' activists. Some 'Eastern Turkestan' armed terrorists have also appeared in Chechnya, Afghanistan and other Central Asian nations. Therefore, it is not hard to understand why the 'Peace Mission-2010' military drill, in which all SCO members will participate, is to be held in the Otar range near the border of China and Kazakhstan.[76]

Finally, in another "first," small elements from Chinese "mountain troops" and the Romanian armed forces conducted a mountain training event in western Romania from September 14-23, 2009. The training was reported to focus on "climbing, shooting, mountain rescues, and field drills."[77] Reporting does not indicate the parent organization of the Chinese troops.

OTHER COMBINED GROUND FORCE TRAINING ACTIVITIES

PLA personnel have taken part in numerous other training events with foreign countries that go beyond military diplomacy and routine visits and exchanges. Such activities include participation in international military skills competitions and topical workshops, as well as receiving and providing military training in foreign countries. These events allow the PLA to observe and learn from others and for outsiders also to learn about PLA doctrine and capabilities.

Small PLA SOF or reconnaissance teams participated in the Estonian Erna long-range reconnaissance competition from 1998 to 2005. Teams from all over the world compete in tasks lasting from 2 days to a week including day and night cross-country movement (orienteering), escape and evasion from enemy forces, weapons handling, and soldier's skills such as day and night live fire, first aid, minefield cross-ing, etc.[78] The PLA apparently has not sent teams to Erna since 2005 when they placed fifth and sixth out of 26 teams (in 2002, they had come in first and second places). In 2009, the Jinan SOF Group sent two 4-man teams for the first time to the "Antropoid 2009" International Military Competition in Zilina, Slovakia. Events included parachuting, overcoming water obstacles, mountaineering, hand-to-hand combat, and shooting. Though a Czech team won, China finished second and third. Other teams came from Belgium, Britain, Croatia, the Netherlands, Slovakia, and the United States.[79]

China also has hosted workshops on functional topics. For example, in June 2008, the PLA hosted a 3-day "ASEAN+3 international disaster relief workshop" at the Shijiazhuang Army Command College.[80] There the Chinese proposed a tentative plan for standard operating procedures for cooperation in disaster relief efforts by armed forces of ASEAN plus China, Japan, and the Republic of Korea (ROK). The participants also watched a field drill by the Bethune Military Medical College.[81] Most recently, for the first time China hosted a meeting of the Pacific Area Senior Officer Logistics Seminar (PASOLS). General Liao Xilong, director of the General Logistics Department (GLD), made a speech at the opening ceremony, and Liu Weiping, deputy chief of staff of the GLD, gave the keynote speech on joint logistics support.[82]

The PLA and PAP also send officers to foreign countries for specific job-related training and to miscellaneous exercises as required. In particular, several PLA SOF personnel have attended the "Hunter School" in Venezuela, including officers whose units participated in "Friendship-2006" and "Peace Mission-2009." As for PAP training in Russia, "39 Chinese specialists, including 14 anti-terrorism chiefs, trained in Russia in 2005 alone. The [Ministry of Interior] leadership also invited representatives of the PAP and the Ministry of Public Security of the People's Republic of China (PRC) to take part in a special anti-terrorism exercise that will take place at the training center of the Ministry of the Interior (MOI) Interior Troops' Novosibirsk Military Institute (Siberia, Russia) from September 25 to October 2, 2006."[83] In April 2009, an unspecified contingent of PLA representatives were among officers from 14 states, such as Russia, the United States, Korea, and Great Britain, who participated in a "joint command and staff exercise" called "Security-2009" in the Batken region of Kyrgyzstan.[84]

China's White Paper on African Policy states, it "will continue to help train African military personnel."[85] For example, since the 1960s, China has trained at least 20 Zimbabwean officers each year in China.[86] In addition to training African military personnel in China, this commitment also includes dispatching PLA training teams to the continent. In one of its most efficient efforts, the PLA has a team of Chinese military instructors at the Zimbabwe Staff College where they teach officers and civilians from Zimbabwe, Botswana, Tanzania, Malawi, Zambia, Namibia, Lesotho, and Mozambique.[87] China also provides directly the Armed Forces for the Defense of Mozambique with "logistical assistance and training [of] personnel at various levels and with different specialty requirements."[88]

Additionally, over the past 10 years, China has trained "about 300 mine clearers for 15 countries and offered various kinds of humanitarian mine clearing assistance for nearly 20 countries." In September 2009, the PLA University of Science and Technology began a 2-month course for 40 Afghani and Iraqi officers in mine clearing operations.[89]

These examples are not included among combined exercises that are the main subject of this chapter, but they provide a degree of insight into PLA relations with other countries and topics of contemporary interest to the Beijing leadership.

CONCLUSIONS

In general, Chinese armed forces training focuses on accomplishing "diversified military tasks." According to a December 2008 article in *Guofang Bao*, diversified military tasks "cover both war operations and non-war military actions." The PLA's *core mission* is preparing to win local wars under informatized conditions. Nonwar military actions include deterrence; counterterrorism; safeguarding stability; border closing and control; emergency response; disaster rescue; peacekeeping; sea and air security protection; and nuclear, biological, and chemical protection and rescue. Based on conclusions attributed to the U.S. Army, this report also states that "improving the capability to perform non-war military actions does not necessarily mean improvement in, and may even negatively impact, the core military capability."[90] Despite this warning, the PLA leadership believes the risk to performing the core mission is worth the gain that comes from training in non-war actions – missions that the Chinese armed forces have found themselves actively and increasingly undertaking in the real world.

Combined training with foreign countries contributes to improving PLA capabilities both to fight local wars and to conduct nontraditional security missions, but only to limited degrees for the former. Combined ground force training, which has focused exclusively on non-traditional security missions with anti-terrorism at the fore, requires detailed staff planning, implementation of multinational command and control procedures, often long-distance rail or air deployment, and logistics support and sustainment of troops frequently in austere environments. These tasks are necessary for warfighting, so some operational benefit accrues to the PLA in these aspects. Many non-traditional security missions, especially anti-terrorist operations, also include the execution of tactical procedures that have important warfighting applications, such as reconnaissance and surveillance, the tactical use of helicopters, close quarter battle drill, sniper operations, chemical defense, and medical evacuation, to name a few topics.

Yet, the combined exercise scenarios have been carefully constructed for the most part to deal with relatively small, ill-equipped, and immobile terrorist or criminal forces. The enemy is more the "Terrorist Version One" bad guy who takes hostages and hides out in the hills than the various forms of flexible, thinking foes that have emerged on contemporary battlefields. So far, Chinese forces and their exercise partners apparently have not had to contend with the use of improvised explosive devices, suicide bombers, rocket and mortar attacks, rocket-propelled grenades fired at low-level helicopters, or unsecure supply lines, rear area logistics bases, and command posts. Movements into the exercise zone have been conducted administratively with time allotted for arriving troops to acclimate, orient themselves to their new situation, and rehearse battle drills. Friendly forces have had total control of the air and sea or achieve it with little enemy resistance.

Exercise artificialities, such as compressing the battlefield so it can be observed from nearby reviewing stands, limited timeframes (often counted in minutes or hours), daylight operations (so that VIPs can see the festivities), result in many exercises devolving into heavily scripted tactical drills or firepower demonstrations. Because the demonstrations take place in daylight, night operations have not been required. Since these exercises are over within hours, supplies of batteries are not expended, vehicles do not run out of fuel, troops and commanders do not need to sleep in the field, and the enemy does not vary much from its initial disposition. When the battlefield is confined to what can be seen from the reviewing stand, SOF and airborne forces are not employed in the enemy's rear when and where they would be in actual operations. When the exercise is completely preplanned, commanders follow timelines instead of making decisions based on actual conditions. In other words, the military operations on display at most of the larger combined exercises lack the reality of modern combat against either an unconventional enemy or larger, modern military opponent.

Nonetheless, some training value is generated as staffs plan and monitor initial operations, troops practice combat drills, and logistics personnel maintain equipment and support troops away from base. Ironically, individual soldiers probably improve their own skills most during the smallest combined exercises where they are teamed up with foreign forces and test themselves in extended exercises.

The PLA is attempting to rectify similar shortcomings in its own unilateral exercises by emphasizing realistic conditions (currently operations in a complex electro-magnetic environment is the buzzword), increasing time and distance traveled, employing force-on-force (confrontational) maneuvers, and incorporating all services, reserve forces, and civilian support in many training scenarios. Perhaps in the future some of these same realities will be applied to combined exercises. As National Defense University professor Ouyang Wei recently told a reporter, "in the future, joint military exercises between China and foreign countries will focus more on pragmatic cooperation and on resolving ways to jointly deal with actual security issues. For example, to jointly deal with terrorism and separatism, it is necessary to aim at actual needs in organizing a joint military exercise in terms of exercise subjects, use of troops, application of tactics, performing command, and providing support for action."[91]

Most combined exercises China has conducted are tiny compared to the combined exercises NATO conducted during the Cold War or the United States and the ROK conducted for decades. For example, in 1990, 55,000 troops took part in the Return of Forces to Germany (REFORGER) exercise "compared with the 97,000 soldiers that took part in the 1988 REFORGER."[92] Or, as reported by *GlobalSecurity.org*, "about 200,000 U.S. and South Korean service members participated in Team Spirit."[93] These numbers varied from year to year, but the scale of such exercises was exponentially larger than the largest Chinese combined exercise to date.

The limitations described above, particularly the carefully prescribed enemy which does not require fighting a war at sea, in the air, or with ballistic missiles, support the official Chinese contention that combined exercise scenarios are not directed at any third party such as Taiwan reinforced by U.S. forces. Many combat actions, mandated by PLA doctrine for fighting a local war, have not been included in China's combined exercises. Moreover, it is unlikely that any of China's exercise partners, Russia specifically but also the other land-locked SCO members, would agree to be associated with actual practice to invade Taiwan or fight the United States at sea and in the sky and space.

In the eyes of the senior Chinese leadership, combined exercises and allowing observers to watch unilateral PLA exercises contribute to the specific foreign policy goal of establishing "a fine image of our military as open, confident, and transparent and reached the goals of advancing troop development, deepening pragmatic cooperation with foreign countries, and improving communications."[94] Nontraditional security exercises and real world missions are viewed as contributing to the cause of "world peace and development." Many exercises also have the stated goal of deterrence towards the "three evils" of "terrorists, separatists, and extremists" to ensure both regional and domestic stability.

The Chinese propaganda machine has become more sophisticated in supplying the media with content to get its message to both internal and external audiences. The amount of newspaper, television, and internet information about recent large combined exercises has skyrocketed since 2002, especially the amount of material available in English. While there is plenty of fluff within this mass of information, many useful details are also included so that limited judgments on capabilities can be made.

The PLA and PAP have been at this task for less than a decade. Based on recent experience, the steady stream of exercises is likely to continue with scenarios becoming more challenging, complex, and realistic.

As such, they present outsiders an opportunity to better understand both China's military capabilities as well as its intentions.

Beijing appears to be willing to discuss the possibility of conducting combined ground humanitarian or disaster relief exercises with U.S. forces (Army or Marines). It seems feasible that American military planners and operators could construct a worthwhile training event within the parameters set by the National Defense Authorization Act. There is no doubt the militaries of both countries will be involved in humanitarian or disaster relief operations in the future, possibly in third countries in adjacent areas at the same time. Prior practice on the training field may permit greater efficiencies in getting that future mission accomplished while contributing to mutual understanding and trust between the nations.

ENDNOTES - CHAPTER 8

1. In U.S. military terminology "combined exercises" involve forces from two or more countries. They may or may not be "joint exercises," involving two or more services, such as Army and Air Force. In most cases, the Chinese use only the term "joint" (lian-he, 联合) for both types of exercises the United States defines as "combined" or "joint." Most Chinese lists of "joint exercises" with foreign forces include only PLA exercises. Adding PAP exercises to the list, as is done in this chapter, significantly increases the number of exercises. Since 2002, the Chinese *Defense White Papers* have listed combined exercises but have not provided much detail, if any, about their content. Chinese media sources (newspapers, internet, and television) have provided increasingly more detailed reports of many of these exercises. Frequently, official sources like *PLA Daily* or *Xinhua* will compile numerous exercise reports and photos on dedicated webpages. However, no Chinese source available has attempted a comprehensive analysis of this series of exercises, and no Chinese source includes every exercise described in this chapter.

2. Nanjing MR is located directly across from Taiwan and is considered the PLA's main force preparing for Taiwan contingency operations. As such, many foreign exercise partners may be hesitant to be involved in an exercise that could be construed to threaten Taiwan. With the improvement of cross-Strait relations in recent years, Beijing may also seek to avoid the appearance of looking for allies in a cross-Strait military scenario. Finally, Nanjing MR shares no land borders with foreign countries and thus is less inclined to be involved in ground exercises with China's neighbors.

3. "Nontraditional security" missions are also known as Military Operations Other Than War (MOOTW) or "nonwar/noncombat operations."

4. Ballistic missile forces are frequently included in unilateral PLA joint operations training as part of the joint firepower campaign, but are not appropriate for most nontraditional security missions. Ground attack cruise missiles with greater accuracy, which are now entering the PLA inventory, might be useful and suitable for some nontraditional security scenarios, such as attacking terrorists in caves or other isolated shelters.

5. China's lack of formal military alliances influences the number, focus, and duration of these combined exercises. Countries which maintain active military alliances routinely conduct combined exercises with much greater frequency, size, and intensity than the Chinese exercises untaken to date.

6. Hu Jintao's Speech on China's Diplomatic Direction, CPP20090805710012, Beijing, China, *Liaowang* in Chinese, July 27, 2009, No. 30, p. 58, translated by the Open Source Center (OSC).

7. Charlie Reed, "Casey: U.S., China to begin joint humanitarian relief training," *Stars and Stripes*, August 26, 2009, available from *www.stripes.com/article.asp?article=64377&section=104*. Section 1201 of the National Defense Authorization Act For Fiscal Year 2000 Public Law 106-65 prohibits U.S. exchanges and contacts with the PLA that "would create a national security risk due to an inappropriate exposure" in force projection operations, advanced combined-arms and joint combat operations, advanced logistical operations, and chemical and biological defense capa-

bilities, among other subjects. However, the act contains the exception for "any search-and-rescue or humanitarian operation or exercise."

8. A list of reports on many combined exercises is found at the *PLA Daily* webpages, "Chinese Military Open and Transparent" available from *english.pladaily.com.cn/site2/special-reports/ 2007zgjdgjtm/node_15213.htm* and *english.pladaily.com.cn/site2/ special-reports/2007zgjdgjtm/node_15414.htm*. The 2002, 2004, 2006, and 2008 Chinese *Defense White Papers* also carry very brief descriptions of the combined exercises held during their reporting periods.

9. "China's National Defense," July 1998, available from *www. china.org.cn/e-white/5/index.htm*. The threats identified here eventually became a large part of nontraditional security missions.

10. "China's National Defense in 2000," September 2000, available from *english.gov.cn/official/2005-07/27/content_17524.htm*.

11. PRC Article Discusses Upcoming SCO Joint Exercise, CPP20030606000230, Beijing, China, *Huanqiu Shibao (Internet Version-WWW)* in Chinese, June 2, 2003, translated by OSC.

12. "China: 'Peace Mission 2005' Exercises Reflect Growing Sino-Russian 'Mutual Trust'," CPP20050827000080, Beijing, China, *Jiefangjun Bao (Internet Version-WWW)* in Chinese, August 27, 2005. Of note, this exercise was framed as a result of the "birth of the Shanghai Cooperation Organization in 2001."

13. PLA border defense units are light infantry elements, organized into regiments, battalions, and companies. They are considered "local forces," not "main force units" which are the subject of most foreign analysis.

14. "PRC: Details of 'Coalition 2003' SCO Joint Military Exercise," CPP20031128000177, Urumqi, China, *Renmin Jundui* in Uyghur, August 30, 2003; and "PLA Daily Gives On-The-Spot Coverage of Stage Two of 'Coalition-2003' Exercises," CPP20030818000110, Beijing, China, *Jiefangjun Bao (Internet Version-WWW)* in Chinese, August 18, 2003, p. 11, translated by OSC.

15. "PRC: Details of 'Coalition 2003' SCO Joint Military Exercise."

16. "PLA Daily Gives On-The-Spot Coverage of Stage Two of 'Coalition-2003' Exercises."

17. "Details of PRC-Pakistan Joint Antiterrorism Exercise 'Friendship-2004'," CPP20040809000097, Beijing, China, *Zhongguo Qingnian Bao* (Internet Version-WWW) in Chinese, August 7, 2004, translated by OSC.

18. According to "China's National Defense in 2008," January 2009, available from *english.gov.cn/official/2009-01/20/content_1210227.htm*, Army border defense units have "carried out extensive exchanges and cooperation on border defense with neighboring countries."

19. JFJB Article on "Background, Rationale of PRC-Indian Joint Antiterror Exercise," CPP20071220710001, Beijing, China, *Jiefangjun Bao (Internet Version-WWW)* in Chinese, December 20, 2007, p. 5, translated by OSC; "Twelve Military exercises: A Chronology," *People's Daily*, August 19, 2005, available from *english.peopledaily.com.cn/200508/19/eng20050819_203469.html*, gives the date of this exercise as August 28, 2004.

20. "China: 'Peace Mission 2005' Exercises Reflect Growing Sino-Russian 'Mutual Trust'."

21. *Ibid.* The term "terrorists on a global scale" parallels President George W. Bush's formulation enunciated his address to Congress on September 20, 2001, "Our war on terror begins with al-Qaida, but it does not end there. It will not end until every terrorist group of global reach has been found, stopped, and defeated."

22. "Scenario for Russian-Chinese Military Exercise Outlined," CEP20050824949010, Moscow, Russia, *Krasnaya Zvezda* in Russian, August 24, 2005, translated by OSC.

23. For a more detailed description of "Peace Mission-2005," see Dennis J. Blasko, "PLA Ground Force Modernization And Mission Diversification: Underway In All Military Regions,"

in Roy Kamphausen and Andrew Scobell, eds., *Right Sizing The People's Liberation Army: Exploring The Contours Of China's Military*, Carlisle, PA: Strategic Studies Institute, U.S. Army War College, September 2007, pp. 325-331, available from *www.strategicstudiesinstitute.army.mil/pdffiles/PUB784. pdf. PLA Daily* has a webpage for this exercise available from *english.chinamil.com.cn/site2/special-reports/2005zelhjy/index. htm.*

24. "PRC Security Official on Ties With Kazakhstan, SCO's Antiterrorism Challenge," CPP20060826004006, Beijing, China, Xinhua Domestic Service in Chinese 1036 GMT, August 26, 2006, translated by OSC.

25. "PRC Troops Maneuver 26 Aug in 2nd Phase of Sino-Kazakhstan Anti-Terrorism Drill," CPP20060826004009, Hong Kong, *Zhongguo Tongxun She*, in Chinese 1201 GMT, August 26, 2006, translated by OSC. *Xinhua* has a webpage dedicated to the exercise available from *news.xinhuanet.com/mil/2006-08/25/ content_4988812.htm.*

26. "Chinese Defense Ministry Official on China-Tajikistan Antiterrorism Exercise," CPP20060923706021, Beijing, China, *Jiefangjun Bao* (Internet Version-WWW) in Chinese, September 23, 2006, translated by OSC.

27. *Ibid.*

28. *PLA Daily* has a webpage devoted to this exercise with links to very brief reports available from *english.chinamil.com.cn/ site2/special-reports/ctjate/index.htm.* The photo page available from *english.chinamil.com.cn/site2/special-reports/ctjate/node_9812.htm* gives some feel for the type of demonstrations conducted.

29. "PLA: Chengdu MR 'Cheetah' Brings 'Outstanding' Reputation to PRC-Pakistani Drill," CPP20061221710013, Beijing, China, *Zhongguo Guofang Bao* (Internet Version-WWW) in Chinese, December 19, 2006, p. 1, translated by OSC.

30. PRC Embassy in Islamabad, Pakistan, "Pakistan-China military exercise concludes" available from *pk.chineseembassy. org/eng/zbgx/t284215.htm.* A CCTV-9 report is available from

www.youtube.com/watch?v=6zIN75Jtwa4&feature=related. A compilation of still photos set to music (probably from a Pakistani source) is available from *www.youtube.com/watch?v=Jm_uHKmcvBI&feature=fvw.*

31. "China'a [sic] first joint military training" available from *english.chinamil.com.cn/site2/special-reports/2008-01/17/content_1093048.htm.* Note from the headline of this report, the editors did not understand the distinction between "joint" and "combined" Zhang was trying to make. This is one report from a *PLA Daily* webpage on joint training in 2007, available from *english.chinamil.com.cn/site2/special-reports/2007zgjsyx/index1.htm.*

32. PRC Paper on "Final Part of Sino-Thai Joint Military Training," CPP20070730530005, Guangzhou, China, *Guangzhou Ribao* (Internet Version-WWW) in Chinese, July 30, 2007, translated by OSC. Also see "The Chinese officers and men taking part in the joint training stated that the joint training of special operation detachments was carried out in mixed formations," in "Chinese and Thai special troops hold joint training," *PLA Daily,* available from *english.chinamil.comcn/site2/special-reports/2008-01/17/content_1093053.htm.*

33. PRC Paper on "Final Part of Sino-Thai Joint Military Training."

34. "Anti-Terror Elites—Sketches of Chinese Troops Participating in 'Peace Mission 2007'," CPP20070815338003, Beijing, China, Xinhua Domestic Service in Chinese, 1343 GMT, August 15, 2007; "JFJB Details Performance of PLA Troops in Peace Mission-2007 Exercise," CPP20070817710008, Beijing, China, *Jiefangjun Bao* (Internet Version-WWW) in Chinese, August 17, 2007, p. 4; "Over 90 Aircraft Of Russia, China AF To Take Part In SCO Exercise," CEP20070716950112, Moscow, Russia, ITAR-TASS in English, July 16, 2007. *PLA Daily* webpages dedicated to this exercise are available from *english.chinamil.com.cn/site2/special-reports/2007peace/index.htm* and *www.chinamil.com.cn/site1/2007ztpdb/hpsmlhfkjy/index.htm.*

35. "China's National Defense in 2008."

36. "PRC Defense Minister Liang Guanglie Examines China's Military Diplomacy," CPP20081223702009, Beijing, China, *Jiefang-*

418

jun Bao Online in Chinese, December 23, 2008. p. 7, translated by OSC. Though this was an all-SCO exercise, Kazakhstan denied the PLA permission for its troops to transit the country by rail. This resulted in units from Xinjiang travelling some 10,000 kilometers via rail (back to northeast China and then through the Trans-Baykal) instead of the roughly 2,000 kilometer straight line distance to the training area in Russia. See "Russia Seen at Odds with China Over SCO's Future," CEP20070822025001, Moscow, Russia, *Izvestiya (Moscow Edition)* in Russian, August 20, 2007, p. 6.

37. "Chinese soldiers heading for anti-terror drill in Russia," *People's Daily*, July 25, 2007, available from *english.people.com. cn/90001/90776/90786/6223968.html*.

38. "Anti-Terror Elites—Sketches of Chinese Troops Participating in 'Peace Mission 2007'."

39. "Russia: Successful Outcome of Peace Mission 2007 Exercise Detailed," CEP20070822358010, Chelyabinsk, Russia, *Vecherniy Chelyabinsk* in Russian, August 21, 2007, translated by OSC.

40. "RF-China Language Barrier At SCO Exercise Being Coped With (Adds)," CEP20070811950131, Moscow, Russia, *ITAR-TASS* in English, 1649 GMT, August 11, 2007.

41. "'Cooperation 2007' wraps up successfully," *People's Daily*, September 7, 2007, available from *english.chinamil.com.cn/site2/ special-reports/2008-01/17/content_1093039.htm*.

42. "武警 '雪豹突击队' 赴俄参加反恐演习" ("PAP 'Snow Leopard Commando Unit' Goes to Russia to Participate in an Anti-terrorist Exercise"), August 30, 2007, available from *www. chinamil.com.cn/site1/jbzsc/2007-08/30/content_934533.htm*.

43. "Sino-Russian anti-terror exercise kicks off," *PLA Daily*, September 4, 2007, available from *english.chinamil.com.cn/site2/ special-reports/2008-01/17/content_1093038.htm*.

44. "India, China Conduct Counter-Terrorism Exercise; Details on PLA's 14 Group Army," SAP20080106342003, New Delhi, India, *Force* (Internet Version-WWW) in English, January 1, 2008.

45. "Delhi Commentary Discusses India-PRC Joint Military Exercise in Yunnan Province," SAP20071223428016, New Delhi, India, *The Indian Express* (Internet Version-WWW) in English, December 23, 2007.

46. "Xinhua: PRC Major General Liu Yongxin on China-India Joint Antiterror Training," CPP20071222004009, Beijing, China, *Xinhua* Asia-Pacific Service in Chinese, 1018 GMT, December 22, 2007, translated by OSC.

47. "Summary: PLA, Thai Military Hold Joint Anti-Terrorism Training in N. Thailand," CPP20080724172020, Beijing, China, *Xinhua Domestic Service* in Chinese, 1346 GMT, July 24, 2008; and "Xinhua: China, Thailand Conclude 'Strike-2008' Anti-Terror Joint Exercise," CPP20080729172020, Beijing, China, *Xinhua* Domestic Service in Chinese, 1437 GMT, July 29, 2008, translated by OSC.

48. "India-China Joint Military Exercises Indicate 'Concerns' on Terrorism in Asia," SAP20081207531003, Noida, India, available from *zeenews.com* in English, December 7, 2008.

49. "ZTS: China-India Army Joint Anti-Terror Exercise Will Increase Mutual Trust," CPP20081205172022, Hong Kong, *Zhongguo Tongxun She* in Chinese, 1119 GMT, December 23, 2008, translated by OSC; "India-China Joint Military Exercises Indicate 'Concerns' on Terrorism in Asia."

50. "PRC: 2008 China-India Joint Anti-terror Military Training," CPP20081206718004, Beijing, China, *Jiefangjun Bao Online* in Chinese, December 6, 2008, p. 4, translated by OSC.

51. *Ibid.*

52. "First China-Russia joint border blockading and controlling military exercise held," *PLA Daily*, March 2, 2009, available from *english.chinamil.com.cn/site2/news-channels/2009-03/02/content_1671910.htm.*

53. "China and Russia hold first boundary river emergency joint exercise," *PLA Daily*, August 19, 2009, available from *eng.chinamil.com.cn/news-channels/photo-reports/2009-08/19/content_4024757.htm.*

54. "First Sino-Russian port emergency drill held in N China," *PLA Daily*, September 1, 2009, available from *eng.chinamil.com.cn/news-channels/photo-reports/2009-09/01/content_4031341.htm*.

55. "SCO Forces To Train Repelling Afghan Terrorists In Tajikistan," CEP20090417950003, Moscow, Russia, *ITAR-TASS* in English, 0032 GMT, April 17, 2009; and "Shanghai bloc's antiterror drills end in Tajikistan," CEP20090418950052, Moscow, Russia, Interfax in Russian, 0935 GMT, April 18, 2009, translated by OSC.

56. "China dispatches troops to participate in joint disaster relief exercise in Russia," *PLA Daily*, May 19, 2009, available from *english.chinamil.com.cn/site2/news-channels/2009-05/19/content_1768906.htm*.

57. "新闻背景：中国国际救援队" ("News Background: China International Search and Rescue Team"), *Xinhua*, October 9, 2005, available from *news.xinhuanet.com/world/2005-10/09/content_3597669.htm*.

58. See photos available from *video.xinmin.cn/zuoke/2009/06/04/2048541.html* and *www.119.cn/xftpk/node_503864.htm*.

59. "Chinese servicemen attending SCO joint disaster relief exercise return," *PLA Daily*, May 25, 2009, available from *english.pladaily.com.cn/site2/special-reports/2009-05/25/content_1777399.htm*.

60. "China-Gabon joint humanitarian medical rescue operation kicks off," *PLA Daily*, June 22, 2009, available from *english.chinamil.com.cn/site2/news-channels/2009-06/22/content_1808459.htm*. The PLA Bethune International Peace Hospital is located in Shijiazhuang and the Academy of Military Medical Sciences is located in Beijing. Though they are situated in the Beijing MR, they fall under the auspices of the General Logistics Department system.

61. "Chinese medical team participating in 'Peace Angel 2009' returns to Beijing," *PLA Daily*, July 3, 2009, available from *english.chinamil.com.cn/site2/special-reports/2009-07/03/content_1826063.htm*.

62. "Chinese and Singaporean militaries hold first joint security and guard training," *PLA Daily*, June 23, 2009, available from *english.chinamil.com.cn/site2/news-channels/2009-06/23/content_1809830.htm*; and "SAF, PLA conduct counter-terrorism training exercise," Channel NewsAsia, June 18, 2009, available from *www.channelnewsasia.com/stories/singaporelocalnews/view/436866/1/.html*.

63. "China, Mongolia to hold joint peacekeeping exercise," *Xinhua*, June 25, 2009, available from *news.xinhuanet.com/english/2009-06/25/content_11601106.htm*; and "China, Mongolia launch joint peacekeeping exercise," *Xinhua*, June 28, 2009, available from *news.xinhuanet.com/english/2009-06/28/content_11615899.htm*.

64. "China's military opens first peacekeeping training center near Beijing," *Xinhua*, June 25, 2009, available from *news.xinhuanet.com/english/2009-06/25/content_11602519.htm*.

65. "PLA Officers Discuss Experiences of Sino-Russian 'Peace Mission 2009' Exercise," CPP20090731710007, Beijing, China, *Zhongguo Qingnian Bao Online* in Chinese, July, 31, 2009; and "Video: PLA Air Force Battle Group in 'Peace Mission-2009' Complete Prep Work," CPM20090910017028, Beijing, China, *CCTV-7* in Mandarin, 1130 GMT, July 16, 2009, translated by OSC. *People's Daily* has a Chinese webpage dedicated to the exercise available from *military.people.com.cn/GB/8221/69693/150099/index.html*. It has a pie chart that shows the PLA contingent was broken down into two equal parts, Army and Air Force. That breakdown might be accurate if Army Aviation assets are added to Air Force personnel involved in the exercise.

66. "'Peace Mission-2009' improves anti-terror response, Chinese military officer," *People's Daily*, July 24, 2009, available from *english.peopledaily.com.cn/90001/90776/90883/6709137.html*.

67. "PLA Daily Sums Up Features of 'Peace Mission' Sino-Russian Exercise," CPP20090727710012, Beijing, China, *Jiefangjun Bao Online* in Chinese, July 27, 2009, p. 4, translated by OSC.

68. "Coordination of PRC, Russian Forces in Exercise Peace Mission 2009," CPP20090727710011, Beijing, China, *Jiefangjun Bao Online* in Chinese, July 27, 2009, p. 2; "PRC: Interpretation of New Concepts in Exercise 'Peace Mission 2009'," CPP20090726005011, Beijing, China, *Xinhua Domestic Service* in Chinese, 1248 GMT, July 26, 2009; "PRC: Exercise Director Explains 'Peace Mission 2009'," CPP20090723716001, Beijing, China, *Xinhua Domestic Service* in Chinese, 0109 GMT, July 23, 2009, translated by OSC.

69. "PRC: Exercise Director Explains 'Peace Mission 2009'."

70. "PLA Officers Discuss Experiences of Sino-Russian 'Peace Mission 2009' Exercise."

71. *Ibid.*

72. "PRC: Interpretation of New Concepts in Exercise 'Peace Mission 2009'."

73. "PLA Officers Discuss Experiences of Sino-Russian 'Peace Mission 2009' Exercise."

74. "Camp village of 'Peace Mission 2009' ready for soldiers," *PLA Daily*, July 13, 2009, available from *eng.mod.gov.cn/SpecialReports/2009-07/13/content_4007512.htm*. Webpages for the exercise are available from *eng.mod.gov.cnSpecialReports/2009 peaceze.htm* and *tp.chinamil.com.cn/zt/2009/hpsm.htm*.

75. "SCO's Peace Mission Anti-terror Drill to Be Held in Kazakhstan in Sept 2010," CEP20090624964102, Moscow, Russia, Interfax in English, 1133 GMT, June 24, 2009.

76. "Peace Mission-2010 to focus on exercises combating "Eastern Turkestan" forces," *People's Daily*, July 29, 2009, available from *english.peopledaily.com.cn/90001/90776/90883/6713667.html*.

77. "China, Romania start joint military mountain training," *People's Daily*, September 15, 2009, available from *eng.chinamil.com.cn/news-channels/today-headlines/2009-09/15/content_4040340.htm*; "罗中两军举行联合训练," ("Romania and China Hold Joint Exercise"), *People's Daily*, September 15, 2009, available from *chn.*

chinamil.com.cn/xwpdxw/2009-09/15/content_4040472.htm. The exact number of participants is unclear. The English-language report said, "Both armies dispatched one squad to take part in the training." However, the Chinese-language report said each side sent a *"fendui"* (分队), which can range in size from a squad to battalion. About 10 personnel from each side is a reasonable estimate.

78. See the Erna webpage, available from *www.erna.ee/ en/?Erna_Raid*.

79. *PLA Daily*, "Chinese special operation members win laurel in 'Antropoid 2009'," July 8, 2009, available from *english. chinamil.com.cn/site2/news-channels/2009-07/08/content_1829048.htm*; and "Czechs win Anthropoid paratrooper competition in Slovakia," July 3, 2009, available from *praguemonitor.com/2009/07/03/czechs-win-anthropoid-paratrooper-competition-slovakia*.

80. "Armed forces of ASEAN+3 hold disaster relief workshop in Shijiazhuang," *PLA Daily*, June 11, 2008, available from *eng.mod. gov.cn/Database/RegionalCooperation/2008-06/11/content_3100531. htm*.

81. "China proposes disaster relief cooperation plan available from 10+3 workshop," *Xinhua*, June 12, 2008, available from *eng.mod.gov.cn/Database/RegionalCooperation/2008-06/12/ content_3100533.htm*. The article includes an outline of the main points of the standard operating procedures.

82. "38th PASOLS meeting opens in Beijing," *PLA Daily*, September 9, 2009, available from *eng.chinamil.com.cn/news-channels/ china-military-news/2009-09/09/content_4036905.htm*.

83. Russian Ministry of Interior, "Russian Minister of Interior, Chinese Minister of Public Security Met in Moscow," RF MOI Press, July 24, 2006, available from *eng.mvdrf.ru/news/2609/*.

84. "Kyrgyz leader, security ministers attend military drills in south," CEP20090425950016, *Bishkek Kabar* in Russian, 0416 GMT, April 25, 2009, translated by OSC.

85. "Full text: China's African Policy," *People's Daily Online*, January 12, 2006, available from *english.peopledaily.com. cn/200601/12/eng20060112_234894.html*.

86. "China, Zimbabwe To Strengthen Military Ties," *Xinhua*, August 1, 2006, available from *news.xinhuanet.com/ english/2006-08/01/content_4901960.htm*.

87. "Botswana Defense Forces Soldiers Graduated From Zimbabwe Staff College in Harare," AFP20081126567007, *Gaborone Mmegi* in English, November 25, 2008.

88. "Mozambique Defense Minister Visits China, Turkey; China Grants $3 Million," AFP20090605517002, *Noticias Online* in Portuguese, June 3, 2009, translated by OSC.

89. "China launches mine-clearing training course for Afghanistan, Iraq," *PLA Daily*, September 15, 2009, available from *eng.chinamil.com.cn/news-channels/2009-09/15/content_4040807. htm*.

90. "Summary: ZGB: Diversified Military Tasks Not Equal To Non-War Military Actions," CPP20081212088003, Beijing, China, *Zhongguo Guofang Bao Online* in Chinese, December 11, 2008, p. 3, translated by OSC. In this article, "nontraditional security" tasks appear to be a subset of "nonwar military actions." For most purposes, the two terms are synonymous and include a wide range of missions.

91. "PRC Expert: Joint Exercises 'Important Channels' for PRC-Foreign Military Exchanges," CPP20090719005005, Beijing, China, *Xinhua* Domestic Service in Chinese, 1223 GMT, July 19, 2009, translated by OSC.

92. "REFORGER 1990 - "Centurion Shield" WEEK ONE" available from *www.3ad.com/history/cold.war/feature.pages/reforger. 1990.htm*. Wikipedia says "Reforger 1988 was billed as the largest European ground maneuver since the end of World War II as 125,000 troops were deployed." Those 125,000 deployed troops were in addition to the units already forward-deployed which took part in the exercise.

93. "Team Spirit," available from *www.globalsecurity.org/military/ops/team-spirit.htm*. These numbers include U.S. and ROK forces stationed on the peninsula as well as American reinforcements from the United States or Japan.

94. "PRC Defense Minister Liang Guanglie Examines China's Military Diplomacy."

APPENDIX - CHAPTER 8

CHINESE COMBINED GROUND EXERCISES
WITH FOREIGN FORCES

Name	Dates	Participants	Operational Location	Total # of Personnel; # of Chinese	Major Chinese Unit (elements of)
Exercise-01	October 10-11, 2002	China, Kyrgyzstan	China-Kyrgyzstan border region	Several hundred; # of Chinese not specified	Xinjiang MD border troops
Apprehension of Illegal Border Crosser Exercise	January 2003	China, Russia	Heilongjiang border region	Unknown	Heilongjiang MD border troops
Coalition-2003 (also called Joint-2003)	August 6-12, 2003	China, Kazakhstan, Kyrgyzstan, Russia, Tajikistan	Ucharal, Kazakh-stan and Yining, Ili, Xinjiang	About 1,300; 700 Chinese	Xinjiang MD mechanized infantry, SOF, PAP, militia, and police
Friendship-2004	August 6, 2004	China, Pakistan	Tajik County, Xinjiang	More than 200	Xinjiang MD border troops
Joint Mountaineering Training	August 24, 2004	China, India	Purang County, Tibet	24; 12 Chinese	Tibet MD border defense unit
Peace Mission-2005	August 18-25, 2005	China, Russia	Multiple locations in Shandong	10,000; 8,000 Chinese	Jinan MR "Ye Ting" Regiment/127th Light Mechanized Division/54th Group Army; SOF unit; PLAN 1st Marine Brigade battalion; 15th Airborne Army mechanized infantry company
Tianshan-1	August 24-26, 2006	China, Kazakhstan	Almaty, Kazakh-stan; Yining, Xinjiang	Over 700 Chinese	Xinjiang PAP border troops; Xinjiang PAP Anti-Terror Recon-naissance Unit
Friendship-2006	December 11-18, 2006	China, Pakistan	Abbottabad, Pakistan	More than 400; 100 Chinese	Chengdu MR SOF unit
Strike-2007	July 16-29, 2007	China, Thailand	Military Sports Comprehensive Training Base, Guangzhou MR	30; 15 Chinese	Guangzhou MR SOF unit
Peace Mision-2007	August 9-17, 2007	China, Kazakhstan, Kyrgyzstan, Russia, Tajikistan, Uzbekistan	Chelyabinsk, Russia	More than 7,500; 1,600 Chinese	Xinjiang MD, two Mechanized Infantry Divisions; airborne company; SOF company; two Army Aviation Regiments

CHINESE COMBINED GROUND EXERCISES
WITH FOREIGN FORCES (Continued)

Name	Dates	Participants	Operational Location	Total # of Personnel; # of Chinese	Major Chinese Unit (elements of)
Cooperation-2007	September 4-6, 2007	China, Russia	Moscow, Russia	1,000; 600 Chinese	PAP Beijing Zongdui Snow Leopards
Hand-in-Hand 2007	December 19-27, 2007	December 19-27, 2007	Kunming, Yunnan	206; 103 Chinese	Chengdu MR 14th Group Army Recon Company +
Hand-in-Hand 2008	December 5-14, 2008	China, India	Belgaum, India	About 270; 137 Chinese	Chengdu MR 14th Group Army Infantry Company
Border Blockade Exercise	February 26, 2009	China, Russia	Heihe- Blagove-schensk border area	Unknown	Heilongjiang MD border troops
Nurek-Antiterror-2009	April 2009	Russia, Tajikistan, Kazakhstan, China, Kyrgyzstan	Fakhrabad, south of Dushanbe, Tajikistan	1,000; Russia, Tajikistan in lead	(Small PLA SOF participation?)
Bogorodsk Disaster Relief Exercise	May 19-22, 2009	China, Russia, Kazakh-stan, Tajikistan	Noginsk, Mos-cow, Russia	200; 20 Chinese	China International Search and Rescue Team (Earthquake Administration, PLA, and PAP); China Emergency Fire Rescue Team (PAP)
Peace Angel 2009	June 17-30 2009	China, Gabon	Ogooué-Ivindo Province , Gabon	70; 60-66 Chinese	Bethune International Peace Hospital; Academy of Military Medical Sciences (located in Beijing MR)
Cooperation-2009	June 18-26, 2009	China, Singapore	Guangzhou MR Comprehensive Training Base, Guilin, Guangxi	122; 61 Chinese	Guangzhou MR anti-chemical regiment and Center for Diseases Control and Prevention
Peacekeeping Mission-2009	June 26 -July 4, 2009	China, Mongolia	Beijing, Huairou Peacekeeping Training Center	91; 46 Chinese	Probably Beijing MR UN PKO Engineer Brigade
Peace Mission-2009	July 24-26, 2009	China, Russia	Taonan Combined Arms Training Center, Jilin Province	2,600; 1,300 Chinese	Shenyang MR 190th Mech Infantry Brigade; SOF unit; and Army Aviation Regiment/39th Group Army
River/port Emergencies Exercises	August 18 and 31, 2009	China, Russia	Heihe, Heilongji-ang and Bla-goveshchensk, Russia	240	Heilongjiang PAP border troops
Friendship Operation-2009	September 14-23, 2009	China, Romania	Western Romania	About 20; about 10	PLA mountain troops

CHAPTER 9

MILITARY EXCHANGES WITH CHINESE CHARACTERISTICS: THE PEOPLE'S LIBERATION ARMY EXPERIENCE WITH MILITARY RELATIONS

Heidi Holz and Kenneth Allen

INTRODUCTION

In the last 2 decades, the People's Liberation Army (PLA) has interacted with the international community in more ways, more often, and more effectively. The increased frequency and sophistication of China's employment of military diplomacy as a tool of statecraft mirrors trends in overall Chinese diplomacy as the People's Republic of China (PRC) becomes increasingly engaged in the international community.

This chapter discusses the role of PLA military diplomacy in China's foreign relations.[1] It examines the various activities encompassed by PLA military diplomacy and the ways in which these activities help to fulfill China's larger foreign policy objectives. It begins by discussing the current strategic objectives that guide Chinese foreign policy and the role that military diplomacy plays in fulfilling those objectives. It then seeks to identify trends and key themes in the PLA's conduct of each of the activities that constitute its foreign military relations program. Finally, it examines the role that PLA military diplomacy plays in PRC foreign relations.

This chapter concludes that, within the context of the PRC's overall diplomatic efforts, China uses PLA military diplomacy to:

- Reassure select countries;
- Enhance China's image as a responsible member of the international community;
- Gain access to foreign military technology and expertise;
- Deter threats to stability by demonstrating the PLA's improving capabilities.

MILITARY DIPLOMACY IN THE CONTEXT OF PRC FOREIGN RELATIONS

Current Chinese leaders share certain overarching strategic objectives that shape both their domestic and foreign policies. Key among those objectives is that of preserving the rule of the Chinese Communist Party (CCP) in the face of the declining popularity of communist ideology. The CCP sees modernizing China's economy and improving living standards as crucial to maintaining domestic stability and ensuring regime survival.[2] A second objective is to establish China as a leading power in Asia, making it capable of influencing the policies of other countries in the region. In keeping with this goal, Chinese leaders seek to build China's global influence and prestige.[3] Chinese foreign policy is therefore guided by a strategy that emphasizes the need for a stable international and regional environment in which it is free to pursue economic growth and development and expand its influence abroad.[4] Since the mid 1990s, China has become increasingly engaged in the international system and progressively more adept at promoting its influence and protecting its interests.[5]

China's swift rise in economic and diplomatic influence, in conjunction with the PLA's rapid modernization, has caused anxiety among the international community concerning the PRC's intentions and aspirations as a rising power. This is one of the key drivers behind the Chinese government's decision to adopt a general policy of reassurance and "good neighborliness" toward other nations. Part of this reassurance effort consists of characterizing China's rising power in nonthreatening terms such as "peaceful development."[6] PLA military diplomacy plays a vital role in these reassurance efforts. It also serves to further a number of other PRC foreign policy objectives.

What is PLA Military Diplomacy?

The *PLA Encyclopedia* defines military diplomacy as "diplomatic activities that represent the military interests of the nation."[7] According to David Finkelstein and Michael McDevitt, "The PLA's conduct of foreign military relations is considered a strategic-level activity that is expected to help achieve the national security objectives of the People's Republic of China."[8] Based on these definitions, PLA military diplomacy is a strategic political activity conducted for the purpose of furthering the Chinese government's national objectives.[9] The following statement from *Xinhua*, the PRC's state-run news agency, further supports this assessment:

> China's military diplomacy will continue to be an *independent foreign policy of peace, serve the state's overall diplomacy and the national defense and army modernization drive*, further increase mutual understanding, friendship and cooperation with the armed forces of other countries so as to contribute still more to world peace and stability and common development.[10]

Although, the *Xinhua* article quoted above describes China's military diplomacy as an "independent foreign policy of peace," the PLA is not free to conduct foreign military relations on its own, as indicated by the directly following statement that military diplomacy "serve[s] the state's overall diplomacy." Evidence suggests that, although the PLA is responsible for managing and carrying out foreign military relations, it is required to coordinate and consult with PRC state and Party bureaucracies.[11] According to the *PLA Encyclopedia*, military diplomacy is a "major component of the nation's foreign relations" that is overseen by both the national foreign affairs apparatus and the military leadership.[12]

What Are the Goals of PLA Military Diplomacy?

PLA military diplomacy has its own subset of objectives that fall within the overarching mandate to further the Party-State's broader diplomatic, economic, and security agendas. According to the 2002 supplemental to the *PLA Encyclopedia*, PLA military diplomacy has at least nine main goals:

1. To uphold national sovereignty, unity, territorial integrity, and security;

2. To conduct military diplomatic activities that counter Taiwan independence, promote unification, and uphold the one-China principle;

3. To oppose imperialism, colonialism, hegemonism, aggression, and expansion and to uphold world peace;

4. To strengthen unity and cooperation with the militaries of developing countries;

5. To pursue an independent and peaceful foreign policy and to oppose military interventionism, gunboat policies, and Cold War policies;

6. To independently develop military relations based on the five principles of peaceful coexistence with all countries;

7. To send military experts and military diplomats to participate in bilateral and multilateral discussions related to the definition of national boundaries;

8. To participate in multilevel, multichannel regional bilateral and multilateral security dialogue and cooperation, and to actively participate in international arms control; and,

9. To use various foreign policy channels to increase exchanges with the defense ministries, armed forces, military academies, scientific research establishments, and defense industries of countries around the world.[13]

It is interesting to note that some of what Western observers might consider the major components of foreign military relations — military dialogue, cooperative activities, and exchanges — rank relatively low on the PLA's list of diplomatic priorities, well behind countering threats to China's sovereignty, deterring Taiwan independence, and opposing imperialism. Indeed, the first five goals are strategic-level goals that are to be supported by the following four operational-level activities. This further illustrates that PLA military diplomacy is not regarded as a freestanding set of activities with its own intrinsic value, but rather as a vehicle for furthering the Party-State's strategic national objectives. The recurring use of the words "peace," "peaceful," and "cooperation" is representative of China's efforts to use military diplomacy as a vehicle for implementing its general policy of reassurance.

Military Diplomacy in Practice.

The PLA interacts with the international community and foreign militaries through a number of channels. PLA military diplomacy includes, but is not limited to, the following activities:

- Strategic security dialogues;
- The exchange of military attaché offices and the establishment of embassy/consulate websites;
- The establishment of a Ministry of National Defense Information Office and spokesman system;
- High-level military exchanges.
- Functional and educational military exchanges;
- PLA Navy port calls;
- Combined exercises with foreign militaries;
- The opening of military exercises and operational units to foreign observers;
- Peacekeeping and antipiracy operations;
- Humanitarian operations.

The PLA's recent conduct of each of these activities is described in detail in the sections below.

Strategic Dialogues and Consultations. China uses strategic dialogues and consultations, as a mechanism for "promoting better mutual trust and understanding," with those countries it perceives as being vital to maintaining regional and international stability. Strategic dialogues and consultations play an important role in China's military diplomacy. China uses high-level consultations to promote cooperation with countries with which it shares strategic interests and to manage relations with countries with which it has conflicting interests.[14] The Chinese purportedly view defense consultations as an important mechanism for promoting "better mutual trust and mutual exchange and cooperation."[15] The frequency with which China has participated in security consultations in recent years underscores the emphasis that the central government places on maintaining a stable regional and international environment. China reportedly participated in a total of 46 security consultations with at least 20 different countries in 2005-06.[16] The countries that engage in defense consultation with China include Japan, the United States, France, the United Kingdom (UK), Australia, Greece, Russia, Thailand, Malaysia, India, and Poland.[17]

The PLA does not always participate in strategic dialogues and consultations. Therefore, new developments or changes in the level of direct PLA participation can be indicators of improvement or deterioration in China's relations with a given country. A significant development occurred during the fifth round of the China-U.S. Strategic Dialogue in January 2008. Major General Ding Jingong, deputy director of the Foreign Affairs Office of the Chinese Ministry of National Defense, became the first Chinese military official to participate in the dialogues. His American counterpart, Assistant Secretary of Defense James Shinn, was the first Department of Defense (DoD) representative to attend the dialogues.[18] Although PLA officials have participated in consultations with other countries, including Greece, France, and Germany, they had not previously participated in dialogues with the United States. This development took place during a relatively positive period in U.S.-China military relations.

Military Attaché Offices and Embassy/Consulate Websites. As China has become increasingly engaged in the international community, it has correspondingly increased its exchange of military attachés with other nations. Attaché offices represent direct channels through which the PLA can communicate with foreign militaries. In addition, PRC embassy and consulate websites represent a new mechanism for managing perceptions of the PLA.

PRC military attaché offices and embassy and consulate websites represent a key channel for military diplomacy. China's exchange of military attachés with other countries has expanded greatly in the last 2 decades, and the websites represent a completely new channel of communication. Five of the six national defense white papers published by China to date have given prominent mention to the number of attaché offices that China has around the world and the number of foreign attaché offices in China. From 1988 to 2008, the number of Chinese military attaché offices abroad has grown from 58 to 109, and the number of foreign countries with attaché offices in Beijing has more than doubled from 44 to 100.[19] Based on this data, it appears that China has markedly expanded its exchange of attachés with other countries within the last 2 decades.

The majority of China's military attachés abroad are Army officers, most of whom are career intelligence officers. This is in large part a reflection of the PLA's ground-force dominated culture. In early 2009, the PLA had naval attaché billets in only 3 countries (United States, UK, and Germany) and air force attaché billets in only 2 countries (United States and UK).[20] In contrast, 21 of the 100 countries with military attaché offices in China in early 2009 had air force attachés and 20 had naval attachés assigned to their embassies in Beijing. Based on discussions with current and former U.S. military attachés stationed in Beijing, it appears that foreign naval and air force attachés stationed in Beijing do not have many opportunities to interact with PLA Navy (PLAN) and PLA Air Force (PLAAF). In fact, the only opportunity that they and other foreign attachés have to interact with PLA officials is when they escort a visiting delegation or when they arrange for a PLA delegation to visit their country.

Many PRC embassies and consulates abroad also use their websites to provide yet another channel for the PLA to communicate with the international community. Each website offers information in Chinese and at least one other language. The websites offer general information about the PLA, as well as information about Chinese military exchanges with that particular host country.[21]

It appears that at least some of the information carried by individual embassy and consulate websites is used as a tool for portraying the desired image of the PLA. For example, the PRC embassies in Cape Town, South Africa, and the Republic of Albania each carried the same article about the PLA Navy's history following the PLAN's 60th anniversary in April 2008.[22] The article painted a highly positive picture of the PLAN, placing particular emphasis on its role as an international envoy of "world peace." In addition, the websites of the PRC embassies in Grenada and Latvia published short articles showcasing senior PLA delegations that visited those countries during 2006.[23]

Ministry of National Defense Information Office and Website. The new Ministry of National Defense (MND) Information Office serves as a perception management tool by creating a direct interface between the PLA and the international media. The MND Information Office and spokesman system represent a relatively new channel for PLA military diplomacy. In early January 2008, the MND announced that it was in the process of creating an information office that would provide information concerning China's military for both domestic and international news media.[24] The spokesman of the new Information Office, Senior Colonel Hu Changming, made his debut on the afternoon of May 18, 2008, at a press briefing concerning the recent Sichuan earthquake.[25] At present, the MND does not hold regularly scheduled press briefings. Press briefings are organized on an ad hoc basis. On August 20, 2009, MND launched an official website to serve as a new platform for releasing military and defense related information.[26]

The establishment of an information office has been touted as a step forward in the PLA's transparency toward the international community. PLA sources argue that it represents an effort to create an interface between China's defense establishment and both domestic and foreign news media.[27] In August 2008, Hu arranged for 103 domestic and foreign journalists to visit the PLA's 6th Armored Division.[28] During the visit Hu pointed out: "Several years ago, it was unimaginable for us to have an exchange opportunity like what we are having today."[29] The 2008 *National Defense White Paper* states that the new spokesman system is intended to "further military exchanges and cooperation, and enhance mutual military confidence."[30] However, it is equally likely that the MND Information Office and spokesman system represents an effort to enhance centralized control over the release of defense and military information under the guise of transparency.

MND Website. The MND website appears to be similar to the embassy/consulate websites in that it communicates a positive and reassuring image of the PLA. The new website came online on August 20, 2009, and there are both Chinese and English versions of the website. Each website displays a different format, and the content varies somewhat between the two sites.[31] Information about PLA diplomacy can be found on the English website in the section on "Military Exchanges." One can also search for examples of military diplomacy by looking at the "Leadership" section, which contains information about each of the 10 military leaders in the CMC. For example, the information for Chief of the General Staff (CGS) General Chen Bingde includes his biography plus links to approximately 40 articles describing his travel abroad and his meetings with visiting military delegations since he became CGS.[32]

High-level Military Exchanges. While the PLA has markedly increased other forms of international engagement, the number of senior officer delegations that it sends abroad each year has remained constant for at least the last 10 years. Visits by senior PLA leaders are often conducted in coordination with other aspects of the PRC's overall diplomatic efforts.

High-level military exchanges play an important role in PLA military diplomacy. Based on the 1998 *Defense White Paper*, the PLA defines foreign "high-ranking military delegations" as being led by "defense ministers, commanders of the three services, and chiefs of the general staff."[33] The *Defense White Papers* refer only to "senior PLA delegations" without specifying the positions of the members of each delegation.[34] According to the 2008 *Defense White Paper*, the purpose of these exchanges and other forms of cooperation is "to create a military security environment featuring mutual trust and mutual benefit."[35] According to various

PLA officials, another key purpose of these delegations is to learn about how foreign militaries organize,
train, and equip their forces. These officials lamented
the fact that the visits are generally brief and the information that they are able to gather is limited.

During each visit abroad, PLA delegations meet
with senior civilian and military leaders, sometimes
including the president of the host country, and visit
various military headquarters, academies, and units.[36]
High-level military exchanges between China and the
United States from 2007-09 have included:

- The March 2007 visit of General Peter Pace, U.S.
  Chairman of the Joint Chiefs of Staff, to China;
- The April 2007 visit of PLA Navy Commander
  Admiral Wu Shengli to the United States;
- The November 2007 visit of U.S. Secretary of
  Defense Robert Gates to China;
- The May 2008 visit of Admiral Timothy Keat-
  ing, commander of U.S. forces in the Pacific, to
  Beijing;
- The April 2009 visit of the Chief of Naval Op-
  erations Admiral Gary Roughead to attend the
  60th anniversary of the PLAN;
- The August 2009 visit of the Chief of Staff of the
  Army General George Casey to China.

Figure 1 provides information for 2001-08 about the
number of countries senior PLA delegations visited
and the number of foreign countries that sent high-
level delegations to China.[37]

Years	Number of Foreign Countries Visited	Number of Foreign Countries that Sent Delegations to China	Number of Foreign Delegations Hosted
2001-02	60	60	90
2003-04	60	70	130
2005-06	60	90	Not Identified
2007-08	40	60	Not Identified

Figure 1. PLA High-Level Exchanges: 2001-08.

The decreased number of exchanges in 2007-08 does not necessarily represent a downswing in overall, long-term engagement. A possible explanation for the decrease in exchanges during the 2007-08 period is that the military's (and China's) attention was focused on the 2007 17th Party Congress, which resulted in several military leadership changes, and the 2008 Olympics. Other factors could have been the diversion of resources to responding to natural disasters, such as the snowstorms in southern China and the Sichuan earthquake, and dealing with civil unrest in Tibet.

A review of senior PLA officer visits abroad indicates that those senior PLA officers who travel abroad do so an average of once per year. In terms of the number of trips abroad by a single officer, only the Minister of Defense and the Chief of the General Staff (CGS) have averaged more than one trip abroad per year. The Minister of Defense averages two to three trips annually, one of which is usually spent participating in the Shanghai Cooperation Organization's (SCO's) annual Defense Minister's Conference (see Appendix A).[38] Most other senior officers did not travel abroad each year or traveled only once per year (see Appendix B).

Although observers tend to focus on the leader of a delegation, it is worth paying attention to the other members as well. It appears that participation in a major delegation abroad can be an indicator that an officer has been selected for promotion. For example, after Liu Shunyao accompanied Minister of Defense and CMC Vice Chairman Chi Haotian to the United States in November 1996, he was promoted from deputy commander of the PLAAF to commander the next month. In September 1998, PLAAF Deputy Political Commissar Qiao Qingchen accompanied CMC Vice Chairman Zhang Wannian to the United States and became the political commissar 3 months later.

Visits by senior PLA leaders are often conducted in coordination with other aspects of the PRC's overall diplomatic efforts. For example, as part of an expansion in its relationship with South Korea, China sent 14 high-level PRC officials to Seoul during the period 2001-06. Visiting officials included President Hu Jintao, the Chairman of the National People's Congress (twice), the foreign minister and vice foreign minister, the minister of defense, the chief and deputy chiefs of the general staff, the commander of the PLAAF, the commandant of the National Defense University, and a military region commander and political commissar.[39] In addition, the PLAN conducted its first-ever port call to South Korea.

Functional and Educational Exchanges. A wider range and greater number of PLA personnel are participating in functional exchanges with an increasing number of countries.[40] Functional exchanges provide PLA officers with first-hand knowledge of foreign militaries that inform decisions about PLA modernization efforts.[41]

According to the 1998 *Defense White Paper*, functional exchanges include exchanges and cooperation with foreign militaries in "the fields of scientific research, academic studies, military education, armed forces administration, culture, sports, and medical and hygiene work."[42] Functional exchanges rarely receive the sort of high-profile media coverage that high-level exchanges and ship visits do. As a result of this dearth of information, the conclusions that can be drawn about the nature and content of the visits are limited.

In recent years, China has been sending an increasing number of military students overseas. In 1999 and 2000, the PLA sent around 200 military personnel to study abroad.[43] During 2007 and 2008, the PLA sent over 900 military students to more than 30 countries — a 450 percent increase in 8 years.[44] As of early January 2007, the PLAAF alone had sent a total of 13 groups of mid- and senior-level officers to study abroad. In addition, the PLAAF Command College had received air force delegations from 43 different countries.[45] Moreover, 20 military educational institutions in China have established exchange programs with counterpart institutions in over 20 countries, including the United States, Russia, Japan, and Pakistan.

Meanwhile, the number of foreign military students studying in PLA academic institutions is also increasing rapidly. For example, the following number of foreign military personnel studied in PLA colleges and universities from 2003-08:

- 1,245 from 91 countries in 2003-04;
- More than 2,000 from more than 140 countries in 2005-06; and
- Approximately 4,000 from more than 130 countries during 2007-08.[46]

A specific example is that of the PLAAF Command College which, as of June 2009, had foreign military students from 34 countries.[47] Meanwhile, delegations of graduating students from the Command College's Campaign Command Course had visited more than 10 countries, including the United States, Russia, the UK, France, Germany, Italy, and Singapore.[48] Educational exchanges between the United States and China are no exception to this trend. In October 2000, the PLA's National Defense University invited two U.S. military officers to attend the 1-month International Security Symposium.[49] Since then, several U.S. military officers, including attaché-designates to USDAO Beijing, have attended the course. Although the course is held at NDU's Changping campus, which is not co-located with the main campus, PLA officers also attend the course.

The PLA has also begun to engage in junior and mid-level officer exchanges. For example, in November 2005, the PLA sent its first delegation of brigade and division commanders to the United States, where they visited Hawaii and Alaska.[50] In March 2006, the U.S. Pacific Command reciprocated by sending 20 field-grade officers to China, where they visited Beijing, Shanghai, Nanjing, Hangzhou, and Ningbo. Each of the U.S. and PLA delegations was led by a flag officer. In addition, in September 2008, the PLA sent a delegation of 15 company-grade officers to visit Japan.[51] The visit was initiated by PRC President and CMC Chairman Hu Jintao during his visit to Japan in May 2008.

Finally, the PLA has begun to engage in enlisted force exchanges. An example of a high-profile exchange took place in June 2008, when the U.S. Pacific Command's Senior Enlisted Leader, Air Force Chief

Master Sergeant James A. Roy, led the first delegation of 12 noncommissioned officers (NCOs) from all three services to the PRC for 5 days.[52] The delegation visited an infantry battalion in Nanjing and an Army NCO Ordnance School in Wuhan. Even though the U.S. delegation was explicitly aimed at creating engagement between U.S. and PLA enlisted personnel, most of the PLA personnel who interacted with the American NCOs were officers. When PACOM hosted a return visit to Hawaii in October 2008, the 13-member "enlisted" delegation was led by a major general and included only three NCOs.[53] This exchange of visits highlights the difference between the ways in which the U.S. military and the PLA view their enlisted force. It appears that the PLA does not have enough confidence in its enlisted personnel to allow them much of a role in military diplomacy.

PLA Navy Port Calls. The PLAN has actively used foreign port calls to further the stated objectives of military diplomacy, including "upholding territorial integrity," "strengthening unity and cooperation with the militaries of developing countries," and to "increase exchanges with armed forces around the world."[54] These port calls also serve to demonstrate the PLAN's growing operational capabilities to the international community.

PLA Navy port calls abroad often receive considerable publicity in both the Chinese and foreign press. This is in large part due to the fact that the PLAN averages only a couple of port calls annually. Moreover, port calls represent a departure from the PLAN's traditional habit of rarely venturing beyond China's territorial waters. PLAN port calls offer a relatively rare opportunity for foreign navies to interact with the PLAN and to observe its vessels.

The PLAN did not make its first foreign port call until 1985, when it visited Pakistan, Sri Lanka, and Bangladesh. From 1985-2008, a total of 31 PLAN task forces conducted 77 port calls abroad.[55] This number does not include the counterpiracy task force sent to the Horn of Africa in late 2008. Of the 31 task forces, 21 were dispatched during the 2000s; however, there is no discernible pattern for the number of visits per year, which ranged from none in 2004 to five in 2007. In terms of the number of countries visited and the distance covered by a single task force, the voyage around the world to 10 countries in 2002 is the most significant.[56]

Some of the visits have been arranged so that the PLAN could participate in various anniversaries, such as Indonesia's 50th anniversary, the 35th anniversary of the Sino-DPRK friendship treaty, the 30th anniversary of Sino-Canadian diplomatic relations, the 50th anniversary of Sino-Pakistan relations, the 100th anniversary of the Philippine Navy, and Russia for the 50th anniversary of the end of World War II and the 300th anniversary of the Russian Navy.[57] At the same time that it is paying its respects to a foreign military, the PLAN is also demonstrating its growing capabilities and establishing a visible presence abroad.

These port calls, especially to distant countries, help PLAN ships prepare to remain out of port for longer periods than they would normally experience during training, to expand beyond their normal operating areas, and to practice replenishment at sea. During these visits, the ships gain experience establishing communications links back to their home base, the fleet, and to PLAN Headquarters. These visits also serve as morale-builders in the PLAN, allowing participating personnel a chance to gain confidence in their ability to venture beyond China's territorial waters.

Combined Exercises with Foreign Militaries. Combined exercises serve several functions. Similar to PLAN port calls; combined exercises offer the PLA an opportunity to demonstrate its improving capabilities to the international community. They also offer an opportunity to observe and learn from foreign militaries in an operational environment. Finally, the exercises serve as a vehicle for building trust and solidifying security cooperation with select countries.

The PLA's participation in combined exercises is a relatively recent development and has received a great deal of attention in China's official press and in the biennial national *Defense White Papers.*[58] The PLA's willingness to engage in combined military exercises with foreign militaries represents a radical departure from previous practice. A mere 10 years ago, Finkelstein and McDevitt wrote, "As a general policy, the PLA does not conduct combined activities such as training or exercises with any foreign militaries."[59] Three years later, in October 2002, China participated in a combined exercise with a foreign military for the first time, when it conducted a joint anti-terrorism military exercise with Kyrgyzstan.[60]

During the 2000s, China has conducted a number of what the international community refers to as "combined," but the PLA calls "joint," exercises with foreign countries. According to an article by PLA Major General Luo Yuan, between 2002 and late 2007, the PLA conducted 18 joint exercises with 11 foreign nations, all of which were covered by the news media.[61] Since 2007, the PLA has reportedly held 29 joint military exercises or joint training exercises with a number of different countries, including Russia, Thailand, India, the United States, France, Pakistan, and several Central Asian countries.[62] The PLA Navy has also been conducting combined search and rescue exercises (SAREXs) at home and abroad and hosted an international fleet review in April 2009 to celebrate its 60th anniversary.

Combined Exercises: Manifestations of Military Alliances or Partnerships? China continues to profess an aversion to alliances yet increasingly engages in alliance-type activities with foreign countries. It appears to want the benefits of a military alliance without the responsibility.

China has consistently stated that its growing military cooperation with foreign countries, including combined exercises, is a partnership not an alliance. An alliance can be defined as "the relationship that results from a formal agreement (e.g., treaty) between two or more nations for broad, long-term objectives that further the common interests of the members," or as "a union to promote common interests."[63] China's aversion to alliances is based in no small part on the fact that it strongly associates them with Cold War diplomacy. In 1998, China's *Defense White Paper* stated, "History has proved that the concepts and systems of security with military alliances as the basis and increasing military might as the means could not be conducive to peace during the Cold War."[64]

Today, the closest that China comes to having an alliance is the SCO, which was created in 2001 on the basis of the 1996 Shanghai Five organization. According to China's 2002 *Defense White Paper*, "The Shanghai Cooperation Organization (SCO) has made outstanding progress in building mutual trust and developing a state-to-state relationship based on partnership rather than alliance, as well as in anti-terrorism cooperation." According to the Council on Foreign Relations (CFR), the SCO created itself as a confidence-building mechanism to resolve border disputes among the six participating countries—China, Russia, Kazakhstan, Kyrgyzstan, Tajikistan, and Uzbekistan—but it is not yet a strong organization because of internal divisions.[65]

China and Russia conducted the "Peace Mission 2005" joint exercise in August 2005, which involved 10,000 army, navy, and air force personnel. Even though only China and Russia participated, they conducted the exercise under the SCO umbrella.[66] Following the exercise, the SCO member states signed the "Agreement on Conducting Joint Military Exercises" and the "Agreement on Cooperation of Defense Ministries."[67] The agreements paved the way for the "Peace Mission" 2007 and 2009 joint counterterrorism exercises that have continued to increase in complexity.[68]

Although the "Peace Mission" exercises are under the SCO umbrella, they have not occurred without problems. For example, during the 2007 exercise, Kazakhstan troops participated but failed—either because of a reluctance or lack of time—to pass legislation allowing foreign troops to cross its territory. As a result, PLA troops had to make 10,000 kilometers detour through Mongolia to get to the exercise area.[69]

PLA Navy Participation in Combined Exercises. The PLAN is expanding the scope of its participation in SAREXs, but not combat exercises. Participation in these SAREXs is part of the PLAN's transformation into an "open ocean navy" (yuanhai or yuanyang haijun). Surprisingly, it appears that the PLAN currently sees a practical use for improving its ability to participate in SAR operations, but not for learning to conduct combat operations with other navies.

The SCO "Peace Mission" combined exercises that have been conducted to date have mostly involved the Army and Air Force, perhaps because there is not much of a role for the Navy in dealing with the security concerns shared by the members of the organization. The PLAN has been left to seek out partners with whom to conduct combined exercises. China's involvement in international naval exercises began with an unprecedented move in 1998 when the PLA Navy accepted an invitation from Washington to send PLAN officers to observe "RIMPAC 98," the major multinational Pacific Ocean naval exercise.[70] Little movement was seen, however, until May 2002, when the PLAN sent observers to the "Cobra Gold" joint military exercises staged by the United States, Thailand, and Singapore.[71] China's 2002 *Defense White Paper* provided a clue that the situation was beginning to change when it stated, "China intends to selectively and gradually participate in more multilateral joint military exercises."

The international exercises in which the PLAN has participated have primarily consisted of search and rescue exercises (SAREXs), but a few exercises have involved antipiracy and counter-terrorism training that included live firing against surface targets.[72] Although the PLAN has conducted its own intra-service SAREXs, it has gradually added several SAREX "firsts" with foreign navies:

- In December 1998, a PLAN Houjian-class missile patrol boat from the Hong Kong Garrison participated for the first time in a SAREX organized by Hong Kong and the United States, Brunei, Singapore, Thailand, and Macau sent observers to the exercise. According to media reports, "The goal of the exercise was to provide training and familiarization in search and rescue techniques for SAR-qualified air traffic controllers, aircrews, and other units likely to be involved in such operations with Hong Kong units."[73]

- Chinese reporting states that the joint SAREX it conducted off the coast of Shanghai in October 2003 with a visiting Pakistani naval vessel was the first SAREX held in Chinese territorial waters with a foreign counterpart.[74]

- The PLAN reportedly conducted its first SAR-EX in foreign waters separately with Pakistani, Indian, and Thai naval forces in November and December 2005.[75] In September and November 2006, the PLAN and the USN conducted joint maritime SAREXs in the offshore waters of San Diego and in the South China Sea, respectively.[76]

- According to the 2008 *Defense White Paper*, "During 2007-2008, the Chinese Navy held bilateral joint maritime training exercises with the navies of 14 countries, including Russia, Singapore, Australia, New Zealand, the United Kingdom, France, the United States, Pakistan, India, and South Africa."[77]

By 2009, the PLAN had expanded the scope of its SAREXs. For example, in March 2009, Pakistan's navy conducted Aman 09 (Peace 09), which was a multinational maritime joint exercise in the Arabian Sea off of Karachi Port aimed at "combating international sea menaces of pirates, drug and human trafficking, and terrorism."[78] A total of 20 warships from 12 countries, including the PLA Navy's *Guangzhou* destroyer from the South Sea Fleet, participated.[79] The exercise consisted of three phases—planning, operational exercise, and post-exercise review. During the operational exercise phase, the ships conducted an open sea surface firing competition against targets seven to eight nautical miles away.[80]

According to two retired USN rear admirals who observe the PLAN on a regular basis, participation in these SAREXs is part of the PLAN's transformation into an "open ocean navy" (*yuanhai* or *yuanyang haijun*).[81] Rear Admiral (RADM) Pendley states that one needs to make a distinction between participating in a SAREX and participating in bilateral or multilateral naval operations or exercises. Participating in a SAREX has a practical value for the PLAN, particularly in supporting their expanding operations outside of home waters and developing the ability to work together and communicate with other navies. Participation in multilateral naval exercises at sea, however, is different. These types of naval exercises are designed to enhance interoperability and thus have the most value for navies that intend to operate together in actual military operations at sea. RADM Pendley believes that the PLAN's participation in combat-related naval exercises, such as RIMPAC, is far less valuable to them and probably will not greatly expand.

RADM Pendley also argues that, as the PLAN increases its competence and operations outside home waters, we should expect it to increase its participation in SAREXs. RADM McVadon supports this view, adding that it is time for the U.S. Navy and PLAN to move beyond rather rudimentary SAREXs and undertake humanitarian assistance and disaster relief (HA-DR) exercises in preparation for a cooperative effort during an actual catastrophic event.

Foreign Observers. The PLA still carefully selects and manages the opportunities it gives foreign officers and news media to observe it up close. It also appears that the PLA is becoming increasingly sophisticated in its ability to interact with foreign observers, using demonstration both to reassure and to deter.

In recent years, the PLA has begun to invite foreign news media and a greater number of military personnel to observe exercises and demonstrations. Since the 1980s, the PLA has been allowing foreign military attachés and some visiting military delegations to observe small-scale exercises at various "model" units. The PLA first began inviting journalists and foreign military officers other than attachés to observe its large-scale exercises in August 2003, when it invited officers from 15 countries to observe the Beijing Military Region's joint exercise, "Northern Sword."[82] The exercise took place at the PLA's largest combined-arms training base, which is located in Inner Mongolia.[83]

The PLA has significantly increased the number of units it has allowed foreigners to visit since the early 1980s, but visits to most units remain highly restricted. Examples of visits by U.S. military delegations to PLA units during the 2000s include:

- The Chairman of the Joint Chiefs' visit to the PLA's Combined-Arms Training Center in Nanjing (November 2000);
- The PACOM commander's visit to a reserve infantry unit to observe a live-fire exercise in Sichuan (December 2002);
- The Chairman of the Joint Chiefs was the first foreigner to visit the Beijing Aerospace Control Center (January 2004);
- The PACOM commander was the first U.S. official to visit the 39th Group Army (May 2006);

- The Chairman of the Joint Chiefs was the first U.S. official to sit in a PLAAF Su-27 fighter and T-99 tank (March 2007).

Meanwhile, no U.S. military officials have been allowed to visit the PLA's command center in the Western Hills near Beijing, even denying a specific request by the Secretary of Defense during his visit to China in October 2005.[84]

Although it is opening up somewhat to the outside world, the PLA still carefully selects and manages the opportunities it gives foreign officers and media to observe it up close. Indeed, it appears that the PLA is becoming increasingly sophisticated in its ability to interact with foreign observers as exemplified by the April 2009 naval demonstration off the coast of Qingdao. During the demonstration, which marked the 60th anniversary of the PLA Navy, PRC President Hu Jintao met with the heads of 29 foreign navy delegations, including the U.S. Navy's Chief of Naval Operations, Admiral Gary Roughead.[85] Following maneuvers and a parade by 52 PLA Navy vessels and aircraft off the coast, 21 vessels from 14 countries lined up for a review.[86] The demonstration also marked the first time that the PLA had publicly displayed its nuclear submarines; however, they were the older Xia- and Han-class submarines rather than the newer Shang-, Jin-, and Yuan-class submarines.[87] A deputy commander of the PLA Navy, Vice Admiral Ding Yiping, told *Xinhua* that foreign "suspicions about China's being a 'threat' to world security . . . would disappear if foreign counterparts could visit the Chinese navy and know about the true situations [sic]."[88] The naval demonstration could serve as a reassurance measure, as suggested by Vice Admiral Ding, but it could also represent a display of power for the sake of deterrence.

"Operational Diplomacy": Peacekeeping and Anti-piracy. The PLA's participation in peacekeeping and antipiracy operations represents an effort to promote an image of China as a "responsible stakeholder" in the international system. Both efforts also serve to highlight the PLA's gradual development of the capabilities necessary to protect China's expanding global interests.

The PLA's contributions to peacekeeping operations (PKOs) and, most recently, its participation in antipiracy operations in the Gulf of Aden represent a more "operational" side to PLA foreign military relations. Rather than sending a message or promoting a desired image through dialogues, exchanges, and combined exercises, the PLA has begun participating in active, real-world military operations to demonstrate China's commitment to being a "responsible power."[89]

When it assumed its seat on the United Nations Security Council (UNSC) in 1971, China was firmly opposed to peacekeeping operations on the grounds that they constituted interference in the internal affairs of other countries.[90] During the 1980s—the period of reform and opening—China gradually shifted its position to offering limited support. Since 2000, China's participation in PKOs has surged.[91] At present, China is now the second largest contributor of peacekeepers among the five permanent members of the UNSC.[92] It is important to note that not all Chinese peacekeepers are PLA personnel. In fact, a significant proportion of them are policemen. Since it began deploying peacekeepers in 1991, the PLA has sent over 10,000 non-combat personnel on missions abroad. The majority of PLA peacekeepers are engineering, medical, communications, transportation, and logistics personnel.[93]

In June 2009, the PLA opened its first Peacekeeping Training Center located near Beijing, that cost $29 million. The center provides training for Chinese and international peacekeepers, as well as serving as a venue for international peacekeeping conferences.[94]

The January 2009 deployment of three PLA Navy vessels—two destroyers and a replenishment ship—to participate in counter-piracy operations in the Gulf of Aden marked an historic event: It was the first time that PLA naval vessels had been deployed outside of Asia.[95] The deployment presented an opportunity for the PLA to cultivate China's image as a responsible power that is committed to international security.[96] In addition, it highlights China's expanding global interests and its gradual development of military capabilities that can protect those interests.[97]

Humanitarian Operations. Humanitarian assistance and disaster relief operations have the potential to serve as a new tool of China's military diplomacy; however, at present, the PLA's humanitarian assistance and disaster relief operations are almost exclusively domestic. To date, the PLA's only involvement in international humanitarian efforts involves demining assistance, including holding demining training courses and donating demining equipment to several countries.[98] With the exception of demining activities, the PLA has been noticeably absent from significant international HA-DR efforts. For example, the PLA was largely an observer to the tsunami response in Southeast Asia in 2004, choosing not to deploy abroad, delivering donated supplies by civilian charter aircraft, and sending only a handful of military and civilian personnel to aid in relief efforts.[99]

There is speculation that the PLA Navy could possibly use its new type-920 hospital ship, which the

PLAN launched in 2007, for HA-DR efforts in the future.[100]

Arms Sales, Technical Cooperation, and Military Assistance. Based on the limited data available, the PLA is no longer directly involved in the sale of major weapons systems. The PLA's role in arms sales appears to be limited to training foreign militaries to use weapons once they have been purchased from Chinese defense conglomerates.

From the mid 1980s to late 1990s, the PLA competed with China's state-owned defense conglomerates to sell major weapon systems and other types of arms abroad and to provide after-sales logistics and maintenance support.[101] In 1998, then CMC Chairman Jiang Zemin ordered the PLA to divest itself of many business ventures, including the sale of major weapons systems abroad.[102] In recent years, China has been increasing its sales of major weapons systems to other countries, based on the small amount of data available; it appears that the PLA's direct involvement in these transactions is limited.[103]

According to Dr. Paul Hotom at the Stockholm, Sweden, International Peace Research Institute (SIPRI), China was the ninth largest exporter of major conventional weapons from 1999 through 2008, during which time it exported major conventional weapons to 35 states. The SIPRI data also notes that China has joint weapon systems development and production cooperation programs with countries such as Pakistan, Egypt, and Sudan.[104]

Although China's defense conglomerates are currently selling more arms abroad, however, the link between the PLA and the arms sales is not clear. The PLA still has various arms import and export companies, including Poly Technologies and the General

Armament Department's (GAD's) Bureau of Military Equipment and Technology Cooperation (BOMETEC); however, in recent reports, these companies are only mentioned in relation to the sale of small arms and munitions. One case that received a great deal of media attention occurred in mid-2008, when Poly Technologies attempted to deliver 77 tons of AK-47 ammunition, rocket-propelled grenades, and mortar rounds worth $1.245 million to the war torn government in landlocked Zimbabwe. South Africa and other ports turned the ship carrying the munitions away, and the ship finally had to return to China with the arms still onboard.[105] With the exception of this case, however, there do not appear to be any specific references in the available literature to direct PLA involvement in the sale of major weapons platforms or in any cooperative weapon system research and development programs.

Although the PLA does not seem to be involved in the sale of major weapons systems, it does appear to be involved in training recipients of Chinese weapons systems. In some cases, such as the 2002 contract with Bangladesh, China has signed a contract to sell arms and to have the PLA train the receiving military to use them.[106] According to reports in November 2009, the aviation industry conglomerates' China National Aero-Technology Import and Export Corporation (CATIC) was in discussions at the Dubai Air Show with about six countries from Africa, the Middle East, and South America that are interested in purchasing the L-15 trainer and JF-17 fighter, but no mention was made of PLA involvement.[107] If the sales occur, however, it is possible that the PLAAF will be involved in training the receiving air force's pilots.

It is also possible that China is taking advantage of visits by senior PLA officials to help promote the sale of Chinese arms abroad and to discuss acquiring certain weapons-related technologies. For example, the Minister of Defense visited 12 of the 35 countries China sold arms to during the 2000s, while GAD leaders (the director, deputy directors, and political commissar) visited 4 of the 35 countries.[108] Although none of the news media reports about the trips discussed arms sales or technology transfer, it is possible that these topics were on the agenda.

The Role of PLA Military Diplomacy.

Based on the preceding analysis of each of the major activities encompassed by PLA diplomacy, the PRC utilizes the tools of military diplomacy in at least four key ways:

1. **China uses PLA military diplomacy as a tool of reassurance to offset the repercussions of China's rapid and extensive military modernization program and to maintain the stability necessary for continued economic growth.** Through direct interaction with foreign officials via security dialogues, high-level military exchanges, functional military exchanges, and other military diplomatic venues, the PLA seeks to reassure other countries, particularly those along its periphery, and reduce the potential for misunderstandings that could lead to conflict.[109]

2. **China uses PLA military diplomacy to enhance China's image abroad by carrying out activities that make China look like a responsible member of the international community.** Participation in peacekeeping and counterpiracy operations, as well as in other forms of security cooperation, fosters the perception among the international community that China is as-

suming responsibility for international security that is commensurate with its status as a rising power.

3. **China uses PLA military diplomacy to secure access to the foreign military technology and expertise necessary to continue rapid military modernization.** Functional exchanges provide the PLA with opportunities to learn about foreign military technology, doctrine, force structure, logistics, training, and professional military education.[110]

4. **China uses PLA military diplomacy as a deterrent by demonstrating the PLA's improving capabilities.** The PLA showcases its growing capabilities to the outside world through port calls, participation in antipiracy and peace-keeping operations, fleet reviews, and other high-visibility activities. These activities often serve the dual roles of reassurance and deterrence.

CONCLUSION

PLA military diplomacy plays an important role in furthering China's foreign policy and national security agendas. The PLA's foreign military relations program has expanded significantly in the last 2 decades to include increasing numbers of foreign attaché offices in China and Chinese attaché offices abroad; participation in more frequent high-level and functional exchanges; the conduct of combined exercises with foreign militaries; increased contribution to peacekeeping operations; and participation in counterpiracy operations. Through all of these activities, the PLA is furthering relations with other countries, while acquiring the tools to further its modernization drive. The knowledge, experience, and technology that the PLA gains through interactions with foreign militaries make it a more formidable fighting force.

The increasing scope and sophistication of PLA military diplomacy is representative of a larger trend in Chinese foreign relations. Since the mid-1990s, as China has become increasingly engaged in the international system and progressively more adept at promoting its influence, so too has the PLA.[111] As a result, China could challenge U.S. interests more effectively than it has in the past. The question U.S. policymakers must consider is to what extent is Chinese military diplomacy being used to further China's interests at the expense of or in competition with U.S. interests.

ENDNOTES - CHAPTER 9

1. Only a few authors have written detailed papers about the PLA's foreign relations over the past 15 years. Kenneth W. Allen and Eric A. McVadon, *China's Foreign Military Relations*, Washington, DC: The Henry L. Stimson Center, October 1999; David Finkelstein and Michael McDevitt, *Engaging DoD: Chinese Perspectives on Military Relations with the United States*, Alexandria, VA: The CNA Corporation, October 1999; Kenneth Allen, *Showing the Red Flag: The PLA Navy as an Instrument of China's Foreign Policy*, Alexandria, VA: CNA, April 2003, CME D0008244.A1/Final; Kenneth Allen, "PLA Air Force Foreign Relations," in *Chinese Military Update*, Vol 3, No. 1, London, UK: RUSI, November 2005; Shirley A. Kan, *U.S.-China Military Contacts: Issues for Congress*, Washington, DC: Congressional Research Service, August 6, 2009.

2. Robert G. Sutter, *Chinese Foreign Relations: Power and Policy Since the Cold War*, New York: Rowman & Littlefield Publishers, Inc., 2008, p. 37; Phillip C. Saunders, *China's Global Activism: Strategy, Drivers, and Tools*, Washington, DC: Institute for National Strategic Studies, National Defense University, October 2006, pp. 1, 3.

3. Sutter, p. 38.

4. Saunders, p. 3.

5. Evan S. Medeiros and Taylor Fravel, "China's New Diplomacy," *Foreign Affairs*, Vol. 82, Issue 6, November/December 2003, p. 22.

6. Simon Rabinovitch, "The Rise of an Image Conscious China," *China Security*, Vol. 4, No. 3, Summer 2008, pp. 33-47; David M. Lampton, *The Three Faces of Chinese Power: Might, Money, and Minds*, Berkeley, CA: University of California Press, 2008, p. 61.

7. *Chinese Military Encyclopedia* (*Zhongguo Junshi Bailiao Quanshu*), Supplemental Volume, Beijing, China: Academy of Military Science Press, November 2002, pp. 280-282.

8. David Finkelstein and Michael McDevitt, *Engaging DoD: Chinese Perspectives on Military Relations with the United States*, Alexandria, VA: The CNA Corporation, 1999, p. 6.

9. Kristen Gunness, "China's Military Diplomacy in an Era of Change," presented at National Defense University's Pacific Symposium, June 2006, p. 2.

10. "China's Military Diplomacy Forging New Ties," *Xinhua*, October 28, 2002. Emphasis added.

11. Finkelstein and McDevitt, p. 10; Liang Guanglie, "Chinese Military Foreign Diplomacy Is in Step with the Times," *Jiefangjun Bao* in Chinese, December 23, 2006, available from *www.pladaily.com.cn/site1/big5/.../content_1594931.htm*. In his article, Liang states that military foreign diplomacy is, from beginning to end, launched under the correct leadership of the CCP Central Committee and the CMC.

12. *Chinese Military Encyclopedia*, pp. 280-282.

13. *Ibid.*

14. Gunness, p. 3.

15. *China's National Defense in 2004*, Beijing, China: Information Office of the State Council of the People's Republic of China, December 27, 2004.

16. "Appendix III: Participation in Security Consultations, 2005-2006," *China's National Defense in 2006*, Beijing, China: Information Office of the State Council of the People's Republic of China, December 29, 2006.

17. *China's National Defense in 2006.*

18. Bai Jie and Chang Lu, "China Sends Military Representative to Attend Fifth Sino-US Strategic Dialogue," *Xinhua*, January 17, 2008. "PRC Analysts Consider Attendance of Chinese General at China-US Strategic Dialogue," *Xinhua*, January 17, 2008.

19. Information about the number of attaché offices in 1988 comes from the files of Kenneth Allen, who was assigned to the U.S. Defense Attaché office in Beijing at the time. In 1998, China reportedly had military attaché offices in more than 90 Chinese embassies abroad, and approximately 60 countries had military attaché offices in China. For information on the number of attaché offices in 1998, see *China's National Defense in 1998*, Beijing, China: Information Office of the State Council of the People's Republic of China, July 1998. For a list of the foreign military attaché offices in Beijing in 1988 and 1998, see Kenneth W. Allen and Eric A. McVadon, *China's Foreign Military Relations*, Appendix B, Washington DC: The Henry L. Stimson Center, October 1999, p. 95. Based on correspondence with the U.S. Embassy in Beijing, 100 countries had attaché offices in Beijing in early 2009.

20. This information is based on correspondence with the U.S. Embassy in Beijing in April 2009.

21. A list of 135 Chinese embassy websites and 49 Chinese consulate websites abroad is available from *uk.china-embassy.org/eng/yqlj/zgqtzwslg/t25286.htm*.

22. "Chinese Navy over Past Six Decades," Consulate General of the People's Republic of China in Cape Town, available from *capetown.china-consulate.org/eng/zt/navy60/t575981.htm*"; China in Photos—Chinese Navy over Past Six Decades," Embassy of the People's Republic of China in the Republic of Albania, available from *al.china-embassy.org/eng/xwdt/t575287.htm*.

23. "People's Liberation Army Delegation Visits Latvia," Embassy of the People's Republic of China in Latvia, June 14, 2006,

available from *fmprc.gov.cn/ce/celv/chn/xwdt/t257939.htm.* "People's Liberation Army Delegation Visits Grenada," Embassy of the People's Republic of China in Grenada, August 9, 2006, available from *gd.china-embassy.org/chn/sbgx/t266852.htm.*

24. "China's Defense Ministry Information Office Under Preparation," *Xinhua*, January 12, 2008.

25. "PRC Defense Ministry Spokesman Makes Debut at News Briefing on Earthquake Rescue," *Xinhua*, May 18, 2008.

26. "PRC Ministry of National Defense Prepares to Open Website for Military Transparency," *Ta Kung Pao*, May 8, 2008. "China's defense ministry launches official website," *China Daily* in English, August 20, 2009, available from *www.chinadaily.com/cn/china/2009-08/20/Content_8592527.htm.* The Chinese version of the new MND website is *www.mod.gov/cn*; the English version is *eng.mod.gov.cn/.*

27. "China's Defense Ministry Information Office under Preparation."

28. Zhang Chongfang and Li Zhihui, "PRC Ministry of Defense Vows to Crush All Terrorist Plots," *Xinhua*, August 1, 2008.

29. Li Hui and Zou Weirong, "JFJB Article on Media Tour of Sixth Armored Division, PLA's Transparency," *Jiefangjun Bao*, August 2, 2008.

30. *China's National Defense in 2008*, Beijing, China: Information Office of the State Council of the People's Republic of China, January 2009.

31. There are two Chinese versions—one using traditional characters, which are used in Taiwan, and one using simplified characters, which are used in China.

32. Available from *eng.mod.gov.cn/Database/Leadership/Chen.htm.*

33. *China's National Defense in 1998.*

464

34. *China's National Defense in 2002*, Beijing, China: Information Office of the State Council of the People's Republic of China, December 9, 2002; *China's National Defense in 2004*, *China's National Defense in 2006*, and *China's National Defense in 2008*. Based on a review of the information in the four *Defense White Papers*, it appears that "senior PLA delegations" refer to delegations led by the vice chairmen and members of the CMC, as well as the commanders and political commissars of the Navy, Air Force, Second Artillery, Academy of Military Science, National Defense University, and each of the seven military regions, plus the deputies of the four General Departments.

35. *Ibid.*

36. Liu Wanyuan, ed., "Serbian President meets China's PLA General Staff chief," *Xinhua*, September 13, 2008, available from *eng.mod.gov.cn/Database/Leadership/2008-09/13/content_4005439. htm.*

37. *China's National Defense in 2002; 2004; 2006; and 2008.*

38. There were no defense ministers' conferences in 2004 and 2005. Of note, the Minister of Defense has yet to attend the Shangri-La Dialogue that has been held annually in Singapore since 2002 and currently involves defense ministers, chiefs of staff and other senior security policy-makers from 27 countries. Two U.S. Secretaries of Defense—Donald Rumsfeld and Robert Gates—have attended and given speeches. China has sent a Deputy Chief of the General Staff to participate in the 2007, 2008, and 2009 conferences.

39. Kenneth Allen, "PLA Diplomacy in Asia: Content and Consequences," unpublished paper presented at a conference in Taiwan, December 2006. China and South Korea established diplomatic relations in 1992.

40. In this case, "mid-level officers" refers to officers from the rank of lieutenant colonel to major general (1 star).

41. Interviews with PLA officers over several years.

465

42. *China's National Defense in 1998*.

43. *China's National Defense in 2000*, Beijing, China: Information Office of the State Council of the People's Republic of China, October 16, 2000.

44. *China's National Defense in 2008*.

45. Zhang Jinyu and Liu Xingan, "PLA Air Force Officers' Foreign Study Tours Represent 'New Openness,'" *Jiefangjun Bao*, January 8, 2007. The length of study abroad was not identified.

46. *China's National Defense in 2004; 2006; and 2008*.

47. "PLA Air Force Command College," PLAAF Net, June 6, 2009, available from *www.plaaf.net/html/14/n-24214.html*.

48. The period was unspecified but probably covers about a decade. Students visited the United States in 1998, Australia and New Zealand in 1999, and India in 2003.

49. Shirley A. Kan, *U.S.-China Military Contacts: Issues for Congress*, Congressional Research Service, Report to Congress RL32496, August 6, 2009, p. 43.

50. *Ibid.*, p. 49.

51. "Our Military's Young Officer Delegation Visits Japan," *Jiefangjun Bao*, September 12, 2008, available from *www.tysb.gov.cn/news/news_show.asp?newsid=505*. The article did not state what organizations the PLA officers came from.

52. Jim Garamone, "Enlisted Delegation Visits Chinese Counterparts," American Forces Press Service, July 11, 2008, available from *www.defenselink.mil/news/newsarticle.aspx?id=50476*.

53. Stephanie L. Carl, "USPACOM Hosts First-Ever PRC Enlisted Delegation," U.S. Pacific Command, October 8, 2008, available from *www.pacom.mil/web/Site_Pages/Media/archives/PR009-08%20PRC%20Enlisted%20 Delegation.shtml*.

54. *Chinese Military Encyclopedia*, pp. 280-282.

55. "Major overseas visits of PLA naval ships," available from *english.chinamil.com.cn/site2/special-reports/2008-03/12/content_1737716.htm*; *China's National Defense in 2008*. For detailed information on the individual port calls through 2006, see Chapter 15, "Foreign Relations, in the USN Office of Naval Intelligence's China's Navy 2007," available from *merln.ndu.edu/archive/china/dod/chinanavy2007.pdf*.

56. This voyage lasted 4 months and covered 30,000 nautical miles.

57. China's Navy 2007, Chapter 15.

58. Chen Gang, "*Xinhua* 'Yearender' on Successes in Military Diplomacy," *Xinhua*, December 29, 2003; *China's National Defense in 2004*, p. 44; *China's National Defense in 2006*, p. 56.

59. Finkelstein and McDevitt, p. 6.

60. *China's National Defense in 2002*.

61. Luo Yuan, "The 'Sunshine-ization' of the Chinese Military," *Outlook Weekly*, Vol. 37, September 10, 2007, pp. 42-43.

62. *China's National Defense in 2008*; Li Xuanliang and Bai Ruixue, "PRC Expert Says Joint Military Exercises Have Become Important Channels for China-Foreign Military Exchanges," *Xinhua* in Chinese, July 19, 2009.

63. U.S. Department of Defense, *Department of Defense Dictionary of Military and Associated Terms*, JP 1-02 (as amended), Washington, DC: U.S. Government Printing Office, May 30, 2008, p. 31; *The Merriam Webster Dictionary*, 1998, p. 14.

64. *China's National Defense in 1998*.

65. Andrew Scheineson, "The Shanghai Cooperation Organization," Washington, DC: Council on Foreign Relations, March 24, 2009, available from *www.cfr.org/publications/10883/*. Other countries have observer status, including Mongolia, Iran, Pakistan, and India.

66. Marcel de Haas, *The 'Peace Mission 2007' Exercises: The Shanghai Cooperation Organization Advances*, London, UK: Defence Academy of the United Kingdom, Advanced Research and Assessment Group, September 2007, p. 6, available from *www.clingendael.nl/publications/2007/20070900_cscp_paper_haas.pdf*.

67. *China's National Defense in 2008.*

68. "China, Russia conclude joint military drills," *Xinhua* in English, August 26, 2005, available from *english.sina.com/china/p/1/2005/0826/43761.htm*; "China, Russia kick off joint anti-terror exercise," *Xinhua* in English, July 22, 2009, available from *english.sina.com/china/p/2009/0721/257432.html*. While all three exercises involved the Army and Air Force, only the 2005 exercise involved the Navy.

69. de Haas, *The 'Peace Mission 2007' Exercises*, p. 6.

70. Jiang Yuanliu, "China's Master-Degree Captain Watches US Naval Exercise," *Jiefangjun Bao*, October 22, 1998, Pacific Rim, *RimPac*, is a multinational, biennial naval exercise that has been held since 1971 during the summer months in the vicinity of Hawaii.

71. *China's National Defense in 2002.*

72. "'Aman 09' naval exercises in Pakistan," Press TV, September 13, 2009; available from *www.presstv.ir/detail.aspx?id=87869&sectionid=35102040*; "The Thrill that was Aman," *Pakistan Navy News*, April 2009, available from *www.pakdef.info/forum/showthread.php?t=10207*.

73. Hong Kong's Civil Aviation Department (CAD) has been conducting SAREXs with the U.S. Navy since 1976. Hong Kong participants have included the CAD's air traffic control personnel, the Hong Kong Marine Police, the Fire Services Department, and the Government Flying Services and Civil Aid Services, available from *forum.apan-info.net/summer99web/hksarex.htm*.

74. "China: PLA Navy Celebrates 60th Anniversary," *Marine News*, April 23, 2009, available from *www.marinebuzz.com/2009/04/23/china-pla-navy-celebrates-60th-anniversary/*.

75. *Ibid.; China's National Defense in 2006.*

76. *China's National Defense in 2006;* "U.S. Pacific Fleet Commander Visits China," U.S. Pacific Fleet Public Affairs, November 13, 2006, available from *www.navy.mil/search/display.asp?story_id=26570;* "Chinese and US navies stage first-ever joint maritime search-and-rescue exercise," *PLA Daily,* September 22, 2006, available from *english.chinamil.com.cn/site2/special-reports/2006-09/22/content_596467.htm.*

77. *China's National Defense in 2008.*

78. The PLAN first participated in Aman 07 along with ships from only eight other countries. "'Aman 09' naval exercises in Pakistan," Press TV, September 13, 2009.

79. "'Guangzhou' warship returns to Sanya military port," *PLA Daily,* March 27, 2009, available from *english.chinamil.com.cn/site2/special-reports/2009-03/27/content_1705296.htm;* "Second phase of Aman 09 military exercise begins," *China Defense Mashup,* March 10, 2009, available from *china-defense-mashup.com/?p-3024.*

80. "The Thrill that was Aman," *Pakistan Navy News,* April 2009.

81. Interview with William T. Pendley (RADM, USN Retired), former Deputy Assistant Secretary of Defense (DASD) for East Asia and the Pacific, and Eric McVadon (RADM, USN Retired), former Defense and Naval Attaché in Beijing and currently Director of the Asia-Pacific Studies at the Institute for Foreign Policy Analysis. See Frederic Vellucci, Jr., "Extending the First Line of Defense: China's Naval Strategy and Development Prospects," *PLA Navy Build-up and ROK Navy-US Navy Cooperation,* Seoul: Korea Institute of Maritime Strategy, 2009, pp. 237-285. According to Vellucci,

> While there is no official U.S. Navy definition of the term 'blue water navy.' There is a general consensus that a blue water navy is one that is capable of operating in one or more locations anywhere in the world for an indefinite amount of time. While there is little consensus with-

in Beijing as to the ultimate operational characteristics of an 'open ocean navy,' it appears to be evolving as a more limited concept than the U.S. version of 'blue water'.

82. *China's National Defense in 2004.* When one of this paper's authors, Kenneth Allen, was an attaché in Beijing, the attaché corps was invited to observe an exercise in the Guangzhou MR in 1988. An interview with Dennis Blasko (LTC, USA Ret.), an attaché in Beijing during the 1990s, indicates that attachés and visiting delegations often visited units to observe small training events, exercises, and demonstrations.

83. Shirley A. Kan, *U.S.-China Military Contacts: Issues for Congress*, Washington, DC: Congressional Research Service, Report to Congress RL32496, August 6, 2009, p. 46.

84. *Ibid.*, pp. 43-48.

85. "China Concludes Celebration of Navy Anniversary With Grand Fleet Review," *Beijing Review*, April 24, 2009, available from *www.bjreview.com.cn/quotes/txt/2009-04/24/content_192515. htm*; Rebekah Blowers, "CNO Visits China, International Fleet Review," *Navy.mil*, April 21, 2009, available from *www.navy.mil/ search/ display.asp?story_id=44555.*

86. Kathrin Hille, "China Parades its Naval Prowess," *Financial Times*, April 24, 2009. According to the *Beijing Review*, the 21 foreign ships lined up in the order of combatant ships, landing craft, auxiliary ships, and a training ship. "China Concludes Celebration of Navy Anniversary With Grand Fleet Review," *Beijing Review*, April 24, 2009.

87. The two submarines displayed were the Long March 6 Xia-class, type 092 (SSBN) and the Long March 3 Han-class, type 091, nuclear-powered attack submarine (SSN). "China Concludes Celebration of Navy Anniversary With Grand Fleet Review," *Beijing Review*, April 24, 2009.

88. Edward Wong, "Naval Show to Feature Submarines from China," *The New York Times*, April 22, 2009.

89. "China's Growing Role in UN Peacekeeping," *Asia Report No. 166*, International Crisis Group, April 17, 2009, pp. 12-13; Andrew S. Erickson and Lieutenant Justin D. Mikolay, "Welcome China to the Fight Against Pirates," *Proceedings*, Annapolis, MD: U.S. Naval Institute, p. 35.

90. "China's Growing Role in UN Peacekeeping," p. 1.

91. *Ibid.*, pp. 5-6.

92. *Ibid.*, p. 1. However, in 2006, the PRC began emphasizing that it was the largest UNSC contributor to peacekeeping missions. See *www.gov.cn/misc/2006-09/28/content_401811.htm*.

93. "China's Growing Role in UN Peacekeeping," pp. 27-28.

94. "China Opens 1st Peacekeeping Training Center," *China Daily*, June 25, 2006, available from *www.chinadaily.com.cn/china/2009-06/25/content_8324367.htm*.

95. Phillip C. Saunders, "Uncharted Waters: the Chinese Navy Sails to Somalia," *Pacnet*, No. 3, Honolulu, HI: Pacific Forum CSIS, January 14, 2009.

96. Erickson and Mikolay, p. 37.

97. Saunders.

98. *China's National Defense in 2004*; and *2008*. The 2006 white paper did have any mention about humanitarian assistance. The countries involved include Angola, Mozambique, Chad, Burundi, Guinea-Bissau, Sudan, Egypt, Peru, Ecuador, and Ethiopia.

99. Drew Thompson, "International Disaster Relief and Humanitarian Assistance: A Future Role for the PLA?" *China Brief*, Vol. 8, Issue 11, June 6, 2008.

100. "Type 920 Hospital Ship," *GlobalSecurity.org*, available from *www.globalsecurity.org/military/world/china/type-920.htm*; "Type 920 Hospital Ship," available from *sinodefence.com. www.sinodefence.com/navy/support/type 920.asp*.

101. During the 1980s and 1990s, the State Council authorized the PLA to sell arms that it already had in its inventory. To accomplish this, the PLA's General Staff Department's Equipment Department created Poly Technologies, Inc., aka the Poly Group, in 1984 as one of its import-export arms. Poly Technologies was responsible for selling 36 DF3-s, CSS-2s, from the PLA's inventory to Saudi Arabia in the late 1980s. "Poly Technologies Corporation," NTI, June 1998, available from *www.nti.org/db/china/baoli. htm*; "China's Missile Exports and Assistance to Saudi Arabia," NTI, no date, available from *www.nti.org/db/china/msarpos.htm*. We were unable to find any information that indicated whether Poly Technologies remained subordinate to the General Staff Department or was resubordinated to the newly established General Armament Department in 1998.

102. Harlan Jencks, "COSTIND is Dead, Long Live COSTIND! Restructuring China's Defense Scientific, Technical, and Industrial Sector," in James C. Mulvenon and Richard H. Yang, eds., *The People's Liberation Army in the Information Age*, Santa Monica, CA: RAND Corporation, 1999, pp. 59-77.

103. In 1998, then CMC Chairman Jiang Zemin ordered the PLA to divest itself of many business ventures, because of their negative effect on the PLA's focus on preparing for combat. Jencks, pp. 59-77.

104. This information came from correspondence with Dr. Paul Hotom, who is an Arms Transfers Programme Leader at SIPRI. The specific information on the arms transfers for 1999-2008 can be found at SIPRI's Arms Transfers Database, available from *armstrade.sipri.org/*.

105. Russell Hsiao, "Chinese Soldiers and Arms Exports Embroiled in Zimbabwe's Electoral Impasse," *China Brief*, Vol. 8, Issue 9, August 5, 2008, available from *www.jamestown.org/ single/?no_cache=1&tx_ttnews%5Btt_news%5D=4883*.

106. "Sino-Bangladesh Ties," *Central Chronicle*, September 22, 2007, available from *www.centralchronicle.com/20070922/2209302. htm*. The article did not specify whether a state-owned conglomerate or the PLA was the arms seller.

107. Siva Govindasamy, "Dubai 09: China Eyes International Military Market," *Flight Daily News*, November 17, 2009.

108. The Minister of Defense visited Argentina, Cambodia, Egypt, Indonesia, Kenya, Kuwait, Nepal, Pakistan, Saudi Arabia, Tanzania, Thailand, and Venezuela. GAD leaders visited Algeria, Bangladesh, Indonesia, and Namibia.

109. Finkelstein and McDevitt, p. 7.

110. *Ibid.*, p. 8.

111. Evan S. Medeiros and Taylor Fravel, "China's New Diplomacy," *Foreign Affairs*, Vol. 82, Issue 6, November/December 2003, p. 22.

APPENDIX A - CHAPTER 9

PRC MINISTER OF DEFENSE TRAVEL ABROAD
2001-08

This appendix provides information from the 2002 through 2008 biennial Chinese *Defense White Papers* and other news media reports concerning travel by the PRC's Minister of Defense. Altogether, the two Ministers of Defense (Generals Cao Gangchuan and Liang Guanglie) took 21 trips to 47 different countries. They visited some countries, such as Russia, more than once, although some of those visits were to participate in the SCO Defense Ministers' Conference.[1]

- January-February 2001: Vietnam, Laos, Cambodia, and Nepal;
- August-September 2001: Venezuela, Colombia, Trinidad, Tobago, Cote d'Ivoire, and Nigeria;
- March-April 2002: Germany, Greece, Croatia, Norway, and Romania;
- May 2002: Russia (SCO Defense Ministers' Conference);
- May 2003: Russia (SCO Defense Ministers' Conference);
- October 2003: United States;
- December 2003: Russia;
- March 2004: Pakistan, India, and Thailand
- October 2004: France, Belgium, Switzerland, and Belgium;
- April 2005: Egypt, Tanzania, Netherlands, and Denmark;
- September 2005: Russia;
- September 2005: Tajikistan and Kazakhstan;
- April 2006: North Korea, Vietnam, Malaysia,

- December 2007: Kenya, Kuwait, and Thailand;
- January 2008: Brunei, Indonesia, and Saudi Arabia;
- May 2008: Tajikistan (SCO Defense Ministers' Conference);
- September 2008: Italy, Germany, Belarus, and Hungary.

ENDNOTES - APPENDIX A - CHAPTER 9

1. No SCO Defense Ministers' Conferences were held in 2004 and 2005.

APPENDIX B - CHAPTER 9
SENIOR PLA OFFICER VISITS ABROAD 2001-2008[1]

Position	Year and Number of Trips/Year and Countries Visited								Total Trips/ Countries Visited
	2001	2002	2003	2004	2005	2006	2007	2008	
CMC Vice Chairmen	2/3			1/3	1/2	1/2			5/10
Minister of Defense	2/9	2/6	3/3	2/7	3/7	2/9	4/11	3/8	21/60
Chief of General Staff	2/7	2/5	2/6	2/7	1/4	2/6	1/3	1/2	13/40
GPD Director			2/4	1/2		1/2	1/2		5/10
GLD Director	1/2								1/2
GLD PC	1/3	1/2	1/3	1/2	1/2	1/2	1/2	1/1	8/17
GAD Director	1/1	1/3			1/3	1/2	2/4		6/13
GAD PC	1/2	1/1	1/3	1/1	1/1	1/2	1/2	1/2	8/14
PLAN Commander	1/1	1/2	1/2				1/3	1/4	5/12
PLAN PC			1/2				1/2		2/4
PLAAF Commander	1/4		1/3		1/3	1/3	1/2	1/3	6/18
PLAAF PC	1/3					1/2	1/3		4/10
2nd Artillery Commander				1/2	1/2	1/2		1/2	4/8
2nd Artillery PC								1/2	1/2
7 MR Commanders	4/9	2/6	2/4	5/10	4/8	2/4	4/6	4/7	27/54
7 MR PCs	2/5	6/14	2/5	4/7	3/5	5/9	3/7	3/6	26/58
AMS President		1/2	1/1		1/2	1/2	1/3	1/2	6/12
AMS PC		1/2	1/2	1/1				1/2	4/7
NDU President	1/3	1/3	1/1	2/5		1/2		1/3	7/17
NDU PC				1/2	1/1	2/3	1/2		5/10
TOTAL	20/52	19/40	19/40	22/49	19/40	23/52	24/54	20/44	

ENDNOTES - APPENDIX B - CHAPTER 9

1. *China's National Defense in 2002; 2004; 2006;* and *2008.*

APPENDIX C - CHAPTER 9

SENIOR PLA OFFICER COUNTRIES VISITED:
2001-2008

This appendix provides information about the names and number of countries and number of times each country was visited by senior PLA officers from 2001 through 2008.[1]

Chief of the General Staff (35 countries). Argentina, Australia (2), Bangladesh, Belarus, Brunei, Cambodia, Cuba, Denmark, Germany, India, Kampuchea, Kenya, Laos, Malaysia, Maldives, Mongolia, Morocco, Myanmar (2), New Zealand (2), Norway (2), Pakistan (2), Republic of Korea [ROK] (2), Russia (2), Serbia, Singapore, South Africa (2), Slovakia, Tanzania (2), Thailand, Turkey, Ukraine, Uruguay, the United States, Vietnam, and Zambia.

Deputy Chiefs of the General Staff (46 countries). Angola, Argentina (2), Australia (3), Bangladesh (2), Brazil (3), Cambodia, Cameroon, Chile (3), Columbia, Cuba, Denmark, Egypt (3), Fiji, Finland (2), France (3), Germany, Greece, Hungary, India (3), Israel, Lesotho, Mexico (2), Mozambique, Myanmar (3), Namibia (2), Nepal, New Zealand (2), Norway, Nigeria, Portugal, ROK (3), Romania, Russia, Singapore, Syria, Tajikistan, Tanzania (2), Tonga, Trinidad and Tobago, Tunis, Turkey (2), Uruguay, the United States (2), Venezuela, Vietnam, Yemen, and Zimbabwe.

General Political Department (GPD) Director and Deputies (33 countries). Argentina (2), Belarus, Brazil, Bulgaria, Cameroon, Cuba (2), Czech, Ecuador (2),

Egypt, Finland (2), Greece, Hungary, Laos (2), Mexico, Morocco, Mozambique, North Korea (2), Poland (2), Portugal, Romania, Slovakia, Spain, Switzerland, Syria, Thailand, Tunisia, Uganda (2), the UK, Venezuela, Vietnam (2), Yemen, Zambia, and Zimbabwe.

General Logistics Department (GLD) Director and Deputies (16 countries). Belgium, Bulgaria, Cuba, Czech, Egypt, Finland, Germany, Kenya, Morocco, Philippines, Poland, Sweden, Tanzania (2), Tunisia, the UK (2), and Zambia.

GLD Political Commissar (PC) and Deputies (18 countries). Austria, Bolivia, Brazil, Chile, Cuba, Egypt, Ethiopia, Greece, Mongolia, Romania, Slovakia, Syria, Tanzania, Tunisia, Uruguay, Venezuela, Zambia, and Zimbabwe.

General Armament Department (GAD) Director and Deputies (13). Austria, Bangladesh, Belarus, Brunei, France, Indonesia, Italy (3), Poland, Russia, South Africa (4), the UK, and Ukraine.

GAD PC and Deputies (11 countries). Algeria, Brazil, Chile, Cuba (2), Czech, Greece, Indonesia, Italy, Malaysia, Namibia, and Slovakia.

Military Region (MR) Commanders (41 countries). Angola, Belarus, Belgium, Brunei, Bulgaria (2), Canada, Chile, Columbia, Croatia (2), Cuba, Eritrea, Ethiopia, Finland (2), Greece, Guinea, Holland, Hungary (2), Iran, Jordan (2), Kenya, Kuwait, Lebanon (2), Mali, Mauritania, Moldova (2), Mongolia, Namibia, Oman, Peru, Philippines, Romania (2), Russia (4), Rwanda, Saudi Arabia, South Korea, Sudan, Sweden, Thailand, Uruguay, the United States, and Zambia.

MR PCs (35 countries). Australia (2), Belarus, Benin (2), Botswana, Cambodia, Cameroon, Croatia (2), Cuba (2), Czech (2), Djibouti, Egypt (3), Ethiopia, Gabon, Greece (2), Hungary (2), India, Jordan, Laos, Madagascar, Mexico, Mongolia, Myanmar, New Zealand (2), Poland (4), Romania (4), Russia (3), Slovakia (3), South Korea (2), Sudan, Syria (3), Tanzania, Togo, Uganda, Vietnam, and Zambia.

ENDNOTES - APPENDIX C - CHAPTER 9

1. *China's National Defense in 2002, 2004, 2006*, and *2008*.

CHAPTER 10

EMERGING GRAND STRATEGY FOR CHINA'S DEFENSE INDUSTRY REFORM

Eric Hagt

THE DECISION TO PURSUE CMI

China has embarked on yet another round of transformative change to its defense industrial complex. The Chinese leadership's strategic sights are set on civil-military integration (CMI [军民一体化]) as the centerpiece of future defense reform.[1] The decision to pursue CMI is the result of a decade of intensive study of international trends and a comprehensive self-assessment that past efforts to retool the industry have not met the needs of the Chinese People's Liberation Army (PLA) in preparing for future warfare.[2]

The government's long-term commitment to CMI appears firm. Since the 3rd Plenum of the Chinese Communist Party (CCP)'s 16th Party Congress in 2003 when defense industry transformation and CMI was included as a strategic goal for China's national economic development, all major political and defense documents have since reiterated these goals.[3] Also importantly, CMI is deeply embedded in China's Medium and Long term National Plan for Science and Technology Development 2006-2020. The plan not only stresses CMI as a primary goal, but approximately half of the 16 items prioritized for development in this document have clear civil-military dual-use features.[4] Officials in various ministries have also taken pains to reiterate the government's commitment to

CMI, a sign of broader policy unity across political and bureaucratic lines.[5] Perhaps more telling of the central government commitment is its ability to marshal the nation's resources for specific CMI goals. Although the picture is still mixed, positive trends are surfacing. There is a great diversity of central funding projects and supporting institutions that have varying relevance to CMI.[6] Many small to medium projects both inside and outside the defense industry are directly linked to dual-use activities. While many larger, national, projects do not carry the CMI tag, the evidence suggests that it is emerging as an integral goal.

CMI is described as the "integrated and coordinated development of the defense and civilian technology economies (国防建设与经济建设协调发展)."[7] There are a number of driving forces behind CMI, some explicit in official publications, others implicit and suggested in nonofficial analysis. The first is economic and one clearly spelled out in the 2008 *Defense White Paper* and other documents. In short, China may simply not be able to afford separate civilian, commercial, and military research and development (R&D)/productions streams. The demand on financial resources to meet the growing needs of military modernization—particularly in pushing the revolution in military affairs (RMA)—are becoming apparent. Moreover, broader access to the market through direct investment opportunities and injection of assets into the stock market holds huge potential for China's defense industry to raise capital. A second driver is acquiring the capacity and talent to innovate in order to meet the needs of a high-tech, networked PLA fighting force. As the 2008 *Defense White Paper* describes, with the defense research institutes and enterprises as the backbone, basic and applied research in institutes of higher learning and other civilian entities will be a new vital force for independent innovation. This means that although much of the capacity to build a modern army resides within the defense industry, the human resources and industrial innovation of the civilian sector has greater potential in many fields of science and technology, upon which a modern fighting force will be built. A third driver is strategic in nature. China's ability to leap frog in high-tech military capabilities is a factor of the nation's overall science and technology (S&T) system and its ability to innovate, itself dependent on the enterprise and other institutional R&D centers that are closely connected to the global economy. In other words, the transfer of technology from abroad, upon which China still heavily relies, is far better facilitated in an environment that is not solely dedicated to military purposes. Another strategic consideration is the advantage of developing certain defense technologies within a CMI framework, such as space assets or components of the command, control, communications, computers, intelligence, surveillance, and reconnaissance (C4ISR) network. They are at reduced physical risk since competitor nations are less likely to view systems that also serve nonmilitary interests as threats.[8]

If successful, CMI will fundamentally change the relationship between the defense and civilian economies not only by impelling reform within the defense industry through greater competition, oversight, and transparency, but also by enlisting the civilian sector to participate in construction of national defense development. Elements of a national CMI plan to achieve these goals are emerging. Yet, it is premised on the fact that past reforms have been inadequate in meeting the demands of China's defense ambitions. If this is so, why has China still produced many technological breakthroughs over the past decade? To see why this may be we turn to a brief review of past reforms.

REDUCING THE GAP: PAST REFORMS

In the mid-1990s, China's defense economy was in a perilous state. It reached its nadir in 1998, over 60 percent of the defense industry was in deficit, totaling 6.4 billion in losses,[9] and it was producing outmoded equipment nearly across the board.[10] The defense sector has long been a bloated and inefficient military production system that was largely based on an outdated Soviet model.[11] But the effects resulting from opening up and reform have also taken a toll. Under a relatively benign international security environment, Deng Xiaoping decided to focus on rebuilding the economy. Defense development was subordinated to national economic development and placed last of the "Four Modernizations." The defense industry's forays into commercial enterprises and military conversion business helped offset a decrease in funding, which plummeted to a mere 1.74 percent of the gross domestic product (GDP) in 1987.[12]

A number of factors triggered the far-reaching reforms to the military-industry complex beginning in the mid-1990s. China's national security conditions had changed dramatically. China saw the Gulf War in 1991 as the "the first modern information war," a war waged and won on the strength of U.S. technological superiority. This event led to a period of self-reflection and military audit that lasted into the mid-1990s and concluded that China was falling dangerously behind in RMA and had to rapidly catch up since future wars would likely be high-tech, fast-paced, of short duration, and would depend heavily on information and electronic systems.[13] This more sober assessment was exacerbated by developments across the Taiwan Strait, culminating in the 1996 crisis, with a humiliating denouement for China.[14]

The latest phase of major reform began with the shakeup of the industry in 1998-99 and is characterized by fiscal, policy, organizational, and enterprise restructuring. Critically, defense funding was dramatically raised. The military budget roughly grew an average of 15 percent per annum from 1994-2009, leading to a nine-fold increase in the budget.[15] Spending on equipment and weapons procurement has increased the most.[16] This portion of the budget was readjusted from a low of 16 percent early in the 1990s to roughly one-third, where it stands today.[17] More funding has also been made available to basic R&D. Defense R&D likely reflects national figures, which have nearly quadrupled since 2000 and currently amount to 1.5 percent of GDP.[18] Greater funding within the defense sector has also been directed toward weapon development management, innovation, and application of basic technologies and the talent needed to implement it.[19] Improved finances are also manifest in the salary increases of key personnel in the defense sector during the past decade.[20]

The reorganizing of the Commission on Science, Technology, and Industry for National Defense (COSTIND) was key as well. The old COSTIND had nearly total control over defense production planning from setting goals and priorities, to investment, R&D, production, and testing. In this pivotal position, it exerted undue influence over the defense-procurement process. On the other hand, the purchasing of equipment was dispersed among several bodies, including the Equipment Bureau of General Staff Department and the Ordinance Office of General Logistics Department. The result was inefficiency, corruption, and an inability to meet the needs of the military. All procurement functions, as well as the military research and facilities, was transferred to the newly created General Armaments Department (GAD) and the new diminutive COSTIND—now strictly under State Council authority—were limited largely to regulatory oversight and management of the defense industry. With the creation of the defense production industries into 10 major group corporations,[21] these reforms separated the buyers from the builders, with COSTIND playing a regulatory and administrative role. This allowed for a more contract-based procurement system that instilled a degree of competition, helping forge a system better equipped to fulfill the demands of the military. In sum, the restructuring was internal to the defense industrial complex and did little to create real competition among themselves, much less open it to the civilian or nonstate sectors, but the organizational and policy reforms have significantly improved the overall health of defense sector.

Reform of the defense R&D system has further spurred progress. In addition to an increase in funding as mentioned above, the dismantling of some of the stove piping between R&D institutes and their separation from production has led to better coordination in bringing basic and preliminary weapons research efforts to development. For example, the PLA's General Armaments Department has instituted a series of national-level coordinating entities to help identify key technologies, establish priorities, and manage planning of R&D programs. There are many such groups comprised of experts from the military research institutions, defense companies, universities, and civilian high-tech enterprises. They identify new technologies and provide feasibility studies on various fields such as nanotechnology, satellite applications, simulation technology, integrated electronic warfare, and precision guidance.[22] This has improved the supervision and increased linkages between the various elements of the R&D cycle, likely having an appreciable impact on bringing key technologies into defense development.

There are a number of other important—possibly critical—factors as to why China's defense industry has performed better in the past decade. At the top of the list is the access to foreign military technology, particularly from Russia.[23] This help has been substantial and wide-ranging; however, as Stockholm International Peace Research Institute (SIPRI) has reported, military sales from Russia to China dropped off sharply in 2007. China and Russia may be reaching a divergence. With China's emphasis on technology transfer and indigenous innovation, it likely has less and less to glean from military trade with Russia. On the other hand, Russia is increasingly careful of selling ever more advanced systems to China. Regardless of the precise reasons, China's continued advancement against the backdrop of slowed sales from Russia and other countries demonstrates that foreign assistance plays less of a critical role to China's defense industrial progress. The aforementioned progress in research, design, and production (and foreign purchases) may explain why many of the recent weapon systems have recently come on line, since most of them have been in the procurement pipeline for many years.

At first blush, it is clear that in the past decade China has made headway on a range of weapon systems including its J-10 and J-11 fighter aircraft, new missile destroyers, land-attack cruise missiles, Jin and Shang Class nuclear subs, or the anti-satellite weapons systems (ASAT) and anti-ship ballistic missiles (ASBM). On balance, however, while the reforms to date have led to significant progress, they do not constitute a paradigm shift away from the industry's traditionally closed and largely monopolized operating philosophy. Does China's current military industrial complex possess the means to meet the far more demanding requirements of equipping the PLA for the future? Or does it require a fundamental reorientation that allows it to integrate with the national economy and create the synergies to help innovate for future high-tech and informationalized warfare? China has concluded that deeper reform is needed.

MARRYING TECHNOLOGY AND INDUSTRY

While civil-military integration has become a catchword for the overall guiding strategy going forward, specific implementation or directives on how to achieve it are far less clear. Few of the current efforts fall squarely into a CMI framework. Some of the vagueness is a result of the vast scale of the objectives. A number of current reforms are a continuation of past efforts; others are new initiatives with a visible CMI label; but most fall somewhere in between. All, however, should be considered as long-term goals to combine military and civilian economies for national defense construction. The reorganization of the management of defense and civilian industry is instructive here.

The creative destruction of bureaucracies are often as much about a power struggle amongst interest groups as they are about rationalizing and streamlining government agency functions. The changes wrought by the formation of Ministry of Industry and Information Technology (MIIT [工业和信息化部]) appear consistently so. On paper, this is a super-ministry that brings together the former Ministry of Information Industries, COSTIND,[24] the informatization responsibilities under the National Development and Reform Commission (NDRC), the State Council Informatization Office, and the State Tobacco Monopoly Administration.[25] Under this new ministry, COSTIND is clearly demoted, at least in an administrative sense, to the State Administration for Science, Technology, and National Defense (SASTIND [国家国防科技工业局]). COSTIND has been in power struggles with several agencies including the NDRC and the Ministry of Science and Technology (MoST [科学技术部]).[26] The NDRC is the arch powerful decisionmaking body over macro national economic and development goals, while COSTIND has traditionally decided defense industry economic planning, often leading to duplication and confusion.[27] Its contest with MoST was often manifested in implementing and allocating R&D projects, which led to a phenomenon of "two channels."[28] But the principle turf battle has been with GAD, which has long pushed for its abolition. GAD would prefer to have all of COSTIND's activities under its control and turn its defense S&T management system into something more akin to the U.S. model of Defense Advanced Research Projects Agency, a smaller and military-dependent entity.[29] It is logical that the demise of COSTIND was in part to break the monopoly of the defense industry, a goal that could be crucial to achieving CMI.

The anatomy of the new super-ministry suggests there are larger strategic implications at play. MIIT will bring together the majority of the nation's industrial and technology capacity under one roof.[30] Theoretically, this will allow for better central coordination and formulation of industrial policies, which have been slow to adapt from the traditional heavy industry sectors to the fast-paced electronics, computer, communications, and digital network sectors. Furthermore, MIIT will serve the specific purpose of uniting the civilian information industries with those of the military. Previously, many parts of this sector (electronics for instance) were spread throughout the former Ministry of Industry and Information, COSTIND, and a number of military's research institutes.[31] As China's military doctrine is now "fighting local wars under conditions of informatization," digitizing the defense industry is a crucial objective.[32] With the civilian information industry well ahead of the military both in technology and industrial capacity, this organizational union accelerates that process and will help extend it to all areas of the military including nuclear, space, aviation, shipping, and ordnance.[33]

MIIT also creates an administrative structure that is coherent with the mandate of integrating the civilian and military economies. In essence, this move will bring a closed, protectionist, monopoly-ridden defense industry alongside the larger, dynamic civilian and nonstate economic sectors. The defense industries were not only shielded from competition, but largely deprived of benefiting from the civilian sector's modes of innovation, modern manufacturing techniques as well as the access to capital. Greater comprehensive planning will in theory better allocate R&D and production resources and rationalize standards. This is a far-sighted strategic move to create an environment for dual-use activity. To aid in this endeavor, the Dual-use Promotion Office was also established with the creation of MIIT. This office's primary task is to identify areas for civil-military convergence and to act as intermediary for marketing dual-use opportunities.[34] Efforts to achieve integration between the military and civilian sectors are not new, but they have never been placed at the nexus with central decisionmaking on the economy, industrial policy, and national innovation directives, where central and local governments, the military, and industry can come together to negotiate their strategic interests.[35]

On paper, this organizational restructuring looks impressive for the task of CMI. It demonstrates that China is serious about creating a viable institutional environment for promoting integration. On-the-ground performance and implementation is, of course, the ultimate judge of success, and the results so far appear mixed. SASTIND's current director is also deputy minister of MIIT and a former COSTIND official is also in charge of the dual-use office. Moreover, SASTIND remains largely in tact as an agency, with three-quarters of its original 400 staff still employed.[36] Therefore, SASTIND's institutional influence over the defense industry remains formidable and, if it proves resistant to change, could cause problems for the ministry's mandate.[37]

Despite the creation of this super-ministry, the nation's industrial policy and planning remains divided. NDRC and the State-owned Assets Supervision and Administration Commission (SASAC), China's state-owned asset watchdog, as well as local governments and state-owned enterprises (SOEs), persist in holding the purse strings that will have a significant impact on funding and carrying out plans under MIIT's diverse interest groups. For this reason, some have suggested that China needs an even stronger, centralized, hierarchical leadership to direct CMI at levels no lower than the Central Military Commission (CMC) and the State Council. This would resemble the U.S. system which is directed by presidential offices and congressional committees, with offices throughout the government and defense establishment to execute it.[38] However, the U.S. system took roughly 10 years to put in place, and we should not expect China's messy organizational oversight, local-central power struggles, the legacy of a monopolized defense industry, and conflicting regulatory and policy directives to take any less time.

INCENTIVE BUILDING

The recent bout of policy reforms arrived in dribbles and without fanfare begining in 2002, and continues until the present. Individually, they are almost indiscernible, but collectively they may be more revolutionary than those of 1998-99. A number of factors have led up to their onset. It was clear to the leadership, both political and military, that the 1998-99 restructuring of the management and operation over the defense enterprises were not sufficient to bring China's entrenched defense industry up to par with the global leaders. Military conversion spin-offs remained the dominant form of dual-use activity, while spin-on and more comprehensive technology diffusion between civilian and military sectors was generally anemic and confined to a few narrow fields. Second, the international trends were clear. After the end of the cold war, global military powers were decisively moving toward "composite defense-economic" characteristics (United States) or already had successful dual-use economies (Japan) in place.[39] China studied other countries closely and made the decision to follow suit.[40]

Procurement.

One critical component to the new policy initiatives was the decision by the military to reform the outdated procurement process and open up bidding to the civilian sector. This was a task under the purview of the military, and it set to work devising regulations.[41] The first and most authoritative law was published in 2002 by the CMC.[42] Five more detailed regulations quickly followed in its wake, released by GAD in 2003.[43] The basic framework of the reforms is to dramatically open up military procurement to the civilian enterprises based on competitive bidding (see Appendix A).[44]

Along with the new regulations, a restructuring of the procurement management system under the newly established GAD was underway.[45] Mainly due to legacies of China's military command structure, GAD is in charge of comprehensive planning of many general use items, as well as much of procurement for the army.[46] However, the Air Force, Second Artillery, and Navy manage much of their own procurement, and the General Staff Department purchases basic training equipment. Actual implementation of procurement can also involve COSTIND, testing centers, and regional military commands. This is in part due to how central military funds are disbursed. It remains based on a quota system where once funds are allocated to various departments, military areas, and services, they largely make their own acquisition decisions.

Through these measures, the military was keen to achieve two procurement reform goals. One was to bring as many acquisition programs as possible under a competitive bidding system — both among defense enterprises and with civilian enterprises. The military saw the costs of weapon systems sky-rocketing beyond budget increases between the 1970s and 2000s, affecting their ability to purchase needed systems — in the military's appraisal, partly due to rising sophistication of weapon systems but also due to lack of competition.[47] A second goal was to centralize procurement of general use items under GAD, thereby achieving scale of purchase and savings.[48]

Civilian enterprises are winning substantial contracts and are even beating out other SOEs, including defense industries — both bellwethers of success. Cases remain rare, but are on the increase. For instance, the Delixi Group of Zhejiang bid to provide low voltage electric apparatuses for Jiuquan rocket-launch base and the Shenzhou spacecraft. It was the only civilian enterprise submitting a tender and won over 20 other SOEs.[49] Also, after a successful competitive bidding competition, the civilian enterprise, Sanxin Steel Structure Ltd. Co., was awarded the contract to produce radio telescope towers, a component of China's most advanced deep space ground station and enabling data transmission for the Chang'e-1 mission.[50]

Other less glamorous examples of successful bids include large quantity computer purchases with reported savings of 28 percent, refueling ships with savings of 20 percent, and ship production with cost gains estimated in the hundreds of millions of yuan.[51] In 2004, savings through centralizing purchases of general use items are estimated to be 7 percent of funds spent on these, however, this amounts to a mere 1 percent of the overall budget for equipment.[52]

More broadly, the reform has fallen far short of expectations. To date, only 20 percent of acquisition is done through competitive bidding. That does not compare favorably to 80 percent in the United States.[53] Moreover, competitive bidding as defined by the new rules includes open bidding but it also includes other forms of "closed bidding" (negotiation, invitation, and single supplier) all of which are less standardized, harder to regulate, and therefore vulnerable to irregular activity. Thus fair and transparent bidding is likely under 20 percent.

Furthermore, the "playing field" is tipped further in the defense enterprises' favor in a number of other ways. The military was keen to open up bidding to as many general use and nonkey weapon systems as possible, but not at the expense of maintaining secrecy. To participate in R&D and the production of military related items, all nondefense enterprises must pass three approvals: for confidentiality, quality control, and for "product security" — the latter being a euphemism for strict requirements to maintain a long-term stable product line.[54] While such constraints plague defense contracts elsewhere, China's secretive defense establishment makes this approval process especially onerous. In March 2009 Inspur Company Ltd won the approvals to produce computer security and hardening equipment for the PLA Navy (PLAN) only after several years of effort.[55] Many do not make the grade even after years of effort.[56]

Even more serious are the various costs to doing business that discriminate against civilian enterprises. Military enterprises are exempted from value-added tax (up to 18 percent), business tax, and land-use taxes, all of which can add up to 25 percent of the total project value.[57] There are also intangible costs such as the government's decision in 2005 to do a sweeping upgrade of the defense industry's manufacturing and design facilities, an investment project that was not available even to civilian enterprises engaged in defense production.[58] Another problem is pricing reform. Prices for many military products, which form the basis for bidding, are drafted by the military, but with production and R&D separated in accounting ledgers, prices often do not include the costs of R&D.[59] Civilian enterprises naturally have to incorporate such costs in doing business.

Other issues such as continuing asymmetry of information continue to exist. The process of publicizing various forms of competitive bidding remains incomplete. Another complaint often heard is the lack of a platform for communicating to civilian enterprises the needs of the military; and vice versa, improving the military's understanding of available technologies and products in the civilian sector. The case of Wuhan-based Pangu Tech Co. is instructive: it developed a technology for heavy vehicle shock absorption — highly useful to the military — but was unknown until a low level technician discovered it in a publication.[60]

The result of these tangible and intangible barriers has led to the vivid image of civilian enterprise activity in the defense industry as "gnawing on bones."[61] The real meat is still mainly reserved for the defense enterprises. In 2005 and 2009, the CMC and GAD published several more regulations to "deepen procurement reform."[62] However, without evidence of more contracts going to the nondefense sector, procurement reform will remain inconsequential as a tool to bring greater competition in the defense industry.

Shareholding Reform.

Probably the far more dramatic policy transformation efforts have been the exposure of the defense industry to shareholding reform. The central government's initiatives to overhaul the inefficient SOE system through asset restructuring began in 1993 and concentrated on the civilian sector SOEs.[63] It has gradually gathered steam within the defense industry as well and has already enhanced the sector's access to market capital, though its impact on how the defense industry is managed and run remains unproven. There are many barriers that are likely to be a source of inertia.

The defense sector's experience with market-based reform has unfolded in three stages.[64] From 1993-2005, initial public offerings (IPOs) from the defense industry flowered, numbering about 54 by the end of this period. The vast majority of these listed companies were spin-offs from the institutes under the defense industry involved in purely civilian production.[65] This phenomenon started prior to the reorganization of the six defense industrial sectors into 11 major defense group corporations in the 1999-2002 timeframe,[66] but IPOs continued after that in the form of subsidiaries of the group corporations.[67]

A second phase was kick-started by a document published by the State Council in 2005, which turned out to be path-breaking in that it officially sanctioned private, nonstate enterprise and even foreign capital investment in the state defense sector.[68] This was closely followed up in early 2007 by two documents published by COSTIND, the NDRC, and the recently established SASAC,[69] elaborating on nondefense and nonstate participation in the defense industry.[70] However, around the same time, the overheated markets led the China Securities Regulatory Commission (CSRC) in 2006 to issue tightened controls on the new stock listings, making IPOs an unattractive option for the defense industry.[71] Nevertheless, SASAC's mandate was to aggressively push ahead with SOE reform and so, rather than go through the route of applying for new IPOs, the defense industry began injecting more of its assets into its already existing IPOs. Since most of the defense group corporations had already listed their military conversion assets as subsidiaries on the market, the emergence of real defense assets began to appear around 2005-06.[72] These new defense assets are highly attractive since their performance on the stock market is impressive and generally superior to the spin-off IPOs.[73] Defense related assets are expected to raise an estimated 50 billion by 2010.[74]

A third stage began near the end of 2008 and is characterized as consolidation through mergers and acquisitions (M&As), principally through existing IPOs within defense group corporations (see Appendix A). According to some specialists, the current phase of intra-group corporation consolidation will continue and be completed by the end of the 12th Five Year Plan, after which time, M&As across group corporations could begin.[75]

These changes to the defense industry's market participation point to a number of conditionally optimistic trends. The reforms have begun to open up the defense sector to capital markets—not only for its military conversion spin-offs, but for defense assets as well. In looking to a long-term strategy to wean the defense enterprises off central government largesse, the potential of the stock market is proving to be a formidable tool to raise the necessary capital. This process has been encouraged through greater and diversified shareholder participation.[76] According to COSTIND, nearly a thousand enterprises out of several thousand under China's 11 defense group corporations (majors) would be allowed to receive nonstate and foreign investment.[77] Yet by the end of 2005, only a handful of small, commercialized subsidiaries, largely producing spin-off products, could be detected in the stock markets. The average percentage of assets in the defense industry in the market at that time was 5 percent.[78] This level is now estimated to be up to 40 percent in AVIC, and 15 percent in CASC, but it still pales in comparison to the civilian SOEs, which is over 65 percent.[79] Despite the limited progress, by December 2008, in total they had raised over 118 billion yuan in capital on the stock market.[80] As lucrative defense assets emerge in the market, the capital raised could be phenomenal considering the 11 majors are valued at over a trillion yuan.[81]

Perhaps most significantly, the opening up of the defense industry to the stock markets offers the potential to fundamentally alter the way the group corporations operate and are managed — traditionally, bloated, inefficient, and laden with insider transactions — through "corporate restructuring" and shareholder demands for efficient and transparent management. The CSRC is responsible for evaluating and ensuring compliance with reporting measures including ratifying IPOs, valuating stock offerings and supervising adherence with public listing requirements.[82] The M&As observed to date have shown signs that restructuring is positively affecting efficiency and operation, particularly in rationalizing the geographically and organizationally dispersed nature of the defense research and development infrastructure. As one important example in this regard, CASC has consolidated a large group of satellite R&D/production facilities and institutes around the country under China Spacesat Co Ltd, effectively reducing duplication, streamlining supply chains, and improving linkages between design and manufacturing. These facilities are now primarily concentrated in Xi'an and Beijing and produce both civilian and military small satellites.[83] Many analysts believe that with the success of these changes, further consolidation of large satellite platforms could be next on the agenda.[84]

As many experts point out, the process of public listing has also exacted its own demands on the transparency of the formerly closed defense industries. For instance, industry reports and annual reports of the defense companies that have been listed include information on the institutes and facilities that have been merged along with their scope of operations, their worth, new R&D projects, total profits of military products and how the capital raised through the stock markets is spent.[85] Still, the information available on the defense assets entering the market is slow to appear, and most often, far from comprehensive, since declared information must also pass strict criteria for secrecy and national security.

While the process of M&As promises a degree of change, transformation of the operation and management of the defense corporations will likely be slow. They are increasingly opening up to the market in their need to raise capital. However, the trend at present is to consolidate assets within a group corporation and maintain a controlling share, a phenomenon that will likely continue to increase in the future.[86] This is the result of certain factors which reveal the limited impact of shareholding reform on defense enterprise operations. First of all, SASAC was mandated to ramp up SOE privatization in 2003, including the defense industry.[87] These assets were divided into 3 categories which provided greater investment opportunities for civilian SOEs, nonstate, and even private enterprises.[88]

In reality, however, numerous limitations remain. First, although weakened in terms of oversight of corporation assets, SASTIND maintains the review of national security status of defense assets and as a conservative body could hold back the opening up of large portions of the industry.[89] In addition to secrecy issues, there are further difficulties to opening up many institutes. Core R&D/production facilities under the group corporations were never formed into subsidiary companies but have always been categorized as "shi-ye dan-wei" (事业单位), making approval for their stock listing a far more complicated process.[90] An estimated 20 percent of the defense industry's facilities are involved in core defense R&D/production—not an insignificant amount. According to one study of the space sector, roughly 60 percent of institutes are engaged in both civilian and noncore military production, thus potentially opening them up to diversified investment and ownership by nondefense state-owned entities.[91] Yet, the defense industry is consolidating by maintaining a controlling share in the majority of assets placed on the market, making the prospects for organizational and management reforms limited. In the small percentage of assets where nonstate and foreign private investments are allowed, special approval is required for shareholding that exceeds 5 percent, entailing a fairly stringent barrier for minority ownership. Moreover, CEOs and other key leaders of the defense group corporations are certified by SASAC only after SASTIND and the Organization Department of CCP Central Committee decide on candidates.[92]

Other barriers exist that prevent the defense industry from listing new assets on the stock market. They must meet basic criteria for profitability and market fairness according to guidelines enforced and ratified by SASAC and CSRC. The defense industry however is known for problems such as intra-industry competition and affiliated transactions, which put minority shareholders at a disadvantage.[93]

In sum, while shareholding reform holds out the future potential to improve the organization, corporate structure, and transparency of the defense industry, currently, little progress has been made and the evolving trends of consolidation within the industry do not augur well. Yet, this reform is highly pertinent to the trends of CMI in the greater access of the defense industry corporations to market capital, an increasingly critical factor as China's need for defense funding grow.

NATIONAL STRATEGY: GATHERING MOMENTUM

The current reshaping of institutions and policies establish the potential to fundamentally change the relationship between the defense and civilian economies. But they are only the building blocks. They are merely improving the environment for reform. The critical question remains whether a coherent national strategy exists to translate the long-term goals of CMI into reality. A comprehensive overview of the contributing elements is beyond the scope of this writing; however, a number of broader themes are emerging.

Funding and Management.

Arguably, the most telling of central government commitment to CMI strategy is the ability to marshal and effectively manage the state's resources in service of this goal. The implementation of CMI—to combine defense and civilian research and industrial bases so that common technologies, manufacturing lines, facilities, and personnel can be applied to both military and commercial needs—involves complex economic and industrial engineering. As such, while Beijing is undoubtedly committed to this goal, national initiatives often do not carry a CMI label (see Appendix B).[94] The relevant initiatives range from specialized projects involving specific technology transfer and innovation funds to broader financial tool directed by the NDRC to invest in large scale technology-industry clusters. An analysis of these sampled items reveals two general trends. First, a growing number of funds have specific CMI goals, particularly the more narrowly focused projects (e.g., Defense Fundamental Research Project Fund). Yet, even many of the broader national funding initiatives, such as the Industry Investment Funds (IIF), have explicit CMI content.[95] Judging from the 10 IIFs approved since 2007, at least 5 of them, worth nearly 80 billion yuan, are related to CMI in some degree.[96] A second trend is that CMI-related funding is ramping up from smaller, sector-specific projects to national-level support such as with the IIFs, with commensurately higher levels of appropriation.

On the other hand, the management of funding associated with CMI raises concerns about effectiveness in implementation. MIIT is ostensibly tasked with executing and managing CMI, mainly through SAS-TIND and the Dual-use Promotional Office. However, the list of government ministries and commissions involved in overseeing a range of funds includes the NDRC and SASAC, both of which approve and ratify most large-scale funding. The Ministry of Science & Technology, Ministry of Finance, Ministry of Education, GAD, and Chinese Academy of Science (CAS) also play key roles.[97] Managing funding also requires close coordination with a number of state-owned assets, enterprises, banks, and local governments, which often raise the actual moneys. It is unclear whether this complex process is feasible for a national strategy to direct funding for CMI activity.

Since the NDRC approves national projects worth more than 5 billion yuan, most industry funding is organized and ratified by the NDRC. This includes large-scale national projects such as the IIFs as well as sector-specific key projects.[98] In 2008, the NDRC also approved 30 national high-tech industrial bases around the country, 20 of which had direct or indirect relevance to CMI.[99] The NDRC was also responsible for establishing national engineering labs to research leading technologies including dual-use concerns since 2007.[100] On the other hand, local governments and enterprises have also founded hundreds of dual-use industrial parks in the past 4 years of their own accord. Zhejiang province alone is planning to build 16 CMI industrial bases in 2009.[101] Moreover, there are a variety of CMI-related funding projects under MoST, MIIT as well as local governments. The result is a highly diverse and complex range of initiatives that call into question the level of coherency as a national strategy.[102]

Central Priorities, Local Interests.

To be successful, CMI will require the cooperation of provincial and local governments.[103] While comprehensive planning and funding are ratified at the highest levels of the central government, much of the national economy is under provincial and local management. This includes many key SOEs, land development decisions, taxes, regional industry development planning, etc.[104] Simply put, the central government does not have the capacity to manage most of the concrete economic activity. As such, the NDRC does not administer the funds, nor do they come from NDRC coffers, it merely approves central and local state-owned entities such as banks, insurance agents, securities enterprises to provide them. A major task of the central government is to negotiate the discrepancies between national strategic goals and local interests.

Failures with the IIFs are testament to the difficulties in harmonizing central and local interests. As of July, 2009, only a portion of the capital had been raised for just two of the approved projects: the Bohai Rim Industry Investment Fund and the Mianyang S&T City Industry Investment Fund (both of which have significant dual-use potential). While both Bohai and Mianyang declared CMI activities as part of their portfolio in order to win approval for the projects, worth 20 billion and 6 billion yuan respectively, both invested in other more lucrative high-profile projects (commercial bank in Bohai or agricultural projects in Mianyang). Bohai IIF, the project furthest along has already been judged by the NDRC as unsuccessful. In fact, Tianjin withdrew its proposal during the second stage funding negotiations for the Bohai project. This indicates a strong disagreement with NDRC directives for the project.[105]

Flexibility in CMI Models.

Another pattern that can be discerned is the adaptation of the civilian-military integration efforts to different parts of the national economy. This means that different models are being applied to various regions, depending on their industrial capacity and specialization, their regional legacy of the state-owned economy and the particular relationship between the central and local government.[106]

The first model is one characterized by consolidation of defense assets in those regions with a strong legacy of defense enterprises. This applies to areas whose local economy is largely dominated by the defense sector, and engages in dual-use activity primarily in the form of spin-off, or military conversion (possibly with a lower degree of two-way technology diffusion). Furthermore, such a model is more applicable to more remote regions — western interior and the northeast — where there is physical distance from centers innovation and higher concentrations of industrial activity. This approach is a way to concentrate formerly dispersed resources and institutes into a spatial clustering of that allows for more complete technology-industrial interactions and supply chains. If such an economic base is sustainable, it will draw in other enterprises; attract local and nonstate investment capital and talent. This is described as a "vertical strategy," requiring central government guidance, large defense SOE participation, as well as local government funding and policy support.

In the past few years, the establishment of industrial parks has become a popular method to attract central funding, but many such experiments have not been successful. The Mianyang Technology City is one such example.[107] The reasons for its failure are complicated, but encompass an inability to attract a critical mass of small and medium technology enterprises to form a larger and more sustainable and diversified innovation and industry cluster. Its heavy reliance on two large entities, Changhong Corporation and the

China Academy of Engineering Physics and its subsidiaries (with a great deal of high level expertise but lacking in smaller scale industry and commercial application) undercut its ability to diversify.

One example of the new approach described above is the "Xi'an National Civilian Aerospace Industry Base."[108] The Shaanxi government the China Aerospace Science and Technology Corporation (CASC) are working together (up to 30 billion yuan in funding) to create a self-sustaining industry cluster.[109] CASC has long been heavily engaged in military conversion, but this project is a far more dramatic consolidation of its assets that will focus on dual-use activity, particularly in the business of small satellite development, productions, and applications. It is expected to generate 30 billion yuan in revenue and will entail mergers and acquisitions by a range of investors, both state and nonstate. This could be the start of an even greater consolidation of CASC at other levels (large satellites, for instance). With such a concentration of resources, the plan is to create a self-sustaining industrial chain, which will then further attract talent, enterprises, and the necessary capital to thrive independently.

A second model is the spontaneous development of CMI activity that arises as a result of strong civilian industrial capacity and defense demand. These regions do not exhibit a high degree of technology diffusion between civilian and military sectors; rather the civil-military relationship is dominated by a sharing of industrial and manufacturing capacity. While local governments may actively solicit such dual-use opportunities—which are often lucrative—they occur more organically and are sustained through natural comparative advantage of the civilian or nonstate sector. A typical example of this model is occurring in Zhejiang. This province holds the nation's most robust nonstate sector—accounting for 90 percent of its GDP—and is particularly strong in manufacturing. Zhejiang does not have a legacy defense industry, yet it has been hugely successful in attracting key defense production contracts.[110] The province is currently establishing 16 CMI industry bases, has set up research institutes and joint ventures, and has 81 enterprises providing hardware for the military ranging from clothes to large military aircraft, unmanned aerial vehicles (UAVs) and electronic components.[111] This arrangement is a marriage between private capital (Wenzhou alone has 600 billion yuan in investment capital) and military demand.

A third emerging model is the introduction of CMI activity into zones of established economic and industrial excellence. In this environment, the military is far more open to working closely with the civilian sector in exchange for substantial technological payoff. This model is dominant in the rapidly developing IT industry, principally located in the three main "information technology clusters": Pearl River Delta, Yangtze River Delta, and the Bohai Rim. With the military's current emphasis on information warfare, the interest in the civilian IT sector is growing on a large scale.

Despite having deep connections with many of China's IT leaders, such as Langchao, Zhongxing, Legend, Huawei, and Hai'er—with a substantial rise in the military's level of technology to show for it—the defense industry's integration with the bulk of China's civilian IT sector remains circumscribed. Shenzhen is illustrative here. As the nation's number one IT economy, Shenzhen makes up one-sixth of the national output.[112] Yet, less than 2 percent of Shenzhen's IT output has military value. Thus, in July 2009, a new Defense Industry Alliance was established with the organizational assistance of the Shenzhen municipal government.[113] The Alliance brings together any enterprise in the defense industry or the civilian sector willing to sign on to military or dual-use economic activity under the principles of "voluntary participation, equality and cooperation." This is a novel concept because it organizes a highly atomized and dispersed, yet innovative and fluid IT industry (epitomized by Shenzhen) into a collective body with which the defense industry can interact. Many IT enterprises are too small, and so individually their access to defense contracts is constrained. Through this common platform, many of the barriers to communication and cooperation, such technical exchange, integrated R&D efforts, are drastically reduced.[114]

THE S&T CATALYST

China's national science and technology system stands at the heart of China's goal to transform itself into a globally innovative power, and by extension the ability to indigenously innovate for national defense purposes. In the span of 3 decades, China has gone from being a nominal to a formidable player in the world-wide technology revolution. The body of China's national S&T program covers a vast array of commercial, civilian, and defense-specific programs, funded and overseen by an equally diverse range of government, military, academic, and enterprise institutions. These efforts range from targeted programs like Key technologies R&D Program, 863, 973, Torch, and Spark,[115] but also includes far more broad-based efforts such as the 80 engineering R&D centers spread around the country in defense labs and academic institutes, the dozens of technology transfer centers, defense preliminary research projects and technology transformation programs.[116] Of particular import have been the 54 national new and high-tech industry parks,[117] containing 30,000 high-tech enterprises, and hailed as the future engines of growth for China's economy and its technological prowess.[118] Civil-military integration has increasingly become central to the planning of China's S&T system.[119]

China has also become the one of the largest recipients of technology focused foreign investment, importers of equipment, and a base for many of the world's best technology innovation companies. Over 8,000 foreign high-tech enterprises were set up in China by 2007 (37 percent of total high-tech enterprises in China[120]), and more than 1,200 foreign R&D centers by 2008.[121] China has increasingly formulated favorable taxation policies for foreign enterprises to establish high-tech investment and manufacturing bases in China—including CMI technologies.[122] In fact, most officials openly acknowledge the benefit of foreign advanced technology to assist in the in China's strategic industry development.[123]

Do the sum of these interactions with the global economy and indigenous efforts put China on the path to becoming a superpower in science and technology? What are the impacts on the defense industry and military modernization? Certainly, China's defense industry has made considerable gains through direct access to foreign technology. China has reportedly purchased R&D know-how outright from Russia, particularly in aviation and missile technology.[124] However, as a number of studies have shown, the impact of foreign transfers on China's indigenous weapons R&D capabilities depends on how well they are absorbed and combined with in-house R&D activities.[125] This is difficult to assess for lack of evidence, and despite a number of notable examples, their affect on defense innovation appears to be limited. China may also acquire sensitive technologies through its global interactions within the S&T related enterprises, however that also appears to be limited.[126] China has also imported RBM 35 billion in high-tech imports, 85 percent of which were in CMI relevant fields including electronics, computers, telecommunications, and opto-electronics.[127] Moreover, in terms of indices measuring domestic S&T progress, China currently ranks near the top in R&D spending per GDP, and published papers and output of S&T graduates.[128] The spillover to the defense industry is almost certainly substantial. Reportedly, one-third of 40,000 top graduates from seven of COSTIND-affiliated universities go to the defense industry.[129]

While considerable progress in a number of areas has been made, China's broader prospects for indigenous innovation or leapfrog in key scientific areas (and their diffusion to the defense industry) remain uncertain due inherent weaknesses in China's S&T workforce and infrastructure.[130] A primary issue is the degree of focus on original R&D activity and enterprise-centered innovation. According to current statistics, enterprises account for 70 percent of R&D spending.[131] Yet, few companies have the financial resources to carry out innovative R&D.[132] This problem is exemplified by the state of China's high-tech parks, where firms spent 1.9 percent of their sales on R&D, far below the 5 percent minimum standard. R&D expenditure is even lower outside high-tech parks. Overall, China's high-tech parks have largely served as distributions, procession, and trading centers for foreign technology rather than undertake the slow, hard work of true technology innovation.[133] Since importing technology has quicker payoffs for productivity increases, R&D money is often misspent. China's large high-tech import expenditure also masks the fact that almost 80 percent is actually purchases by enterprises wholly foreign-owned (63 percent) or joint-invested companies (16 percent) rather than Chinese firms, which make up just 19 percent.[134]

While the number of China's engineering and science graduates looks impressive at face value, it disguises the problems for indigenous S&T development. The level of education for a sizable percentage of China's 1.34 million "engineering students" is significantly lower than their western counterparts.[135] Furthermore, China's professional community is very young, often deficient in practical training and lacking the requisite experience, particularly for more senior leadership positions in the R&D system. There is also a serious brain drain challenge where multinationals operating in China compete (favorably due to higher wages and better opportunities) with domestic firms for the "best and the brightest," which could in the future lead to a talent war and affect foreign direct investment (FDI) and China's own S&T development.

China's S&T system suffers from a number of other failings such as an imperfect Intellectual Property Rights regime. While on paper, regulations and legal protection for patents appear robust, enforcement, particularly at the local level is often impossible. China will need to generate its own IPRs to cultivate sustainable indigenous innovation.

There is a deficit of institutional support that may hinder not only financial incentives but innovation-oriented ways of thinking. Similar to the way in which

China's defense establishment organized its nuclear weapons and missile and satellite programs, the heavy hand of government management is also evident with high-tech initiatives, as seen with the experience of *Zhongguancun* (中关村) high-tech zone.[136] The stifling effect of government can also be seen in the control over important ingredients of innovation—autonomy, free access to and flow of information, even dissent, both scientific and political. As one observer of China's S&T culture notes, "if researchers and entrepreneurs are not able to think outside the box . . . the success of the innovation strategy is called into question."[137]

IMPACT ON MILITARY MODERNIZATION

This chapter has attempted to address two basic issues: China's decision to pursue CMI, and its emerging strategy to achieve it. But what impact will it have on China's military modernization ambitions? How do we measure its progress and what is the end-game?

There is no question that China's past reforms have already produced substantial results across a broad spectrum of weapon systems. But the most impressive achievements have been primarily in legacy defense industries such as missiles, shipping, and aviation. Whether it is China's anti-satellite weapons, the anti-ship ballistic missile, DH-10 cruise missile, or the *Shang* class nuclear attack submarine, these are formidable weapons. But, while they may have acute strategic implications—even U.S. game changers in specific theatres of potential conflict—they do not constitute leap-ahead technologies or disruptive innovations that permanently alter U.S. military superiority. For the most part, these weapons are upgrades and incremental improvements on systems that have been in development for a long time.[138] Moreover, since these are products arising from the legacy defense industries, one should expect these advances to continue with or without CMI.

Rather, the measure of CMI's success will be in those areas where leap-ahead and disruptive innovations are most likely to occur; that is, in C4ISR systems, advanced electronic components, high-end integrated circuits, next generation broadband wireless mobile communications, precision guidance, and its tracking and targeting assets, situational awareness, connectivity, digital simulation facilities, etc.[139] Highly representative of these capabilities, IT and space will be two of the most decisive sectors.[140] These technologies may adjust the power balance in a more fundamental way since, if successful, China would begin to compete (or close the gap) with the United States where it is strongest—such as advanced net-centric warfare, high-speed communication links, and interoperable data systems.[141] It is in these areas that will make by far the highest demands in human and monetary resources as well as industrial capacity, and where the dynamic and large scale of the civilian sector will be most critical.[142]

Space.

If talent and capital are the primary ingredients to success, how is the space sector faring? China's space industry is operating in a unique environment. First, the legacy of past policies have left it (China Aerospace Science and Technology Corporation and China Aerospace Science and Industry Corporation) dispersed, bloated, and located in geographically isolated regions. As a result, the primary strategy of the space industry is consolidation and concentration of its dual-use assets (mainly in CASC) such as with the establishment of the Xi'an National Aerospace Industry Base. Here, CASC is ramping up its spin-off for its small satellite technology and applications. By concentrating these resources in an industrial base, as described earlier, it has won central funding and through a restructuring is attracting outside investment. Already, after 2 years of operation, numerous other aerospace related businesses have moved to the Xi'an base in areas of chip production, inertial guidance, spatial information systems, and new energy sources and so on, attracting talent and investment. The base is expected to earn 300 billion yuan by 2020.[143]

This strategy holds great promise for CMI synergies since a spatial concentration of assets to produce satellites and related technology for both military and civilian purposes help create the potential for spin-on activity and two-way technology diffusion. Virtually every space technology being pursued is of interest to both military and civilian end-user; from position/navigation, microsatellites, communication satellites to remote sensing, and even manned space. For instance, advances in autonomous proximity maneuvering and virtual detection technology greatly aid in allowing a number of smaller satellites to fly in formation, comprising a network of satellites, making disruption difficult, and replacement far easier than if one large orbiting asset was disabled.[144] The same technology is applicable to co-orbital, anti-satellite activity.

However, many obstacles exist to CMI in this sector. While the application of most satellites are dual-use in nature, and while CAS, universities, enterprises, and other civilian agencies are increasingly involved in upstream (manufacturing, launch services) and downstream (satellite application) activities;[145] R&D, production, and design for space systems remains dominated by defense industry.[146] Moreover, the large upfront cost of developing and producing a space system often constitutes an extremely high entry barrier for government agencies (much less nonstate enterprises) Despite participation of the civilian sector and the stock market to raise capital, the price tag for putting hundreds of more satellites in orbit — to achieve a space capability comparable to the United States — will require far more than is currently being invested and may be prohibitively high.

IT Industry.

The benefits to the military through its strategic relationship with China's robust civilian, and nonstate IT sectors that have evolved since the late 1990s has been described in detail.[147] It has been characterized as intimate, expansive, and centrally supported resulting in substantial progress. This chapter will neither challenge nor repeat those findings. However, with the vast demands to increase virtually every aspect of information technology to push forward China's defense modernization plans, a "paradigm shift" in civil-military cooperation appears far from complete. While there are many examples of successes in electronics, telecommunications, and computer technologies, there are also failures. One telling example is the limited success of China's indigenous semi-conductor and integrated circuit industries, after almost a decade of intensive effort to translate its initial chip manufacturing success into a seamless upstream/downstream industrial scale production.[148] Early in this decade, China first attempted to adopt the Integrated Device Manufacturer (IDC) industrial model similar to the

United States but failed. It then turned to the Taiwanese strategy, a Merchant-Foundry model, where design and production of chips were specialized and separated into separate systems. This attempt was not successful either leaving China's chip makers disconnected and atomized. The result is that while China's domestic semi-conductor market is now worth 540 billion yuan, 80 percent of chips are still imported. That should be a sobering conclusion for the military, considering it is two to three generations behind the civilian sector in IT sector and depends highly on semiconductors and integrated circuits for most weapon categories (see Figure 1).

Weapon system	Naval vessel	Vehicles	Aircraft	Missiles	Satellites
IC as % cost of unit	22%	24%	33%	45%	66%

Figure 1. Percentage of Semi-Conductors and Integrated Circuits per Weapons Category.

The industry is looking to the military to play a role in securing central funding for larger projects, as it does through numerous dual-use basic research and application projects such as 863, Torch, 909, etc. But the government has become more resistant to providing significant central funding to major private sector dominated industries, including semi-conductor production. This is being partly redressed by the NDRC's recent decision to make 40 billion yuan available for "core electronic components, high-end general-use chips, and fundamental software."[150] In short, it is imperative to the military that the civilian industry succeeds. Yet, the defense industry's progress in CMI depends on a relationship that allows the private sector a free hand to continue innovation yet support it enough to succeed.

IMPLICATIONS FOR THE UNITED STATES: NEW APPROACHES

The prospects for success of China's new strategic direction in defense industry reform remain decidedly uncertain, though not for lack of vision or effort. The highest rungs of leadership in the military, political, scientific, and industrial bureaucracies have committed to forge ahead with civil-military integration as the cornerstone of future defense reform. However, the difficulty of harmonizing the very disparate economies and cultures of China's closed, massive military industrial complex and its dynamic but vast civilian economy will hold significant barriers to fashioning a comprehensive and coherent strategy. To date, CMI is best characterized as *"jiu long zhi shui"* ([九龙治水] nine dragons to tame the floods). That is, an air of trial and error pervades the various attempts to mold policy, institutional, programmatic, and funding efforts into a feasible plan.

Yet, the same doubts have long persisted regarding China's ability to tame a large and unwieldy defense sector and effect real change. This was the case after the 1998-99 reforms, and yet, over the last decade, China has succeeded in developing a new generation of weapons that have deep strategic significance for the United States. While many structural impediments remain to further progress in China's defense reform, a degree of success is all but guaranteed. It has already succeeded in certain sectors such as space, nanotechnology, and telecommunications.[151] Even moderate progress in achieving CMI and the indigenous innovation that would result would inevitably bring profound challenges for the United States.

In terms of meeting those challenges, U.S. strategic planners would do well to better understand the broader trends and benchmarks of China's ongoing defense reform. To date, the study of China's military modernization has been largely dominated by investigative research and reportage — based on a close scrutiny of defense related literature — to track capabilities and their specific strategic implications. The hallmark of this approach is the Pentagon's annual military report on the PLA, and the result is usually surprise when a new system or capability surfaces. As defense reform proceeds, and especially as CMI specifically picks up steam, such strategic shockers will emerge with greater frequency. More importantly, advances in China's defense industry input will grow harder to detect and evaluate with several consequences. First, it will be increasingly difficult to parse the specific military application of China's highly dual-use space or telecommunications infrastructure.[152] Moreover, China's growing capability to conduct information-based warfare will largely depend on breakthroughs in more amorphous C4ISR components, many of which will be difficult to assess.[153] Finally, and perhaps most significantly, tracking technological progress for national defense purposes, will be complicated as CMI blurs the lines between civilian and military entities participating in weapons R&D and productions.

All of these factors will require additional methods to better measure and assess defense industry reform at a systemic level. One example is to use a more traditional approach. Rather than just looking at the end-product weapon system (or the defense institute responsible for applying a technology or developing a core component), one may need to look further up the R&D/production chain. This will require a closer scrutiny of high-tech parks, R&D centers, and S&T talent.[154] Benchmarks for progress may also include events further removed from defense reform measures, for instance: a central funding grant in support of a large-scale civilian industry cluster engaged in CMI activity; or perhaps the successful consolidation of a defense group corporation (like CASC); or an nondefense SOE winning a bid for a major defense contract; maybe legislation requiring a defense group to diversify its management; or possibly policies that require greater transfer of technology. Individually and collectively, these developments may accumulate to have a profound long-term impact on China's ability to innovate and produce for national defense objectives.

A second approach to analyzing defense reform and China's military effectiveness will involve more analytical rigor than has characterized the bulk of past studies. The amount of information on the PLA, its activities, capabilities, and modernization developments (and our access to it) is reaching the point where it can be useful to new methodologies of research. Transferring this information into more useful data sets could facilitate better research where specific variables can be established and where causal inferences and general propositions can be tested.[155] Such analytical studies would help shift away from short-term, incident specific analysis and worst-case assumptions of China's defense modernization to more systematic hypothesis testing. The result would inevitably be a clearer and deeper understanding of both larger trends and specific developments.[156]

In short, understanding China's military modernization and its strategic impact for the United States will grow increasingly difficult and will require commensurately more varied and sophisticated tools. We need to be able to peer further into the future to both aid specific military planning as well as allow more time to adjust psychologically to the inevitable strategic shift that China's defense industry reform will beget.

ENDNOTES – CHAPTER 10

1. This chapter builds on a number of excellent studies. The RAND study of China's aerospace, aviation, shipping, and electronics/information defense sectors broadly covers defense industry reform from the 1998-99 reforms until 2005. For the most comprehensive treatment of China's civil-military integration strategy, see Tai Ming Cheung, *Fortifying China: The Struggle to Build a Modern Defense Economy*, Ithaca, NY: Cornell University Press, 2009. Defense reform more generally is covered well in Evan Medeiros *et al.*, *A New Direction for China's Defense Industry*, Washington, DC: Washington, DC: RAND Corporation, 2005; Keith Crane *et al.*, *Modernizing China's Military: Opportunities and Constraints*, Washington, DC: RAND, 2005. Other related works on reform of the defense industry include Richard A. Bitzinger, *Towards a Brave New Arms Industry?* Adelphi Paper No. 356, London, UK: International Institute for Strategic Studies/Oxford University Press, 2003; and "Reforming China's Defense Industry: Progress in Spite of Itself?" *Korean Journal of Defense Analysis*, Fall 2007; Arthur S Ding, "Civilian-Military Relationship and Reform in the Defense Industry," *Institute of Defense and Strategic Studies*, Singapore, June 2005; David Shambaugh, *Modernizing China's Military: Progress, Problems, and Prospects*, Berkeley: University of California Press, 2002. In addition, a number of works associated with defense industry reform include topics on the reform of China's S&T culture by Cong Cao, including "China's Innovation Challenge," *China's Galloping Economy: Prospects, Problems and Implications for the United States*, Washington, DC: Woodrow Wilson's Asia Program; and "Zhongguancun and China's High-tech Parks in Transition: Growing Pains or Premature Senility?" *Asian Survey*, Vol. 44, No. 5, September/October, 2004, pp. 647-66; Denis Fred Simon and Cong Cao, *China's Emerging Technological*

Edge: Assessing the Role of High-end Talent, New York: Cambridge University Press, 2009.

2. Hu Jintao (胡锦涛),"Report to the 17th CCP National Congress," *Xinhua News Agency*, October 24, 2007, available from *news.xinhuanet.com/newscenter/2007-10/24/content_6938568_8. htm*; *The White Paper of China's Defense in 2008*(2008年中国的国防), State Council Information Office of China (国务院新闻办公室), January 2009, available from *www.gov.cn/zwgk/2009-01/20/content_1210224.htm*; "国家中长期科技发展规划纲要2006年-2020年" ("National Medium and Long Science and Technology Development Plans 2006-2020"), State Council of China, 2006, available from *www.most.gov.cn/kjgh/*; "Eleventh Five-Year Development and Reform Thoughts of National Defense Science and Technology Industry," State Council of China, 2006, available from *www.china-spacenews.com/n435777/n435778/n435790/29083.html*. There are dozens of related articles published in the past 30 years. For instance, Liang Jun, Yuan Lin, "着眼核心军事能力建设，大力推进武器装备发展" ("Building a Core Military Capacity, Promoting Weapon Equipment Development"), 国防科技工业 (*National Defense S&T Industry*), Issue 3, 2009. Also see Ren Haiping, "寓军于民，统筹经济与国防建设的大趋势" ("On the Integration of Military Industry with Civilian Industry"), 军事经济研究 (*Military Economic Research*), Issue 2, 2005.

3. Includes the 11th FYP Defense White Papers and MLP for Science, Technology and Industry for National Defense; "Hu Jintao's Report to the 17th Party Congress," *Xinhua News Agency*, October 24, 2007, available from *news.xinhuanet.com/newscenter/2007-10/24/content_6938568_8.htm*; *The White Paper of China's Defense in 2008*, State Council Information Office of China, January 2009, available from *www.gov.cn/zwgk/2009-01/20/content_1210224.htm*; "National Medium and Long Science and Technology Development Plans, 2006-2020," State Council of China, 2006, available from *www.most.gov.cn/kjgh/*; "Eleventh Five-Year Development and Reform Thoughts of National Defense Science and Technology Industry," State Council of China, 2006.

4. The core electronic components are high-end general chips, basic software, ultra large-scale integrated circuit manufacturing technology, next-generation broadband wireless mobile communications, high-end CNC machine tools, basic manufacturing

technology, large oil and gas fields, coal-bed methane development, large-scale advanced pressurized water reactor, high temperature gas cooled reactor nuclear power plant, water pollution control and governance, new varieties of genetically modified organism cultivation, new drugs, prevention and treatment of AIDS, viral hepatitis and other major infectious diseases, large aircraft, high-resolution earth observation systems, and manned space flight and lunar exploration. See "国家中长期科学和技术发展规划纲要" ("National Middle and Long Period S&T Development Plan 2006-2020"), Published by the State Council of PRC, 2006, pp. 30-31.

5. Yin Xingtong (尹兴彤) (an official of CMI Promotion Office under MIIT), "Prospects for CMI Development," Speech during the Fourth China International Military and Civil Mutually Use Technologies Exhibition, September 3, 2009.

6. Discussed later and detailed in Appendix B.

7. *Xinhuanet*, CCP Politburo 15th Group Study "Maintaining Principles of Harmonious Development in National Defense and Economic Construction, CCP Politburo 15th Study Group," Beijing, China, July 24, 2004, available from *news.xinhuanet.com/zhengfu/2004-07/26/content_1648021.htm.*

8. Pan Youmu (潘友木), "着眼空天一体化，探索国家空天安全战略" ("Exploring National Aerospace Security Strategies in View of Air and Space Integration"), 中国军事科学 (*China Military Science*), Vol. 19, No. 2, April 1, 2006; Liang Zhaoxian (梁兆宪) and Shen Shilu [沈世禄], "从国际空间法看空间攻防对抗," ("Space Countermeasure in View of International Space Laws"), 装备指挥技术学院学报 (*Journal of the Academy of Equipment Command and Technology*), Vol. 15, No 2, April 1, 2004.

9. Zhang Yufeng (张玉峰), "国防科技工业企业深化改革的几点思考" ("Thoughts of Further Reform in Defense Industry"), 航天技术与民品 (*Aerospace Technology and Civilian Products*) No. 9, 1999.

10. Qian Cunli (钱春丽) and Hou Guangming (候光明), "我国装备采办组织管理体制现状及改革思路" ("Reform Path for China's Equipment Procurement Organization Management System")军事经济研究 (*Military Economic Journal*), No 3, 2008, pp. 51.

11. The defense industry in the Soviet Union was characterized by a centralized, planned model. Each enterprise had an was handed an annual plan specifying what and how much it was to produce, even where its product would go. Supply was similarly dictated. Also, the defense industrial complex was completely segregated from the civilian economy. Defense R&D fared better than the civilian sector as it was given high priority by the state and party. See, for example, Liu Kefu (刘可夫), "欧美苏军工管理模式简介" ("Brief Description of Defense Industry Management Modes among Europe, Soviet Union and United States"), 外国经济与管理 (*Foreign Economies and Management*), Issue 12, 1988.

12. If inflation is factored in from 1978 to 1988, defense expenditure decreased by an average of 4 percent each year between 1978 and 88. Defense expenditure in 1988 was RMB 21.8 billion. See "2008年中国国防" (*China's National Defense in 2008*), Information Office of State Council. Even after 1989, defense expenditure recovered slowly, in 1996, the percentage of defense expenditure in GDP is 1.01 percent, which is its lowest point in the past 60 years. See *China Statistics Yearbook* in 1989; Zhang Lijun (张丽军) and Zhang Cuiping (张翠平), "浅析1978年以来中国国防支出的变化趋势" ("Analysis of Chinese Defense's Industry Trends Since 1978"), 经济研究导刊 (*Economic Research Guide*), Issue 13, 2009.

13. David Finkelstein, "China's National Military Strategy: An Overview of the Military Strategic Guidelines" in Roy Kamphausen and Andrew Scobell, eds., *Right-sizing the People's Liberation Army*, Carlisle, PA: Strategic Studies Institute, U.S. Army War College, 2007.

14. Beijing perceived Taiwan's political actions as moves toward independence, prodded by continued U.S. interference in the issue. China fired missiles off Taiwan's coast which then led to the United States sending two U.S. aircraft carriers to the Strait without any response from China. See Fang Gongli (房功利), "中国国防战略演变研究，1949-2002" ("Development of China's National Defense Strategy from 1949 to 2002"), *Excellent Ph.D. papers of Central Party School in 2004*; "中国军事现代化的转折点—再议96台海危机" ("Milestones for China's Defense Modernization—Rethinking the Taiwan Strait Crisis of 1996"), *BBS of China.com*, October 20, 2009, available from *club.china.com/data/thread/1011/2706/15/94/0_1.html*.

15. Li Zhaoxing (李肇星), at Press Conference of NPC (十一届全国人大二次会议记者招待会), "2009年中国国防预算为4806.86亿元" ("China Defense Budget is 480.686 Billion in 2009"), *Xinhua News Agency*, March 4, 2009.

16. Equipment portion of the budget has increased from 16.3 percent to 33.90 percent over the 1990-2009 period based on official figures. Guo Jia (郭佳) and Lü Ying (吕颖), "我国国防费结构优化的现状判断及实证分析" ("Analysis and Assessment of the Current Situation of China's National Defense Spending Structure Optimization"), 军事经济研究 (*Military Economic Research*), No. 2, 2009.

17. In 1990, the equipment portion of the budget is RMB 5 billion, 16.4 percent of defense budget. In 2007, the equipment portion of the budget increased to RMB 114 billion, 32 percent of defense budget. See *China Statistics Yearbook* in 1991 and *China's National Defense in 2008* published by Information Office of State Council.

18. "科技统计数据 2009" ("China Science & Technology Statistics Data Book, 2009)," Ministry of Science and Technology of The People's Republic Of China. As of 2008, China's total R&D investment amounted to more than U.S. \$65.6 billion, RMB 444 billion, available from *www.sts.org.cn/zlhb/2009/hb1.1.htm#1*.

19. From 2006-09, R&D funds for Electronic Information College under the PLA Information Engineering University increased three times, reaching RMB 100 million in 2009. See, Li Yunming (李玉明) and Cheng Xiangran (程相然) "解放军信息工程大学努力营造人才培养环境" ("PLA Electronic Engineering University Strives for Better Conditions to Train Professionals"), 解放军报 (*PLA Daily*), April 14, 2009; Weapons and Equipment Basic Research Fund. Fund awards are valued at RMB 50,000 − 2 million. Other funding sources include the GAD-managed Defense Technology Cross-Enterprise Fund, the Defense Technology Key Laboratory Fund, the CASC Innovation Fund, and the CASIC Support Fund. See Mark Stokes, "China's Evolving Conventional Strategic Strike Capability: The ASBM Challenge to the U.S. Maritime Operations in the Western Pacific and Beyond" Project 2049 Institute, September 14, 2009, pp. 8-12, available from *project2049. net/documents/chinese_anti_ship_ballistic_missile_asbm.pdf*.

20. PLA officer salaries were on average 20 percent higher than comparable government officials prior to 1994. This was slowly reversed and reached its greatest disparity in 2007, when the average PLA monthly salary was RMB 1,450 and comparable officials' salaries was RMB 5,100 per month. From 2007 to 2009, the PLA twice saw a dramatically increase in salary, now relatively at par with comparable government officials. See *blog.newssc. org/u/10549/archives/2009/79412.html*. Another example is the raise in the percentage of personal expenditure of the budget, including salary, from 31.8 percent in 2002 to 33.7 percent in 2007. In RMB terms, this meant an increase from RMB 54 billion in 2002 to RMB 120 billion in 2007. These changes can be found comparing the National Defense White Paper published from 2003 to 2008.

21. Nuclear, Aerospace, Aviation, Ordnance, and Shipping. In 2002, a third, the China Electronic Technology Group Corporation, was established as the 11th.

22. For GAD Satellite Application Expert Group, see Xu Jianmin (徐建民), "卫星应用现状与发展" ("*Current Application and Development of Satellite*"), Beijing, China: Zhongguo Keji Chubanshe, 2001. For discussion of Precision Guidance Expert Group, also see Stokes "China's Evolving Conventional Strategic Strike Capability," p. 8.

23. Foreign military technology transfer is covered in many works and will not be covered in detail here. For example, "China, Russia: An Evolving Defense Relationship," *Stratfor Global Intelligence*, March 31, 2008. It is also tracked by *SIPRI* in their annual report "Armaments, Disarmament and International Security," available from *www.sipri.org/yearbook/2008/files/SIPRIYB08AnC. pdf*.

24. Except the management of nuclear industry, which will go to the National Energy Commission.

25. "Stipulations for Major Internal organizations and Staffing Requirements of Ministry of Industry and Information Technology of the People's Republic of China," State Council Issuance, No. 72, July 17, 2008, available from *www.miit.gov.cn*.

26. Wang Hongwei (王宏伟), "政府机构改革推进国防科技工业的"两个融合"" ("Government Organizational Reform: Pushing

the National Defense Industry's 'Two Integrations'"), 中国军转民 (*Defense Industry Conversion in China*), No. 8, 2008.

27. "Information Industry Ministry and COSTIND Merge to Promote Industry Integration," State Council's National S&T Strategic Development Research Leading Group, March 1, 2008, available from the *Liao Yi Website*.

28. Lei Zhonghui (雷中辉), "大部制改革将推动跨行业整合" ("Merger of Ministry of Information Industry and Commission of Science, Technology and Industry for National Defense will drive cross-industry integration") 21世纪经济报道 (*21st Century Business Herald*), March 12, 2008.

29. Although it should be noted that at present, COSTIND, or even its diminutive reincarnation, SASTIND, remains a formidable bureaucracy in charge of the entire defense industry and cannot be compared to DARPA, which is responsible for identifying and initiating key defense. Interviews with former GAD officers.

30. Other parts remain under the Ministry of Education and MoST as well.

31. In fact, the MII was born of military, so bringing them together again seems logical.

32. "Informatization" is a term that means the integrating, systematizing of industry, or the military employing digitized networking, communications, computer, and other information technologies.

33. Yu Fuxiu (于付秀) and Wang Huadan (王花丹), "浅谈通过'民技军用实现军民企业双赢'" ("To Achieve a Win-Win for Civil and Defense Enterprises by Using Civil Technology in Military"), 航天工业管理 (*Aerospace Industry Management*), No. 5, 2008.

34. For a sample of the kind of role the dual-use office would play, see Song Binbin (宋斌斌), "将技改与军民结合产业基地建设结合起来" ("Band Technology Transformation and CMI Industrial Bases together"),中国工业报 (*China Industry News*), July 20, 2009.

35. Ma Guojun (马国钧), "军民融合的路还有多远" ("How Far Does CMI Have to Go?"), 中国军转民 (*Defense Industry Conversion in China*), Issue 8, 2008.

36. Zhou Ling (周玲), "工信部三定方案出炉" ("MITT Reform Plans Got Permission"), 东方早报 (*Oriental Morning Post*), July 3, 2008.

37. One should be careful not to see SASTIND as necessarily the more conservative and MIIT the institutional innovator. MIIT largely comes from former MII, itself largely composed of the original Ministry of Post and Tel, the Electronics Industry. The inertia is solely referring to integration and opening up of the closely guarded defense industries.

38. Meaning, an institutional arrangement that goes beyond ad hoc Small Leading Groups, of which there are several. This author is referring to an institutional form that goes beyond permanent or ad hoc small leading groups, of which there are several. Luan Enjie (栾恩杰), "加强顶层设计，促进军民结合" ("Strong Top-level Design to Promote CMI"), COSTIND News Center (航天科工集团信息中心,), March 15, 2007.

39. John Battilega, Randall Greenwalt, David Beachley, Daniel Beck, Robert Driver, Bruce Jackson, *Transformations in Global Defense Markets and Industries: Implications for the Future of Warfare*, Washington, DC: National Intelligence Council, June 2001; Eugene Gholz and Harvey M. Sapolsky, "Restructuring the U.S. Defense Industry," *International Security*, Vol. 24, No. 3, Winter 1999/2000, pp. 5-51.

40. There are a number studies that reach this conclusion. For instance, see Liang Haibing (梁海冰), "中国特色国防研究30年·国防科技工业篇" (*"Chinese* Defense Research in the Past 30 Years, National Defense S&T Industry"), 军事历史研究 (*Military Historical Research*), Issue 3, 2008.

41. PRC Procurement Law was published in 1999, which led the way for CMC to publish specific rules for defense procurement.

42. "江泽民签领颁布　中国人民解放军装备采购条例" ("Jiang Zemin Signed Regulations on Armament Procurement for the

People's Liberation Army"), CMC, 2002, available from *www. chinanews.com.cn/2002-11-01/26/239143.html.*

43. "Regulations of Armament Procurement Plan Management," "Regulations of Armament Procurement Contract Management," "Regulations of Armament Procurement Ways and Procedures Management," "Regulations of Armament manufactory Certification Censorship Management," and "Regulations of Same Type of Armament Collective Procurement Management"), all issued by GAD in December 2003.

44. Li Hongjun (李红军) and Wu Lei (吴磊), "论装备采购方式的选择," "Discussions on Choices for Armament Procurement Methods"), 经济研究导刊, *(Economic Research Journal)*, No. 9, 2009; Liu Hanrong (刘汉荣), Zhang Zhan (张展), and Zhang Hua (张华), "不同装备采购方式的装备价格形成机制探讨," ("Discussions on Pricing Systems for Various Armament Procurement Methods"), 军事经济研究 *(Military Economics Research)*, No. 12, 2008.

45. Qian Chunli (钱春丽) and Hou Guangming (候光明), "我国装备采办组织管理体制现状及改革思路," ("Reform Path for China's Equipment Procurement Organization Management System"), 军事经济研究 *(Military Economic Research)*, No. 3, 2008.

46. Such as mechanized and armored equipment, chemical defenses, army aviation, systems engineering, and amphibious vehicles.

47. During the Eighth Five-Year Plan, 1991-95, budget constraints resulted in major reductions of orders for aircraft and ships for the air force and navy. For example, the order of one particular fighter plane was half of the quantity planned. Chen Tao (陈涛), Bai Haiwei (白海威), and Bai Chenggang (白成刚), "开展招标工作促进舰船采购模式的转变" ("Developing Open Bidding and Promoting Naval Ship Procurement Model"), 装备指挥技术学院学报 *(Journal of Institute of Equipment Command and Technology)*, Vol. 12, No. 1, February 2002.

48. Considering that a significant portion of all official areas of China's military budget is spent on general use items, basic training, administrative supplies, uniforms, maintenance, etc., the savings here could be substantial. See Guo Jia (郭佳) and Lü Ying (吕颖), "我国国防费结构优化的现状判断及实证分析" ("Analysis and

529

Assessment of the Current Situation of China's National Defense Spending Structure Optimization"), 军事经济研究 (*Military Economic Research*), No. 2, 2009.

49. Liu Xia (刘霞), "德力西荣登神舟5号的启示" ("Revelation of Delixi's Products used by Shenzhou Spacecraft Five"), 人民论坛 (*People's Forum*), No. 1, 2004.

50. This source was originally produced by CETC's 54th institute. See Zhou Yang (周扬), "奔月的民企们" ("Civilian Enterprises Racing to the Moon"), 21世纪经济报道 (*21st Century Business Herald*), October 25, 2007.

51. Liu Jianjun (刘建军) and Zhao Bo (赵波), "我军装备采购改革初见成效" ("Initial Successes in PLA's Armament Procurement Reform"), 解放军报 (*PLA Daily*), April 28, 2004.

52. Qian Cunli (钱春丽) and Hou Guangming (候光明), "我国装备采办组织管理体制现状及改革思路" ("Reform Path for China's Equipment Procurement Organization Management System"), 军事经济研究 (*Military Economic Research*), No. 2, 2008, p. 55.

53. Guo Jia (郭佳) and Lü Ying (吕颖), "我国国防费结构优化的现状判断及实证分析" ("Analysis and Assessment of the Current Situation of China's National Defense Spending Structure Optimization"), 军事经济研究 (*Military Economic Research*), No. 2, 2009.

54. Ding Feng (丁锋) and Wei Lan (魏兰), *References of Civil Enterprises Provides Military Products*, Beijing, China: Ordnance Industry Press, 2008, pp. 267-270.

55. "浪潮军品顺利通过海军二方认证审核" ("Inspur Military Products Smoothly Pass the Navy's Approval Inspection"), 腾讯科技 (*Tengxun Technology*), April 27, 2009.

56. In one example, a large Jiangsu Electronics Company in the business of making world-class level semiconductor and integrated circuit technology has tried unsuccessfully to get relevant approvals. Zheng Yuan (郑园), "民营企业参与国防科技工业建设的主要壁垒及对策" ("Barriers and Measures to Civilian Enterpris-

es Entering the Defense Industry Sector"), 国防技术基础 (*Technology Foundation of National Defense*), No. 9, 2007.

57. Gao Junmei (高俊梅), Tian Dasan (田大山) and Li Xiaoning (李小宁), "民参军的政府政策与管理" ("Policies and Management of Civilian Enterprises Participating in the Military Enterprises"), 中国军转民 (*Defence Industry Conversion in China*), No. 8, 2008; Zhou Yang (周扬), "少将解读民企参军五通道" (Major General Deciphers Five Paths for Private Enterprise To 'Participate in the Army'"), 世纪经济报道 (*21st Century Business Herald*), August 7, 2007.

58. Wang Haijiao (王海佼) and Zhang Han (张函), "民用企业应该进入武器装备生产核心领域" ("Civilian Enterprises Should be Allowed to Enter the field of Core Weaponry and Equipment Production)," 军事经济研究 (*Military Economic Research*), No. 10, 2006.

59. Zheng Yuan (郑园), "民营企业参与国防科技工业建设的主要壁垒及对策" ("Barriers and Measures to Civilian Enterprises Entering the Defense Industry Sector"), 国防技术基础 (*Technology Foundation of National Defense*), No. 9, 2007.

60. Song Zhenbing (宋珍兵) and Niu Lingjun (牛灵君), "民营企业参与军品生产存在的问题及应对措施" ("Existing Problems and Measures for Private Enterprises Participating in the Military Production"), 军事经济研究 (*Military Economic Research*), December 2006.

61. Described in Jiang Jinqi (江金骐), "获准'参军'地位提升, 私营企业谨慎面对" ("Private Enterprises Exercise Caution as their Position Strengthens in Permission to 'Participate in Military Production'"), 华夏时报" (*China Times*), August 11, 2007.

62. "Proposal of Developing Armament Procurement Institution Reform," issued by CMC in 2005; "Proposal of Strengthening Competitive Armament Procurement" issued by GAD in 2009. There is also the army procurement reform regulation, "Competitive methods for Army Weapon Armament Model R&D," issued by Army Armament Research and Procurement Office (GAD) in 2006. Ding Feng and Wei Lan, *References of Civil Enterprises Provides Military Products*, Beijing, China: Ordnance Industry Press, 2008, pp. 71-72.

63. The Company Law of 1993 was passed by the National People's Congress to facilitate the corporatization of SOEs. The aim was to transform SOEs into modern enterprises, allowing them to be restructured into three types of companies: wholly state-owned companies, limited liability companies, and joint stock limited companies. Also see Zhang Sunzong (张顺宗), "我国军工企业资产证券化问题探讨" ("Discussion of Defense Enterprises' Assets being Public Listed in Stock Market"), 现代商业 (*Modern Business*), Issue 15, 2009.

64. Yu Xin (喻鑫) and Fan Ruipeng (樊瑞鹏), "我国军工上市公司存在的主要问题及对策" ("Problems and Measures for China's Defense Industry Corporations in the Stock Market"), 军事经济研究 (*Military Economic Research*), July, 2009.

65. Some were engage in CMI R&D/production such as the Huojian Co., which produced CMI sensors used for both missiles and satellites.

66. The five areas of the defense industry (missiles/space, nuclear, ordnance, aviation, shipping) was only restructured into 10 state-owned group corporations in 1999 and the electronics industry into an 11th group corporation in 2002.

67. There were 29 IPOs prior to 1999 and 25 more since then. The statistics comes from Finance Channel of *Baidu.com*; and Chen Gang (陈刚) and Wang Tianyi (王天一), "国防工业整合：国家利益优先" ("Defense Industry Merger: National Interests Take First Place"), Oriental Securities (东方证券), July 7, 2009.

68. "国务院关于鼓励支持和引导个体私营等非公有制经济发展的若干意见" ("Several Opinions by the State Council on Encouraging, Supporting and Guiding Individual Private and other Nonpublic Economic Development"), available from *www.china.com.cn/chinese/PI-c/795128.htm*. "Opinions" published by the State Council are more like principal directives, or prototype legislation.

69. SASAC was established in 2003 to streamline and invigorate SOE asset restructuring.

70.   These two regulations have been termed the "two guides," "关于非公有制经济参与国防科技工业建设的指导意见" ("Guide of Non-state Economy participates in Defense S&T Industry"), COSTIND in 2007, available from *www.china.com.cn/policy/txt/2007-03/01/content_7888427.htm*; "关于推进军工企业股份制改造的指导意见" ("Guide of Promoting Share-holding reform in Defense Industry"), jointly published by COSTIND, NDRC and SASAC, 2007, available from *law.laweach.com/rule_12267_1.html*.

71.   The full name is "首次公开发行股票并上市管理办法" ("Administration of Initial Public Offering and Listing of Shares Procedures"), CSRC, May 2006, available from *www.csrc.gov.cn/n575458/n870280/n4240338/10305328.html*.

72. Asset injection actually began to appear following the State Council Opinions and before the 2007 COSTIND document. See Aerospace Changfeng injection of assets in 2005, as in Figure 1.

73. After defense assets were injected into public listed companies, public profit rate of these companies increased. For example, the profit rate of China North Optical-Electric, Zhongbin Guangdian, increased 38 percent in first quarter of 2009 after defense assets were injected in 2008. Meanwhile, the average profit rate of public listed companies was around 5 percent. Public quarter report of China North Optical-Electric Company Investors of stock markets also welcomed those stocks including defense assets. For example, during 1 week of August 2009, the value of whole stock markets in Shanghai and Shenzhen decreased 4.7 percent. Meanwhile, prices of 20 defense stocks increased over 20 percent. Among these 20, the rising prices of 15 of them were driven by the anticipation of M&A or as defense asset injection. Chen Cai (陈才), "中国军工前线报告：资本运作势不可挡" ("Report on China's Defense Frontier: An Onrush of Operating Capital"), 东方早报 (*Dong Fang Daily*), August 29, 2009.

74. Wu Fenglai (吴风来), (a senior official of COSTIND 国防科工委体制改革司司长), "积极稳妥推进军工企业产权制度改革" ("Promote Property Right Reform for Defense Enterprise"), 中国证券报 (*China Securities Newspaper*), December 25, 2007.

75. Interview with Ye Guoji (叶国际), researcher in Ping'An Securities (平安证券) on November 3, 2009.

76. In late 2008, China North Industries Optica-Electric purchased all military and dual-use production from Beijing China Optical Instruments Ltd. It later went on to raise over 800 million yuan to produce other products and has formed a joint venture with a German company. See *www.cngc.com.cn/NewsDetail. aspx?id=11627*. Ningbo Huaxiang Electronics Co Ltd purchased Liaoning Luping Machinary Plant, Military code 705 Plant) for 660 million yuan to produce dual-use vehicles. See Zhou Yang (周扬), "少将解读民企参军五通道" ("Major General Deciphers Five Paths for Private Enterprise to 'Participate in the Army'"), 21世纪经济报道" (*21st Century Business Herald*), August 7, 2007. There is also the case of 10 different civilian enterprises in Zhejiang investing in Air-to-Air Missile Research Institute (under AVIC-I), and a number of other defense institutes to produce BKZ-904 UAV electro-optical reconnaissance systems and other components. See Zhu Zongwen (朱宗文), "浙江制造业寻求转型之路81家民企涌入军工产业" ("Zhejiang Manufacturing transformation: 81 Civilian Enterprises Enter the Military Industry Sector"), 21世纪经济报道" (*21st Century Economic Journal*), November 25, 2008.

77. Lan Xinzhen and Ding Wenlei, "China to Unleash Market Forces in Arms Sector," *Beijing Review*, July 25, 2007.

78. "Investment Opportunities in the Stock Market for China's Defense Industry," Shanghai Securities Research Center, 2006.

79. Sha Zhinong (沙志龙), "破解军民融合发展的难题" ("Deciphering the Difficulties of CMI Development"), 国防科技工业 (*National Defense S&T Industry*), No. 2, 2009.

80. Yu Xin (喻鑫) and Fan Ruipeng (樊瑞鹏), "我国军工上市公司存在的主要问题及对策" ("Problems and Measures for China's Defense Industry Corporations in the Stock Market"), 军事经济研究 (*Military Economic Research*), July 2009.

81. "Investment Opportunities in the Stock Market for China's Defense Industry," Shanghai Securities Research Center, 2006.

82. Responsibilities of CSRC in official website of CSRC, available from *www.csrc.gov.cn/pub/newsite/zjhjs/zjhjj/200709/t20070918_95176.htm.*

83. Note this consolidation is within CASC, not across group corporations, so it does not include assets from CASIC. CASC is comparatively more engaged in CMI satellite activities while CASIC is more concentrated on missiles and dedicated military technologies. CASIC plays a more supporting role in CMI aerospace industry.

84. "中国卫星：卫星一体化应用实力最强" ("China Spacesat: Strongest Component of Satellite Integrated Application"), 投资者报" (*"Investor Journal"*), Sep.7, 2009.

85. "平等准入　公平竞争　一视同仁－－张嘉浩司长解读　国防科工委关于非公有制经济参与国防科技工业建设的指导意见" ("Director Zhang Jiahao Explains Guide of Non-state Economy participates in Defense S&T Industry"), 中国军转民 (*Defence Industry Conversion in China*), No. 4, 2007; Wang Hongwei (王宏伟), "试析民营经济准入国防科技工业的几个问题" ("Analysis on Civilian Economy Participating in Defense S&T Industry"), 军事经济研究" (*Military Economic Research*), No. 3, 2007.

86. Again, the example of China Spacesat shows that CAST (under CASC) holds 51.32 percent of stocks in China Spacesat. See Hexun Finance website, available from *stockdata.stock.hexun.com/2009_sdgd_600118.shtml.*

87. In the reorganization of COSTIND in 2008, authority for defense asset restructuring was transferred to SASAC.

88. According to the 2007 COSTIND regulations, the three areas included: a first group of key military enterprises producing strategic weapons and equipment directly relevant to national security would remain under sole ownership of the State; a second group, defense industries engaged in the production, general assembly and design of key weapon platforms and core subsystems would be permitted to convert to joint stock companies with the State as controlling shareholder; the remainder could reorganize in any form, including with private and foreign investors as controlling shareholders.

89. Interview with Ping'An Securities on November 3, 2009.

90. This means that in addition to SASTIND and SASAC — the usual ratifying bodies for stock listing approval — the approval of additional oversight bodies like the Ministry of Finance, the State Commission Office for Public Sector Reform, the Ministry of Human Resources and Social Security are also required. This is because of the need to resolve social security support for employees for instance. In addition, transforming to enterprise status automatically reduces or cuts off central government funding. Li Chao (李超) and Xu Ying (徐英), "大军工过槛" ("Defense Industry Will Cross Threshold"), 21世纪经济报道 (21st Century Business Herald), December 13, 2008.

91. Ren Qing (任晴), "试析航空工业体系改革" ("Analyzing the Aeronautics Technology Research Institutes System Reform"), 研究与探讨 (Research & Discussion), No. 5, 2002.

92. Sheng Ruowei (盛若蔚), "中国军工企业揭开"面纱"首次面向全球招聘高管" ("Defense Enterprise looks to Global Recruitment for Senior Manager for First Time"), 人民日报 (People's Daily), February 7, 2009.

93. Intra-industry competition: When a defense asset producing one technology under one defense corporation is listed as an IPO or asset injection, it has to put all facilities of the same category and products into that new concern to adhere to market fairness guidelines. The scattered and dispersed nature of the thousands of enterprises under the defense corporations makes this difficult. For example, in 2007, when China Aviation Optical-Electrical Technology controlled by AVIC planned an IPO, it has to skillfully purchased related assets under AVIC. After dealing with the problems of intra-industry competition, China Aviation Optical-Electrical Technology received permission for an IPO from the CSRC. Zhu Yu (朱宇), "中航光电揭开军工整体上市面纱" ("China Aviation Optical-Electrical Technology Unveils IPO as A Whole"), 中国证券报" (China Securities Daily), December 3, 2007. As for "Affiliated transactions," any transaction conducted within the company, or between it and an affiliated company and/or interested persons, is regarded as a negative thing by the stock market. In the Chinese defense system, however, only 15

percent of defense corporation is unfair from the perspective of stock markets. For example, the IPO Hongdu Air has to sell all exported planes to China National Aero-technology Imported and Exported Company, which is also controlled by AVIC. This trade is unfair in stock markets though it is ruled by government. Yu Xin (喻鑫) and Fan Ruipeng (樊瑞鹏), "我国军工上市公司存在的主要问题及对策" ("Problems and Measures for China's Defense Industry Corporations in the Stock Market"), 军事经济研究 (*Military Economic Research*), July, 2009.

94. There is no single funding list for CMI. These items are gathered from a variety of sources. This list is not meant to be comprehensive but a substantial compilation of programs that are discussed as CMI or CMI-related initiatives in the Chinese literature. See, for instance, the discussion of CMI usage of Mian Yang Industry Investment Funds. Hou Zhiqiang (候治强), "科技城全力推进产业经济高速发展" ("S&T City Promotes Speedy Development of Industry Economy"), 绵阳日报 (*Mian Yang Daily*), February 16, 2009. The discussion of CMI usage of Technology Transformation Fund can be found in, Tu Senlin (屠森林), Director of Dual-use Promotional Office under MIIT (工业技改司局长), "将技改与军民结和产业基地建设结合起来" ("Integrate Technology Transformation with CMI Industry Base"), website of MIIT, July 21, 2009, available from *www.miit.gov.cn/n11293472/n11293832/n11293907/n11368223/12468840.html* .

95. "渤海产业投资基金" (Bohai Rim Industry Investment Fund); 四川绵阳高科技产业基金, (Sichuan Mianyang High-tech Industry Investment Fund ("广东核电及新能源产业投资基金" (Guangdong Nuclear Energy and New Energy Industry Investment Fund), 天津船舶基金 (Tianjin Shipbuilding Industry Investment Fund), 东北装备制造产业投资基金 (Dongbei Equipment Manufacture Industry Investment Fund).

96. The five include: 渤海产业投资基金 (Bohai Rim Industry Investment Fund), 四川绵阳高科技产业基金 (Sichuan Mianyang High-tech Industry Investment Fund), 广东核电及新能源产业投资基金 (Guangdong Nuclear Energy and New Energy Industry Investment Fund), 天津船舶基金 (Tianjin Shipbuilding Industry Investment Fund), and 东北装备制造产业投资基金 (Dongbei Equipment Manufacture Industry Investment Fund). See Zhang

Liang (张良), "发改委将不再推出产业试点基金" ("NDRC won't approve anymore Industrial Investment Funds"), 上海证券报 (*Shanghai Securities News*), August 5, 2008; Li Chao (李超), "产业基金众生相：游戏规则尚待明确" ("Industry Investment is Clearly Discovering the 'Rules of the Game'"), 21世纪经济报道 (*21st Century Business Herald*), March 28, 2009.

97. 863 Projects including CMI items are directed by MoST and financial support is provided by MoF. Some universities, for example Beijing Institute of Technology and Harbin Institute of Technology, funded by GAD and MoST to research military projects, also are directed by MoE. Discussed at 2009 the Exhibition of China Civilian Enterprises Technology and Products listed for Defense Construction, held by China Peaceful Use of Defense Technology Association (中国和平利用军工协会) under SASTIND. GAD, MoST, MoF, MIIT, SASTIND and NDRC were all invited as relevant departments from military and government. Also see 2008 Fourth Exhibition of CMI Technology, available from *www.cq.xinhuanet.com/news/2008-02/26/content_12549710.htm*; and MoST Discusses with Guizhou province to Promote Relevant CMI Activity, available from *www.most.gov.cn/dfkjgznew/200911/t20091118_74272.htm*.

98. One example of its purview over sector-specific projects is the core electronic components, high-level general integrated circuits and fundamental software Announcement by MoST: "核心电子器件、高端通用芯片及基础软件产品" ("Major National Projects in Science and Technology: Core Electronic Components, High-end general-use chips, fundamental software"), September 5, 2009.

99. "国家发展改革委关于建设北京等30个国家高技术产业基地的通知" ("Notification from the NDRC Regarding the 30 national high-tech industrial bases in Beijing and elsewhere"), available from *www.ndrc.gov.cn/zcfb/zcfbtz/2008tongzhi/t20080305_196369.htm*.

100. NDRC, "National Engineering Labs Management Measures," NDRC, 2007, available from *www.ndrc.gov.cn/zcfb/zcfbl/2007ling/t20070801_151722.htm*.

101. "Zhejiang Province Determines to Build 16 CMI Industrial Development Bases," Zhejiang Economics and Information Commission, August 6, 2009.

102. Tang Bailu (汤白露), Xia Xiaobo (夏晓柏), and Peng Liguo (彭立国), "500亿元重构航天产业集群" ("50 Billion Yuan for Restructuring the Aerospace Industrial Clusters"), 21世纪经济报道" (*21st Century Business Herald*), June 10, 2008.

103. Han Sumin, "Study of Western Region CMI Integration Mechanisms under a Super-ministry System," *Journal of Northwestern Polytechnical University, Social Sciences*, Vol. 28, No 2, June 2008.

104. 136 corporations are controlled by central government, available from *www.sasac.gov.cn/n1180/n1226/n2425/index.html.*

105. Li Chao (李超), "产业基金众生相：游戏规则尚待明确" ("Industry Investment is Clearly Discovering the 'Rules of the Game'"), 21世纪经济报道" (*21st Century Business Herald*), March 28, 2009.

106. Mo Zengbin (莫增斌), "军民结合产业基地建设的研究与建议" ("CMI Industrial Base Construction Research and Proposals"), 国防科技工业 (*Defense Science and Technology Industry*), No. 1, 2009.

107. Yang Xiao (杨晓), "成都VS绵阳两个创新区域的发展模式之辩" ("Chengdu vs. Mianyang, Debate of Two Development Modes"), 四川日报 (*Sichuan Daily*), July 3, 2007; Lang Lang (郎朗), "绵阳千亿大戏：主角还是长虹" ("Chang Hong Remains Leading Role in Mianyang's Hundreds of Billions Plan"), 21世纪经济报道 (*21st Century Business Herald*), August 17, 2009.

108. Tang Bailu (汤白露), Xia Xiaobo (夏晓柏) ,and Peng Liguo (彭立国), "500 亿元重构航天产业集群" ("50 Billion Yuan for Restructuring the Aerospace Industrial Clusters"), 21世纪经济报道" (*21st Century Business Herald*), June 10, 2008.

109. Cheng Zhi (成智）and Cheng Hui (程慧), "国家级航空产业基金西安"破冰"" ("Xi'an National Civilian Aerospace Industry Fund Underway"), 西安晚报 (*Xi'an Evening Paper*), July 1, 2009.

110. For example, there are 99 companies and institutions under China North Industry Group Corporation across the whole nation. Among them, there is only one institution, named Ningbo Branch of Ordnance Science Institution, in Zhejiang province. In the document published by Zhejiang government in 2008, it admitted Zhejiang's defense industry is weaker than other provinces. "浙江省促进结合产业发展纲要" ("Outline of Zhejiang Province Promoting CMI Industry Development"), Zhejiang Province in 2008, available from *www.zjjmw.gov.cn/jmzh/zdxx/2008/09/24/2008092400029.shtml*.

111. Zhu Zongwen (朱宗文), "浙江制造业寻求转型之路81家民企涌入军工产业" ("Zhejiang Manufacturing transformation: 81 Civilian Enterprises Enter the Military Industry Sector"), 21世纪经济报道" (*21st Century Economic Journal*), November 25, 2008.

112. "深圳市军工办副主任殷勇在深圳军工项目推介会上的讲话" ("Speech in Shenzhen Defense Projects Presentation by Yinyong, Associate director of Shenzhen Defense Industry Office"), *Jungong Information On-line*, April 3, 2008, available from *www.jungong.info/newsdetail.asp?id=1900*.

113. Du Shun (杜舜), "深圳成立军工产业联盟" ("Defense Industry Alliance Found in Shenzhen"), 南方日报" (*Nanfang Daily*), July 28, 2009.

114. There are other models outlined by various authors such as "designated CMI industrial parks and bases," which are zones newly established due to their uniqueness in terms of location, industrial capacity, their supporting industrial supply chain network and transportation accessibility or because of their close political connections to the central government. An example of this model is Shanghai's National Aerospace Industry Park.

115. For an overview, see *National Programs for Science and Technology*, available from *china.org.cn/english/features/China2004/107131.htm*.

116. Engineering R&D centers are located in defense corporations, enterprises, and academic institutions; technology transfer centers are generally established at universities and CAS insti-

540

tutes, funded by the NRDC; and technology transformation funded projects are usually within enterprises and funded by MIIT See "PRC S&T — Survey of PRC 'Technology Transfer Centers'," Open Source Center, February 12, 2008.

117. Note that in recent official documents there is talk of 30 national high-tech parks. These are not entirely new entities but will be integrated into original high-tech enterprises or projects but with renewed favorable policies and funding. For example, in Beijing, Zhong Guancun information high-tech park will be integrated into Beijing high-tech integration base. "关于建设北京等30个国家高技术产业技术基地的通知" ("Notification for Building 30 National High-tech Industry Bases"), NDRC , 2008. The full text is available from *www.sdpc.gov.cn/zcfb/zcfbtz/2008tongzhi/t20080305_196369.htm*.

118. See Zhang Tingting (张婷婷), "我国高技术产业发展现状" ("Status of China's High-tech Industry Development"), 合作经济与科技 (*Co-Operative Economy & Science*), Issue 1, 2009.

119. Weng Shiyou (翁仕友) and Zhang Xiangdong (张向东), "工信部切分200亿资金首次项目本月下达" ("MITT distributes 20 Billion Technology Reform Funds"), 经济观察报 (*Economic Observer*), May 2, 2009; "高技术产业发展 '十一五' 规划" ("The Eleventh Five Year Plan of High-tech Industry Development"), NDRC, 2007. The full text is available from *www.sdpc.gov.cn/gjscy/cyzhdt/W020070514622304097239.pdf* .

120. "2007年我国高技术产业发展情况分析" ("China High-tech Industry Development in 2007"), S&T Statistics, Development Office under MoST, December 16, 2008.

121. Jia Zhimin (贾志敏), "金融危机之下外资在华设立研发中心趋势不减" ("In the time of Financial Crisis, Numbers of Foreign R&D Centers still Increasing"), 解放日报 (*Jie Fang Daily*), February 12, 2009.

122. In 2003 and 2006, MoST and the Ministry of Commerce jointly published the "鼓励外商投资高新技术产品" ("Catalogue of High-tech Products Encouraged to Be Invested by Foreign Enterprises"), The 2006 catalogue included 596 items of high-tech

products; electronics, IT, aviation and aerospace, nuclear items, and can be used in CMI, most of which is relevant to CMI activity. The full text is available from *www.investteda.org/zcfg/xfsd/gjxfsd/glwstzgxjscpml2006.doc.*

123. Sun Zhifa, "China Publishes Catalogue of High-tech Products Encouraged to Be Invested by Foreign Enterprises," *China News Agency*, July 18, 2003.

124. "中国空空导弹研究院低代价利用外国先进技术" ("China Air-to-air Missile Academy Low Spending on Foreign Advanced Technology"), 中国航空报 (*China AVIC News*), June 26, 2006.

125. See Albert Guangzhou Hu *et al.*, "R&D and Technology Transfer: Firm-level Evidence from the Chinese Industry," *The Review of Economics and Statistics,* November 2005, pp. 780-786.

126. While anecdotal evidence suggests China has acquired a number of sensitive technologies from the United States through its so-called dual-use S&T system, the scope of these technology transfers appear to be limited. In remarks to the U.S. China Business Council in June, 2007, Mario Mancuso, then Undersecretary for Industry and Security, stated that in 2006, "high-tech exports to China grew by 44 percent to $17.7 billion." Of this, only 1.3 percent required a license. See "Enhancing Secure Trade with China," Remarks by Mario Mancuso, Under Secretary of Industry and Security on June 18, 2007, available from *www.bis.doc.gov/news/2007/mancuso06182007.htm.*

127. "2008 年我国高技术产品进出口状况分析" ("Analysis of China's High-tech Products Import and Export in 2008"), Published by Development Office of MoST, July 27, 2009. The full text is available from *www.most.gov.cn/kjtj/tjbg/200908/P020090827541149373539.pdf.*

128. *China Science & Technology Statistics Data Book, 2009*, Ministry of Science and Technology of The People's Republic Of China, available from *www.sts.org.cn/zlhb/2009/hb1.1.htm#1.*

129. Tai Ming Cheung, "Dragon on the Horizon: China's Defense Industrial Renaissance," *The Journal of Strategic Studies*, Vol. 32, No. 1, pp. 29-66, February 2009.

130. Denis Fred Simon and Cong Cao, *China's Emerging Technological Edge: Assessing the Role of High-end Talent*, New York: Cambridge University Press, 2009, pp. i-xi.

131. *China Science & Technology Statistics Data Book, 2008*, Ministry of Science and Technology of The People's Republic Of China, available from *www.sts.org.cn/sjkl/kjtjdt/data2008/cstsm08.htm*.

132. Cong Cao, "China's Innovation Challenge" *China's Galloping Economy: Prospects, Problems and Implications for the United States*, Washington, DC: Woodrow Wilson's Asia Program, No. 140, May 2008.

133. Cong Cao, "Zhongguancun and China's High-tech Parks in Transition: Growing Pains or Premature Senility?" *Asian Survey*, Vol. 44, No. 5, September/October 2004, pp. 647-668.

134. "2008年我国高技术产品进出口状况分析" ("Analysis of China's High-tech Products Import and Export in 2008"), Development Office of MoST, July 27, 2009. The full text is available from *www.most.gov.cn/kjtj/tjbg/200908/P020090827541149373539.pdf*.

135. Cong and Simon, *China's Emerging Technological Edge*.

136. Cong Cao, "Zhongguancun and China's High-tech Parks in Transition."

137. Cong Cao, "China's Innovation Challenge."

138. The DH-10 has been in development for 2 decades (the ASBM, DF-21) since the 1960s, the ASAT since the 1980s, Shang attack sub since 1983, and the J-10 since 1988.

139. These are listed from the 2008 *Defense White Paper* and the 2006 MLP.

140. IT components will constitute the body of technology to informationalize and integrate its combat forces and digitize weapon systems. Space assets will provide the platforms on which this networking will be executed: navigation/positioning,

remote sensing, electronic intelligence, communications, and battlefield awareness.

141. For instance, the various communication link upgrades, from Link-11 to the NATO Improved Link Eleven, Link-16, the Multifunction Advanced Data Link, the Battlefield Airborne Communications Node which would translate between different protocols, the Advanced Extremely High Frequency satellites, beyond-line-of-sight Terminals, etc.

142. Detailed costs of China's individual weapons programs are notoriously hard to come by but the magnitude of the cost of new and high-tech space systems over legacy weapons is apparent. For example, the cost to build two earth resources CBERS satellites ran over a billion RMB, while the cost to build a DF-31 missile was reportedly 3 million USD. Even the cost of building a destroyer is only in the hundreds of millions. For CBERS, "中巴两颗资源卫星及其运载火箭研制投入15亿" ("China and Brazil invest 1.5 billion in developing 2 Resource Satellites and their launch vehicle"), October 21, 2003, available from *CCTV.com*, *www.cctv.com/news/china/20031021/100932.shtml*. Even for cheaper small satellites, China Spacesat has invested over 2.3 billion RMB for early phase R&D, available from *static.sse.com.cn/sseportal/cs/zhs/scfw/gg/ssgs/2009-08-12/600118_2009_z.pdf*. Even the cost of a destroyer is listed as in the mid hundreds of millions RMB, See Chen Tao (陈涛), Bai Haiwei (白海威), and Bai Chenggang (白成刚), "开展招标工作促进舰船采购模式的转变" ("Developing Open Bidding and Promoting Naval Ship Procurement Model"), 装备指挥技术学院学报 (*Journal of Institute of Equipment Command and Technology*), Vol. 12, No. 1, February 2002.

143. Tang Bailu (汤白露), "军转民"推动西安航天产业基地升级" ("CMI Promotes Upgrade of Xi'An Aero-space Industry Base"), 21世纪经济报道 (*21st Century Herald*), April 9, 2008.

144. 2008-11-25 13:19:08, available from *www.fyjs.cn/bbs/htm_data/125/0811/166151.html*.

145. "航天科技集团公司打造航天卫星应用产业集群" ("CASC develops Aero-space Satellite Application Industry Group"), July 14, 2009, available from *www.china-spacenews.com/n435777/n502211/59099.html*.

146. Universities, for example, Tsinghua University, Harbin Institute of Technology, and Zhejiang University, participate in R&D of small satellites. One company, Hangtian Tsinghua Satellite Technology Ltd., jointly founded by Tsinghua University and CASIC, develops and manufactures small satellites. Since its establishment, the company has developed and manufactured five small satellites: Tsinghua-1 micro satellite, KT-1PS/PS2/PS3, and a nano-satellite NS-1. The company was also awarded by GAD as military technology development award in 2007, information available from *www.casic-sat.com.cn/abouts-1.asp*. CAS is less involved in development and production of satellites, but is very involved in running a number of facilities.

147. Evan Feigenbaum, *The Military Transforms China: The Politics of Strategic Technology from the Nuclear to the Information Age*; James Mulvenon, *The Digital Triangle: A New Defense-Industrial Paradigm? A New Direction for China's Defense Industry*.

148. Huang Jie (黄婕), "问计大部制契机: 半导体业谋求产业合力" ("With Founding of Super Ministry, Semiconductor Industry Seeks Integrated Production"), 21世纪经济报道 (*21st Century Herald*), March 29, 2008.

149. *Ibid.*

150. Announcement by MoST: "核心电子器件、高端通用芯片及基础软件产品" ("Major National Projects in Science and Technology: Core Electronic Components, High-end general-use chips, fundamental software"), September 5, 2009.

151. For summary of achievements in these areas, see "Hearing on China's Industrial Policy and its Impact on U.S. Companies, Workers and the American Economy" U.S.-China Security and Economic Review Commission, March 24, 2009.

152. Refer again to the strategic component of DUI.

153. Most likely limited to military exercises such as with Peace Mission 2005. See Tan Yanqi (谭延启), Yin Jianbo (殷建波)

and Ding Jianmin (丁建民), "济南军区测绘信息中心保障中俄军演顺利进行" ("Survey and Mapping Center of Jinan Military Area Guarantees Success in Sino-Russian Joint Military Exercise"), 解放军报 (*PLA Daily*), October 31, 2005.

154. Denis Fred Simon and Cong Cao, *China's Emerging Technological Edge: Assessing the Role of High-end Talent*, New York: Cambridge University Press, 2009.

155. For example, look at the correlation of specific institutional changes or institutional barriers to hardware output to make qualitative inferences about defense industry effectiveness.

156. The author would like to thank Michael Beckley for the point made in this paragraph.

APPENDIX A - CHAPTER 10

M&AS AND ASSET INJECTION IN STOCK MARKET (2006-09)

Enterprise	Sector/Group Corp	Date	Asset Listed (R&D/production area)	Type
China North Optical-Electric 中兵光电-SHA:600435	CNGC	2008	UAVs, inertial navigation, global positioning, seeker systems, inertial guidance, fire control; civil geographic information systems, robots, ship-borne sat antennas.	Injection of CMI assets[157]
Aero-electronics 航天电子-SHA:600879	CASC	2007	aerospace electronic equipment	Injection of Defense assets[158]
		2008	aerospace electronic equipment	M&A within CASC[159]
Aero-engine 航空动力-SHA:600893	AVIC	2007	CMI aviation engine	Injection of Defense assets
Hongdu Aviation 洪都航空-SHA:600316	AVIC	2006	Jet training aircraft.	Injection of Defense assets
AeroSpace Chang Feng 航天长峰-SHA:600855	CASIC	2005	CMI, numeric control systems, computer simulation and precision components	Injection of Defense assets
Aerosun 航天晨光-SHA:600501	CASIC	2006	Special purpose vehicle and guidance systems.	Injection of Defense assets[160]
Westone Information 卫士通-SHE:002268	CETC	2008	CMI information security equipment, cryptography tech.	IPO
AVIC Heavy Machinery 中航重机-SHA:600765	AVIC	2009	Aviation equipment and new energy.	M&A within AVIC[161]
China Ship 中国船舶-SHA 600150	CSSC	2007-2008	bulk cargo ships, oil tankers, semi-submersible drilling platforms, floating production storage and offloading	M&A within CSSC[162]
China Spacesat 中国卫星-SHA:600118	CASC	2007-2008	CMI small satellites.	M&A within CASC
ST Space ST 宇航-SHE:000738	CASC	2009	CMI aviation engine control system assets within AVIC.	M&A within AVIC
Chang'an Automobile 长安汽车-SHE:000625	CSGC	2009	Passenger and commercial vehicles	M&A of spin off assets between CSGC and AVIC[163]
Dong'an Auto Engine 东安动力-SHA:600178	AVIC			
ST Chang'he ST 昌河-SHA:600372	AVIC			
Guihang Stock 贵航股份-SHA:600523	AVIC	2009	automobile and motorcycle components	M&A of CMI aviation assets within AVIC[164]
Xifei International 西飞国际-SHE:000768	AVIC	2009	CMI transportation plane.	M&A within AVIC (not ratified yet)
New Huaguang 新华光-SHA:600184	CNGC	2009	CMI optical glass and solar battery modules	M&A with Xi Guang Corp's Defense assets[165]
Aerospace Hi-Tech 航天科技-SHE:000901	CASIC	2009	automobile electronic products, household electronic products and aerospace products	M&A plan was denied by CSRC in 2008.

547

ENDNOTES - APPENDIX A - CHAPTER 10

1. CNGC injected its CMI assets (all assets in Beijing North Optical-electric Company) into the public listed civil company, North Sky-bird (Beifang Tianniao), which it formerly involved in the manufacture and sale of embroidery machines. After CMI assets injection, the name of stock changed from North Sky-bird to China North Optical-Electric, *Zhongbing Guangdian*.

2. Defense assets injection from Aerospace Times Electronic Technology Co., Ltd., and then name of stock changed from Rocket Stock to Aero-electronics in 2007.

3. The five subsidiaries under Long March Launch Vehicle Tech Co. Ltd. (Shanghai Aerospace Electronics Co., Zhengzhou Aerospace Electronics Tech Co., Guilin Aerospace Electronics Co., Hangzhou Aerospace Electronics Co., and Beijing Aerospace Jintai Survey Co.) were merged by China Aerospace Times Electronics Co.

4. Chongqing Aerospace New Century Satellite Application Technology Co. was injected to the public listed company, Jilin Biochemistry, in 2007. After injection, in 2008 the name of stock changed from Jilin Biochemistry to Aero-engine.

5. After M&A among subordinated of AVIC in 2009, the name of stock changed from LiYuan Yeya to AVIC Heavy Machinery.

6. After 2008 when M&A became a subordinate of CSSC, the stock received a new name of China Ship, under which it is a new company, China CSSC Holdings Limited.

7. Chang'an Automobile under CSGC merged civilian assets of Dong'an and Chang'he under AVIC. AVIC plans to inject other aviation assets into the two public listed companies, Dong'an Auto Engine and ST Chang'he, after they sold their civilian passenger vehicle assets to Chang'an Automobile.

8. Ratified by SASTIND and SASAC, awaiting approval from CSRC.

9. *Ibid.*

APPENDIX B - CHAPTER 10

CURRENT CMI RELATED FUNDING

Fund	Amount (bn ¥)	Organ in charge	Purpose
Industry Investment Fund:	140 bn for 10 industry investment funds[166]	Ratified by NDRC (operated by Fund Management Companies)	Capital from SOEs to invest in key industries including CMI
Bohai Rim	20	Bohai Industrial Investment Fund Man. Co.	Invest in industrial projects in Tianjin (50%), Bohai Rim (30%) and other areas (20%) in China.
Sichuan	6	CITIC Industrial Investment Fund Man. Co.	Invest in financial services, energy and defense industry, mainly located in Mianyang.
Guangdong	10	Guangdong Nuclear Power and New Energy Industrial Invest. Fund Man. Co., Ltd.	Invest in national nuclear energy including dual-use nuclear capacity.
Tianjin	20	China Ships Industrial Investment Fund Man. Co.	Invest in ship building, transport and harbor construction.
Dongbei	20	Controlled by China Development Bank and Liaoning SASAC	Invest in equipment manufacturing in northeast China.
Strategic Industry Venture Capital[167]	9.2	NDRC, local governments and private invest funds.	Support for medium and small enterprises in rising strategic industries including new energy, integrated circuit, etc.
National High-tech Industrial Projects (including 54 [parks and 30 bases)[168]	Taxation advantages and low interests loan.	NDRC and MoST	Transform high technology to applied industries including CMI.
Electronic Information Industry Development[169]	3.9 bn— central government, >200 bn—local governments. (1986-2005)	MITT and local governments	Electronic information industry technology progress and transformation.
Technology Transformation	21.7 bn (783 items, 29 CMI).[170]	MIIT	Enforce tech transformation including CMI technology development.
Innovation Fund for Small Tech-based Firms[171]	>1 billion every year.	MoST and local governments	Facilitate scientific transformation and support technological innovations of Small Technology-based Firms.
863 (National High-tech Research and Development Plan)	>10 billion/year (11th FYP, 10 high-tech areas and 38 special projects.[172])	MoST, GAD, SASTIND	Support high-technology research and development.
973 (National Important Fundamental Research Dev Plan)	8.2 bn from 1998-2008 384 projects, 1998-2008.[173]	MoST, GAD, SASTIND	Support important fundamental science and technology research and development.
Defense S&T Industry Fundamental Research Innovation Fund[174]	No exact amount	SASTIND	Promote research in advanced industrial technology, fundamental technology and civil-military dual use applications.
Defense S&T Prelim Research and National Security Fundamental Research[175]	No exact amount	SASTIND and Defense Corporations	Fund research centers in universities and defense research institutions to enhance defense research.
GAD Weapon Preliminary Research[176]	50,000 – 2 million/year	GAD	Fund universities and defense research institutions to research weapon projects.
National Industrial Tech Innovation and Reform	370 bn[177]	State Council	Remove technology bottlenecks and transfer technology to engineering and industrialization.

ENDNOTES - APPENDIX B - CHAPTER 10

1. Luo Xiao, "社保基金一千亿元投资计划振奋产业基金" ("100 Billion Yuan Investment Plan of Society Insurance Fund Inspires Industry Fund") 新京报 (*New Capital News*), October 30, 2009.

2. Hang Yang, "92 亿 '新兴战略产业' 基金启航" ("9.2 billion Yuan 'Rising Strategic Industry' Fund Begins to Operate"), *21 世纪经济报道"* (*21st Century Business Herald*), November 28, 2009.

3. NDRC, "关于建设北京等30个国家高技术产业基地的通知" ("Notify to build 30 National High-tech Industrial Bases Including Beijing Base"), February 20, 2008.

4. Wang Xudong, "在电子信息产业发展基金成果大会的讲话" ("Speech at Electronic Information Industry Development Fund Achievement Conference"), *Saidi* 网 (*CCID Net*), August 16, 2005.

5. Tu Shenlin, "将技改与军民结合产业基地建设结合起来" ("Integrate Technology Reform with Construction of CMI Industry Bases"), July 21, 2009, available from the official NDRC website, *www.miit.gov.cn/n11293472/n11293832/n11293907/n11368223/12468840.html.*

6. More contents about this fund are available from *www.innofund.gov.cn/index.asp.*

7. Joint office of 863 Plan under MoST, "十一五国家高技术研究发展计划（863计划）申请指南" ("Guidance to Apply Eleventh Five Years' National High-tech Research and Development Plan"), available from the official website of MoST, *www.most.gov.cn/tztg/200703/t20070326_42347.htm.*

8. Official website of 973 Plan, "国家重点技术研究发展计划（973计划）组织实施情况" ("Achievements of 973 Plan") available from *www.973.gov.cn/ReadCont.aspx?aid=419.*

9. CONSTIND, "国防科技工业技术研究传信基金管理暂行办法" ("Temporary Measures of Defense S&T Industry Fundamental Research Innovation Fund Management"), 中华人民共和国国防科学技术工业委员会文告 (Documents of CONSTIND), Issue 12, 2007.

10. Zhao Bo, "武器装备应用技术研究成绩显著" ("Great Achievements of Weapon Equipment Appliance Fundamental Research"), *PLA Daily*, October 17, 2004.

11. "关于申报2008年度武器装备预研基金项目的通知" ("Notify to Apply GAD Weapon Preliminary Research in 2008") Haerbin Institute of Technology, August 20, 2007, available from *today.hit.edu.cn/articles/2007/08-20/08122328.htm*.

12. Liu Xianyun, "自主创新这一年" ("Independent Innovation in 2009") *People's Daily*, December 2, 2009.

CHAPTER 11

TAMING THE HYDRA:
TRENDS IN CHINA'S MILITARY LOGISTICS
SINCE 2000*

Susan M. Puska

INTRODUCTION

> Vast [numbers of] officers and men . . . using support
> methods that were relatively manpower intensive . . .
> made up for the insufficiency in equipment and instru-
> ments. This is a traditional characteristic of the PLA's
> logistics.
>
> > Report from a 2008 Military-Wide Logistics
> > Academic Research Center Seminar[1]
>
> You will not find it difficult to prove that battles, cam-
> paigns, and even wars have been won or lost primarily
> because of logistics.
>
> > General Dwight D. Eisenhower[2]

Throughout much of the history of the People's
Liberation Army (PLA), since the closing days of the
Civil War and the founding of the People's Republic

---

*This chapter examines Chinese military logistics modernization
based primarily on Chinese language sources published since the
late 1990s. It seeks to add to the literature of the last 10 years concerning Chinese military logistics which has been few in number
in openly available publications, many of which focus on organizational and administrative issues. See the section on Military Logistics Research—Secondary Sources of Information. This chapter
addresses the logistics modernization discussion by assessing
developments of operational capabilities that would enable force
projection beyond China's land borders.

of China (PRC) in late 1949, military logistics served as disarticulated systems of independent and redundant support provided by the services[3] and individualized by units, commanders, and locations. China's military logistics system reached into local, nontraditional roles and functions in civil production and resource exploitation. These connections were strengthened during the 1960-70s, when the PLA was directly embedded into the civilian logistics infrastructure to secure and manage distribution networks, commodities, and key resources.

PLA logistics subsequently developed into bloated, multiheaded systems of support. Nonetheless, these proved adaptive and sufficient to support defensive military operations at or near China's border. Logistics support for mobile offensive operations beyond its borders, however, has been deficient. For examples, China's military logistics was inadequate and ill-prepared to support exploitation of the retrograde of United Nations (UN) forces below the 38th parallel in 1950. Almost 30 years later, China's military logistics system proved inadequate to sustain offensive military operations in Vietnam in 1979. Consequently, China's military forces were forced to fall back to positional warfare—along the demilitarized zone, in the case of Korea, and along China's southern border during operations in Vietnam.

After the Third Plenum of the Chinese Communist Party's (CCP) 11th National Congress in 1979, China's military began to withdraw from civil affairs. As a result, the PLA's logistics structure began a protracted process of reduction and regularization in the 1980s. Lucrative commercial opportunities and military budget limitations, however, blunted military logistics reform, as elements of the logistics system slipped into the murky world of PLA, Inc. This state of affairs flourished until divestiture in 1998-99, when, during an anti-smuggling meeting held in July 1998, Jiang Zemin ordered the PLA to withdraw from commercial enterprises.[4]

This chapter examines trends in the modernization of China's military logistics, particularly since divestiture, when modernization efforts began to gain momentum, moving beyond remedial reforms toward that of building capacity to support both defensive and offensive military operations under informationalized conditions. This is a significant turning point for China's logistics modernization because military logistical support, to be successful, must have the capacity to support military force compositions, capabilities, and missions to execute the commander's intent at the strategic, operational, and tactical levels of war.

Even if China's armed forces were designed to only support defensive operations, it would still be necessary to have the capabilities to sustain and increase combat power while under attack from a potential enemy. Offensive operations are even more challenging for logisticians where it is necessary to maintain operational momentum[5] regardless of whether the forces are conducting operations on land, at sea, or in the air, or supporting mobile missiles operations beyond China's border.

If China is to project military power overseas, particularly through the operational domains of the sea and the air, its ability to do so will largely be shaped by its military logistics capacity within four areas addressed in this chapter.

1. Joint and Mobile Logistics,
2. Logistics in High-Tech Warfare Environment,
3. Civil Sector Support, and
4. Sustainment of Units Abroad.

This chapter seeks to provide an overall assessment of the success and shortcomings of PLA logistics reforms, since the late 1990s, in each of these areas and to examine future trends. Finally, this chapter examines implications for U.S. policy, and the author hopes to demonstrate that China's logistics system is steadily moving toward providing increased capability to support China's armed forces in both offensive and defensive operations under informationalized conditions. However, there are also shortcomings and some curious features that co-exist alongside these improvements that provide contradictory indicators about the pace, scope, and potential intent of China's military modernization in general, and particularly its ability to support expeditionary operations beyond its land border.

MILITARY LOGISTICS RESEARCH

Current Sources Of Primary Information.[6]

The sources used in this review were mainly a combination of Chinese professional journal and newspaper articles in Chinese or an English translation. A preliminary survey of selected books and articles published since 2000, on China's military logistics modernization is also introduced as an indicator of the professional development of military logistics in China.

Additionally, openly available[7] secondary sources on China's military logistics system were screened for pertinent information. While secondary sources on China's military logistics modernization have been rather limited, primary Chinese sources have matured and expanded (see Appendix A for a selected bibliographic listing of Chinese publications since 2000, for examples). This development reflects a growing sophistication and professionalization of Chinese researchers and practitioners of military and civil-military logistics support.

A brief examination of Chinese military logistics books published from the mid-1980s illustrates this trend toward increasing sophistication. Between the mid-1980s and early 1990s, general surveys dominated publications, with titles such as, *A Brief Introduction to Military Logistics* (军队后勤管理浅说),[8] *Modern China Military Logistics Work* (当代中国军队的后勤工作),[9] and the *Practical Handbook on Logistics* (实用后勤知识大全),[10] for examples. These books provide general introduction to logistics work, and also introduce the military to U.S. logistics, with a particular focus on U.S. Army logistics operations.

By the mid-1990s military logistics studies in China incorporated analysis of U.S. military (usually Army) logistical operations during the Gulf War. Among these volumes were *Mobilizing Military Logistics* [11] and *Logistics Protection in High-tech War*.[12] As the decade ended, Chinese military logistics studies developed greater depth and breadth: *Logistics Support for Mobile Operations*,[13] *The Study on Campaign Logistics Under The Condition of Information Warfare*,[14] and *Informatization and Military Logistics*[15] illustrate a growing interest in how to incorporate information technology into logistics, as well as how to provide effective operational support. In addition, during this time detailed guides on logistics leadership, supply management, and developing a code of conduct for logisticians[16] also appear.

Since 2000, professional military logistics writings have been deepened by publications in professional journals, such as Logistics Technology (物流技术), Military Logistics (军事物流), and China Military Science (中国军事科学), as well as books published by the Military Sciences Press, General Logistics Department, National Defense University, and the Academy of Military Sciences Press, among others.

Secondary Sources of Information.

Secondary sources on China's military logistics modernization are fragmented throughout broader studies on military modernization. Logistical aspects of these studies have often focused on logistics organization (or reorganization), functions, and reform.[17] Indepth studies of the General Logistics Department (GLD),[18] General Armament Department,[19] and particularly operational capabilities[20] have been limited. Logistics-related studies of the defense industries[21] and defense economy[22] have also formed a special niche of interest, which touch on larger military logistics questions, more than operational aspects.[23]

The scarcity of secondary studies on China's operational logistics modernization can be attributed to at least three factors. First, Chinese sources of information on logistics were limited in number, scope, and depth until the mid- to late-1990s. The ability of China's military to conduct Joint Logistics, for example, appeared highly speculative in 1998 when Joint Logistics was established. Second, hardware studies, which can be more easily quantified and relate directly to assessments of combat power have tended to receive more attention. Third, once the U.S. suspended Foreign Military Sales (FMS), which had generated relatively active bilateral logistics contacts during the 1980s, logistics cooperation became increasingly sensitive and problematic for both sides, which may have also inadvertently discouraged continuing research on the topics.

MILITARY-MILITARY LOGISTICS CONTACTS

After the closeout of the four FMS cases in December 1992—a bitter lesson for both operational and logistical proponents of military cooperation with the United States—bilateral logistics contacts languished until the mid-1990s. When they did resume, they were constrained to seemingly safe areas, such as military medicine.

Three bilateral events occurred between 1995 and 1998. Major General Wen Guangchuan, Assistant Director, GLD, received briefings on U.S. logistics doctrine and systems, and Chinese military officers were allowed to observe military logistics operations during a 1995 visit to the United States at the invitation of the Office of the Under Secretary of Defense for Acquisition and Technology.[24] In March 1996, Assistant Secretary of Defense for Health Affairs Stephen Joseph visited China and signed a "Memorandum of Medical Exchange and Cooperation."[25] GLD Deputy Director Lieutenant General Zhou Youliang conducted a reciprocal visit in September 1996, when possible cooperation between the PLA 301 Hospital and Walter Reed Army Medical Center was discussed.[26]

During March-April 1998, GLD Director General Wang Ke visited the United States at the invitation of the Under Secretary of Defense for Acquisition and Technology. During this trip, Wang Ke visited Aberdeen Proving Ground, Maryland; Warner-Robins Air Logistics Center, Georgia; the Defense Logistics Agency's Defense Supply Center , Richmond, Virginia; the

USS *Abraham Lincoln* aircraft carrier; and USPACOM. Wang Ke received briefings on Department of Defense (DoD) Logistics Systems' organizations, Logistics Modernization Initiatives, Joint Logistics/Focused Logistics, DoD Outsourcing Process and Experiences, DoD Military Retirement Systems, and the Army's Integrated Training Area Management Program.[27]

Since 1998, however, logistics contacts have been even more limited. In early 2001, General Wang Shouye, Director of the Capital Construction and Barracks Department, GLD, for example, visited the United States as the head of a GLD military environmental protection delegation. Although he visited Davis-Monthan Air Force base near Tucson, Arizona, Wang's briefings focused on environmental management.[28] In 2006, a GLD delegation that visited Hawaii as the guest of the USPACOM J-1, Colonel William Carrington, discussed personnel management issues, including salary differences between the U.S. and Chinese military.[29] No bilateral relations with the General Armament Department (GAD) have been reported, and there appear to have been no exchanges of senior visits between DoD and GLD since 2006, although contacts through multilateral logistics events, such as the Pacific Area Senior Officer Logistics Seminar (PA-SOLS), a multilateral organization sponsored by U.S. Pacific Command, have continued since 1995. China hosted the 38th PASOLS, held in Beijing on September 8-10, 2009.[30]

MILITARY LOGISTICS RESEARCH AND APPLICATION

Chinese military researchers at universities, institutes, and Army units have actively studied recent developments throughout the U.S. military logistics system since the 1990s, and particularly since the Iraq War began in 2003. Among the topics of interest for potential application to Chinese logistics systems are bar coding and radio-frequency (RF) tracking, which could greatly improve assets visibility, and enhance information management systems for inventory control and distribution. There also has been special interest in how the U.S. military logistics system leverages contracted civilian support, as well as how streamlined distribution networks provide more agile support to the end user.[31]

Discussions of how to improve China's military logistics have not been limited to military affiliated researchers and active duty personnel, however. Civilian researchers, too, are actively assessing ways to adapt modern logistics methods, including domestic commercial advances such as regional support centers to improve military capabilities. Further, the military is increasingly looking to the civilian logistics sector for ways to enhance military logistics.

While it appears that the PLA logistics system is scurrying to leverage its own civilian logistics know-how, as well as that of more advanced military systems, such as the United States, its ability to generate knowledge and technology into logistics capacity remains a work in progress that requires a combination of more sophisticated knowledge with operational experience, application, and testing of systems and technology to optimize their effectiveness. Additionally, the Chinese military will need a team of expert military and civilian logisticians who can work together to support the commander's intent. As a start point to assess China's logistics capability in terms of practical application such as support to force projection, we will examine China's current logistics terminology, and compare it to the terminology of an advanced expeditionary force, the U.S. military.

CHINA-U.S. COMPARISON OF LOGISTICS TERMS

China's military logistics modernization is largely taking place through the adaptation and exploitation of what can be absorbed from foreign militaries and civilian advanced logistics capabilities. Logistics tests within the Jinan Military Region (MR) provide a basis for developing tested capability and standards that can be radiated out to the entire force. But there are questions that will be further examined about the content and pace of China's military logistics improvements, and what kind of missions these improvements are really designed to provide, which are reflected in three key Chinese terms: Integrated Joint Logistics Support; Comprehensive Support; and Joint Logistics.

Integrated Joint Logistics Support (一体化联合作战保障).

This term is generally defined as the integration of military services' logistics, civil-military compatibility, and the combination of wartime and peacetime functions to support mobilization.[32] The 16th Party Congress (2002) enshrined this concept, authorizing and encouraging civil-military integration of peacetime logistics functions, know-how, and capacity to support wartime requirements that have encouraged advanced planning and coordination through Civil Air Defense organizations, for example. Integration of civil-military logistics support seeks to enhance military operations by leveraging civil capacity.

The U.S. military does not have an exact equivalent to this Chinese term, but the integration of civil support is embedded into U.S. military logistics operational concepts, such as:[33]

- Integrated logistic support (ILS)—"composite of all the support considerations necessary to assure the effective and economical support of a system for its life cycle. It is an integral part of all other aspects of system acquisition and operation."[34]
- Integrated materiel management (IMM)— "exercise of total DoD-level management responsibility for a federal supply group or class, commodity, or item for a single agency. It normally includes computation of requirements, funding, and budgeting, storing, issuing, cataloging, standardizing, and procuring functions." [35]

As a global expeditionary force engaged in multiple long-term operations, the U.S. military logistics system has developed complex and adaptable systems that link together the support capabilities of the various services, federal support, commercial off-the-shelf (COTS) acquisition, host-nation support, contracted support, as well as research, development and acquisition of equipment and systems to support global operational requirements.[36]

Throughout the U.S. military logistics system, a complex set of laws and regulations governing command and control have been developed to integrate civil-military capability for peacetime and wartime operations. At the Joint level, for example, U.S. logistics seek to integrate core Joint logistic capabilities (supply, maintenance operations, deployment and dis-

563

tribution, health service support [HSS], engineering, logistic services, and operational contract support)[37] to provide support according to the operational environment, and to integrate this organic service support with "the strategic sustaining base of the Nation."[38]

While U.S. logistics terms reflect its expeditionary operations outside the continental United States, China's logistics terms appears to focus more on defensive homeland mobilization concepts in the tradition of People's War in which civilian and military capacity can be mobilized to support defense of China during attack. Many of the civil-military mobilization mandates are further under resourced and centrally managed, allowing local experimentation and variations that could undermine effective national mobilization. Logistics support to offensive power-projection capabilities, discussed more below, does not appear to be an urgent priority and/or appreciated requirement to offensive operations, as the gradual implementation of joint logistics based on the Jinan MR tests begun in 2004 seems to indicate.

Comprehensive Support (综合保障).

Differences in American and Chinese military operational concepts, as well as capacity, are also indicated in the Chinese term, comprehensive support. China's concept of comprehensive support may be defined as "a series of support measures . . . to ensure the smooth execution of a campaign and its final victory . . . [including] operational support, logistic support and equipment support."[39]

This term can be compared to the U.S. military's joint logistics concept, which is defined as "the coordinated use, synchronization, and sharing of two or more Military Departments' logistic resources to support the joint force."[40] The U.S. military logistics system includes several core Joint Logistics functions, which support its expeditionary operations worldwide:

- Supply—Management of supply operations; inventory management; management of supplier networks.
- Maintenance Operations—Depot and field maintenance operations to rapidly return systems to the user to enable operational freedom of action; long-term life cycle readiness, maximizing availability and reliability of systems at best value to the military services.
- Deployment and Distribution—Planning, coordinating, synchronizing, moving forces, and sustainment to support military operations. Move forces and materiel.
- Health Service Support—Services that promote, improve, conserve, or restore the mental and physical wellbeing of the force. Casualty management; patient movement; medical logistics; preventive medicine and health surveillance; theater medical information.
- Engineering—Operations that assure mobility provide the infrastructure needed to position, project, protect, and sustain the force and enhance visualization of the operational area across the full range of military operations. Integrates combat, general, and geospatial engineering capabilities.
- Logistics Services—Operations essential to the technical management and support of the joint

force, such as food, water and ice, base camp, and hygiene services in an expeditionary environment.

- Operational Contract Support—Operations that provide the ability to orchestrate and synchronize integrated contract support and management of contractor personnel in a designated operational area.

Joint Logistics (联合后勤).

China military's use of the term "Joint logistics" seems to focus more on staff organization and functions (and streamlining) than operational capability. For example, the China Military Logistics Encyclopedia defines Joint Logistics as "unifying the organization of the services to implement common logistics work. Implementing joint logistics avoids duplicate staffing, organizations and facilities, rationally distributes manpower, material and financial resources to support joint operations and joint activities."[41]

Joint logistics support, at this point in China's military modernization, appears to be driven by cost saving, regularization, and reduction of redundant staffing. It has been limited to managing common use materials and logistical services needed by the troops, ensuring that the armed services support function operate under unified control, while service-unique materials and services remain under the command and control of "their organic support systems."[42]

Military material is managed by the military logistics departments and consists of manufactured products and other related materials that are used during operations or for the purpose of troop building. At the strategic and operational levels, military material support breaks through services' boundaries. Providing common use material support is the responsibility of the joint logistic system. Service-specific material support is provided through the services' organic support entities.[43]

The 16th Chinese Communist Party Congress further elaborated on the organizational, rather than operational, emphasis of Joint Logistics, with initial focus on providing common supplies and services, stating:

Integrating the logistics supply units of the military branches into one means to establish a joint services administrative framework—one in which the logistics supply units of the three military branches are jointly structured, the logistics support forces of the three military branches are used as a whole, and the logistics systems for the three services are organized in light of the overall situation in accordance with the requirements imposed by joint military operations.[44]

Chinese Joint Logistics, subsequently, divides its support between common use material (通用物资) and special-use/service-specific material (专用物资). Common use materials may include some types of ammunition, clothing/uniforms, raw materials (such as metals; glass; heating fuel; petroleum, oils, and lubricants [POL]; and cement), electronics/mechanical material (machinery, industrial ovens, machine tools, and various electronic components[45]), food, barracks material, and common services (financial, medical, transportation, and barrack engineering services).[46] Special-use/service-specific material (专用物资) remained those which are used by one service, such as aircraft tires and ship boiler [steam] engines.

LOGISTICS TRANSFORMATION GOALS AND THE NEW HISTORIC MISSIONS

> For modern armed forces, organizing effective logistics work in the rear is of great significance.
>
> Mao Zedong[47]

> There are many ways of fighting a war, including fighting a war through logistics. Logistics work serves the war proper.
>
> Deng Xiaoping[48]

> The strong fighting capacity of the armed forces cannot do without effective logistics support.
>
> Jiang Zemin[49]

> In a certain sense, modern warfare is to be fought through the confrontation and competition of logistics. Without a powerful comprehensive support capacity, it is hard to win victories in military operations.
>
> Hu Jintao[50]

In 2007, President and Party General Secretary Hu Jintao[51] identified four general objectives for China's military logistics modernization in the new millennium: [52]

1. Cultivation of high-quality logisticians,
2. Mechanization and informatization,
3. Application of science and technology, and
4. Development of an Integrated Logistics Support System for all services with some embedded civil support.

Efforts to improve the quality of logistics personnel have been ongoing over the last 30 years of Chinese military modernization. These have often been hampered by a bias for independent and redundant support provided by each service, which would narrow the logisticians' knowledge and experience. Additionally, a preference for warfighting skills over developing more sophisticated logistics officers and enlisted personnel, would also siphon off better educated personnel into other military specialties.

Corrupt activities of logistics personnel have also likely contributed to the underdevelopment of professional logisticians, particularly in efforts to improve accountability and asset management. General Wang Shouye, who was stripped from his post as Deputy Commander, PLAN,[53] exemplifies a persistent tradition of abuse of military logistics resources for personal gain that hampers the development of a professional core of logisticians. Corruption insidiously works against efforts to improve the Chinese logistics system to make it more efficient and responsive, while undermining personnel development.

RECENT KEY TRENDS IN CHINA'S LOGISTICS MODERNIZATION

The general improvements that President Hu proposes as identified above must be operationalized through concrete improvements to China's military logistics to support potential power projection beyond China's shoreline, including Taiwan and beyond. This section examines China's military logistics modernization in terms of four trends, the success of which will determine China's future ability to support the projection of military power:

1. Joint and Mobile Logistics,
2. Logistics in High-Tech Warfare Environment,

3. Sustainment of Units Abroad, and

4. Civil Sector Support.

Joint and Mobile Logistics.

> Mobility is the true test of a supply system.
>
> Captain Sir Basil Liddel Hart,
> *Thoughts on War*, 1944

Development of Joint Logistics (联合后勤保障, abbreviated as 联合后勤) and Mobile logistics (机动后勤) or mobile support (移动保障) to support China's ability to project military power by applying land, sea, air, and space capabilities has progressed since 1999 when GLD director Wang Ke initiated key logistics reforms.[54] Since 2000, joint logistics reforms have helped eliminate duplicate logistics facilities and services, streamline links in the logistics system, develop a more rational system of distribution of logistics resources, and achieve substantial cost savings. Nonetheless, it remains a work in progress with successes in limited areas of common support, but still lacking effective application to the operational level.

Beginning in the late 1990s, the PLA took concrete steps to develop joint and mobile logistics capabilities.[55] On January 24, 1999, President Jiang Zemin signed the PLA Joint Campaign Program (referred to as the Number 13 PLA Combat Order), which initiated training and organization for Joint Operations. The following year, joint logistics departments were created in all seven MRs. The initial step for developing joint logistics was the "two joining and one base" (两结合一个基础) initiative, which merged MR logistics resources and organizations, as well as common use of support capabilities.[56] After this, General Wang Ke,

Director, GLD, published an article, which established a 10-year program for PLA logistics reform. Key goals that supported the establishment of joint logistics included developing a system that could simultaneously support the needs of army, navy, and air force requirements, standardizing PLA supplies, and scientifically managing military logistic services. [57] Authors of an internally distributed article assessing Wang Ke's strategy divided this effort into three phases:[58]

Phase One:

- Eliminate service branch logistics.
- Reform military region logistics departments to become joint logistics departments and sub-departments subordinate to the GLD.
- The GLD will allocate and manage on an equitable basis logistic support personnel, material, equipment, facilities, and other resources to the MRs and service logistics departments.
- The GLD will directly supply unified troop support to the army, navy, air force and Second Artillery Corps.
- After the services are no longer involved in logistics, a war logistics coordination organization (战勤协调机构) will be established that will be responsible for the logistics work of subordinate units and systems.

Phase Two:

- Form a three-tiered logistics system consisting of the GLD, war zone logistics departments, and regional logistics departments.
- The GLD and war zone logistics departments will be at the same level of leadership.
- The war zone logistics departments and the regional logistics sub-departments will be at the same level of leadership.

Phase Three:
- Under the joint leadership of the GLD, and according to the strategic direction and regional deployments, establish within the country several regional war zone logistics departments that are subordinate to the GLD and responsible for logistics in the war zone and within every war zone establish subordinate war zone logistics department sub-departments.

Joint Logistics Supply Distribution after 2000.

An examination of supply and material distribution after the 2000 reforms incorporated MR Joint Logistics departments and sub-departments provided in Figure 1[59] illustrates how the 2000 reforms affected joint logistics. The chart shows three distinct distribution channels for material flow down to using units. One channel is the distribution of common use material through the MR Joint Logistics Material and Fuel Department, through subordinate (sub) departments to material supply stations and, finally, to using units. The center distribution channel depicts material flow for service-specific items through the military region's service logistics departments and supply stations to using units. The third channel on the right side of the chart depicts the flow of "comprehensively planned material" (统等物流) through the GLD's Military Material Planning Bureau and material storage and delivery stations. Critical commodities, such as rice, are supplied by the GLD through national procurement to military regions that do not have sufficient production capacity to support military needs, such as areas of Qinghai Province, the Xizang Autonomous Region or the Xinjiang Autonomous Region, within the Lanzhou and Chengdu MRs, for example.[60]

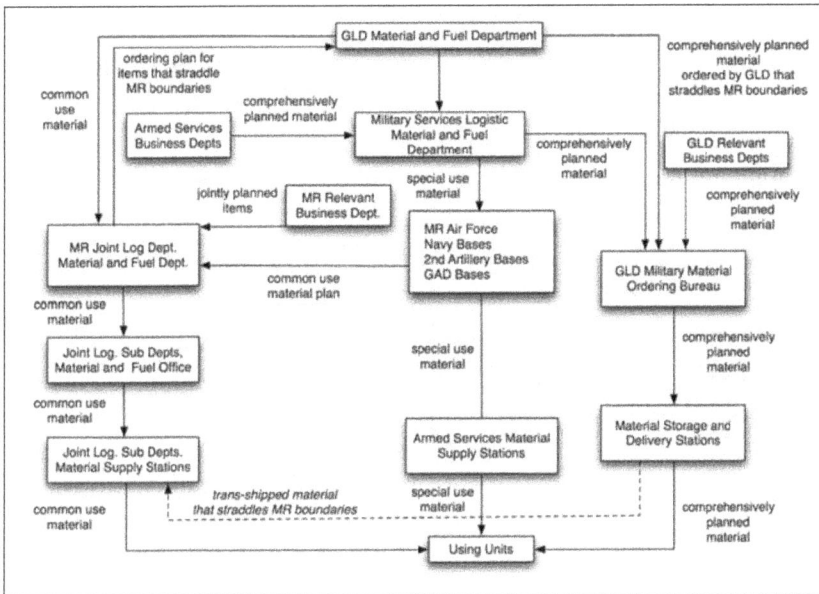

Figure 1. Joint Logistics Supply Distribution (after 2004).

In July 2004, Jinan MR initiated a joint logistics pilot test, combining common use and service-specific supplies.[61] During this test, the Jinan MR Joint Logistics Department was renamed the Jinan War Zone (济南战区) Joint Logistics Department. By "combining regional and organization support and integrating common use and special use (service unique) support (通用保障与专用保障相结合)" the Jinan test eliminated the dual-track common use and service-special support that had been implemented in 2000. Under this reform, the GLD remained in charge of all-army joint logistics. Each MR's joint logistic department exercised responsibility for joint logistics within its "war zone" (战区), while joint logistics sub-departments (联勤分部) bore the responsibility for organizing and implementing regional common use support (通用保障) for all three services.[62]

By 2006, Jinan MR Deputy Commander, Zhong Shengqin, described the pilot as "a good start." He cautioned, however, that the joint support system needed to be "perfected in practice" before the CMC could issue specific plans on how to implement joint logistics reforms to the PLA. Zhong called on Jinan MR personnel to consolidate achievements from the pilot and intensify efforts to solve problems.[63]

Joint logistics supply distribution in the Jinan MR pilot may be depicted as a two-track distribution system (see Figure 2),[64] which eliminates the services' branch logistics departments. One channel distributes common use and service-specific materials. A second channel continues to distribute comprehensively planned material to poorer regions.

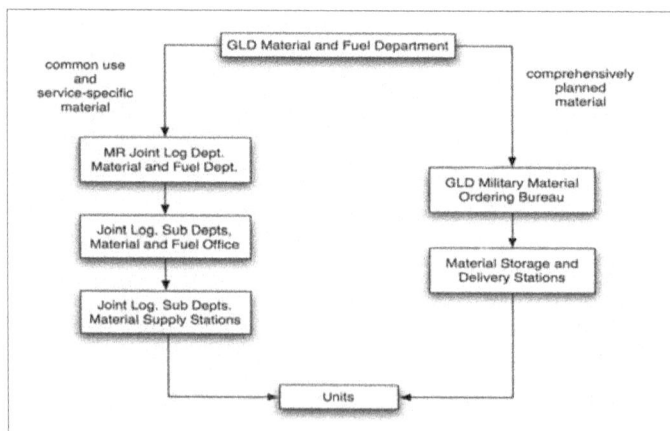

Figure 2. Joint Logistics Supply Distribution in the Jinan MR.

Chinese assessments of the initial reforms to establish JLDs within the MRs indicated some success in creating a logistics system more geared to joint military operations using both horizontal and vertical support links. Common use materials and logistic services were successfully provided by the joint logistics departments. Multiple services logistics units were eliminated, which reduced support redundancy. Duplicate logistic facilities and services were also eliminated. Collectively, these changes helped increase logistics efficiency and achieve higher standards in materials and services provided. Logistics support to units also became more responsive as a number of links within the support system were greatly reduced allowing for closer support, which rationalized support distribution and also speeded up logistics operations. Additionally, significant savings were realized through a reduction in transportation mileage, and the consolidation of rear area warehouses used by the three services.[65]

The Jinan MR joint logistics pilot test beginning in 2004 achieved several positive results, which appear to have promoted more jointness throughout the force. First, as the new JLD changed its name from an MR JLD to MR (War Zone) JLD, the proportion of personnel serving in the JLD from other services was increased. MR-based service logistic commands were eliminated. Service facilities were amalgamated into joint facilities, including war zone-based warehouses, hospitals, convalescent homes, material organizations, and infrastructure that were put under the JLD.[66] The vast majority of units now fall within several tens of kilometers of these facilities.[67]

Among the other achievements recognized in reform arising from the Jinan MR pilot joint logistics test are:

- All supporting facilities in the theater/war zone are centrally managed.
- The support of supplies is provided from the nearest location.
- The PLAAF, PLAN, and Second Artillery logistics commands in Jinan were eliminated.[68]
- There is no longer a differentiation between common/service unique support and materials.
- Supporting facilities, such as warehouses, hospitals and engineering organizations, became centrally managed/constructed.
- Deployment of logistic resources is more rational.
- The speed of logistics operations was increased.
- The percentage of non-army cadres in the department has risen from 12 percent to 40 percent.[69]

The China *Defense White Paper* (2006) highlighted force reductions arising from joint logistics reform, as follows:

> Apart from special purpose depots and general hospitals under the general headquarters/departments, the Navy, Air Force and Second Artillery Force, all other rear depots, hospitals and recuperation centers have been integrated and reorganized into the joint logistical support system. A total of eight joint logistical sub-departments, 94 rear depots, and 47 hospitals and recuperation centers have been closed.[70]

Despite organizational and operational improvements to joint logistics since Joint reforms began in 2000, and the Jinan MR pilot test began in 2004, many barriers continue to impede the development of an effective Joint logistics system throughout the armed forces. As a result, problems in support for mobile operations persist. One author who urged for the transition from fixed storage to military material distribution centers, for example, criticized the excessive levels within the logistics chain of command, which interfere in requisition processing,[71] consequently delaying support to end users. Local barriers also disrupt cross leveling of supplies. Additionally, the lack of information technology undermines the ability to exercise command visibility over logistics assets. As a result, inventory visibility is often limited to independent storage facilities, where PLA supplies and materials remain in static storage.[72] The author recommended application of optical storage cards, bar codes, and radio-frequency technology to accurately assess available supplies and materials and to accurately track distribution.[73]

A 2001 analysis of the logistics challenges to support amphibious operations[74] against Taiwan also frankly discussed logistics challenges to support military operations under the challenging conditions of an amphibious assault across 1,000 kilometers. He concluded that the Chinese military logistics system could not provide all the necessary logistics supplies for island landing operations, and he expressed skepticisms over how civilian ships and fishing boats could assist a forced landing on the island to support combat operations. Consequently, he recommended adapting combat operations according to the logistic limitations and realities. In particular, he recommended logistics operations during the initial phase of the battle be supported by air cover provided by helicopters. Mobilization of civilian ships to support logistics, he wrote, could be achieved during the second and later phases of the operation once China had seized Taiwan and the Strait, and military operations were subsequently reduced. Wary of the cost of military operations, he noted, application of civilian resources would reduce defense expenditures. Among the logistics improvements he recommended, many of which appear to have been adopted as goals, are:

- Establish a wartime command system for logistics.
- Provide support according to the principles of high mobility, high flexibility, smooth operations, and high efficiency.
- Transcend regions, divisions and types of armed forces to achieve an integrated command logistics.
- Strengthen logistics support to become highly efficient, rapid reaction.
- Develop a technical force of logisticians led mainly be reservists.
- Place emphasis on timely and accurate delivery of services at minimum cost and damage, using a smooth command mechanism.

Logistics in High-Tech Warfare Environment.

> The modernization of the armed forces will require a significant input of resources, the process of informatization also requires high input. . . . The contradiction between the needs in defense and army modernization and the relative insufficiency of funds will continue to exist for a long time. Thus, we must, according to the requirements of the scientific development concept, firmly take the course of less input and higher efficiency in the modernization of national defense and the armed forces.
>
> Hu Jintao[75]

Within the overall context of informationalized warfare, the adaptation of information technology to logistics has, so far, concentrated on improving inventory visibility and management; standardization, which would enhance networking of logistics information; tracking of material and equipment throughout the distribution process; and information management. These areas are weaknesses, not only within the military, but also throughout China's growing commercial logistics structure, which could eventually help benefit the military's adaptation of information technology, as improvements are made within the nation-wide logistics system.

Among the technologies of particular interest to the Chinese, which are often based on the study of foreign (often U.S. military) logistics technology and application, are:

- Bar coding (跳码) and Radio Frequency Identification (RFID) (射顿识别)[76]—Logistics Command College (后勤指挥学院) and its Military Logistics Lab (解放军事物流工程实验至) in Beijing; GLD Logistics Science Research Institute (Beijing) (总后后勤科学研究所); and Unit 86599 (Beijing).
- Intelligent Card (IC) (非接触式IC卡)[77]—Department of Air Materials, Xuzhou Air Force College, Xuzhou.

Linked through Global Positioning Systems (GPS), these commercial off-the-shelf technologies, which are already widely used by international civilian and military logistics systems, can assist the military to monitor the location of equipment, shipping containers, vehicles, palletized supplies and material, for example, from their production through distribution to the end user. As a result, these innovations could significantly enhance the military's visibility over logistics assets, cross-leveling, and by increasing the speed of distribution.

Four additional areas of interest to the PLA to enhance China's military logistics operations under informationalized conditions are the application of digital technology to improve standardization,[78] a persistent problem within both military and civilian logistics inventory management;[79] forecasting[80] using a back-propagation (BP) neural net,[81] and simulation[82] to test logistics operations under wartime conditions, for example, which could enhance the logisticians' ability to accurately forecast requirements, enhance standardization, and improve the military's overall logistics modernization.

To integrate this information, military logistics researchers are seeking ways to develop modern command information systems to provide commanders with greater asset visibility over logistics resources within their area of operations in order to facilitate rush support and cross-leveling of assets. This area presently represents a major portion of military logistics research as they seek ways to adapt modern logistics systems and concepts to military operations. Potential integrating management systems that could be adapted to integrate Chinese military logistics information include:

- CALS[83] (Continuous Acquisition and Life-cycle Support[84]).
- Information Fusion.[85]
- DSS (Decision Support System).[86]
- ILS (Integrated Logistics Support).[87]

Acquiring commercial off-the-shelf (COTS) logistics information technology could significantly enhance China's military logistics management and accountability system-wide if implemented effectively. There are no clear indications, however, that the CMC/GLD/GAD has reached a point where software and hardware decisions have been made, or will be made, which would enhance coherent application of information technology to logistics operations. Without top-down direction on selection and development of hardware and software options, a tendency toward independent development and adaptation exists that could create local systems that will not be able share information over the near term, and may require extensive reworking to achieve interconnectedness.

Civil Sector Support.

> To effect the healthy and rapid development of defense and military modernization, we must persist in effecting military and civilian combination, embedding military resources in the civilian sector, and incorporating defense and military modernization deeply in the system of economic and social development. . . . We should adhere to the strategic concept of the people's war, closely rely on the people in building national defense, persist in combining the streamlined elite regular forces with the strong reserve forces, continuously enhance our nation's war potential and defense strength. . . . Actively explore and develop the new way of the people's participation in war and support for the battle front.
>
> Hu Jintao[88]

> As the link between the war front and the home front, the logistic process is at once the military element in the nation's economy and the economic element in its military operations.
>
> Duncan Ballantine[89]

Civil sector support to China's military logistics capability has become a key feature of military modernization through peacetime-wartime integration. It seeks to leverage civilian expertise, scientific innovation, technology, and logistics resources to develop a joint civil-military logistics capability during peacetime that would support wartime military mobilization.

Civil support occurs during mobilization and socialization, or the contracting of goods and services. Mobilization refers to preparations for war, while socialization not only refers to contracting for goods and services in preparation for a potential war, but also to support of the military in its daily peacetime activities. In fact, much of the socialization effort to date has been done in non-operational units, such as schools and headquarters units, in large cities.[90]

Civil-military support was included in the 17th CPC National People's Congress Work Report in 2007 when Hu Jintao identified areas for integration, including: weapons and equipment research and manufacturing, military personnel training, and logistics.[91] Building on the traditions of civil support for a new age, Hu sought to combine national defense and national economic development to "change the mode of logistics building for a quantity and scale pattern to a quality and efficient pattern." Exploiting the resources of the national economy for defense building in peacetime and mobilization in wartime enable the military to utilize the "material and technological foundation of the nation" to help build a "great logistic support capacity" to deter war and respond to crises.[92]

Three of the additional goals that have been identified for civil support in Chinese publications include reducing costs, while improving logistics support capabilities, as well as technology and management. A fourth reason is to provide concealment for military mobilization in civilian activities. [93]

Although mobilization of civil assets plays a key role, to date, no national level law governing mobilization has yet been adopted, but several local mobilization laws have been put into force at the provincial and city level, which indicates that a system is taking shape. The only national level mobilization law that has been established was passed 4 years prior to the 17th CPC National Congress in 2003.This allowed for the mobilization of civilian transportation assets.[94] It permits the military to use abundant local transportation support capabilities and resources to enhance military transportation.[95]

Civil support is still under development and may be encountering some resistance on both sides. Nonetheless, there have some accomplishments reported at local levels with equipment support, for example.

In June 2009, a Xinjiang MD armored regiment signed a "Highway Transportation Agreement for Armored Equipment" and conducted the first emergency call-out exercise using civilian flatbed trucks to transport armored vehicles,[96] which allowed the unit to augment its limited organic capability (two trucks) to respond more quickly. In another example, in May 2009, another unit in Xinjiang MD received repair parts from a distributer in Jinan, Shandong. Five commercial trucks delivered the parts directly to designation distribution centers for closer distribution to users units, which replaced the past practices of storing the repair parts in a central warehouse. The unit negotiated the delivery at no additional transportation cost to using units, which increased efficiency and reduced costs.[97]

Another article frankly evaluating civil-military integration of equipment support noted a number of problems in implementing the change, including a systemic resistance to civilian outsourcing, a lack of macro-level planning for civil-military integration, including an integration mechanism (organization) that would oversee this change in how armament and equipment support is managed.[98]

Despite problems with implementing mobilization and socialization reforms, particularly inadequate regulations and laws, the PLA remains committed to increasing its reliance on the commercial sector. Socialization efforts during peacetime are forcing the military to confront the issue of proper remuneration, something the PLA has not had experience with as it tries to implement contracts relying on very vague regulations that have been issued since 2002.

Civil support will continue to develop domestically, as the military and commercial enterprises figure out how to support the military. These improvements should over time broaden and deepen logistics support domestically, which could strengthen China's defensive posture. At the same time, and perhaps more importantly to China's ability to project power outside its borders, civil support to operations is also developing as the Gulf of Aden mission illustrates.

Sustainment of Units Abroad.

> During the Korean War, the attack by the People's Volunteer Army was described by United Nations forces as a 'one-week attack,' mainly because the quantity of grain and bullets each of the soldiers . . . carried . . . determined the length of combat time. . . . Sooner or later, China is going to have to start acting like a mature power (and establish overseas bases).
>
> Dai Xu, PLAAF Air Force Colonel[99]

> The major powers are withdrawing from the peace-keeping role. . . . China felt it is the right time for us to fill this vacuum. We want to play our role.
>
> Wang Gangya, China's UN Ambassador[100]

Over the last 10 years, a major feature of PLA overseas operational experience has concentrated on participation in UN Peacekeeping Missions. In 2000, China's participation fell well below the top 20 nations,[101] but China has expanded its support from individual observers to the addition of police, and finally adding military personnel, which presently include battalion-sized and larger military units. Figure 3 shows Chinese participation by mission, location and type of personnel provided in July 2009, when China fell within the top 20 contributors. [102]

Date	Mission	Location	Observers	Troops	Police
31-Jul-09	MINURSO	Western Sahara	13	0	0
31-Jul-09	MINUSTAH	Haiti	0	0	144
31-Jul-09	MONUC	Congo	13	218	0
31-Jul-09	UNAMID		0	324	1
31-Jul-09	UNFIL	Lebanon	0	344	0
31-Jul-09	UNMIL	Liberia	2	564	16
31-Jul-09	UNMIS	Sudan	12	444	17
31-Jul-09	UNMIT	Timor-Leste	2	0	27
31-Jul-09	UNMIT	Timor-Leste	2	0	27
31-Jul-09	UNTSO	UN Truce Supervision Organization	4	0	0
Total			53	1894	205

Figure 3. China's Participation in UN Peacekeeping Missions.

Logistics elements from China's military participate in these missions, exposing them to the UN logistics system and other militaries, as well as providing mission-oriented experience. The second batch of Chinese participants in the UNMIL mission in Liberia, for example, included a 240-person transport battalion and a 43-member medical team out of a team of 558, as well as a 275-member engineer battalion. Through the UNMIL mission, these Chinese units worked to facilitate transportation, build roads and bridges, and administer medical treatment in Liberia.[103]

China's ship visits, although limited, have developed within the last 10 years, which help expand PLAN logistics practical experience that is an important development in the long-term development of overseas sustainment capabilities. In July 2000, for example, Rear Admiral Huang Jiang led the first PLA Navy (PLAN) ship, consisting of the *Shenzhen*, China's newest guided-missile destroyer at the time, and the *Nancang* supply ship, to South Africa.[104] In 2002, the

PLAN sent a flotilla around the world.[105] More recently, in November 2008, China sent its navy training ship, *Zheng He*, to the Vietnamese port of Tien Sa, one of two major ports in Danang, for a 5-day visit.[106] In May 2009, the PLAN sent its first ocean teaching-training ship to Taiwan with a contingent of 160 students and teachers from the Dalian Maritime University.[107]

In late 2008, China took a more significant step toward development of maritime operational capabilities, including logistics support at sea, when it announced it would deploy ships to the Gulf of Aden to protect commercial ships transiting near the Horn of Africa.[108] China announced plans to send two destroyers (*Haikou* and *Wuhan*) and a support vessel (*Weishanhu*) from the PLAN's Hainan base near Sanya to conduct a 4-month antipiracy mission in the Gulf of Aden.[109] Admiral Du Jingcheng, the mission commander, was quoted as saying: "Our primary target is not striking but dispelling them. If the pirates make direct threats against the warships or the vessels we escort, the fleet will take countermeasures."[110] Wuhan and Haikou returned to their homeport of Yulin in April, while *Weishanhu* provided support for the relieving vessels, which had departed from South Sea Fleet headquarters in Zhanjiang, and included the destroyer, *Shenzhen*, and the frigate, *Huangshan*.[111]

While the antipiracy mission is providing operational experience to PLAN, its logistics operational experience is also breaking new ground. On June 21, 2009, for example, the flotilla replenished in Port Salalah, which was the first time that PLA Navy warships had berthed in Oman. This was the third in-port replenishment since the mission began in January. Two previous replenishments were conducted in the Port of Aden, Yemen. Fresh water, diesel, and more

587

than 50 kinds of 5 major categories of nonstaple foods, such as poultry meat, vegetables, and fruits were restocked. An advance party of representatives from the PLAN and China's Ministry of Foreign Affairs of the PRC coordinated the replenishment through Chinese agencies in Oman including the West Asia Company of the China Ocean Shipping (Group) Company (COSCO) to procure commercial products.[112]

Yang Weijun, the *Weishanhu* commander, said the main reason for selecting Port Salalah at that time was to further explore and perfect commercial bulk replenishment relying on foreign commercial ports, "so as to accumulate experience for the PLA Navy in carrying out oceanic logistics support during the military operation other than war."[113]

ACCESS VERSUS BASING – CHINA'S ROLE IN INTERNATIONAL PORTS

The possibility of China establishing military bases overseas has long been unthinkable for at least three reasons: (1) the limitations of China's own military capabilities, which have largely relegated it to a landbound army and near-periphery air and sea operations; (2) China's avowed principles of nonalignment and noninterference outside China's territory; and (3) sensitivity to international opinion, which has discouraged Chinese military activity abroad. These conditions could change over time, however, as China's military power projection capabilities mature to provide greater employment options and Chinese leaders see concrete value in deploying military forces to promote their national interests. Domestic pressure could also become a wild card for the decisionmaking of China's leadership if leaders feel pressured to take action to protect China's economic interests and citizens abroad if they face threats and violence. Under such circumstances, Chinese leaders may feel they have no choice but to take action, rather than appear weak to domestic critics. Additionally, as China successfully demonstrates that it is willing to contribute to international security actions in a professional manner, such as China's navy did in the Gulf of Aden mission, resistance to employing China's armed forces overseas may diminish.

An area where a potential shift in China's employment of its armed forces overseas may appear over time at key economic hubs, such as international ports, where economic interests could draw China into more complex security commitments and arrangements to protect and promote its interests. China now makes substantial investments to port improvements around the world to facilitate the flows of goods, materials, and commodities to and from China. In Africa, for example, China Union, in early 2009, signed a contract, which includes improvements to the port of Monrovia, to develop Liberia's Bong iron-ore project at an estimated cost of U.S. $2.6 billion.[114] In Latin America, China has already outstripped Japan as a major trading partner.[115] Investments in shipping infrastructure, such as a reported $10 billion of improvements for the Panama Canal,[116] support China's priorities to ship high volume quickly to and from China.

China's investment in Brazilian ports has grown with the volume of trade, which made China Brazil's major trading partner, displacing the United States.[117] On May 19, 2009, China's Minister of Transport, Li Shenglin, signed a memorandum of understanding with the Minister of Special Secretariat, Pedro Britto that will help to further modernize Brazil's port facilities,[118] while enhancing China's access to commodities, such as soybeans, iron ore, and oil from Brazil.

For now China remains sensitive to potential worries about the presence of Chinese military personnel abroad, in general. In Latin America, however, China has been even more cautious to avoid "becoming entangled in Chavez's larger goal of counterbalancing U.S. influence in the Western hemisphere"[119] or other relationships that would antagonize America.

OVERALL ASSESSMENT: SOME POSITIVES VERSUS NEGATIVES

> Historians record many offensive operations as "the big push." One might well wonder whether any success was due to the combat arms' "pushing" the enemy or the (logistics) support units' "pushing the combat arms. [Logistics units must] maintain the momentum [in the offense] . . . [In the defense,] the role of the logistician. . . . is to *sustain and increase combat power.*

> Major John E. Edwards, USA (Ret.)[120]

The last 10 years of China's logistics modernization have been significant in building up a foundation in the key areas of Joint Logistics, sustainment abroad, logistics informationalization, and the ability to leverage commercial assets to support the military from garrison to operational missions, like China's antipiracy operations in the Gulf of Aden. Looking at these recent advances made to China's military logistics compared to its continuing shortcomings, we can make some observations.

First, military logistics modernization now enjoys the highest priority it has ever had over the past 30 years of defense modernization in China. Nonetheless, higher priority on the purchase of advanced arms and equipment is likely to continue, with logistics falling behind in terms of resources, which will have some effect on the pace of continuing reform. More sophisticated weaponry and equipment demand more sophisticated logistics support, which may ultimately drive faster logistics transformation. Consequently, developments in China's military logistics capacity will remain an important indicator of when and how well China can project power beyond its land borders.

Second, there are a number of positive indicators that evaluate the maturation of China's logistics modernization to support military objectives under informationalized conditions, and they include:

- A Joint logistics system has been established, which provides the basis for further development and potential support to expeditionary forces.
- Once systems and methodologies are established through testing, such as the Jinan MR Joint logistics program, the foundation for accelerated implementation can be achieved, which will significantly speed up the modernization of logistics.
- Preparation for logistics mobilization has been stressed as a key feature of civil-military logistics support, which can help the Chinese leverage civilian support domestically and internationally as it develops a post-"Reform and Opening" Chinese-style military-industrial complex.
- China's ability to support PLAN operations offshore has been enhanced through the development of logistics support vessels; real world experience, such as logistics support to anti-pi-

racy missions in the Gulf of Aden, and logistics support operations during domestic emergencies (floods, earthquakes, etc.), provide the military with operational experience, which can be radiated throughout the military logistics forces as lessons learned and command guidance.

- Military and civilian logistics researchers and organizations, as well as military units, are collaboratively researching, applying, and testing logistics support capabilities, which can help accelerate the adaptation of innovation and improvement to logistics in an informationized environment.
- The trends in China's military logistics modernization appear consistent with advanced capabilities that have already been mastered by the United States and other militaries. Although the PLA trails well behind more advanced military logistics systems, it does appear to be on the right track for significantly advancing China's military logistics capabilities.
- A growing base of knowledge and application of modern logistics capabilities is developing, which can provide a strong platform for advancing the development of a core of professional military logisticians, as well as civilian logisticians who support the military.

Third, "negative" indicators remain, and in some cases contradict points of progress in China's logistics modernization, which indicate limitations in the overall capacity of the logistics force. Among the shortcomings are:

- The rate of change in the modernization of China's military logistics does not reflect a high level of urgency. There is a high tolerance for excessive decentralized innovation and experimentation, which inhibits dissemination of best practices in logistics operations.

- The corps of professional logisticians appears to be insufficient to support the size of the Chinese military and its power projection aspirations; the best and the brightest do not appear to be going to logistics units.
- Standardization remains a significant problem in logistics, which can negatively affect the agility and regenerative capacity of China's military logistics system, particularly when faced with high consumption rates during war, and support to expeditionary forces.
- The ability for Chinese military logistics to support military operations will depend upon how well GLD and GAD support elements can integrate missions, such as resupply of ammunition (GAD function), fuel, food, etc. (GLD function), services, such as medical support (GLD function) and battlefield maintenance, including battlefield repair, evacuation and repair, repair parts supply, etc. (GAD function) to support operational units. Separation between GAD and GLD support during wartime may inhibit the effectiveness of support.
- The PLA and the logistics system are trying to do many things at once, which could overwhelm human capacity and resources, while undermining the potential rate of logistics transformation.
- Funding for logistics reform is insufficient. Overreliance on civil support appears to be needed to fill budget and priority gaps.

- Decentralization versus centralization—logistics reform innovation, testing and application—is happening at local levels throughout the country, creating pockets of innovation that do not appear to be quickly disseminating throughout the armed forces. Central authority does not appear to have the power to mandate change quickly.

FUTURE TRENDS IN CHINESE MILITARY LOGISTICS REFORM

Based on the level of effort and trends of logistics modernization over the last 10 years, we should expect continued operational logistics improvements to support military operations outside China's border. Improvements can be accelerated with command decisions from above, increased sense of urgency to address perceived threats, and application of greater resources and heightened priority.

Nonetheless, Joint Logistics (as understood in the West) will continue to mature, and best practices will radiate throughout the force, although levels of logistics operations may vary from one MR to the next. Logistics capacity to support operational mobility within and near China's land border should improve first, while providing potential capacity to support increases in scope, distance, and duration of overseas operations.

China's civilian logistics system, which is concurrently modernizing and maturing at a significant rate, should help multiply the capacity of the military logistics system through direct support to mobilization and outsourcing (socialization). Additionally, a more robust and sophisticated civilian logistics system should also help improve China's military logistics over time, and continue to feed innovation and adaptation of new and improve logistics systems and practices into the military, as occurs in other countries.

Development of the PLA's ability to globally project force has made a good start with the Gulf of Aden mission. We should expect China to build on this to develop greater capacity for offshore operations and to protect national interests around the world. Long-distance logistics support will require foreign port access for replenishment, which we can expect China to continue to advance.

Foreign basing of Chinese military forces may become more feasible and attractive, even necessary, as China's power and global interests grow. Its continued participation in international efforts to stabilize lawless areas and trouble spots may help promote its self-image as a peaceful and responsible actor, which could dampen criticism and fear of Chinese military deployment. For the near term, however, China is more likely to continue to develop worldwide commercialized "basing" options through the expansion of China's commercial operations in existing and new ports and other commercial nodes around the world.

However, potential disruptions to the military modernization trend line arising from instability within China should not be discounted. Domestic instability and the potential reaction of the Party to preserve its authority and to promote stability, to include using the PLA, remain wild cards overhanging the pace and scope of military reform, including logistics, in the near future.

IMPLICATIONS FOR U.S. POLICY

> Truth is unattractive. Error charms. It holds out all
> manner of false hopes . . . All the shores of the great
> ocean of time are strewn with those whitened skeletons
> of misguided thought.
>
> Lester Ward, *Applied Sociology*[121]

Predicting the effects of China's logistics modernization and commensurate improvements in its power
projection capabilities on U.S. policy defies a simplis-
tic threat, no threat analysis. Concrete improvements
in China's military logistics system would certainly
pose potential concerns for the worldwide operation
of U.S. forces, however, as well as for U.S. obligations
to Taiwan and military alliances. A key indicator of
the potential negative aspects of China's increasing
military reach will be China's ability or inability to
dispassionately adapt to how to handle encounters
between the two militaries at sea and in the air without it escalating into a crisis with damaging effects on
U.S.-China relations.

As discussed in this chapter, improvements to China's military logistics over the last 10 years have moved
steadily toward a higher degree of regional and global
support capacity. Nonetheless, logistics remains an
area of weakness for the PLA. Logistics serves as an
indicator of potential ambition and capability, but it
does not in and of itself provide a clear understanding
of intentions to threaten the United States, let alone to
displace America's global position. China does, however, seek autonomous military capability that could
be used to protect its own national interests, which
will require adaptation from the United States, other
regional and global powers, as well as China itself.

How the United States responds to improvements in China's military capabilities beyond its shores, in general, will be influenced to a large degree by China itself. U.S. military logistics cooperation with China, which has been significantly constrained for most of the last 20 years since the Tiananmen Square incident, could provide an area for development of cooperation and mutual reassurance of intentions.

Continuing a de facto embargo of professional military logistics contacts serves special interests group in both China and the United States who benefit more from a mutual threat perception, than they do from effort to enhance cooperation, transparency, and trust. Although we can expect the U.S. to continue to constrain military logistics contacts due to a perception that operational contacts in logistics mean potential "assistance" to the growth of China's military capabilities, it may be time to rethink the role and purpose of U.S. military contacts with China for two reasons.

First, continuing no contact in military logistics inhibits the development of U.S.-China military contacts, which may not best serve national interests to maintain stability, particularly as China's military becomes more capable and confident. Second, these restrictions do not enhance the U.S. military's understanding of China's growing operational capabilities, while they have had limited to no effect on the pace, scope, and rate of improvement to China's military logistics system.

The United States would be ill advised to make unilateral overtures to China for new bilateral contacts in logistics as well as other areas, until China can take ownership of its own role in promoting substantive military-to-military contacts with the United States, rather than hold them hostage to past grievances and

U.S. commitments to Taiwan. If China is not willing to move into more substantive areas, such as operational logistics, which would potentially expose some of China's operational weaknesses, as well as help to develop a greater level of trust with the United States, the United States should not offer proposals that the Chinese will not respond to.

Over the last 20 years, U.S. military contacts with China were narrowed by the horror of Tiananmen Square, as well as assumptions that military-military relations are always expendable. The latter was especially the case since China's military could be expected to remain inferior to the United States for the foreseeable future. Now that China's military capabilities are making significant progress, it may better serve U.S. national interests to pursue new ways to positively cooperate with China militarily, but the United States cannot do this alone.

For the near term, then, it seems realistic that the possibility of genuine bilateral partnership and reciprocity between the U.S. and Chinese militaries is unrealistic. Despite positive atmospherics, politically, the cost of this effort may be too high for the United States for several reasons.

First, congressional and special interest scrutiny and hostility toward U.S.-China military-to-military logistics cooperation could undermine contacts in this area, making it unsustainable and counterproductive. Critiques could paint even the best managed contacts as reckless, even traitorous acts, arguing that these would enhance China's military power projection capabilities, which would chip away at support inside and outside the U.S. military.

Second, on the Chinese side, logistics cooperation can be expected to continue to be constrained by a sense of past wrongs, such as the disruption of the flow of *Blackhawk* repair parts in 1989, or ongoing military relations with Taiwan. U.S. proposals in this area could be interpreted as signs of weakness requiring more concessions from the United States, which would sooner or later make contacts unsustainable for the United States. Habitual imbalances in reciprocity and transparency can be expected from the Chinese, but these will be increasingly counterproductive for the Chinese as its military capabilities grow. China will have to act more like a responsible military power or the lack of it will undermine the benign perception of its intentions that it is trying to cultivate.

Multilateral contacts in logistics, however, provide a more realistic venue for the two militaries for the foreseeable future and can indirectly contribute to incident avoidance between the two militaries. Consequently, U.S. military efforts to cooperate with Chinese in the area of military logistics should be limited to practical requirements associated with U.S.-China cooperation to support UN and other regional and international missions, such as the Gulf of Aden antipiracy mission. This type of effort offers the most pragmatic area for some level of logistics cooperation based on practical cooperation, rather than bilateral military exchanges.

ENDNOTES - CHAPTER 11

1. "PLA Seminar on Speeding Up Reform of Modern Logistics," *PLA Daily Online,* November 4, 2008.

2. Daniel Hawthorne, *For Want of a Nail: The Influence of Logistics on War*, New York: Whittlesey House, McGraw-Hill, 1948, p. xii.

3. The Army has been the main force of the PLA and continues to dominate PLA leadership. The other services include the PLAN, established at the end of the Civil War when units of the Republic of China Navy defected; the PLAAF, also formally established in 1949, and the Strategic Rocket Forces, established in July 1966. The Marines, which are a separate service within the U.S. military system—although part of the Department of the Navy headed by the Secretary of the Navy, are part of the PLA in the Chinese system.

4. Cheung, Tai Ming, *China's Entrepreneurial Army*, New York: Oxford University Press, 2001, p. 232.

5. Major John E. Edwards (USA, Retired), *Combat Service Support Guide*, 3rd Ed., Mechanicsburg, PA: Stackpole Books, 2000.

6. Special thanks to Rear Admiral Eric McVadon (USN, Ret.), Erin Barker, Bud Cole, and others at the 2009 PLA Conference for their comments on an earlier version of this chapter. The author would also like to thank Daniel Alderman for his research assistance in identifying secondary and primary sources of information. Any errors or oversights are the responsibility of the author alone.

7. Several studies of China's logistics systems that have been developed based on open source research have been classified "For Official Use Only," or higher, which excluded them from consideration in this report.

8. Gong Yude (龚裕德), Beijing, China: PLA Press (解放军出版社), 1986.

9. Jointly published by Xinhua Bookstore Distribution (新华书店经销) and China Social Sciences Press (中国社会科学出版社), Beijing, China, 1990.

10. Zhang Youqing (张有卿) and Pi Zhaokun (皮兆坤), Beijing, China: Legal Press (法律出版社), 1991.

11.Wan Xiaoyuan (万小元), Cheng He (程鹤), Fan Sipeng (范思鹏), *Mobilizing Military Logistics* (军事后勤动员学), Beijing, China: National Defense University Press, 1994.

12. Yu Yongzhe (余用哲), *Logistics Protection in High-tech War* (高技术战争后勤保障), Beijing, China: jointly published by the Military Science Press and the Xinhua Bookstore Distribution, 1995.

13. Wen Guangchun (温光春), *Logistics Support for Mobile Operations* (机动作战后勤保障), Beijing, China: PLA Press, 1997.

14. Gong Fei (龚飞), *A Study on Campaign Logistics under the Condition of Information Warfare* (信息战争战役后勤研究), Beijing, China: National Defense University Press, 1998.

15. Shao Hua (邵华) and Yan Hui (闫辉), *Informatization and Military Logistics* (信息时代与军事后勤), Beijing, China: Modern China Press, 1998.

16. Among these was Sun Xiude (孙秀德) *et al.*, *Selected Material on The People's Liberation Army Supplies* (战略后勤新探；军需史资料选编), Beijing, China: General Logistics Department, Quartermaster Division, 1999; He Yanfang (贺艳方) and Fan Gongsong (樊恭嵩), *Military Expenditures Theory* (军费论), Beijing, China: Military Sciences Press, 1999; Wang Hongyun (王宏运) *et al.*, *Logistics Personnel Conduct Regulations and Control* (后勤人员行为调控法), Beijing, China: 海湖出版社, 1999; and Zhu Hongda (朱洪达) *et al.*, *An Introduction to Logistics Leadership Science* (后勤领导科学概论), Beijing, China: National Defense University Press, 1999.

17. Tai Ming Cheung, "Reforming the Dragon's Tail: Chinese Military Logistics in the Era of High-Technology Warfare and Market Economies," in James R. Lilley and David Shambaugh, eds., *China's Military Faces the Future*, Washington DC: M. E. Sharpe, 1999, pp. 228-246.

18. The 7-year-old publication, *The People's Liberation Army as Organization*, James C. Mulvenon and Andrew N. D. Yang, eds., Santa Monica, CA: Rand, 2002, contains two chapters, "The People's Liberation Army (PLA), General Logistics Department (GLD): Toward Joint Logistics Support," by the author, which provides an organizational history of the GLD; and "The General Armament Department," by Harlan Jencks, which provides an analysis of the organizational history leading to the founding of the GAD in April 1998, and its mission and organization.

19. See, for example, Ngok Lee, *China's Defence Modernisation and Military Leadership*, Sydney: Australian National University Press, 1989; You Ji, *The Armed Forces of China*, New York: I. B. Tauris, 1999; David Shambaugh, *Modernizing China's Military: Progress, Problems and Prospects*, Berkeley: University of California Press, 2002.

20. See Ken Allen, "Logistics Support for PLA Air Force Campaigns," and author's "Rough but Ready Force Projection: An Assessment of Recent PLA Training," in *China's Growing Military Power: Perspectives on Security, Ballistic Missiles, and Conventional Capabilities*, in Andrew Scobell and Larry M. Wortzel, eds., Carlisle, PA: Strategic Studies Institute, U.S. Army War College, 2002; and Lonnie Henley, "PLA Logistics And Doctrine Reform, 1999-2009," in Susan M. Puska, ed., *People's Liberation Army After Next*, Carlisle, PA: Strategic Studies Institute, U.S. Army War College, August 2000.

21. Evan S. Medeiros *et al.*, *A New Direction for China's Defense Industry*, Santa Monica, CA: Rand, 2005; and James Mulvenon, *Soldier of Fortune: The Rise and Fall of the Chinese Military-Business Complex, 1978-1999*, Armonk, NY: M. E. Sharpe, 2001.

22. Tai Ming Cheung, *Fortifying China: The Struggle to Build a Modern Defense Economy*, Ithaca, NY: Cornell University Press, 2008; and "China's Entrepreneurial Army: The Structure, Activities and Economic Returns of the Military Business Complex," in C. Dennison Lane, Mark Weisenbloom, and Dimon Liu, eds., *Chinese Military Modernization*, New York: The AEI Press, 1996, pp. 168-197.

23. Eric A. McVadon raised several logistics operational issues the Chinese faced in the late 1990s, when he wrote that it was not clear if the PLA had "come to grips with the less grandiose concepts of logistics support, preventive maintenance, and timely and efficient repair, "Systems Integration in China's People's Liberation Army," in James C. Mulvenon and Richard H. Yang, eds., *The People's Liberation Army in the Information Age*, Santa Monica: RAND, 1999, p. 241.

24. Shirley, Kan, "U.S.-China Military Contacts: Issues for Congress," *CRS Report for Congress*, August 6, 2009, p. 31.

25. *Ibid.*, p. 33.

26. *Ibid.*, p. 34.

27. *Ibid.*, p. 37.

28. *Ibid.*, p. 43.

29. *Ibid.*, p. 49.

30. PASOLS began in 1971 as a U.S. Army initiative. The seminar was broadened in 1976 when oversight passed from the U.S. Army Component Command to Headquarters, U.S. Pacific Command. It is a multilateral organization of senior logisticians participating from Pacific, Asian, and Indian Ocean area nations. The purpose of the seminar is to promote the exchange of logistics information, pursue bilateral and multilateral initiatives, and encourage a spirit of friendship and regional cooperation. Information available from *www.pasols.org/*.

31. Susan M. Puska, "Learning from Others: A Survey of Chinese Exploitation of U.S. Military Logistics," *Defense Group Inc.*, Washington, DC: Center for Intelligence Research and Analysis, 2007.

32. James Mulvenon, "Chairman Hu and the PLA's 'New Historic Missions'," *China Leadership Monitor*, No. 27, available from *media.hoover.org/documents/CLM27JM.pdf*.

33. See Joint Logistics (Distribution): Joint Integrating Concept Version 1.0, February 7, 2006, Washington, DC: The Joint Staff, available from *www.dtic.mil/futurejointwarfare/concepts/jld_jic.pdf*.

34. *Joint Publication (JP) 1-02, DoD Dictionary of Military and Associated Terms*, Washington, DC: The Joint Staff, last updated October 2009.

35. *Ibid.*

36. See Joint Integrating Concept Version 1.0.

37. Joint core logistics capabilities included supply, maintenance operations, deployment and distribution, health service support (HSS), engineering, logistic services, and operational contract support. See *Joint Publication 4-0, Joint Logistics*, Washington, DC: The Joint Staff, July 18, 2008, available from *www.dtic.mil/doctrine/jel/new_pubs/jp4_0.pdf*.

38. *Ibid.*, p. I-9.

39. Xing Shizhong *et al*, eds., *Military Equipment Studies* (军事装备学), Beijing, China: National University Press, 2000, p. 95.

40. *Joint Publication 4-0, Joint Logistics*, Washington, DC: Joint Chiefs of Staff, July 18, 2008, p. I-2, available from *www.dtic.mil/doctrine/jel/new_pubs/jp4_0.pdf*.

41. Liu Dengrong, Wen Guangchun *et al.*, eds., *China Military Logistics Encyclopedia* (中国军事后勤百科全书), Beijing, China: Jindun Press, 2002, Vol. I, p. 43.

42. Jiang Zemin, quoted in Wang Zhilei and Zhang Haiping, "Reform and Opening Promote Support Might: A Summary of PLA Logistics Development," *PLA Daily*, December 20, 1998.

43. Wei Xianyi, "Issues of Military Material Joint Support (军用物资联勤保障应把的几个问题)," *Military Economic Research* (军事经济研究), September 2000, pp. 66-69. This definition reflects how the Joint Logistics Departments were structured with the reforms that commenced on January 1, 2000, and also reflects the definition of the term as defined in the *China Military Logistics Encyclopedia*.

44. Cheng Ying and Xu Jinzhang, "Interview with Liao Xilong," *Liaowang Dongfang Zhoukan*, January 19, 2006, pp. 33-34.

45. Zhang Zhiyun in Wen Guangchun *et al.*, eds., *China Military Logistics Encyclopedia*, Vol. XI, p. 198.

46. Jia Wansuan in Bo Quanyu *et al.*, eds., *Supplement to the China Military Encyclopedia* (中国军事百科全书增补), Beijing, China: Military Science Press, 2002, p. 467.

47. *Selected Military Works of Mao Zedong*, Vol. 6, p. 339, Beijing, China, Military Science Press, Central Document Press, 1993.

48. *Selected Works of Deng Xiaoping*, Vol. 2, Beijing, China: People's Publishing House, 1994, p. 264.

49. Jiang Zemin, *On Defense and Army Building*, Beijing, China: PLA Publishing House, 2003, p. 86.

50. James Mulvenon, "Chairman Hu and the PLA's 'New Historic Missions'," *China Leadership Monitor*, No. 27, available from *media.hoover.org/documents/CLM27JM.pdf*.

51. Zhang Liansong and Zhou Ling, "Hu Jintao's Theses on Military Logistics," *China Military Science* (中国军事科学), Vol. 5, 2007.

52. Mulvenon, "Chairman Hu and the PLA's "New Historic Missions."

53. "Former navy deputy commander stripped of NPC post," June 29, 2009, available from *www.chinadaily.com.cn/china/2006-06/29/content_629565.htm*.

54. Wang Ke, "On Strongly Promoting Logistics Reform to Raise the Economic Efficiency of our Armed Forces," *China Military Science*, April 20, 2000, pp. 6-11.

55. This section draws upon Robert T. Forte, *et al.*, "PLA Joint Logistics Reform," Washington, DC: Defense Group, Inc., Center for Intelligence Research and Analysis (CIRA), 2007.

56. Zhang Liansong (张连松) and Liu Jing (刘晶,), "From Individual Service Support to Joint Support" ("从军兵种自我保障到筹连和保障"), *Military History Research* (军事历史研究) April 2004, p. 40.

57. Wang Ke, "On Strongly Promoting Logistics Reform to Raise the Economic Efficiency of our Armed Forces."

58. Wang Guanghui and Wang Youlin, "Several Opinions On Our Military's Integrated Logistics Building," *Military Art,* October 2004, pp. 62-65.

59. Based on Wei Xianyi, "Issues of Military Material Joint Support," in Robert T. Forte, *et al.,* eds., *Military Economic Research,* Washington, DC: Defense Group, Inc., Center for Intelligence Research and Analysis (CIRA), 2007, pp. 66-69.

60. Legal Notice, "Management Methods of Managing the Supply of Military Food Items," *People's Daily,* May 13, 1994, available from *www.people.com.cn.*

61. Liu Wei and Liu Mingxue, "Jinan Theater Achieves Initial Success in Reform of Joint Logistics," *PLA Daily,* July 20, 2005. Also see "Briefing of Chinese Joint Logistics," available from *www.pasols.org/joint_log_presentations/china.pdf.*

62. Zhang Xuemeng, "An Exploration into Raising Logistic Support Effectiveness in Future Warfare" ("提高未来战争后勤保障效益初探"), *Soldier News* (战士报), August 24, 2005, p. 2. Also see, "Briefing on China's Joint Logistics System," available from *www.pasols.org/joint_log_presentations/china.pdf.*

63. Highlights, PLA Activities Report, July 1-15, 2006, as reported in *Qianwenbao,* June 30, 2006.

64. Based on Wei Xianyi, "Issues of Military Material Joint Support," pp. 66-69.

65. Wen, "Issues of Military Material Joint Support," p. 67; Shen, "Combined Logistic Service for the Three Armed Services to Officially Start Next Year," p. D1; Ma Shuming, "Speeding Up the Process of Joint Logistics," *PLA Daily,* May 14, 2002, p. 6.

66. Liu Mingxue, "The CMC Decides to Deepen the Reform of the Joint Logistics System," *PLA Daily,* June 26, 2004.

67. Liu Wei and Liu Mingxue, "Jinan War Zone Big Logistics Reform Pilot Project Makes Incremental Accomplishments," *PLA Daily,* July 20, 2005, p. 1.

68. Unattributed, "A Description of the Jinan Joint Logistic Experiment, Internet version, March 19, 2005, available from *news3.xinhuanet.com/mil/2005-03/19/content_271729.htm*. Further evidence of Second Artillery Corps participation in the JLD is provided in Zhang Xinkai and Ma Jinyuan, "Joint Logistics 'Jointness' Produces Combat Ability," *Rocket Force News*, October 25, 2006, p. 3.

69. Liu and Liu, "Jinan Theater Achieves Initial Success in Reform of Joint Logistics"; "Interview with GLD Director, Zhang Zhende," *PLA Daily*, August 31, 2004, p. 270. "China's National Defense in 2006," aka 2006 White Paper, Section IV, available from *www.china.org.cn/english/China/194332.htm*.

71. Wang Fan, "Benefits Opened Up by Distributed Support," *Beijing Bao Online*, January 29, 2009, p. 2.

72. *Ibid.*

73. *Ibid.*

74. Yu Chuanxin, "A Few Issues Concerning Logistic Support for the Cross-strait Amphibious Landing Operation," *Journal of Military Economic Studies*, January 15, 2001.

75. James Mulvenon, "Chairman Hu and the PLA's 'New Historic Missions'," *China Leadership Monitor*, No. 27, available from *media.hoover.org/documents/CLM27JM.pdf*.

76. Wang Ailing and Xia Zhijun, "Research on Combined Application of Bar Code Technology and RFID Technology in Military Logistics," *Logistics Technology*, No. 10, 2005, pp. 231-232, 244; Chen Xinggang, Liu Zhenhua, and Guo Baohua, "Anticipation of RFID and bar code (application)" ("RFID 余条码技术在军事物流领域中的联合应用"), Packaging Engineering, Vol. 27, No. 1, 2006, pp. 87-89; and Zhao Hongtao, "Applications of RFID in Military Logistics," ("论RFID在军事物流领域中的应用"), *Logistics Science and Technology* (物流科技), June 22, 2005. pp. 28-121.

77. Xu Guangyao, Zheng Jinshong, and Chen Hongji, "Untouched Intelligent Card and its Application in Air Material Management at (an) Air Base ("非接触式IC卡"), *Logistics Technology*, No. 2, 2005, pp. 4-5, 98.

78. Feng Yongmin, Zhang Lingling, and Wang Guijing, Military Transportation Institute, Tianjin, "Analysis and Countermeasures on the Present Situation of China's Military Logistics Standardization" ("我军军物流标准化的现状分析及对策"), *Logistics Technology*, No. 7, 2005, pp. 86-88, 91.

79. Liu Haijun, Logistics Command Academy, Beijing, "Application of VMI (Velocity Managed Inventory) Strategy in Military Logistics," ("VMI 策略在军事物流领域中的应用"), *Military Logistics, Academic Edition*, Issue 6, 2004, pp. 63-65; Chang Jiane and Liu Guojing, School of Mechantronic Engineering, Wuhan University of Technology, Wuhan, "Analysis of Air Material Inventory Management Based on SCM, Supply Chain Management)" ("浅谈基于供应链的航材库存管理"); and Li Jie, Chen Huansheng, Sun Ronglin, and Guo Zhenbin, Department of Military Supplies, Xuzhou Air Force Institute, Xuzhou, "Military Inventory Control System Based on MAS, Multi-Agent System) in the Condition of Agile Logistics" ("灵敏后勤条件下基于多智能体的军队库存控制系统研究").

80. Zhang Zhiyong and Kuang Xinhau, School of Management, National University of Defense Technology, Changsha, "Study on the Order Forecasting Method of Military Logistics Based on BP Neural Net" ("其于BP神经网络的军事物流订单预测方法研究"), *Logistics Technology*, No. 12, 2005, pp. 66-69.

81. The BP neural network algorithm is commonly used to predict oil deposits, for example. One Chinese conference paper available in English, describes BP as a "relatively perfect feedforward neural network algorithm." BP is discussed within wide discussion of the development and application of "fuzzy logic" to enhance the ability to predict and forecast resources and requirements. Meng Qingwu, Li Chengbin, Cheng Hu, and Li Ti, "Software Department, Daqing Petroleum Administrative Bureau, Improved BP Network Algorithm Based on Fuzzy Logic and Application in Geophysics," Conference Paper for ESIT 2000, September 14-15, 2000, Aachen, Germany.

82. Chen Yao, Yang Xilong, Wang Jin, and Jiang Honggon, Department of Information Engineering, Logistics Engineering University, Chongqing, "Intelligent Simulation of Military Logis-

tics in Limited War" ("局部战争下军事物流智能仿真初探"), *Logistics Technology*, No. 1, 2005, pp. 83-86.

83. "Information Integrated for Military Logistics According to CALS" ("基于CALS的军事供应链信息集成，管理纵横") *Vertical and Horizontal Management*, date unknown, pp. 82-84.

84. A logistics knowledge integrating system originally developed by the U.S. DoD, formerly called, "Computer Aided Logistics Support." CALS introduced standards (commonly referred to as CALS) to help regularize logistics information systems.

85. Gao Lu, Department of Equipment Command and Management, Ordnance Engineering College, Shijiazhuang, Wang Jian, Beijing Institute of Tracking and Telecommunication Technology, Beijing, and Li Zhen, Department of Equipment Command and Management, Ordnance Engineering College, Shijiazhuang, "Research on Military Logistics Decision Technology Based on Mulit-resource Information Fusion" ("其于多信息融合的军事物流决策研究"), *Logistics Technology* No. 11, 2005, pp. 83-85.

86. Ge Xianjun, Li Yibo, Zhang Haijun, and Jiang Bin, National Aeronautical Engineering Institute (NAEI), "Research Decision Support System Used in Military Logistics" 军事后勤决策支持系统研究, (*Journal of Naval Aeronautical Engineering Institute*), Vol. 20, No. 2, May 2005, pp. 235-238.

87. Song Tailiang, *Integrated Logistics Support Guide* (装备综合保障实施指南), Beijing, China: National Defense Industry Publishing House, 2004.

88. Mulvenon, "Chairman Hu and the PLA's 'New Historic Missions'."

89. Available from *www.au.af.mil/au/awc/awcgate/navy/log_quotes_navsup.pdf*.

90. Kevin Pollpeter, *The Evolving Military-Nexus in PLA Logistics*, Washington, DC: Defense Group Inc., January 2007.

91. *A Reader's Guide to the Report to the 17th CPC National Congress*, Beijing, China: PLA Press, 2007, p. 41, quoted in Fan Jichang,

"A Study of the Strategy of Building a Logistic Support System Based on Military and Civilian integration with Chinese Characteristics," *China Military Science*, May 2008.

92. Fan Jichang, "A Study of the Strategy of Building a Logistic Support System Based on Military and Civilian integration with Chinese Characteristics," *China Military Science*, May 2008.

93. Pollpeter, *The Evolving Military-Nexus in PLA Logistics*.

94. "Civilian Transportation National Defense Mobilization Regulations" ("民用运力国防动员条列"), promulgated by the CMC Standing Committee on September 11, 2003; Pollpeter, *The Evolving Military-Nexus in PLA Logistics*.

95. Lu Shijiao, Zhao Wukui, and Li Zhen, "Comparison Between the Equipment Support Socialization of the Chinese and U.S. Army" ("中美军队装备保障社会化比较"), *Journal of the Academy of Equipment Command and Technology*, April 2006, Vol. 17, No. 2, pp. 14-18.

96. *PLA Daily*, June 5, 2009.

97. *PLA Daily*, May 21, 2009.

98. "Problems Existing in Military-Civilian Integration for Armament Support and Maintenance in Our Armed Forces and Measures for Resolving Such Problems," *Military Economic Research*, May 2009.

99. Dai Xu, "China Should Establish Overseas Bases," Beijing, China: Huanqiu Shibao, February 3, 2009.

100. Quoted in Colum Lynch, "China Filling Void Left by West in U.N. Peacekeeping," *The Washington Post*, November 24, 2006, available from *www.washingtonpost.com/w p-dy n/content/article/2006/11/23/A R2006112301007_pf.html*.

101. Information available from *www.un.org/Depts/dpko/dpko/pub/pko.htm*.

102. Information available from *www.un.org/Depts/dpko/dpko/contributors/2009/july09_1.pdf*.

103. *Xinhua*, available from *english.cri.cn/2946/2008/04/30/1261@352140.htm*.

104. Available from *english.people.com.cn/english/200007/29/eng20000729_46779.html* .

105. "Chinese Naval Ships End Visit to Ukraine," *People's Daily Online*, available from *English.peoplesdaily.com.cn/*.

106. "Chinese naval ship visits Vietnam," SINA English, November 19, 2008, available from *english.sina.com/china/2008/1118/198940.html*.

107. "Mainland training ship visits Taiwan," SINA English, May 15, 2009, available from *english.sina.com/china/p/2009/0515/241471.html*.

108. Xia Hongping and Hou Yaming, "Weishanhu ship berths in Port Salalah for first replenishment," *PLA Daily*, June 24, 2009, available from *english.chinamil.com.cn*.

109. "China navy set for Somalia mission," December 23, 2008; "Chinese navy to patrol Somali coast," December 26, 2008, available from *english.aljazeera.net/news/asia-pacific/2008/12/2008122653142196826.html*; and "Chinese Naval Fleet returned from 4-month escort mission in Africa," April 29, 2009, available from *www.china-defense-mashup.com/?tag=pirates*.

110. *Ibid.*

111. Xia Hongping and Hou Yaming, "Weishanhu ship berths in Port Salalah for first replenishment," *PLA Daily*, June 24, 2009, available from *english.chinamil.com.cn*.

112. "PLA Navy Escort Fleet berths in Port Salalah for first replenishment," July 1, 2009, available from *www.china-defense-mashup.com/?tag=pirates*.

113. *Ibid.*

114. Information available from *ports.co.za/news/article_2009_02_25_5054.html#three*.

115. Antonio Castillo, "China in Latin America," *The Diplomat*, June 18, 2009, available from *www.the-diplomat.com/article.aspx?aeid=13466*.

116. Phil Brennan, "China Filling U.S. Vacuum in Latin America, "available from *archive.newsmax.com/archives/articles/2004/9/11/170621.shtml*.

117. Tyler Bridges, "China's big move into Latin America," July 12, 2009, available from *www.csmonitor.com/2009/0712/p06s10-woam.html*.

118. "China and Brazil sign MOU on Port Cooperation," *www.zgjtb.com*, May 21, 2009, available from *en.mesa.gov.cn/msa/root/0 2/1243216536855/1244689048837*; "Brazil's iron ore sales tumble amid China port woes," available from *www.reuters.com/article/rbssMiningMetalsSpecialty/idUSSEO18139420090602*.

119. Dan Erikson, Inter-American Dialogue, quoted in Tyler Bridges, "China's big move into Latin America," available from *www.csmonitor.com/2009/0712/p06s10-woam.htm?print=true*.

120. Edwards, p. 39.

121. Lester F. Ward, *Applied Sociology: A Treatise on the Conscious Improvement of Society by Society*, Boston, MA: Ginn and Company, 1906, pp. 81-82.

APPENDIX A - CHAPTER 11

LOGISTICS MODERNIZATION TIMELINE

Civil War — people's war within liberated areas — local support (voluntary and involuntary) — multigenerational equipment and weapons (scavenged and acquired) — light infantry basis — peasant conscription army — ingenuity, but lack of professionalism.

Korean War — ill prepared, ill equipped and unable to respond to challenges mainly because of politics and Mao's leadership from Beijing (chain-of-command problem).

1952 — Premier Zhou Enlai and acting Chief of Staff Nie Rongzhen advocated the creation of a joint logistics system (integrated support system) following avoidable defeats during the Third Campaign (December 31, 1950).[1]

Soviet Union influence — evolutionary vice revolutionary change of equipment and weapons

Cultural Revolution

1979 Vietnam Border War

1980s — U.S. flirtation; back to Union of Soviet Socialist Republics (USSR); logistics force structure reductions and reorganizations
- PLAN eliminates three fleet logistics departments (1985)[2]
- Airborne airfields begin supplying PLAAF airborne divisions and regiments

- Three Generation (三代) reform in 1988, developing a joint program in supply, maintenance, and medical support in Shanxi, Jinan, and Hainan; two constants and one adjustment (两个不变一个调整), which permitted units to access the closest support unit available for supply, maintenance and medical support.[3]

1990s — Russia; diversification of mil-mil; reorganization; Joint Logistics develops
- GLD established joint logistics support for material supplies, hospital treatment, maintenance support, and other common logistics services at the Hong Kong Garrison in July 1997.[4]
- More than 100,000 troops from army, navy, and air force units work together to provide emergency logistics support to over three million households in Hunan and Hubei Provinces affected by flooding (1998).[5]
- General Armament Department (GAD) officially created. Changed from the three-department (GLD, GPD, and GSD) organization that had endured since 1957.[6] Equipment and maintenance repair included in April 1998.
- Joint Logistics System established (1998).
- President Jiang Zemin signs the *PLA Joint Campaign Program* (also known as the *Number 13 PLA Combat Order*), which ordered the PLA to begin joint operations training, and organization — stipulates merging MR logistic resources and organizations, as well as common use of support customers under the "two joinings and one base" ("两结合一个基础") program in January 1999.

- General Wang Ke publishes article in April 1999, entitled "On Strongly Promoting Logistics Reform to Raise the Economic Efficiency of our Armed Forces," which maps out a 10-year program for PLA logistics reform, including Joint Logistics reform in the following areas: [7]
  - Build a logistics system capable of supporting all three services simultaneously.
  - Standardize military supplies.
  - Scientifically manage the military's logistics service.

2000s — Leveraging Civilian Commercial Modernization Achievements and Capacity; Enhanced Regulation

- 10-year logistics modernization effort launched by PLA in January 2000 [8]
- PLA Regulations on Armaments (Weaponry) Promulgated by the Central Military Commission; drafted by General Armament Department. [9]
- Joint Logistics Department (JLD) established in each of the seven Military Regions (MRs). [10]
  - Charged with providing common use materials and services. [11]
  - MRs continued to provide service-specific materials, and services continued to be provided by MR services branch logistics departments. [12]
  - Logistics is the first joint system developed by the Chinese military; permanent system, which does not require creation during wartime [13]
  - Joint logistics departments became responsible for leading, managing, plan-

ning, building, and using in a unified way, warehouses, hospitals, supply stations, and other logistic service entities for common use by the three armed services.[14]

— The service branch logistics departments still provided service-specific materials and logistical support through their organic support systems.[15] In addition to unifying supply channels, the JLD system was made joint with a significant increase in the number of non-ground force cadres in the JLD,[16] and the integration of their logistic support resources (e.g. rear depots, hospitals, material supply facilities, etc).[17]

2002

• PLA Regulation on Armament Maintenance (July) Promulgated by CMC; drafted by GAD.[18]

2003

• First regulations since the founding of China passed by the CMC Standing Committee governing national mobilization of civilian means of transportation "Civilian Transportation National Defense Mobilization Regulations" (民用运力国防动员条列) on September 11.

2004

• Hu Jintao issues guidance at an enlarged CMC meeting on optimizing the distribution of strategic resources, including concrete requirements to coordinate resource allocations and use between priority and ordinary units, as well as by units stationed in interior areas and units deployed to coastal areas. Hu Jintao said military logistics needs to develop in both mechanization and informatization.

- Logistics regularizations led to the development of standards, rules, and regulations, as well as prosecutions that took place during 2002-04. Standards and regulations are established to support Joint Logistics reform.[19]
- Jinan MR Pilot begins in July. The Jinan MR JLD provides all services and material to all services' units located in Jinan MR.[20]
  - Personnel representing the PLA Air Force, Navy, and Second Artillery are increased on the MJR JLD.[21]
  - Jinan MR, purportedly, has served as a logistics test bed since 1980s.[22]
- At the end of the year, Hu announces his New Historic Missions (新的历史使命) in support of the three historic tasks: accelerating modernization construction; reunifying the motherland; and maintaining world peace and accelerating common development:[23]
  - Provide an important, powerful guarantee for strengthening the party's ruling position (为党巩固执政地位提供重要的力量保证).
  - Provide a firm security guarantee for safeguarding China's opportunity for strategic development (为维护国家发展的重要战略机遇期提供坚强的安全保障).
  - Provide strong strategic support for safeguarding national interests (为维护国家利益提供有力的战略支撑).
  - Play an important role in safeguarding world peace and in accelerating the development of all (为维护世界和平与促进共同发展发挥重要作用).

617

2005

- Hu Jintao asked military to develop the capability of coping with multiple threats to security and fulfilling diverse military tasks; required logistics personnel to continuously create a new situation in logistics work, and to provide strong support to the armed forces to perform missions in the new stage of the new century.
- Hu and GLD laid down the goal of developing the logistics support system, socializing social form, informatization support means, and enhancing scientific logistics management to promote the compound development of military logistics and lay a solid foundation for building informatized logistics and guaranteeing the winning of an informationized war by 2050.
- Hu Jintao issues new guidelines to place quality and efficiency at the core of logistics modernization and to incorporate defense and army modernization into the overall strategy of national modernization.

2006

- PLA Regulation on Rewarding Professional and Technical Personnel Promulgated by CMC; drafted by GSD, GLD, GPD, and GAD. [24]
- The military appears to have overcome the confusion that began in 2000 over what should be considered a common use item and what must remain service-specific. [25]

2007

- April—PLA officially implemented an integrated (joint) logistics system in the Jinan MR to support army-navy-air force (three services) integration.[26]

2008

- Outsourcing accomplishments highlighted by PLA include:
  - Guangzhou MR established "Evaluation Standards for Logistics Outsourcing Quality and Benefit" to provide standards for evaluating reform achievements.
  - Chengdu MR explored outsourcing of medical support taking advantage of local health providers to provide medical support to local and scattered military units.
  - GSD and GPD intensified supervision of food procurement, transportation, and processing to improve food safety for military units.
  - 5,200 PLA barracks pushed ahead property management outsourcing.
  - About 1,300 PLA units carried out POL outsourcing.
- China announces plans to send two destroyers (*Haikou* and *Wuhan*) and a support vessel from the PLAN's Hainan base to conduct anti-piracy operations off the Horn of Africa, especially in the Gulf of Aden.[27] Admiral Du Jingcheng, the mission commander, was quoted as saying: "Our primary target is not striking but dispelling them. If the pirates make direct threats against the warships or the vessels we escort, the fleet will take countermeasures."[28]

2009

- Jan—Chinese missile-armed warships *Haikou* and *Wuhan* began escort duty in the Gulf of Aden. Including the accompanying supply ship, the crew.
- May 6—Five commercial trucks loaded with automobile repair parts left Jinan, Shangdong Province, to deliver the support directly to Xinjiang MD distribution centers for issue to local military units. In the past, the repair parts were placed in material warehouses and units were required to drive to the central warehouse to pick up the parts. Under this method, civilian transportation distributes the repair parts at no additional cost closer to the using units.[29]
- May 15—Medical Support Exercise. First time the PLAN logistics department conducted a medical exercise with the new Peace Ark medical ship. The 72-hour exercise was conducted with full crew, and tested full capacity support for 300 sick beds. The training served to comprehensively test onboard medical equipment, medical staff, medical services flow, and medicines and medical material when operating at full capacity. Experts at the Field Surgery Research Institute of the PLA, the Second Medical University, and the Third Medical University helped design the content of the training.[30]
- June 4—Xinjiang MR armored regiment signed a "Highway Transportation Agreement for Armored Equipment" and conducted the first emergency call-out exercise using civilian platform trucks to transport armored vehicles.[31]

- June—East Sea Fleet (ESF) tests a new floating dock ship for repair and maintenance support. The dock was issued to a "speedboat flotilla." The dock included a GPS tracker and other advanced support equipment.[32]
- June—South Sea Fleet (SSF) conducts a Comprehensive Support Exercise lasting nearly eight hours that incorporated comprehensive support ships and a medical ship, to provide support to combat ships and dock landing ships 1,000 kilometers away from land in the South China Sea. Food replenishment, maritime first aid, and ammunition replenishment support were tested.
- June—PLAN established the navy's first integrated civil-military vessel equipment center in Guangzhou with civilian equipment development unit. The center has established an equipment support network that can provide technical equipment support to vessels throughout South China. PLAN signed agreements with six factories and institutes. Multiple forward support centers have also been established at key ports to exploit technical workforces dispatched by development units, to enable frontline military ports, base support centers and equipment development factories to provide maintenance support to PLAN vessels.[33]

ENDNOTES - APPENDIX A - CHAPTER 11

1. Colonel Susan M. Puska, "The People's Liberation Army (PLA) General Logistics Department (GLD): Toward Joint Logistics Support," *The People's Liberation Army as Organization: Reference Vol. 1.0*, Santa Monica, CA: RAND, 2002, p. 252.

2. Hu Fuwen, "On Realizing the Prospect's of Our Military's Logistics Leap Frog Development" ("伦实现我军后勤跨越式发展的基本途径"), 军事经济学院学报 (*Journal of Military Economics Academy*), p. 46.

3. In addition to main focus on supply, maintenance, and medical support, the *san dai* experiment also covered military traffic, sanitation, vehicle and ship transportation, fuel, material, and common equipment maintenance. Zhang Liansong (张连松) and Liu Jing (刘晶,), "From Individual Service Support to Joint Support" ("从军兵种自我保障到军联合保障"), *Military History Research* (军事历史研究), April 2004, p. 40.

4. *Ibid.*, p. 41.

5. *Ibid.*

6. Harlan Jencks, "The General Armament Department," in James C. Mulvenon and Andrew N. D. Yang, eds., *The People's Liberation Army as Organization Reference Volume v1.0*, Santa Monica, CA: RAND, 2002, pp. 273-308.

7. Wang Ke, "On Strongly Promoting Logistics Reform to Raise the Economic Efficiency of our Armed Forces," *China Military Science* (中国军事科学), April 20, 2000, pp. 6-11.

8. Robert T. Forte, Johanna G. Cox, and Kevin Pollpeter, *PLA Joint Logistics Reform*, Washington, DC: Defense Group, Inc., Center for Intelligence Research and Analysis (CIRA), 2007.

9. Tai Ming Cheung, *Fortifying China*, Ithaca, NY: Cornell University Press, 2008, pp. 132-133.

10. Forte, Cox, and Pollpeter.

11. *Ibid.*

12. *Ibid.*

13. *Ibid.*

14. *Ibid.*

15. Shen Xiao, "Combined Logistic Service for the Three Armed Services to Officially Start Next Year," *Wen Wei Po,* August 5, 1999, p. D1.

16. The percentage of non-Army cadres rose from 12 percent to 45 percent; Information Office of the State Council of the People's Republic of China, *China's National Defense in 2004,* available from *www.fas.org/nuke/guide/china/doctrine/natdef2004.html.*

17. *Ibid.*

18. Cheung, p. 133.

19. Forte, Cox, and Pollpeter.

20. *Ibid.*

21. *Ibid.*

22. *Ibid.*

23. James Mulvenon, "Chairman Hu and the PLA's 'New Historic Missions'," *China Leadership Monitor,* No. 27, available from *media.hoover.org/documents/CLM27JM.pdf.*

24. Cheung, p. 134.

25. Forte, Cox, and Pollpeter.

26. "PLA Seminar on Speeding Up Reform of Modern Logistics," *PLA Daily,* November 4, 2008.

27. "China navy set for Somalia mission," December 23, 2008; and "Chinese navy to patrol Somali coast," December 26, 2008, available from *english.aljazeera.net/news/asia-pacific/2008/12/2008122653142196826.html.*

28. *Ibid.*

29. *PLA Daily,* May 21, 2009.

30. Ren Pan and Ju Zhenhau, "'Peace Ark' Conducts Medical Support Exercise," *PLA Daily* in English, June 10, 2009.

31. *PLA Daily*, June 5, 2009.

32. Yu Wei, Liao Haifeng and Lu Wenqiang, "Floating dock serves as maritime mobile 'warship hospital'," available from *English.chinamil.*

33. Si Yanwen and Zhou Yawen, "Naval Base establishes vessel equipment support center," *PLA Daily*, June 11, 2009, *English. chinamil.com.cn.*

APPENDIX B - CHAPTER 11

SELECTED CHINESE MILITARY LOGISTICS BOOKS AND PROFESSIONAL JOURNAL PUBLICATIONS, 2000-09

First Author	Title (English Translation)	Title (Chinese)	Year
Song Qing (宋庆)	Logistics Command Information Sciences (海湖出版社, Beijing)	后勤指挥信息学	2009
Ren Min (任民)	National Defense Mobilization Studies (军事科学出版社, Beijing)	国防动员学	2008
Zhou Zhenduo (周振铎)	Research on Army Management Under Informationized Conditions (军事科学出版社, Beijing)	信息化条件下部队管理研究	2007
Zhu Zhigang (祝志刚)	China Military Order and Purchase Goods (国防工业出版社, Beijing)	中国军事订货与采购	2007

Wang Jinghai (王京海)	Military Logistics and Strategic Choices (军事科学出版社, Beijing)	军事后勤与战略选择	2007
Zhao Zhanping (赵占平)	Military Transportation (中国大百科书出版社, Beijing)	军事交通运输	2007
Jiang Dali (姜大立)	Military Logistics System Modeling and Application (中国物资出版社, Beijing)	军事物流系统模型与应用	2006
Liu Yongqiang (刘永强)	Research on National Defense Mobilization Under Informationized Conditions (解放军出版社, Beijing)	信息化条件下国防动员研究	2006
Su Shuyan (苏书岩)	Armed Forces' Logistics Military Training (军事科学出版社, Beijing)	军队后勤军事训练学	2006
Tan Fengxu (谭凤旭)	Comprehensive Research on U.S. Military Logistics S&T Equipment Development (解放军出版社, Beijing)	美军后勤科技装备发展综合研究	2006

Xu Ruyi (许如意)	*A Study of Comprehensive Joint Warfare Logistics Simulation* (Journal of Military Economics Academy, Vol. 13, No. 1, pp. 33-34)	一体化联合作战后勤仿真初探	2006
Wang Jinfa (王进发)	Grand Strategy for China Military Logistics Transformation (Reform) (国防大学出版社, Beijing)	中国军事后勤变革大战略	2005
Jiang Dali (姜大立)	Contemporary Military Logistics (中国物资出版社, Beijing)	现代军事物流	2005
Zhang Lijun (张礼军)	Research on Informationized Logistics (海湖出版社, Beijing)	后勤信息化研究	2005
Wu Jianguo (吴建国)	An Introduction to Ground Force Logistical Operations Command (解放军出版社, Beijing)	陆军作战后勤指挥概论	2005
Zhu Qinglin (朱庆林)	National Economic Mobilization of China (军事科学出版社, Beijing)	中国国民经济动员学研究	2005

Jin Xiuman (金秀满)	Military Vehicle Management Studies (军事科学出版社, Beijing)	军用车辆管理学	2005
Li Yu (李玉)	Military Information Resources Classification (军事科学出版社, Beijing)	军事信息资源	2005
Shao Weizheng (邵维正)	Informationized Joint Logistics Support Political Work (军事科学出版社, Beijing)	信息化战争联勤保障政治工作	2005
Xu Xiangnan (徐向南)	*In Revelation of the U.S. Military Logistics Informatization Regarding the Construction of Our Military's Joint Logistics Informatization* (Journal of Military Economic Academy, Vol. 12, No. 1, pp. 40-45)	美军后勤信息化对我军联勤信息化建设的启示	2005
Zhou Zhengsong (周正嵩)	*Discussion About the Standardized Work of Logistics* (Logistics Science and Technology, Vol. 28, No. 113, pp. 74-75)	关于物流标准化工作的探讨	2005

Gou Chengfu (苟成富)	*The Government How to Develop the Third Party Logistics* (Journal of Shandong Institute of Commerce and Technology, Vol. 5, No. 4, pp. 6-8)	政府应当怎样推动第三方物流的发展	2005
Zhang Lanfang (张兰芳)	*The Study of Agile Supply Chain Strategy* (Logistics Technology/No. 10, pp. 47-49)	敏捷供应链的战略研究	2005
Chen Yao (陈瑶)	*Intelligent Simulation of Military Logistics in Limited War* (Logistics Technology/No. 1, pp. 83-86)	局部战争下军事物流只能仿真初探	2005
KU Guisheng (库桂生)	New Revolution in Military Logistics (解放军出版社, Beijing)	军事后勤新变革	2004
Jiang Dali (姜大立)	Military Logistics (中国物流出版社, Beijing)	军事物流学	2004
Wang Fuchen (王福臣)	Transportation Mobilization Studies (军事科学出版, Beijing)	交通动员学	2004

Chen Guoshu (陈国书)	PLA Combined Forces Logistics Deputy Staff Officer Applied Training Material (解放军出版社, Beijing)	中国人民解放军合成军队师旅团后勤参谋助理员应用训练教材	2004
Li Guangren (李广仁)	Research on Ground Force Tactics for Logistics Support (解放军出版社, Beijing)	陆军战术后勤保障研究	2004
Song Tailiang (宋太亮)	Integrated Logistics Support Guide (国防工业出版社, Beijing)	装备综合保障实施指南	2004
Li Zhiyun (李志云)	High-Tech Warfare Logistics Support Political Work (军事科学出版社, Beijing)	高技术战争后勤保障政治工作	2004
Liu Yuanyue (刘远跃)	The New Revolution in Military Affairs and Informationized Logistics (海湖出版社, Beijing)	新军事革命与信息化后勤	2004
Liu Yang (刘洋)	A Study on The Military Strategy and Military Expenses Management (国防大学出版社, Beijing)	军事战略与军费管理	2004

Cao Mingdu (曹明都)	*Exploration on Equipment Support of the USA-UK Troops in Iraq War* (Journal of the Academy of Equipment Command & Technology/Vol. 15/No. 2, pp. 18-21)	伊拉克战争中美英联军装备保障透析	2004
Ding Guoqin (丁国勤)	*Establishment and Analysis on Incentive Model of Military Oil Social Support* (Logistics Technology/No. 7, pp. 62-65)	军队油料社会化保障游励模型的建立和分析	2004
Wang Beisheng (王北生)	The Study of Military Logistics Innovation (海湖出版社, Beijing)	军事后勤创新学	2003
Liu Yuejun (刘粤军)	Informationized Military Knowledge Reader (长征出版社, Beijing)	信息化军事知识读本	2003
Tang Xiaoping (唐小平)	Transport Vehicle Defense Command (军事科学出版社, Beijing)	汽车运输防卫指挥	2003

631

Li Wanjun (荔万俊)	An Introduction to Socialization of Military Logistics Support (解放军出版社，Beijing)	军队后勤保障社会化概论	2003
Han Jin (寒金)	The Military Logistics Behind the Iraq War (China Water Transport/ Vol. 6 , pp. 26-27)	对伊战争背后的军事物流	2003
Xian Yangbao (线杨保)	A Summary of the U.S. Military (Army) Revolution in equipment Maintenance Support (National Defense Technology Base / No. 3, pp. 31-32)	美军装备维修保障改革综述	2003
Yang Xuechang (杨学强)	A Summary of the Main Logistics Theories of the U.S. Military (Overseas Logistics/No. 7, pp. 55-56)	美军主要军事物流力论综述	2003
Zhang Nian (张念)	Third Party Logistics Trend in China (Logistics Management/Vol. 26/No. 95, pp. 21-24)	我国第三方物流发展方向	2003

Jiang Luming (姜鲁鸣)	An Introduction to the Study of Modern National Defense Economics (国防出版社, Beijing)	现代国防经济学导论	2002
Zhan Guoqiao (占国桥)	Cold, Altitude and Mountainous U.S.: Border Counterattack Operational Logistics Support Research (2 Vol.) (解放军出版社, Beijing)	高寒山地： 边境反击作战后勤保障研究（2 Vol.）	2002
Jia Xianwen (贾宪文)	Joint Logistics Theory Research (解放军出版社, Beijing)	联勤理论研究	2002
Wu Jianguo (吴建国)	Ground Force Joint Combat Logistics Support Army (解放军出版社, Beijing)	陆军合同战斗后勤保障	2002
Sun Xiude (孙秀德)	Military Logistics Studies (解放军出版社, Beijing)	军事后勤学	2002
Sun Zhiping (孙智平)	An Introduction to Air Force Wartime Economic Support (军事科学出版社, Beijing)	空军作战经济保障概论	2002

Guo Qinmao (郭钦茂)	21st Century Provincial Military Region Logistics Building and Development (海湖出版社, Beijing)	21世纪初省军区后勤建设与发展	2002
Wang Benhong (王本宏)	The Application of punitive Damages on the Field of Contact (Journal of Anhui Electric Power University For Staff/Vol. 7/No. 2, pp. 88-91)	论惩罚性赔偿在合同领城的适用	2002
Li Yanbin (李言斌)	China War Zone Geography and Logistics Support (2 Vol.) (解放军出版社, Beijing)	中国战区地理与后勤保障 (2 Vol.)	2001
Wang Libing (王立兵)	An Introduction to Military Logistics Reform (金盾出版社, Beijing)	军队后勤改革概论	2001
Wang Yixing (王益兴)	A Discussion of Contemporary Military Provisions (金盾出版社, Beijing)	现代军队给养论	2001
Geng Xianyou (耿宪友)	Handle Sudden Outbreaks: Research on Logistics Support Methods (解放军出版社, Beijing)	处置突发事件后勤保障法研究	2001

Wan Xiaoyuan (万小元)	Strategic Logistics Studies (解放军出版社, Beijing)	战略后勤学	2001
Yu Gaoda (余高达)	Battle Logistics Studies (解放军出版社, Beijing)	战役后勤学	2001
Liu Shengjun (刘胜俊)	Strategic Studies of Military Logistics Development (金盾出版社, Beijing)	军事后勤发展战略学	2000
Huang Wenshou (黄文寿)	Contemporary Research on Foreign Militaries' Logistics (金盾出版社, Beijing)	当代外军后勤研究	2000
Peng Zhizhong (彭志忠)	An Integrated Logistics and Supply Chain Management Strategy (Logistics Technology/No. 1, pp. 36-38)	一体化物流与供应链管理战略分析	2000

ABOUT THE CONTRIBUTORS

DANIEL ALDERMAN is a Bridge Award Fellow at The National Bureau of Asian Research (NBR). Prior to joining NBR, he was a 2008-09 National Security Education Program Boren Fellow in Beijing, China. He is the author of "The PLA at Home and Abroad: Assessing the Operational Capabilities of China's Military," *2009 People's Liberation Army Colloquium Brief* (Carlisle, PA: Strategic Studies Institute, U.S. Army War College, 2010). Mr. Alderman is currently a master's candidate at the Elliott School of International Affairs at the George Washington University and holds a B.A. in history and political science from Presbyterian College.

KENNETH ALLEN at the time the conference was held, Mr. Allen was a Senior China Analyst at CNA China Studies; however, he is currently a Senior China Analyst at Defense Group Inc. (DGI). He is a retired U.S. Air Force officer with many years of analytic work on China. His extensive service abroad includes a tour in China as the Assistant Air Attache, plus assignments in Taiwan, Japan, and Berlin. The author of numerous articles and three major monographs on Chinese military affairs, including China's Foreign Military Relations, he also authored the seminal English-language monograph on the PLA Air Force that remains the cornerstone for research on the Chinese Air Force. A Chinese linguist, he holds an M.A. in international relations from Boston University.

DENNIS J. BLASKO is a retired U.S. Army lieutenant colonel who now works as an independent analyst. He served 23 years as a Military Intelligence Officer and Foreign Area Officer specializing in China. Lieutenant Colonel Blasko was an Army attaché in Beijing and Hong Kong from 1992-96. He also served in infantry units in Germany, Italy, and Korea, and in Washington at the Defense Intelligence Agency, Headquarters Department of the Army (Office of Special Operations), and the National Defense University War Gaming and Simulation Center. Lieutenant Colonel Blasko has written numerous articles and chapters on the Chinese military and is the author of the book, *The Chinese Army Today: Tradition and Transformation for the 21st Century* (Routledge, 2006). Lieutenant Colonel Blasko is a graduate of the United States Military Academy and the Naval Postgraduate School.

ANDREW S. ERICKSON is an Associate Professor in the Strategic Research Department at the U.S. Naval War College and a founding member of the department's China Maritime Studies Institute (CMSI). He is an Associate in Research at Harvard University's Fairbank Center for Chinese Studies, a Fellow in the National Committee on U.S.-China Relations' Public Intellectuals Program (2008-11), and a member of the Council for Security Cooperation in the Asia Pacific (CSCAP). Dr. Erickson previously worked for Science Applications International Corporation (SAIC) as a Chinese translator and technical analyst. He has also worked at the U.S. Embassy in Beijing, the U.S. Consulate in Hong Kong, the U.S. Senate, and the White House. Proficient in Mandarin Chinese and Japanese, Dr. Erickson has traveled extensively in Asia. His research, which focuses on East Asian defense, foreign policy, and technology issues, has been published widely in such journals as *Journal of Strategic Studies*, *Orbis*, *Joint Force Quarterly*, and *Proceedings*. He is coeditor of, and a contributor to, the Naval Institute Press book series, "Studies in Chinese Maritime Development." Dr. Erickson graduated magna cum laude with a B.A. in history and political science from Amherst College, and an M.A. and Ph.D. in international relations and comparative politics from Princeton University.

PAUL H. B. GODWIN retired as professor of international affairs at the National War College, Washington, DC, in 1998. His research specialties focus on Chinese defense and security policies. Among Professor Godwin's recent publications are: "The Cradle of Generals: Strategists, Commanders and the PLA National Defense University," in Roy Kamphausen, Andrew Scobell and Travis Tanner, eds., *The "People": in the PLA: Recruitment, Training and Education in China's Military* (Carlisle, PA: Strategic Studies Institute, U.S. Army War College, 2008); "China's Emerging Military Doctrine: A Role for Nuclear Submarines?" in Andrew S. Erickson, Lyle J. Goldstein, William S. Murray, and Andrew R. Wilson, eds., *China's Nuclear Submarine Force* (Annapolis, MD: Naval Institute Press, 2007); "China as a Major Asian Power: The Implications of its Military Modernization," in Andrew Scobell and Larry M. Wortzel, eds., *Shaping China's Security Environment: The Role Of the People's Liberation Army* (Carlisle, PA: Strategic Studies Institute, U.S. Army War College, 2006); "Decisionmaking Under Stress: The Unintentional Bombing of China's Belgrade Embassy and the EP-3 Collision," in Andrew Scobell and Larry Wortzel, eds., *Chinese National Security Decisionmaking*

Under Stress (Carlisle, PA: Strategic Studies Institute, U.S. Army War College, 2005); "Change and Continuity in Chinese Military Doctrine: 1949-1999," in Mark A. Ryan, David M. Finkelstein, and Michael A. McDevitt, eds., *Chinese Warfighting: the PLA Experience Since 1949* (Armonk, New York: M. E. Sharpe, 2003). Professor Godwin is now a consultant and serves as a nonresident scholar for the Foreign Policy Research Institute. He graduated from Dartmouth College with a degree in international relations, and holds a Ph.D. in political science from the University of Minnesota.

ERIC HAGT is the director of the China Program at the World Security Institute in Washington, DC. He manages research projects at the Program's Beijing office covering a range of traditional and nontraditional security issues in China with an emphasis on space, the defense-industry, energy security, and crisis management. He was a visiting researcher at the Freeman Chair in Studies at the Center for Strategic and International Studies and has studied and worked in Taiwan and Mainland China for 8 years. Mr. Hagt has authored publications in journals such as *Naval War College Review, Survival, Central Asia-Caucasus Analyst,* and *China Security,* and has testified before Congress's U.S.–China Economic and Security Review Commission. Mr. Hagt holds a master's degree in international policy and China studies from the University of California Berkeley.

HEIDI HOLZ is a China analyst at CNA China Studies. Prior to joining CNA, she worked as a bio defense analyst and China specialist with the Division of Integrated Bio Defense at Georgetown University's Imaging Science and Information Systems Center, where she analyzed the frequency and causality of infectious diseases in various parts of China. An accomplished linguist, Ms. Holz was previously a staff member at the Voice of America's Mandarin Service, where she wrote programming in both Chinese and English, to include broadcast programs for teaching English to VOA's Chinese audience. Ms. Holz has studied Mandarin Chinese in Beijing at Peking University and Tsinghua University. She is a graduate of Georgetown University's School of Foreign Service where she studied Chinese and East Asian history. She is currently completing a master's degree in security studies at Georgetown University.

ROY D. KAMPHAUSEN is Vice President for Political and Security Affairs and Director, Washington, DC, The National Bureau of Asian Research. A retired U.S. Army China Foreign Area Officer, Mr. Kamphausen served as the China Country Director in the Office of the Secretary of Defense, China Branch Chief in the Directorate for Strategic Plans and Policy for the Joint Chiefs of Staff, and at the Defense Attaché Office of the U.S. Embassy in the People's Republic of China. He has served as a consultant for the Office of the Secretary of Defense, Department of State and other U.S. government agencies. His areas of professional expertise include China's Peoples Liberation Army (PLA), U.S.-China defense relations, U.S. defense and security policy toward Asia, and East Asian security issues. Mr. Kamphausen co-authored the chapter, "Military Modernization in Taiwan," in *Strategic Asia 2005-06: Military Modernization in an Era of Uncertainty*, with Michael Swaine; wrote the chapter, "PLA Power Projection: Current Realities and Emerging Trends," in *Assessing the Threat: The Chinese Military and Taiwan's*

Security (2007) with Justin Liang; edited the volume, *Right-Sizing the People's Liberation Army: Exploring the Contours of China's Military* (2007), with Andrew Scobell; and edited the volume, *The "People" in the PLA: Recruitment, Training, and Education in China's Military* (2008), with Andrew Scobell and Travis Tanner.

DAVID LAI is Research Professor of Asian Security Studies at the Strategic Studies Institute (SSI) of the U.S. Army War College. Before joining the SSI, Dr. Lai was on the faculty of the U.S. Air War College. Having grown up in China, Lai witnessed China's "Cultural Revolution," its economic reform, and the changes in U.S.-China relations. His teaching and research interests are in international relations theory, war and peace studies, comparative foreign and security policy, U.S.-China and U.S.-Asian relations, and Chinese strategic thinking and operational art. Dr. Lai holds a bachelor's degree from China and a master's degree and Ph.D. in political science from the University of Colorado.

KEVIN POLLPETER is China Program Manager at Defense Group Inc.'s Center for Intelligence Research and Analysis. Previously, he was a researcher at the Rand Corporation. Mr. Pollpeter is widely published on China national security issues and focuses on the Chinese space program. He has travelled widely in Asia, including China, where he lived for 2 years. Mr. Pollpeter has advanced Chinese language skills and holds a master's degree in international policy studies from the Monterey Institute of International Studies.

SUSAN M. PUSKA, a retired U.S. Army Colonel, is a researcher at the Defense Group, Inc., Center for Intelligence Research and Analysis (CIRA). She currently investigates Chinese dual-use RDA, military modernization, and mobilization issues. Colonel Puska served as the U.S. Army Attaché in Beijing during 2001-03, and an assistant Army attaché during 1992-94. She attended The Johns Hopkins-Nanjing University Center for Chinese and American Studies as a China Foreign Area Officer (FAO) in 1988-89. Colonel Puska's publications include "Resources, Security and Influence: The Role of the Military in China's Africa Strategy," *China Brief*, May 30, 2007, "*Assessing America at War: Implications for China's Military Modernization and National Security*," in *Shaping China's Security Environment: The Role of the People's Liberation Army*, (Carlisle, PA: Strategic Studies Institute, U.S. Army War College, 2006), and "*SARS 2002-2003: A Case Study in Crisis Management*," in *Chinese National Security: Decisionmaking Under Stress* (Carlisle, PA: Strategic Studies Institute, U.S. Army War College, 2005). Colonel Puska holds an B.A. in archaeology and an M.A. in China studies from the University of Michigan.

ANDREW SCOBELL is Senior Political Scientist at the RAND Corporation. Prior to this he was Associate Professor of International Affairs at the Bush School of Government and Public Service at Texas A&M University located in College Station, Texas. From August 1999 until August 2007, he was Associate Research Professor in the Strategic Studies Institute at the U.S. Army War College and Adjunct Professor of Political Science at Dickinson College, both located in Carlisle, Pennsylvania. He is the author of *China's Use of Military Force: Beyond the Great Wall and the Long March*

(Cambridge University Press, 2003) and other publications. Dr. Scobell holds a Ph.D. in political science from Columbia University.

HAROLD TANNER is an associate professor at the University of North Texas, where he teaches undergraduate and graduate courses on ancient, medieval, and modern Chinese history and U.S.-China diplomatic history. His publications and research include *China: A History* (Hackett Publishers, 2009), *Strike Hard: Anti-crime Campaigns and Chinese Criminal Justice, 1979-1984* (Cornell East Asia Series, 1999), and several articles on Chinese criminal justice, as well as articles and conference papers on Chinese Communist strategy and operations in the war against the Nationalist armies in Manchuria between 1945 and 1948. Dr. Tanner holds an M.A. in area studies from the School of Oriental and African Studies, University of London, and a Ph.D. in Chinese history from Columbia University.

YOU JI is reader/associate professor in School of Social Science, the University of New South. He has published widely on China's political, military, and foreign affairs. He is author of three books, including *The Armed Forces of China*, 1999. He wrote numerous articles, including "Politics as the Foundation for Health Balance of Power," *Asia Policy*, No. 8, 2009; "The 17th Party Congress and the CCP's Changing Elite Politics," in Dali Yang and Zhao Litao (eds.), *China's Reform at 30* (Singapore: World Scientific, 2009); "The Soviet Military Model and the Breakdown of the Sino-USSR Alliance," in Thomas Bernstein and Hua-yu Li, eds., *The Soviet Influence on China in the 1950s* (Rowman & Littlefield, 2009); "China's New Diplomacy, Foreign Policy and Defense Strategy," in Stuart Harris, Qin Yaqing & Pauline Kerr, eds., *China's New Diplomacy: Tactical or Fundamental Change?* (Palgrave Macmillan, 2008); "Revolution in Military Thinking," in Bo Huldt & Masako Ikegami, eds., *The Strategic Yearbook on East Asian Security* (The Swedish National Defence College and the Finnish Defence University, 2008); "Dealing with Malacca Dilemma: China's Effort to Protect its Energy Supply," *Strategic Analysis*, Vol. 31, No. 3, 2007. You Ji is a member of the editorial board of the *China Journal*; *Provincial China*; *East Asia Policy*; and *Journal of Contemporary China*; and a Member of advisory board for the series on contemporary China, *World Scientific Publisher*, Singapore.

www.ingramcontent.com/pod-product-compliance
Lightning Source LLC
Chambersburg PA
CBHW080041280326

41935CB00014B/1750